Cracking the

TASC

Test Assessing Secondary Completion™

The Staff of The Princeton Review

PrincetonReview.com

Penguin
Random
House

The Princeton Review
24 Prime Parkway, Suite 201
Natick, MA 01760
E-mail: editorialsupport@review.com

Published in the United States by Penguin Random House LLC, New York, and in Canada by Random House of Canada, a division of Penguin Random House Ltd., Toronto.

Some of the content in *Cracking the TASC Test Assessing Secondary Completion*™ has previously appeared in the following titles, published as trade paperbacks by Random House, an imprint and division of Penguin Random House LLC.

Cracking the AP Biology Exam, 2016 Edition
Cracking the AP Economics Macro & Micro Exams, 2016 Edition
Cracking the AP English Language & Composition Exam, 2016 Edition
Cracking the AP English Literature & Composition Exam, 2016 Edition
Cracking the AP Environmental Science Exam, 2016 Edition
Cracking the AP Human Geography Exam, 2016 Edition
Cracking the AP U.S. Government & Politics Exam, 2016 Edition
Cracking the AP U.S. History Exam, 2016 Edition
Cracking the AP World History Exam, 2016 Edition
Cracking the GED® Test, 2016 Edition
Cracking the SAT Biology E/M Subject Test, 15th Edition (2014)
Cracking the SAT Literature Subject Test, 15th Edition (2014)
Cracking the SAT Math I Subject Test (2014)
Cracking the SAT Physics Subject Test, 15th Edition (2014)
Cracking the SAT U.S. History Subject Test (2014)
Cracking the SAT World History Subject Test (2014)

Terms of Service: The Princeton Review Online Companion Tools ("Student Tools") for retail books are available for only the two most recent editions of that book. Student Tools may be activated only twice per eligible book purchased for two consecutive 12-month periods, for a total of 24 months of access. Activation of Student Tools more than twice per book is in direct violation of these Terms of Service and may result in discontinuation of access to Student Tools Services.

ISBN: 978-1-101-88209-2
eBook ISBN: 978-1-101-88210-8
ISSN: 2380-6737

TASC Test Assessing Secondary Completion™ is a trademark of McGraw-Hill School Education Holdings, LLC, which does not sponsor or endorse this product. McGraw-Hill Education is not affiliated with The After-School Corporation, which is known as TASC. The After-School Corporation has no affiliation with the Test Assessing Secondary Completion ("TASC test") offered by McGraw-Hill Education, and has not authorized, sponsored or otherwise approved of any of McGraw-Hill Education's products and services, including TASC test.

The Princeton Review is not affiliated with Princeton University.

Editor: Meave Shelton
Production Editors: Kathy G. Carter and Harmony Quiroz
Production Artist: Deborah A. Silvestrini

Printed in the United States of America on partially recycled paper.

10 9 8 7 6 5 4 3 2 1

Editorial
Rob Franek, Senior VP, Publisher
Casey Cornelius, VP Content Development
Mary Beth Garrick, Director of Production
Selena Coppock, Managing Editor
Meave Shelton, Senior Editor
Colleen Day, Editor
Sarah Litt, Editor
Aaron Riccio, Editor
Orion McBean, Editorial Assistant

Random House Publishing Team
Tom Russell, Publisher
Alison Stoltzfus, Publishing Manager
Melinda Ackell, Associate Managing Editor
Ellen Reed, Production Manager
Kristin Lindner, Production Supervisor
Andrea Lau, Designer

Acknowledgments

Many thanks to the following contributors: Josh Nagel, David Stoll, Zoe Gannon, Erik Kolb, Eliz Markowitz, Linda Kelley, Gina Donegan, Christina Bartley, Clarissa Constantine, Chris Chimera, Anne Goldberg, and Sara Kuperstein.

Special thanks to Adam Robinson, who conceived of and perfected the Joe Bloggs approach to standardized tests, and many of the other successful techniques used by The Princeton Review.

Contents

Register Your

1 Go to **PrincetonReview.com/cracking**

2 You'll see a welcome page where you can register your book using the following ISBN: 9781101882092.

3 After placing this free order, you'll either be asked to log in or to answer a few simple questions in order to set up a new Princeton Review account.

4 Finally, click on the "Student Tools" tab located at the top of the screen. It may take an hour or two for your registration to go through, but after that, you're good to go.

NOTE: If you are experiencing book problems (potential content errors), please contact EditorialSupport@review.com with the full title of the book, its ISBN number (located above), and the page number of the error.

Experiencing technical issues? Please e-mail TPRStudentTech@review.com with the following information:

- your full name
- e-mail address used to register the book
- full book title and ISBN
- your computer OS (Mac or PC) and Internet browser (Firefox, Safari, Chrome, etc.)
- description of technical issue

Book Online!

Once you've registered, you can access...

- A second full-length practice test, with detailed answer-explanations
- Extra practice drills for the most challenging topics
- Sample responses to the essay prompts in the practice tests
- "Further skills and concepts" lessons covering less-frequently-tested topics
- Tutorials for the technology-enhanced and constructed-response questions
- Printable scoring tables and custom answer sheets for both practice tests
- A tally of any updates to this book and/or the TASC test

Look For These Icons Throughout The Book

 Online Practice Test

 Online Articles

 Online Practice Drills

 More Great Books

The **Princeton Review**®

Part I
Introduction

Chapter 1
How to Use This Book to Achieve a Passing (or CCR) Score

In this chapter, you will assess your goals and learn how to most effectively use this book to ensure you perform your best on the TASC test.

CONGRATULATIONS!

You are reading this book because you want to make a better future for yourself, and that future begins with obtaining the equivalent of a high school degree. The doors that will open depend on your personal and professional goals, as the many successful people who earned a high school equivalency certificate—including some famous people listed nearby—can tell you. We admire your motivation and congratulate you on your decision.

We are also delighted that you have chosen to use this book to prepare for the TASC test. We have helped millions of people achieve their goals, and we are honored to have the privilege of helping you. Your road to a passing—or even a College and Career Readiness (CCR)—score involves a combination of content, reading skills, writing skills, test-taking skills, practice, and self-evaluation.

The chapters in this book address the content and skills you need, and it is your job to learn the content and practice the skills. Most chapters contain drills that will help you assess your mastery. Answers and explanations are available to download when you register your book at **PrincetonReview.com/cracking**. Moreover, there's a full-length practice test (along with answers and explanations) in Part VII, and a second test online. You should take these tests under simulated testing conditions. In the next section, we suggest when you should take each test.

Of course, we understand that your needs may differ from someone else's, and we want to ensure that you get exactly what you need from this book. To that end, this chapter will guide you on the proper use of this book based upon your knowledge, needs, and goals.

Please begin by answering the following three questions and reading the Road Map that follows.

Famous People Who Earned a High School Equivalency Certificate

Wally Amos, founder of Famous Amos Cookies
Augusten Burroughs, bestselling author
Ben Nighthorse Campbell, former U.S. Senator
Dr. Richard Carmona, former U.S. Surgeon General
Michael Chang, tennis champion
Eminem, rapper, actor, and record producer
Drake, rapper, songwriter, and actor
D. L. Hughley, political commentator and comedian
Bishop T. D. Jakes
Peter Jennings, journalist and news anchor
Honorable Greg Mathis, U.S. District Court judge
Ruth Ann Minner, former Governor of Delaware
F. Story Musgrave, NASA shuttle astronaut
Danica Patrick, auto racing champion
Mary Lou Retton, Olympic gold medalist
Michelle Rodriguez, actor and screenwriter
Chris Rock, comedian and actor
Hilary Swank, Academy Award–winning actor
Dave Thomas, founder of Wendy's
Mark Wahlberg, actor and producer

SELF-ASSESSMENT: MY FAMILIARITY WITH THE TASC TEST AND MY TEST-TAKING ABILITIES

1. I am familiar with the structure of the TASC test, how it is scored, and how to register for the test. ☐ *Yes* ☐ *No*
2. I am familiar with the look and feel of the TASC test. ☐ *Yes* ☐ *No*
3. I want to learn or to improve my ability to apply relevant test-taking strategies that an effective tester utilizes. ☐ *Yes* ☐ *No*

Road Map

- If you answered *No* to either of questions 1 or 2, read Chapter 2 (or the relevant parts of Chapter 2) *before* you complete this chapter.
- If you answered *Yes* to question 3, complete Chapter 3.
- Even if you answered *Yes* to all three questions, we encourage you to read the Other Resources section in Chapter 2. You may do so now or after you complete this chapter.

Next, proceed through the following steps.

Step One: Answer each group of questions that follow.
Step Two: Take the first practice test (Chapter 30).
Step Three: Review and, if appropriate, change your answers to the questions that follow.
Step Four: Read and follow the Road Map that follows each group of questions that follow.

SELF-ASSESSMENT: MY LEVEL OF MASTERY— READING

4. I want to improve my mastery of answering reading questions relating to main ideas, evidence, and conclusions. ☐ *Yes* ☐ *No*
5. I want to improve my mastery of answering reading questions relating to analyzing arguments. ☐ *Yes* ☐ *No*
6. I want to improve my mastery of answering questions relating to literary devices and how authors achieve effects. ☐ *Yes* ☐ *No*
7. I want to improve my mastery of answering questions relating to multiple passages. ☐ *Yes* ☐ *No*

Pace Yourself
Doing a little studying each day is much better than trying to cram it all into one week.

Custom Answer Sheets!
Available to download and print out when you register your book online.

Road Map

- If you answered *Yes* to question 4, complete Chapters 4 and 5.
- If you answered *Yes* to question 5, complete Chapters 4 and 6.
- If you answered *Yes* to question 6, complete Chapters 4 and 7.
- If you answered *Yes* to question 7, complete Chapters 4 and 8.
- Even if you answered *No* to any of questions 4 through 7, we recommend that you complete Chapter 4, as well as the drills in Chapters 5 through 8.

SELF-ASSESSMENT: MY LEVEL OF MASTERY— WRITING

8. I want to refine my knowledge about one or more of the following concepts of structure and related topics. ☐ *Yes* ☐ *No*
    - Sentence construction
    - Punctuation and capitalization
    - Subject/verb agreement
    - Pronoun/noun agreement
    - Proper pronoun usage
    - Modifiers
    - Word choice and spelling
    - Joining thoughts
    - Logic and clarity
9. I want to improve my ability to revise text appropriately. ☐ *Yes* ☐ *No*
10. I want specific advice on how best to write an effective TASC test essay. ☐ *Yes* ☐ *No*

Road Map

- If you answered *Yes* to question 8, complete Chapter 9 and all or the relevant parts of Chapter 10.
- If you answered *Yes* to question 9, complete Chapters 9 and 11.
- If you answered *Yes* to question 10, complete Chapters 9 and 12.
- Even if you answered *No* to any of questions 8 through 10, we recommend that you complete Chapter 9, as well as the drills in Chapters 10 through 12.

SELF-ASSESSMENT: MY LEVEL OF MASTERY— MATHEMATICS

11. I want to refine my mastery of one or more of the following concepts of arithmetic. ☐ *Yes* ☐ *No*
    - The number line
    - Positive and negative number operations
    - Order of operations (PEMDAS)
    - Decimal place value and rounding
    - Fraction essentials
    - Operations with fractions
    - Distance as a function of rate and time
    - Cost: discounts, markups, commission, and profit
    - Probability
    - Ratios and proportions
    - Percents

12. I want to refine my mastery of one or more of the following concepts of algebra. ☐ *Yes* ☐ *No*
    - Understanding and working with polynomials
    - Understanding and working with exponents
    - Equations and inequalities involving variables
    - Quadratic equations (FOIL)
    - Translating words into math
    - Systems of equations

13. I would like to learn a test-taking strategy that may, on certain algebra problems, make those problems easier to solve. ☐ *Yes* ☐ *No*

14. I would like to refine my mastery of one or more of the following concepts of functions. ☐ *Yes* ☐ *No*
    - Inputs and outputs
    - Function notation: $f(x)$
    - Graphing functions and understanding graphs of functions

15. I want to refine my mastery of one or more of the following concepts of geometry. ☐ *Yes* ☐ *No*
    - Triangles (types, area, and perimeter)
    - Pythagorean theorem
    - Four-sided figures (types, areas, and perimeter)
    - Circles (circumference and area)
    - Arcs and interior angles of circles
    - Similar triangles and other figures
    - Combined figures and shaded regions
    - Volume and surface area of 3-D figures
    - The coordinate plane
    - Equation of a line, slope, and y-intercept
    - Systems of equations on the coordinate plane

16. I would like to refine my mastery of one or more of the following concepts of trigonometry. ☐ *Yes* ☐ *No*
    - Trigonometry identities and terms
    - The Unit Circle
    - Connecting Trigonometry and the Pythagorean theorem

Road Map

- If you answered *Yes* to question 11, complete Chapter 13 and all or the relevant parts of Chapter 14.
- If you answered *Yes* to question 12, complete Chapter 13 and all or the relevant parts of Chapter 15.
- If you answered *Yes* to question 13, read the "Why Plug In" section in Chapter 15.
- If you answered *Yes* to question 14, complete Chapter 13 and all or the relevant parts of Chapter 16.
- If you answered *Yes* to question 15, complete Chapter 13 and all or the relevant parts of Chapter 17.
- If you answered *Yes* to question 16, complete Chapter 13 and all or the relevant parts of Chapter 18.
- Even if you answered *No* to any of questions 11 through 16, we recommend that you complete Chapter 13, as well as the drills in Chapters 14 through 18.

SELF-ASSESSMENT: MY LEVEL OF MASTERY— SOCIAL STUDIES

17. I want to refine my mastery of geography. ☐ *Yes* ☐ *No*
18. I want to refine my mastery of United States history. ☐ *Yes* ☐ *No*
19. I want to refine my mastery of world history. ☐ *Yes* ☐ *No*
20. I want to refine my mastery of economics. ☐ *Yes* ☐ *No*
21. I want to refine my mastery of civics. ☐ *Yes* ☐ *No*

Road Map

- If you answered *Yes* to question 17, complete Chapter 19 and all or the relevant parts of Chapter 20.
- If you answered *Yes* to question 18, complete Chapter 19 and all or the relevant parts of Chapters 21 and 22.
- If you answered *Yes* to question 19, complete Chapter 19 and all or the relevant parts of Chapter 23.
- If you answered *Yes* to question 20, complete Chapter 19 and all or the relevant part of Chapter 24.
- If you answered *Yes* to question 21, complete Chapter 19 and all or the relevant parts of Chapter 25.
- Even if you answered *No* to any of questions 17 through 21, we recommend that you complete Chapter 19, as well as the drills in Chapters 20 through 25.

SELF-ASSESSMENT: MY LEVEL OF MASTERY— SCIENCE

22. I want to refine my mastery of one or more of the following concepts of life sciences. ☐ *Yes* ☐ *No*
    • Organisms and cells
    • Life and ecosystems
    • Heredity and evolution
23. I want to refine my mastery of one or more of the following concepts of earth and space sciences. ☐ *Yes* ☐ *No*
    • The universe and our solar system
    • The Earth
    • Humans and the Earth
24. I want to refine my mastery of one or more of the following concepts of physical sciences. ☐ *Yes* ☐ *No*
    • Atoms and molecules
    • Reactions
    • Forces
    • Energy and heat
    • Waves

Road Map

• If you answered *Yes* to question 22, complete Chapter 26 and all or the relevant parts of Chapter 27.
• If you answered *Yes* to question 23, complete Chapter 26 and all or the relevant parts of Chapter 28.
• If you answered *Yes* to question 24, complete Chapter 26 and all or the relevant parts of Chapter 29.
• Even if you answered *No* to any of questions 22 through 24, we recommend that you complete Chapter 26, as well as the drills in Chapters 27 through 29.

SELF-ASSESSMENT: MY SCORE GOALS

25.   My goal is to achieve a *Passing/CCR* score.

Road Map

- If you answered *CCR*, we recommend that you complete all chapters in this book, without regard to the Road Maps.

After you have completed the chapters according to your Road Map, you should take the second practice test. If the test indicates areas on which you should try to further improve, revisit the appropriate chapters.

Also, remember that you have access to other resources as described on page 19.

If you follow the steps outlined above, are diligent in your work, and assess your progress throughout your preparation, by the time you sit for the TASC test, you should find it familiar and manageable, and you should be able to take it with confidence!

When you register your book online at **Princeton-Review.com/cracking**, you can download and print out Practice Test 2 and its answers and explanations. Custom answer sheets for both tests are also available.

Chapter 2
All About the
TASC Test

This chapter will summarize the structure, scoring, and look and feel of the TASC test, and provide important information about other available resources.

WHAT IS THE TASC TEST ASSESSING SECONDARY COMPLETION™?

The TASC test is a high school equivalency test created by McGraw-Hill Education CTB, in partnership with several U.S. states that have decided to use the TASC test. The test is made up of five sub-tests, one each in Reading, Writing, Mathematics, Social Studies, and Science. The test was gradually changed between 2014 and 2016 to reflect the Common Core State Standards. The book you are holding comprehensively addresses how those standards are reflected on the TASC test, based on the information available at the time of publication. To ensure you have the most up-to-date information, please access the online content available when you register this book and utilize the other resources noted on page 19.

Three test assessments are given each year. The same test is currently given in two formats: paper-and-pencil and online. A particular test center in your state may offer one or both of these formats. In addition, the test is offered in both English and Spanish. Test-takers with relevant documented disabilities may apply for applicable testing accommodations such as extra time, large print test booklets, and many others.

The cost to take the TASC test is $52. Your state may offer subsidies to offset some or all of that cost.

*Future assessments may be offered only online. Check your Online Tools or **TASCtest.com** for updates.*

What Is a Passing Score?

To pass the TASC test, you must obtain a passing score of 500 on each of the five sub-tests, as well as a score of at least 2 out of 8 on the essay portion of the Writing test. According to the TASC test website, a passing score reflects "a level of knowledge and skill that meets or surpasses approximately 60 percent of graduating high school seniors."

If you have taken the old GED® test, check to see whether your state still honors your scores. If so, you may not need to pass every TASC sub-test but rather only the subjects that you did not pass on the GED® test.

The sub-test scores are based on the number of questions you answer correctly. No points are deducted for wrong answers, so be sure to record an answer to every question, even if you are making a guess. The range of possible scores is 300 to 800. Your essay will be graded on a scale from 0 to 4 by two graders. Those two scores will be added if they are the same or differ by one. If they differ by more than one, the essay will be graded by a third person.

You must take the entire TASC test in one sitting.

If you do not pass one or two of the sub-tests, you may retake that or those sub-tests for free within the testing year. If you need to retake additional sub-tests, the cost for each such test is $10.40. We are confident, though, that you will not need to retake any of the sub-tests if you use this book to its fullest extent!

The TASC test creators are developing a College and Career Readiness (CCR) score for each sub-test. Those who achieve this higher threshold for a particular subject are predicted to earn at least a C grade in a college course for credit in that subject. For updated information on the status of the CCR, check your online content or visit **TASCtest.com**.

How Is Each Sub-Test Structured?

1. **Reading Literacy**
   75 minutes (English), 80 minutes (Spanish)

   Number of questions and format
   - 48 computer-based or 49 paper-based multiple-choice questions
   - One constructed-response (open-ended, not multiple-choice) item
   - One technology-enhanced item (on computer-based test only; for example, drag-and-drop answer choices rather than traditional multiple choice answers)
   - Up to eight passages

The questions relate to informational texts (70%) and literary texts (30%). Informational texts are drawn from literary nonfiction, history/social studies, science, technical texts, and workplace and community texts. Literary texts are drawn from novels, poetry, and drama.

Questions will test your understanding of what the passage says (comprehension), your examination of how and why details are used (analysis), your ability to transfer ideas from one context to another (application), and your ability to put ideas together to understand a larger meaning (synthesis). Specific question areas include key ideas (30%), craft (30%), integration of knowledge (30%), and vocabulary acquisition and use (10%).

As of the time of this book's publication, there was limited information on the nature of the constructed-response and technology-enhanced items. For the latest updates, please check your online content for supplementary tutorials on these question types.

You can also check out the online demo of the tech-enhanced questions at **TASCtest.com/ preparing-for-tasc- test-for-test-takers. html**

2. **Writing**
    105 minutes, including 45 minutes for essay writing (English)
    110 minutes, including 45 minutes for essay writing (Spanish)

    Number of questions and format
    - 50 computer-based or 51 paper-based multiple-choice questions
    - One constructed-response item
    - One technology-enhanced item (computer-based)
    - One writing prompt based on two passages

Section 1 of the Writing sub-test is Language Use and Conventions. Questions relate to writing (15%), grammar usage (30%), capitalization/punctuation/spelling (25%), and knowledge of language (30%). Texts are drawn from how-to documents, informative writing, and workplace correspondence.

Section 2 is the Writing Essay. It is scored on a scale of 0 to 8 based on clarity of expression; clear and strategic organization; complete development of ideas; and sentence structure, punctuation, grammar, word choice, and spelling.

3. **Mathematics**
   50 minutes for Section 1; 55 minutes for Section 2 (English)
   55 minutes for Section 1; 60 minutes for Section 2 (Spanish)

   Number of questions and format
   - 42 computer-based or 43 paper-based multiple-choice questions
   - 11 gridded-response items
   - One constructed-response item
   - One technology-enhanced item (computer-based)

Both sections test the following mathematical concepts: numbers and quantity (13%), algebra (26%), functions (26%), geometry (23%), and statistics/probability (12%). Section 1 permits a calculator, while Section 2 does not. You will receive a page of mathematical formulas to use during the test (this reference sheet is available online at **http://ctbassessments.com/pdfs/TASCTest_MathRefSheet.pdf**).

The test focuses on your ability to select and apply math procedural skills, recognize and apply math concepts and principles, and use strategies to solve problems and judge the reasonableness of solutions.

The test writers recommend the *TI-30XS calculator* for Section 1. If you are using a different calculator, ensure that it has trigonometry and logarithm functions and that it does not have graphing or programming capabilities.

Visit **TASCtest.com/ tasc-test-calculators- for-test-takers.html** for a list of other approved calculators.

4. **Social Studies**
75 minutes (English), 80 minutes (Spanish)

Number of questions and format
- 48 computer-based or 49 paper-based multiple-choice questions
- One constructed-response item
- One technology-enhanced item (computer-based)
- Passages, charts, graphs, and illustrations

Questions relate to
- U.S. History (25%), including the Civil War and Reconstruction (1850–1877), the development of the industrial United States (1870–1900), and post-war United States (1945–1970s)
- World History (15%), including the age of revolutions (1750–1914), a half century of crisis and achievement (1900–1945), and the 20th century since 1945 (promises and paradoxes)
- American Civics and Government (25%)
- Geography (15%)
- Economics (20%)

Questions will test your understanding of what you read (comprehension), your ability to transfer ideas from one context to another (application), your examination of the logical structure of ideas and drawing conclusions from various types of data (analysis), and your judgment of fact versus opinion and the reliability of information (evaluation).

5. **Science**
   85 minutes (English), 90 minutes (Spanish)

   Number of questions and format
   - 48 computer-based or 49 paper-based multiple-choice questions
   - One constructed-response item
   - One technology-enhanced item (computer-based)
   - Paragraphs, graphs, maps, tables, figures, and charts

Questions relate to
- Physical sciences (36%), including matter, motion and stability, energy, and waves
- Life sciences (36%), including structures and processes of molecules and organisms, ecosystems, heredity, and evolution
- Earth and space sciences (28%), including Earth's place in the universe, Earth's systems, and Earth and human activity.

Questions will test your understanding of what you read (comprehension), your use of information in a concrete situation (application), your exploration of relationships among ideas (analysis), and your judgment of the soundness or accuracy of scientific information or methods (evaluation).

Paper-and-Pencil Versus Online Testing

You have likely encountered paper-and-pencil multiple-choice tests before, but even if the TASC test is your first such test, you will become familiar and comfortable with the test format by using this book. Indeed, the in-chapter drills and full-length practice tests are specifically designed to help you achieve a passing (or even CCR) score on the TASC paper-and-pencil test.

You may be curious about the computer-based test, or perhaps it is the only option available to you. While only limited information about the look and feel of the online TASC test was available at the time of publication, the test writers have offered assurances that the computer interface will be easy to use. Please visit the following link for a demonstration of the computer skills needed for the online test: **http://www.brainshark.com/ctb/vu?pi=zCjz6UudQz0z0.**

While the current edition of this book will help you to master the content tested on the TASC test, it is designed to help you become familiar and comfortable with the paper-and-pencil format *only*. We will update your online content as additional information about the computer test is made available, and you may continue to make use of the resources described on page 19.

How Do I Register for the TASC Test—and When Do I Receive My Scores?

If you do not have Internet access, call the CTB Customer Care group at 888.282.0589.

Registration procedures differ by state. Some will use their own systems, while others will use the official CTB system established for the TASC test. To find out what locations are available near you, visit **TASCtest.com/test-center-locations-for-test-takers.html.**

If you take the paper-and-pencil test, scores will load into the reporting system within 10 business days. If you take the computer-based test, your score should load within 24 hours and likely within three hours. Your Candidate Report will include information on what topics you should study if you need to retake any of the sub-tests.

TEST DAY—AND THE NIGHT BEFORE

Good Test Snacks
- Apples
- Energy bars
- Raisins

If you are taking the test in the morning, make sure that you get up early enough to have a good breakfast. Your brain uses more calories than you think, and after several hours of concentration, it is very easy to "hit the wall" when your blood sugar drops. Take a snack with you—the best snacks contain a good balance between protein, fat, and sugar. Most state test examiners give breaks in between the sections of the test, so you will have a chance to eat your snack, go to the bathroom, and walk around to get your circulation moving.

Take a printout of the registration form you received by email. If you didn't get one, call your testing center or CBT Customer Care group at 888-282-0589 to make sure the testing center is expecting you. Dress casually. You are going to be spending a number of hours sitting at a desk and you want to be comfortable. Be sure to dress in layers so you can adjust to temperature changes —the rooms are often colder than you expect. You will need to show two pieces of identification before you are allowed to take the test. A driver's license, social security card, birth certificate, green card, or passport are all acceptable. If you don't have two pieces of identification, be sure to discuss this with your local examiner before the actual test date.

No Cheating!
While cheating may be the furthest thing from your mind, we do want to mention that the testing center has sophisticated equipment to monitor your behavior and ensure that you are taking the test honestly. There are video cameras throughout the room, and the proctors are trained to sniff out suspicious behavior. You could get in serious trouble if you are found cheating on the TASC test.

When one sub-test ends, put it behind you, even if you are disappointed with how you think it went. Most people in the middle of taking the TASC test are not good judges of how they are doing. Besides, if it did go badly, the next test will cover an entirely different topic and be graded separately. Even if you didn't pass one test, you can still pass all the others and have to take only the one test over again.

Finally, be sure to get a good night's sleep the night before. Hopefully, you have prepared over several weeks or even months, and you are feeling confident! Staying up late—or worse, all night—to cram is likely to have a negative effect on your score. If you sleep well, you will be more focused.

OTHER RESOURCES

If you are looking for additional support, here are several resources.

PrincetonReview.com—If you register this book at PrincetonReview.com, you will have access to ongoing updates on the TASC test, including the computer-based question types, as this information becomes available. You'll also find extra practice drills for the most challenging topics, sample essays for the Writing prompts, and "further skills and concepts" content lessons to enhance your understanding of some of the topics covered in this book.

If you're thinking about college, the college section of PrincetonReview.com contains detailed profiles of colleges, ranking lists, and a free dynamic search engine to help you identify your *best fit* college. We also publish several books on colleges that you may find useful.

TascTest.com—The official site for the TASC test provides practice questions for each of the five sub-tests. You may find these at **TASCtest.com/practice-items-for-test-takers.html.**

In addition, you will find links to other useful pages, such as a resources page, a blog, detailed guidelines for essay scoring, a demonstration of the computer interface for online testers, and other information, at **TASCtest.com/preparation-materials-for-test-takers.html.**

Finally, if you have any questions that are not answered elsewhere, you may call or email TASC Test Customer Support at 888-282-0589 or **TASC_Helpdesk@cbt. com**, respectively.

Need more practice? Try our online drills!

The TASC test, the GED® test, and the HiSet® exam are all tests of high school equivalency. No one test is superior to the others. A given state may offer only one of the tests, or more than one. Check to make sure your state offers whatever test you decide to prepare for.

Chapter 3
The Habits
of Effective
Test Takers

In this chapter, we'll show you how to boost your score with key skills designed to maximize your performance.

Taking a standardized test involves more than knowledge. You need to approach the test with strategy and learned skills. Effective test takers adopt certain habits that help to reduce stress and increase points. Here are some suggestions that we've found to be helpful.

1. Answer the Easy Questions First

Depending on your specific skill set and how comfortable you are with the range of difficulty on the test, some questions will be easier for you than others. It's important to remember that within each section, all of the multiple-choice and grid-in questions are worth approximately an equal number of points, which means that getting a difficult question wrong is not going to cost you more than missing an easy question. Likewise, getting a difficult question correct does not give you any more points than getting an easy question correct. You also have the freedom to answer the questions in any order you like. So, to maximize your score, first answer all of the questions with which you are comfortable, and come back to the more challenging problems later. If you are running out of time, it is best to have already completed all of the "easy" problems so you can spend your remaining minutes guessing on the difficult ones.

It may feel more natural to do the problems in the order they are presented. However, you want to be able to see all of the questions on a section and know that you have worked through all of the questions you could in the time allotted. Simply circle skipped questions on the paper test or mark skipped questions on the computer test, and you will be able to find them quickly during your second pass through the section. Do mark an answer on a skipped question, though, in case you don't have time to come back to it later. Remember: **Skip early and skip often.**

2. Use Your Pencil to Stay on Task

Whether you are taking the paper test or computer test, you will have the ability to take notes—either on the test booklet or on a separate sheet of paper. While you are preparing for the TASC test, be sure to use your pencil aggressively.

Keeping your hand moving while you focus on the physical task of writing is an essential way to stay focused on the test itself. If your brain has to communicate with your hand, then it is engaged and active and less likely to be distracted, which can force you to reread a question multiple times.

In addition to keeping your brain focused and on task, writing can help you to stay on target with the techniques presented in this book. Having something to write down, such as a summary of a reading passage or a math formula, may be just the push your brain needs to get it moving in the right direction. That is, writing is not only for math questions. Use your pencil to help you identify key information in passages and other visual items across subjects, spot grammar errors, and eliminate wrong answers.

3. Move On When You Are Stuck

It is inevitable that at some point during the test you will encounter a question that you don't understand, or one that you *think* you understand...but the answer you want isn't an option. Often, the problem is that you have misread the problem or made a small calculation error. Research shows that once you have misread a problem, you are likely to keep reading it in the same way, no matter how many times you try. Meanwhile the clock is ticking, and you aren't getting any closer to an answer. If you get stuck, the best thing to do is to skip the question for now and move on. Distracting your brain by doing other problems is often just what you need in order to come back and read the problem with fresh eyes. And when you do come back to skipped problems, you may find them easier than you thought—or you may realize that in the given time left, you were better off guessing.

4. Pacing

Many wrong answers are the result of simply going too fast and reading too quickly. However, most test takers feel they have to rush through the "easy" problems because they won't have time on the more difficult ones. Try a few questions untimed, and you will make fewer mistakes. You'll also probably work more quickly than you think. The questions don't get harder when you add a timer, but somehow, test takers tend not to score as highly.

The trick is to take the TASC test at an even pace, recognizing when a question is more difficult and should be saved for later. Work for accuracy, because doing all the problems will not get you a higher score unless you do them correctly. Slow down and make sure that you are (a) choosing to do the questions you understand first and (b) giving them enough time, attention, and focus to answer them correctly. If you run into a question that feels like a brick wall, move on to an easier question.

The only exception to this rule is in the last few minutes of any section. This is the time to quickly complete any remaining questions, revisit skipped questions if you have time, and ensure that you have left nothing blank.

Eliminate the Out-of-Scope Answers

Q: What's the capital of Malawi?

A Paris
B Dukhan
C London
D Lilongwe

Turn the page for the answer.

In each sub-test of the computer-based version, one question may look different—for example, an interactive "drag-and-drop" question—but you can still guess from the given options! You can even guess on math grid-in questions; although the odds of gaining a point are low, leaving a question blank can't ever help.

5. Guessing and Process of Elimination

The TASC test does not penalize you for an incorrect answer; there is never any deduction for getting a question wrong. So regardless of whether you know the answer to any given problem, it is to your advantage to record an answer to every problem. Thus, guessing on problems that you don't know how to solve, or that you don't have time to work through, can actually add points to your score.

Pick a "Guess Letter"

If you had a one-in-four chance to win $10 (and entering didn't cost you anything), you would enter, right? The multiple-choice questions on the TASC test are very much like that $10 chance. On any single multiple-choice question your chance of correctly guessing is 25 percent, but if you randomly guess a different answer for each question, those odds probably won't add up to as many points as you had hoped. However, if you choose the same answer for every multiple-choice question on which you randomly guess, you are likely to get one in four of the answers correct. Those are pretty good odds, and simply choosing a consistent "guess letter" can improve your score.

But what if you could increase your odds even more?

Process of Elimination (POE)

For questions that stump you, try using a technique we call Process of Elimination, or POE, to help you guess more accurately. Oftentimes it is easier to spot incorrect answer choices than to know the correct answer. To use this technique, first read all of the possible responses, even if you think you know the answer right away, just to make sure you aren't missing something. If no answer choice is clearly correct, eliminate as many as you can by actually crossing them off in the test booklet, and then consider those that seem the most likely. After you have eliminated as many as you can, select an answer from the remaining choices. Every time you get rid of one answer choice, the odds of selecting the correct answer go up significantly.

Try the following question:

1. **Read the list in the box. Then answer the question that follows.**

> - **Long summer days and winter nights**
> - **Cold climate**
> - **Sparse vegetation**
> - **Home to oldest known rocks on Earth**

Which country is described by the list in the box?

You don't know? The good news is that the TASC test would never ask such a question. Or rather, if it did, you would be given a reading passage in which the answer could be found. The purpose of this example question is to show what you can do if you have a few extra seconds to add to your guessing on a multiple-choice question.

If this were a fill-in-the-blank question, and you did not have time to read the passage, you would have to guess, but the likelihood of your getting it correct would be very small. Now, consider the same question in multiple-choice format.

1. **Read the list in the box. Then answer the question that follows.**

   > - **Long summer days and winter nights**
   > - **Cold climate**
   > - **Sparse vegetation**
   > - **Home to oldest known rocks on Earth**

   Which country is described by the list in the box?

   A United States of America

   B Greenland

   C Mexico

   D Croatia

Now the question looks a little easier, right? You know that all of America doesn't satisfy all the items on the list, so you can eliminate (A). You also know that Mexico is south of the United States. Even if you don't know a lot about Mexico, you probably are aware that it is not a cold climate, so you can eliminate (C) too. You may not know much about Croatia or Greenland, but at least you were able to narrow the answers down to two. This leaves you with as fifty-fifty shot at getting the right answer! While process of elimination may not guarantee a correct answer, you should embrace anything that improves your guessing odds on hard questions.

Try one more.

2. **There are 10 students in a class, and their average score on a test is 79 out of 100. If a new student is added to the class, what is the minimum score he would need to achieve in order to bring the class average up to 80 out of 100?**

   A 1

   B 79

   C 85

   D 90

This problem may seem fairly complex to figure out. Don't worry if you don't know how to do averages; we will teach you all you need to know in the Mathematics chapters. However, you can understand that if a student's score has to bring up the class average, it would have to be higher than the class average to begin with. With this information you could eliminate (A) and (B), and you would have a fifty-fifty chance of guessing the correct number, which is (D).

Eliminate the Out-of-Scope Answers
A: The capital of Malawi is Lilongwe, but you didn't need to know that to eliminate choices (A) and (C).

6. Let It Go

No one question is that important to your score. If you read a question and aren't immediately sure how to answer it, mark it and move on. Do not spend any time beating yourself up for not knowing how to do the problem, as everyone is likely to find at least some questions they don't know how to do. If a problem is taking too much time to figure out, fill in a guess and move on. Keeping track of how many questions you think you got correct, or getting upset because you think you aren't doing well, can only impact your score negatively. Know that you have made the right decision for your overall score at every stage, and move forward to deal with the next question relaxed and confident.

More Great Books
Thinking about college? Check out our guide books, including *Colleges That Pay You Back, The Complete Book of Colleges,* and *Paying for College Without Going Broke.*

Focus on Your Strengths

Sometimes the questions on this test may seem confusing, especially if you have been away from school for a long period of time. It is important to notice the strengths that you bring to this test; they can help you to achieve the score you are looking for. Implement the six habits to take control of your testing experience. To this foundation, add the preparation and practice from the rest of this book.

By focusing on your strengths, you can maintain the proper perspective. The TASC test is only that—a test. It doesn't measure your worth as a human being. It measures how effectively you have acquired a few skills and how you make use of that knowledge in a timed, stressful situation. Use the test's own limitations to your advantage, and with a little hard work, you can earn your high school equivalency certificate.

Happy studies and best wishes for a successful future!

Part II
Reading

Chapter 4
Reading Overview

In this chapter, we will provide an overview of the Reading portion of the TASC test. In the following chapters, we will explore the specific content areas of this sub-test in more detail.

The Reading Literacy section on the TASC test is 75 minutes long. During that time, you are more likely to encounter informational (nonfiction) texts than literary passages, which is good news if you've ever had to grapple with abstractions, symbolism, and complex language as the clock is ticking. Only 30 percent of the Reading passages will be literary; 70 percent will be informational material, which tends to be more straightforward, with concrete language and clearer presentation.

READING LITERACY AND THE REAL WORLD

The focus on informational material reflects the TASC test's emphasis on the skills required for a career or college. Employees in every industry and at all levels are expected to respond appropriately to the information they receive, and college students need to work with large volumes of information. That's why the reading passages and questions, with their emphasis on informational material, is considered so important in predicting readiness for a career or for college. Therefore, the Reading section is all about critical thinking and active reading—analyzing and questioning the passage as you go through it instead of just passively absorbing what it says. You'll see up to eight passages or sets of passages, and you will need to show not only that you understand the material, but also that you can do something with it—summarize it, find reasoning flaws in it, or make inferences from it, for example. (We'll get into that in more detail when we discuss the types of questions you can expect.) Taking this test gives you a chance to develop and demonstrate critical thinking and analytical skills for potential employers or college admissions officers. The strategies you'll discover as you work through this book will help you prepare, so you'll walk into the testing center knowing what to expect and feeling confident of your abilities.

WHAT KIND OF PASSAGES ARE ON THE READING LITERACY TEST?

The TASC test is intended to test an examinee's ability to understand the information presented in excerpts from newspapers, magazines, novels, short stories, poetry, drama, and business or legal text passages. The Reading test includes both literary and informational texts.

What are they about? Well, informational passages could cover a broad range of topics, as long as they're nonfiction. Such readings are drawn from literary nonfiction, history/social studies, science, technical texts, and workplace and community texts. Literary texts, on the other hand, are drawn from novel excerpts, poetry, and drama excerpts.

WHAT KIND OF QUESTIONS ARE ON THE TEST?

The TASC test is very systematic about the reading skills it assesses, following a detailed set of criteria called the Common Core Readiness Standards (CCRS). So what? So now we know what reading skills the test writers are looking for, which determines the passages they select and the questions they ask. The questions will appear in two formats. Most will be multiple-choice questions, with four choices. As always, Process of Elimination is your friend with multiple-choice questions. If you start by looking for what's clearly wrong, you should find you can eliminate a couple of the choices, and then look for the right answer in the other two—or, worst case, guess at which one is right. By using Process of Elimination to get rid of two of the four choices, you've just increased your chances of making a correct guess to 50 percent instead of the original 25 percent.

> **Where Are the Answers?**
> They're in the reading passages, although they may not always be obvious. You're expected to use your critical thinking skills, analyze the text, dig beneath the surface, and make inferences. Don't draw on your own knowledge and experience; they could lead you astray. Rely only on the information in the passages.

WHAT, EXACTLY, IS TESTED ON THE READING SECTION?

Between the informational and literary texts, there are four main "sub-domains" that are actually being tested:

Key Ideas and Details (30%). This sub-domain requires focus on the main idea(s) and supporting details of a text. You will be expected to know what a text says and be able to determine how those ideas are supported.

Craft and Structure (30%). This sub-domain asks you to pay attention to the structure of a text. This could include the structure of sentences, paragraphs, verses, chapters, or other section. You will also be expected to pay attention to choices the author made when crafting a text, such as the use of literary devices, language choice, and point of view.

Integration of Knowledge and Ideas (30%). This sub-domain asks you to review and critique the success of a writer's argument in a text. You may be asked to do this through comparing and contrasting multiple texts on the same topic or texts that contain a similar theme. This might also require you to cite sources, which we will discuss later in this section of the book.

Vocabulary Acquisition and Use (10%). This sub-domain asks you to identify not only the meaning of words, but also how words are used in a specific context. You may be asked to identify the secondary definition, rather than the primary definition, of words in a certain context.

INFORMATIONAL TEXTS

Use critical thinking skills with the information that fills your own life, too.

Think about it—what do you spend more time reading and listening to in a typical day? News reports, advertisements, political speeches and similar nonfiction material, or literary stories? Nonfiction, right? Life is filled with informational material that you need to deal with in some way (even if only to decide to tune it out), so that's what the TASC test emphasizes. In fact, 70 percent of the reading passages are classified as informational. The critical thinking and active reading skills you'll gain in preparing for the reading passages will help you sort through the informational material that fills your life outside the test, too. With those skills you'll learn to question, identify flaws in reasoning, recognize a legitimate argument when you see it, and, in short, become a wiser, more discriminating consumer of information.

What Kind of Informational Passages Are on the Test?

How about an article explaining how wind turbines work? Or a speech from a company's president outlining the great opportunities for growth—and profit—that lie ahead? Or perhaps the results of a study on which foods are the best choices for good cholesterol?

Since the TASC test aims to measure readiness for career and college, subjects can be drawn from both the workplace and the academic worlds. That's a pretty big target, and indeed, the range of real-world subjects is broad.

From the workplace, you could see letters or ads aimed at customers, corporate policy statements, executive speeches, or community announcements about events the company is sponsoring. From the academic world, subjects focus on science (especially energy, human health, and living systems) and on social studies. Those social studies subjects are built around what's called the Great American Conversation, which includes documents created when the United States was founded as well as later discussions about American citizenship and culture. There, you might see editorials or essays, speeches, biographies, letters written by famous people, government documents, court decisions, or contemporary articles.

Informational texts come from the real world of the workplace and from the fields of science and social studies.

Readings could be in the public domain, which means they're old enough that any copyright has expired and they sport the long sentences and flowery language characteristic of earlier styles of writing. That doesn't necessarily make them too difficult to follow when you put your critical thinking skills in gear. Try this Great American Conversation excerpt, for instance:

Excerpt from *A Defense of the Constitution of Government of the United States of America*

by John Adams, 1786

If we should extend our candor so far as to own, that the majority of men are generally under the dominion of benevolence and good intentions, yet, it must be confessed, that a vast majority frequently transgress; and, what is more directly to the point, not only a majority, but almost all, confine their benevolence to their families, relations, personal friends, parish, village, city, county, province, and that very few, indeed, extend it impartially to the whole community.

⎯⎯⎯⎯⎯⎯⎯◯⎯⎯⎯⎯⎯⎯⎯

That's how people wrote back in 1786. Once you break this long sentence into pieces, skip over the parts that don't make a direct statement, and substitute simpler words in the parts that do, you end up with a pretty straightforward summary: "Even if we say that most men mean well, we have to admit that almost all of them limit their kindness to the people around them." The context should help you take a good guess at the meaning of words that may not be familiar, such as "candor," "benevolence," and "transgress," as well as the unusual meaning of "own." After you've tossed out the extra words and phrases, though, the only one of these words really needed for your straightforward summary is "benevolence," and the pairing of that word with "good intentions" makes its meaning fairly obvious.

What you won't see among the informational readings are objective, neutral passages that simply describe or explain something, such as you'd find in an encyclopedia or a product instruction manual. The TASC test's informational passages are more complex than that. They will have a "voice"—an author with a specific point of view and purpose. The author might be trying to persuade readers to boycott a particular company, for instance, or the author may be giving a speech criticizing a new government policy. These passages will draw on your analytical and critical thinking skills to discover not only the author's purpose but also what techniques the author uses to support a position, what assumptions the author has made, and whether the argument is logical and sound.

> Informational passages are written by an author who has a specific purpose and point of view.

How Should I Read Informational Passages on the Test?

First, keep your mind actively engaged with the passage and second, think critically instead of simply accepting the passage at face value.

While you may not have time for full-blown active reading strategies, you'll still need to use them (and your scratch paper) to some extent in order to seize control of the passage and make it give you what you need, instead of letting the passage run the show. You're on a mission—you have questions to answer in a limited amount of time—and passively absorbing (or worse, skimming through) the passage will only force you to keep going back and rereading it.

How do you read actively? In a nutshell, keep asking questions and looking for specific things as you go through the passage. Hunt for the flaws and gaps that weaken an argument; recognize the strong support and smooth organization that strengthen it. When you read each section or paragraph, summarize quickly, in your own words, what it's saying.

You'll need to do a lot of this in your head—that's about all you have time for—but you can scribble a couple of words to capture a main idea, or a one-word-per line list of what happens first, second, and so on. You won't need to get far into the passage before you'll know what's important. For many people, just writing something down helps them remember, even if they don't look at their scratch paper again, and searching for words that would be important enough to jot down can force you into active reading mode. You can try using this technique with the drills and practice tests in this book and online to see how much it helps you.

Using scratch paper can remind you to read actively and help you take control of the passage.

> **Questions to Ask As You Read Informational Passages**
>
> - What does the author want readers to do or to think after they read this?
> - Who is the intended audience?
> - What is the author's main point?
> - How, and how well, is the main point supported?
> - Does the author have an obvious bias or point of view?
> - What assumptions does the author make?
> - What is the author's tone?
> - Is the author's reasoning logical?
> - Is the piece complete, or does it leave unanswered questions?
> - Are the language and sentence structure appropriate for the audience and for the time in which the author was writing?

Answering those questions as you read will put you in command of just about any informational piece, whether it's from a workplace or an academic context. Then you can start cracking the questions.

Putting It All Together

Let's go through a couple of examples that will help you practice reading actively and approaching the different question tasks.

Excerpt of a CD Review

from Soul Blues *Magazine*

1   Even by genre standards, Texas bluesman Sam "Lightnin" Hopkins released a stupefying amount of material during his lengthy career. As a guitar player, he was never what one would call a perfectionist: few of his recordings are free of off-notes or mis-fretted chords, and he had no compunction about putting out version after version of the same song, either under the same or different titles.

2   For such reasons, many fans feel that Hopkins is better served by "Best of" compilations than by individual albums. But how is one to choose which tracks to include on a compilation CD, when there is such a surfeit of material? How can one select the best, say, "Mojo Hand," when there are 30-odd recordings of it floating around? Seemingly every time he sat down to record, he'd do another run through of "Mojo Hand." Every time he recorded the song he played it a little differently: each has its recommendations, each its shortcomings. And every one of those takes has been released at some point over the years.

3   Since so many versions of the song were released, none sold appreciably better than the others—making "popular acclaim" a moot point. No particular recording can be called a "Greatest Hit," even though the song itself is probably his best-known composition.

4   So, when it's time to put out another "Lightnin" Hopkins compilation CD, that means it's time to decide upon a "Mojo Hand" to include on it.

5   It would seem that all the intrepid compiler can do is choose one version of "Mojo Hand" that is just as good as (although admittedly no better than) many others … and then do the same for "Katie Mae," and again for "Lightnin's Boogie," and on and on … thus rendering any purported "Best of" album less representative of Sam "Lightnin" Hopkins than of the person putting it together.

6   So it is with this most recent album: the song titles are there, and a fan finds few surprises among them. But do you need this album? Do you need these particular versions, culled from various sessions spanning five decades? Do you need yet another "Lightnin" Hopkins CD titled—you guessed it—MOJO HAND?

Let's look at how to read this passage actively by asking yourself questions as you go through it.

What does the author want readers to do or to think after they read this? The overall impression, by the time you reach the end of the review, is summed up in the question, "do you need this album?" (paragraph 6). The author wants readers to understand that, if they already have a selection of "Lightnin" Hopkins's huge roster of albums, they probably don't need this one, too.

Who is the intended audience? You can tell by the casual tone, lack of musical terminology (except for "mis-fretted chords" in paragraph 1) and absence of background information on the singer or the songs mentioned that the reviewer is writing for people who are probably not professional musicians but who are familiar with Hopkins' work.

What is the author's main point? That's in the references to the number of versions of a song Hopkins habitually recorded, and in the conclusion that so many versions makes "any purported 'Best of' album less representative of Sam 'Lightnin' Hopkins than of the person putting it together" (paragraph 5).

How, and how well, is the main point supported? The difficulty of compiling a truly representative "Best of" album is well supported. The author says that Hopkins "had no compunction about putting out version after version of the same song" (paragraph 1) and that "each [version] has its recommendations, each its shortcomings" (paragraph 2). There is no objective yardstick for selecting what to include, leading to subjective decisions by the person making the selections.

Does the author have an obvious bias or point of view? The author clearly thinks Hopkins was sloppy in creating his body of work ("few of his recordings are free of off-notes or mis-fretted chords, and he had no compunction about putting out version after version of the same song" (paragraph 1).

What assumptions does the author make? The lack of background information about the artist and the songs mentioned reveals an assumption that readers are already familiar with Hopkins' work.

What is the author's tone? You can tell from opinions such as "never what one would call a perfectionist" (paragraph 1) and "all the intrepid compiler can do is choose one version of 'Mojo Hand' that is just as good as (although admittedly no better than) many others" (paragraph 5) that the author is critical of both the singer's careless approach and the objective of creating a "Best of" compilation.

Is the author's reasoning logical? Yes; the author builds a logical chain of reasoning from too many versions of a song, with none standing out as superior, to a compilation that relies on the subjective opinions of an unknown compiler and is therefore of questionable value in representing the best of an artist's work.

Is the piece complete, or does it leave unanswered questions? Since the author places so much weight on the person selecting which version of each song to include, it would be helpful to know who actually made the compilation. Was it someone who had followed Hopkins' career for a long time? Someone who is well versed in that genre of music?

Are the language and sentence structure appropriate for the audience and for the time in which the author was writing? Yes; the language is appropriate for an educated audience well versed in this genre of music but not professional musicians. The sentence structure is contemporary and varied, making the piece interesting to read.

LITERARY TEXTS

These passages should keep your interest up if you're not the type of person who prefers the real-world grounding of informational passages. The literary selections are more fanciful, imaginative, and for some people, easier to read. On the other hand, though, fictional passages leave a lot more scope for complexity—flashbacks, dream sequences, raving mad narrators, multiple layers of meaning—and can challenge your active reading and critical thinking skills more than informational passages drawn from the real world.

What Kind of Literary Passages Are on the Test?

From the modern era or from an older time, with lots of dialogue or with paragraphs of lengthy descriptions—you could find it all in the literary selections. These passages don't fall into clear categories as the informational passages do. What the literary selections have in common is good storytelling—a strong plot line and well developed characters—and the use of literary elements such as imagery and rich language. Beyond that, though, it's the Wild West and you could encounter just about any topic or type of literature. Like the informational passages, they may represent earlier eras when different styles of writing—such as the long, intricate sentences of Victorian novels—were common. Take a look at this one, for instance:

Excerpt from *The Pickwick Papers*

by Charles Dickens, 1837

They had no sooner arrived at this point, than a most violent and startling knocking was heard at the door; it was not an ordinary double-knock, but a constant and uninterrupted succession of the loudest single raps, as if the knocker were endowed with the perpetual motion, or the person outside had forgotten to leave off.

Yes, that's all one sentence and yes, essentially it just says "someone kept banging on the door." Early Victorian writers were not known for getting straight to the point, though, and this lengthy description adds vivid images of sight and sound that a modern version would lack. So while literary passages can indeed be filled with complex layers, they can also (as in this example) be simple, written in a style that's completely in keeping with the writer's era. The active reading technique of summarizing in your own words will help you see the difference between real complexity and writing styles that may look complex but really aren't.

Greater length can also lead to more complexity, though. Now there's room for things like flashbacks, knocking events out of sequence, or for different levels of meaning. (For instance, when is a house a place to live and when does it symbolize a particular culture's claim to a stretch of land?)

Even though literary passages tell interesting stories, you still need to read them actively and think critically about them on the test.

Consider this brief excerpt, drawn from a literary source that is classified at a level appropriate for grades 9 and 10:

Excerpt from *Candide, Or The Optimist*

by Voltaire

1   The French captain soon saw that the captain of the victorious vessel was a Spaniard, and that the other was a Dutch pirate, and the very same one who had robbed Candide. The immense plunder which this villain had amassed, was buried with him in the sea, and out of the whole only one sheep was saved.

2   "You see," said Candide to Martin, "that crime is sometimes punished. This rogue of a Dutch skipper has met with the fate he deserved."

3   "Yes," said Martin; "but why should the passengers be doomed also to destruction? God has punished the knave, and the devil has drowned the rest."

———————————○———————————

Even from this short exchange, you can guess that something more is going on than the simple sinking of a ship in battle. There are indications of much broader concepts of justice, retribution, and good and evil. You can expect layers of meaning like that in many of the literary passages.

How Should I Read Literary Passages on the Test?

You can't just relax and soak up a story the way you can when you're reading a novel for entertainment. You're taking a test and need to seize control and shake the right answers out of the passage. That means active reading again. The questions to ask yourself as you go through the passage will be different than they were for informational texts, though.

> **Questions to Ask As You Read Literary Passages**
>
> - What's happening?
> - Who are the main characters?
> - Who is telling the story?
> - What is the setting?
> - What is the mood?
> - Who is the intended audience?

Putting It All Together

Let's work through a couple of examples that will help you practice reading actively and approaching the different question tasks in literary passages.

Excerpt from *The Necklace*

by Henri Albert Guy De Maupassant

1   One evening, her husband returned home with a triumphant air and holding a large envelope in his hand. "There," said he, "here is something for you."

2   She tore the paper sharply, and drew out a printed card which bore these words: "The Minister of Public Instruction and Mme. Georges Ramponneau request the honor of M. and Mme. Loisel's company at the palace of the Ministry on Monday evening, January 18th.

3   Instead of being delighted, as her husband had hoped, she threw the invitation on the table with disdain, murmuring, "What do you want me to do with that?"

4   "But my dear, I thought you would be glad. You never go out, and this is such a fine opportunity. I had awful trouble to get it. Everyone wants to go; it is very select, and they are not giving many invitations to clerks. The whole official world will be there."

5   She looked at him with an irritated eye, and she said, impatiently, "And what would you want me to wear?"

6   He had not thought of that; he stammered. "Why, the dress you go to the theater in. It looks very well to me." He stopped, distracted, seeing that his wife was crying. Two great tears descended slowly from the corners of her eyes toward the corners of her mouth. He stuttered, "What's the matter? What's the matter?"

7   But, by a violent effort, she had conquered her grief, and she replied, with a calm voice, while she wiped her wet cheeks, "Nothing. Only I have no dress, and therefore I can't go to this ball. Give your card to some colleague whose wife is better equipped than I."

8   He was in despair. He resumed "Come, let us see Mathilde. How much would it cost, a suitable dress, which you could use on other occasions, something very simple?"

9   She reflected several seconds, making her calculations and wondering also what sum she ask without drawing on herself an immediate refusal and a frightened exclamation from the economical clerk. Finally, she replied hesitatingly, "I don't know exactly, but I think I could manage it with four hundred francs."

10   He had grown a little pale, because he was laying aside just that amount to buy a gun and treat himself to a little hunting vacation with several friends. But he said "All right. I will give you four hundred francs. And try to have a pretty dress."

This passage is rich in the development of characters, undertones, and unstated implications. Did you pick up those characteristics as you were reading through it? Let's explore the active reading questions for literary passages to find some clues to what's going on under the surface. To sharpen your active reading skills, note your answer on some scratch paper (or at least *think* of your answer) before you read the one below the question.

Summarize in your own words by answering the classic news questions: who, what, when, where, why, and how?

What's happening? Imagine a friend comes up to you and asks, "What are you reading"? "A book," you answer helpfully. Not satisfied, your friend goes on, "What's it about"? Ah, now we're getting to the heart of this active reading question: a summary of the passage. If you can summarize it in your own words—ideally as you're reading it, not just after—then you're in control. A good place to start is to answer as many as possible of the classic news reporter questions: who, what, when, where, why, and how? In this passage, a man is bringing his wife an invitation to a social event. That's on the surface. However, there are many indications that more is going on under the surface: the wife's unhappy reaction to receiving such an invitation, for instance, and the husband's emotional reaction to the request for four hundred francs to buy his wife a dress.

Who are the main characters, and what do we know about them? There are two in this passage, and they reveal a great deal about the passage's undertones. The husband, M. Loisel, appears as a simple, well-meaning husband who is eager to make his wife happy. We learn later on that he may not be as economical as his wife thinks, as he is saving money for his own selfish interests. His wife seems a great deal less eager to please her husband; she meets his initial offering of the invitation with cold rejection. Mathilde then goes on to prove herself calculating, although sensitive to the economic constraints of their family, when selecting a value to request for her new dress.

First-person ("I") narrators may not be reliable or objective in telling their stories.

Who is telling the story? Is it a nameless, faceless, fly-on-the-wall narrator, as in this passage? In that case, the narrator is probably objective and giving a trustworthy account of the action. On the other hand, first-person narrators (the "I" narrators) are always suspect. They could be as objective as the third-person narrator just described, but they could be highly biased or just plain crazy, too. You need to pay close attention to what they reveal about themselves in order to judge whether you can take the story they're telling at face value.

What is the setting? Sometimes the setting (place and time) can add a lot to your grasp of the passage, and sometimes it doesn't reveal much. In this passage, the place does not give too much away. The reader is told in the first sentence that M. Loisel is returning home. However, knowing that this exchange between husband and wife is so cold while in the privacy of their own home, rather than say in a public setting, could indicate how strained their relationship is.

What is the mood? The mood in this passage is tense, reflected on the surface by the unhappiness of Mathilde and the desire of M. Loisel to please her. In other passages, the mood could be lighthearted or neutral; it could add a lot to your understanding of the passage or it might not be very helpful. It all depends on the passage.

Who is the intended audience? You might not be able to guess from the passage; it's not as easy with literary texts as it is with informational pieces. If you *can* get a picture of the intended audience, though, you'll have another layer of insight into the passage. Perhaps it's intended for young readers. That would explain fairly black-and-white characters and straightforward action. Identifying the intended audience may help determine the undertones that may be present in a passage.

OUR APPROACH

In the next three chapters, we'll look at informational and literary reading passages in more detail as we discuss and tackle different question types. You will have a drill at the end of each chapter to try on your own. You can check your work in the Chapter Drill Answers and Explanations supplement, available online.

As you go through the following chapters, you will want to keep in mind the Habits of Effective Test Takers that were covered in Chapter 3. Let's review how they specifically relate to the Reading Literacy test before moving on.

1. Answer the Easy Questions First. There will be a variety of question types on the Reading Literacy test. How difficult the questions are may be determined by the difficulty of the passage, but mostly how difficult a question is depends on you. If you prefer a certain question type over another, such as a detail or evidence question, do those first!

There are several things to keep in mind when it comes to selecting which questions to answer first:

- Look for questions that direct you back to a specific area of the passage. For example:

    "In the final paragraph, what feeling does the author express towards the future?"

    Where will you find the answer to this question? In the final paragraph. What information do you need to find to answer the question? What feeling the author expresses about the future.

- Look for short questions and short answer choices. Usually the less complex the question and answers, the easier it is to at least eliminate incorrect answers.

- Save the general questions for last. It is very difficult to answer questions on the main point, tone, or argument approach of a passage right at the start. Instead, spend time with easier, more detail-oriented questions to familiarize yourself with the passage before going on to the general questions.

2. Use Your Pencil to Stay on Task. It may seem as though reading questions are just about reading a passage and then feeling your way to an answer choice. That's just not true on a standardized test. The reading questions are problems that need solving—active solving. Treat them just like you would a math problem: Rather than keeping all the work in your head, write it down on your scratch paper! Having something to write down, such as a summary of a reading passage, may be just the push your brain needs to get it moving in the right direction.

3. Move On When You Are Stuck. Reading tests can be tough for a variety of reasons: confusing language, an unclear plotline, a dull topic. It is likely that you will encounter a question on the Reading test that you don't feel confident answering. If that happens, skip the question and come back to it. It may be that by reading a little more of the story and answering other questions, that tough question becomes easier to tackle.

4. Pacing. Many wrong answers are the result of simply going too fast and reading too quickly. There is no point in rushing through the easy reading questions—it will be that much more difficult to answer the harder questions later on. Make sure you are taking the time to be careful!

5. Guessing and Process of Elimination. Because reading is a very subjective area of knowledge, some questions may not have clearly correct answers. Sometimes you may not agree immediately with any answer choice you're given. If you are ever stuck, eliminate answer choices that you know must be wrong based on the passage and then guess and move on.

6. Let It Go. No one question is that important to your score. If after you have read a question and reviewed the passage you really can't eliminate a single answer choice on a question, let it go. Do not spend any time beating yourself up for not knowing the answer to a question, as everyone is likely to find at least some questions they are completely unsure of. If a question is taking too much time to figure out, fill in a guess and move on.

Chapter 5
Main Ideas,
Evidence, and
Conclusions

This chapter will focus on three ways in which you'll be expected to identify information in Reading passages on the TASC test. Following the content lessons, we'll give you some practice questions.

All written works, whether informative or literary, are written with the same goal in mind: to convey information to the reader. Authors do this by providing supporting details or evidence for the topic they are writing about, drawing conclusions based on that evidence, and establishing an overall, main idea of the text in the readers' minds. On the Reading test you will be expected to find the evidence, conclusions, and main idea that are written in a passage. In this chapter, we will review how you will be asked about evidence, conclusions, and main ideas and how to find the answers!

FINDING THE MAIN IDEA

This is what we like to call a "helicopter question," because it asks you to take the 10,000-foot view of the passage (or perhaps of one or more paragraphs in it). At first, don't get tangled up in all of the details and supporting points and writing techniques the author has used. When you look out the helicopter window and see them all together below, what overall main idea or theme do they convey?

The main idea is the gist, or the big picture. For example, suppose there's a passage about all the different ways a man is stingy, how he cheats his best friend out of an inheritance, and scrimps on food around the house so badly that his kids go to bed crying from hunger every night. The passage goes on for 50 or 60 lines describing this guy. The main idea is that this guy is an evil, greedy miser. If the passage gives a reason for the miser's obsession with money, you might include that in your mental picture of the main idea: This guy is an evil, greedy miser because he grew up poor. No doubt the passage tells you exactly how he grew up and where (in an orphanage, let's say), and exactly what kind of leftover beans he eats (lima) and exactly how many cold leftover lima beans he serves to his starving kids each night (three apiece), but those are details, not the big picture. Use the details to build up to the big picture.

> In main idea questions, look at the forest, not the trees.

The question will probably then ask you to *do* something with that big-picture overview you've gained—identify the details that support it, for instance, or draw a conclusion by stitching together the main ideas of a few different paragraphs. Whatever task the question sets, your first step is to get a clear view of that main idea or theme.

Finding the main idea is an essential step to understanding the text you're reading. When you are reading to find the main idea, look for answers to the following questions:

1. What is the topic of the passage?
2. What is the most important thing the author says about the topic?
3. Do sentences in the passage either lead up to or support this idea?

Let's go through the following example and try to answer the preceding questions.

Excerpt from *Madam Bovary*

by Gustave Flaubert

1   Meanwhile, in the depths of her soul, she was waiting for something to happen. Like a sailor in distress, she kept scanning the solitude of her life with anxious eyes, straining to sight some far-off white sail in the mists of the horizon. She did not know how it would come to her, what wind would bring it to her, to what shores it would carry her, whether it would be a launch or a towering three-decker, laden with sorrow or filled to the gunwales with bliss. But every morning when she awoke she expected it to arrive that day; she listened to every sound, periodically leapt to her feet with a start and was surprised when she saw it had not come; then, at sundown, sadder than ever, she longed for the next day.

2   Spring came again. She had difficulty in breathing during the first warm days, when the pear trees were blossoming.

3   Early in June she began to count on her fingers how many more weeks were left till October, thinking that the Marquis d'Andervilliers might give another ball at La Vaubyessard. But the whole month of September went by without a single letter or visitor.

4   After the chagrin of this disappointment, her heart was once more left empty, and the series of identical days began all over again.

---

1.   What is the topic of the passage?

   In this passage, the topic is an unnamed woman.

2.   What is the most important thing the author says about the topic?

   Well, the passage says a lot of things about the woman, but the thing that keeps being focused on is how she is *waiting for something to happen* and that she is *sadder than ever* as she *longed for the next day*.

3.   Do sentences in the passage either lead up to or support this idea?

   The rest of the passage is a long description of how she feels while she is waiting, a possible event she is waiting for (that doesn't end up happening), and that in the end *her heart was once more left empty*.

Now that you have seen finding the main idea in action, try it again with another example.

Excerpt from *Waste Burial in Arid Environments*

by the U.S. Department of the Interior—U.S. Geological Survey

1   Accumulation and management of waste is a pressing problem facing the United States today. Improper disposal of hazardous wastes poses a threat to public health and environmental quality. As arid sites increasingly are being sought for disposal of the Nation's radioactive and other hazardous wastes, concern about the potential effect of contaminants on water resources in the arid western United States is being raised. In addition, volumes of locally generated municipal and industrial wastes are increasing because of rapid population growth and industrialization of the region.

2   The suitability of a waste-burial site or landfill is a function of the hydrologic processes that control the near-surface water balance. Precipitation that infiltrates into the surface of a burial trench and does not return to the atmosphere by evapotranspiration from the soil and plants can percolate downward and come in contact with buried waste. Water that contacts the waste can enhance the release of contaminants for subsequent transport by liquid water, water vapor, or other gases.

1. **The author's main purpose in this article is to**

   A   stress that solving the population growth issue will help to decrease waste contamination

   B   discuss the dangers that current waste management approaches pose to water resources

   C   offer a suggestion for a suitable waste disposal site

   D   persuade people to put more time and effort into recycling

Here's How to Crack It

Think about how you would answer those three main idea questions we tried earlier. What is the topic of the passage? Waste and contamination of water resources. What is the most important thing that the author says about the topic? That waste can contaminate our water, which is not a good thing. Do other sentences in the passage lead up to or support this idea? Yes, the author makes it clear in the last paragraph that there are several ways in which harmful contamination can occur. Using POE, (A) can be eliminated since the problem of population growth was not part of the main purpose of this passage; it was merely mentioned. Choice (D) can be eliminated since the author never mentioned recycling. Although the author does discuss the sites generally used for waste disposal, at no point does he or she suggest a site for use, so (C) is also incorrect. That leaves (B), which matches the answers we had for determining the main idea for this passage.

FINDING EVIDENCE AND EXCERPT QUESTIONS

Finding Evidence—Evidence-based questions (a.k.a. specific questions) direct you to a specific place in the passage and ask about your comprehension of the details.

Excerpt Questions—Many specific questions give you an excerpt from the passage with which to work. We call these questions excerpt questions. For excerpt questions there are three things you need to keep in mind:

- Reread the lines in question.
- Keep the main idea of the passage in mind, and use POE whenever possible.
- If you're stuck, go back to the passage and read at least one full sentence before the excerpt and one full sentence after the excerpt.

Keep in mind that a word or phrase you are being asked to define may not have the meaning you would infer from the wording of the question. It is important that you refer to the context if you are at all unsure of the answer.

Take a look at an excerpt question based on the excerpt from the passage below.

Excerpt from *The Methods of Ethnology*

by Franz Boas

During the last ten years the methods of inquiry into the historical development of civilization have undergone remarkable changes. During the second half of the last century evolutionary thought held almost complete sway and investigators like Spencer, Morgan, Tylor, Lubbock, to mention only a few, were under the spell of a general, uniform evolution of culture in which all parts of mankind participated. The newer development goes back in part to the influence of Ratzel, whose geographical training impressed him with the importance of diffusion and migration. The problem of diffusion was taken up in detail particularly in America, but was applied in a much wider sense by Foy and Graebner, and finally seized upon in a still wider application by Elliot Smith and Rivers, so that, at the present time, at least among certain groups of investigators in England and also in Germany, ethnological research is based on the concept of migration and dissemination rather than upon that of evolution.

Read the following excerpt.

[Excerpt] During the second half of the last century evolutionary thought held almost complete sway and investigators like Spencer, Morgan, Tylor, Lubbock, to mention only a few, were under the spell of a general, uniform evolution of culture in which all parts of mankind participated.

[Question] What is the purpose of the list of names included in these lines?

Reread the lines in question. What does this line say about the men listed? Well at the beginning of the sentence, the author states that *during the second half of the last century evolutionary thought held almost complete sway*. The author then follows with a list of these men and says that they *were under the spell of a general, uniform evolution of culture*. Based on this sentence alone, it appears that the list serves as an example of those who were under the spell of evolutionary thought.

Does this match the main idea of the passage? The first part of the passage, in which the men are listed, is discussing the old approach to culture. The rest of the paragraph discusses the newer developments that are occurring, and lists different men as examples of those who are grouped with those schools of thought. Based on the fact that using the men as a list of examples matches the rest of the passage, now would be a time to do some POE!

Try the next on your own.

Excerpt from "Feuerbach: Opposition of the Materialist and Idealist Outlook"

by Karl Marx and Friedrich Engels

The third form of ownership is feudal or estate property. If antiquity started out from the *town* and its little territory, the Middle Ages started out from the *country*. This different starting-point was determined by the sparseness of the population at that time, which was scattered over a large area and which received no large increase from the conquerors. In contrast to Greece and Rome, feudal development at the outset, therefore, extends over a much wider territory, prepared by the Roman conquests and the spread of agriculture at first associated with it. The last centuries of the declining Roman Empire and its conquest by the barbarians destroyed a number of productive forces; agriculture had declined, industry had decayed for want of a market, trade had died out or been violently suspended, the rural and the urban population had decreased. From these conditions and the mode of organization of the conquest determined by them, feudal property developed under the influence of the Germanic military constitution.

2. Read the following excerpt:

> The last centuries of the declining Roman Empire and its conquest by the barbarians destroyed a number of productive forces; agriculture had declined, industry had decayed for want of a market, trade had died out or been violently suspended, the rural and the urban population had decreased. From these conditions and the mode of organization of the conquest determined by them, feudal property developed under the influence of the Germanic military constitution.

According to these lines, how did feudal property come to develop under the influence of the Germanic military constitution?

A Through the German overthrow of the Roman Empire

B Through the decline of trade

C Through the deterioration of many facets of life in the Roman Empire

D Through the barbaric nature of Roman society

Here's How to Crack It

The Germanic military constitution is discussed in the last line of the excerpt. According to this line, it was under this influence that feudal property began to develop. What the question wants to know is how did that come to happen? To answer that, you need to go to the previous lines. So let's reread those lines. In the previous line of the excerpt, the passage states the decline of the Roman Empire and a conquest by barbarians *destroyed a number of productive forces*; the sentence then goes on to list how several areas of life, including agriculture, industry, trade, and population, were decreasing or destroyed entirely. The sentence that introduces the topic of Germanic military influence opens with *from these conditions*, referring to those declined or destroyed areas of Roman life. Choice (A) does not refer to any of these conditions; it refers to a German overthrow of the Roman Empire. Since these lines refer to a gradual decline and a conquest by barbarians, not an overthrow by Germans, this is not the correct answer. Choice (B) does reference one of the declining areas of the Roman Empire, trade, but that is just one small part of the fall of Roman Empire and doesn't account for how a whole new Germanic militarism influence took over. Eliminate (B). Choice (D) refers to the Romans as the barbarians, not the people who conquered their Empire, so that choice is also incorrect. The only choice left is (C), which states that it was due deterioration of many facets of life in the Roman Empire. Since this matches what we read in the lines, that it was that list of conditions that resulted in the Germanic militarism influence, this is the correct answer.

ALMOST-EXCERPT QUESTIONS

Sometimes evidence-based questions are excerpt questions in disguise. They don't provide an excerpt or mention a specific line number, but nonetheless offer clues as to where you can find the answer. Usually there's one word or phrase from the passage that will help:

The author mentions *the guillotine* in order to

In a case like this, just scan the text for the word "guillotine" (conveniently italicized). Then reread the passage—five lines above and five lines below—for the context.

Here's another example:

The colonists consider the trade tariffs unfair because

Now you'll have to scan the text for the word "colonists" or "tariffs." Despite the fact that no excerpt is given, this question is still an evidence-based question, and the answer should be relatively easy to locate in the passage. For these questions there are only two things you need to keep in mind:

- Go back to the passage and read at least one full sentence before the excerpt and one full sentence after the excerpt. Look for clues from the question (lead words, names, dates, italics, and other clues) to help find the right area of the passage.
- Keep the main idea in mind, and use POE whenever possible.

Let's try it out on the following passage and question.

Saving Lives Through Better Design Standards

by the U.S. Department of the Interior—U.S. Geological Survey

1   When the 1989 Loma Prieta earthquake struck, 42 people tragically lost their lives in the collapse of a half-mile-long section of the Cypress structure, an elevated double-decker freeway in Oakland, California. Yet adjacent parts of this structure withstood the magnitude 6.9 temblor—why? The part that collapsed was built on man-made fill over soft mud, whereas adjacent sections stood on older, firmer sand and gravel deposits. Following the collapse, scientists set out instruments in the area to record the earthquake's many strong aftershocks. These instruments showed that the softer ground shook more forcefully than the firmer material—even twice as violently.

2   The collapse of the Cypress freeway, built in the 1950's, emphasized the importance of having accurate knowledge of the destructive forces a structure may face. Before 1932, the strength of ground shaking near large earthquakes had not been recorded. At that time, seismographs were used primarily to record weak motions from distant earthquakes and were overloaded by the intense shaking of large, nearby shocks. In 1932, scientists began to install special instruments to accurately record strong shaking in earthquake-prone regions of the United States. In the 1960's, the number of these instruments totaled only about 100, but it has now grown to more than 3,000. The vast majority are operated by the United States Geological Survey (USGS) and the California Division of Mines and Geology. This expanding network of instruments is yielding large numbers of strong-motion records. The records provide an ever more complete picture of how strong and how varied shaking can be in a large earthquake.

> **The strength of ground shaking near earthquakes was not recorded prior to 1932 because**

In order to answer this question, you will need to go back to the passage to find the answer. What words or phrases in the question help guide you to the right area of the passage? 1932.

Going back to the passage we find 1932 discussed a little over halfway through. Reread those lines:

> Before 1932, the strength of ground shaking near large earthquakes had not been recorded. At that time, seismographs were used primarily to record weak motions from distant earthquakes and were overloaded by the intense shaking of large, nearby shocks. In 1932, scientists began to install special instruments to accurately record strong shaking in earthquake-prone regions of the United States.

The question asked why the strength of ground shaking was not recorded prior to 1932. What does this part of the passage say about that time period?

> At that time, seismographs were used primarily to record weak motions from distant earthquakes and were overloaded by the intense shaking of large, nearby shocks.

So why weren't there recordings of the strength of ground shaking near earthquakes before 1932? Well, the author tells us that the seismographs were *overloaded by the intense shaking of large, nearby shocks* and that they *were used primarily to record weak motions from distant earthquake.* Does this information fit in with the main idea of the passage? Yes, the passage is reviewing historical information regarding earthquakes, as well as the history and importance of the tools used to measure earthquakes. So the answer to this question will match that information.

Try the next one on your own.

Excerpt from *Emma*

by Jane Austen

1   Emma Woodhouse, handsome, clever, and rich, with a comfortable home and happy disposition, seemed to live a wonderful life, and had lived nearly twenty-one years in the world with very little to distress or vex her.

2   She was the younger of the two daughters of an affectionate, indulgent father; and had, since her sister's marriage, been mistress of his house from a very young age. Her mother had died too long ago for her to remember her; and her mother's place had been taken by an excellent woman as governess, who had become much like a mother in her affection.

3   Sixteen years had Miss Taylor been in Mr. Woodhouse's family, less as a governess than a friend, very fond of both daughters, but particularly fond of Emma. Between *them* it was more the intimacy of sisters. Even before Miss Taylor had stopped holding the title of governess, her mildness had hardly allowed her to impose any restraint on Emma. The shadow of her authority over Emma being now long gone, the two had been living together as friends, very mutually attached, and Emma doing just what she liked; highly valuing Miss Taylor's judgment, but directed chiefly by her own.

4   The real evils, indeed, of Emma's situation were the power of her having her own way somewhat too often, and a disposition to think a little too well of herself; these were the disadvantages which threatened to harm her many enjoyments. The danger, however, was at present so unperceived, that they did not by any means seem like misfortunes to her.

3.   **According to the passage, Emma and Miss Taylor's relationship can best be described as**

   A   almost like family

   B   not as strong as Emma's relationship with her sister

   C   that of a pupil and a teacher

   D   more business than friendship

Here's How to Crack It

The question is asking for a description of Emma and Miss Taylor's relationship. Go back to the passage, looking for where Emma and Miss Taylor mentioned near one another. This first occurs at the beginning of the third paragraph. According to these lines of the passage, Miss Taylor, the governess of the family, was *less as a governess than a friend, very fond of both daughters, but particularly fond of Emma*. Since this line states that she is less a governess and more a friend, eliminate (C) and (D) since those answer choices stress the governess aspect of the relationship. The following lines say that *between **them** it was more the intimacy of sisters*. Since *them* refers to Emma and Miss Taylor, it is they who are like sisters, not Emma and her real sister, so eliminate (B). As the passage states that Emma and Miss Taylor have the intimacy of sisters, the correct answer is (A).

SUPPORTING TEXT QUESTIONS

Rather than asking you to choose an answer that is supported by the text of the passage, a question may just give you a statement in the question itself, and ask you to support it with statements straight from the passage. For example:

> **Which of the following statements from the text supports the idea that the Nineteenth Amendment of the United States Constitution was long overdue?**

> **What detail from the text tells you that the polar bears are increasingly endangered?**

The nice thing about these questions is that half of the work is done for you—they are telling you what they want to know! Your job is to just pick the statement from the passage that supports what they want supported.

When you see one of these questions, keep the following steps in mind:

1. Be clear on what you are being asked to support. If you are confused about what the question is you to do, read it again.
2. Check all four answer choices, making sure you can find the statement in the text and connect it directly to the information in the question.

Try it out on the following excerpt.

Excerpt from *Meditations on First Philosophy*

by Rene Descartes

Several years have now elapsed since I first became aware that I had accepted, even from my youth, many false opinions for true, and that consequently what I afterwards based on such principles was highly doubtful; and from that time I was convinced of the necessity of undertaking once in my life to rid myself of all the opinions I had adopted, and of commencing anew the work of building from the foundation, if I desired to establish a firm and abiding superstructure in the sciences. But as this enterprise appeared to me to be on of great magnitude, I waited until I had attained an age so mature as to leave me no hope that at any stage of life more advanced I should be better able to execute my design.

Which of the following statements from the text supports the idea that the author was older when he attempted to rid himself of false knowledge?

You need to be clear on what this question is asking. It is asking you to support that the author was **older** when he tried to **rid himself of false knowledge**.

You need to select an answer choice that supports those above points. You should use the answer choices to help you do this. If an answer choice is not connected to either of these ideas, you should eliminate it.

A The author has had false opinions since his youth.

Does this statement support the fact that the author was **older** when he tried to **rid himself of false knowledge?** No, it is saying the author has had false opinions since a young age. No indication of trying to rid himself of those opinions at an older age in this statement. POE this choice.

B The author believes all of his opinions and knowledge can be called into doubt.

Does this statement support the fact that the author was **older** when he tried to **rid himself of false knowledge?** No, it is saying the author doubts the validity of his opinions and knowledge. There is no reference to age or wishing to rid himself of his opinions. POE this choice.

C The author wishes to build a firm knowledge foundation in the sciences.

Does this statement support the fact that the author was **older** when he tried to **rid himself of false knowledge?** No, it is saying the author wished to build a firm knowledge foundation in the sciences. No mention of age or ridding himself of knowledge. POE this choice.

D The author waited until a mature age so he would be well equipped to build new knowledge.

Does this statement support the fact that the author was **older** when he tried to **rid himself of false knowledge?** Yes! It states that the author wished to build new knowledge, ridding himself of his knowledge, at an older age so he would be prepared for such a task. This is the only answer that connects back to what you were asked to support in the question.

Try this one on your own.

───────────○───────────

Arsenic in Ground Water in Sanilac County, Michigan

by the U.S. Department of the Interior—U.S. Geological Survey

1   **INTRODUCTION—SOURCE OF ARSENIC** Previous studies of ground-water resources in Michigan by the Michigan Department of Community Health (MDCH), the Michigan Department of Environmental Quality (MDEQ), and the U.S. Geological Survey (USGS) indicate that in several counties in the southeastern part of the State the concentrations of arsenic in ground water may exceed the U.S. Environmental Protection Agency (USEPA) maximum contaminant level (MCL) of 50 micrograms per liter [μg/L].

2   **HEALTH EFFECTS OF ARSENIC FOR MORE INFORMATION REFERENCE** The Agency for Toxic Substances and Disease Registry (ATSDR, 1998) Toxicological Profile for arsenic describes some possible health effects of arsenic exposure. Consumption of arsenic doses greater than 60,000 μg/L in food or water can be lethal (ATSDR, 1998). Doses between 300 and 30,000 μg/L may cause stomach pain, nausea, vomiting or diarrhea (ATSDR, 1998). Long-term exposure to arsenic may produce other effects. Arsenic is classified as a known human carcinogen by the USEPA, and it has been linked to skin, bladder, lung and prostate cancer. In addition, non-cancer effects of long-term exposure may include darkening and thickening of the skin (especially on the palms of the hands, the soles of the feet, and the torso) as well as numbness of the feet and hands, anemia or cardiovascular changes. The concentrations of arsenic that result in these long-term effects have not been clearly established.

4.   **What detail from the text tells you that people may die from consuming arsenic?**

A   Doses between 300 and 30,000 μg/L may cause stomach pain, nausea, vomiting or diarrhea.

B   Arsenic has been linked to skin, bladder, lung, and prostate cancer.

C   The levels of arsenic in the ground water in Michigan may exceed EPA standards.

D   Consuming a dose of arsenic greater than 60,000 μg/L may be fatal.

Here's How to Crack It

The question asks for the detail that states people die from consuming arsenic. Since (C) only references that arsenic has been found in Michigan but nothing about health effects such as death, it can be eliminated. Choice (A) does reference negative health effects that result from consuming, but it does not indicate that they would result in death eventually. Eliminate (A). Choice (B) references much more serious health conditions, cancers, which are caused by arsenic, but once again the passage does not actually say that people die from these conditions. Eliminate (B) as well. The only choice that does reference death is (D), which notes that at a certain level arsenic doses can be fatal. Choice (D) is the only choice that directly connects to the question.

DRAWING CONCLUSIONS

Many questions on the TASC test will ask you to draw conclusions. There is no one set type conclusion question—they may ask about the theme or structure, tone, or style of the piece as a whole. They may or may not ask a question about the attitude of a character, the author, or the author's intentions. Take a look at the examples below:

What is the most likely reason for including the information presented in the fourth paragraph?

How do you think Mr. Bennett feels about the change of heart Lizzy has had towards Mr. Darcy?

According to this passage, why might the historian choose to ignore a contributing factor to the Civil War?

Pick an answer only if you can point to the specific place in the text that supports your answer. (If your justification is "I don't know where, but I feel like it's in there," you're probably not choosing the right answer, or you need to look harder in the text.)

If you answer these questions after you answer specific, evidence based questions, you should have a good idea of what the passage is about—you may not even have to go back to the text. Don't worry if you need to consult the passage, however. That's what it's there for.

Let's practice on the following excerpt.

Excerpt from *An Ideal Husband*

by Oscar Wilde

1 LORD GORING: Robert you love your wife, don't you?

2 SIR ROBERT CHILTERN: I love her more than anything in the world. I used to think ambition the great thing. It is not. Love is the great thing in the world. There is nothing but love, and I love her. But I am defamed in her eyes. I am ignoble in her eyes. There is a wide gulf between us now. She has found me out, Arthur, she has found me out.

3 LORD GORING: Has she never in her life done some folly—some indiscretion—that she should not forgive your sins?

4 SIR ROBERT CHILTERN: My wife! Never! She does not know what weakness or temptation is. I am of clay like other men. She stands apart as good women do—pitiless in her perfection—cold and stern and without mercy. But I love her, Arthur. We are childless, and I have no one else to love, no one else to love me. Perhaps if God had sent us children she might have been kinder to me. But God has given us a lonely house. She has cut my heart in two. Don't let us talk of it. I was brutal to her this evening. But I suppose when sinners talk to saints they are brutal always. I said to her things that were hideously true, on my side, from my stand-point, from the standpoint of men. But don't let us talk of that.

Which of the following can be inferred about Sir Robert Chiltern?

This is a VERY open-ended question. A LOT can be inferred about Sir Robert Chiltern. But don't worry! Even though this may seem like it involves a lot of guesswork on your part, the answer will still be based on evidence from the passage.

Hopefully, this is a question we would answer after having answered several specific, evidence-based questions on this passage. But since that isn't the case here, let's go through the passage and note what it tells up about Sir Robert Chiltern:

LORD GORING: Robert you love your wife, don't you?

What do we learn about Sir Robert from this line? That he is married!

SIR ROBERT CHILTERN: I love her more than anything in the world. I used to think ambition the great thing. It is not. Love is the great thing in the world. There is nothing but love, and I love her. But I am defamed in her eyes. I am ignoble in her eyes. There is a wide gulf between us now. She has found me out, Arthur, she has found me out.

What do we learn about Sir Robert from these lines? That he loves his wife, that he cares more about love than ambition, and that his wife has found out something bad about him.

> LORD GORING: Has she never in her life done some folly—some indiscretion—that she should not forgive your sins?

It may not look like it, but we do learn a little more about Sir Robert in these lines. Lord Goring is asking Sir Robert about being forgiven for his *sins*. It seems more and more clear that Sir Robert has done something bad.

> SIR ROBERT CHILTERN: My wife! Never! She does not know what weakness or temptation is. I am of clay like other men. She stands apart as good women do—pitiless in her perfection—cold and stern and without mercy. But I love her, Arthur. We are childless, and I have no one else to love, no one else to love me. Perhaps if God had sent us children she might have been kinder to me. But God has given us a lonely house. She has cut my heart in two. Don't let us talk of it. I was brutal to her this evening. But I suppose when sinners talk to saints they are brutal always. I said to her things that were hideously true, on my side, from my stand-point, from the standpoint of men. But don't let us talk of that.

What do we learn about Sir Robert from these lines? Quite a bit! We know that he thinks his wife is perfect, but also cold and stern. We know that he and his wife are childless. We know that he has said terrible things to his wife.

Let's say you have an answer choice that reads "It can be inferred that Sir Robert has lost the love and trust of his wife." Where would you point to support that answer? You could point to the second paragraph, specifically to lines such as *there is nothing but love, and I love her. But I am defamed in her eyes. I am ignoble in her eyes. There is a wide gulf between us now. She has found me out, Arthur, she has found me out.* We could also point to the fourth paragraph, specifically to lines such as *she has cut my heart in two. Don't let us talk of it. I was brutal to her this evening. But I suppose when sinners talk to saints they are brutal always. I said to her things that were hideously true, on my side, from my stand-point, from the standpoint of men.*

See? There is lots of evidence waiting right there in the passage to help solve conclusion questions. Just be sure you always know exactly where to point to prove your answer.

Try the next passage and on your own.

"Unemployment Cost $3,000,000,000 a Year"

from The New York Times, *1920*

1   Unemployment annually costs this country $3,000,000,000, according to Dr. N. I. Stone, economist and labor manager of the Hickey-Freeman Company, Rochester, whose estimate, based on the figures of the census, was presented yesterday to several hundred economists at a meeting of the American Association for Labor Legislation in the Hotel Astor. Other speakers said that is was obligatory for employers to join with labor and the public to adopt practical means for avoiding the evils of irregular production.

2   Professor Henry R. Seager, formerly Secretary of the President's Industrial Conference, who presided at the meeting, asserted that the passage of the pending Nolan bill by Congress for a national public employment service was one of the first essential steps. Sidney Hillman, President of the Amalgamated Clothing Workers of America, maintained that industry should either guarantee continuous employment or provide for insurance against unemployment, for which the public eventually was compelled to pay. Otto T. Mallery, Executive Secretary of the Pennsylvania Public Works Commission and a member of the Pennsylvania State Industrial Board, said that unemployment and depression would be unnecessary during the coming year.

5.   **According to this article, why should industry be required to provide insurance against unemployment?**

   A   because the lack of unemployment insurance will keep people in poverty

   B   because without it the public eventually pays the cost incurred by unemployment

   C   because the lack of unemployment insurance costs the government over $3,000,000,000 a year

   D   because unemployment can result in depression in future years

Here's How to Crack It

The passage says a great deal about unemployment, but this question is actually asking a very specific question: Why should industry be required to provide insurance against unemployment? Insurance against unemployment is mentioned in the second paragraph, so that is the most likely spot you will find evidence to support an answer choice. The only information we are given in regards to insurance against unemployment is that currently it is the public who must pay for unemployment. This supports (B) as the correct answer. There is no support for (A) since poverty is never mentioned in the passage. Although it may seem as though there is support for (C) and (D) in the passage, be careful! Choice (C) repeats the same amount as what unemployment costs; the passage doesn't state that this is the cost to the government. Choice (D) repeats the word *depression* and references the future as seen in the last line of the passage, but there is no indication in that line, or anywhere else in the passage, that unemployment results in depression. The only possible answer that is supported by the passage is (B).

Main Ideas, Evidence, and Conclusions Drill

Over to you now. Ask yourself the active reading questions as you go through this passage, and make sure your critical thinking skills are in gear. Then try the questions, using your knowledge of the question types we just reviewed (the order of those tasks is mixed up in this drill, as it will be on the test). To check your answers, register your book at **PrincetonReview.com/cracking** and download the Chapter Drill Answers and Explanations supplement.

Directions **Read the text. Then do Numbers 1 through 6.**

Companies use statements of Corporate Social Responsibility (CSR) to explain the values and principles that govern the way they do business, and to make a public commitment to follow them. These documents typically have high-level support from management and the board of directors, and are made available to all stakeholders, from employees to investors, customers to government regulators.

Pine Trail Timber Statement of Corporate Social Responsibility

1   In carrying out our mission to supply the residential construction industry with the highest quality products from sustainably managed sources, Pine Trail Timber adheres to the following commitments to its stakeholders, to the communities in which it does business, and to the environment.

Responsibility to Stakeholders

2   Our stakeholders place their trust in us, and we work every day to merit that trust by aligning our interests with theirs.

3   All employees deserve a safe, supportive work setting, and the opportunity to achieve their full potential. We stress safety training, prohibit any type of discrimination or harassment, and support employees' efforts to enhance their job-related skills. In return, we expect our employees and officers to devote themselves to fulfilling our commitments to other stakeholders.

4   Investors have a right to expect transparency, sound corporate governance, and a fair return on their investments. We pride ourselves on full disclosure, adherence to the most rigid standards of ethical oversight, and a track record of profitable operations, as our rising stock chart and uninterrupted five-year series of dividend increases show.

5   Our valued customers are entitled to exceptional value and service. Our product innovation and wise management of resources ensure that they receive both.

6   Our suppliers rely on us for fair dealing in specifying our requirements and in meeting our obligations. We consider our suppliers to be our partners—when we succeed, they succeed.

7   We meet the expectations of government and industry regulators by complying with all applicable laws of the countries in which we carry out our business operations, and cooperating in all authorized investigations.

8   We fulfill our duty to the media and the public through providing timely information about any events that might have an impact beyond our operations, and making senior spokespeople available on request.

Support for Local Communities

9   We aim to enhance our host communities. Our presence provides training and jobs, and contributes to the local economy.

10   In the field and in our processing facilities, we recognize the impact our activities may have on local groups. We strive for open communication in order to build relationships, and create opportunities for consultation to foster understanding of our plans.

11   In urban centers where we have administrative operations, we match charitable donations made by our employees and run programs that give employees a block of time off work to volunteer with local organizations. Pine Trail Timber routinely forms one of the largest volunteer groups in the annual Arbor Day activities in several countries, planting trees and teaching other participants how to care for them.

Respect for the Environment

12   We recognize that our current and future success depends on the wise use of renewable resources. We value our reputation as a conscientious steward of the lands that furnish our products.

13   All of our production and processing operations worldwide are certified by the Forest Stewardship Council (FSC) as meeting its rigorous standards for responsible resource management. The FSC certification assures our stakeholders and host communities of independent verification of our operations.

14   Through constant process innovation, we aim to make the least possible use of non-renewable resources in our production.

15   We strive to leave the smallest possible footprint and, where necessary, carry out prompt and thorough remediation. After we finish our operations in an area but before we leave, we ensure that the land is returned to a state where it can produce abundant crops, offer a welcoming home for wildlife, and provide outdoor enjoyment for local residents.

We're Listening

16   If you have any questions or comments about our Corporate Social Responsibility commitments, we invite you to contact Mr. Joseph d'Argill, our Chairman and Chief Executive Officer.

1.   **The CSR statement specifies that employees are expected to "devote themselves to fulfilling our commitments to other stakeholders" (paragraph 3) because**

   A   the authors of the CSR statement are worried that they can't take responsibility themselves for the promises they're making

   B   the authors know that stakeholders will usually be dealing with lower level employees instead of with the senior executives and board members who created the CSR statement

   C   the authors want to exert additional influence on employees through this public statement that stakeholders can expect everyone who works for Pine Trail Timber to fulfill these commitments

   D   employees work in many different locations and countries, far from the home office where the senior executives and directors behind the statement work

2. Read this excerpt from the text. Then answer the question.

> Investors have a right to expect transparency, sound corporate governance, and a fair return on their investments. We pride ourselves on full disclosure, adherence to the most rigid standards of ethical oversight, and a track record of profitable operations, as our rising stock chart and uninterrupted five-year series of dividend increases show.

What is the author saying about his company?

A that his company is a good one for people to put their money into

B that the company has more pride than is usually found at other companies

C that investors don't always get what they deserve

D the company tells investors only what they need to know

3. The authors wrote and published this CSR statement because

A government regulations require them to do it

B they want to present a public image of Pine Trail Timber as a responsible, ethical, trustworthy company

C all of their competitors in the forestry industry have one

D they want to explain the company's mission

4. Considering the overall theme of the CSR statement, what conclusion can you draw from the last two paragraphs in the "Responsibility to Stakeholders" section (paragraphs 7–8)?

A The company sometimes fails in its goals of being a trustworthy steward and improving the areas in which it has operations.

B Responsibilities to regulators and to the public are considered less important than responsibilities to employees and other stakeholders.

C The company fosters close relationships with governments and the media.

D There is a strong sense of responsibility to stakeholders who are not directly involved with the company's business operations.

5. What is the most significant contribution made by the mention of Arbor Day (paragraph 11) to the company image portrayed in the CSR statement?

A It reinforces the global nature of the company's operations, since Arbor Day is celebrated in many different countries.

B It supports the company's claim of giving employees time off work to volunteer for charitable activities.

C It would help attract potential employees who want to preserve the environment.

D It demonstrates the company's wise use of resources, since participation in Arbor Day would replace some of the trees the company takes.

6. Which of the following statements from the text supports the idea that the company follows externally set standards?

A The company engages in Arbor Day activities by planting trees and providing instruction on their care.

B The company strives to leave the smallest possible footprint.

C The company aims to use few non-renewable resources production.

D The company is certified by the Forest Stewardship Council (FSC).

Chapter 6
Analyzing Arguments

This chapter will focus on how an author makes his or her case as well as some common logical fallacies to look out for. Following the content lessons, we'll give you some practice questions.

ANALYZING ARGUMENTS (OR REASONING)

Yes, you, the TASC test taker, get to analyze whether the author has done a thorough, reliable, persuasive job of making his or her case. How's that for giving you power and letting you show off your critical-thinking skills?

Analyzing questions ask you to judge the author's evidence, reasoning, or assumptions.

To begin, of course, you need to travel through the passage to create a map of the argument as the author moves from Point A to Point B to Point C to arrive at a final conclusion. Only then will you be able to do what the questions ask you to do with that argument. For analyzing questions, those tasks generally fall into three categories.

First, you could be asked to analyze the evidence the author uses to support claims. Is the evidence trustworthy—the opinion of a well-known expert in the field, perhaps, or the results of a professional research study? Is the evidence directly applicable to the claim, or does it sound good but really not have much to do with the author's point? Does the author provide *enough* evidence to support a claim, or perhaps no evidence at all?

Second, the question might ask you to analyze whether the author's reasoning is sound. Here you're looking for what are called logical fallacies—major flaws in reasoning that may not be apparent until you really think about it. Like rhetorical techniques, logical fallacies come in a long list of creatively named types. In this case, the TASC test writers won't expect you to know those names, but they will expect you to recognize faulty reasoning when you see it.

One logical fallacy you might find familiar is called the slippery slope. Politicians often use it to gain support for their positions by generating fear. For example, "If we allow the Bank of Broad River to refuse loans to any company that hasn't been profitable for the past 10 years, pretty soon all of the banks will be refusing those loans and small business in the state will collapse." The first act is the beginning of a snowballing slide down towards destruction. But wait a minute—who said any other banks would adopt the same policy? What evidence does the author provide to support that claim? The chain of reasoning from one bank's change in policy to the annihilation of small business in the entire state is unreliable.

Third, you might need to dig out the assumptions behind the author's argument and judge whether they're valid. For instance, say a candidate for mayor is trying to persuade voters to support her because her top priority is expanding the mass transit system to reduce traffic gridlock. What are the underlying assumptions? She's presuming that most voters use mass transit or that they even care about it enough to fund it with their tax dollars. She's thinking they would choose mass transit as a solution instead of adding traffic lanes or a new bypass highway. In a large, sprawling city where many businesses and shopping areas are miles away and constructing long rail or subway lines could be very expensive, her assumptions might not be valid. She could just have lost a large group of potential supporters.

Some Common Logical Fallacies

Ad Hominem: If you can't refute the opponent's argument, attack the opponent. An ad hominem fallacy might concede that a prominent scientist's latest published theory "seems to sound promising, but don't forget that this is the author who was suspected of plagiarizing other researchers' work a few years ago."

Appeal to Emotion: In appealing for donations, a charity often tells heartbreaking stories of the people it has helped. But do these emotional appeals perhaps hide the fact that the organization is paying its executive director a huge salary, or that it uses half of the money it raises to pay for more fundraising campaigns?

Begging the Claim: The conclusion that the writer should prove is validated within the claim.

> *Example:* Overly processed, high-calorie foods should be banned.

Arguing that overly processed, high-calorie foods are harmful for a population's health and thus should be banned would be logical. But the very conclusion that should be proved, that processed food causes enough of a health risk to warrant banning its use, is already assumed in the claim by referring to it as "overly processed, high-calorie".

Circular Argument: This restates the argument rather than actually proving it.

> *Example:* Donald Trump is a good communicator because he speaks effectively.

In this example, the conclusion that Trump is a "good communicator" and the evidence used to prove it "he speaks effectively" are basically the same idea. Specific evidence such as using everyday language, breaking down complex problems, or illustrating his points with humorous stories would be needed to prove either half of the sentence.

Either/or: This is a conclusion that oversimplifies the argument by reducing it to only two sides or choices.

> *Example:* We can either stop allowing gun sales or have increased gun violence.

Continued

You won't need to memorize the names of these logical fallacies, but be prepared to recognize them in a text!

Some Common Logical Fallacies—Continued

Hasty Generalization: This is a conclusion based on insufficient or biased evidence. In other words, you are rushing to a conclusion before you have all the relevant facts.

> *Example:* As soon as the credits started to roll, I knew that coming to this movie was going to be a huge waste of time and money.

In this example, the author is basing his evaluation of the entire movie going experience on only the opening credits, which is never the best part of any movie. To make a fair and reasonable evaluation the author should watch more of the movie and read articles or critical reviews in order to have sufficient evidence to base a conclusion on.

Moral Equivalence: This fallacy compares minor misdeeds with major atrocities.

> *Example:* Watching reality TV is like being tortured.

In this example, the author is comparing the relatively harmless action of watching reality TV with the horrific action of torture. This comparison is unfair and inaccurate.

Red Herring: This is a diversionary tactic that avoids the key issues, often by avoiding opposing arguments rather than addressing them.

> *Example:* The level of greenhouse gases produced by coal use may be harmful to the environment, but what will coal farmers do to support their families?

In this example, the author switches the discussion away from the quality of the environment and talks instead about an economic issue, the livelihood of those mining coal. While one issue may affect the other, it does not mean we should ignore environmental issues because of possible economic consequences to a few individuals.

Slippery Slope: In an attempt to persuade people to do (or not to do) something, this technique claims the result of inaction (or action) will be widespread disaster, but doesn't provide evidence to support that conclusion. Wars have been started this way: "If we don't stop this dictator now, he'll take over every country in the whole region."

Straw Man: This technique exaggerates or misstates an opponent's argument so it's easy to knock it down.

> *Example:* Advocates of compact fluorescent light bulbs want us all to die from mercury poisoning in order to save energy.

Analyzing argument questions will not ask directly for you to name these logical fallacies, but you should be prepared to identify them when they appear in text. Questions will ask a variety of things about an author's argument. Here are some examples:

- Why did an author use a certain statement to support an argument?
- What can be inferred from an author's argument?
- How does the author use a specific statement to support his or her argument?

When you are asked about an author's argument, ask yourself the following questions:

- What is the author arguing for or against?
- What exactly does the author say about that topic?
- What proof or statement does the author give to support his or her side?

Let's look at a logical fallacy in action. Read the following excerpt:

Barry Goldwater's Presidential Nomination Acceptance Address, 1964

Now, fellow Americans, the tide has been running against freedom. Our people have followed false prophets. We must, and we shall, return to proven ways—not because they are old, but because they are true. We must, we shall, set the tides running again in the cause of freedom. And this party, with its every action, every word, every breath, and every heartbeat, has but a single resolve, and that is freedom—freedom made orderly for this Nation by our constitutional government; freedom under a government limited by the laws of nature and of nature's God; freedom balanced so that order lacking liberty [sic] will not become the license of the mob and of the jungle.

What is the author arguing for or against? The author is arguing for freedom, arguing that *we must, we shall, set the tides running again in the cause of freedom.*

What exactly does the author say about that topic? At the beginning the author says the *tide has been running against freedom*. In order to get back to freedom we must *return to proven ways.*

What proof or statement does the author give to support his or her side? The only "proof" or support the author offers for why we must return to the proven ways that will bring us back to freedom is *because they are true.*

What logical fallacy does this fall under? This sounds like begging the question, in which the conclusion an author should validate is stated in the claim. Why will the proven ways bring us back to freedom? Because they are true. The very claim that they are true, which is what the author should be proving, is implied in the fact that they are the proven ways we must return to.

Give the following excerpt and question a try on your own.

———————◯———————

The following excerpt is taken from a speech by Huey Pierce Long. Best known for his Share the Wealth campaign, Long served as Governor of Louisiana from 1928 to 1932 and was an outspoken opponent of exploitation and unfair banking practices.

Share Our Wealth

by Huey Pierce Long, 1935

Ladies and gentlemen, it has been publicly announced that the White House orders of the Roosevelt administration have declared war on HUEY LONG. The late and lamented, the pampered ex-crown prince, Gen. Hugh S. Johnson, one of those satellites loaned by Wall Street to run the Government, and who, at the end of his control over and dismissal from the NRA, pronounced it "as dead as a dodo," this Mr. Johnson was apparently selected to make the lead-off speech in this White House charge begun last Monday night. The Johnson speech was followed by more fuss and fury on behalf of the administration by spellbinders in and out of Congress. In a far-away island, when a queen dies, her first favorite is done the honor to be buried alive with her. The funeral procession of the NRA* (another one of these new-deal schisms or isms) is about ready to occur. It is said that General Johnson's speech of Monday night to attack me was delivered on the eve of announcing the publication of his obituary in Red Book Magazine.

* The **National Recovery Administration** was a prime New Deal agency established by U.S. president Franklin D. Roosevelt (FDR) in 1933. The goal was to eliminate "cut-throat competition" by bringing industry, labor and government together to create codes of "fair practices" and set prices.

1. **Read the excerpt:**

> **The late and lamented, the pampered ex-crown prince, Gen. Hugh S. Johnson, one of those satellites loaned by Wall Street to run the Government, and who, at the end of his control over and dismissal from the NRA, pronounced it "as dead as a dodo", this Mr. Johnson was apparently selected to make the lead-off speech in this White House charge begun last Monday night.**

Why does the author mention that Mr. Johnson was dismissed from his position at the NRA?

A to diminish the public's trust in both Mr. Johnson and the White House administration

B to provide the credentials of a presidential selection to a committee

C to point out that he, the author, would be a better fit for giving the speech

D to give as many biographical details in his eulogy as possible

Here's How to Crack It

Remember the three questions to ask. The author is arguing against the current White House administration, saying they have declared war on him. The author also refers disparagingly to the NRA. The author brings up Gen. Johnson specifically, referring to him as a pampered ex-crown prince. He then goes on the mention that Gen. Johnson was fired, which was intended to further demonstrate what a poor choice his appointment by the administration was. This best supports (A); the author is trying to smear the reputation of Gen. Johnson and the White House administration by focusing on these negative facts. He is not merely providing Gen. Johnson's credentials, he is trying to discredit him, so eliminate (B). At no point does the author indicate that he wishes he were the one selected for the speech and job; in fact he seems against the whole situation. Eliminate (C). Although (D) may look like a good answer choice at first since the passage does reference "funeral" several times, there is no indication that the author is providing a eulogy here, making (D) incorrect as well.

The type of logical fallacy used in the speech was ad hominem—attacking an opponent directly rather than the attacking his or her argument. But you didn't have to know the name of it because the question didn't ask for that; you just had to be able to notice it!

Analyzing Arguments Drill

Remember to ask yourself the active reading questions as you go through this passage, and make sure your critical thinking skills are in gear. Then try the questions, using your knowledge of the question types we just reviewed in this chapter and in the previous chapter. To check your answers, register your book at **PrincetonReview.com/cracking** and download the Chapter Drill Answers and Explanations supplement.

Excerpt from "Failing Our Children: Implications of the Third International Mathematics and Science Study"

from the National Science Board, 1998

1   The Third International Mathematics and Science Study (TIMSS) reports disturbing findings about the performance of U.S. secondary school students in science and mathematics, ranking them well below the international average. Together with an array of related national data, the TIMSS results raise serious concerns about the state of U.S. education.

2   No nation can afford to tolerate what prevails in American schooling: generally low expectations and low performance in mathematics and science, with only pockets of excellence at a world-class level of achievement. Formal education has traditionally been the path to productive careers, upward mobility, and the joy of lifelong learning. If we do not arm our children with appropriate tools, we fail them.

3   It is the conviction of the National Science Board that world class achievement in science and mathematics education is of critical importance to our Nation's future. In the new global context, a scientifically literate population is vital to the democratic process, a healthy economy, and our quality of life.

4   The National Science Board urges all stakeholders in our vast grass-roots system of K-12 education to develop a nation-wide consensus for a common core of knowledge and competency in mathematics and science.

5   The TIMSS report and other studies of education practices here and abroad make a compelling case for rigor and depth as essential components of mathematics and science instruction. A clear message of the data is that in-depth study of a few topics within a subject each year yields far better results than the broad, repetitive, superficial coverage of many topics that characterizes current U.S. curricula.

6   For a mobile population, local schools are *de facto* national resources for learning. Students often move several times during their K-12 education, encountering varying curricula and instructional materials that cover an increasing number of topics while sacrificing depth and rigor. Student access to exemplary teachers and support also suffers. Without better coordination across districts and States on common elements in each year of schooling, progress in students' mathematics and science knowledge and skills will not be achieved.

1. **Read the following excerpt. Then answer the question.**

   Formal education has traditionally been the path to productive careers, upward mobility, and the joy of lifelong learning.

   The author includes this line in order to

   A demonstrate that formal education is the only way students learn

   B explain that it is important to keep traditions alive in school

   C stress that formal education has been a fundamental part of becoming successful

   D offer a new solution to a historical problem

2. **Which of the following statements from the text creates a sense of necessity in her argument?**

   A If we do not provide students with what they need, we will fail them.

   B World class achievement in science and math is very important.

   C Students are moving away.

   D America is not alone in its poor testing performance.

3. **The author says students perform poorly on the TIMSS and at science and math in general because of**

   A increased mobility and various curricula

   B unfair testing practices

   C the fact that America is well below average compared to other countries

   D the lack of a clear message in data

4. **Why does the author reference the Third International Mathematics and Science Study?**

   A as an example of how many tests students have to take

   B to compare the U.S. students success to the rest of the globe

   C to discredit the study before others introduce it later

   D to support her argument by providing factual information

5. **What is the author's tone in the passage?**

   A indifferent

   B disturbing

   C authoritative

   D relaxed

Chapter 7
Literary Devices
and How Authors
Achieve Effects

This chapter will focus on literary devices and structure, theme, and language use questions. Following the content lessons, we'll give you some practice questions.

As you just reviewed in the Analyzing Arguments chapter, authors write in order to make a point. They use different types of arguments to make that point, but arguments aren't the only tools that authors have available to them. They have several different ways of using language to help express their ideas. In this chapter, we will review those additional tools and how they come up on the TASC test.

LITERARY DEVICES

Some questions might ask what literary devices the author uses to achieve his or her purpose more effectively. What are literary devices? They're simply tools that writers use, like hammers or wrenches, to get the job done better.

One common literary device is analogy—comparing something to another thing that will be more familiar to readers, in order to help them understand the author's point and increase the chance that they will agree with it. For instance, the passage might explain that "a Hemi engine is more powerful than a flathead engine because the Hemi is designed to minimize heat loss and unburned fuel, in much the same way as a toaster oven is more energy efficient than a full-sized oven."

Another common literary device is repetition. Think of the last ad you saw for a new car. How many times, in how many different ways, did the ad tell you that you would be powerful, free, safe, and environmentally responsible if only you would buy this car?

If you wanted to be an extremist, you could find ridiculously long lists of obscure literary devices (*paraprosdokian*, anyone?). The TASC test, however, is not extremist. The test writers expect you to recognize only a few of the most commonly used literary devices, and you can often guess a device's name just by looking at what it does. Try this one:

> **In your SnoSqual parka, you'll enjoy unmatched protection from the cold, unrivalled flexibility for your gear, and unsurpassed style on the slopes.**

Now the question:

> **The writer creates a positive image and desire for a SnoSqual parka through the use of**
>
> **A** alliteration
>
> **B** parallelism
>
> **C** hyperbole
>
> **D** repetition

Remember Process of Elimination, or POE? You can get rid of "repetition"—the sentence doesn't say the same thing over and over. Check out "Some Common Literary Devices" below, and you'll see that "alliteration" and "hyperbole" are eliminated. So "parallelism" is left, and indeed that's the technique the author uses.

However, you could also have chosen "parallelism" based simply on what the author's description does: It presents the SnoSqual parka's three advantages (warmth, flexibility, and style) in parallel structures (each starting with an "un-" description and ending with a phrase, such as "from the cold," that puts the advantage in context). The end result is a product claim that sounds organized, trustworthy, and appealing, and would advance the author's purpose of making readers want this coat.

Since you don't want to rely on POE by itself, review the list of the most commonly used and tested Literary Devices:

Some Common Literary Devices

Alliteration: creating rhythm through repeating initial consonant sounds. *Example:* "The *store's spectacular sales season* yielded enormous profits."

Analogy: enhancing readers' understanding by comparing two things that have similar features. *Example:* "A jet pump *works much like a drinking straw* in a glass of soda."

Hyperbole: exaggerating a statement to make a point. *Example:* "I've tried *a million* different ways to open the file you sent, but it's broken."

Imagery: Imagery is an author's use of descriptive and figurative language used to create a picture in the reader's mind's eye.

Irony: An expression of meaning that is the opposite of the literal meaning. *Example:* "Here's a pleasant little ditty by Megadeth."

Stories can be ironic as well when they end in a way that is the opposite of what you would have expected. A story about an obsessively clean man who is killed by a garbage truck is ironic. O. Henry's classic story "The Gift of the Magi" is a classic example of dramatic irony. The husband sells his watch to buy his wife an ornate hair comb for Christmas, only to find out that she has sold her hair to buy him a watch chain.

Metaphor: Describing something by saying it's the same as an otherwise unrelated thing. *Example:* "The empty *highway was a ribbon* stretching over the distant mountains."

Parallelism: Stringing together phrases or sentences with similar structures. *Example:* "First push the power button, then select fan mode, and then select the fan speed."

Continued

Some Common Literary Devices—Continued

Personification: Assigning human attributes to something nonhuman. *Examples:* "I hope that fortune will smile on me when I take my exam." "My car always seems so miserable when I let someone else drive."

Qualifying Statement: Toning down what sounds like an extreme statement. *Example:* "That's the worst lasagna I've ever eaten—*since I had Aunt Mabel's lasagna last week*, that is."

Repetition: Stating the same thing in different ways to emphasize a point. *Example:* "A snow shovel with a curved handle *puts less strain on your back*. It *makes shoveling easier* and *minimizes the risk of injury*."

Simile: Adding impact to a description by comparing one thing to another unrelated thing using the word "like" or "as." *Example:* "His stare was *as cold as ice*."

Structure: The framework of a work of literature; the organization or overall design; often provides clues to character and action.

Theme: The central meaning or dominant idea in a literary work; theme provides a unifying point around which the plot, characters, setting, point of view, symbols, and other elements of a work are organized.

Understatement: Making something sound less significant than it really is to achieve an effect. *Example:* "The country has a *minor* trade deficit of $3 trillion."

Literary device questions won't necessary ask you to name a literary device that is being used, but it will reference specific literary devices and ask why they are being used or what effect they create.

Let's take a look at an example. Read the article and question that follow.

"America in the World"

from The New York Times, *1923*

The chief and critical item in the Administration's new statement of its foreign policy is the frank abandonment of the notion that the United States can stand aloof from the rest of the world. "We cannot," declares Secretary Hughes, "dispose of these problems by calling them European." Names do not sway things. "They are world problems," adds the American Secretary of State, "and we cannot escape the injurious consequences of a failure to 'settle them.'" Thus the fond idea of isolation crashes to the earth. America wakes from her two years' dream to find that she is in and of the whole world.

In the last sentence, what is the effect of the author's use of personification?

In order to answer this question, we need to find the author's use of personification in the last line. What is being personified? America. How is America being described? As waking up after dreaming for two years. What point is this making? That America has been asleep, or inattentive, to the matter at hand for the last two years.

Try it on your own. Read the following excerpt and question.

Excerpt from *The Picture of Dorian Gray*

by Oscar Wilde

1   The studio was filled with the rich odor of roses, and when the light summer wind stirred amid the trees of the garden there came through the open door the heavy scent of the lilac, or the more delicate perfume of the pink-flowering thorn.

2   From the corner of the divan of Persian saddle-bags on which he was lying, smoking, as was his custom, innumerable cigarettes, Lord Henry Wotton could just catch the gleam of the honey-sweet and honey-colored blossoms of the laburnum, whose tremulous branches seemed hardly able to bear the burden of a beauty so flame-like as theirs; and now and then the fantastic shadows of birds in flight flitted across the long tussore-silk curtains that were stretched in front of the huge window, producing a kind of momentary Japanese effect, and making him think of those pallid jade-faced painters of Tokyo who, through the medium of an art that is necessarily immobile, seek to convey the sense of swiftness and motion. The sullen murmur of the bees shouldering their way through the unmown grass, or circling with monotonous insistence round the dusty gilt horns of the woodbine, seemed to make the stillness more oppressive. The dim roar of the London was like the bourdon note of a distant organ.

1.   The author includes what in his use of imagery in this passage?

    A   detailed visual description of the anatomy of certain plants

    B   sensory descriptions, including smell, sight, and hearing

    C   a thorough description of Lord Henry Wotton

    D   a review of different cultural styles of art

Here's How to Crack It

This excerpt is filled with description, so this is a very open-ended question—use POE! Although the passage does include information about the plants, different kinds, colors, movement, there is no technical anatomy description. Eliminate (A). Lord Henry Wotton is certainly mentioned in the passage, but he is barely described at all, so eliminate (C) as well. Choice (D) may look good at first glance, but the passage mentions Japanese art and artists only briefly. So (D) should also be eliminated. Choice (B) refers to sensory descriptions that include smell, sight, and hearing. All three of these senses are addressed in the passage, with scent referenced in the first paragraph, sound referenced at the end of the second paragraph, and sight included throughout. This makes (B) the correct answer.

Structure

Structure questions could ask what a particular part of the passage adds to the author's purpose or to the development of the author's ideas. In other words, why is it there? That's the question to ask yourself with structure questions. Why did the author put a particular description or instruction, sentence or paragraph in the passage, and why does it appear where it does?

Hunting for transitional or signal words will be a big help here. What are those? They're words that indicate a change (or transition)—perhaps from one opinion to another—or that signal a relationship—perhaps between two statements.

Consider the following examples:

> I prefer living in a big city because there are so many things to do. *On the other hand,* (change to the opposite point of view) a small town offers warmth and a sense of community that big cities lack.

> Frosty-Man air conditioners are the most energy-efficient units on the market. *In addition,* (signal that the author is going to build upon a previous point), with an average lifespan of 15 years, they are the most reliable.

In the first example above, the transition to the opposite opinion reveals something important about the character making the statements—he or she may be indecisive or confused or perhaps weak. In the second case, the author is strengthening the goal of promoting Frosty-Man air conditioners by building a list of their advantages. Transition and signal words help give the reader a smoother ride through the author's points.

Let's see an example.

Lines

by Emily Bronte

Far away is the land of rest
Thousand miles are stretched between
Many a mountain's stormy crest
Many a desert void of green

Wasted worn is the traveler
Dark his heart and dim his eye
Without hope or comforter
Faltering faint and ready to die

Often he looks to the ruthless sky
Often he looks o'er his dreary road
Often he wishes down to lie
And render up life's tiresome load

But yet faint not mournful man
Leagues on leagues are left behind
Since your sunless course began
Then go on to toil resigned

If you still despair control
Hush its whispers in your breast
You shall reach the final goal
You shall win the land of rest

Where does a shift in tone occur in the passage?

This question is asking about a shift in tone, so look out for words that indicate a structural shift in the passage. The most clear indicator that there is a shift is the word "but" at the beginning of the fourth stanza. Read the first three stanzas—what is their tone? Hopeless, despair, dark. Read the last two stanzas—what is their tone? Hopeful, winning, goal-oriented.

Try the next one on your own.

Excerpt from *Julius Caesar*

by William Shakespeare

ANTONY: Friends, Romans, countrymen, lend me your ears!
I come to bury Caesar, not to praise him.
The evil that men do lives after them,
The good is often buried with their bones;
So let this be true for Caesar. The noble Brutus
Has told you Caesar was ambitious;
If it were true, it was a terrible fault,
And terribly has Caesar suffered for it.
Here, with the approval of Brutus and the rest—
For Brutus is an honorable man;
So are they all, all honorable men—
I come to speak at Caesar's funeral.
He was my friend, faithful and fair to me;
But Brutus says he was ambitious,
And Brutus is an honorable man.
Caesar returned many captives home to Rome,
And filled the treasury with reward money.
Did this in Caesar seem ambitious?
When the poor have cried, Caesar has wept;
Ambition should be made of sterner stuff:
Yet Brutus says he was ambitious,
And Brutus is an honorable man.
You all saw that, at the festival,
I thrice presented him a kingly crown,
Which he did thrice refuse. Was this ambition?
Yet Brutus says he was ambitious,
And sure he is an honorable man.
I speak not to disprove what Brutus spoke,
But here I am to speak what I do know.
You all did love him once, not without cause;
So what cause keeps you from mourning for him?
O Judgment, you must have gone to mindless beasts,
Because people have lost their common sense. Bear with me;
My heart is in the coffin there with Caesar,
And I must pause till it come back to me.

2. The author's use of the words "yet" and "but" throughout the poem demonstrates

   A   that Brutus is a highly argumentative character

   B   the author cannot make up his mind as to whether or not Caesar was ambitious

   C   there are two points of view at odds with one another in regards to Caesar

   D   that Antony loves Caesar and Brutus equally

Here's How to Crack It

The passage opens up the scene of Caesar's funeral. We learn that Brutus accused Caesar of being ambitious, and that he has allowed Antony to speak at the funeral for Caesar. Next, it goes on to list the good things that Caesar has done, which seem to be at odds with what Brutus has said about him. The words "but" and "yet" are applied to the conflicting facts we are given regarding the good acts of Caesar and Brutus' statements, and how honorable Brutus is. This best supports (C), as clearly Brutus and Anthony have conflicting views of Caesar and his ambition. The author is using the conflicting statements Antony makes regarding Caesar to make this point, not because he is unsure if Caesar was ambitious, so eliminate (B). Since it is Antony that is arguing, not Brutus, (A) can be eliminated. Antony only expresses a love for Caesar (my heart is in the coffin), not both Caesar and Brutus so eliminate (D) as well.

Theme

A theme is a general idea contained in a text; the theme may be stated explicitly or only suggested. A theme is not just an idea; it is an idea that is developed, often over the course of a chapter or an entire book. Usually, one can identify a central theme and several minor ones. Sometimes both are overtly stated, as in the example that follows.

> *Example:* Many scholars agree that the central theme in *Adventures of Huckleberry Finn* is the conflict between nature and civilization. But clearly, the book contains other themes, such as the worth of honor and the voyage of self-discovery.

Read the following passage, and see if you can identify a central theme.

We now touch on civilization's most sensitive spot; it is an unpleasant task to raise one's voice against the folly of the day, against chimeras that have caused a downright epidemic. To speak against the absurdities of trade today means to expose oneself to anathemas, just as much as if one had spoken against the tyranny of the popes and the barons in the twelfth century. If it were a matter of choosing between two dangerous roles, I think it would be less dangerous to offend a sovereign with bitter truths than to offend the mercantile spirit that now rules like a despot over civilization—and even over sovereigns! And yet a superficial analysis will prove that our commercial systems defile and disorganize civilization and that in trade, as in all other things, we are being led further and further astray. The controversy on trade is barely half a century old and has already produced thousands of books, and yet the participants in the controversy have not seen that the trade mechanism is organized in such a way that it is a slap in the face to all common sense. It has subordinated the whole of society to one class of parasitic and unproductive persons: the merchants. All the essential classes of society—the proprietor, the farmer, the manufacturer, and even the government— find themselves dominated by a non-essential, contingent class, the merchant, who should be their subordinate, their employed agent, removable and accountable, and who, nevertheless, directs and obstructs at will all the avenues of circulation.

What is the theme of this passage?

What would you say the theme is here? It should not surprise you that the title of the essay that this passage is excerpted from is "On Trade." In his essay, the French socialist Charles Fourier develops a central theme: Merchants, through trade, have both corrupted society and become its tyrant. Many of the passages on the TASC test are long enough to permit you to identify at least one central theme, and you will almost certainly be asked to do so.

Excerpt from "The Raven"

by Edgar Allan Poe

Once upon a midnight dreary, while I pondered, weak and weary,
Over many a quaint and curious volume of forgotten lore—
While I nodded, nearly napping, suddenly there came a tapping,
As of someone gently rapping—rapping at my chamber door.
"'Tis some visitor," I muttered, "tapping at my chamber door—
Only this and nothing more."

Ah, distinctly I remember, it was in the bleak December,
And each separate dying ember brought its ghost upon the floor.
Eagerly I wished the morrow; vainly I had sought to borrow
From my books relief of sorrow—sorrow for the lost Lenore—
For the rare and radiant maiden whom the angels name Lenore—
Nameless here for evermore.

And the silken sad uncertain rustling of each purple curtain
Thrilled me—filled me with fantastic terrors never felt before;
So that now, to still the beating of my heart, I stood repeating
"'Tis some visitor entreating entrance at my chamber door—
Some late visitor entreating entrance at my chamber door;
This it is and nothing more."

Presently my soul grew stronger; hesitating then no longer,
"Sir," said I, "or Madam, truly your forgiveness I implore;
But the fact is I was napping, and so gently you came rapping,
And so faintly you came tapping—tapping at my chamber door,
That I scarce was sure I heard you"—here I opened wide the door:
Darkness there and nothing more.

Deep into that darkness peering, long I stood there wondering, fearing,
Doubting, dreaming dreams no mortal ever dared to dream before;
But the silence was unbroken, and the darkness gave no token,
And the only word there spoken was the whispered word, "Lenore?"
This I whispered, and an echo murmured back the word, "Lenore!"
Merely this and nothing more.

3. Read this stanza.

> Ah, distinctly I remember, it was in the bleak December,
>
> And each separate dying ember brought its ghost upon the floor.
>
> Eagerly I wished the morrow; vainly I had sought to borrow
>
> From my books relief of sorrow—sorrow for the lost Lenore—
>
> For the rare and radiant maiden whom the angels name Lenore—
>
> Nameless here for evermore.

Which words help create a tone of melancholy?

A bleak, dying, sorrow

B rare, radiant, lost

C relief, angels, evermore

D separate, nameless, December

Here's How to Crack It

The question asks specifically about which words help create a tone of melancholy, so eliminate any choices with positive words in it. This includes (B) and (C), since "radiant" and "relief" do not match melancholy. Although the words in (D) are not positive, they are not necessarily negative. The only choice with only negatively words with connotations that match melancholy is (A).

Language Use

Ah, the old "guess an unfamiliar word's meaning from its context" trick. You could find some readings where knowing the vocabulary is important to understanding the passage. However, these words won't be obscure technical terms that only a master electrician or an economist would understand. They'll be words that aren't specific to any particular field of study—words such as "specificity" and "formulate" (in informational material) or "unabashedly" and "faltered" (in literary passages). Look at what the context is telling you, try substituting a word you know for the unfamiliar word, and see if it makes sense. Here's an example.

Although the mayor and town council were initially ardent supporters of a new public library building, their position faltered when the cost estimates started coming in.

What does the context tell you about "ardent" and "faltered"? Well, the cost estimates were apparently higher than expected, causing local officials to reconsider. If you guessed from that a meaning of "enthusiastic" or "passionate" for "ardent" and "weakened" for "faltered," you'd be right.

Language use questions might go further, too, and ask you what impact the author's word choice has on the tone or the meaning of the passage. For example, someone who offers to "assist you in reaching out to a competent attorney" is setting a more formal tone than someone who offers to "help you find a good lawyer."

Let's look at an example.

Science-Based Strategies for Sustaining Coral Ecosystems

by the U.S. Department of the Interior—U.S. Geological Survey

Coral ecosystems and their natural capital are at risk. Greenhouse gas emissions, overfishing, and harmful land-use practices are damaging our coral reefs. Overwhelming scientific evidence indicates that the threats are serious, and if they are left unchecked, the ecological and social consequences will be significant and widespread. Although the primary stressors to coral ecosystems are known, science-based strategies are needed to more accurately explain natural processes and forecast human-induced change. Collaborations among managers and scientists and enhanced mapping, monitoring, research, and modeling can lead to effective mitigation plans. U.S. Geological Survey scientists and their partners assess coral ecosystem history, ecology, vulnerability, and resiliency and provide study results to decision makers who may devise policies to sustain coral resources and the essential goods and services they provide.

In the first line, what does the term natural *capital* mean?

The passage tells us that both coral ecosystems and their natural capital are at risk. So you know that the natural capital is something that coral ecosystems are in possession of. Think about what kinds of things a coral reef possesses? What lives in that ecosystem? What does it produce?

Most likely, the answer here would be something like "fish," "plant-life," and/or "coral." Luckily, once you get to the point of having an idea of what the answer needs to match, you will be able to go to the answer choices and use POE.

Try it out on your own.

Lead Poisoning in Wild Birds

by the U.S. Department of the Interior—U.S. Geological Survey

Lead in its various forms has been used for thousands of years, originally in cooking utensils and glazes and more recently in many industrial and commercial applications. However, lead is a potent, potentially deadly toxin that damages many organs in the body and can affect all animals, including humans. By the mid-1990s, lead had been removed from many products in the United States, such as paint and fuel, but it is still commonly used in ammunition for hunting upland game birds, small mammals, and large game animals, as well as in fishing tackle. Wild birds, such as mourning doves, bald eagles, California condors, and loons, can die from the ingestion of one lead shot, bullet fragment, or sinker. According to a recent study on loon mortality, nearly half of adult loons found sick or dead during the breeding season in New England were diagnosed with confirmed or suspected lead poisoning from ingestion of lead fishing weights.

4. **What is the meaning of the word *potent* in the second sentence?**

   A very strong

   B strong smelling

   C possible

   D an indication

Here's How to Crack It

Since this is asking about a specific word, look at the context around that word. You know that "potent" is describing lead, and that lead is a potentially deadly toxin. Potent is included in that description, so it needs to match the context that lead is a potentially deadly toxin. Going to the answer choices, see what you can POE right away. It doesn't seem likely that smell is an important fact to include when describing lead as a potentially deadly poison, so eliminate (B). Possible would be redundant with *potentially*, so eliminate (C) as well. Potent is being used to describe lead, not as something that means an indication in and of itself—eliminate (D). The only good descriptive word that also makes sense as describing a potentially lethal poison is strong, (A).

Literary Devices Drill

Try these questions, using your knowledge of the question types we just reviewed in this chapter and from previous chapters. To check your answers, register your book at **PrincetonReview.com/cracking** and download the Chapter Drill Answers and Explanations supplement.

Excerpt from *The Leopard Man's Story*

by Jack London

1   He was the Leopard Man, but he did not look it. His business in life, whereby he lived, was to appear in a cage of performing leopards before vast audiences, and to thrill those audiences by certain exhibitions of nerve for which his employers rewarded him on a scale commensurate with the thrills he produced.

2   As I say, he did not look it. He was narrow-hipped, narrow-shouldered, and anemic, while he seemed not so much oppressed by gloom as by a sweet and gentle sadness, the weight of which was as sweetly and gently borne. For an hour I had been trying to get a story out of him, but he appeared to lack imagination. To him there was no romance in his gorgeous career, no deeds of daring, no thrills—nothing but a gray sameness and infinite boredom.

3   Lions? Oh, yes! he had fought with them. It was nothing. All you had to do was to stay sober. Anybody could whip a lion to a standstill with an ordinary stick. He had fought one for half an hour once. Just hit him on the nose every time he rushed, and when he got artful and rushed with his head down, why, the thing to do was to stick out your leg. When he grabbed at the leg you drew it back and hit him on the nose again. That was all.

4   With the far-away look in his eyes and his soft flow of words he showed me his scars. There were many of them, and one recent one where a tigress had reached for his shoulder and gone down to the bone. I could see the neatly mended rents in the coat he had on. His right arm, from the elbow down, looked as though it had gone through a threshing machine, what of the ravage wrought by claws and fangs. But it was nothing, he said, only the old wounds bothered him somewhat when rainy weather came on.

5   Suddenly his face brightened with a recollection, for he was really as anxious to give me a story as I was to get it. "He was a little, thin, sawed-off, sword-swallowing and juggling Frenchman. De Ville, he called himself, and he had a nice wife. She did trapeze work and used to dive from under the roof into a net, turning over once on the way as nice as you please.

6   "De Ville had a quick temper, as quick as his hand, and his hand was as quick as the paw of a tiger. The word went around to watch out for De Ville, and no one dared be more than barely civil to his wife. And she was a sly bit of baggage, too, only all the performers were afraid of De Ville.

7   "But there was one man, Wallace, who was afraid of nothing. He was the lion-tamer, and he had the trick of putting his head into the lion's mouth. He'd put it into the mouths of any of them, though he preferred Augustus, a big, good-natured beast who could always be depended upon.

8   "As I was saying, Wallace—'King' Wallace we called him—was afraid of nothing alive or dead. He was a king and no mistake.

9   "Madame de Ville looked at King Wallace and King Wallace looked at her, while De Ville looked at them darkly. We warned Wallace, but it was no use. He laughed at us, as he laughed at De Ville.

10   "But I saw a glitter in De Ville's eyes which I had seen often in the eyes of wild beasts, and I went out of my way to give Wallace a final warning. He laughed, but he did not look so much in Madame de Ville's direction after that.

11   "Several months passed by. Nothing had happened and I was beginning to think it all a scare over nothing. We were West by that time, showing in 'Frisco. It was during the afternoon performance, and the big tent was filled with women and children.

12   "Passing by one of the dressing tents I glanced in through a hole in the canvas: in front of me was King Wallace, in tights, waiting for his turn to go on with his cage of performing lions. I noticed De Ville staring at Wallace with undisguised hatred. Wallace and the rest were all too busy to notice this or what followed.

13   "But I saw it through the hole in the canvas. De Ville drew his handkerchief from his pocket, made as though to mop the sweat from his face with it (it was a hot day), and at the same time walked past Wallace's back. The look troubled me at the time, for not only did I see hatred in it, but I saw triumph as well. "De Ville will bear watching," I said to myself, and I really breathed easier when I saw him go out the entrance to the circus grounds. A few minutes later I was in the big tent. King Wallace was doing his turn and holding the audience spellbound. He was in a particularly vicious mood, and he kept the lions stirred up till they were all snarling, that is, all of them except old Augustus, and he was just too fat and lazy and old to get stirred up over anything.

14   "Finally Wallace cracked the old lion's knees with his whip and got him into position. Old Augustus, blinking good-naturedly, opened his mouth and in popped Wallace's head. Then the jaws came together, *crunch*, just like that."

15   The Leopard Man smiled in a sweetly wistful fashion, and the far-away look came into his eyes.

16   "And that was the end of King Wallace," he went on in his sad, low voice. "After the excitement cooled down I watched my chance and bent over and smelled Wallace's head. Then I sneezed."

17   "It . . . it was . . .?" I queried with halting eagerness.

18   "Snuff—that De Ville dropped on his hair in the dressing tent. Old Augustus never meant to do it. He only sneezed."

1.   **The overall structure of this passage most closely resembles which of the following?**

   A   an inverted pyramid

   B   a maze

   C   a frame within a frame

   D   a spiral

2.   **Why does the author give such a lengthy description of the Leopard Man's attitude towards the work he does?**

   A   to show that any profession can get boring after a while

   B   to reveal how aging can affect someone's enthusiasm for life

   C   to highlight the contrast between the Leopard Man and Wallace

   D   to reflect one of the main ideas in the story that the Leopard Man tells

3. When the narrator speaks of the "ravage wrought by claws and fangs" (paragraph 4), he is referring to

A the result of performing with leopards throughout the Leopard Man's career

B the Leopard Man's advancing age

C the damage caused by the big cats the Leopard Man fights

D the Leopard Man's lack of excitement about his career

4. Compare the Leopard Man's attitude toward De Ville with Wallace's. Which of the following statements is true?

A Both the Leopard Man and Wallace let their guard down.

B The Leopard Man believed warnings were needed; Wallace completely ignored warnings.

C Wallace underestimated De Ville; the Leopard Man did not.

D Wallace thought his physical strength made him invincible; the Leopard Man knew that De Ville's cleverness was more dangerous than physical strength.

5. Which event in the passage has the *weakest* support from the other descriptions and events in the passage?

A the Leopard Man repeatedly warning Wallace about De Ville

B De Ville waiting so long for revenge when the cause of his anger had stopped

C Wallace not being afraid of De Ville

D Augustus biting off Wallace's head

6. The moral of this passage is

A brains are better than brawn

B don't try to fight nature

C honesty is always the best policy

D the grass is never greener

Chapter 8
Multiple Passages

This chapter will focus on how to approach sets of multiple passages on the Reading portion of the TASC test. Following the content lessons, we'll give you some practice questions.

MULTIPLE PASSAGES

You will encounter at least one set of "Multiple Passages," or two passages that are somehow related. Not to worry! These passages are no more difficult than any other kind.

The main thing to keep in mind when you see a set of Multiple Passages is that you want to take it one passage at a time:

1. Do all the questions that deal with Passage 1 first.
2. Do all the questions that deal with Passage 2 second.
3. Finally, do the remaining questions that ask about both passages together.

The questions that focus on one passage only are exactly like all the questions reviewed in the previous chapters. Once you have answered all of those, you will be well acquainted with both passages and ready to answer the questions that deal with both passages at the same. It is important to know as much as you can about the two passages before answering the questions on both, since those questions will be asking you to compare the two passages.

Comparison (of Different Passages That Deal with Similar Topics)

In comparison questions, you're looking for what's different and why. Those differences will fall into three broad categories.

First, the two readings could present the same information in different formats. Think, for instance, of a computer blog's feature article about a new tablet and the technical spec sheet for that same product on the manufacturer's website. Both pieces probably include such information as processor speed and memory size, but the two formats will present it in quite different ways. Why? Think about the purposes, audiences, and tone of the two pieces. The article aims to interest a more general audience—readers who are perhaps just investigating tablet brands—and will have more casual tone. The spec sheet, on the other hand, is designed to give detailed technical information to more knowledgeable readers who are seriously considering a purchase, and will have a neutral, objective tone to inspire confidence in the accuracy of the information.

Second, the two pieces might treat a similar topic differently because they were written in different eras, when writing styles and cultural values differed. Consider, for example, these two quotes about education:

"I know no safe depository of the ultimate powers of the society but the people themselves; and if we think them not enlightened enough to exercise their control with a wholesome discretion, the remedy is not to take it from them, but to inform their discretion by education."

—Thomas Jefferson

"What does education often do? It makes a straight-cut ditch of a free, meandering brook."

—Henry David Thoreau

Jefferson, one of the Founding Fathers, writes in the lengthy, complex, formal sentence structure of his era and his status, at a time when the young democracy was defining itself and establishing its legitimacy. In plain language, he's saying that ordinary people are the only safe source of power and if you don't think they'd exercise it wisely, then educate them to do it. Thoreau, on the other hand, writes with the simplicity of a naturalist during the American Romantic era and sees man-made institutions, including education, as threats to nature. Even if you weren't familiar with these two authors or the times in which they wrote, you would be able to see the differences in their writing styles and in the values they consider important. Those more general differences are what the questions would target.

The third and trickiest type of comparison questions will present opposing viewpoints on a topic and ask you to delve down to see how the arguments rely on different interpretations of the same facts, or how they emphasize different evidence that supports their positions. Look for authors with rigid opinions who select evidence to support conclusions they've already reached. Fracking (or hydraulic fracturing) is a good example of a topic that has generated so much data from the shale gas industry on one side and environmental groups on the other that an author could easily construct a strong pro or con argument just by selecting the right research results or expert statements. The TASC test question could expect you to detect that type of bias.

Let's look at a set of multiple passages and questions that may accompany them.

Excerpt from *Pride and Prejudice*

by Jane Austen

1   "Well," said Charlotte, "I wish Jane luck with all my heart; and if she were married to him tomorrow, I should think she had as good a chance of happiness as if she were to be studying his character for a twelve-month. Happiness in marriage is entirely a matter of chance. If the dispositions of the parties are ever so well known to each other, or ever so similar beforehand, it does not advance their felicity in the least. They always continue to grow sufficiently unlike afterwards to have their share of vexation, and it is better to know as little as possible of the defects of the person with whom you are to pass your life."

2   "You make me laugh Charlotte; but it is not sound. You know it is not sound, and that you would never act in this way yourself."

Excerpt from *Mansfield Park*

by Jane Austen

1   "Everybody is taken in at some period or other."

2   "Not always in marriage, my dear Mary."

3   "In marriage especially. With all due respect to such of the present company as chance to be married, my dear Mrs. Grant, there is not one in a hundred of either sex who is not taken in when they marry. Look where I will, I see that it is so; and I feel that it must be so, when I consider that it is, of all transactions, the one in which people expect the most from others, and are least honest themselves."

4   "You have been in a bad school for matrimony, in Hill Street."

5   "My poor aunt had certainly little cause to love the state; but, however, speaking from my own observation, it is a maneuvering business. I know so many who have married in the full expectation and confidence of some one particular advantage in the connection, or accomplishment or good quality in the person, who have found themselves entirely deceived, and been obliged to put up with exactly the reverse! What is this but a take in?"

All multiple text passages will have questions that are specific to one passage only as well as questions on both passages. The best approach to these passages is as follows:

1. Look at the questions to see if there are more questions specific to one passage than the other—read that passage first and answer the questions only on it.
2. Read the other passage and answer the questions only on it.
3. Keeping the main idea of each passage in mind, answer the questions on both passages.

Try out the specific passage questions.

Don't forget to use your paper! Writing down the main idea for each passage as you read it will help you answer the questions that ask about both passages.

1. **In _Pride and Prejudice_, what does Charlotte mean when she says "Happiness in marriage is entirely a matter of chance"?**

    A Knowing your future spouse well does not guarantee they will remain the same in marriage.

    B Marriages are generally bad.

    C You may be being deceived by your partner, or you may not.

    D Happiness in marriage is a choice people make.

Here's How to Crack It

In this story Charlotte is arguing that no matter how well acquainted someone is with their future spouse it is likely that person will change over time, and so marriage is always up to chance. This best matches (A). There is no indication that Charlotte thinks more marriages are bad than good, just that you can never be certain of how happy you will be prior to being married. Eliminate (B). Deception is not mentioned in this passage; it is mentioned in the other one. Since (C) is not mentioned in this passage at all, eliminate it as well. And at no point does Charlotte indicate that people choose to be happy or choose not to, only that they will be or they won't. Choice isn't involved at all in terms of their being happy later on. Choice (D) is incorrect as well.

2. **In the third paragraph of *Mansfield Park,* what opinion does Mary give regarding marriage?**

    A Honesty is essential to having a happy marriage.

    B Many marriages are rushed into.

    C People are likely to change after they are married.

    D People often misrepresent themselves to their future spouses.

Here's How to Crack It

In the third paragraph Mary says that marriage is the one transaction in which *people expect the most from others, and are least honest themselves.* This best matches (D), that people often misrepresent themselves when they marry. Although Mary is speaking about people being dishonest here, she does not actually state that people must be honest to have a happy marriage, so eliminate (A). Choice (C) can be eliminated as it refers to the other passage. The same rule applies to (B); the timing of marriage is only discussed in the other passage.

Now that you have answered just one question on each passage, you should have an idea of how the main ideas of the two passages differ. These passages are by the same author and on the same topic, but they differ greatly in their treatment of that topic. To make sure you are ready to move on to the questions on both passages, answer the following questions:

What is the topic of the passages? Marriage.

How does the first passage treat that topic? In the first passage, Charlotte indicates that it does not matter how well or long one knows his or her spouse prior to being married; spouses are likely to change throughout a marriage.

How does the second passage treat that topic? In the second passage, Mary states that people are generally dishonest when they are looking for a spouse, and misrepresent themselves. This is commonly the case, and so many people who are married end up being disappointed when they discover the truth.

Now let's look at a question on both passages.

    Both Charlotte and Mary would like agree that

You just noted the differences between the two passages and those characters. Charlotte is focused on people changing after they are married, while Mary is focused on how they deceive people prior to marriage. But either way they both agree on what? Well, since the only topic they both discuss is marriage, focus on that. Their opinions on marriage seem to be less romantic and more practical; they both seem to think that marriages are as likely to end up disappointing people as they are to make people happy.

Try the next one on your own.

———————○———————

3. **Both passages include**

   A   a person who is married as part of the conversation

   B   a character who disagrees with the opinion being expressed

   C   a rhetorical question

   D   a marriage proposal

Here's How to Crack It

This is a very open-ended answer choice, so POE is the best approach. Since the question is asking about both passages, make sure you are checking the answer against both passages as you use POE. For (A), it may be that Mrs. Grant is married in Passage 2 since Mary references her when offering all due respect to those who are married. But in Passage 1 there is no indication whatsoever that either of the people are married. Since you can't point to clear evidence in both passages, eliminate (A). There are two characters in each passage, and both do express disagreement with the opinions given in both of the passages; Charlotte is told her opinion is not sound in Passage 1 and Mary is told people are not always taken in by marriage in Passage 2. Choice (B) is supported by both passages. Choice (C) asks for a rhetorical question, which is a question that is asked to make a point rather than be answered. The only question we see, rhetorical or otherwise, is in in Passage 2. Since both passages do not include this literary device, eliminate (C). And although (D) may seem good at first glance since the passages are both on marriage, there is no marriage proposal in either passage. The only possible answer is (B).

———————○———————

Data Representation

Another way that you may see information in two different ways on the TASC test is with data representation. Data representation refers to a visual way of telling readers facts, such as through bar graphs, lines graphs, pie charts, timelines, and so on. Using data representation can make things easier on both the author and readers. Authors don't have to spend as much time trying to explain relationships or relate dry, number-based information through text. Readers can more easily digest information when it is a graph or table than they can from text.

There will not be very many data representation questions on the TASC test, but you can expect at least one or two. These are not any more difficult than other reading questions—they are still asking for you to find information based on something you have read.

One type of data representation question could ask you for information just from the figure. The only difference will be that you are reading a graph, table, figure, or chart, instead of a piece of text.

The other type of question will ask you to integrate information from both the figure and the text. This is just like a multiple passages question—take it one step at a time.

Let's take a look at this type of question. To make things easier, let's use a passage you have already seen before.

Companies use statements of Corporate Social Responsibility (CSR) to explain the values and principles that govern the way they do business, and to make a public commitment to follow them. These documents typically have high-level support from management and the board of directors, and are made available to all stakeholders, from employees to investors, customers to government regulators.

Pine Trail Timber—Statement of Corporate Social Responsibility

1   In carrying out our mission to supply the residential construction industry with the highest quality products from sustainably managed sources, Pine Trail Timber adheres to the following commitments to its stakeholders, to the communities in which it does business, and to the environment.

Responsibility to Stakeholders

2   Our stakeholders place their trust in us, and we work every day to merit that trust by aligning our interests with theirs.

3   All employees deserve a safe, supportive work setting, and the opportunity to achieve their full potential. We stress safety training, prohibit any type of discrimination or harassment, and support employees' efforts to enhance their job-related skills. In return, we expect our employees and officers to devote themselves to fulfilling our commitments to other stakeholders.

4   Investors have a right to expect transparency, sound corporate governance, and a fair return on their investments. We pride ourselves on full disclosure, adherence to the most rigid standards of ethical oversight, and a track record of profitable operations, as our rising stock chart and uninterrupted five-year series of dividend increases show.

5   Our valued customers are entitled to exceptional value and service. Our product innovation and wise management of resources ensure that they receive both.

6   Our suppliers rely on us for fair dealing in specifying our requirements and in meeting our obligations. We consider our suppliers to be our partners—when we succeed, they succeed.

7   We meet the expectations of government and industry regulators by complying with all applicable laws of the countries in which we carry out our business operations, and cooperating in all authorized investigations.

8   We fulfill our duty to the media and the public through providing timely information about any events that might have an impact beyond our operations, and making senior spokespeople available on request.

Support for Local Communities

9   We aim to enhance our host communities. Our presence provides training and jobs, and contributes to the local economy.

10   In the field and in our processing facilities, we recognize the impact our activities may have on local groups. We strive for open communication in order to build relationships, and create opportunities for consultation to foster understanding of our plans.

11   In urban centers where we have administrative operations, we match charitable donations made by our employees and run programs that give employees a block of time off work to volunteer with local organizations. Pine Trail Timber routinely forms one of the largest volunteer groups in the annual Arbor Day activities in several countries, planting trees and teaching other participants how to care for them.

Respect for the Environment

12   We recognize that our current and future success depends on the wise use of renewable resources. We value our reputation as a conscientious steward of the lands that furnish our products.

13   All of our production and processing operations worldwide are certified by the Forest Stewardship Council (FSC) as meeting its rigorous standards for responsible resource management. The FSC certification assures our stakeholders and host communities of independent verification of our operations.

14   Through constant process innovation, we aim to make the least possible use of non-renewable resources in our production.

15   We strive to leave the smallest possible footprint and, where necessary, carry out prompt and thorough remediation. After we finish our operations in an area but before we leave, we ensure that the land is returned to a state where it can produce abundant crops, offer a welcoming home for wildlife, and provide outdoor enjoyment for local residents.

We're Listening

16   If you have any questions or comments about our Corporate Social Responsibility commitments, we invite you to contact Mr. Joseph d'Argill, our Chairman and Chief Executive Officer.

Look at the table; then answer the question.

Number of employees	North America	Central America	Africa	Southeast Asia
In production jobs	54,200	17,054	3,214	9,875
In remediation jobs	1,210 [2.2%]	651 [3.8%]	55 [1.7%]	62 [0.6%]
Earned safety certification	11,254 [20.8%]	1,675 [9.8%]	424 [13.2%]	681 [6.9%]
On worker safety committees	325 [0.6%]	153 [0.9%]	107 [3.3%]	31 [0.3%]
Designated as safety representatives	22 [0.04%]	103 [0.6%]	28 [0.9%]	3 [0.03%]
Refused dangerous work	318 [0.59%]	122 [0.72%]	116 [3.6%]	19 [0.02%]

4.   **Compare the figures in the table above to the overall company image portrayed in the CSR statement. From the answer choices below, identify the *most significant* similarity or difference in topics covered by *both* of the two sources. (Assume the percentages shown in the table are correct; you do not need to calculate them.)**

A   The table suggests the safety and remediation commitments made in the CSR statement apply unevenly to different geographic locations.

B   The table reinforces the extensive worldwide operations suggested in the text statement.

C   The table reveals that workers have more control over their safety than the text statement says.

D   The table confirms the CSR statement's commitment to restoring the land after the company's work there is complete.

Here's How to Crack It

This question asks you to compare information about Pine Trail Timber given in two different formats—text and figures in a table. However, that information does not portray quite the same company image.

The text statement presents a company committed to responsible resource management and concern for employees, including workers' safety. The table tells a rather different story. Even in Pine Trail Timber's largest operations (North America), only 20.8% of the workers have earned safety certification, and the largest percentage of remediation workers (still only 3.8%) is found in Central America, which is only the company's second largest area of activity.

Now to find the *most significant* difference or similarity, use Process of Elimination. Choice (C) is eliminated because the text statement doesn't say anything about workers controlling their own safety, let alone being able to refuse dangerous work, as the table shows. Read the question carefully—you're comparing topics covered by *both* of the two sources. While (B) has some truth, it's hardly the most significant issue raised in a comparison. Choice (D) is also a weak similarity; having fewer than four percent of the workforce involved in remediation in even the area with the highest percentage isn't much of a commitment to restoring the land. Choice (A) is the correct answer, and you can see it more easily from the percentages than from the absolute numbers. Southeast Asia lags the other three areas on all measures of concern for workers' safety, for instance, while Africa has been more successful than the other areas in giving workers a voice in safety (through workers' committees and representatives, and through exercising the right to refuse dangerous work).

Multiple Passages Drill

Your turn. Try the questions, using your knowledge of the question types we just reviewed in this chapter and previous chapters. To check your answers, register your book at **PrincetonReview.com/cracking** and download the Chapter Drill Answers and Explanations supplement.

The Gettysburg Address

by Abraham Lincoln

1   Four score and seven years ago our fathers brought forth on this continent, a new nation, conceived in Liberty, and dedicated to the proposition that all men are created equal.

2   Now we are engaged in a great civil war, testing whether that nation, or any nation so conceived and so dedicated, can long endure. We are met on a great battle-field of that war. We have come to dedicate a portion of that field, as a final resting place for those who here gave their lives that that nation might live. It is altogether fitting and proper that we should do this.

3   But, in a larger sense, we cannot dedicate—we cannot consecrate—we cannot hallow—this ground. The brave men, living and dead, who struggled here, have consecrated it, far above our poor power to add or detract. The world will little note, nor long remember what we say here, but it can never forget what they did here. It is for us the living, rather, to be dedicated here to the unfinished work which they who fought here have thus far so nobly advanced. It is rather for us to be here dedicated to the great task remaining before us—that from these honored dead we take increased devotion to that cause for which they gave the last full measure of devotion—that we here highly resolve that these dead shall not have died in vain—that this nation, under God, shall have a new birth of freedom—and that government of the people, by the people, for the people, shall not perish from the earth.

Excerpt from "I Have a Dream"

by Martin Luther King Jr., 1963

I am happy to join with you today in what will go down in history as the greatest demonstration for freedom in the history of our nation. Five score years ago, a great American, in whose symbolic shadow we stand today, signed the Emancipation Proclamation. This momentous decree came as a great beacon light of hope to millions of Negro slaves who had been seared in the flames of withering injustice. It came as a joyous daybreak to end the long night of their captivity. But one hundred years later, the Negro still is not free. One hundred years later, the life of the Negro is still sadly crippled by the manacles of segregation and the chains of discrimination. One hundred years later, the Negro lives on a lonely island of poverty in the midst of a vast ocean of material prosperity. One hundred years later, the Negro is still languished in the corners of American society and finds himself an exile in his own land. And so we've come here today to dramatize a shameful condition.

1. **What phrase does Lincoln use to give an impression of the setting of his speech?**

    A a reference to the continent and country of which he is speaking

    B they are meeting on a great battlefield

    C the symbolic shadow they are standing in

    D he is unable to consecrate the ground on which they stand

2. In the second paragraph, what is the meaning of the phrase "can long endure"?

A can withstand pain

B can defeat their enemies

C can remain unified

D can stomach war

3. It can be inferred from Martin Luther King Jr.'s speech that he speaking to

A people attending a demonstration

B the United States Government

C Abraham Lincoln

D his church congregation

4. What is the purpose of the repetition of the phrases "one hundred years later' in Martin Luther King Jr.'s speech?

A to dramatize the condition of African Americans

B to point out how long these demonstrations have been occurring

C to stress how long African Americans have been enslaved in America

D to emphasize how little has changed for the African American population since the Civil War

5. How do the tones differ?

A Passage 1's tone is more respectful, while Passage 2's tone is more rallying.

B Passage 1's tone is more depressed, while Passage 2's tone is more hopeful.

C Passage 1's tone is more apologetic, while Passage 2's tone is more vengeful.

D Passage 1's tone is more assertive, while Passage 2's tone is more subdued.

6. The authors of both passages would most likely agree on which of the following statements?

A Memorials and consecrated grounds are the most important tribute paid in our society.

B More must be done to accomplish full equality for all Americans.

C Bloodshed is an unfortunate but necessary part of the fight for freedom.

D Segregation has had a negative effect on the ability of African Americans to succeed.

7. What do both passages contain?

A the name of a signed government document

B a reference to religion

C repetitive sentence structure

D a reference to time

Part III
Writing

Chapter 9
Writing Overview

In this chapter, we will provide an overview of the Writing portion of the TASC test. In the following chapters, we will explore the specific content areas of this sub-test in more detail.

The TASC Writing test is 105 minutes long. The first 60 minutes you will work on Section 1 of the Writing test, Language Use and Conventions. Questions relate to writing (15%), grammar usage (30%), capitalization/punctuation/spelling (25%), and knowledge of language (30%). Texts are dawn from how-to documents, informative writing, and workplace correspondence. The remaining 45 minutes of the Writing test you will work on Section 2, The Essay. It is scored on a scale of 0 to 8 based on clarity of expression; clear and strategic organization; complete development of ideas; and sentence structure, punctuation, grammar, word choice, and spelling.

ENGLISH AND THE REAL WORLD

What would you think of an employer who posted a job ad full of obvious grammar mistakes? Does that sound like someone who might mess up your paycheck too? Or how about a political candidate who dropped off a "vote for me" flyer filled with spelling errors? Is that someone you would trust to be careful with your tax dollars?

Proper use of the English language isn't just about grammar or punctuation—it's about clarity and credibility. It's about getting your message across and inspiring confidence in the skill and accuracy people can expect from you. If you don't care whether your résumé is written clearly and correctly, why should an employer spend time figuring out what it says? If you don't bother putting proper sentences together on a loan application, why would the lender trust you to make the effort to repay it on time? Your language use can reveal a lot about yourself; you want it to make the best impression.

LANGUAGE USE AND CONVENTIONS: WHAT KIND OF QUESTIONS ARE ON THE TEST?

The TASC test has two different question formats on the Language Use and Conventions section of the test. The first type is Structure questions—these questions will ask you about the structure of a sentence or other various grammar rules. It asks you to check for a grammar rule in a set of answer choices. For example:

Which of the following sentences is punctuated correctly?

A   She found it difficult to read the entire book there were many plot twists that confused things.

B   She found it difficult: to read the entire book there were many plot twists that confused things.

C   She found it difficult to read the entire book, there were many plot twists that confused things.

D   She found it difficult to read the entire book; there were many plot twists that confused things.

The second type is Revision questions. Revision questions will give you either a line or a short paragraph to read and ask you to make revisions to it. For example:

> **One upon a time, on a day that was both lovely and beautiful but also for many days, there lived a young woman who being that she was parentless had been mistreated to a great degree by her adoptive family.**

> **Which of the following revisions is most correct and concise?**

> **A**   Once upon a time, there lived a young orphaned woman who was mistreated by her adoptive family.

> **B**   A young woman, parentless, mistreated, once upon a time there was.

> **C**   A young woman was sad in that she was mistreated, once upon a time, by her adopted family.

> **D**   Once upon a time, on days that were both lovely and beautiful, of which there were many, lived a mistreated by her family women who had lost her parents previously.

Both of these questions will ask about a specific set of grammar rules, which we will review in the following chapter.

OUR APPROACH

In the next two chapters, we'll look at both structure and revision questions in more detail as we discuss and tackle different grammar rules that will be tested on them. You will have a drill at the end of each chapter try on your own.

As you go through the following chapters, you will want to keep in mind the Habits of Effective Test Takers that were covered in Chapter 3. Let's review how they specifically relate to the Writing test before moving on.

1. Answer the Easy Questions First. There will be a variety of question types on the Writing test. How difficult the questions are may be determined by the type of question asked and the grammar it involves, but mostly how difficult a question is depends on you. If you prefer a certain question type over another, if you are better at recognizing a certain grammatical error more quickly than another, do those questions first!

2. Use Your Pencil to Stay on Task. It may seem as though English questions are just about reading a bunch of sentences and then deciding which answer choice "sounds good." That's just not true on a standardized test. The Writing questions are problems that need solving—active solving. Treat them just like you would a math problem: Rather than keeping all the work in your head, write it down on your scratch paper! Having something to write down, an error you note right away or what answer choices you can eliminate immediately, may be just the push your brain needs to get it moving in the right direction.

3. Move On When You Are Stuck. English questions can be tough. Many grammar rules are very specific and hard to spot, and you may be asked about several grammar rules in a single question. It is likely that you will encounter a question on the Writing test that you don't feel confident answering. If that happens, skip the question and come back to it. No sense in wasting time when you can be moving on to questions you *can* answer.

4. Pacing. Many wrong answers are the result of simply going too fast and reading too quickly. There is no point in rushing through the easy grammar questions—it will be that much more difficult to answer the harder questions later on. Make sure you are taking the time to be careful!

5. Guessing and Process of Elimination. Because there are several different ways to fix grammatical errors in a sentence, and because some errors are very easy to miss, some questions may not have clearly correct answers. If you are ever stuck on a grammar question, let the answers help you! You don't need to know how the sentence might change—the test is changing it for you in the answer choices. Compare the answer choices and note the difference between them. Then ask yourself what grammar rules are being tested and check the answer choices for those rules. If you still have two or three answer choices left, guess and move on!

6. Let It Go. No one question is that important to your score. If after you have read a question and compared the answer choices, you really can't eliminate a single one of them, let it go. Do not spend any time beating yourself up for not knowing the answer to a question, as everyone is likely to find at least some questions they are completely unsure of. If a question is taking too much time to figure out, fill in a guess and move on.

THE ESSAY: WHAT KIND OF QUESTIONS ARE ON THE TEST?

The Essay will consist of one writing prompt based on two passages. According to the TASC test you will write an essay that either states and supports a claim or provides information about a topic of interest. Examinees plan, write, and revise their essays. Scoring is based on the following criteria:

- Clarity of expression
- Clear and strategic organization
- Complete development of ideas
- Sentence structure, punctuation, grammar, word choice, and spelling

The Essay will most likely ask you to read two passages and assess the construction of the authors' arguments and the effectiveness of those arguments. The text could be from a variety of sources, including novel excerpts, poetry, drama excerpts, educational passages, research or news articles, and so on.

The Essay will be reviewed in the last chapter of this section.

Chapter 10
Structure

This chapter will break down the areas of language use you'll need to know and the kinds of errors you should be able to identify. Following the content lessons, we'll give you some practice questions.

WHAT WILL I NEED TO KNOW ABOUT LANGUAGE?

The TASC Writing multiple-choice questions target nine areas of language use that have been identified as the most important for a career or college. Don't panic when you see the list below—you're about to learn how the question format on the TASC test makes it easier to reach the correct answer.

Language Skills on the TASC Test

- **Sentence construction:** Avoiding wordiness, run-on sentences, and fragments
- **Punctuation and capitalization**
- **Agreement**: Of subject and verb, of noun and pronoun
- **Pronoun use:** Clear antecedents, correct case
- **Parallelism:** Similar phrases within a sentence should have the same grammatical structure
- **Modifiers:** Correctly placed
- **Word choice and spelling**: Avoiding words that are often confused or used in a nonstandard way, and the correct spelling of words
- **Joining thoughts:** Proper coordination, subordination, and parallel construction
- **Logic and clarity:** Effective use of words and phrases that mark a clear path for the reader

---

You don't even need to know the names of any of these areas of language use, either. For the Writing test, you simply need to be able to recognize when something is wrong—for whatever reason—and when it's correct. Looking at the nine target areas simply shows you what kind of errors you can expect to see on the test so you can eliminate them more quickly from the four answer choices.

Of course, you'll also be expected to know how to express your ideas clearly and concisely when you write your essay response. Reviewing the language skills covered in this chapter can you help improve your essay score, too, because part of the essay is evaluated on how well you demonstrate these skills.

We will review the first seven language skills listed above in this chapter, and the following two in the next chapter.

Sentence Construction

Sentence construction involves the structure of sentence. The TASC test focuses on three main things when it comes to sentence construction: wordiness, run-on sentences, and sentence fragments. All three can torpedo a clear, concise expression of your ideas.

Wordiness

Let's start with wordiness. Here's part of a letter from a cellist who blew her audition for the local symphony orchestra:

> I hope you will reconsider and think again about giving me another chance to audition. I was extremely tired and nervous that day because I hadn't slept much the night before. I was too anxious and excited to sleep. If you'll just give me another chance, I'll show you how well I can play because I won't be as nervous the second time.

Now how's that for saying the same thing several times in slightly different ways? That's wordiness, and it puts readers to sleep. Say it once, say it concisely, and move on.

Try it out:

---

1. **Read this sentence:**

> **Abigail had a long and unending day, because of that reason she decided to go to bed early.**

Which revision of the sentence best expresses the idea precisely and concisely?

A Having had a long and unending day, the decision was made by Abigail to go to bed early.

B Because Abigail had a long day, she decided to go to bed early.

C In that she had a long day, Allison made the decision to go to bed early.

D Going to bed early was the result of Allison having had a long day.

Here's How to Crack It

There are a couple of wordy areas in the first sentence: "a long and unending day" and "because of that reason." Choice (A) repeats the "a long and unending day" wordiness, so eliminate it. Choice (C), although more concise than the original creates new wordiness with "made the decision to." Since it would be more concise to the "decided to," eliminate (C). Choice (D) creates new wordiness with the phrase "having had a long day," so eliminate it as well. Only (B) contains no original or new wordiness in it, so it is the best answer!

Run-on Sentences

Run-on sentences can also put a reader to sleep:

> Ingrid might make a good addition to the volleyball team, I guess, except that she hasn't been playing for very long and she doesn't have a car, so someone else would always have to bring her to out of town games and besides, she never has any money so she couldn't go out with us after the games, so maybe we shouldn't ask her to join the team after all.

There are several separate sentences in that monster run-on, and that's how they should be presented.

Watch out, too, for separate sentences that are being held together by a comma, like this:

> Industries are using less coal, natural gas is often the replacement of choice.

There should be a period after "coal" and a new sentence starting with "Natural" or, if the writer *really* wants to stress the connection between the two ideas, a semicolon after "coal." A comma never connects two separate sentences.

Fragments

Sentence fragments are the opposite of run-ons: Instead of having too much in them, fragments aren't all there. A complete sentence needs a subject and a verb, at minimum, and it must stand on its own.

Fragments don't have both a subject and verb (sometimes they don't even have either one), and they need something else added before they can stand alone.

> The conductor ran. (That's a complete sentence.)

> Being cold and wet from the howling storm that threatened the train's very survival. (That's not—there is no subject and no verb.)

Try these grammar rules out on the following question:

2. **Which of these sentences is grammatically correct?**

A   I find the best way to sleep is on my side it is impossible for me to sleep on my stomach.

B   My favorite thing to do in the morning is drink a cup of coffee I always make sure to add a lot of sugar.

C   I used to have a great deal of trouble waking up in the morning, but now I get up with no trouble at all.

D   Although many say the best way to start the day is with a big breakfast.

Here's How to Crack It

Remember you are looking out for run-ons and fragments here, so check the full sentences. Choice (A) has two complete sentences in it "I find the best way to sleep is on my side" and "it is impossible for me to sleep on my stomach," so eliminate that. Choice (B) does the same thing with "my favorite thing to do in the morning is drink a cup of coffee" and "I always make sure to add a lot of sugar," so eliminate it as well. Choice (D) contains a fragment because of the inclusion of the word "Although" at the beginning of the sentence. The only answer choice that is grammatically correct is (C), with a complete sentence at the beginning joined to an incomplete sentence at the end. It is neither a run-on nor a fragment.

Punctuation and Capitalization

There are even more basic parts to a sentence's structure though, such as capitalization and punctuation. Every sentence starts with a capital letter and ends with a period, of course.

Capitalization: In English we capitalize the names of specific people, places, national holidays, months, days of the week, titles when used with a person's name (Dr. O'Reilly)—you know all of that.

So why does the TASC test ask about capitalization? Because it is easy to miss if you are rushing and not reading carefully. Read the answer choices carefully; don't let time pressure trick you into missing the lower case "t" on "tuesday." The TASC assessment could very well have a question like that because the ability to take in and process information carefully is very much part of readiness for a career or college.

Whenever you are asked about capitalization, look at one answer choice at a time and note what is capitalized in each, and what is not. If anything looks odd, make a note to come back to it later.

Punctuation: In addition to capitalization rules, the TASC test focuses on four specific punctuation items.

One is the correct use of an **apostrophe** in possessives. "The banker's bonus" (apostrophe "s" if the noun is singular) and "the boys' skateboards" ("s" apostrophe if the noun is plural) are fairly straightforward cases. How about "the people's choice," though? Even though there are a lot of individuals in that noun, "people" doesn't end in an "s"; therefore the possessive form is apostrophe "s," just as if the noun were singular. Another special case is possessive pronouns (such as hers, theirs, and its); these do not have apostrophes.

A second focus is the use of **commas** in a series or in apposition (we'll explain that one):

> She stopped off at the grocery store for bread, eggs, milk, and cheese. (That's a series of three or more items separated by commas.)

> Wheeling General, the largest employer in town, is building another new plant next year. (That's apposition: "Wheeling General" and "the largest employer in town" both refer to the same thing and share the same function in the sentence—both work as the subject. "The largest employer in town" is *in apposition* to "Wheeling General" and needs commas around it.)

A third focus the TASC test highlights is punctuation between clauses. An **independent clause** stands alone (it could be a separate sentence); a **dependent clause** doesn't (it depends on the independent clause for its existence). You need a comma between two independent clauses that are joined by a word such as "but" or "and" (a coordinating conjunction):

> Fire destroyed six houses on the street, but the corner store suffered only minor damage.

You also need a comma when a dependent clause comes before an independent clause, but not when it comes after. In the following example, the dependent clause comes first, so you need a comma after "street."

> Even though fire destroyed six houses on the street, the corner store suffered only minor damage.

This example, by contrast, doesn't require a comma—the independent clause comes first.

> The corner store suffered only minor damage even though fire destroyed six houses on the street.

As you read earlier, two independent clauses can be separated by a conjunction such as "and" or "but" along with a comma. Two complete clauses can also be separated by either a **period** or a **semicolon**:

All squares are rectangles. Not all rectangles are squares.
All squares are rectangles; not all rectangles are squares.
All squares are rectangles, but not all rectangles are square.

All of the above sentences are grammatical correct. The period, semicolon, and comma + "but" all correctly separate these two independent clauses.

The **colon** works a little differently. A colon must have an independent clause before it and a list or example after it. The list or example that comes after can be an independent clause or a dependent clause; that doesn't matter. As long as there is an independent clause before the colon, the colon is correct:

There is not much you need in order to learn how to ride a bike: just a bike, a helmet, and a little motivation.

The fourth and final focus for punctuation on the TASC test is the **hyphen**. A hyphen separates compound words. What does that mean? The evolution of creating new words out of two words usually goes in this order: two words are separate, then joined by a hyphen, then joined altogether. For instance, life time changed to life-time, and then to lifetime.

Rules for hyphens:

- If the pair of words forms an adjective that comes before the noun, use a hyphen.

  First-class work
  Full-time employee

- If the adjective pair comes after the noun it is describing, you don't need a hyphen.

  His work is always first class.
  She is one of our employees who works full time.

- Use the hyphen for fractions and compound numbers 21 through 99.

  He ate two-thirds of the pie in one sitting. (Exception: fractions acting as nouns, such as "Two thirds of the pie have now been eaten.)
  She will be turning forty-five next Friday.

- Sometimes a hyphen is used to differentiate certain words:

  He recollected that he had a doctor's appointment the next day.
  She re-collected all the tests from the students who fixed what they missed.

Try out a few questions to practice:

---

3. **Which of these sentences has an error in capitalization?**

    A I think I may run to Target to get some dr. pepper.

    B I went to Mount Everest recently on a school trip.

    C *On the Origin of Species* is one of the best books written on evolution.

    D I am planning a vacation to Hawaii, specifically Honolulu.

Here's How to Crack It

The question is asking specifically about capitalization errors, so focus on the capitals in each choice. Since "Mount Everest" is a proper name, (B) is grammatically correct. Since prepositions in titles are not capitalized, (C) is grammatically correct. And since places like cities, states, and countries are capitalized, (D) is grammatically correct. Brand and company names, like Target, must be capitalized. So the fact that Dr. Pepper is not capitalized is the error here. Choice (A) is the correct answer.

---

4. **Which of these sentences is grammatically correct?**

    A Julia has three requests when she turns thirty-one: no party, no balloons, and no cake.

    B I need to be finished by three o'clock in the after-noon; but not a minute before.

    C The peoples' reaction to the actors skills was not good.

    D The dance was not very exciting, even though the music selection was awesome.

Here's How to Crack It

Go one answer choice at a time and note the different punctuation. Choice (A) has a hyphen; is it being used correctly? Yes! It is separating a compound number. This choice also has a colon; is it being used correctly? Yes! It has a complete sentence in front of it and a list after it. This is a grammatically correct sentence. But just to be sure, let's check the others. Choice (B) has a semicolon; is it being used correctly? No! A semicolon can only separate two complete sentences, and this one separates a complete sentence and a fragment. Choice (C) has an apostrophe; is it being used correctly? No. It should read "people's" rather than "peoples,'" since "people" is already plural. Also, there should be an apostrophe on actors since it was their skills people thought were not good. And in (D) there is a comma; is that being used correctly? No. There should be no comma in this sentence because the dependent clause is at the end. The only correct answer is (A).

Agreement

Subject-verb agreement is fairly straightforward: If the subject is singular, so is the verb. Here are some examples:

> John *learns* quickly.

In the sentence below there are two subjects, so the subjects and the verb are plural:

> Beth and Marc *learn* more slowly.

The following example is a little tricky. There are two subjects, but when you see "neither," or "either," you're dealing with only one singular subject at a time. So use the singular form of the verb.

> Neither Sam nor Anita *learns* much at all.

And in this example, the subject "class" is singular, so the verb is also singular. Don't get tripped up by the words stuffed in between the subject and the verb.

> The entire class, which will be going on a camping trip this weekend, *is learning* how to read a compass.

Noun-pronoun agreement is a common difficulty, though. Try this one:

> The company released _____ quarterly results before the board members announced _____ intention to raise the dividend.

The first answer is "its" because "company" is singular. The second is a plural pronoun, "their," because we're talking about more than one board member. If the sentence said "...before the board of directors announced...," the pronoun would again be "its" because "board" is singular. "Board" is the subject; "of directors" is simply a phrase that describes it.

Another common error occurs when people try to avoid using "his or her":

> Each student should buy _____ own books.

If you said "their," you're making that common mistake. The answer is actually "his or her own books" because we don't know the gender of the student. The student is singular, though, so the pronoun must be singular, too. If you find "his or her" awkward, you can avoid using it by making the subject plural: *Students* should buy *their* own books.

Try a couple on your own:

5.   **Which of these sentences contains a grammatical error?**

   A   Wearing her new yellow dress, Kate were feeling quite beautiful.

   B   Margot and Ben were very angry that rain made the company baseball game impossible.

   C   Joe is going to the baseball game on Friday, unless it is called off on account of rain.

   D   After they come back from the camping trip, Marguerite and Tyler are going straight to sleep.

Here's How to Crack It

Whenever you are asked an open-ended grammar question, check for agreement. In this case, all of the answer choices agree completely but (A). Choice (A) has a singular subject, Kate, and a plural verb, were. Since a singular subject and a plural verb do not agree, (A) is grammatically incorrect.

6.   **Which of these sentences is grammatically correct?**

   A   Campaign managers will do anything to ensure his candidate's election.

   B   An actor's appearance may the reason they do not get a part in a move.

   C   Each of the guests to the baby shower is expected to bring a gift of her choosing.

   D   When marketing to a specific demographic, it is important to take their interests into account.

Here's How to Crack It

Once again, whenever you are asked an open-ended grammar question, check for agreement. In this case, there are issues with noun-pronoun agreement in three of the answer choices. In (A), the noun is "campaign managers" and the pronoun is "his," which doesn't agree. In (B) the noun is "actor" and the pronoun is "them," which doesn't agree. And in (D) the noun is "demographic" which is singular, but the pronoun is "their," which is plural. This also doesn't agree. In (C) the subject is "each of the guests," which is singular because of the word "each." The pronoun is "her" which is singular as well. Choice (C) is the answer!

Pronoun Use

There are a couple of flavors of correct pronoun use on the TASC test. The first is a clear **pronoun antecedent** (the noun that the pronoun is replacing). Things can get pretty confusing when it's difficult to figure out which noun should be paired with the pronoun. Consider the following example:

> Jorge asked Tony if he had found his wallet yet.

Well, whose wallet is missing? Has Tony been searching for his own wallet, or had he offered to find Jorge's wallet for him? The antecedent of "his" (Jorge or Tony) isn't clear.

The other aspect of pronoun use is correct **pronoun case**. The old comedy line "*Whom* shall I say is calling?" is actually incorrect. Reword the sentence "I shall say whom is calling," and it becomes apparent that the correct version would be "I should say *who* is calling," because "who" is the subject of the verb "is calling." (Similarly, it would be correct to write, "I should say she is calling," using the subjective "she.") On the other hand, in another phrase—"To *whom* am I speaking?"—the pronoun "whom" is in the objective case, because it is the object of the preposition "to."

Try these on your own:

---

7. **Which of these sentences is grammatically correct?**

A He and her are going to go the store later.

B Sara and Zoe both ordered the same appetizer, but only she ordered dessert.

C Greg is planning to go to the movie with Kelly and I.

D Between you and me, I avoid running errands until I absolutely have to.

If you are ever confused if you need "I" or "me" in a sentence, cross out the extra person and read it. Would you say "go the movie with I" or "go to the movie with me"?

Here's How to Crack It

Since there are pronouns in all of the answers, check for antecedents and case. Choice (A) has a case error; "her" should be "she" since "He and she" are the subject of the sentence. Choice (B) has the correct case for the pronoun at the end, but an unclear antecedent: Did Sara or Zoe order dessert? Choice (C) has a pronoun case issue. "I" should be "me," so eliminate this choice. That leaves (D), which has no antecedent or case errors.

Parallelism

Parallel construction is an important grammar rule, and you can see it most easily in bulleted lists. To guide the reader smoothly through the list, each bullet point should be built the same way. Try to figure out which bullet point needs to be changed in this example:

When you go on the wilderness survival course, you'll learn

- how to start a campfire
- how to identify edible plants
- how to build a shelter, and
- hunting.

There are three "how to" bullets and one oddball "…ing" bullet, which needs to be changed to "how to hunt" in order to make the structure of the bullets the same, or parallel.

---

8. **Which of these sentences contains a grammatical error?**

   A The summer camp will teach you how to tie knots, will take you on hikes, and will give you badges for certain skills.

   B Clarissa wanted to make a lot of money, buy a lot of stock, and she wanted to retire early.

   C Our plans for the evening are watching a show, eating a meal, and then going to bed.

   D After catching a fish you need to take the hook out, hold on tight, and get your knife ready.

Each of these answer choices has a list of actions in it, so make sure to check for parallelism. All of the choices are in parallel form except for (B). In (B) the actions go from ". . . **make** a lot of money, **buy** a lot of stock, and **wanted to retire** early." Since those three are not parallel, this is the incorrect one. Choice (B) is the answer.

—————————◯—————————

> If you have trouble on parallelism questions, try listing the actions in bullet point form on your scratch paper like the example on the previous page.

Modifiers

A modifier describes a noun, as in "the golf ball *that went into the sand trap.*" It's not the golf ball in the caddy's hand or the one at the bottom of the water feature; it's the one in the sand trap. The problem arises if a modifier is misplaced—not clearly beside the noun it's (there's that "it is" contraction again) modifying. That can make things confusing for the reader. Take a look at this example:

> The delivery man left a package at the door *that looked as if it had been used as a football by the night crew.*

Just what was the night crew kicking around here—the door or the package? To fix this confusing sentence, you could either omit "at the door" (after all, where else would he leave it?) or else start a new sentence ("The beaten-up package looked as if...").

That's called a misplaced modifier—it's placed too far away from what it's describing.

Just as confusing is the dangling modifier. That occurs when a sentence starts with a modifier but the thing that comes right after it is not, in fact, what the modifier is describing. The modifier just dangles there at the beginning of the sentence without being attached to anything sensible. Here's an example:

> *Determined to cut the budget, salaries* were lowered by 12 percent after the new governor took office.

So the salaries are determined to cut the budget? No; those words must be describing the new governor, not the salaries:

> *Determined to cut the budget, the new governor* lowered salaries by 12 percent after she took office.

Try it on your own:

———————————○———————————

9. **Which of these sentences is grammatically correct?**

A To make a good grade, hard work is required.

B Having so much fun at the party, dancing and board games went on until dawn.

C As hungry as a horse, the pizza was delicious.

D Running at top speed, I felt my hat fly off.

Here's How to Crack It

All of the answers have an introductory phrase, which is a good indicator that you have a misplaced modifier question. Check the subject that comes immediately after each descriptive phrase. In (A) it is the "hard work" that must make a good grade, which is not correct. In (B) it is "dancing and board games" that had so much fun at the party, which is not correct. In (C) it is the "pizza" that is hungry as a horse, which is incorrect. In (D) it is "I" who was running at top speed, which is correct. The only correct choice is (D).

———————————○———————————

Other Commonly Confused Words
accept/except
allusion/illusion
cite/site
complement/compliment
fewer/less
ensure/insure
principal/principle
stationary/stationery
whose/who's

Other Nonstandard Uses
anyway (not "anyways")
couldn't care less (not "could care less")
a couple of (not just "a couple")
regardless (not "irregardless)
supposed to (not "suppose to")
would have (not "would of")

Word Choice and Spelling

Spelling mistakes are common errors we make every day, and it hasn't gotten any easier with predictive texting and autocorrect. The TASC test will ask one or two questions about spelling, but they will let you know that is what they are testing by bringing it up specifically. For these questions, read slowly and check each word in each answer choice before picking your answer.

Word Choice. Some words are commonly confused or easily used in a nonstandard way, especially when you're working under time pressure. Here are some examples:

They're (contraction for "they are") putting *their* (possessive) coats over *there* (location).

The *effects* (noun) of climate change will *affect* (verb, action) us all.

It's (contraction for "it is") amazing how quickly the tree shed *its* (possessive) leaves when *it's* (contraction for "it is") still so warm at night.

That report is due on Friday. If you submit it *then* (a point in time), the boss will be more willing to consider a raise *than* (a comparison) if you hand it in late. If you're even later *than* (a comparison) Steve usually is, *then* ("in that case") you can probably forget about any raise this year.

You should *try to see* ("to see" is the infinitive form of the verb "see") him before he leaves. (not "*try and see*...," which is a nonstandard, incorrect use)

You're the best one to make a list of the words that you sometimes confuse or use incorrectly. Research them in a good grammar book or online resource before the test, so you can choose the correct word with confidence, in spite of the time pressure.

Structure Drill

Now try a structure drill on your own. Review the seven language use areas from this chapter before you start; the errors you see will be in those areas. Remember to read the answer choices carefully, too, so you won't miss a small difference between a wrong answer and one that's correct. To check your answers, register your book at **PrincetonReview.com/cracking** and download the Chapter Drill Answers and Explanations supplement.

1. **Read this sentence. Then answer the question.**

   The lawyer, left in the glove compartment, picked up the papers.

   Which revision of the sentence best expresses the idea precisely and concisely?

   A Left in the glove compartment, the lawyer picked up the papers.

   B Picked up by the lawyer, the glove compartment had papers left in it.

   C Picking up the glove compartment, the lawyer left the papers.

   D The lawyer picked up the papers left in the glove compartment.

2. **Which of these sentences is grammatically correct?**

   A The passenger's possessions was lost at sea.

   B Neither Tom nor Jerry is a very good role model.

   C Constantly sending text messages are a very annoying habit.

   D Each of the fortune cookies are completely wrong.

3. **Which one of these sentences contains a misspelled word?**

   A In order to be succesful you must be willing to work very hard.

   B It is not necessarily true that more is always better.

   C It has been shown that driving while tired can adversely affect your driving abilities.

   D It is impossible to achieve all of your goals all at once in life.

4. **Read this sentence. Then answer the question.**

   I don't know what to say when I receive compliments from others so I just blush.

   What change should be made to correct the sentence's punctuation?

   A I don't know what to say; when I receive compliments from others so I just blush.

   B I don't know what to say when I receive compliments; from others so I just blush.

   C I don't know, what to say, when I receive compliments from others so I just blush.

   D I don't know what to say when I receive compliments from others, so I just blush.

5. **Which of these sentences is punctuated correctly?**

A The one thing that will help you dress well: buy clothes cut for your body.

B You wish to dress well, your clothes must fit your body.

C Here's how to dress well; clothes that fit your body.

D In order to dress well you should follow one rule: wear clothes that are cut to fit.

6. **Which one of these sentences contains an error in capitalization?**

A Do you want to go to the Cubs' baseball game today?

B Everything you say has a Shakespearean theme to it.

C I enrolled in Psychology 101 yesterday when registering online.

D Just like the novel, I feel this will be the Winter of our Discontent.

Chapter 11
Revision

This chapter will focus on the best ways to edit sentences or paragraphs on the Writing portion of the TASC test. Following the content lessons, we'll give you some practice questions.

REVISION

In the last chapter you reviewed seven out of the nine language skills tested on the TASC test. In this chapter you will review the final two language skills tested: Joining Thoughts and Logic and Clarity. These skills require you not only to fix grammatical errors in a sentence but also to think about the *best way* to edit a sentence or paragraph.

Once again, you don't need to know the names of these areas; you simply need to be able to recognize when something is wrong—for whatever reason—and when it's correct.

Joining Thoughts

Joining thoughts is really just coordination and subordination. What's the difference between coordination and subordination? Well, in coordination, the two thoughts are equally important; in subordination, one is more important than the other. The choice of coordination or subordination—and the choice of which thought is subordinated—can have a profound impact on the meaning.

Take a look at two brief statements that someone might be including in a cover letter for a job application:

> I have no paid work experience in marketing.

> I chaired the volunteer marketing committee for a charity.

Coordinating those two thoughts (using "and") would just plain confuse the employer:

> I have no paid work experience in marketing, and I chaired the volunteer marketing committee for a charity.

What is this applicant trying to tell the employer? By coordinating the two facts, the applicant is presenting them as equal in importance. It seems as if the statements on either side of the "and" are fighting each other, though. Now see what a different impression you can create by subordinating each of those statements:

> Although I chaired the volunteer marketing committee for a charity, I have no paid work experience in marketing.

What does the employer see and remember? "No paid work experience in marketing."

Now consider this sentence:

> Although I have no paid work experience in marketing, I chaired the volunteer marketing committee for a charity.

Now what does the employer see and remember? This applicant is being honest about his lack of paid experience, but he's downplaying it by subordinating it (with "although"), and highlighting his volunteer leadership experience instead.

You may see several different questions that ask about subordination and coordination in joining thoughts. Here are two possible questions you may encounter on the test:

> Which of these is the most accurate and effective revision to the sentence?

> Which revision best expresses the ideas precisely and concisely?

These questions will have answer choices that contain grammatical errors you reviewed in the previous chapter, but it is important to pay attention to how the thoughts are related to one another as well.

Combination Questions

One specific question type you will see that will also require you to think about joining thoughts is a combination question. Pay attention to how ideas are related to one another and check to make sure the punctuation is correct. Consider these two sentences:

> One of the biggest complaints workers have about working in an office is the lighting. No one looks good under the bright glare of fluorescent lights.

To combine these sentences, you must determine both the main point and the supporting point. The main point is that people don't like the lights, and the supporting point is that the reason they dislike them is that no one looks good under them. Do these ideas fit together or are they going against one another? They fit together! So a possible combination could be the following:

> Once of the biggest complaints workers have about working in an office is the lighting, since no one looks good under bright glare of fluorescent light.

Try one on your own:

---

1. **Read these sentences:**

> **Another thing people hate is the lack of privacy while in a cubicle. There is no fourth wall, no door, and no escape from passersby.**

How could these sentences best be combined?

A Another thing people hate is the lack of privacy while in a cubicle, there is no fourth wall, no door, and no escape from passersby.

B The lack of a fourth wall, no door, and no escape from passersby is what people hate about offices: their privacy.

C Another thing people hate is the lack of privacy while in a cubicle, and there is no fourth wall, no door, and no escape from passersby.

D Another thing people hate is the lack of privacy while in a cubicle: no fourth wall, no door, and no escape from passersby.

Here's How to Crack It

The easiest thing to check for first in combination questions is the punctuation. Check for any punctuation errors, since you can eliminate answers without having to think about the other changes. Choice (A) has two complete sentences separated with only a comma, so it can be eliminated. Choice (C) has a comma with a conjunction, which is grammatically correct. But is the best way to join these ideas with the word "and"? No, so eliminate (C) as well. Choice (B) is also grammatically correct, but it changes the meaning of the sentences; it is saying that what people hate is their privacy. Eliminate that one as well. The only choice left is (D), which is both grammatically correct and retains the meanings of the original sentences.

Logic and Clarity

Communication that is clear and logical is easy for the reader to follow. It guides the reader with transition and signal words that indicate a change in direction, perhaps, or a more detailed explanation of a point just made. The skilled use of these road signs allows the reader to concentrate on the writer's argument instead of struggling to figure out exactly what that argument is. See how easy you find it to read this example:

> Deep water drilling promises to unlock rich sources of untapped energy. There are environmental concerns. A major storm could damage a drilling rig, leading to an oil leak that would threaten the surrounding ecosystem.

Now see how much more sense that example makes if you simply add "however" before the second sentence and "for example" before the third, telling the reader that you're changing direction and then that you're going to elaborate on a point.

There are three types of questions that really stress logic and clarity.

Some Common Transition and Signal Words

Changing course:
- alternatively
- however
- nevertheless
- on the other hand
- otherwise

Adding:
- also
- in addition
- furthermore
- moreover
- not only ... but also

Reaching a conclusion:
- accordingly
- as a result
- consequently
- on the whole
- therefore

Making a Break

Certain questions on the TASC test will ask where it makes most sense to add a paragraph break. In order to answer these questions, focus on where a shift is happening in the paragraph. Consider this example:

> Scarlett hated Rhett Butler with a fiery passion. She wanted nothing to do with his carpet-bagging ways. She had no interest in him romantically, no matter how many times he asked her to marry him. She was in love with Ashley after all this time, and there was nothing Rhett could say to change her mind. But she needed money to save Tara.

Where do you see a shift in the above paragraph? At the "but." The focus shifts from Scarlett's feelings regarding Rhett and Ashley over to her need for money.

Try it on your own:

Directions Read the following paragraph.

Excerpt from *Narrative of the Life of Frederick Douglass, An American Slave*

by Frederick Douglass

(1) I do not remember having ever met a slave who could tell me his birthday. (2) A lack of information about my own has been a source of unhappiness to me, even when I was a child. (3) The white children could tell their ages. (4) I could not tell why I should be deprived of the same privilege. (5) I was not allowed to make any inquiries of my master about it. (6) He deemed all inquiries on the part of a slave improper and evidence of a restless spirit. (7) The nearest estimate I can give makes me now between twenty-seven and twenty-eight years of age. (8) I figured this out, from hearing my master say, sometime during 1835, I was about seventeen years old. (9) My mother's name was Harriet Bailey. (10) She was the daughter of Isaac and Betsey Bailey, both colored, and quite dark.

2. **Where might the author add a paragraph break to better organize the text?**

A between sentences 5 and 6

B between sentences 6 and 7

C between sentences 7 and 8

D between sentences 8 and 9

Here's How to Crack It

As you read the paragraph look out for where there is a shift in what the author is discussing. In this paragraph the first 8 lines are dedicated to the author's lack of knowledge surrounding his birthday. Starting at line 9 the author begins to speak of his mother, and birthdays and age are no longer mentioned. This is the most clear shift that occurs in the paragraph, which makes (D) the best answer.

Adding On

Another type of question that will require you to pay attention to logic and clarity are the adding-on questions. These come in two versions:

> Which of the following would be the most effective addition to start the paragraph?

> Which of the following would be the most effective addition to conclude the paragraph?

Whenever you are asked to add on a sentence at either the end or the beginning of a paragraph, pay close attention to the ideas in the paragraph. What is the main topic, and what is the author saying about that person or thing? Do you see any of the transitional words reviewed earlier mentioned in the paragraph?

Practice on the following paragraph:

> These were the opening words for a talk with Secretary of Agriculture Wilson, in response to a request to give to the readers of *The New York Times* some comments and opinions on the departing and arriving years. "A great ending, with every man who wants work employed at good wages, with plenty to eat and clothes better than ever before at the prices, the country getting around to unanimous conviction on sound money, and even the timid philanthropists awakening to the fact that expansion will expand not only our physical limits but enlarge our appreciation of and ability to encounter greater responsibilities.

What is the main point of this paragraph? The previous year. What is being said about the previous year? That it went very well, many great things happened, and it perhaps created possibilities for the future.

So what would you want to add to the beginning of this paragraph? Well, the first words we read are "These were the opening words," so probably some opening words. Since the opening words were given by Wilson in response to being asked about the previous and coming years, should the words we pick be positive or negative? Positive! They should match his positivity later in the passage.

Try one on your own:

Directions **Read this paragraph.**

In Louisiana the sales of malt liquors have decreased during the past fiscal year 51,972 barrels, or upwards of 20 percent of the total output, which is due to the substitution for heavily taxed lager beer and ale as popular beverages, of un-taxed domestic wines and cider, which contain a much larger percentage of alcohol and are sold at a much lower price than malt liquors. At present there are strong indications that there will be a considerable increase in the sales of lager beer and ale during the year 1900, attributable to the phenomenal prosperity of the country, especially the manufacturing interests, mechanics and the laboring classes being the principal consumers.

3. **Which of the following would be the most effective addition to conclude the paragraph?**

   A However, it is immoral for a Christian nation to consume such beverages at all.

   B This increase would be greatly aided by the repeal of the alcohol tax.

   C In Texas, the statistics are relatively the same, although in Oklahoma they are not nearly as high.

   D Note that it is usually men who drink alcoholic beverages, although women do drink wine.

Here's How to Crack It

The first sentence in the paragraph is focused on the increase of sales of un-taxed alcoholic beverages as opposed to the heavily taxed lager and ale beverages. The second sentence is focused on the fact that lager and ale sales are expected to increase due to the prosperity of the nation as a whole and those who buy such beverages. Since no shift has occurred here, the answer you select should continue on this topic. Choice (A) is a clear shift from the passage, stating that alcoholic beverages are wrong, so it should be eliminated. Choices (C) and (D) do not shift as sharply, but they introduce the new topics of different states and women versus men, which are also not on point here. Eliminate both of those choices. The only choice that stays on the topic of increasing sales is (B).

Fill in the Blank

The last question type that will require you to pay close attention to logic and clarity are Fill in the Blank questions. They will not ask you for any old word, but they will ask you for a word that accomplishes a specific task in the sentence or paragraph. Pay attention to what the question is asking for and you will be fine on these! Let's look at an example:

> **Read these sentences:**
>
> The city of Austin has made several advancements in order to deal with the stress of traffic on the city's infrastructure. They built a light rail for commuters, which has _____ in ridership since starting in 2013. These increased uses of mass transit have made a noticeable, although still small, dent in Austin's transportation problem.
>
> **Which word, when added to the blank, would best stress the advancements Austin has made?**

What exactly is the question asking you to do? Stress the advancements Austin has made in addressing their traffic problem. So should this word be something positive about the light rail ridership, or something negative? Positive! Our answer would likely be something like increased, doubled, or grew.

Try this one on your own:

---

4.   **Read these sentences:**

> There was a long discussion at yesterday's meeting over the bill requiring all engineers in the state to be licensed by the state board. Several engineers have _____, fearing that if the bill should be passed it would place their current contracts in jeopardy.
>
> **Which word, when added to the blank, would best stress the engineer's disapproval of the bill?**

A   protested

B   agreed

C   read

D   scoffed

Here's How to Crack It

The question asks for you to stress the engineer's disapproval. Eliminate anything that doesn't match disapproval, which are (B) and (C). Both (A) and (D) do match disapproval, but only (D) fits into the sentence, matching "fear." Choice (A) is the best answer.

Remember: Do What They Ask

Just like with the Fill in the Blank questions, you may see other questions that ask you to pick an answer choice that accomplishes a specific goal. You may be asked to emphasize a point, you may be asked to stress a point, or you may be asked to match a point.

Regardless of how these questions are phrased, remember: Answer the question that is being asked! Just like in the last practice problem, focus on what the question asks you to focus on and use POE.

Revision Drill

Now try a revision drill on your own. Review the two language use areas from this chapter before you start; the errors you see will be in those two main areas and will cover the question types we just discussed. Remember to read the answer choices carefully, too, so you won't miss a small difference between a wrong answer and one that's correct. To check your answers, register your book at **PrincetonReview.com/cracking** and download the Chapter Drill Answers and Explanations supplement.

Directions **Read the draft of a paragraph. Then do Numbers 1 and 2.**

(1) Mauna Loa on the Island of Hawaii is the world's largest volcano. (2) People residing on its flanks face many hazards that come with living on or near an active volcano, including lava flows, explosive eruptions, volcanic smog, damaging earthquakes, and local tsunami (giant sea waves). (3) The County of Hawaii is the fastest growing County in the State of Hawaii. (4) Its expanding population and increasing development mean that risk from volcano hazards will continue to grow.

Source: U.S. Department of the Interior—U.S. Geological Survey

1. **Which sentence would be the most effective addition to the end of the paragraph?**

    A This is why people should not live on Hawaii.

    B Despite the fact that people live so close to danger, it is most likely well worth it due to the other amenities a location like Hawaii offers.

    C Scientists at the Hawaiian Volcano Observatory (HVO) closely monitor the volcano to enable timely warning of hazardous activity and help protect lives and property.

    D There is also another very large volcano, Kilauea, nearby.

2. **How could sentences 3 and 4 best be combined?**

    A The County of Hawaii, the fastest growing County in the State of Hawaii, expanding population and increasing development mean that risk from volcano hazards will continue to grow.

    B The County of Hawaii is the fastest growing County in the State of Hawaii; this increased development means that risk from volcano hazards will continue to grow.

    C The County of Hawaii is the fastest growing County in the State of Hawaii, growing the risk from volcano hazards.

    D Expanding population and increasing development mean that risk from volcano hazards will continue to grow.

Read the draft of a paragraph. Then do Numbers 3 and 4.

(1) In 2003, eighty-three percent of Americans lived in metropolitan areas, and considerable population increases are predicted within the next 50 years. (2) Nowhere are the environmental changes associated with urban development more evident than in urban streams. (3) Contaminants, habitat destruction, and increasing streamflow flashiness resulting from urban development have been associated with the _____ of biological communities, particularly the loss of sensitive aquatic biota. (4) Every stream is connected downstream to other water bodies, and inputs of contaminants and (or) sediments to streams can cause degradation downstream with adverse effects on biological communities and on economically valuable resources, such as fisheries and tourism. (5) Understanding how algal, invertebrate, and fish communities respond to physical and chemical stressors associated with urban development can provide important clues on how multiple stressors may be managed to protect stream health as a watershed becomes increasingly urbanized.

Source: U.S. Department of the Interior—U.S. Geological Survey

3.   **Which word would best fit in the blank in sentence 3 to clarify the danger of urban development to streams?**

   A   destruction

   B   rehabilitation

   C   highlighting

   D   mischief

4.   **Where might the author add a paragraph break to better organize the text?**

   A   Between sentences 1 and 2

   B   Between sentences 2 and 3

   C   Between sentences 3 and 4

   D   Between sentences 4 and 5

Chapter 12
The Essay

This chapter will cover the two types of Essay prompts that you might see on the Writing portion of the TASC test. Following the content lessons, we'll give you some practice drills.

Anyone can learn to write an essay. Yes, anyone. You need a plan to follow (which we'll give you in this chapter) and confidence (which will increase as you get more practice writing and evaluating your own work).

You can use our method to help you analyze the arguments you encounter in everyday life beyond the test, too. Try it the next time you get a message from someone urging you to buy something or do something. Switch into active reading (or active listening) mode right away and start looking for the main arguments and how well they're supported. You'll soon know if you should consider the request or not.

As you saw in the Writing Overview chapter, you will be asked to write one essay during a 45-minute period. The essay is scored on a scale of 0 to 8 based on clarity of expression; clear and strategic organization; complete development of ideas; and sentence structure, punctuation, grammar, word choice, and spelling. Let's look at how they grade those skills more closely.

SCORING

Although the essay is assigned as a grade from 0–8, the scoring rubric is based on a scale of 0–4. This is because two separate people will read and score your essay from a 0–4, and those scores will be added for a score of 0–8. You'll need to earn at least 2 out of these 8 points to pass.

Review the scoring rubric in order to better understand what you need to accomplish in your essay:

Score	Informational Essay	Argumentative Essay
4	The response is a well-developed essay that examines a topic and presents related information from both texts. • Effectively introduces the topic to be examined • Uses specific facts, details, definitions, examples, and/or other information to develop the topic fully • Uses an organizational strategy to present information effectively • Uses precise and purposeful word choice • Uses words, phrases, and/or clauses that effectively connect and show relationships among ideas • Uses and maintains an appropriate tone • Provides a strong concluding statement or section that logically follows from the ideas presented • Has no errors in usage and conventions that interfere with meaning	The response is a well-developed essay that develops and supports an argument. • Effectively introduces a claim • Uses logical, credible, and relevant reasoning and evidence to support the claim • Uses an organizational strategy to present reasons and relevant evidence • Acknowledges and counters opposing claims, as appropriate • Uses precise and purposeful word choice • Uses words, phrases, and/or clauses that effectively connect and show relationships among ideas • Uses and maintains an appropriate tone • Provides a strong concluding statement or section that logically follows from the ideas presented • Has no errors in usage and conventions that interfere with meaning

3	The response is a complete essay that examines a topic and presents information. • Clearly introduces the topic to be examined • Uses multiple pieces of relevant information to develop the topic • Uses an organizational structure to group information • Uses clear word choice • Uses words and/or phrases to connect ideas • Uses an appropriate tone • Provides a concluding statement or section that follows from the ideas presented • Has few, if any, errors in usage and conventions that interfere with meaning	The response is a complete essay that develops and supports an argument. • Clearly introduces a claim • Uses reasoning and evidence to support the claim • Uses an organizational structure to present reasons and relevant evidence • Attempts to acknowledge and/or counter opposing claims, as appropriate • Uses clear word choice • Uses words and/or phrases to connect ideas • Uses an appropriate tone • Provides a concluding statement or section that follows from the ideas presented • Has few, if any, errors in usage and conventions that interfere with meaning
2	The response is an incomplete or oversimplified essay that examines a topic. • Attempts to introduce a topic • Develops the topic, sometimes unevenly, with mostly relevant information • Attempts to use an organizational structure • Uses simple language, which sometimes lacks clarity • Provides a weak concluding statement or section • May have errors in usage and conventions that interfere with meaning	The response is an incomplete or oversimplified essay that develops and supports an argument. • Attempts to establish a claim • Develops, sometimes unevenly, reasons and/or evidence to support the claim • Attempts to use an organizational structure • Makes little, if any, attempt to acknowledge or counter opposing claims • Uses simple language, which sometimes lacks clarity • Provides a weak concluding statement or section • May have errors in usage and conventions that interfere with meaning
1	The response provides evidence of an attempt to write an essay that examines a topic. • May not introduce a topic, or topic must be inferred • Provides minimal information to develop the topic • May be too brief to demonstrate an organizational structure • Uses words that are inappropriate, overly simple, or unclear • Provides a minimal or no concluding statement or section • Has errors in usage and conventions that interfere with meaning	The response provides evidence of an attempt to write an essay that offers an argument. • Weakly states or alludes to a claim • Has minimal support for the claim • May be too brief to demonstrate an organizational structure • Makes no attempt to acknowledge or counter opposing claims • Uses words that are inappropriate, overly simple, or unclear • Provides a minimal or no concluding statement or section • Has errors in usage and conventions that interfere with meaning
0	The response is completely irrelevant or incorrect, or there is no response.	The response is completely irrelevant or incorrect, or there is no response.

Looking at the rubric, you no doubt noticed that there are *two* types of essay prompts that you may encounter: Argumentative and Informational. Let's now examine the differences between the two by looking at the possible prompts. Both types of prompts consist of four parts.

ARGUMENTATIVE PROMPT

Part 1: The Question

You will be given a topic and a question to write an essay on. You will be provided with two passages that are related to that topic. You are then expected to read the essays and select a stronger side to write about.

Here is an example topic and question.

> There is an ongoing debate in the public domain as to whether or not the government should have more oversight and regulation of the "sharing economy." What are the pros and cons to having an unregulated open marketplace? Is it in our best interest to implement government oversight over voluntary financial interactions?

> **Weigh the claims on both sides, and then write an argumentative essay supporting either side of the debate in which you argue for or against government regulation of the shared economy. Be sure to use information from both texts in your argumentative essay.**

Part 2: Go Read, and What To Read For

The prompt will instruct you read the passage. You should follow this advice. Even if it is a passage you have seen earlier in the test, always go back and read it again.

The prompt will also give you advice on what to pay attention to while you are reading.

> **Before you begin planning and writing, read the two texts:**

> 1. When Sharing is Not Caring: The Hidden Evils of the Sharing Economy

> 2. Mi Casa, Su Casa: The Rise of Sharing Economy

> As you read the texts, think about what details from the texts you might use in your argumentative essay. You may take notes or highlight the details as you read.

Take their advice. Use your pencil and scratch paper or highlighter to take notes.

Part 3: Plan, and How To Plan

After reading the texts, create a plan for your argumentative essay. Think about ideas, facts, definitions, details, and other information and examples you want to use. Think about how you will introduce your topic and what the main topic will be for each paragraph.

This is all good advice. As you read, you should be doing all the things listed above, and you should certainly be planning before you write your essay. Without a plan, how do you know what you are going write?

Part 4: Tasks

Finally, you will be asked start writing the essay. You will also be asked to accomplish certain tasks in the essay. This list is pretty comprehensive:

Now write your argumentative essay. Be sure to:

- Introduce your claim.

- Support your claim with logical reasoning and relevant evidence from the passages.

- Acknowledge and address alternate or opposing claims.

- Organize the reasons and evidence logically.

- Use words, phrases, and clauses to connect your ideas and to clarify the relationships among claims, counterclaims, reasons, and evidence.

- Establish and maintain a formal style.

- Provide a concluding statement or section that follows from and supports the argument presented.

INFORMATIONAL PROMPT

The informational prompt will come in the same format as the argumentative prompt, but you will see a few key differences. Read the example below and note how it differs from the previous prompt:

Many people believe that high schools should be focused not only on college readiness but career and job readiness as well. They propose that apprenticeship programs should be implemented in schools to prepare those students who do not plan to attend college with a skill set and practical experience that could be applied to a trade or job immediately upon graduation. Opponents of this argument believe that by providing such a curriculum within schools students would be less encouraged to attempt to attend college or that a "class system" could emerge within schools. Could such a program be implemented successfully?

Read both texts and then write an informational essay detailing a plan that a school district could use to implement apprenticeship programs, without the pitfalls the opponents fear could happen. Be sure to use information from both texts in your essay.

Before you begin planning and writing, read the two texts:

1. The Lost Art of Apprenticeship

2. Depreciating Dreams though Apprenticing

As you read the texts, think about what details from the texts you might use in your essay. You may take notes or highlight the details as you read.

After reading the texts, create a plan for your essay. Think about ideas, facts, definitions, details, and other information and examples you want to use. Think about how you will introduce your topic and what the main topic will be for each paragraph.

Now write your informational essay. Be sure to:

- Use information from the two texts so that your essay includes important details from both texts.

- Introduce the topic clearly, provide a focus, and organize information in a way that makes sense.

- Develop the topic with facts, definitions, details, quotations, or other information and examples related to the topic.

- Use appropriate and varied transitions to create cohesion.

- Clarify the relationship among ideas and concepts.

- Use clear language and vocabulary to inform about the topic.

- Provide a conclusion that follows the information presented.

Note that there are differences between the two assignments. For argumentative prompts you are asked contrast two different arguments and then select one side and support it based on your contrast. For informational prompts you are asked to synthesize information from two opposing sides in order to create something original and new.

Let's review how to answer the argumentative essay first, since you will use the same approach to the argumentative essay as you will the informational essay.

HOW DO I BUILD MY ARGUMENT?

While these may seem like very different prompts, they are actually asking you to do a lot of similar things.

From studying the prompt (the test writers call it "unpacking the prompt"), you know what you need to do:

1. Analyze the arguments in the two passages to decide which author provides stronger support.
2. Write your own argument about which one is better supported, using evidence from the passages.
3. Be objective; consider the support, not the topic.
4. Do it in 45 minutes.

Remember active reading from the Reading Overview chapter? That's where you summarize and ask questions as you read, forcing the passage to give you what you need from it. And that's where you'll start assembling the points and evidence for your argument, whether you are making a completely new argument for informational or a supporting argument for argumentative.

Let's try active reading with a brief example. *While you are reading* the following excerpt (not after you're done), determine the author's argument and the support he provides for it, and note them briefly on your scratch paper. You'll likely find it helpful to make a quick chart for yourself, such as this one:

Argument	Support

Excerpt from *The New Freedom*

by Woodrow Wilson

For indeed, if you stop to think about it, nothing could be a greater departure from original Americanism, from faith in the ability of a confident, resourceful, and independent people, than the discouraging doctrine that somebody has got to provide prosperity for the rest of us. And yet that is exactly the doctrine on which the government of the United States has been conducted lately. Who have been consulted when important measures of government, like tariff acts, and currency acts, and railroad acts, were under consideration? The people whom the tariff chiefly affects, the people for whom the currency is supposed to exist, the people who pay the duties and ride on the railroads? Oh, no! What do they know about such matters! The gentlemen whose ideas have been sought are the big manufacturers, the bankers, and the heads of the great railroad combinations. The masters of the government of the United States are the combined capitalists and manufacturers of the United States.

That was published in 1913 so yes, the sentences are a bit long, but the author's points are still clear. Your chart might look like the one below:

Use active reading and scratch paper to boil the passage down to the evidence you need for your essay.

Argument	Support
U.S. government is being run by leaders of business and finance instead of by the people, as originally intended (paragraph 1)	Three examples: tariff, currency, and railroad acts. (paragraph 1)

On the test, of course, you'll be working with several paragraphs in each passage, so you would also note the number of the paragraph that contains each point so you can find it again quickly. And since you're under a strict time limit, your chart would contain short forms and abbreviations that are meaningful to you.

What's the value of this chart? It boils an article, or a news release, or a letter—any of the different types of documents you might encounter in a passage—down to one common bare-bones list of the arguments and support points you need for your essay. It saves you the time of rereading and flipping from page to page just to find something again. And it gives you a clear picture of the support in each passage, making it easier to decide which one provides the best. That's the topic of your essay, after all.

Later on in this chapter, we'll give you some examples that will let you practice active reading and boiling the passages down into argument/support charts.

HOW DO I ORGANIZE MY ARGUMENT?

You've read both passages actively, and now you've got a couple of quick charts listing the authors' arguments and the support for those arguments. You can make a clear case for which author provides better support for his or her position. In other words, you have the broad strokes of what you want to say for the essay prompt. Now what?

Let's work through an example of how you would organize and develop your essay. Suppose one of the two passages on the test is a letter to the editor from a local consumers' group complaining about the large, unexplained car insurance rate hike imposed on drivers in that city. The other is a response from a local association of insurance brokers arguing that, after three years of flat rates, an increase was overdue.

The Essay Template

First let's look at the template—or framework—for the essay. We'll discuss the pieces in more detail later, but first we need a picture of what the whole structure looks like.

In 45 minutes you won't be able to produce a polished essay. Even the test writers regard this as an "on-demand draft" and expect that it will contain some errors. However, if you have a concept of how an ideal essay would be structured, you'll have a plan for where to start and what to write in the limited time available.

The essay has a beginning, a middle, and an end. Well of course, you may say. However, it isn't quite as simple as it sounds. The essay has a *specific* beginning, middle, and end. You might be familiar with the classic advice given to people who have to make a speech: "Tell them what you're going to tell them, tell them, and tell them what you told them." That's a pretty good outline of the beginning, middle, and end of the essay, too.

The Beginning

This is the first paragraph, which sets expectations about what readers will find in the rest of the essay. It has three components.

The Attention-Getter Ideally, the first paragraph begins with an attention-getter—something that would make a human reader want to see what's in the rest of your essay. Although you don't have a human reader for the TASC Essay, an attention-getter will still get your essay off to a strong start for the robo-reader. Remember, everything it knows, it learned from human graders.

The essay begins with a three-part paragraph:

- An attention-getter, which makes the reader want to keep going
- A thesis statement, which outlines what the essay will prove
- A big picture outline of the arguments that prove the thesis statement

What would capture a reader's attention?

- You could begin with a question—for example, "Why have car insurance rates gone up so much?"
- You could start with what's called the "startling fact." For instance, "The average U.S. driver pays about $900 in car insurance premiums." (You can probably find a good startling fact candidate in the two passages.)
- You could open with a quotation (if one pops into your head without spending time thinking of one). It doesn't have to be a direct quote, using the exact words of whoever said it. You could paraphrase it instead. For example, a paraphrase such as "Abraham Lincoln claimed that it was impossible to fool everyone all of the time" would avoid trying to remember Lincoln's exact words. In this example, you'd need to add a sentence tying that quote to the passages: "However, in its letter to the editor, the consumers' group complains that car insurers seem to be trying to do just that—fool all of their customers into accepting unexplained rate hikes."

If you can't think of an attention-getter quickly, then you could simply begin with a statement about the two passages: "Rising car insurance premiums are drawing complaints from consumers and forcing the industry to defend itself, as these two passages reveal." This leads readers into the essay rather than hitting them over the head right at the start, and it's a much stronger opening than "This essay will discuss ..." or "The subject of this essay is ...."

You're not writing about car insurance premiums, though; you're writing about which side (consumers or brokers) makes the stronger case in the passages. The thesis statement, which we'll discuss next, makes the topic of your essay clear.

The Thesis Statement After the attention-getter comes the thesis statement, which makes the claim that you intend to prove in the rest of your essay. In this case, the claim is that passage X provides the stronger support for its position. The thesis statement might read as follows:

> In the dispute between drivers and insurance brokers, the consumers' group provides stronger evidence for its position that the steep rise in car insurance premiums is both unfair and unnecessary.

Depending on your attention-getter, you might need to add some type of transition sentence to tie that first sentence to the thesis statement.

Although it's called a statement, the thesis can be more than one sentence long. It should be specific: The example above mentions the two sides and the subject of the dispute, as well as notes the stronger side's position. The thesis statement should also cover *only* what you will support with evidence in your essay.

The Big Picture Arguments Finally, the first paragraph ends with a high-level list of the evidence that supports your thesis statement and which you'll explain in detail in the middle paragraphs. You've already got a list of this evidence (the authors' arguments in the chart you made up during your active reading of the passages). Sticking with the car insurance topic, let's say you found three pieces of evidence that make the "stronger" side's support better. You would finish the introductory paragraph by listing those three arguments:

> As the consumers' group points out, insurance companies made record profits last year, while the average driver had to cope with a 10 percent increase in gas prices but only a one percent rise in wages.

The Middle

In the next few paragraphs (likely the same number as the number of points you outlined in the "big picture arguments" part of the first paragraph), you'll provide evidence to support each argument that proves your thesis. Be sure to explain *why* or *how* it proves your thesis. Remember, too, that you need to incorporate some evidence from the less-supported passage, too. Deal with one point per paragraph, and start each paragraph with a topic sentence.

The Topic Sentence The topic sentence is just what it says—a sentence that introduces the topic of the paragraph. Like transition and signal words (see Chapter 11), it guides the reader through your essay and demonstrates your skill in organizing and developing your argument, traits on which you'll be graded. It does not give details about the topic (such as dollar amounts or dates or specific examples). Those come later in the paragraph.

Let's take the example of the consumers' first argument in the car insurance case.

> They say that car insurance companies already made record profits last year.

Read the paragraph below and see how you think it flows. Remember that it would be the next paragraph after the introductory paragraph.

> The consumers' argument that the car insurance industry recorded $10 billion in profits last year, more than any year in the past decade, proves that the insurance companies don't really need extra money.

The brokers' position (here we're drawing in some evidence from the less-supported passage, too) is much weaker because it doesn't address the industry's financial success. Three years of flat premiums do not justify raising prices, as the brokers argue, when the insurance companies have already made so much money.

The essay writer just jumped into that first argument. Now see how much more smoothly this writer glides into the argument by using a topic sentence before getting into specific details such as $10 billion in profits.

The consumer group refutes the brokers' claim about cash-poor insurance companies. The consumers' argument that the car insurance industry recorded $10 billion in profits last year....

The next paragraph (the third one) could then begin with a topic sentence introducing the consumers' second argument and making a smooth transition to the new point.

On the other hand (this signals a transition), the consumers argue, they are already paying more to drive.

Following that topic sentence, you would provide details about this second argument (the 10 percent increase in gas prices), and point out what makes it stronger (likely the brokers ignored the issue).

The fourth paragraph would repeat this formula with the third argument, which says consumers' wages haven't increased enough to cover the extra driving costs they already face.

The Evidence The rest of each middle paragraph will give details about the "relevant and specific" (as the prompt says) piece of evidence you're explaining in that particular paragraph. Again, this information is in the chart you made during the active reading phase. So, continuing on from the topic sentence, you'll

- describe the author's argument and the support he or she provides for that argument in the passage; remember to be specific
- explain why that evidence proves your thesis that one passage has the better support (in other words, explain why it's relevant)

Here's the complete paragraph describing the consumer group's first argument, with notes pointing out what function each part of the paragraph performs.

> The consumer group refutes the brokers' claim about cash-poor insurance companies (the topic sentence). The consumers' argument that the car insurance industry recorded $10 billion in profits last year, more than any year in the past decade, (the argument and support for it) proves that the insurance companies don't really need extra money (how this argument proves the thesis that the consumers' case has better support). The brokers' position is much weaker because it doesn't address the industry's financial success (evidence brought in from the other passage). Three years of flat premiums do not justify raising prices, as the brokers argue, when the insurance companies have already made so much money (how this argument is weaker, which again proves the thesis that the consumers' case has better support).

Quoting and Paraphrasing Evidence How you incorporate evidence into your essay is important. You can't quote directly from the passage unless you put the author's words in quotation marks. Without the quotation marks, it's called

Be specific. If the passage says the price of cabbages fell by two percent, use that product and figure. Don't be vague and say the price of vegetables is lower.

plagiarism. In many colleges, that earns you a black mark on your record the first time and expulsion the second. Adults well into their careers have lost their jobs when plagiarism from decades earlier was exposed. So it's a good idea to get into the habit of avoiding plagiarism.

How do you include evidence from the passages, then? Most of the time, the answer is paraphrase—rephrase the evidence in your own words. For example, let's say the brokers' passage contains the following argument and support for the argument:

> Insurance companies report little or no increase in average premiums during the past three years. However, claims payouts have risen, on average, by three percent in each of those years.

Try rephrasing that in your own words. Did you end up with something like, "The brokers argue that premium revenue has remained flat for three years, while claims expenses have kept increasing"?

Next, you need to explain *why* that paraphrased piece of evidence is important to your thesis.

The brokers weaken their own case by mentioning rising claims costs but failing to acknowledge the other side of the story: the record profits that more than cover the insurance companies' higher claims payouts.

When should you use a direct quote (in quotation marks, of course)?

- When the passage author's exact words are important for proving your thesis
- When the author phrases an idea in such a unique way that a paraphrase wouldn't convey its true meaning accurately

Both cases will be rare in the passages you're likely to encounter in the Essay section, so you should usually count on paraphrasing your evidence. Of course, you would also mention which side of the debate offered the evidence you're using.

Paraphrasing Exercise Imagine the following statements are made in a passage. Try paraphrasing them so you can use them as evidence in your essay. Some possible paraphrases are below the list of statements.

1. A landmark study conducted in Antarctica found that penguins were thriving despite the evidence of the toll taken by climate change on other facets of the environment.
2. In its report, the commission concluded, "We should all learn from the experiences of First Nations people, who are trying to strike a balance between their traditional customs and the change demanded by industrial development."
3. Although fish farming increases the supply of fish, there is alarming evidence that it lowers the quality.

There is no one "correct" paraphrase. An acceptable paraphrase should be in your own words and should convey the content of the original statement accurately.

Below are some possible ways to paraphrase these statements.

1. Penguins in Antarctica are flourishing, according to a pioneering study, even though climate change is causing environmental damage elsewhere on the continent.
2. The commission's report highlighted the lessons to be learned from the conflict between the growth of new industries and the traditional way of life for First Nations.
3. Evidence suggests that fish farms lead to higher production but lower quality.

The End

Ideally, the final paragraph concludes your argument by restating your thesis *in different words,* and reminding readers of the arguments that prove your thesis. Your final paragraph will be stronger if you simply say it and avoid starting with "In conclusion, ..."

> Because it considers both consumers and the insurance industry, and backs up its claims with actual figures, the consumer group's letter to the editor provides the best support. (This topic sentence introduces the main arguments and restates the thesis.) The group draws a strong contrast between the industry's record profits on the one hand and, on the other, a 10 percent increase in drivers' fuel costs that must be financed with only a one percent average increase in wages. The brokers' weak argument that a premium increase is overdue, and their failure to consider consumers' financial hardship, make their position the weaker of the two. (These sentences remind readers of the main arguments in the passages.)

WHERE YOUR OPINION COUNTS—THE INFORMATIONAL ESSAY

At last—a chance to make your own argument, without being limited by the source documents you're given. Here you get to take a stand and present your point of view on the topic in the prompt. This should be an essay you look forward to!

Even better, there is no "right" or "wrong" answer. All that matters is how effectively you argue and back up your position. If you like to debate, this is your opportunity to really shine.

The informational essay isn't a license to ramble on about your own personal views, though. To get a high score, you need to do three things:

- Take a definite position, so no one would question where you stand on the topic of the prompt.
- Develop an argument that builds and moves forward instead of simply repeating the same point several times in different ways.
- Support the points in your argument with evidence drawn from your own knowledge, reading, experiences, and observations.

> ## The Essay Template
>
> ### The Beginning
> - Introductory paragraph
>   - Attention-getter
>   - Thesis statement
>   - Big picture list of evidence that proves the thesis statement
>
> ### The Middle
> - One paragraph for each piece of evidence that proves the thesis statement
>   - Topic sentence
>   - Evidence from the passages
>   - Explanation of how the evidence supports the thesis statement
>
> ### The End
> - Restatement of the thesis in different words
> - Reminder of the pieces of evidence that prove the thesis

Lower-scoring essays tend to simply summarize what the author says in the passage, or wander aimlessly through an impassioned list of the student's own beliefs without giving any evidence to support them. The concept of a conversation with the author is helpful. If you were talking with this author and either agreeing, disagreeing or giving a "yes...but" (qualifying) opinion, how would you argue your position? What evidence would you offer to back it up?

Suppose you have the same situation as before: One of the two passages on the test is a letter to the editor from a local consumers' group complaining about the large, unexplained car insurance rate hike imposed on drivers in that city. The other is a response from a local association of insurance brokers arguing that, after three years of flat rates, an increase was overdue.

But this time you are not asked to choose a side, but to offer a plan of how the public should have been informed of a rate increase on car insurance.

The Beginning

The Attention-Getter Just as you saw before, the first paragraph in this type of essay begins with an attention-getter—something that would make a human reader want to see what's in the rest of your essay.

If you can't think of an attention-getter quickly, then you could simply begin with a statement about the two passages: "Rising car insurance premiums are drawing complaints from consumers and forcing the industry to defend itself, as these two passages reveal." This leads readers into the essay rather than hitting them over the head right at the start, and it's a much stronger opening than "This essay will discuss ..." or "The subject of this essay is ...."

You're not writing about car insurance premiums, though; you're writing about a new plan based on the information in the two passages. The thesis statement, which we'll discuss next, makes the topic of your essay clear.

The Thesis Statement After the attention-getter comes the thesis statement, which makes the claim that you intend to prove in the rest of your essay. In this case, the claim is that passage X would have been the best way to inform the public of the insurance rate increase. The thesis statement might read as follows:

> The way to introduce the public to a plan is to provide them with the reasoning behind such a decision and offer them a good deal of lead time to raise objections and prepare themselves for the cost.

Depending on your attention-getter, you might need to add some type of transition sentence to tie that first sentence to the thesis statement.

Although it's called a statement, the thesis can be more than one sentence long. It should be specific: The example above mentions the two sides and the subject of the dispute. The thesis statement should also cover *only* what you will support with evidence in your essay.

The Big Picture Arguments Finally, the first paragraph ends with a high-level insight as to why your plan is necessary. Highlight why you are right. For example you might write the following sentences:

> Clearly the unhappiness of the public indicates that the current method of providing information by the car insurance industry is not working. In order to make life easier for both consumers and insurance providers, a new approach to communication is necessary.

The Middle

In the next few paragraphs (likely the same number as the number of points you outlined in the "big picture arguments" part of the first paragraph), you'll provide evidence to support the plan in your thesis. Be sure to explain *why* or *how* your plan is correct. Remember, too, that you need to incorporate some evidence from both passages. Deal with one point per paragraph, and start each paragraph with a topic sentence.

The Evidence The rest of each middle paragraph will give details about the "relevant and specific" (as the prompt says) piece of evidence you're explaining in that particular paragraph. Again, this information is in the chart you made during the active reading phase. So, continuing on from the topic sentence, you'll

- describe the various sides or events that have led to the issue you are addressing; remember to be specific
- explain how the evidence proves that your plan addresses the concerns of both parties

The End

Ideally, the final paragraph concludes your argument, or plan, by restating your thesis *in different words,* and reminding readers of the arguments that prove your thesis. Once again, your final paragraph will be stronger if you simply say it and avoid starting with "In conclusion, ..."

The Five-Paragraph Essay

This is the classic template. You might even remember it from earlier years in school.

The first paragraph is the introduction (the beginning described above).

Along with the attention-getter and the thesis statement, it gives three high-level reasons why the thesis statement is true.

Each of the next three paragraphs provides details about one of those three reasons.

The second paragraph begins with a topic sentence covering the first reason you mentioned, and explains details about it. The third paragraph does the same for the second reason, and the fourth paragraph for the third reason. Those paragraphs are the middle described above.

The fifth paragraph is the conclusion (the end). It wraps up the thesis statement and the details from the middle section, and concludes your argument neatly. It doesn't simply restate the introduction, though, because by now you've added details that put meat on the bare bones of the introduction.

There is no set length of number of paragraphs for your essay.

Of course, your essay doesn't *have* to be five paragraphs. You might have four reasons for your thesis statement, or only two. There might be six reasons, but two of them are so weak they're not worth discussing. There is an expectation that the essay will be more than one paragraph, but that's the only guideline the test writers give. The essay can be as long or as short as the time and doing a good job of the prompt task allow.

Prewriting

The template above gives you an organizational structure into which you can pour your essay (remember, organization is one of the traits on which you'll be graded) and a plan to follow in developing your argument about which passage has stronger support.

The template also explains why you don't just jump in and start writing. Your essay will sound like you just jumped in and started writing. For a coherent, persuasive essay that responds to the prompt, "hangs together" well, and gets a high score, you first need to plan it. That's where prewriting comes in.

Understanding your task through upfront thinking and planning has a tremendous impact on the quality of the final product (your Essay, in this case). As one of the world's great minds said,

> If I had an hour to solve a problem I'd spend 55 minutes thinking about the problem and 5 minutes thinking about solutions.

We're certainly not advocating that you spend more than 90 percent of the time thinking about the task in the prompt, but do spend five minutes or so thinking about why one passage provides stronger support, and planning the order in which you'll discuss the evidence from the passages. Use scratch paper to jot down any ideas you have for a strong opening paragraph and conclusion. Write a number beside each point in your argument/support chart to remind yourself which claim you want to cover first, second, and so on. You can cross off each one as you finish discussing it, so you'll see the progress you're making.

Taking a few of your 45 minutes to plan will save you from getting 40 minutes into writing and realizing you're badly off track. It will also leave you a couple of minutes at the end to review your essay so you can improve it and fix errors.

Your goal with prewriting is to have the whole essay essentially done—in your head, in thin air, on your scratch paper, wherever. It's just not written down yet, and that's all you need to do with the next 30 or so minutes, leaving yourself a couple of minutes at the end to review and improve what you've written.

HOW CAN I IMPROVE MY WRITING?

You already encountered several ways to improve your writing: the nine areas of language use targeted on the TASC test, and the use of a topic sentence to begin each paragraph.

Here are two more tips to make your writing stronger, more interesting, and easier to read.

Dividing Up Your Time
  5 minutes—Actively reading the two passages, noting the main arguments and supporting points on the chart
  5 minutes—Prewriting
35 minutes—Writing
  5 minutes—Reviewing and improving the essay
50 minutes

Use Active Verbs

As the name implies, with an active verb, the subject is performing the action. With a passive verb, the subject is passive; the action is being done to it. Take a look at these stripped-down examples:

> John closed the door. (That's an active verb. The subject, John, is doing the closing.)

> The door was closed by John. (That's passive. The subject, the door, is getting the action done to it.)

Recognizing active and passive verbs gets a bit more complicated when phrases and clauses enter the picture:

> Tired, cold, and hungry from their frightening adventure in the dark woods, the *three boys began devising a plan* to return home without attracting the attention of anyone in the house. (That's active—the wayward boys are devising the plan.)

> Although the antique mahogany piano weighed a ton and would have sold for a fortune, *it was unloaded* from the moving van quickly and carelessly, in complete defiance of its great value. (Here's a passive verb—the subject, the piano, is getting the action of being unloaded done to it.)

There are a few cases in which you might want to use a passive verb. Let's say the owner of the small company where you work forgot to pay the computer service contract fee last month, leading the service company to cancel its contract. What do you tell Sofia in accounting when she asks why she can't get her computer fixed? Do you say, "Our idiot boss forgot to pay the computer service invoice last month"? (That's an active verb, by the way—the subject is doing the forgetting.) No, not likely. You might say something like, "The bill wasn't paid on time last month." That's passive—the subject is the one getting acted upon (in this case, not being paid). By using a passive verb, you can focus on the action and avoid blaming the one who carried out that action (the boss).

Cases in which a passive verb is a better choice are rare, though. Your writing will be stronger and more interesting to read if you use active verbs most of the time.

Active Verb Exercise

Try turning the passive verbs in the following sentences into active verbs. You'll find answers below. After you've finished, compare the active and passive versions.

Notice how much stronger and easier to read the active version is.

1. An umbrella was purchased by Juanita because of the weather forecast for several days of rain.
2. Since it was clearly dying, the tree was felled by city maintenance workers.
3. After receiving a prize for the best children's book of the year, the author was honored at a lavish reception given by the local literary society.
4. The house was renovated during the winter by electricians, plumbers, and painters.

Here are some possible answers:

1. Juanita bought an umbrella because the weather forecast called for several days of rain.
2. City maintenance workers felled the tree because it was clearly dying.
3. The local literary society held a lavish reception to honor the author of the best children's book of the year.
4. Electricians, plumbers, and painters renovated the house during the winter.

Use Variety in Sentence Length and Structure

How many paragraphs like the one below could you read?

> Carrots are a root vegetable. Carrots are healthy. Carrots contain beta-carotene. Beta-carotene is an antioxidant. Carrots have Vitamin A. Vitamin A is good for vision.

Are you tired of those short, choppy sentences yet? They're all the same structure and all about the same length. They soon become boring, and they make the topic they're describing sound boring, too.

Look what happens when you combine these short sentences in different ways, though. Now the subject is interesting and the writing is more engaging.

> Carrots, a root vegetable, are healthy because they contain the anti-oxidant beta-carotene. They also have Vitamin A, which is good for vision.

Carrots are loaded with beta-carotene, an antioxidant. This root vegetable is also healthy because it contains Vitamin A, a vision-boosting nutrient.

Carrots, a member of the root vegetable family, provide the vision and health benefits of Vitamin A and the antioxidant beta-carotene.

Health and vision benefits come from carrots, a root vegetable, because of the beta-carotene (an antioxidant) and Vitamin A they provide.

As those examples show, you can combine short sentences into more interesting structures in several ways.

- By coordinating or subordinating thoughts from two or more sentences (see Chapter 11)
- By using phrases ("Carrots, a member *of the root vegetable family,* ...")
- By using a series of words ("...beta-carotene and Vitamin A")
- By using compound subjects or verbs ("*Health and vision benefits* come from carrots...")

Sentence Variety Exercise

Try your hand at combining the following short sentences into more varied structures. See how many different solutions you can create. One possible answer is below the short sentences.

The house was painted white. The house was old. The paint was faded. The stairs were crooked. The porch floor had a hole. Some windows were broken. The house was empty. The house was not welcoming.

There are many possible ways to combine those sentences into a more interesting description of the house. Here's just one way:

The old house, with its faded white paint and broken windows, stood empty. Its crooked stairs and unsafe porch floor made it seem unwelcoming.

HOW DO I IMPROVE MY COMPLETED ESSAY?

Because you planned your essay before you started writing, you should have about three minutes left to review it. The test writers don't expect a perfect job in 45 minutes (*they* probably couldn't do a perfect job in 45 minutes, either). However, you should use the extra time to improve your essay as much as you can, revising and editing it as you read through it.

Revising

When you revise your work, you're making changes to the content. No, you won't have much time to do this, but you can check to make sure that you've supported each of your arguments with evidence drawn from the passages, and that you've explained how the evidence proves your thesis (that one passage is better supported than the other). If you notice a statement that seems unclear, see if there's a better way to say what you intended.

Editing

Editing involves simply correcting language and spelling errors, without changing the content of your essay. Watch for the nine language use points explained in Chapters 10 and 11. Remember, too, that you can't rely on spelling or grammar checkers in the test.

PUTTING IT ALL TOGETHER

Let's use a fairly straightforward example to work through the process of building and organizing an argument. The first passage is a flyer for a seminar at which modern urban cave dwellers can learn about the Paleo diet, the diet of the hunter-gatherers who roamed the earth before the birth of agriculture and the domestication of livestock. The second is a warning notice on the bulletin board of a sports medicine clinic that has many patients who do CrossFit training, a program that recommends the Paleo diet.

Flyer

Are you living in an unheated, unlit basement cave but still eating like it's the 21st century?

1   Embrace the Paleo diet and harmonize your lifestyle!

What is the Paleo diet?

2   It's a way of eating that's close to that of primitive humans. It means eating the foods that our bodies evolved to consume.

3   The Paleo diet eliminates all foods that were not available in Paleolithic times. It avoids many staples of the modern American diet, such as grains, dairy, high-fat meats, starchy vegetables, legumes, sugars, salty foods, and processed foods. It includes foods that are as similar as possible to foods available to Paleolithic man. That means grass-fed beef and free-range bison instead of the corn-fed meat readily available at most grocery stores.

What makes it good for you?

4

- By eliminating legumes, grains, and processed foods, the Paleo diet results in a healthy weight loss for most people. In a study of 14 participants, those who followed a strict Paleo diet lost an average of five pounds after three weeks on the program.

- Debilitating diseases such as cancer, arthritis, multiple sclerosis, and diabetes are a modern problem, brought on partly by cultivated crops. These illnesses were unknown in Paleolithic times, when people ate a diet rich in meat and in the berries, fruits, and nuts that grew naturally around them.

- The Paleo diet is "clean." It doesn't contain additives, preservatives, or chemicals that have been linked to lower energy levels and problems focusing on detailed tasks. The plant nutrients in the Paleo diet have significant anti-inflammatory benefits, and the higher red meat intake leads to an increase in iron. Followers find they can accomplish more in their day.

- The Paleo diet promotes a natural rotation of nutrients in harmony with the seasons and the landscape. By eating only what would have been available in a particular season and location, people following the Paleo diet avoid overworking their digestive systems with out-of-synch foods, such as fresh oranges in the depths of the Wisconsin winter.

Want to learn more?

5   Join us for a free seminar to

- see the Paleo diet creator, Dr. Loren Cordain, on video as he explains the theory and benefits of eating the Paleolithic way

- hear real-life stories from fans who will never go back to a modern diet

- sample some Paleo staples Tuesday night at 7:30 p.m. Charming Gulf District School auditorium at the corner of Relling & 184th St.

Warning Notice

Don't just live like our ancestors—eat like them too!

1   The medical staff at Sutton Sports Medical Centre cautions patients about the harmful effects of the Paleo diet, which many of you are following.

2   The potential risks include the following concerns:

3   **Nutritional imbalance**—Even with a very long list of allowed foods, the Paleo diet does not provide guidance on a balanced approach to nutrition. It also does not guarantee that people following the plan get enough of certain nutrients that are necessary to optimal health.

4   **Weight gain**—Because many of the allowed foods (such as nuts) are very high in calories, some people may find that following the Paleo diet actually causes weight gain instead of the rapid weight loss promised by the program. For instance, calorie consumption becomes a problem if a person eats five pounds of nuts in the course of one day.

5   **Suboptimal athletic performance**—The diet is restrictive in carbohydrates, which may be inadequate for athletes who use carbohydrates as a source of energy when exercising. Athletes need between three to six grams of carbs per pound of body weight per day; this is very difficult to achieve when consuming only the foods allowed by the Paleo diet. Thus, athletes may be faced with suboptimal performance.

6   **Bone and heart problems**—Removing all dairy products from your diet can cause a significant decrease in calcium and Vitamin D. A reduction in these essential nutrients can be harmful to bone health. In addition, the diet's focus on red meat can cause heart problems; a 2012 study confirmed that red meat consumption is associated with an increased risk of cardiovascular disease.

7   The clinic's resident nutritionist, Dr. Arpad Geuin, is available to create a diet plan customized to your nutritional needs and athletic goals.

Here's How to Crack It

Follow the steps we've explained.

1. Build your argument, using active reading to extract evidence (the authors' arguments and how they support those arguments), and note them on the chart.
2. Decide on your thesis (which passage is best supported).
3. Plan how you will organize the evidence.
4. Fill in the essay template to write your essay.
5. Review and improve your work.

Building the Argument

This example makes it easy to find the arguments each side uses to make its case. In most of the passages you'll encounter in the Extended Response section, the arguments will be "buried" in text paragraphs instead of clearly laid out in bullet points.

The charts you filled in during your active reading might look like the ones below. (Of course, given the limited time you have on the test, yours would contain a lot of short forms and abbreviations.)

Pro side (flyer):

Argument	Support
weight loss (paragraph 4)	study (paragraph 4)
no modern illnesses (paragraph 4)	unknown in Paleolithic times (paragraph 2)
followers get more done (paragraph 4)	more energy, better focus (paragraph 4)
followers don't overwork digestive systems (paragraph 4)	natural rotation of nutrients (paragraph 4)

Con side (warning):

Argument	Support
nutritional imbalance (paragraph 3)	no guidance on balanced nutrition (paragraph 3)
weight gain (paragraph 4)	nuts example (paragraph 4)
lower athletic performance (paragraph 5)	amount of carbs needed (paragraph 5)
bone and heart problems (paragraph 6)	red meat study (paragraph 6)

Now you have a bare bones list of the evidence you need. Each side presents four arguments, all of them supported. Two of the arguments are contradictory (weight loss/weight gain). Which passage is better supported?

Choosing Your Thesis

In this case, you might choose the warning. It cites one study (as the flyer does), but also gives specific figures (the nuts and carbs) for two other arguments. Its author is familiar enough with the diet to know that it doesn't include advice on balanced nutrition. (Showing an understanding of the other side's position boosts credibility.) The warning's support is more specific and credible than the support offered in the flyer, too. In two cases, the flyer supports arguments with only the vague experiences of unidentified "followers" of the diet.

The strongest reason for choosing the warning side, though, lies in the authors and their purposes. The flyer's author is trying to promote a seminar, and is making the assumption that urban cave dwellers want to eat like the real thing—not necessarily a valid assumption. The promotional tone of the flyer and the benefits offered (free food samples, video) undercut the credibility of the "pro" side's argument. The warning's author, on the other hand, has the credibility of being a medical professional. This author's purpose is to prevent the clinic's patients from damaging their health with a harmful diet, and the underlying assumption that patients are concerned about their health is valid.

Organizing Your Argument

From the chart, you can see that you'll end up with a six-paragraph essay: the introduction (the beginning), one paragraph for each of the four arguments (the middle), and a conclusion (the end).

You have two choices for the order in which you'd discuss the arguments. You could stick with the order in which they're listed in the better-supported passage (the warning), or else start with the warning's strongest argument (either the heart issue, which is supported with a specific study, or else the low athletic performance, which would be important to the warning's audience). Here, too, there is no right or wrong answer; choose the order you think you could do the best job of covering in the middle four paragraphs. Remember to start each paragraph with a topic sentence and use transitions (such as "in addition" or "furthermore") to guide readers smoothly through your discussion of the four pieces of evidence.

Writing the Essay

Now you've got everything you need to write your essay. You have your thesis (that the warning provides the best support), the evidence that supports your thesis (the arguments from the chart), and the template to follow in presenting your points. So let's get started on the writing.

The Introduction This example would work well with a question attention getter:

> Should modern urban cave dwellers and athletes be eating like Paleolithic man?

Then you would tie that question to the topic of your essay, state your thesis, and give the big picture outline of the arguments:

> The promoter of a Paleo diet seminar thinks they should. However, a sports medicine clinic's warning about the diet's nutritional, health, and athletic dangers is better supported than the arguments in favor of eating like our ancient ancestors.

The Middle Here you'd give the evidence from the passage (one argument per paragraph), and explain why it proves your thesis that the case against the Paleo diet is better supported.

For instance, if you're following the order used by the better-supported side, you would begin with the evidence about nutritional imbalance, which is supported by a medical professional's familiarity with the Paleo diet and its lack of guidance about nutrition. You could also point out the weakness of the corresponding argument from the seminar promoter: The vague statements about a natural rotation of nutrients and not overworking the digestive system aren't credible from someone who isn't a professional nutritionist.

The next three paragraphs would deal with the next three arguments, always explaining how each one contributes to proving your thesis that the warning is better supported.

The End Here you would restate your thesis in different words, and remind readers of the main pieces of evidence that prove your thesis. This concluding paragraph might say something like this:

> Based on the credibility of the medical professional who wrote the warning and the specific support for the arguments given, the case against the Paleo diet is better supported. Detailed figures back up the arguments about health dangers (weight gain and cardiovascular problems) as well as the argument about lower athletic performance.

This author has also made the effort to learn about the Paleo diet, and has noted its failure to provide nutritional guidance. The seminar promoter, on the other hand, cites only one study and is clearly trying to entice people to attend by mentioning the goodies that will be available.

Reviewing Your Work

Now, while you're practicing, you have time to assess your own work. During the test, of course, you won't. Then, you'll simply be reviewing your essay to revise it (is something not clear? is there a better way to say it?) and edit it (correcting grammar or spelling errors).

Essay Drills

Now *you* try building and organizing your argument and writing an essay on your own. There are two essay tasks below. (Remember, the more practice you get, the better you'll become at doing these essays.)

The first task, about electric vehicles, will give you some experience digging evidence out of the text paragraphs in two very different types of documents. The second, about antibiotics in farm animal feed, provides an example of unequally weighted evidence (one main argument on one side, several on the other). Depending on your opinion about this issue, it might also allow you to exercise the discipline of arguing for a position with which you don't agree.

Use active reading to extract the authors' arguments and support as you read, and note them in a chart. Then plan, write, and review your essay. To check your reasoning, register your book at **PrincetonReview.com/cracking** and download the Chapter Drill Answers and Explanations supplement.

Argumentative Essay Drill

Below are two passages: a government document about the benefits of electric vehicles and a letter from a father to his daughter, urging her not to buy an electric car because of the dangers.

Weigh the claims on both sides, and then write an argumentative essay supporting either side in which you argue for or against electric vehicles as a replacement for gasoline-powered vehicles. Be sure to use information from both texts in your argumentative essay.

Before you begin planning and writing, read the two texts:

1. Benefits and Considerations of Electricity as a Vehicle Fuel

2. Letter from a Concerned Parent

As you read the texts, think about what details from the texts you might use in your argumentative essay. You may take notes or highlight the details as you read.

After reading the texts, create a plan for your argumentative essay. Think about ideas, facts, definitions, details, and other information and examples you want to use. Think about how you will introduce your topic and what the main topic will be for each paragraph.

Now write your argumentative essay. Be sure to:

- Introduce your claim.

- Support your claim with logical reasoning and relevant evidence from the passages.

- Acknowledge and address alternate or opposing claims.

- Organize the reasons and evidence logically.

- Use words, phrases, and clauses to connect your ideas and to clarify the relationships among claims, counterclaims, reasons, and evidence.

- Establish and maintain a formal style.

- Provide a concluding statement or section that follows from and supports the argument presented.

Benefits and Considerations of Electricity as a Vehicle Fuel

Note: The following document uses these short forms (or acronyms) in discussing different types of vehicles powered by electricity: EV (electric vehicle), HEV (hybrid electric vehicle) and PHEV (plug-in hybrid electric vehicle).

1   Hybrid and plug-in electric vehicles can help increase energy security, improve fuel economy, lower fuel costs, and reduce emissions.

Energy Security

2   In 2012, the United States imported about 40% of the petroleum it consumed, and transportation was responsible for nearly three-quarters of total U.S. petroleum consumption. With much of the world's petroleum reserves located in politically volatile countries, the United States is vulnerable to price spikes and supply disruptions.

3   Using hybrid and plug-in electric vehicles instead of conventional vehicles can help reduce U.S. reliance on imported petroleum and increase energy security.

Fuel Economy

4   HEVs typically achieve better fuel economy and have lower fuel costs than similar conventional vehicles.

5   PHEVs and EVs can reduce fuel costs dramatically because of the low cost of electricity relative to conventional fuel. Because they rely in whole or part on electric power, their fuel economy is measured differently than in conventional vehicles. Miles per gallon of gasoline equivalent (mpge) and kilowatt-hours (kWh) per 100 miles are common metrics. Depending on how they're driven, today's light-duty EVs (or PHEVs in electric mode) can exceed 100 mpge and can achieve 30–40 kWh per 100 miles.

Infrastructure Availability

6   PHEVs and EVs have the benefit of flexible fueling: They can charge overnight at a residence (or a fleet facility), at a workplace, or at public charging stations. PHEVs have added flexibility, because they can also refuel with gasoline or diesel.

7   Public charging stations are not as ubiquitous as gas stations, but charging equipment manufacturers, automakers, utilities, Clean Cities coalitions, municipalities, and government agencies are establishing a rapidly expanding network of charging infrastructure. The number of publicly accessible charging units surpassed 7,000 in 2012.

Costs

8   Although fuel costs for hybrid and plug-in electric vehicles are generally lower than for similar conventional vehicles, purchase prices can be significantly higher. However, prices are likely to decrease as production volumes increase. And initial costs can be offset by fuel cost savings, a federal tax credit, and state incentives.

Emissions

9   Hybrid and plug-in electric vehicles can have significant emissions benefits over conventional vehicles. HEV emissions benefits vary by vehicle model and type of hybrid power system.

10   EVs produce zero tailpipe emissions, and PHEVs produce no tailpipe emissions when in all-electric mode.

Source: Office of Energy Efficiency and Renewable Energy (EERE), U.S. Department of Energy (Abridged)

Letter from a Concerned Parent

1   My dear Melissa,

2   I'm so proud of you for completing your dental technician course and graduating with such exceptional grades!

3   As promised when you first returned to school, I'm transferring enough money to your account to allow you to buy a reasonably priced new car. You deserve this reward for your perseverance and hard work.

4   The choice of car is up to you. However, I know you want to "live green" and I'm concerned you might be thinking of an electric vehicle. If you are, I want to urge you to buy a regular gasoline-powered car instead. Your safety is very important to me, and there are just too many dangers with an electric vehicle.

5   First, you could find yourself stranded on a dark highway in the middle of nowhere. Electric cars have such a limited range (an average of about 80 miles) and even the state with the most public charging stations, California, has only about 5,000. Assuming you can find a public charging post when you need one, a charge can take hours if it's not a rapid-charge station. I have visions of you hanging around some station alone at night for up to eight hours.

6   Second, parts and repairs for electric cars are much more expensive. And the batteries need to be replaced after about five years, at a cost of thousands of dollars. That's on top of the initial price of the car, which can be as much as twice the cost of a gasoline-powered car.

7   Third, with a top speed of about 70 miles per hour, electric cars aren't safe for highway driving. What if you had to pass someone quickly, or speed up suddenly to get away from a dangerous situation? That means you wouldn't be able to drive home to visit your mother and me.

8   And finally, I've been seeing news reports of a few electric vehicles catching on fire while they're just sitting in the owner's garage or driveway. No one seems to know what causes them to ignite, but I don't want to be worrying about you every night asleep in your ground-floor apartment while your car is burning away just outside.

9   I hope you enjoy your well-deserved reward, and that you'll use it wisely and choose a gasoline-powered car.

10   —Your loving father

Informational Essay Drill

Below are two passages: a government media release about a voluntary ban on antibiotics in farm animal feed, and a posting on a farmers' online forum warning about the negative effects such a ban would have on farmers, consumers, and the economy.

Read both texts and then write an informational essay detailing a way in which the government and farmers might work together to reach a compromise on antibiotic use in animals. Be sure to use information from both texts in your essay.

Before you begin planning and writing, read the two texts:

1. FDA Implements Voluntary Plan to Phase Out Antibiotics

2. Ban the FDA's Antibiotic Ban!

As you read the texts, think about what details from the texts you might use in your essay. You may take notes or highlight the details as you read.

After reading the texts, create a plan for your essay. Think about ideas, facts, definitions, details, and other information and examples you want to use. Think about how you will introduce your topic and what the main topic will be for each paragraph.

Now write your informational essay. Be sure to:

- Use information from the two texts so that your essay includes important details from both texts.
- Introduce the topic clearly, provide a focus, and organize information in a way that makes sense.
- Develop the topic with facts, definitions, details, quotations, or other information and examples related to the topic.
- Use appropriate and varied transitions to create cohesion.
- Clarify the relationship among ideas and concepts.
- Use clear language and vocabulary to inform about the topic.
- Provide a conclusion that follows the information presented.

FDA Implements Voluntary Plan to Phase Out Antibiotics

1   The Food and Drug Administration (FDA) is implementing a voluntary plan with industry to phase out the use of certain antibiotics for enhanced food production.

2   Antibiotics are added to the animal feed or drinking water of cattle, hogs, poultry, and other food-producing animals to help them gain weight faster or use less food to gain weight.

3   Because all uses of antimicrobial drugs, in both humans and animals, contribute to the development of antimicrobial resistance, it is important to use these drugs only when medically necessary. Governments around the world consider antimicrobial-resistant bacteria a major threat to public health. Illnesses caused by drug-resistant strains of bacteria are more likely to be potentially fatal when the medicines used to treat them are rendered less effective.

4   FDA is working to address the use of "medically important" antibiotics in food-producing animals for production uses, such as to enhance growth or improve feed efficiency. These drugs are deemed important because they are also used to treat human disease and might not work if the bacteria they target become resistant to the drugs' effects.

5   "We need to be selective about the drugs we use in animals and when we use them," says William Flynn, DVM, MS, deputy director for science policy at FDA's Center for Veterinary Medicine (CVM). "Antimicrobial resistance may not be completely preventable, but we need to do what we can to slow it down."

6   Once manufacturers voluntarily make these changes, the affected products can then be used only in food-producing animals to treat, prevent, or control disease under the order of or by prescription from a licensed veterinarian.

7   Bacteria evolve to survive threats to their existence. In both humans and animals, even appropriate therapeutic uses of antibiotics can promote the development of drug-resistant bacteria. When such bacteria enter the food supply, they can be transferred to the people who eat food from the treated animal.

Why Voluntary?

8   Flynn explains that the final guidance document made participation voluntary because it is the fastest, most efficient way to make these changes. FDA has been working with associations that include those representing drug companies, the feed industry, producers of beef, pork, and turkey, as well as veterinarians and consumer groups.

Source: U.S. Food and Drug Administration (Abridged)

Ban the FDA's Antibiotic Ban!

The following posting appeared on the FairToFarmers.org forum.

1   The FDA is banning the use of antibiotics in animal feed. Food producers will be barred from adding antibiotics to feed or water unless an animal is sick and threatens the health of the rest of the herd or flock. Even then, a veterinarian's order will be required.

2   The FDA fails to realize that the regular use of antibiotics *prevents* disease, and prevention is much cheaper than curing an illness that has taken root on the farm. Antibiotics not only maintain animal health; they also promote faster growth, and therefore faster time to market. In addition, antibiotics lead to more efficient growth, since less feed is required to reach the desired weigh.

3   The FDA's reasoning is that antibiotic use in food animals *might* contribute to the development of antibiotic-resistant "superbugs." Scientific studies have so far been inconclusive, and some point to doctors overprescribing antibiotics for human patients as the cause, together with unsafe food handling practices by consumers. The FDA made the ban voluntary for the present; but if the scientific evidence were clear, the ban would have been mandatory right away.

4   European countries that have banned antibiotics in animal feed have not seen a decline in antibiotic-resistant diseases, but they have seen a significant increase in meat and poultry prices and a reduction in export sales. Food animals take several days longer to reach the desired weight and consume more feed before they do, increasing farmers' costs.

5   Each American farmer today feeds an average of 155 people, *six times* more than in 1960. Advances in agricultural practices, including the regular use of antibiotics in animal feed, have made that possible. Without antibiotics, American farmers will not be able to meet the food needs of a growing population.

6   Do people want enough food? Do they want affordable food? Do politicians want a thriving agricultural economy? Then we must end this voluntary ban on antibiotics in animal feed while we still can, before it becomes mandatory.

7   Add your voice to the petition to ban the FDA's ban on antibiotics in animal feed. Simply click on the button below. The petition will be delivered to the FDA when we have 100,000 signatures.

Part IV
Mathematics

Chapter 13
Mathematics
Overview

In this chapter, we will provide an overview of the Mathematics portion of the TASC test, as well as give you some tips and strategies to help you out on test day. In the following chapters, we will explore the specific content areas of this sub-test in more detail.

If the TASC Mathematics test covered all the math topics they teach in high school, it would be an overwhelming test. Fortunately, it doesn't, and it isn't. The TASC test writers concentrate on a few areas very heavily, which means that by reading the chapters that follow and working through the practice questions we provide, you should be able to score very well—even if you've always hated math.

ABOUT THE MATHEMATICS TEST

To score well on this sub-test, you first need to know what to expect on test day. First, there are two versions of the Mathematics test: a computer-based version and a paper-based version. On the English and Spanish versions of the Mathematics test, you'll have 105 and 115 minutes, respectively, to complete the following.

Computer-Based	Paper-Based
42 Multiple-Choice Questions	43 Multiple-Choice Questions
11 Gridded-Response Items	11 Gridded-Response Items
1 Constructed-Response Item	1 Constructed-Response Item
1 Technology-Enhanced Item	

The questions on this test will be either word problems that involve real-world situations or problems that require you to interpret data presented in charts, graphs, diagrams, and tables.

According to the TASC creators, questions will test your *procedural skills*, or the ability to select and apply procedures correctly; *conceptual skills*, or the ability to recognize and apply math concepts and principles; and *application and problem-solving skills*, or the ability to use strategies to solve problems and evaluate the solutions.

What's on the Mathematics Test?

The paper-based version Mathematics section on the TASC test consists of two math sections: one 50 minute section that allows the use of a calculator and one 55 minute section that does not allow students to use a calculator.

The areas covered in the Mathematics test are as follows:

Numbers and Quantity	13%
Algebra	26%
Functions	26%
Geometry	23%
Statistics and Probability	12%

Check out our supplementary tutorials on the constructed-response and tech-enhanced items when you register your book at **Princeton-Review.com/ cracking**!

There are no calculus, pre-calculus, or proofs on the Mathematics test. There won't be any surprise topics on the exam, either, so if you have a solid grasp of the subject matter listed above, you should be good to go!

Question Types

On the paper-based version Mathematics test, you will encounter 43 multiple-choice questions, 11 gridded-response questions, and 1 constructed-response item.

If you choose to take the computer-based version of the Mathematics test, you will need to answer 42 multiple-choice questions, 11 gridded-response questions, 1 constructed-response item, and 1 technology-enhanced item.

Gridded-Response Questions

Unlike multiple-choice questions, gridded-response questions won't give you four possible answers to choose from. Instead, you'll be presented with a question followed by a grid. Here's an example.

Pluto's radius is 736.9 miles. What is its circumference? Use 3.14 as pi, and solve to the nearest whole mile.

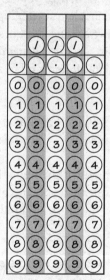

Answer the question by bubbling in the correct answer. Decimal points and fraction bars are provided in the top two rows. (We'll show you how to solve this problem in Chapter 14.)

The Calculator

The 43-question Mathematics test is broken up into two sections. In the first part, you will be allowed to use a calculator. In the second part, you will *not* be allowed to use one.

You may think that the first section will be easier than the second, but there's one hitch: You'll need to use an approved calculator. The preferred model for the TASC test is the Texas Instruments TI-30XS Multiview™ Calculator, shown below.

Although you'll be provided with a calculator reference sheet to use with both the print and online versions of the test, it is vital that you familiarize yourself with this particular model ahead of time. Why spend your valuable test time figuring out how to use the calculator when you could be actually solving the questions? We strongly recommend that you buy (or borrow) this specific calculator and practice with it for several weeks before the test. It is available in most office supply stores or online for about $18.

Visit **TASCtest.com/tasc-test-calculators-for-test-takers.html** to download the official calculator reference sheet. Also listed on this page are alternate scientific calculators that meet the approval criteria for the TASC test.

There are two major features of the Texas Instruments TI-30XS that can be pretty confusing. They are the arrow keys and the green "2nd" key.

The arrow keys (located at the top right) can be used to move within a function on the screen or to exit a function and return to the main expression you are calculating. You will use the arrow keys to input fractions, mixed numbers, or numbers in scientific notation.

Pushing the "2nd" key (located at the top left) before another key accesses the function that is written above the key. You will use this to input mixed numbers and to calculate roots and percentages.

Let's take a look at how you would input the mixed number $12 \frac{1}{2}$:

You can see why we are telling you to get the calculator in advance and become familiar with it.

The Mathematics Reference Sheet

One of the helpful items that the TASC test creators have included for use on the Mathematics test is a reference sheet. You will be given a list of the more complicated formulas to use during both sections of the exam. So, in case you don't remember a specific formula, you can just look it up! However, other formulas—such as $A = lw$ for the area of a rectangle—will *not* be on the reference sheet, so you will have to know those yourself. Once you've worked through the Geometry section of this book, you should have those formulas embedded in your brain by test day.

You can download and print the reference sheet directly from the TASC test's website at **TASCtest.com/assets/mathrefsheet.pdf.** Take the time to familiarize yourself with it—and keep it on hand as you work through the drills in the upcoming chapters and the practice tests. That way, you'll know what's on there and what isn't, and you can be sure to memorize any formulas that are not included.

TIPS AND STRATEGIES

Ballparking

We've already introduced you to Process of Elimination earlier in this book, and we've explained that there's no guessing penalty on the TASC test. On the Mathematics test, you can use POE to eliminate any out-of-scope answer choices, leaving just the answers that make sense. This is what we call **ballparking**, and it is especially useful for answering those difficult questions that you may not know how to solve!

You may once have encountered a problem on a math test that looked like this:

1. **This month, 1,500 new members joined a particular health club. The club's goal for this month was 2,000 new members. What percentage of the club's goal was achieved?**

If you weren't sure how to solve this problem during that test, you were pretty much out of luck. It certainly wouldn't have made sense to guess, would it? For example, if you had closed your eyes and picked a number at random ("…uh, 14!"), the chances that you would happen to pick the right answer would have been pretty slim.

But on the TASC Mathematics test, most of the problems are in the multiple-choice format. Here's how that question would look:

1. **This month, 1,500 new members joined a particular health club. The club's goal for this month was 2,000 new members. What percentage of the club's goal was achieved?**

   A   75%

   B   82%

   C   112%

   D   150%

You may be saying, "Big deal. Same problem." But, in fact, this is not the same problem at all—it gives you more information than the first. Even if you didn't know how to do it, you would have an enormous advantage because you would no longer have to guess at random. In the multiple-choice question format, there are only four possible answers, and one of them has to be right. Just by guessing among the four answer choices, you have a 25 percent chance of answering the question correctly. But we can do even better than that. Many TASC Mathematics answer choices aren't reasonable at all. Let's just think about that problem above. The health club's goal was 2,000 new memberships, but they actually got only 1,500 new memberships. Did they reach their goal? No way. Putting this in the language of percentages, let's restate the question: Did they reach 100 percent of their goal? The answer is still no.

That means the correct answer to this problem must be *less* than 100 percent. So even if you are unsure how to calculate the exact percentage, you can see at a glance that two of the answer choices don't work. Look at (D), 150%. This answer implies that the club not only met its goal, but it exceeded it as well. That's not right. Look at (C), 112%. Again, this is just wrong—the correct answer must be less than 100%. Both of these answers are out of the ballpark.

We have eliminated two answer choices. This means the correct answer to this question is either (A) or (B). All of a sudden, your odds of getting this question correct are much better: You now have a fifty-fifty chance of being right. Pick one. If you picked (A), you just got the question correct.

Okay, let's say you *do* know how to solve a problem. Should you bother to ballpark it first? Definitely. Taking a test does funny things to people. You might be a math whiz ordinarily, but if you're feeling stressed, you might not be thinking as clearly as you do when you're relaxing at home. Or you might feel pressed for time and make a mistake that you would never normally make. You can prevent lots of careless errors by stepping back from a math problem and saying, *Wait a minute. Before I even start multiplying or dividing, which answers don't make sense?*

Once you've gotten rid of the out-of-the-ballpark answer choices, you can start solving the problem. And if your calculations happen to lead you, mistakenly, to one of those out-of-the-ballpark answer choices—well, you'll know you just made a mistake, and you'll be able to figure out what went wrong. You'll find that once you start looking at TASC questions in this way, you'll spot many opportunities to ballpark. This is because the test writers construct their incorrect answer choices not to be reasonable but to anticipate common errors that test takers make when they're in a hurry.

Partial Answers

The test writers know that a stressed test taker tends not to read the question carefully enough, or solves only some of what the question asks. These mistakes can lead you to wrongly choose a *partial answer* (even though you may be on the right track). Let's look at another multiple-choice problem.

2. **Dayanara buys a coat from a mail-order catalog. The coat costs $140, plus an $8 shipping charge and a $2 handling fee. If there is a 10% sales tax on the entire amount, what would be the total cost of buying the coat?**

    A $135

    B $150

    C $160

    D $165

Like many problems on the Mathematics test, this requires several steps. What is the first thing you would do if you were actually buying this coat? We add up the costs we have so far:

$$
\begin{array}{lr}
\text{the coat} & \$140 \\
\text{shipping} & \$8 \\
\text{handling} & +\ \ \$2 \\
\hline
 & \$150
\end{array}
$$

We are already up to $150, and we haven't even added in the tax yet. Do you see any answer choices we can cross out? If you said (A) and (B), you are right on the money. The correct answer must be greater than $150, which means there are only two possibilities left: (C) and (D). Look at that—we just created another fifty-fifty chance of guessing the correct answer.

Why did the test writers choose two answers that didn't make sense? Because they wanted to include some answers that many test takers are likely to pick by mistake. For example, let's say that you were doing this problem, and you got to the point we have already reached: You added up the numbers and got $150. If you were in a hurry, you might look at the answer choices, see (B), $150, figure that you must be done, and select (B). However, this number is only a partial answer to the question.

To find the correct answer to this question—(D), $165—you must do three separate calculations. First, add up the cost of the coat and the postage and handling. Check. Second, calculate the tax. To compute this, you find 10 percent of $150, which turns out to be $15. Third, add the tax to the previous total. If a test taker chose (B), $150, it was not because he made a mistake in his calculations. The answer to step one of this problem is $150. And if a test taker chose (A), $135, it was likely due to subtracting the tax instead of adding it.

On the TASC test, you will frequently find partial answers lurking in wait for you. To avoid getting taken in by one of these, you have to read the problem very carefully the first time and then read it again just as carefully right before you select your answer.

Because the test writers employ partial answers so often on the Mathematics test, you can actually use the partial answers as clues to help you find the final answer. For example, working on a two-step problem, you may find that the answer to the first step of the problem is also one of the answer choices. This is a good sign. It means you are on the right track. If the answer to your first step is close to one of the answer choices, but just a little off, you might try redoing the calculation to see if you made a mistake.

Don't Get Stuck, Just Move On

There are always going to be problems that, for whatever reason, you just can't get. It might be a mental block, or maybe you never learned a particular type of problem, or maybe the question was simply written so poorly that it is impossible to understand. No matter how easy you think the problem ought to be, don't dig your heels in. Even if you can't do the very first problem, there are plenty of others waiting for you, and you will find that many of them are pretty easy.

The Two-Pass System

Of course, it isn't necessary to solve every problem to do very well, and in fact, you will see that by skipping the problems you don't know how to do, you can actually increase your score. Here's how.

The Mathematics test is made up of two separately timed sections: the Calculator Session and the Non-Calculator Session. You have to finish the first before proceeding to the second. Apart from that, you have the freedom to answer the questions in any order you like.

So, we recommend that you take each section in two passes. On your first pass, start at the beginning of the section and do every problem that comes easily to you. If you read a question and know just what to do, then it is a first-pass problem. However, if you read a problem and have no idea of how to solve it, make a note of it and move on. Don't worry—you have not skipped this problem for good. You are merely saving it for later, after you've locked in all the easy points.

First pass: Do the questions you KNOW you can get right.

When you finish your first pass, you can then move on to the second pass, during which you attempt the questions you had initially marked. Hopefully, you will be able to conquer the question the second time around. If not, don't worry: You won't be penalized for an incorrect answer, so you have nothing to lose by guessing. Pick a "guess letter" and move on. Remember: Don't leave any questions unanswered!

Now that you have a bird's-eye view of the Mathematics test, along with some tried-and-true strategies to help you out on test day, let's zoom in on subject areas you'll need to know well.

Chapter 14
Arithmetic

In this chapter, we'll introduce you to the key topics related to arithmetic on the TASC Mathematics test. We'll discuss number sense, decimals, fractions, probability, proportions, and percents. Following the content lessons, we'll give you some practice questions.

In this chapter, we're going to show you all the basic arithmetic topics that come up on the TASC Mathematics test. With each topic, we'll first show you the concept behind the topic, then illustrate it with typical examples, and finally give you a small drill so you can practice the concept on your own. At the end of the entire chapter, there will be a drill that will evaluate your ability to handle the concepts we've shown you. The purpose of this is to give you some practice recognizing the different types of questions when they are all mixed together—just as they are on the real TASC test.

NUMBER SENSE, DECIMALS, AND FRACTIONS

You probably remember learning about numbers, decimals, and fractions in elementary school. Unlike the arithmetic tests you took in school, which probably required you to regurgitate information, questions on the Mathematics test are more relevant to real life. Consequently, you won't find any questions on the more theoretical aspects of arithmetic—properties of integers, for example. Nor will there be any questions about prime numbers or any of the other terms that generally go under the name "axioms and fundamentals." Instead, the test focuses on practical math. Several of the questions will be word problems that try to evoke situations you might find in everyday life.

The basic arithmetic concepts that we will cover in this section include the following.

- The Number Line
- Positive and Negative Number Operations
- Decimal Place Value and Rounding
- Fraction Essentials
- Operations with Fractions
- Word Problems Step by Step
- Distance as a Function of Rate and Time
- Cost: Discounts, Markups, Commission, and Profit

The Number Line

The number line is a visual way of studying positive and negative numbers in relation to one another.

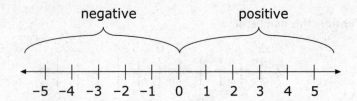

Positive numbers are to the right of zero on the number line above, while negative numbers are to the left of zero on the number line above. Zero itself is neither negative nor positive, and is often referred to as *nonnegative*.

Note that positive numbers get bigger as they move away from zero, and negative numbers get smaller as they move away from zero. For example, −3 is smaller than −1. A number line can extend infinitely to the left or right, but the number lines on the TASC test generally look like the example above, with a fairly small number of position points. Let's try identifying some points on the number line.

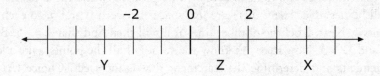

Find point X on the number line. What number does point X represent? If you said 4, you were absolutely right! How about points Y and Z? If you said −3 and 1, respectively, you were right again!

Let's take a look at a number line problem you might encounter on the Mathematics test.

———————————○———————————

1. **Consider this number line.**

Which statement is <u>not</u> true?

A The distance between points A and B is greater than the distance between points C and D.

B The absolute value of point B is equal to that of point C.

C The sum of points B and C is less than the sum of points A and D.

D The distance between points A and D is double the distance between points B and C.

Here's How to Crack It

Whenever you encounter a number line, start at zero and orient yourself, remembering that values to the right of zero will be positive, while those to the left of zero will be negative. Here, there are five spaces between 0 and 5, so each space represents 1. Next, label the number line. You will then find that A = –5, B = –2, C = 2, and D = 3. Now that you know the values of all the points, take a look at the statements and determine the statement that is incorrect. Choice (A) states that the distance between points A and B is greater than the distance between points C and D. In order to determine distance, you can count the spaces between the points; here, there are 3 spaces between A and B. Alternatively, you can take the absolute value of the difference between the two points; e.g., the distance between points A and B is $|-5 - (-2)| = |-5 + 2| = |-3| = 3$. Since the distance between points A and B is greater than the distance between points C and D, which is 1, (A) is true and can be eliminated. Choice (B) states that the absolute value of point B is equal to that of point C; the value of point B is $|-2| = 2$ and the value of point C is 2, so this statement is also true and should be eliminated. Choice (C) states that the sum of points B and C is less than the sum of points A and D. The sum of points B and C is equal to $-2 + 2 = 0$, while the sum of points A and D is equal to $-5 + 3 = -2$; since 0 is greater than –2, this statement is false. Choice (D) states that the distance between points A and D is double the distance between points B and C. The distance between points A and D is 8, while the distance between points B and C is 4, so this statement is true and can be eliminated. Accordingly, the only false statement is (C).

———————————○———————————

Positive and Negative Number Operations

Positive and negative numbers, which can be visualized on the number line, form the basis of math.

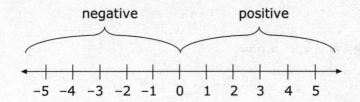

Adding and Subtracting Positive and Negative Numbers

Lots of people have trouble adding and subtracting negative numbers. There is a very easy way to do this, using the number line.

When you add two positive numbers, you are actually counting over to the right on a number line. For example, let's add 2 + 3. To find two on the number line, count over two places to the right of zero. That's 2. Now let's add three, by counting over three more places to the right. Thus, 2 + 3 = 5.

Okay, okay, we know that's pretty simple. But the great thing is that it's just as simple to add or subtract negative numbers. Let's add a positive number and a negative number: 5 + (–3). Find 5 on the number line by counting over five places to the right from zero. Now, to add –3, count over three places to the left. Where are you? That's right,

$$5 + (–3) = 2$$

By the way, adding a negative number is exactly the same thing as subtracting a positive number. Thus, the addition problem above could also have been written this way:

$$5 – 3 = 2$$

Now, let's add two negative numbers: (–2) + (–1). First, find –2 by counting over two places to the left of zero on the number line. Now, to add –1, count over one more place to the left.

$$(–2) + (–1) = –3$$

Again, we could have written this as

$$(–2) – 1 = –3$$

Multiplying and Dividing Positive and Negative Numbers

Multiplication is actually just the process of adding a number several times. For example, to multiply 4 by 3, you are actually just adding 4 three separate times

$$4 \times 3 = 4 + 4 + 4 = 12$$

or adding 3 four separate times

$$3 \times 4 = 3 + 3 + 3 + 3 = 12.$$

To multiply 5 by 2, you are actually just adding 5 two separate times

$$5 \times 2 = 5 + 5 = 10$$

or adding 2 five separate times

$$2 \times 5 = 2 + 2 + 2 + 2 + 2 = 10.$$

Of course, it's a lot quicker to use the multiplication (times) tables. We just wanted to remind you of the theory behind multiplication. If your times tables are a little rusty, don't worry. You're going to get lots of opportunity to practice over the next three chapters.

There are four rules regarding the multiplication of positive and negative numbers.

positive $\times$ positive = positive

positive $\times$ negative = negative

negative $\times$ positive = negative

negative $\times$ negative = positive

We have provided the following multiplication table for you to fill in to refresh your memory. Try to memorize this multiplication table before the Mathematics test; you will be able to work through questions much more quickly if you do!

	1	2	3	4	5	6	7	8	9
1									
2									
3									
4									
5									
6									
7									
8									
9									

Division is actually the opposite of multiplication. If we multiply 2 by 3, we get 6. If we divide 6 by 2, we are actually asking what number times 2 equals 6?

$$6 \div 2 = 3. \text{ You can also write this as } \frac{6}{2} \text{ or } 2\overline{)6}$$

The same four rules of multiplication apply to the division of positive and negative numbers.

> positive ÷ positive = positive
>
> positive ÷ negative = negative
>
> negative ÷ positive = negative
>
> negative ÷ negative = positive

Multiplying and Dividing: Is My Answer Positive or Negative?
SAME sign? The answer will be POSITIVE. DIFFERENT signs? The answer will be NEGATIVE.

Let's take a look at a question that tests your number skills.

---

2. **If x is equal to the sum of two negative integers, y is equal to the product of two negative integers, and z is the product of x and y, which of the following statements about z is true?**

   A $z = 0$

   B z is positive

   C $z = x + y$

   D z is negative

Here's How to Crack It

The question provides information regarding x, y, and z, and requires you to find out information about z. In order to solve for z, however, you must first solve for x and y. Here, you know that x is equal to the sum of two negative integers. Based on the properties of numbers, you know that the sum of a negative number and a negative number will be a negative number; thus, x is negative. (If you forget these rules, just plug in easy numbers; e.g., $-2 + (-2) = -4$.) Next, you are told that y is the product of two negative integers. Based on the properties of numbers, you know that the product of a negative number and a negative number will be a positive number; so, y is positive. Finally, you are told that z is the product of x and y. Since x is a negative number and y is a positive number, the product of x and y will be negative. Accordingly, the only answer choice that is accurate about z is (D); z is a negative number.

Order of Operations

In a problem that involves several different operations, the operations must be performed in a particular order. There's an easy way to remember the order of operations:

Please **E**xcuse **M**y **D**ear **A**unt **S**ally

First, you do operations enclosed in Parentheses; then you take care of Exponents; then you Multiply and Divide; finally you Add and Subtract. We're going to save exponents for the next chapter, but let's try out PEMDAS with a couple of problems.

$$((-5) + 4)\left(\frac{8}{2}\right) + 4 =$$

How about this one?

$$(3) + \left(\frac{8}{2}\right)(4 - 5) + 1 =$$

If you did these in the correct order, you should have gotten the same answer both times: 0.

Note that Multiply and Divide are *actually the same step*; so are Add and Subtract. Many people assume that you always have to multiply before dividing, or add before subtracting. But this isn't so. Take the following example:

$$18 - 4 + 8 =$$

If you thought you were supposed to add first, you'd begin with 4 + 8 = 12, and then subtract 12 from 18 to get 6.

However, when you're given an equation that's made up of equal steps, perform the operations from left to right. In this case, 18 − 4 = 14, and 14 + 8 = 22. That's a very different answer! It's also the correct one.

Commutative and Distributive Properties

The Commutative Property: When you add a string of numbers, you can add them in any order you like. The same thing is true when you are multiplying a string of numbers.

4 + 5 + 8 is the same as 8 + 5 + 4.

6 × 7 × 9 is the same as 9 × 7 × 6.

> The Commutative Property applies ONLY to addition and multiplication. It does NOT pertain to subtraction or division.

The Distributive Property: The TASC test writers will sometimes use an equation that can be written in two different ways. They do this to see if you know about this equation and if you can spot when it is in your interest to change the equation into its other form.

The distributive property states that

$$a(b + c) = ab + ac \text{ and } a(b - c) = ab - ac$$

Example: $3(4 + 2) = 3(4) + 3(2) = 18$

Example: $3(4 - 2) = 3(4) - 3(2) = 6$

If a problem gives you information in "factored" format—$a(b + c)$—you should distribute it immediately. If the information is given in distributed form—$ab + ab$—you should factor it. Take the following example:

$$\frac{1}{2}(5) + \frac{1}{2}(3) =$$

Finding $\frac{1}{2}$ of 5 and $\frac{1}{2}$ of 3 is a bit troublesome because the answers do not work out to be whole numbers. It isn't that you can't find half of an odd number if you have to (or at least you will be able to, after our review of fractions later in this chapter), but why do more work than necessary?

Look at what would happen if we changed this distributed equation into its factored form instead:

$$\frac{1}{2}(5 + 3) =$$

Isn't that a lot easier? One half of 8 equals 4. Always be on the lookout for chances to do less work on the TASC test. It's a long test, and you need to conserve your strength.

Decimal Place Value and Rounding

All numbers are made up of digits. In the number 2,364, there are four digits: 2, 3, 6, and 4. In this case, the 4 is in the ones' place. The 6 is in the tens' place, the 3 is in the hundreds' place, and the 2 is in the thousands' place.

In the number 0.85, there are two digits: 8 and 5. In this case, the 8 is in the tenths' place and the 5 is in the hundredths' place.

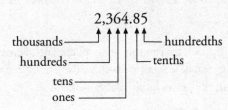

2,364.85

thousands ——
hundreds ——
tens ——
ones ——

—— hundredths
—— tenths

Digit and Decimal Place Quiz
Q: Which digit is in the hundreds place of 65,420?

Turn the page for the answer.

The Mathematics test may ask you to round off a number. The problem might read, "To the nearest thousand, how many…" or "What number to the nearest tenth…"

Whether you round to the nearest thousand or the nearest tenth, the process is exactly the same. Let's begin by rounding to the nearest dollar. If you have up to $1.49, then to the nearest dollar you have $1. If you have $1.50 or more, then to the nearest dollar you have $2.

Exactly the same principles hold true when you round any type of number.

1. Identify the place you are rounding to.
   • For example, let's round 6,342.57 to the nearest ten.
   • Which digit is in the tens place? The 4 is in the tens place.

Since we are rounding to the tens place, draw a number line that counts by tens:

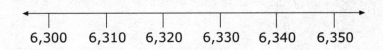

6,300   6,310   6,320   6,330   6,340   6,350

2. Look at the digit that comes *after*.
   In our example, what is the digit after 4? The next digit is 2.
   • If that digit is 0, 1, 2, 3, or 4, you will round the tens place down. (Keep the 4.)
   • If that digit is 5, 6, 7, 8, or 9, you will round the tens place up. (Change the 4 to a 5.)

Let's look at this on the number line. Make a mark where the original number lies.

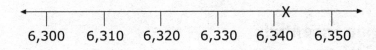

6,300   6,310   6,320   6,330   6,340   6,350

Is it closer to 6,340 or to 6,350? In this case, it is closer to the smaller amount, 6,340.

**Digit and Decimal
Place Quiz**
A: 4

4 is the digit is in the hundreds place of 65,**4**20.

3. Replace any digits after the rounding place with zeros.
   - Which digits will we replace with zeros? The 2, 5, and 7 all get replaced.
   - So our number now looks like 6,340.00.

Do we need the zeros after the decimal point? Nope. Go ahead and drop those off to get the final answer: 6,340.

Let's take a look at how this concept might be tested on the TASC test. You may remember the following question from Chapter 13.

---

3. **Pluto's radius is 736.9 miles. What is its circumference? Use 3.14 as pi, and solve to the nearest whole mile.**

Here's How to Crack It

The question tells you that Pluto's radius is 736.9 miles, and you need to solve for Pluto's circumference. Circumference is equal to $2\pi r$, so Pluto's circumference is $2\pi(736.9) = 4{,}627.732$. Since the question asks you to use 3.14 as π and solve to the nearest whole mile, the rounded circumference is 4,628 miles.

Fraction Essentials

On the TASC test, you may encounter questions that incorporate fractions. While fractions may seem tricky, don't let them psych you out. Let's take a deeper look at fractions and how they work.

Fractions

A fraction is part of a whole. We write a fraction as $\dfrac{(PART)}{(WHOLE)}$, where the top number is the number of parts we are referring to and the bottom number is the total number of parts that make up one whole. Take a look at the pie below.

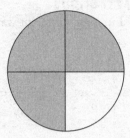

This pie has been divided into four equal pieces. Three of the four pieces are shaded. If we wanted to express the part of the pie that is shaded, we would say that $\dfrac{3}{4}$ of the pie is shaded. If we wanted to express the part of the pie that is not shaded, we would say that $\dfrac{1}{4}$ of the pie is not shaded.

A fraction is always a part over a whole.

$$\dfrac{1}{2} \quad \dfrac{(PART)}{(WHOLE)}$$

In the fraction $\dfrac{1}{2}$, we have one part out of a total of two equal parts.

In the fraction $\dfrac{3}{7}$, we have three parts out of a total of seven equal parts.

Another way to think of a fraction is as just another kind of division. The expression $\dfrac{1}{2}$ means 1 divided by 2. The fraction $\dfrac{x}{y}$ is nothing more than x divided by *y*. A fraction is made up of a numerator and a denominator. The **numerator** is on top; the **denominator** is on the bottom.

$$\frac{1}{2} \quad \frac{\text{numerator}}{\text{denominator}}$$

Reducing (Simplifying) Fractions

Every fraction can be expressed in many different ways:

$$\frac{1}{2} = \frac{2}{4} = \frac{3}{6} = \frac{4}{8} \ldots \text{ and so on.}$$

Each of these fractions means the same thing. To reduce a fraction with large numbers, see if the numerator and the denominator share a number that divides evenly into both of them. For example, both the numerator and the denominator of $\frac{2}{4}$ can be divided by 2, which reduces the fraction to $\frac{1}{2}$. With larger fractions, it may save time to find the largest number that will divide evenly into both numbers, also known as the *greatest common factor* (*GCF*). You can still reduce a fraction using any common (shared) factor, but you will probably have to reduce several times. Using the GCF guarantees that you will have to reduce only once! So how can you find the GCF of your numerator and denominator? Look at the factors of each. Let's take the fraction $\frac{8}{12}$. What are the different ways to make 8? $1 \times 8 = 8$ and $2 \times 4 = 8$.

So the factors of 8 are 1, 2, 4, and 8.

Now, what are the different ways to make 12? $1 \times 12 = 12$, $2 \times 6 = 12$, and $3 \times 4 = 12$.

The factors of 12 are 1, 2, 3, 4, 6, and 12.

To find our GCF, we compare these two lists. What is the largest number that occurs in both? That's right—4 is your GCF. Now divide both your numerator and denominator by 4 and you have the simplest (most reduced) form of your fraction.

$$\frac{8}{12} = \frac{8 \div 4}{12 \div 4} = \frac{2}{3}$$

Get used to reducing all fractions (if they can be reduced) before you do any work with them. It saves a lot of time and prevents errors that crop up when you try to work with big numbers.

Comparing Fractions

Sometimes a problem will involve deciding which of two fractions is bigger.

Which is bigger, $\frac{2}{5}$ or $\frac{4}{5}$? Think of these as parts of a pie. Which is bigger, two parts out of five, or four parts out of five? The fraction $\frac{4}{5}$ is clearly bigger. In this case, it was easy to tell because they both had the same whole, the same denominator.

It's more complicated when the fractions have different denominators. Which is bigger, $\frac{2}{3}$ or $\frac{3}{7}$? To decide, we need to find a common whole, or denominator. How do you decide what your new denominator should be? It's called the *least common denominator* (*LCD*), and is the smallest number that all of your denominators can divide into. How do you find the LCD? Start by listing the multiples of each denominator. Let's find the LCD of 3 and 7. What are the multiples of 3?

Count by threes: 3, 6, 9, 12, 15, 18, 21, 24, 27, 30, 33, 36, 39, 42, ...

Don't go on forever; just write down a few and if you need to add more later on you can. Now what are the multiples of 7?

Count by sevens: 7, 14, 21, 28, 35, 42, 49, ...

Do we have a number that is common to both of these lists? Yes—21 and 42 appear in both lists. But which number is the smaller of the two? The smaller number, 21, is our LCD.

Let's change the denominator of $\frac{2}{3}$ into the number 21. To get 3 to equal 21, we have to multiply it by 7. Of course, anything you do to the denominator, you have to do to the numerator, so we also have to multiply the numerator by 7.

$$\frac{2 \times 7}{3 \times 7} = \frac{14}{21}$$

The fraction $\frac{14}{21}$ still has the same value as $\frac{2}{3}$ (it would reduce to $\frac{2}{3}$) because we multiplied the fraction by $\frac{7}{7}$, or one.

Let's change the denominator of $\frac{3}{7}$ into 21 as well.

$$\frac{3 \times 3}{7 \times 3} = \frac{9}{21}$$

The fraction $\frac{9}{21}$ still has the same value as $\frac{3}{7}$ (it would reduce to $\frac{3}{7}$) because we multiplied the fraction by $\frac{3}{3}$, or one.

Now we can compare the two fractions. Which is bigger, $\frac{14}{21}$ or $\frac{9}{21}$? Clearly $\frac{14}{21}$ (or $\frac{2}{3}$) is bigger than $\frac{9}{21}$ (or $\frac{3}{7}$).

Let's do it again. Which is bigger, $\frac{2}{3}$ or $\frac{3}{5}$?

First we look at the two denominators, 3 and 5.

The multiples of 3 are 3, 6, 9, 12, 15, 18, 21, ...

And the multiples of 5 are 5, 10, 15, 20, 25, ...

This time, the least common denominator is 15.

$$\frac{2}{3} \qquad \frac{3}{5}$$

$$\frac{2}{3} \times \frac{5}{5} = \frac{10}{15} \qquad \frac{3}{5} \times \frac{3}{3} = \frac{9}{15}$$

So $\frac{2}{3}$ is bigger than $\frac{3}{5}$.

The Bowtie

Sometimes you will need to add and subtract fractions without the help of a calculator. The Bowtie is a shortcut that finds a common denominator and converts the numerators for you. Let's compare the last two fractions again. First, we get the common denominator by multiplying the two denominators together:

$$\frac{2}{3} \quad \frac{3}{5} = \frac{}{15}$$

Then, we get the new numerators by multiplying using the bowtie-shaped pattern shown below:

$$\text{⑩}\frac{2}{3} \times \frac{3}{5} \text{⑨} = \frac{}{15}$$

Finally, compare the fractions. Once again, we see that $\frac{10}{15}$ (or $\frac{2}{3}$) is bigger than $\frac{9}{15}$ (or $\frac{3}{5}$).

Converting to Fractions

A normal number, such as 8, can always be expressed as a fraction by making that number the numerator and 1 the denominator: $8 = \frac{8}{1}$.

Sometimes the TASC test gives you numbers that are mixtures of normal numbers and fractions, for example, $3\frac{1}{2}$. These numbers are called mixed fractions (or mixed numbers). It is often easier to work with these numbers by converting them completely into fractions. Here's how you do it: Because the fraction is expressed

Fraction Quiz

Q: Which is bigger,

$\frac{8}{9}$ or $\frac{7}{8}$?

Turn the page for the answer.

in halves, let's convert the normal number into halves as well: $3 = \dfrac{6}{2}$. Now just add the $\dfrac{1}{2}$ to the $\dfrac{6}{2}$. You get $\dfrac{7}{2}$.

There is also a shortcut for converting mixed fractions. Multiply the denominator by the whole number, and then add the numerator. This number becomes your new numerator and you keep the original denominator.

$$3\frac{1}{2} = \frac{3 \times 2 + 1}{2} = \frac{7}{2}$$

Now that you know how to compare fractions, let's see how this concept might be tested on the TASC test.

4. **Which of the following fractions has the least value?**

   A $\dfrac{36}{8}$

   B $\dfrac{37}{6}$

   C $\dfrac{36}{7}$

   D $\dfrac{37}{9}$

Here's How to Crack It

The question asks you to find the greatest value, so you need to determine the value of each fraction. Start by converting the fractions into mixed numbers; choices (A), (B), (C), and (D) will be $4\frac{1}{2}$, $6\frac{1}{6}$, $5\frac{1}{7}$, and $4\frac{1}{9}$, respectively. Since you are looking for the least value, and (B) and (C) are greater than 4, (B) and (C) can be eliminated. Next, you need to compare (A) and (D), both of which had 4 as the coefficient in the mixed number. If you compare the fractions $\frac{1}{2}$ and $\frac{1}{9}$, you will find that $\frac{1}{2}$ is greater. Accordingly, the least value is $4\frac{1}{9}$ or $\frac{37}{9}$, so select (D).

Note
The Bowtie does not always find the least common denominator. Because of this, you should always look to reduce your answer.

Operations with Fractions

Now that you know the structure and function of fractions, you need to know how to work with fractions. On the TASC test, you will encounter questions that require you to add, subtract, divide, and multiply fractions. Don't panic; read on to learn how to handle operations with fractions.

Adding and Subtracting Fractions

Now that we've reviewed finding a common denominator, adding and subtracting fractions is simple. Let's use the Bowtie to add $\frac{2}{5}$ and $\frac{1}{4}$.

$$\underset{5}{\overset{2}{8}} \times \underset{4}{\overset{1}{5}} = \frac{8+5}{20} = \frac{13}{20}$$

Let's use the Bowtie to subtract $\frac{2}{3}$ from $\frac{5}{6}$.

$$\underset{6}{\overset{5}{15}} \times \underset{3}{\overset{2}{12}} = \frac{15-12}{18} = \frac{3}{18} = \frac{1}{6}$$

Multiplying Fractions

To multiply fractions, line them up and multiply straight across.

$$\frac{5}{6} \times \frac{4}{5} = \frac{20}{30} = \frac{2}{3}$$

Was there anything we could have canceled or reduced *before* we multiplied? You betcha. We could cancel the 5 on top and the 5 on the bottom. What's left is $\frac{4}{6}$, which reduces to $\frac{2}{3}$.

Fraction Quiz

A: Use the Bowtie! The fraction $\frac{8}{9}$ is bigger than $\frac{7}{8}$.

Sometimes people think they can cancel or reduce in the same fashion *across an equal sign*. Consider this example:

$$\frac{\cancel{5}x}{6} = \frac{4}{\cancel{5}} \text{ No!}$$

You *cannot* cancel the 5's in this case or reduce the $\frac{4}{6}$. When there is an equal sign, you have to cross-multiply, which we will cover in the chapter on algebra, Chapter 15.

Dividing Fractions

To divide one fraction by another, just invert the second fraction and multiply.

$$\frac{2}{3} \div \frac{3}{4} \text{ is the same thing as } \frac{2}{3} \times \frac{4}{3} = \frac{8}{9} \ .$$

You may see this same operation written like this:

$$\frac{\frac{2}{3}}{\frac{3}{4}}$$

Reciprocal Fact

Dividing by 6 is the same thing as multiplying by $\frac{1}{6}$.

Again, just invert and multiply. Try the next example.

$$\frac{6}{\frac{2}{3}}$$

Think of 6 as $\frac{6}{1}$, and so we do the same thing.

$$\frac{6}{1} \times \frac{3}{2} = \frac{18}{2} = 9$$

Now that you know how to manipulate fractions, let's see how this concept might appear on the TASC test.

5. It takes Moose $1\frac{3}{4}$ of an hour to build a cathouse. How many completed cathouses can Moose build in $14\frac{1}{2}$ hours?

A 6

B 7

C 8

D 9

Here's How to Crack It

First, don't panic; this will be straightforward. Whenever you see compound fractions, you probably want to covert them into normal fractions. So, $1\frac{3}{4} = \frac{7}{4}$ and $14\frac{1}{2} = \frac{29}{2}$. So, it takes Moose $\frac{7}{4}$ hours to complete one cathouse, and you want to know how many cathouses can be made in $\frac{29}{2}$ hours. In other words, $\frac{29}{2} \div \frac{7}{4} = \frac{29}{2} \times \frac{4}{7} = \frac{58}{7} = 8\frac{2}{7}$. Therefore, in $14\frac{1}{2}$ hours, Moose can complete 8 cathouses.

Word Problems with Fractions

Test takers are often intimidated by word problems, but you should realize that beneath all those words there lies a simple math problem. Before you even read these word problems, there should be one thing you notice right away: There are fractions in the problem. That can mean only one thing. This is a fraction problem.

On the TASC test, the only things you are ever asked to do with fractions is add them, subtract them, multiply them, divide them, or compare them—and you've just learned how to do all those things, if you didn't know them already.

So, let's tackle a fraction-based word problem that you may see on the Mathematics test.

6. A group of students is asked about their favorite sports. If $\frac{1}{4}$ of the students prefer baseball and $\frac{1}{3}$ of the students prefer volleyball, what fraction of the group prefer neither baseball nor volleyball?

A $\frac{1}{6}$

B $\frac{5}{12}$

C $\frac{7}{12}$

D $\frac{5}{6}$

Here's How to Crack It

Just like with any word problem, you want to break the question into bite-sized pieces. Here, we are told that $\frac{1}{4}$ of the students prefer baseball and $\frac{1}{3}$ of the students prefer volleyball. In short, the question wants to know the fraction of the students that remain after removing the students who prefer volleyball and baseball.

Let's use the Bowtie method to add up the fractions that we know.

$$\frac{1}{4} \diagdown\!\!\!\!\diagup \frac{1}{3} = \frac{3+4}{12} = \frac{7}{12}$$

So, if $\frac{7}{12}$ of the students prefer either volleyball or baseball, the remaining students comprise $1 - \frac{7}{12} = \frac{5}{12}$ of the group. Therefore, the correct answer is (B).

Distance as a Function of Rate and Time

On the Mathematics test, you may encounter questions that provide you with a rate and ask you to find the distance between two points. These are known as rate questions. Thankfully, it's easy to spot rate problems: They almost always use the word "per" in the question stem.

You may not think so, but you already know the formula to solve every rate problem. Don't believe us? Let's say you drive in a car for 2 hours at 50 miles per hour. How far have you traveled? That's right: 100 miles. Fifty miles per hour is the rate at which you traveled, 2 hours is the time it took you to travel, and 100 miles is the distance you traveled.

The formula looks like this:

$$Rate \times Time = Distance$$

Or like this:

$$Rate = \frac{Distance}{Time}$$

Using the formula, the previous example would be solved as follows:

$$50 \text{ miles per hour} \times 2 \text{ hours} = 100 \text{ miles}$$

Regardless of the format, both equations are the same and can be used to find a rate, time, or distance. Once you've identified two parts of the formula, you can calculate the remaining part. Memorizing this formula can save you a headache later on when you aren't sure whether to divide or multiply.

When working with rate questions, make sure you always check your units! Minutes must go with minutes and hours must go with hours. So, if the previous example had said that you drive in a car for 120 minutes at 50 miles per hour, you would have to convert the minutes to hours prior to solving for the distance.

Let's see how rates may appear on the Mathematics test.

Rate Problem Quiz
Q: How do you spot an
$R \times T = D$ problem?

Turn the page for
the answer.

---

7. **If a cougar runs at a speed of 45 miles per hour for 150 minutes, how many miles does the cougar travel?**

A 6,750.0

B 180.0

C 112.5

D 3.3

Here's How to Crack It

As you do with all problems, you want to break the question into bite-sized pieces. Here, you are asked to find the distance the cougar travels if he moves at a speed of 45 miles per hour for 150 minutes. Since the question is asking about distance, and provides the rate and time, you want to use the formula Rate × Time = Distance. Before you plug in numbers to the formula, however, you need to make sure your units align. Because the cougar's speed is given in miles per hour and the time is given in minutes, you must convert the time into hours; in this case, 150 minutes is 2.5 hours. Now, you can plug in the speed and time into the formula to find that the cougar travels 45 miles per hour × 2.5 hours = 112.5 miles. Thus, the correct answer is (C).

Cost

You will probably encounter questions on the Mathematics test that deal with real-world situations like buying, selling, or receiving a discount on items. In short, these questions deal with money and almost always involve work with percentages. There are four main cost-question concepts you should know for the TASC test: discounts, markups, commissions, and profits.

Have you ever gone to the store and seen signs advertising "50% off everything?" This is an example of a **discount**, which is the amount of money saved from the original purchase price. Oftentimes, you will be given the original price and the discounted price of an item, and will need to calculate the percent discount on that item.

Problems with Percents?
For a more in-depth look at how to deal with percents, take a look at the percents section later in this chapter!

Whenever you need to calculate percent change, whether it is an increase or a decrease, you will want to use the **percent change formula**:

$$\frac{Difference}{Original} \times 100 = Percent\ Change$$

Imagine that you went to buy a television that originally cost $500. When you get to the store, the sales associate tells you that the television you want is on sale for $436. If you wanted to find the percent discount of the television, you would need to first find the difference between the two prices:

$$\$500 - \$436 = \$64.$$

Then, simply plug in the relevant information into the percent change formula, to find that the percent discount is

$$\frac{64}{500} \times 100 = \frac{16}{125} \times 100 = 12.8\%$$

You may also encounter a scenario in which you need to calculate the amount of the discount. For example, say the sales associate told you that there was a 12.8% discount on the $500 television. Here, you need to just calculate 12.8% of $500:

$$\frac{1280}{100} \times \$500 = \$64$$

Another concept that may be tested on the Mathematics test is **markup**, which is the percent or the amount of money added to the original cost of an item. For example, if an electronics store purchases a television for $80 and then adds a 32% markup, the markup would be

$$\frac{32}{100} \times \$80 = \$25.60$$

In order to find the price after markup, simply add the original price and the markup together. Here, the new price would be

$$\$80 + \$25.60 = \$105.60$$

You can also calculate the percent markup using the percent change formula. Just like with discounts, plug in the provided information into the formula for markups to find the answer you need.

Sometimes you will see questions on the TASC test that deal with a sales associate's **commission**, or the amount of money a sales associate receives for selling a product. For example, let's say that the television sales associate receives 5% commission on every television he sells. If the sales associate sells only one television, and it costs $500, his commission would be

$$.05 \times \$500 = \$25.$$

What if he sells 14 televisions, 10 that cost $500 each and 4 that cost $1,000 each. First, you would need to find the total amount of the televisions he sold:

$$(10 \times \$500) + (4 \times \$1,000) = \$9,000.$$

Then, just like before, calculate the commission:

$$.05 \times \$9,000 = \$450.$$

The last cost-related concept that you should be able to calculate is **profit**, the amount of money earned after accounting for expenses. For example, let's assume that the electronics shop can buy a television for $320 and sell it for $500. If the shop buys 48 televisions and sells 40 of them, what would be the shop's profit? To solve this, you would first need to calculate the amount of money the shop initially spent on the televisions:

$$48 \times \$320 = \$15,360$$

Next, find the amount of money the shop made from selling the televisions:

$$40 \times \$500 = \$20,000$$

Finally, determine the profit by calculating the difference:

$$\$20,000 - \$15,360 = \$4,640$$

At times, you may need to determine the **percent profit**, or the ratio of profit to expenses. To find percent profit, you want to use a variation of the percent change formula, the percent profit formula:

$$\frac{Profit}{Expenses} \times 100 = Percent\ Profit$$

So, if you wanted to calculate the percent profit for the electronics shop, you would plug into the formula to find

$$\frac{4,640}{20,000} \times 100 = 23.2\%$$

Accordingly, the shop made a profit of 23.2% on televisions.

Let's try a question that you may see on the TASC test.

───────────────○───────────────

8.   Shanita works at a rock-climbing gym and makes a 12% commission on every pair of rock-climbing shoes and an 8% commission on every carabineer she sells. Shanita sells 14 pairs of shoes and 22 carabineers on Tuesday, 4 pairs of shoes and 52 carabineers on Wednesday, and 10 pairs of shoes and 16 carabineers on Thursday. If shoes cost $68 a pair and carabineers cost $6 each, how much did Shanita make in commission over the three days?

   A $1,746.40

   B $271.68

   C $228.48

   D $43.20

Here's How to Crack It

There are a lot of words in this question—make sure you break the question down into bite-sized pieces. Since the question asks for Shanita's total commission, start by adding up the number of shoes and carabineers she sold. Shanita sold a total of 14 + 4 + 10 = 28 pairs of shoes and 22 + 52 + 16 = 90 carabineers. Next, calculate the commission for the shoes. Shanita makes 12% commission on every pair of shoes, so she makes 28 × (.12 × $68) = 28 × ($8.16) = $228.48 commission on shoes. Now, calculate the commission for the carabineers. Shanita makes 8% commission on every carabineer sold, so she makes 90 × (.08 × $6) = 90 × ($0.48) = $43.20 commission on carabineers. Finally, add the two commissions together to find that Shanita's total commission was $228.48 + $43.20 = $271.68. Thus, the correct answer is (B).

PROBABILITY, PROPORTIONS, AND PERCENTS

The basic arithmetic concepts that we will cover in this section include the following.

- Simple Probability
- Multiple Event Probability
- Ratios
- Proportions
- Percents
- Percent Word Problems

Simple Probability

If you flip a coin, what are the odds that it's going to come out tails? If you said anything but "$\frac{1}{2}$," "1 out of 2," or "50 percent," then you may want to avoid betting money at a casino. This is an example of probability, which can be expressed as a fraction, percent, or decimal. Probability indicates the likelihood that an event will happen and is a value between 0 and 1, where 0 is the probability that an event will *never* happen and 1 is the probability that an event will *always* happen.

On the Mathematics test, probabilities are generally expressed as fractions. The number of possibilities that one thing could happen is the numerator. The number of total possibilities is the denominator. In short, you can think of simple probability as

$$\frac{What\ you\ want}{What\ you\ got} \quad or \quad \frac{The\ number\ of\ possibilities\ that\ fulfill\ the\ desired\ outcome}{Total\ number\ of\ possibilities}$$

For example, let's take that coin we just mentioned. If you toss the coin once, how many chances are there on this one toss that it will be heads? One chance. And how many total possible outcomes are there? There are two possible outcomes—heads or tails. Therefore, you have a 1 out of 2, $\frac{1}{2}$, or 50 percent chance of seeing tails.

Let's assume that you have two blue books, four red books, five green books, and six black books, and you want to find the probability that you would randomly select a blue book. In this scenario, you want to determine *what you want* and *what you got.* You want a blue book, and you have two blue books. You also have a total of 2 + 4 + 5 + 6 = 17 books. Therefore, the probability of randomly selecting a blue book would be $\frac{2}{17}$. What would be the probability of randomly selecting a black book? If you said $\frac{6}{17}$, you are absolutely right!

Now that you've mastered simple probability, let's try a problem.

———————◯———————

9. **Ru received six black socks, eight blue socks, four polka-dot socks, and two yellow socks on National Sock Day. If Ru randomly selects a sock from her sock drawer, what is the probability that she would pick a polka-dot sock on her first try?**

A $\dfrac{1}{2}$

B $\dfrac{2}{5}$

C $\dfrac{3}{10}$

D $\dfrac{1}{5}$

Here's How to Crack It
Just like before, you want to determine *what you want* and *what you got*. You want a polka-dot sock, and Ru has four polka-dot socks. Ru also has a total of 6 + 8 + 4 + 2 = 20 socks. Therefore, the probability that Ru would pick a polka-dot sock on her first try would be $\dfrac{4}{20} = \dfrac{1}{5}$. Therefore, the correct answer is (D).

———————◯———————

Multiple Event Probability
When we discussed simple probability, we were talking about the probability of only one event; i.e., what is the probability of randomly selecting a book from a pile of books. However, you may be asked to find the probability of multiple events. For example, you may be asked to find the probability of picking a blue book *and* a black book, or the probability of selecting a blue book *or* a black book. These are examples of multiple event probability, or **compound probability**.

When working with multiple event probability questions, you will need to determine whether the two events are independent or dependent. If the probability of one event does not affect the probability of a second event, the two events are considered **independent**. If the probability of one event does affect the probability of the second event, the two events are considered **dependent**.

There are two types of compound probability that you will need to know for the Mathematics test: **and** probability and **or** probability.

"And" Probability

And probability refers to the probability that multiple events will happen—e.g., the probability that one event *and* another event will happen. To calculate and probability, simply find the probability of each event and multiply the two events together.

Let's take another look at our book example from the simple probability section. Again, assume that you have two blue books, four red books, five green books, and six black books. However, you now want to find the probability that you will pick a blue book first *and* a red book second, without replacement.

Before you dive into solving this question, you need to determine whether the events are independent or dependent of one another. Since there is no replacement, the total number of books will go down after selecting a blue book. This, in turn, will affect the probability of selecting a red book, indicating that the two events are dependent.

Just like before, start by finding the probability of randomly selecting a blue book. Since there are two blue books and 17 total books, the probability of randomly selecting a blue book would be $\frac{2}{17}$.

Next, find the probability of randomly selecting a red book. Since you have already removed a book from the pile, the total number of books is now 16. Therefore, there are four red books and 16 total books, so the probability of randomly selecting a red book would be $\frac{4}{16}$ or $\frac{1}{4}$.

Now that you have the probabilities for each event, simply multiply the individual probabilities together.

$$\frac{2}{17} \times \frac{1}{4} = \frac{2}{68} = \frac{1}{34}$$

Thus, the probability of selecting a blue book first and a red book second is $\frac{1}{34}$.

"Or" Probability

Or probability refers to the probability that one event *or* another event will happen. To calculate or probability, simply find the probability of each event and add the two events together.

Let's get back to our multi-colored books! Just like before, assume that you have two blue books, four red books, five green books, and six black books. However, you now want to find the probability that you will pick a blue book *or* a red book. Since you are looking at the probability of one event or another event, the two events are independent from one another.

Just like before, start by finding the probability of randomly selecting a blue book.

Since there are two blue books and 17 total books, the probability of randomly selecting a blue book would be $\frac{2}{17}$.

Next, find the probability of randomly selecting a red book. There are four red books and 17 total books, so the probability of randomly selecting a red book would be $\frac{4}{17}$.

Now you have the probabilities for each event. Remember that if you are solving for the probability of one event *or* another event occurring, you simply add the individual probabilities together.

$$\frac{2}{17} + \frac{4}{17} = \frac{6}{17}$$

Accordingly, the probability of selecting a blue book or a red book is $\frac{6}{17}$.

Okay! You are a multiple probability master! Now let's take a look at a question that you might see on the Mathematics test.

———————————○———————————

10. Xi decides to get a new pet and goes to a pet store that has 16 goldfish, 8 kittens, 4 puppies, and 2 geese. If Xi randomly selects an animal from the pet store's selection, what is the probability that Xi will pick either a goose or a kitten?

A $\frac{1}{4}$

B $\frac{1}{3}$

C $\frac{1}{2}$

D $\frac{2}{3}$

Here's How to Crack It

First, you want to identify whether this is *and* or *or* probability and whether the events are dependent or independent of one another. The question asks you to find the probability that Xi will pick either a goose *or* a kitten, so this is *or* probability and, in turn, the events are independent of one another.

Next, you want to find the probability of each individual event. There are two geese and a total of 16 + 8 + 4 + 2 = 30 animals. Therefore, the probability of randomly selecting a goose is $\frac{2}{30} = \frac{1}{15}$. Then you want to find the probability of randomly selecting a kitten. Since there are 8 kittens and 30 animals, the probability of randomly selecting a kitten would be $\frac{8}{30} = \frac{4}{15}$.

Finally, you want to add the individual probabilities together to find the probability that Xi will pick either a goose or a kitten.

$$\frac{1}{15} + \frac{4}{15} = \frac{5}{15} \text{ or } \frac{1}{3}$$

Therefore, the probability that Xi will pick either a goose or a kitten is $\frac{1}{3}$, or answer (B).

Ratios

If you've ever cooked, you've worked with ratios. For example, if you were making brownies that needed 2 cups of flour for every 3 eggs, the ratio of flour to eggs would be 2:3 or $\frac{2}{3}$. Unlike a fraction, which compares a part to a whole, a **ratio** shows the relationship between two parts of a whole.

Imagine that you had 4 coffees, 5 teas, and 6 sodas at your house. If you wanted to express the ratio of coffee to tea to soda, you would write the ratio as 4:5:6.

Now, imagine that the ratio of coffee to tea to soda was 4:5:6, but you had a total of 75 drinks at your house. How could you find out the actual number of coffee, tea, and sodas you have? Well, you could construct a ratio box.

A **ratio box** allows you to organize the information you are given and find the actual number of beverages you have. A ratio box will always have three rows: the ratio row, where you put the ratio, the multiplier row, which indicates the amount by which the ratio should be multiplied, and the actual number row, which indicates the actual number of items you have.

So, for this example, your initial ratio box would look like this:

	Coffee	Tea	Soda	Total
Ratio	4	5	6	
Multiplier				
Actual Number				75

Next, add the numbers in your ratio row together to find the ratio total.

	Coffee	Tea	Soda	Total
Ratio	4	5	6	15
Multiplier				
Actual Number				75

Then, you can find the multiplier by determining what 15 must be multiplied by to equal 75. Since $15 \times 5 = 75$, the multiplier is 5. Note that the multiplier is the same across the entire row in order to maintain the ratio.

	Coffee	Tea	Soda	Total
Ratio	4	5	6	15
Multiplier	5	5	5	5
Actual Number				75

Finally, you can multiply the ratio for each item with the multiplier to find the actual number of each beverage; i.e., $4 \times 5 = 20$, $5 \times 5 = 25$, and $6 \times 5 = 30$.

	Coffee	Tea	Soda	Total
Ratio	4	5	6	15
Multiplier	5	5	5	5
Actual Number	20	25	30	75

Accordingly, there are 20 coffees, 25 teas, and 30 sodas in the house.

By using the ratio box, you can transform tricky ratio questions into simple arithmetic questions.

Now that you are a ratio rockstar, let's try a question!

---

11. **A farmer has planted tomato, cucumber, and lettuce crops in a ratio of 4:3:8. If the farmer ends up with 48 heads of lettuce, what is the total number of tomatoes, cucumbers, and lettuces produced?**

A 90

B 24

C 18

D 6

Here's How to Crack It

Just like before, start by creating a ratio box and filling in the information you are given.

	Tomatoes	Cucumbers	Lettuce	Total
Ratio	4	3	8	
Multiplier				
Actual Number			48	

Next, add the numbers in your ratio row together to find the ratio total.

	Tomatoes	Cucumbers	Lettuce	Total
Ratio	4	3	8	15
Multiplier				
Actual Number			48	

Then, you can find the multiplier by determining what 8 must be multiplied by to equal 48. Since $8 \times 6 = 48$, the multiplier if 6.

	Tomatoes	Cucumbers	Lettuce	Total
Ratio	4	3	8	15
Multiplier	6	6	6	6
Actual Number			48	

Finally, you can multiply the ratio total with the multiplier to find the total number of tomatoes, cucumbers, and lettuces produced. So, 15× 6 = 90.

	Tomatoes	Cucumbers	Lettuce	Total
Ratio	4	3	8	15
Multiplier	6	6	6	6
Actual Number	24	18	48	90

Accordingly, there are a total of 90 vegetables produced; i.e., the correct answer is (A).

Proportions

As we discussed in the fractions section of this text, fractions can be expressed in many different forms. For example, $\frac{1}{2} = \frac{2}{4} = \frac{3}{6}$ and so on. A proportion problem simply asks you to express a particular fraction in a slightly different form.

For example, imagine that you are looking at a map that uses a scale in which 1 inch = 250 miles. If two cities that are separated by 6 inches on the map, you would simply need to set up a proportion to find the actual distance between the two cities. Here, the question is indicating a relationship between inches and miles, which can be expressed as

$$\frac{1 \text{ inch}}{250 \text{ miles}}$$

As you can see, the relationship between inches and miles is expressed as a fraction. Now, you need to set up the proportion with both the information you are given and the information that is unknown. Your proportion would be set up as follows:

$$\frac{1 \text{ inch}}{250 \text{ miles}} = \frac{6 \text{ inches}}{x \text{ miles}}$$

In English, this proportion shows that if 1 inch equals 250 miles, 6 inches equals an unknown quantity, x. Finally, cross-multiply to solve for the unknown quantity, the number of miles represented by 6 inches:

$$1x = 6 \times 250$$

$$x = 1,500$$

As you can see, after cross-multiplying, you will find that x, the unknown quantity, is equal to 1,500. Therefore, the distance of 6 inches on the map is equivalent to 1,500 miles in the real world. In order to check your work, simply ensure that your new relationship, $\dfrac{6 \text{ inches}}{1,500 \text{ miles}}$, reduces to $\dfrac{1 \text{ inch}}{250 \text{ miles}}$. Since $\dfrac{6 \text{ inches}}{1,500 \text{ miles}}$ does, in fact, reduce to $\dfrac{1 \text{ inch}}{250 \text{ miles}}$, you have correctly solved for the unknown quantity.

Now that you are a proportion pro, let's try out a question!

———————————○———————————

12. **If a froglet can capture 15 flies in 30 minutes, how many flies can the froglet capture in $4\dfrac{1}{2}$ hours?**

   A   67.5

   B   100

   C   135

   D   540

Here's How to Crack It

Notice that, just like in the previous question, you can set up a proportion and solve for an unknown. The froglet captures 15 flies in 30 minutes, and you need to find how many flies the froglet can capture in $4\dfrac{1}{2}$ hours. Therefore, you should set up a proportion.

However, before you set up the proportion, make sure that your units are aligned. The question uses both minutes and hours, so in order to create an accurate proportion, convert the hours into minutes. Since there are 60 minutes in an hour, there are 270 minutes in $4\dfrac{1}{2}$ hours. Now, you can set up your proportion.

$$\frac{15 \text{ flies}}{30 \text{ minutes}} = \frac{x \text{ flies}}{270 \text{ minutes}}$$

When you cross multiply you will find that

$$30 \times x = 15 \times 270$$

$$30x = 4{,}050$$

$$x = 135$$

Accordingly, the froglet catches 135 flies in 270 minutes; the correct answer is (C).

Percents

A percent is really just a fraction whose denominator happens to be 100.

$$20\% = \frac{20}{100} \qquad 45\% = \frac{45}{100} \qquad 37.5\% = \frac{37.5}{100}$$

Like any fraction, a percentage can be converted to a decimal and vice versa. Percentage/decimal conversion is even easier than converting a normal fraction because both percentages and decimals are almost invariably already being expressed in hundredths.

$$30\% = \frac{30}{100} = 0.30 \qquad 54\% = \frac{54}{100} = 0.54$$

To convert a regular fraction into a percent, you can first convert the fraction to a decimal, which, as we just said, is very close to a percentage already.

There are some fractions, decimals, and percentages that come up so often that it's worth memorizing them. We've filled in some for you. Practice your conversions on a separate piece of paper to fill in the remaining boxes. Check your work with a calculator afterwards.

Ballparking Percent Quiz
Q: Roughly speaking, what's 20% of 410?

Turn the page for the answer.

You can use your calculator to help calculate percents quickly. To find 50 percent of a number, multiply the number by 0.50. To find 25 percent of a number, multiply the number by 0.25. To find 5 percent of a number, multiply the number by 0.05.

Fraction	Decimal	Percent
		1%
$\frac{1}{50}$		
	0.05	
$\frac{1}{10}$		
		11.11%
	.2	
$\frac{2}{9}$		
		25%
$\frac{1}{3}$		
$\frac{2}{5}$		
		44.44%
	.5	
$\frac{5}{9}$		
		60%
$\frac{2}{3}$		
	.75	
$\frac{7}{9}$		
		80%
$\frac{8}{9}$		
	1	

When working with percents, you can translate words into mathematical expressions and vice-versa. For example, the word *percent* indicates a fraction with 100 in the denominator, the word *of* always means multiply, the word *what* indicates the unknown quantity, or variable, and the words *is, are, were, did,* and *does* indicate an equals sign. So, if the TASC test asks, "What is 36 percent of 350," it would be written

$$? = \frac{36}{100} \times \frac{350}{1}$$

You could then cancel out factors (that is, divide 100 and 350 by 50) to find

$$\frac{36}{2} \times \frac{7}{1} = 18 \times 7 = 126$$

So, let's tackle a percent problem that you may see on the Mathematics test.

---

13. **A store has 5,500 fish and 30% of fish have blue fins. How many fish do <u>not</u> have blue fins?**

A 3,850

B 3,300

C 2,750

D 1,650

Here's How to Crack It

In order to solve this question, you need to figure out how many fish do not have blue fins. If 30% of the fish have blue fins, 70% of the fish do not have blue fins. Then, you need to find 70% of 5,500. Using the rules of translating words to math, you would find that 0.70 × 5,500 = 3,850. Therefore, the correct answer is (A).

Word Problems with Percents

On the TASC test, it's possible that you will encounter word problems that deal with percents. First of all, don't panic when you see these problems. While they may appear to be extremely difficult, you will use the same techniques as you do on other percent questions: Break the question into bite-sized pieces, translate the words into math, and solve.

Outta Here!

In the following question, find the answers that are out of the ballpark.

Q: Andrew McCutchen hits three home runs of lengths 375 feet, 380 feet, and 400 feet. What was the average length of his home runs?

A 385 feet
B 405 feet
C 420 feet
D 1,155 feet

Turn the page for the answer.

Now that you know your percents, let's try a word problem that you may see on the Mathematics test.

————————————○————————————

14. **A drone is on sale for 18% off its normal price of $420. If the sales tax is 8%, what is the cost of the drone?**

   A $453.60

   B $371.95

   C $344.40

   D $27.55

Outta Here!

A: Choice (D), 1,155 is WAY out of the ballpark—it's the sum of all three numbers in the question. So are (B) and (C) because the average length can't be bigger than the largest number being averaged. The correct answer is (A).

Here's How to Crack It

Just like with any word problem, you want to break this question down into bite-sized pieces. Start with the sale price of the drone. Here, you are told that the drone is on sale for 18% off its normal price of $420. So, you are interested in finding 18% of $420. By translating the words to math, the operation you need to perform is $\frac{18}{100} \times \$420 = \$75.60$. Therefore, if the drone is reduced by $75.60, the new price of the drone is $420 − $75.60 = $344.40. Next, you need to find the sales tax, or 8% of $344.40. Using the same concept as before, you will find that the sales tax is $\frac{8}{100} \times \$344.40 = \$27.55$. Finally, you need to add the sales price and the sales tax to find that the cost of the drone is $344.40 + $27.55 = $371.95. Accordingly, the correct answer is (B).

————————————○————————————

Arithmetic Drill

Now try these questions. To check your answers, register your book at **PrincetonReview.com/cracking** and download the Chapter Drill Answers and Explanations supplement.

1. François goes to the local farmer's market to buy some cherimoyas. Originally priced at $1.50 each, cherimoyas are on sale for 20% off of the original price. If François purchases 4 cherimoyas, and pays a 5% sales tax, how much did he money did he spend at the farmer's market?

   A $1.26

   B $4.80

   C $5.04

   D $5.10

2. Hakim has 13 pineapple, 10 cherry, 8 strawberry, 5 muscat, and 4 lychee flavored gummy bears. What is the probability that Hakim will randomly select a muscat gummy bear followed by a pineapple gummy bear?

   A $\dfrac{13}{320}$

   B $\dfrac{1}{24}$

   C $\dfrac{1}{8}$

   D $\dfrac{9}{20}$

3. ChiknBitz purchases baby chickens for $0.22 each and sells them to loving owners for $1.69 each. How much would ChiknBitz make in profit from the sale of 148 chickens?

   A $282.68

   B $250.12

   C $217.56

   D $32.56

4. If x is the smallest prime number, y is a nonnegative integer less than 1, and z is the difference between x and y, which of the following is the value of z?

   A   3

   B   2

   C   1

   D   0

5. Consider this number line.

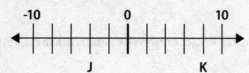

In the number line above, point *L*, not shown, is located midway between points *J* and *K*. If point *M*, not shown, is equal to half the distance between points *J* and *L*, what is the value of *M* ?

A   –1

B   1

C   2

D   5

6. Zori can travel at an average speed of 35 miles per hour on her hoverboard. If she needs to travel the 804 miles between Houston, Texas and Chihuahua, Mexico, approximately how many hours will the journey take? (Rate × Time = Distance)

A   24

B   23

C   22

D   21

7. Which of the following statements is true?

A   The product of two negative numbers is always negative.

B   The sum of an odd number and an even number is always even.

C   The difference between two even numbers will always be zero.

D   The product of a negative number and a positive number is always negative.

8. Skyler has 10 bags of salted, 8 bags of salt and vinegar, 5 bags of sour cream and onion, and 3 bags of barbecue potato chips. If Skyler has already eaten one bag of salted and one bag of barbecue chips, what is the probability that Skyler would randomly select a bag of salt and vinegar potato chips and then select a bag of salted chips?

A $\dfrac{1}{12}$

B $\dfrac{3}{23}$

C $\dfrac{1}{3}$

D $\dfrac{9}{23}$

9. If Fabian can bake 8 loaves of bread in 90 minutes, how many loaves of bread could he bake in 4.5 hours?

A 480

B 36

C 24

D 16

10. A tablet that was originally $720 is reduced to $635. By approximately what percent did the price of the tablet decrease?

A 11

B 12

C 13

D 85

11. If Paula runs for 45 minutes at a speed of 8 miles per hour, how many miles did she run?
(Rate×Time = Distance)

A 5.625

B 6

C 8

D 360

12. In a bowl of 60 candies, there is a 7:8 ratio of blue to red candies. How many blue candies are in the bowl?

A 28

B 30

C 32

D 60

13. In a band, $\frac{1}{4}$ of the members play the saxophone, $\frac{1}{3}$ of the members play the trumpet, and the remaining members play the guitar. What fraction of the band plays the guitar?

A $\frac{3}{12}$

B $\frac{4}{12}$

C $\frac{5}{12}$

D $\frac{7}{12}$

14. Elijah works at a car company where he gets 8% commission on the new cars he sells and a 5% commission on the used cars he sells. On Tuesday, Elijah sells two new cars for $20,000 each and one used car for $10,000. On Thursday, Elijah sells three used cars for $8,000 each and one new car for $30,000. What was the total amount that Elijah made in commission on Tuesday and Thursday?

A $3,700

B $4,400

C $7,120

D $7,300

15. Which of the following statements is true?

A The product of a nonnegative number and a positive number is positive.

B The sum of a fraction and its reciprocal is zero.

C The product of a nonnegative number and a positive number is negative.

D The result of dividing any number by zero is undefined.

Chapter 15
Algebra

In this chapter, we'll walk you through the key topics related to algebra on the TASC Mathematics test and explain how to approach equations and expressions. Following the content lessons, we'll give you some practice questions.

POLYNOMIALS AND EXPONENTS

The Nature of Polynomials and Terms

One of the tricky parts of algebra is understanding all of the math vocabulary. We'll define these words as we go, and you can also find a glossary at the end of this chapter.

First, the term **expression**. Think of the usual meaning of the word: It's something someone says. In math, an expression is a phrase that's said using math symbols. It's not a whole sentence—that would involve an equals sign. Below are some examples of expressions:

$$3x + 1 \qquad\qquad 9 \times 5 \qquad\qquad 4z^2 + 7z - y$$

Notice that each of these expressions consists of two or more things separated by operation symbols such as a plus sign. Each of those things is called a **term**. In the first expression above, $3x$ is a term. 1 is also a term. In the third expression, $4z^2$ is a term, and so are $7z$ and y. Anything that is stuck together before or after a +, −, or × is a term. Division is not normally used in expressions because division problems are usually written as fractions, and a fraction goes together as a term.

Many expressions can also be described as **polynomials**. A polynomial is an expression that consists of two or more terms. More specifically, an expression with two terms, such as $3x + 1$, is known as a **binomial**. The prefix *bi-* means two. Something like 9×5 is not considered a polynomial or a binomial because it can be written as 45, since that's what 9×5 equals. 45 is just one term, so it's not a polynomial. An expression with three or more terms, such as $4z^2 + 7z - y$, is simply known as a polynomial, since the prefix *poly-* means many.

Combining Like Terms

Sometimes you will see an expression that includes **like terms**. Like terms are ones that can be put together because they are the same type of term. For instance, in the previous example, 9 and 5 are like terms, since they are both just numbers, so we can go ahead and multiply them together. In its simplest form, a polynomial should not include any like terms because they should have already been combined together.

Numbers by themselves are "like terms." So are **variables**, or letters that represent numbers, if they are the same letter. For example, $x + x = 2x$. The number in front of the variable x is called a **coefficient**. The prefix *co-* means "with," so a coefficient goes with the variable, right in front of it. It is being multiplied by the variable, so it shows how many of that variable there are. Variables with coefficients are easy to add or subtract: $4y + 7y = 11y$. $20a - 25a = -5a$. Simply add or subtract the coefficients. Keep in mind, though, that the variables must be the same to do this.

$3x + 4y$ cannot be combined because the two terms in the binomial are unlike terms. The expression cannot be written in any simpler way.

Terms that involve exponents can also be combined if they have the same **degree**, which means the same exponent. We will talk more about exponents in a few pages, but for now, understand that $2x^2$ and $7x^2$ are like terms and can be added or subtracted. $2x^2$ and $7x^3$ are not like terms because one is to the second power and the other is to the third power. They cannot be added or subtracted. Remember that the same is true when the variables are different: $2x^2$ and $7y^2$ cannot be combined because even though they have the same exponent, the variables must be the same for them to be like terms.

Here is a sample problem on combining like terms.

1. **What is the simplest form of the expression $5x + 12 - 3x^2 + 2x^2 - 6x + 2 + 10$?**

    A $17x - x^2 - 4x + 10$

    B $x^2 + x + 2$

    C $-x^2 - x + 24$

    D $3x^2 - x + 12$

Here's How to Crack It

Notice which terms can be combined here: numbers, x, and x^2. Start by combining the x^2. Ignore the other terms and pay careful attention to addition and subtraction. The terms given are $-3x^2$ and $+ 2x^2$. $-3 + 2 = -1$, so this is $-1x^2$, or just $-x^2$. (Notice at this point you could go ahead and pick (C) since it's the only one that has that.) Now combine the x: $5x - 6x = -1x = -x$. Now combine the numbers: $12 + 2 + 10 = 24$. Last, put it all together: $-x^2 - x + 24$. The answer is (C).

It is conventional for polynomials to be written in this descending order, starting with the highest power and going down to just numbers, if applicable.

Adding and Subtracting Polynomials

Adding and subtracting polynomials simply means combining the like terms.

———————◯———————

2. $(3z^2 - 12z + 7) + (-5z^2 + z + 6) =$

A $-2z^2 - 11z + 13$

B $8z^2 - 11z + 13$

C $-2z^2 - 13z + 13$

D $8z^2 - 13z + 13$

Here's How to Crack It

Since the polynomials are being added together, simply ignore the parentheses and rewrite like this: $3z^2 - 12z + 7 - 5z^2 + z + 6$. Remember that adding a negative is the same as subtracting. Now combine like terms. $3z^2 - 5z^2 = -2z^2$. $-12z + z = -11z$. $7 + 6 = 13$. The result is $-2z^2 - 11z + 13$, which is (A).

———————◯———————

Subtracting polynomials is the same except you have to be careful with the negatives.

———————◯———————

3. $(-10b^2 + 6b + 2) - (-4b + 1) =$

A $-10b^2 + 2b + 1$

B $-10b^2 + 10b + 3$

C $-10b^2 + 2b + 3$

D $-10b^2 + 10b + 1$

Here's How to Crack It

Again rewrite without the parentheses, but this time the negative must be distributed to every term in the second set of parentheses. Remember that two negatives equal a positive. This looks like $-10b^2 + 6b + 2 + 4b - 1$. Now combine like terms to get $-10b^2 + 10b + 1$, which is (D).

———————◯———————

Exponents and MADSPM

We've seen exponents in expressions. Now let's take a break from working with expressions to see how exponents work and what their rules are.

An exponent is shorthand for multiplication. The expression $4 \times 4 \times 4 \times 4 \times 4$ can also be written as 4^5. This is expressed as "4 to the fifth power." The large number (4) is called the **base**, and the little number (5) is called the **exponent** or **power**.

Always remember that exponents cannot be added or subtracted. This is to say, $4^5 + 4^2$ does not equal 4^7. You should know this already because they are not like terms and only like terms can be added or subtracted. Exponents that have the same base and the same power can be put together, but that involves adding or subtracting the coefficients only, not the powers themselves.

What operations can be done with exponents? One is multiplication.

When you multiply numbers that have the same base, you simply add the exponents.

$$6^2 \times 6^3 = 6^{(2 + 3)} = 6^5$$

Why is this true? Let's write this out in long form:

$$6^2 = 6 \times 6 \qquad 6^3 = 6 \times 6 \times 6$$

$$\text{so, } 6^2 \times 6^3 = 6 \times 6 \times 6 \times 6 \times 6 \text{ or } 6^5$$

Exponents can also be divided. When you divide numbers that have the same base, you simply subtract the bottom exponent from the top exponent.

$$\frac{6^3}{6^2} = 6$$

Why is this true? Let's write it out in long form:

$$\frac{6^3}{6^2} = \frac{6 \times 6 \times 6}{6 \times 6} = \frac{6}{1} = 6$$

One other thing that can be done with exponents is raising an exponent to another power like this: $(5^3)^5$. In this case, the powers are multiplied, so here the result is 5^{15}.

Why is this true? Let's write it out in long form:

$(5^3)^5 = (5^3)(5^3)(5^3)(5^3)(5^3) = (5 \times 5 \times 5)(5 \times 5 \times 5)(5 \times 5 \times 5)(5 \times 5 \times 5)$
$(5 \times 5 \times 5)$

There are a total of 15 fives, so it is 5^{15}.

A good way to remember what can be done with exponents and how to do those operations is with the acronym **MADSPM**. When you multiply exponents, add the powers. When you divide exponents, subtract the powers. When you raise a power to another power, multiply the powers.

M—Multiply
A—Add
D—Divide
S—Subtract
P—Power
M—Multiply

Remember that all of this is true only when the exponents have the same base, whether it is a number or a variable.

Special Exponent Rules

Anything to the zero power is 1.

$$4^0 = 1 \quad x^0 = 1$$

Anything to the first power equals that number.

$$4^1 = 4$$
$$-3^1 = -3$$

You would expect that raising a number to a power would increase that number, and usually it does, but there are exceptions.

• If you raise a positive fraction of less than 1 to a power, the fraction gets smaller.

$$\left(\frac{1}{2}\right)^2 = \frac{1^2}{2^2} = \frac{1}{4}$$

- If you raise a negative number to an odd power, the number gets smaller.

$$(-3)^3 = (-3)(-3)(-3) = -27$$

(Remember –27 is smaller than –3.)

- If you raise a negative number to an even power, the number becomes positive.

$$(-3)^2 = (-3)(-3) = 9$$

---

4. **Which is a simplified version of $(x^3)^{-4} + \dfrac{x^6}{x^2}$?**

    A $x^{-12} + x^4$

    B x^{-8}

    C x^8

    D x^2

Here's How to Crack It

Start with the first term. Remember that raising a power to another power requires multiplying the powers. $3 \times (-4) = -12$, so the first term can be written as x^{-12}. Then figure out the second term. Dividing exponents means to subtract the powers, so do $6 - 2$ to get x^4. Now we have $x^{-12} + x^4$. Can we add these together? No! They are not like terms, so they can't be added or subtracted. Leave it the way it is and choose (A).

Fractional Exponents and Roots

You may also see exponents that contain a fraction in the power, like this:

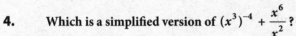

$$9^{\frac{1}{2}}$$

Fractional exponents are another way of writing roots. The one-half power means the square root—the opposite of squaring. So $9^{\frac{1}{2}} = \sqrt{9}$. You can solve roots on the calculator, but for the non-calculator section, you will have to understand how they work. Since square root is the opposite of squaring, ask yourself what number multiplied by itself equals 9. The answer is 3 because 3×3 or 3^2 equals 9. Here is a trickier fractional exponent:

$$8^{\frac{2}{3}}$$

The three on the bottom of the exponent means the cube root, the opposite of cubing. The two at the top of the exponent is a regular second power, meaning squaring. So this really refers to the cube root of 8^2, which can be written like this: $\sqrt[3]{8^2}$. First square 8 to get 64. Now take the cube root of 64. Ask yourself what number cubed equals 64. You can always guess and check. $2^3 = 2 \times 2 \times 2 = 8$. That's too small. $3^3 = 3 \times 3 \times 3 = 27$. Still too small. $4^3 = 4 \times 4 \times 4 = 64$, so the answer is 4. It is also fine to take the cube root of 8 first and then square the answer. You will get the same result.

EQUATIONS AND INEQUALITIES

Introduction to Algebra

If an expression is a mathematical phrase, what's a mathematical sentence? An **equation**. An equation is more than an expression because it includes an equals sign. It finishes the sentence by telling what the expression is equal to.

Most problems with algebra involve equations. With an equation, it is possible to solve for a variable, meaning to know what number the variable represents. Here's an example:

$$x + 6$$

This is an expression, so x could be any value. There is no information telling us what x is.

$$x + 6 = 10$$

This is an equation, so we can solve for x. In a simple equation like this, think of x like a question mark or mystery box. What number is added to 6 to get 10? Of course, the answer is 4, so $x = 4$.

Solving for *x*

In the previous example, think about how we could find the value of *x*. In such a simple equation, it's easy to look at it and know instantly what *x* must be. But if *x* is 4, what is the relationship between it and the other terms? 4 is the same as $10 - 6$. To solve for *x*, we subtract 6 from both sides to be left with just *x* on the left side and 4 on the right side, leaving us with the equation $x = 4$.

Think of an equation like a balanced scale. Both sides always have to be equal. Whatever we do to one side, we must also do to the other side.

Let's try another equation.

$$2x + 8 = 20$$

In this equation, it isn't immediately obvious what *x* is. Solve it step by step. The main goal in solving an equation is to *isolate the variable*. This means to have *x*, or whatever the variable is, alone on one side. To do this, we need to get rid of everything else on the left side. The first thing to get rid of is the + 8. In order to "get rid of" it, we can subtract it. But, we need to do that on the right side as well to keep the equation equal. The result is then $2x = 12$. Now think about, two groups of what number equal 12? The answer is 6. Really, you got that by dividing 12 by 2. Again we are doing the opposite operation. Since the 2 is being multiplied by *x*, we divide both sides by 2 to get rid of it.

One- and Two-Step Equations

Here is another example of a one-step equation.

$$\frac{y}{4} = 20$$

Here's How to Crack It

The goal, as always, is to get *y* alone. In order to do that, we must get rid of the 4 that *y* is being divided by. What's the opposite of division? Multiplication. Multiply both sides by 4 to get $y = 80$.

Here is another example of a two-step equation.

---○---

$$9z - 6 = 21$$

Here's How to Crack It

Always start by getting rid of the addition or subtraction. Since 6 is being sub-tracted on the left side, add 6 to both sides. The result is $9z = 27$. Next, the 9 is being multiplied by z. Do the opposite and divide both sides by 9. This results in $z = 3$.

---○---

Equations with Combining Like Terms

Sometimes you may be given "extra stuff" in the equation—"like terms" that need to be combined first. You already know how to combine like terms, so this shouldn't throw you off.

---○---

5.   **What is the solution to the equation $3x + 4 - x = 9 + 3$?**

    A 1

    B 2

    C 3

    D 4

Here's How to Crack It

Start by combining like terms. $3x - x = 2x$. $9 + 3 = 12$. Now the equation is $2x + 4 = 12$. Next, get x by itself. Subtract 4 from both sides to get $2x = 8$. Now divide both sides by 2 to get $x = 4$, which is (D). Notice here that the question asks for the solution, or the value of x. There are only 4 possibilities since this is mul-tiple choice. Another possible strategy is to guess and check the answer choices, but it's always a good idea to combine like terms before doing this. Some algebra problems will be grid-ins, so you won't be able to use the guess-and-check strategy.

---○---

Equations With x on Both Sides of the Equals Sign

Sometimes you will see an equation that has x on both sides. These work the same way: Get x by itself on one side and combine like terms on each side first if possible.

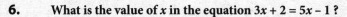

6.   **What is the value of x in the equation $3x + 2 = 5x - 1$?**

     A $-\dfrac{3}{2}$

     B $-\dfrac{2}{3}$

     C $\dfrac{2}{3}$

     D $\dfrac{3}{2}$

Here's How to Crack It

Try to get everything with an x on the left side and the numbers on the right side.

Start by subtracting $5x$ from both sides to get rid of it from the right side. The result is $-2x + 2 = -1$. Now get rid of the 2 on the left side by subtracting it from both sides to get $-2x = -3$. Now solve for x by dividing both sides by -2 to get $x = \dfrac{3}{2}$. The correct answer is (D).

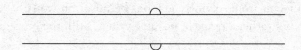

7.   **Consider this equation.**

       $4(x + 2) = 3x - 1$

     What is the value of x that makes this equation true?

     A -9

     B -3

     C 3

     D 9

Here's How to Crack It

The 4 on the outside of the parentheses means it is being multiplied by the binomial in the parentheses. It is necessary to **distribute** the 4 by multiplying it by each term in the parentheses. The result is $4x + 8$. Now the equation is $4x + 8 = 3x - 1$. Subtract $3x$ from both sides to get $x + 8 = -1$. Now subtract 8 from both sides to get $x = -9$, or (A).

Inequalities

Another vocabulary word to know is **inequality**. The prefix *in-* means "not," so an inequality is a mathematical sentence that does not involve an equals sign. Instead it has a greater than sign ($>$), a less than sign ($<$), a greater than or equal to sign ($\geq$), or a less than or equal to sign ($\leq$).

Be careful with the directions of the signs. It's easy to make a mistake on a timed test. You can remember that the wider part of the sign is in the direction of the bigger thing.

A problem might tell you something like this:

$$x > 0$$

This means x is greater than 0, meaning it is a positive number. It cannot be zero unless a greater than or equal to sign ($\geq$) is used. But other than that, we don't know exactly what x is.

You may see some problems that require you to solve an inequality. Solving inequalities is different from solving equations because you won't be left with a single value for x, but rather a range of possible values. Still, the process is the same.

---

8. Which of the following is the solution for $3x + 9 < 3$?

    A $x < 0$

    B $x < -2$

    C $x > 0$

    D $x > -2$

Here's How to Crack It

Do the same as for an equation: Get the x by itself. First subtract 9 from both sides to get $3x < -6$. Next divide by 3 to get $x < -2$, or (B).

The only difference when working with inequalities is if you have to multiply or divide by a negative number.

> An inequality is just like an equality EXCEPT when multiplying or dividing by a negative number. In this case, the inequality sign flips!

9.   If $-3x + 6 < 18$, then which of the following expressions gives all the possible values of x?

   A $x > -4$

   B $x < -4$

   C $x > 2$

   D $x < 2$

Here's How to Crack It

Start by solving the normal way. Subtract 6 from both sides to get $-3x < 12$. Now divide by -3 to get x on the left side and -4 on the right side. But, since we divided by a negative the less than sign changes to a greater than sign. The result is $x > -4$, or (A). And that's the only difference between solving equations and solving inequalities!

QUADRATIC EQUATIONS

First, Outside, Inside, Last (FOIL)

You should already be familiar with the distributive property, meaning that in an expression like $3(x + 4)$, the 3 must be multiplied by both of the terms in the parentheses. But what happens when you have two sets of parentheses multiplied together? That looks like this:

$$(x + 2)(2x + 5)$$

Each term must be multiplied by each other term. A good way to remember to do this is to follow the order of FOIL, which stands for First, Outside, Inside, Last.

Start by multiplying the two terms that come FIRST in the parentheses: $x \times 2x = 2x^2$

Then multiply the two terms that are at the OUTSIDE of the parentheses: $x \times 5 = 5x$

Next multiply the two terms that are on the INSIDE of the parentheses: $2 \times 2x = 4x$

Finally, multiply the two terms that come LAST in the parentheses: $2 \times 5 = 10$

Now put it all together: $2x^2 + 5x + 4x + 10$. Combine like terms to get $2x^2 + 9x + 10$.

It is helpful to draw curves as you go to make sure you multiply everything correctly. Your work should look something like this:

1. $(x + 2)(2x + 5)$
    $2x^2$

2. $(x + 2)(2x + 5)$
    $2x^2 + 5x$

3. $(x + 2)(2x + 5)$
    $2x^2 + 5x + 4x$

4. $(x + 2)(2x + 5)$
    $2x^2 + 5x + 4x + 10$

---

10. **Which of the following is equal to $x^2 + 6x + 8$?**

    A $(x + 2)(x + 1)$

    B $(x - 3)(x + 4)$

    C $(x + 1)(x - 3)$

    D $(x + 4)(x + 2)$

Here's How to Crack It

You now know how to FOIL, so you can use the answer choices and FOIL each one to see which one gets the expression that is given. To save some time, though, notice that the number by itself must be 8. The number by itself is represented in the LAST step of FOIL. By multiplying just the LAST numbers in the parentheses, we can see that (A) is going to be 2, (B) is –12, (C) is –3, and (D) is 8. Since (D) is the only one that is 8, it must be the correct answer. If we use FOIL on (D), we multiply the FIRST terms (x and x) to get x^2, multiply the OUTSIDE terms (x and 2) to get $2x$, multiply the INSIDE terms (4 and x) to get $4x$, and multiply the LAST terms (4 and 2) to get 8. The result is $x^2 + 2x + 4x + 8 = x^2 + 6x + 8$.

Factoring

Another way to get the answer to the previous question is by factoring. Factoring is the opposite of using FOIL. It takes a polynomial, or a **quadratic** when it looks like the ones we've just seen, and puts it into the two sets of parentheses.

Let's take a look at $x^2 + 6x + 8$ again. To factor it, draw two sets of parentheses:

$$(\qquad)(\qquad)$$

The first two terms will usually be x and x. You might sometimes have a number before one or both of them, but in this case there isn't a number before the x^2 so they are both just x.

$$(x\qquad)(x\qquad)$$

Now we need to figure out what the numbers are. The number by itself in this quadratic is 8. We get this number by multiplying the "last" terms in the parentheses, so the two numbers in this case must multiply together to equal 8. Think about what equals 8: 1×8 or 2×4. As we saw before, we find the second term in the quadratic, the x, with the "outside" and "inside" terms that are added together after being multiplied. So the two numbers must add or subtract to equal 6 since that is the number before the x in the second term of this quadratic. One and 8 cannot add or subtract to equal 6, but 2 and 4 can if they are added. Thus the parentheses look like this:

$$(x + 2)(x + 4)$$

You can and should always use FOIL to check that your factors multiply together to equal what you started with.

Let's try an example that involves negatives.

$$x^2 - 4x - 12$$

Start with the parentheses and x in each one:

$$(x\qquad)(x\qquad)$$

Now list the factors of 12: 1×12, 2×6, and 3×4. Ask yourself which one could add or subtract to equal -4. Keep in mind that since they multiply to equal -12, one will be positive and one will be negative because two positives or two negatives multiply together to equal a positive. The only two that could add or subtract to equal -4 are 2 and 6.

$$(x \quad 2)(x \quad 6)$$

Now determine which is positive and which is negative. If it is $+6$ and -2, the sum will be positive 4. It needs to be -4, so that will be -6 and $+2$. The quadratic factored is as follows:

$$(x + 2)(x - 6)$$

One type of question you may see involves an equation, not just an expression like the previous examples. You may have to factor a quadratic and also solve for x. Using the same example, the problem might look like this:

---

11. **Consider this equation:**

$$x^2 - 4x - 12 = 0$$

What is the positive solution to the above equation?

Here's How to Crack It

Finding the solution to an equation that looks like this always requires factoring first. We've already done this above and determined that it was $(x + 2)(x - 6) = 0$. Don't forget to write the $= 0$ part at the end. Notice now that we have two binomials multiplied together that the problem tells us equals 0. How could this equal 0? Well, if the first or the second binomial equaled 0, the whole thing would equal 0 because any number times 0 equals 0. Set the first binomial equal to 0:

$x + 2 = 0$. Now subtract 2 from both sides to get $x = -2$. This is one solution. Now set the second binomial equal to 0: $x - 6 = 0$. Add 6 to both sides to get $x = 6$. The two solutions are $x = -2$ and $x = 6$. Usually these problems will have two solutions. In this case the question asks for the positive solution, so you would grid in 6. You may also see a multiple-choice question that asks for both solutions or it may even ask for something like the sum or the product of the solutions. Regardless, the method is the same.

Note: If the equation doesn't equal 0 but does involve an x^2 and an x like the polynomials we've seen in this section, be sure to subtract everything from the right side so it equals 0 before factoring.

TRANSLATING ALGEBRA

Creating Equations

Sometimes a problem may ask you to create your own equation. The simplest kind is like this:

3 more than a number is 10

Translate this into math. We don't know what the number is, so that is represented by a variable, say x. "3 more than" tells us to add, so we can start with $x + 3$. The problem tells us that that *is* 10—the word "is" in math means to write an equals sign. So we write down $x + 3 = 10$ and from there we could solve as usual.

---

12. Marjorie makes an investment and doubles her money. If she ends up with $480, which equation below could be used to discover the amount of her original investment of x dollars?

   A $\dfrac{x}{2} = 480$

   B $x - 2 = 480$

   C $x + 2 = 480$

   D $2x = 480$

Math/English Dictionary
- "is" means "="
- "of" means "×"
- "more than" means "+"
- "less than" means "−"

Here's How to Crack It
The gist of the problem is this: Marjorie put her nest egg into an investment that doubled her money.

You need to express this in mathematical terms, and the key, as always, is the variable. In this case, the variable *x* represents the money Marjorie had *before* she invested. The $480 represents the money she had *after* she invested. Mathematically, what do you have to do to *x* in order to double it? That's right: 2*x*. And after it was doubled, how much money did she have? That's right: $480. The equation should read as follows:

$$2x = 480$$

The correct answer is (D).

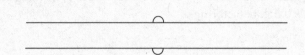

13. A certain cell phone messaging plan costs $5.00 for 200 text messages. If a customer goes beyond the 200 text messages, there is a charge of $0.25 for each additional message. If *C* represents the cost of the plan and *m* represents the number of messages beyond the 200 allowed, which of the following is an equation for a customer's messaging charge under this plan?

A $C = 5$

B $C = 0.25 + 5m$

C $C = 5 + 0.25m$

D $C = 5 + 0.25$

Here's How to Crack It
Try to write your own equation first; then check the answer choices. The flat fee is $5.00. The customer has to pay at least that. Then added on to that is $0.25 for each additional message, represented by *m*. Thus, this should look like $5 + 0.25m$ because "for each" tells us to multiply by the number of messages. This expression equals the total cost for messaging, or *C*. The complete equation is $C = 5 + 0.25m$, which is (C).

Systems of Equations
Some problems will require you to deal with two equations together. Take a look at this equation:

$$x + y = 10$$

What are *x* and *y*? They could be 6 and 4, or 2 and 8, or even something weird like 9.8 and 0.2 or –2 and 12. There is not enough information to know what either variable actually equals. But when we add a second equation, we will be able to solve for both variables.

> The number of variables corresponds with the number of equations that are needed to solve for the variables. Two equations are needed to solve for two variables, three equations for three variables, and so on.

Let's add a second equation.

$$x + y = 10$$

$$2x + 5y = 23$$

Now that we have more than one equation, this is known as a system of equations.

Solving Using Substitution

The usual way to solve is by using substitution. To do this, get one equation so it has just one variable on one side. We'll use the top equation since the variables don't have any coefficients. Let's keep x on the left side and get rid of y by subtracting it from both sides. This results in $x = 10 - y$. Now we know something that x equals. If x equals $10 - y$, we can substitute $10 - y$ when we see x in the second equation. That looks like this:

$$2(10 - y) + 5y = 23$$

Now we have one equation with only one variable, so we will be able to solve for y. First distribute the 2.

$$20 - 2y + 5y = 23$$

Now combine like terms.

$$20 + 3y = 23$$

Subtract 20 from both sides.

$$3y = 3$$

And divide by 3 to solve for y.

$$y = 1$$

Now that we know what y equals, we can put that in for y in either of the original equations to solve for x. Use the first one because it's simpler. $x + 1 = 10$, so $x = 9$. Now we know $x = 9$ and $y = 1$.

14. Consider this system of linear equations.

$$x - 2y = 14$$

$$x + 3y = 9$$

What is the solution to the system of linear equations?

A $x = 12; y = -1$

B $x = -1; y = 12$

C $x = -12; y = 1$

D $x = 1; y = -12$

Here's How to Crack It

First get x alone in one equation. Let's use the first one. Add $2y$ to both sides to get $x = 2y + 14$. Now substitute that for x in the second equation: $2y + 14 + 3y = 9$. Then combine like terms: $5y + 14 = 9$. Subtract 14 from both sides: $5y = -5$. Divide by 5 to get $y = -1$. Now substitute that for y in either equation. Let's use the second one. $x + 3(-1) = 9$. Next multiply to get $x - 3 = 9$. Add 3 to both sides to get $x = 12$. The solution is $x = 12$ and $y = -1$, or (A).

Why Plug In?

Plugging In converts algebra problems into arithmetic problems. No matter how good you are at algebra, you're better at arithmetic. Why? Because you use arithmetic every day, every time you go to a store, balance your checkbook, or tip a waiter. Chances are you rarely use algebra in your day-to-day activities.

Plugging In is oftentimes more accurate than algebra. When you plug in real numbers, you make the problems concrete rather than abstract. Once you're working with real numbers, it's easier to notice when and where you've messed up a calculation. It's much harder to see where you went wrong (or to even know you've done something wrong) when you're staring at a bunch of x's and y's.

Notice another option in the previous problem is to guess and check the answer choices. If you're given a multiple-choice problem, it may be a faster and easier way to plug in the options from the answer choices as the values of x and y to see which one gives you the correct result for both equations.

Solving Using Addition and Subtraction

Another neat way to solve systems of equations is to add or subtract the whole equations. This works best when you have something in the two equations that is the same or the opposite (like $3x$ and $-3x$). For instance, in question 14 above, both equations include x, so we can subtract the equations and the x will cancel out. Start by stacking the two equations:

$$x - 2y = 14$$
$$- (x + 3y = \quad 9)$$

Now subtract, but just be careful to remember that everything is being subtracted. $x - x = 0$, so that variable cancels out. $-2y - 3y = -5y$. $14 - 9 = 5$. We're left with $-5y = 5$. Divide by -5 to get $y = -1$, just as we did before. And as before, we plug that into one equation to solve for x.

Some problems may be easier to solve using this strategy rather than using substitution.

Word Problems

Here is an example of how systems of equations can be tested in a word problem.

———————◯———————

15. **A concert venue sells tickets for floor seats and balcony seats. Floor seats cost $30 and balcony seats cost $20. One day, the venue sells a total of 500 tickets and brings in $12,200. If f represents the number of floor seats sold and b represents the number of balcony seats sold, which of the following systems of equations could be used to find the number of each type of seat sold?**

   A $f + b = 12,200$
   $30f + 20b = 500$

   B $f + b = 500$
   $20f + 30b = 12,200$

   C $f + b = 12,200$
   $20f + 30b = 500$

   D $f + b = 500$
   $30f + 20b = 12,200$

Here's How to Crack It

Write your own system of equations. First, we know that 500 tickets were sold. This is the total of the floor seats and the balcony seats, so this means that $f + b = 500$. Eliminate (A) and (C) because they don't have this. Next, we have the price for each ticket. 30 times the number of floor seats will give us the dollar amount for those tickets, and 20 times the number of balcony seats will give us that dollar amount. This means $30f$ and $20b$. The total of those must equal 12,200 since the problem says that's the total dollar amount. The second equation is $30f + 20b = 12,200$. The answer is (D).

———————◯———————

Algebra Glossary

Here's a handy table to help you remember the terms discussed in this chapter.

Expression	A mathematical phrase that includes two or more terms
Term	A number, variable, or anything else that can come before or after +, −, or × symbols
Polynomial	An expression with two or more terms
Binomial	An expression with exactly two terms
Like terms	Terms that have the same variables and powers; like terms can be added or subtracted
Variable	A letter that represents an unknown number
Coefficient	A number that is being multiplied by a variable
Degree	The exponent given to a number or variable
Equation	A mathematical sentence that includes an equals sign
Inequality	A mathematical sentence that includes <, >, ≥, or ≤
Quadratic	An expression that involves squaring, usually in the form $ax^2 + bx + c$

Algebra Drill

Now try these questions. You can use a calculator for all of them EXCEPT the ones that have a "no calculator" icon above them. To check your answers, register your book at **PrincetonReview.com/cracking** and download the Chapter Drill Answers and Explanations supplement.

1. **Which of the following is equivalent to $8x - 5 + 2y^2 + 3x + 12 - 5x^2$?**

    A . $-10xy^2 + 11x + 7$

    B $3x + 2y^2 + 15x - 5x^2$

    C $5x^2 - 2y^2 + 11x + 7$

    D $-5x^2 + 11x + 7 + 2y^2$

2. $(9z^2 + 4z) - (-3z^2 + 2z + 12) =$

    A $12z^2 + 2z - 12$

    B $-12z^2 + 2z - 12$

    C $12z^2 + 2z + 12$

    D $-12^2 + 2z + 12$

3. $25^{\frac{3}{2}} =$

    A $\sqrt[3]{25^2}$

    B $25^{\frac{2}{3}}$

    C 5

    D 125

4. **If $2x - 6 = 11$, then $x =$**

    A $\dfrac{5}{2}$

    B 5

    C $\dfrac{17}{2}$

    D 17

5. Evaluate $3x^2 - 4y$, if $x = 2$ and $y = 3$.

A 24

B 6

C 0

D −6

6. Consider this equation.

$$8x - 6 + 4x = 4 + 5x - 2$$

What is the value of x that makes this equation true?

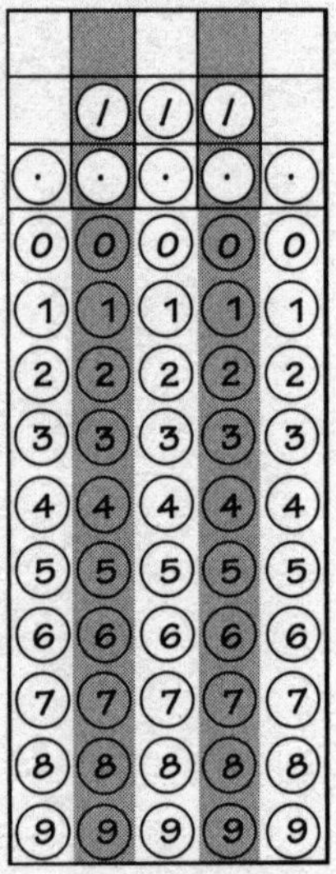

7. If $3m + 7 < 28$, then which of the following expressions gives all the possible values of m?

A $m < 9$

B $m < 7$

C $m > -5$

D $m > -7$

8. Multiply.

$$(4x - 8)(x + 2)$$

A $4x^2 - 16$

B $-4x + 2$

C $4x^2 + 16x - 16$

D $5x - 6$

9. Which of the following is a factor of $x^2 - 4x + 3x - 12$?

A $(x + 4)$

B $(x - 4)$

C $(x - 3)$

D $(x - 2)$

10. What is the sum of the solutions of the equation $5x - 10 + x^2 - 2x = 0$?

A -3

B 2

C 3

D 5

11. If $x = 2y + 5$ and $x = 3y - 6$, what is the value of x?

A 11

B 22

C 27

D 33

12. If $4x - 3y = 15$ and $5x = 12 - 3y$, what is the value of x?

A -3

B -1

C 1

D 3

13. At a certain fruit stand, apples cost 25 cents and bananas cost 30 cents. If Bill buys a total of 8 apples and bananas for $2.15, how many bananas did Bill buy?

A 3

B 4

C 5

D 6

Chapter 16
Functions

In this chapter, we'll guide you through the key topics related to functions on the TASC Mathematics test, including solving and graphing functions. Following the content lessons, we'll give you some practice questions.

FUNCTIONS: INPUTS AND OUTPUTS

Functions are not nearly as scary as they seem. Think of a machine that has an input and an output. You can liken a mathematical function to a machine that produces one distinct output for every input introduced.

Input → [Machine] → Output

If any input produces more than one output, then it is not a function. Let's say that for every time 6 is the input, 12 will be the output. While 12 might be the outcome for other inputs, it will always be the outcome for an input of 6 for this particular function. Therefore, 6 in this function will only yield a result of 12. If you input 6 and can also get another outcome, then it is not a function.

Functions are often expressed in terms of coordinates, graphs, and equations, which we will look at more in detail. For now, let us consider (x, y) ordered pairs, in which x represents the input to the function and y represents the corresponding output. We will discuss the xy-coordinate plane later on in the chapter, but for now let us call x the input and y the output in the ordered pairs. Remember, every input must yield one and only one output.

Let's give it a try.

---

1. **Which set of ordered pairs represents a function?**

   A (5, 6), (–4, 2), (–3, 2), (–4, 4)

   B (7, 2), (7, –1), (10, –5), (14, –11)

   C (8, 8), (–14, 4), (7, 2), (–8, –14)

   D (–3, 5), (5, 3), (–1, 2), (–1, –3)

Here's How to Crack It

The definition of a function is that for every input, there is one distinct output. Therefore, each x-input must have a distinct y-output in each of the ordered pairs. In (A), (5, 6) and (–3, 2) are distinct because the x-value is only given once. However, when $x = -4$, there are two different corresponding outputs or y-values (2 and 4 respectively). Therefore, (A) is wrong. Choice (B) contains the same error in the pairs (7, 2) and (7, –1), in which the input is the same and yields two different outputs. Choice (D) makes the same error when the input is –1, so the correct answer is (C). Each of the x-values in this answer choice is distinct, making it a valid function.

---

x and *f*(*x*)

Just as functions can be expressed as ordered pairs, there is a specific mathematical expression that shows the input and output more clearly. Functions are usually expressed by the mathematical expression $f(x)$, in which the x is the input to the formula, and $f(x)$ is the corresponding output, or y-value. For example, in the function $f(x) = 4x^3 + 3x - 2$, the x represents the number to plug into the equation, whatever that number might be. If a question were to ask the value of, say, $f(6)$, you would simply plug 6 in every time x appears: $f(6) = 4(6)^3 + 3(6) - 2$. Functions can have any variable, $f(t)$, $f(s)$, $f(n)$, etc., but the variable inside the parentheses is always the input of the function, and the entire "$f(x)$" represents the outcome. x and $f(x)$ can be shown in lists, as formulas, expressed as different variables, but all these different expressions mean the same thing: For every input, there is one and only one output.

Let's give it a try.

---

2.   **Consider the equation $f(x) = 5x^2 + 4x - 7$. What is $f(3)$?**

    A   20

    B   34

    C   50

    D   54

Here's How to Crack It

Since the question is giving an input for x, plug in the value given every time x appears:

$$f(x) = 5x^2 + 4x - 7$$

$$f(3) = 5(3)^2 + 4(3) - 7$$

From here, solve using order of operations (remember your PEMDAS!)

$$f(3) = 5(9) + 4(3) - 7$$

Multiply before adding and subtracting:

$$f(3) = 45 + 12 - 7$$

Combine like terms with addition and subtraction last:

$$f(3) = 50$$

The correct answer is (C). Once you have a number to plug into the formula, in this case 3, simply plug that number into the formula every time x appears and follow the order of operations until you are left with the final answer. If you forgot to square the 3 before multiplying by 5, you would arrive at (A), so be careful with your order of operations. Similarly, be careful of your signs, that you don't add 7 instead of subtract, which would lead you to answers (B) or (D).

Let's try another example.

3. **Which of the following lists is NOT a function?**

A

x	f(x)
-3	11
-1	3
0	2
1	2
3	11
4	18

B

x	f(x)
0	6
1	8
-1	6
3	8
1	0
5	3

C

x	f(x)
-2	-8
-1	-1
0	0
1	1
2	8
3	27

D

x	f(x)
0	-2
1	1
-1	-6
2	12
-3	-38
4	74

Here's How to Crack It

Even though the question presents a series of charts instead of ordered pairs, the concept is the same as in example 1. Here, the ordered pairs are expressed as x and $f(x)$, though they still represent the inputs and the outputs, respectively, just like x and y. Since the question asks which of the sets is NOT a function, look for two x-values that yield different $f(x)$ values. Though there are repeating $f(x)$ values, (A) has all distinct x values, so it is a function. Choice (B) has x equal to 1 twice, the first time the ordered pair appears as (1, 8), and the second time as (1, 0). Since the same input cannot produce multiple outputs, this is not a function, and therefore is the correct answer. Repeating the same process for (C) and (D), the x-values all are distinct from one another and therefore are considered to be functions.

GRAPHING FUNCTIONS

Okay, let's get back to the notion of x and y as ordered pairs. Just as a function can be expressed as (x, y) or x and $f(x)$, this information can be shown on an xy-coordinate plane. x and $f(x)$ are the same as x and y, so the ordered pair would look like $(x, f(x))$ or (x, y) if using this type of notation. Each of these ordered pairs may be graphed on the xy-coordinate plane. Here is a sample function on the xy-coordinate plane, in which the x-axis runs horizontally (left to right) and the y-axis runs vertically (up and down).

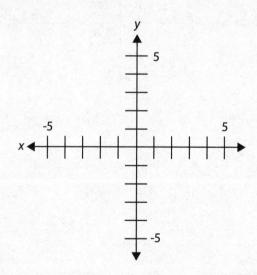

You can see that the x- and y-axes cross at 0, and extend infinitely in positive and negative directions. As the x-axis extends more to the right from zero, it represents positive values, while to the left of zero represents the negative values. Similarly, the y-axis above zero represents the positive outputs and below zero lie the negative output values. Since the ordered pairs representing the inputs and outputs of a function can be expressed as (x, y), they can be plotted along the xy-coordinate plane. Consider this function:

$$y = x^2$$

From this function, you can generate the following set of ordered pairs by plugging in various x-values:

x	y
−2	4
−1	1
0	0
1	1
2	4

By plotting the points on the xy-coordinate plane, you will get the following results:

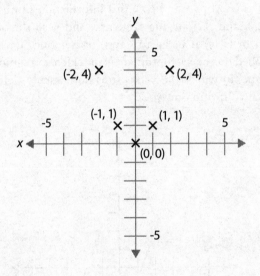

By connecting the points together, the graph will consist of all possible values of x and y, since most functions work for all real numbers (we will take a look at a few exceptions in a bit). By connecting the points above, the graph of $y = x^2$ will look like so:

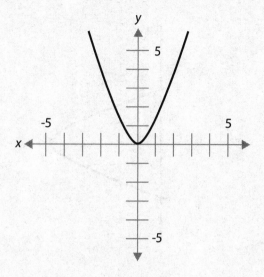

Remember, any function must have only one output (y) for every input (x). Notice in the graph above that at any point, x, there is only one value for y.

A simple way to check if a graph is a function is to draw a vertical line. Using the same graph of $y = x^2$, let's draw a vertical line at $x = -2$.

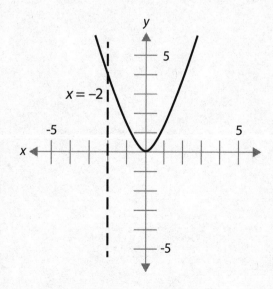

A vertical line test is a simple way to test if the graph is indeed a function. Since the graph above touches the line $x = -2$ at only one point, then it is considered a function. If the graph touches the vertical line at two or more places, then it is not considered a function:

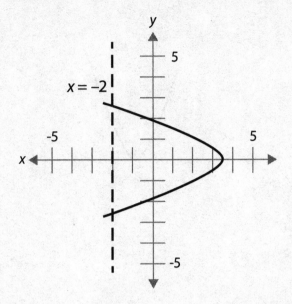

Now, you might notice that this graph appears to be similar in shape to the function $y = x^2$, but notice that here it crosses the vertical line $x = -2$ twice. Because of this, the above graph is not a function.

Let's try an example.

4. **Which of the following graphs represents a function?**

A

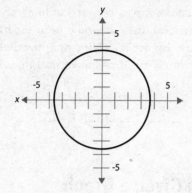

B

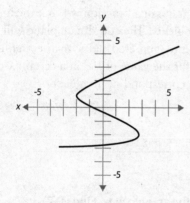

C

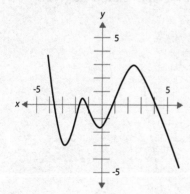

D

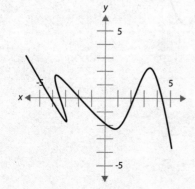

Here's How to Crack It

While all these graphs are interesting and visually appealing, not all of them are functions. Draw vertical lines over each of the graphs. The graph that passes the vertical line test, no matter where it is drawn, is (C). Choice (D) is tempting, but the portion in the negative *x*–range does not pass the vertical line test. In (A), the only time the circle would pass the vertical line test would be at the lines tangent on either side. Similarly, (B) would overlap a vertical line multiple times, depending on where it is placed. If you get stuck, try drawing vertical lines in different places to double check.

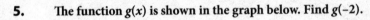

Solving Functions When Given a Graph

Often, the TASC test might give the graph of a function without the formula. Not to worry if you come across these problems. The coordinate plane will be defined by units, which will help you to identify ordered pairs on the graph to answer questions. The TASC test might ask for the value of *f*(*x*) at a certain *x*-coordinate, and the grid will help you to find the corresponding *y*-value, or *f*(*x*).

Let's try an example.

---

5. The function *g*(*x*) is shown in the graph below. Find *g*(–2).

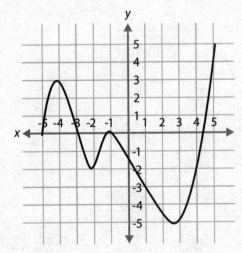

A   3

B   0

C   –2

D   –4

Here's How to Crack It

At $x = -2$, $y = -2$. The variables y and $g(x)$ are interchangeable, so do not worry that the formula for the graph is unknown. Since $g(x)$ is graphed, simply find where the graph crosses $x = -2$. Another way to approach this problem is by drawing the vertical line $x = -2$. Then, find where the line intersects the graph, which happens to be at $y = -2$. The correct answer is (C).

Let's try one more.

6. The function $f(x)$ is shown in the graph below. What is the value of x when $f(x) = -1$?

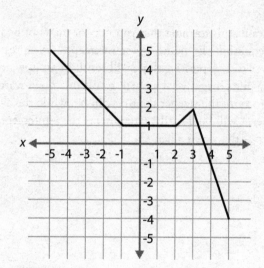

Here's How to Crack It

This question has a twist from the last question: Now, it asks for the *x*-value instead of *f*(*x*). Instead of a vertical line, draw a horizontal line at $y = -1$ to signify the desired outcome. You will find that the graph crosses this line at $x = 4$. Since that is the only place the line crosses, you are all set!

Graphing Linear Functions

The TASC test often tests linear functions in the form of ordered pairs and formulas. Linear functions are simply straight lines, as opposed to functions that are curved or irregular in shape. The most common formula for a linear function is slope intercept form, $y = mx + b$, in which *x* and *y* are the ordered pairs that you are now used to working with.

There are two other variables in this formula that you may or may not be familiar with, and which give the equation the name "slope-intercept." *m* represents the slope of the line, the rise over run. A positive slope will result in an upward trending line from left to right, while a negative slope will result in a downward trend. The further the slope is from zero, the steeper the line will be, while the closer the slope is to zero, the shallower it will be. Finally, *b* represents the *y*-intercept, which is simply the point that crosses the *y*-axis when $x = 0$.

Let's try an example.

7. Which of the following graphs represents the function $f(x) = 2x - 4$?

A

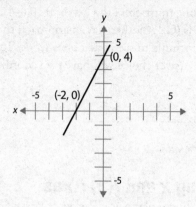

B

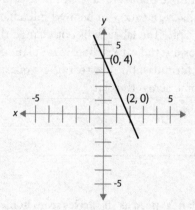

C

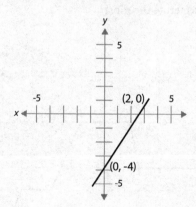

D

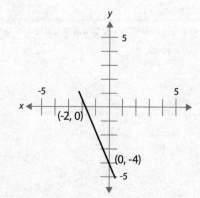

Here's How to Crack It

There are a few ways to approach this question. One way is to identify one part of the slope-intercept form to eliminate answer choices. The slope, *m*, is 2, which means it must be a positive, upward trend, eliminating (B) and (D). Similarly, the *y*-intercept is −4, meaning that the line must cross the *y*-axis at (0, −4). Therefore, eliminate (A) and the correct choice is (C). Another way to approach this is to plug the points from the graphs into the formula to see which ones work. This will lead you to the same answer, as only one answer choice will have two coordinate points that work in the equation.

_____○_____

Graphing Functions Using *x* and *f*(*x*) Axes

Sometimes, the axes on the *xy*-coordinate plane are labeled not as *x* and *y*, but as *x* and *f*(*x*). Since you know already that *y* and *f*(*x*) can be used interchangeably, do not worry if you see this on your graph. The labels will not change the way you treat the graph; continue to treat it as a standard *xy*-coordinate plane. The graphs may or may not be accompanied by formulas, but just treat these questions as any other graphing question you have come across thus far.

Let's try an example.

_____○_____

8. The function *f*(*x*) represents Jane's speed as she drives from home to work. At which interval does she accelerate the most?

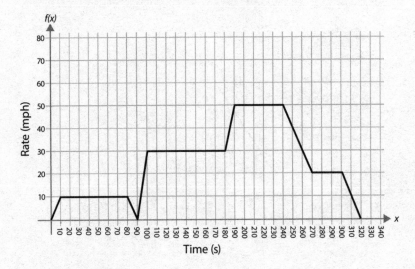

A   0–10 seconds

B   90–100 seconds

C   180–190 seconds

D   240–270 seconds

Here's How to Crack It

Find the slope of each of the sections of the graph to see which is the largest (which will indicate the greatest acceleration). From 0–10 seconds, the mph changes from 0–10. The slope would be 10 mph/10 seconds = 1 = m in (A). In (B), the change in time is still 10 seconds, but the acceleration is from 0 to 30 mph. Through the same process, the slope would be 30 mph/10 seconds = 3 = m. Since this slope is greater than in (A), you may eliminate (A). In (C), the change in time is still 10 seconds, and the acceleration is from 30 to 50, which results in a change of 20 mph. This might seem like a tempting answer because the car is traveling at its fastest during this time, though the *acceleration* is 20 mph. Therefore, 20 mph/10 seconds is less of a slope than in (B), so eliminate (C). In (D), the change in time is 30 seconds and the car decelerates 30 mph, from 50 to 20. –30 mph/30 seconds creates a slope of –1, so this is less than (B) as well. Choice (B) is correct.

Exceptions to a Range of "All Real Numbers"

There are some instances, depending on the formula, in which the function will not produce real numbers. In some equations, the output for a given x-value is undefined because it creates an undefined mathematical equation, usually zero in the denominator of a fraction. Since anything divided by zero is undefined (think about it—how can you divide something into zero equal parts?), there will either be a hole at a specific value or the graph will get close to a value but never reach it, which we call an asymptote. Don't worry too much about memorizing the vocabulary for these special cases, but rather recognize when an equation will not work. Ask yourself how you could get the denominator to equal zero if the question asks for an undefined or unreal output.

Let's try an example.

---

9. At which value of x will the equation $f(x) = \dfrac{1}{x}$ **not** equal a real number?

    A –1

    B 0

    C .00001

    D 1

Here's How to Crack It

Since there are real numbers in the answer choices, plug the answers into the equation. In (A), $f(-1) = \dfrac{1}{(-1)}$, which is equal to –1, which is a real number. However, in (B), $f(0) = \dfrac{1}{(0)}$. This answer is undefined because zero is in the denominator.

Since zero is in the denominator, this value for the function is undefined. If you look at the table of points in a graphing calculator, you will find an error at this x-value.

Let's try another.

10. **At which value of x does the equation $f(x) = \dfrac{(x + 3)}{(x - 5)}$ not equal a real number?**

    A   –5

    B   –3

    C   3

    D   5

Here's How to Crack It

The only way that the equation will not equal a real number is if the denominator equals zero. The denominator, $x - 5$, will equal zero when $x = 5$. Therefore, if $x = 5$ is inserted into the equation, the result will be $f(5) = \dfrac{(5 + 3)}{(5 - 5)}$, or $f(5) = \dfrac{(8)}{(0)}$. Since $\dfrac{8}{0}$ is undefined, (D) is the correct answer.

Functions Drill

Now try some questions. To check your answers, register your book at **PrincetonReview.com/cracking** and download the Chapter Drill Answers and Explanations supplement.

1. For the function $f(x) = 3x^2 + 2x + 6$, what is $f(3)$?

   A 21

   B 24

   C 38

   D 39

2. Which set of ordered pairs represents a function?

   A (5, 8), (−5, 8), (0, 2), (1, 2)

   B (5, 8), (6, 9), (7, 10), (5, 11)

   C (−6, 2), (−6, 4), (5, 2), (−5, 2)

   D (−3, 1), (1, 3), (−1, 3), (1, −3)

3. **Which of the following is <u>not</u> a function?**

A

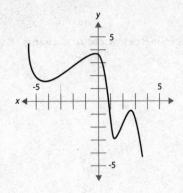

C

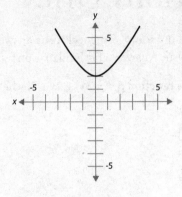

B

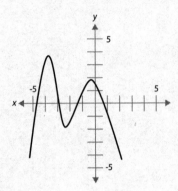

D

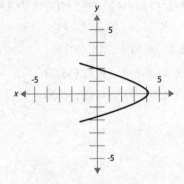

4. What is the value of x when the function $f(x) = -3x^2 + 4x + 42$ is equal to 10?

A   −3

B   −2

C   3

D   4

5. On the graph below, for how many values does $f(x) = 4$?

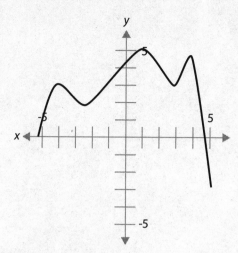

6. For which value of x is $f(x) = \dfrac{(x-1)}{(x+3)}$ **not** a real number?

A –3

B –1

C 1

D 3

7. What is the slope of the function represented in the table below?

x	$f(x)$
3	34
5	26
7	18
9	10
11	2

A −8

B −4

C $-\dfrac{1}{4}$

D 2

8. A car rental company charges a flat rate of $25 dollars for the first day, and $10 dollars per day for each subsequent day that a customer rents a car. What is the function, f, that represents the amount of d dollars that a customer would pay for a rental car x days long?

A $f(d) = 25 + 10x$

B $f(d) = (25 + 10)x$

C $f(d) = 25 + 10(x - 1)$

D $f(d) = 10 + 25x$

9. Which graph models the function that contains (–3, 0), (–1, 2), and (2, –1) included in its solution set?

A

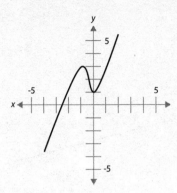

C

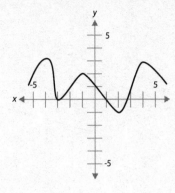

B

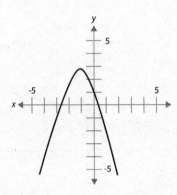

D

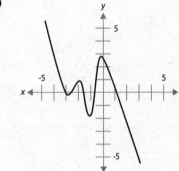

10. For the function $g(x) = \dfrac{5}{6}x - 4$, what is $g(18)$?

11. Which of the following graphs represents the function $f(x) = -\dfrac{1}{4}x + 4$?

A

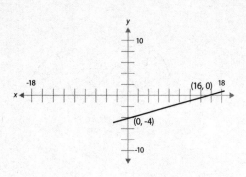

C

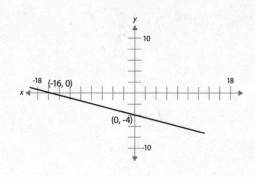

B

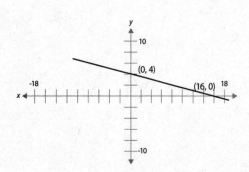

D

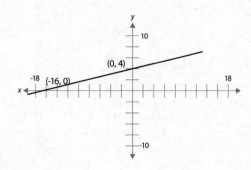

12. The graph $f(x)$ lies on the coordinate plane below. Find $f(-2)$.

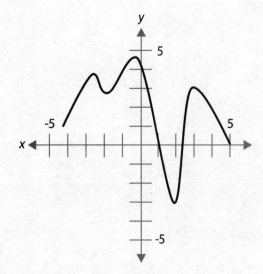

A −3

B −2

C 2

D 3

13. An attendant fills a pool over a 15-minute period. The graphed function $f(x)$ models the rate at which the water fills the pool in gallons per minute (GPM).

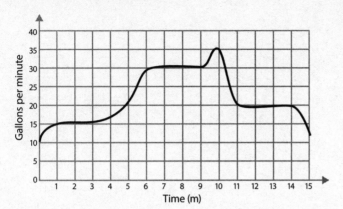

During which time period does the flow rate increase the most?

A   0 to 1 minute

B   5 to 6 minutes

C   6 to 9 minutes

D   9 to 10 minutes

14. What is one zero of the function $y = (x + 4)(x - 7)$?

A   –7

B   –4

C   4

D   –28

15. For which of the following functions does $f(5) = 38$?

A $f(x) = (-8/5)x^2 + 4x + 5$

B $f(x) = -2x^2 + (8/5)x + 14$

C $f(x) = (4/5)x^2 + 4x - 2$

D $f(x) = 3x^2 - 4x - 2$

Chapter 17
Geometry

In this chapter, we will guide you through the key topics related to geometry on the TASC Mathematics test, from triangles and quadrilaterals to circles and 3-D figures. Following the content lessons, we'll give you some practice questions.

GEOMETRY ON THE TASC TEST

There are more geometric concepts than can be counted; however, fortunately, most of them are not going to show up on the TASC test. About 25% of the questions on the TASC test will be geometry-based, so this can be a bit scary. The good thing is that this chapter will encompass nearly every topic you should come across on the TASC test that is geometry-related.

Measuring Diagrams

On the TASC test, you may find yourself with a picture for some geometry questions. Figures are very helpful for geometry, as they allow for better visualization of the question or process at hand. As a general rule, figures are not drawn specifically in order to deceive; however, that does not mean they are perfectly drawn to scale. So while a protractor or ruler may not be of use, if two lines do look equal, they probably are equal or almost equal. Therefore, don't rely on your eyes to determine equality or exact numbers, but using them for ballparking purposes works out very well.

What If No Picture is Given?

When you hear the term "geometry," shapes typically come to mind, and with good reason. Therefore, if no image is provided, you should go ahead and draw your own. Don't worry about how good or bad the drawing is; no one will see your drawings but you! Just draw an image since it is much easier to work with an actual picture than the one in your head. Even if your drawing doesn't look the best, all that matters is that you know what the image should be.

The Reference Sheet

For both the Calculator and Non-Calculator Sessions, you will be given a reference sheet with many equations. For starters, most 3-D figures have equations provided in that box. Volume equations are given for cylinders, spheres, pyramids, and cones. Also, the intersecting chords theorem and relationships between inscribed and central angles in circles are provided, as are the distance and midpoint formulas. However, the only 2-D equation given besides that is the Pythagorean theorem, so if you cannot remember the area of a quadrilateral or circumference of a circle formulas, study them prior to testing.

PLANE GEOMETRY I

Angles in Triangles

A **triangle** is a geometric figure with three sides. There are many important aspects that could be tested with regard to triangles, though—let's start with the angles.

> In any triangle, the total number of degrees is 180°.

1. **A given triangle has angle measures as given. What is the value of *x*?**

    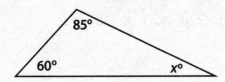

    A 35

    B 55

    C 125

    D 155

Here's How to Crack It

Since the total number of degrees in any triangle is 180°, the sum of the three angles given must be 180°. This gives 60 + 85 + *x* = 180; solving for *x* gives an angle measure of 35°, (A).

Ballparking would also be helpful here; the angle is clearly not obtuse, which would allow (C) and (D) to be eliminated. Testing out (B) would give a sum of 200°, which is too large; this leaves (A).

Types of Triangles

There are two ways to classify triangles—based on their angle measures and based on their side lengths.

When comparing triangles based on angles, the terms used are **acute, right,** and **obtuse.** Triangles classified as **acute** contain only angles that are acute; that is, all angles are less than 90°. Triangles that contain one angle measuring exactly 90°, or a **right angle**, are considered to be right triangles. If a triangle contains one **obtuse angle**, or angle with a measure greater than 90°, it is considered an obtuse triangle.

Triangles are also classified based on their side lengths. If all three sides are the same in length and all angles equal, **equilateral** is the term used to describe the triangle. If two of the sides and the angles opposite those sides are equal, the triangle is then **isosceles**. If no two sides share the same length and no two angles measure the same, the triangle is considered **scalene**.

---

2.   In triangle *DEF* below, $DE \cong DF$ what is the value of *x*?

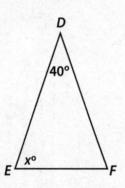

    A   40

    B   70

    C   110

    D   140

Here's How to Crack It

Since sides *DE* and *DF* are the same, the angles opposite them must be the same as well. Therefore, $40 + 2x = 180$. Solving for *x* would give a measure of 70° per angle. Another way to do this is by using POE; plug in each answer as *x* for the two missing angles, and see whether the sum is 180°. Be sure not to fall for the trap answer here; angle *EDF* is 40° but that is opposite *EF*, which is not one of congruent sides.

3. **If a given triangle with sides of length 6 and 7 is scalene, which of the following could NOT be the length of the unknown side?**

    A 5

    B 7

    C 9

    D 11

Here's How to Crack It

A scalene triangle has three sides that are all different. For this reason, sides of length 5, 9, and 11 would all be fine, but a side with length 7 would not be since one of the sides provided was 7. Therefore, the answer is (B). Whenever dealing with a question asking which could NOT be true, always be sure to read carefully; if you rush, you may choose the first answer if it works, rather than continuing to find the one that does not work and therefore answers the question.

Perimeter of Triangles

The **perimeter** any figure is the distance around the outside edge of the two-dimensional object. The perimeter of a triangle is therefore the sum of the sides of the triangle. To find the perimeter given the sides, add the three sides together—that's all there is to it!

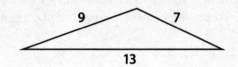

4. Triangle *GHI* has side lengths as shown. What is the perimeter of the figure?

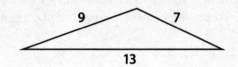

$$9 \qquad 7$$
$$13$$

    A 16

    B 20

    C 22

    D 29

Here's How to Crack It

Since the perimeter is the sum of all the known sides, the perimeter would be found by adding 9 + 13 + 7. That gives a total of 29, so the perimeter is 29, (D). If you add only two of the sides, you will get any of the incorrect answers—all of them are the sums of only two sides, so be sure you add all three together!

5. An isosceles triangle has a perimeter of 45. If one of the sides has a length of 21 and the other two sides are equal, what is the measure of each of the other sides?

    A 12

    B 24

    C 33

    D 66

Here's How to Crack It

Since the triangle is isosceles, two sides are equal. The question specifies that the equal side lengths are the unknown ones, so let's call them x; therefore, $45 = 21 + 2x$. The lengths of the unknown sides would be $\frac{45 - 21}{2}$, which is 12, (A). Be careful when working the problem; if you accidentally forget to cut the difference between 45 and 21 in half, the result is (B).

Area of Triangles

The formula for the area of a triangle is $\frac{1}{2}$(base × height). Another way this is frequently written is $\frac{(\text{base} \times \text{height})}{2}$. In both cases, the base is the length of the bottom side of the triangle, and the height is the length of a line perpendicular from the base of the triangle to its highest point. In a right triangle, the two legs are the sides used; if a triangle is not a right triangle, always be careful to ensure you are using the correct sides.

The formula itself is not given, so make sure you have it memorized.

$$\text{Area of a triangle} = \frac{1}{2}(\text{base} \times \text{height})$$

6. Given triangle *JKL* provided, determine the area of the triangle.

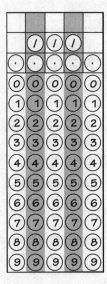

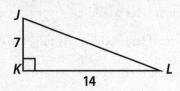

Here's How to Crack It

Use the formula for area of a triangle. Since the base shown is 14 and the height is given as 7, the area will be $\left(\dfrac{1}{2}\right)(14)(7)$, which is 49. Make sure you take half of the product; if the question were multiple choice, there would likely be an answer of 98 there, since that is the product of 7 and 14.

That one wasn't so bad, was it? Try another one:

7. If the length of *MO* is 13, what is the area of triangle *MON*?

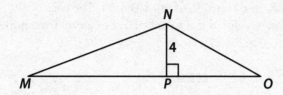

- **A** 17
- **B** 26
- **C** 34
- **D** 52

Here's How to Crack It

You're given 4 as the height, so multiply that by the base—which is 13, the length of *MO*—to get 52. Using the formula for the area of a triangle, divide 52 by 2, and you're left with 26, or (B).

Sometimes, a question may involve both area and perimeter. Be careful to use the right formula and in the right order to answer such questions correctly.

8. Triangle *PQR* has sides with lengths as shown. What is the ratio of the area to the perimeter of the triangle?

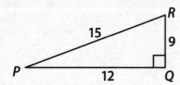

- **A** 1:3
- **B** 2:3
- **C** 1:1
- **D** 3:2

Here's How to Crack It

First, find the perimeter. Perimeter is calculated by adding together all side lengths; in this case, that is 9 + 12 + 15, which is 36. Then, calculate the area of the figure by taking half the product of the base and height. The base of 12 and the height of 9 have a product of 108, so the area (half of that) is 54. The ratio of the area to the perimeter is then 54:36, which reduces to 3:2, (D). Be careful here; notice that (B) is the same two numbers, but backwards.

The Pythagorean Theorem

No triangle lesson or review would be complete without mentioning the Pythagorean theorem. Over 2,000 years ago, a guy named Pythagoras realized there was a relationship that was always true for right triangles: The sums of the squares of the legs always was the same as the square of the hypotenuse. The **legs** were defined as the shorter sides of the right triangle, the sides that formed the right angle; the **hypotenuse**, on the other hand, is the length of the longest side, the one across from the right angle. This formula is so important, it's even one of the ones given to you in your reference box; however, it helps having it memorized, so here it is again below.

$a^2 + b^2 = c^2$, where a and b are the legs and c is the hypotenuse of a right triangle

---

9. **Given a right triangle with legs of length 5 and 12, what is the hypotenuse?**

A 7

B $\sqrt{119}$

C 13

D 17

Here's How to Crack It

Use the Pythagorean theorem! Since the legs have lengths of 5 and 12, the Pythagorean theorem becomes $5^2 + 12^2 = c^2$. The value of 5^2 is 25, and the value of 12^2 is 144; these have a sum of 169, so $c = \sqrt{169}$, which is 13, (C). Make sure you plug the numbers into the equation properly; if instead of adding 25 and 144 you take the square root of the difference, (B) is the result. If the two known sides are simply added or subtracted, (A) and (D) are obtained; make sure you always answer exactly what the question asks.

———————————◯———————————

See that right triangle? It's one of the most common ones that is seen, and therefore if you can memorize it, do so. Another one that is often seen is the 3-4-5 triangle (one whose sides are in a 3:4:5 ratio), or its multiple, the 6-8-10. Being on the lookout for those can save time when working with right triangles, as shown in this next question.

———————————◯———————————

10.   **A right triangle has a hypotenuse length of 5. If one of its legs has a length of 4, what is the length of the other leg?**

A   3

B   5

C   6

D $\sqrt{41}$

Here's How to Crack It

Again, time to pull out the Pythagorean theorem…or do we need to? Notice the hypotenuse is given as 5, and the leg is given as 4; therefore, knowing the 3-4-5 triangle can save quite a bit of time. If that triangle is not known, plug the numbers into the theorem. That would give $a^2 + 4^2 = 5^2$. Since 4^2 is 16 and 5^2 is 25, the missing side must be $\sqrt{25 - 16}$, or 3, (A). Also, ballparking works wonders here; since the legs must be shorter than the hypotenuse, the answer had to be less than 5—and only (A) actually is.

———————————◯———————————

Often, questions will require knowledge of side lengths to answer questions about perimeter or area. Other times, questions will not work out quite so prettily in terms of the math.

11. What is the perimeter of triangle *STU*?

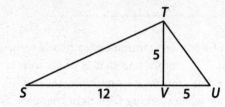

A $10 + 5\sqrt{2}$

B 30

C $30 + 5\sqrt{2}$

D 42.5

Here's How to Crack It

The hypotenuse of each triangle must be determined in order to figure out the perimeter of the figure. Triangle *STV* is one that may be known—the 5-12-13 triangle—but if it's not memorized, the Pythagorean theorem will solve it; the side would be equal to $\sqrt{5^2 + 12^2}$, which is 13. Use the Pythagorean theorem again for the next triangle; this time, the unknown length *TU* would be $\sqrt{5^2 + 5^2}$, which is $\sqrt{50}$ or $5\sqrt{2}$. Adding all sides together then would give 12 + 5 + $5\sqrt{2}$ + 13, which gives a total of $30 + 5\sqrt{2}$. The wrong answers do not answer the question posed; (A) is the perimeter of only triangle *TUV*, (B) is the perimeter of triangle *STV*, and (D) is the area of the figure.

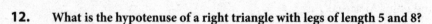

12. What is the hypotenuse of a right triangle with legs of length 5 and 8?

A 3

B $\sqrt{89}$

C 13

D 40

Here's How to Crack It

Since the triangle has legs of length 5 and 8, plug those into the Pythagorean theorem. $\sqrt{5^2 + 8^2} = \sqrt{89}$, so that is the answer. Not a pretty number, no, but notice the answer is given as a radical—not some messy decimal.

Four-Sided Figure Types

Any four-sided figure is called a **quadrilateral**. The quadrilateral is one of the most common types of shapes that will be seen, since there are simply so many different types of them.

If a quadrilateral is composed of two sets of lines that are parallel to one another, the figure is called a **parallelogram**. If the quadrilateral has one set of lines that are parallel and another set of lines that are not, the quadrilateral is considered a **trapezoid**.

Parallelograms can be broken down further in some special cases. Most parallelograms have the two sets of parallel lines that meet and create "big" and "small" angles, as shown.

However, sometimes, the angles that are formed are all the same. In such cases when the sets of parallel lines meet to form four equal angles, the shape is called a **rectangle**. Furthermore, each angle in a rectangle is equal to 90°.

Rectangles have even another step to go. If the rectangle has four equal sides, and each of its angles are 90°, the shape is then a **square**.

One more special type of parallelogram is a cross between a square and a parallelogram, and is called a **rhombus**. The shape of a rhombus is created by two sets of parallel lines that intersect one another and do not form 90° angles—but do have four equal side lengths. If all sides are equal, the shape is a rhombus.

Wow, that was a lot of terminology! Let's try a question involving the terms themselves.

13. **Which of the following statements concerning quadrilaterals is true?**

   A   All rhombuses are squares.

   B   All parallelograms are trapezoids.

   C   All rectangles are rhombuses.

   D   All squares are rectangles.

Here's How to Crack It

Rhombuses do not have equal angles, whereas squares do; this eliminates (A). Trapezoids are only a subset of quadrilaterals, so nothing involving trapezoids and any other quadrilateral subset is correct, eliminating (B). Rhombuses are a subset of parallelograms that are NOT rectangles, eliminating (C). However, squares are rectangles with equal sides, making (D) the correct response.

Knowing the relationships between quadrilateral types is very useful, but more often than not, questions will be about aspects of the shapes rather than relationships between them.

Perimeters and Areas of Four-Sided Figures

Perimeters of any quadrilateral are the same as those of triangles: They are the total lengths around the shape, and can be found by adding all sides together, at times using special formulas. Areas though are determined slightly differently, since area is the total 2-D space something takes up. Formulas for area and perimeter of four quadrilaterals are given below.

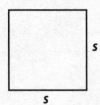

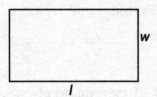

Area = s^2
Perimeter = $4s$

Area = $l \times w$
Perimeter = $2l + 2w$

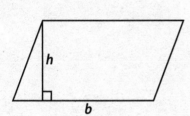

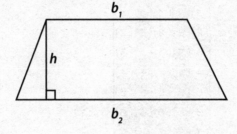

Area = $b \times h$

Area = $\dfrac{(b_1 + b_2) \times h}{2}$

Let's try a sample problem.

14. **What is the area of a square if its side length is 6?**

   A   12

   B   24

   C   36

   D   48

Here's How to Crack It

Since the formula for area of a square is given by the square of the side length, the area of a square with a side length of 6 would be 6^2. This gives 36, (C). Choice (B) is a trap; that would be the perimeter, not the area. Also, if you accidentally double 6 rather than square it, (A) is obtained—be careful!

That wasn't so bad, was it? Try another:

15. **What is the perimeter of a square if its area is 49?**

Here's How to Crack It

Since the area of the square is 49, and that must be equal to the square of the side length, $49 = s^2$. Solving for the value of s would give 7; however, don't stop there! The question asked for the perimeter, which must be the sum of all the sides of the square. If the square has four sides that are 7 each, the perimeter would be 7×4, which is 28.

Let's toughen up the image and try with a slightly less friendly quadrilateral.

---

16. **A rectangle has a perimeter of 24. If the length is twice the width, what is the length?**

A 4

B 6

C 8

D 12

What technique would be helpful for this question?

Here's How to Crack It

Try the answer choices! Start with (B). If the length is 6, and the length is twice the width, the width is 3. Since the width is 3, the perimeter would be 6 + 3 + 6 + 3; this is 18, which is too small. Both (B) and (A) are eliminated; next, try (C). If the length is 8, then the width is 4; the perimeter would be 8 + 4 + 8 + 4 = 24, so that is the correct answer. This could also be done algebraically; since the length is twice the width, $l = 2w$. Since the perimeter would be $2l + 2w$, it would be $2(2w) + 2w = 6w = 24$, so $w = 4$. Since the question asked for the length, double that number to get the answer of 8. Notice the width is an answer too, so make sure you answer exactly what the question asked!

---

17. **What is the area of the figure shown with side lengths given?**

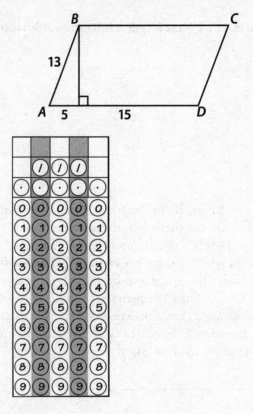

What shape is this? What is needed in order to find the area? How can you get there?

Here's How to Crack It

This figure is a parallelogram, which means its area is the product of the base and the height. Though the base is 5 + 15 = 20, the height needs to be calculated. Fortunately, *ABE* is a right triangle, so we can use the Pythagorean theorem (or remember this special triangle) to determine the length of *BE*. Since $5^2 + b^2 = 13^2$, $b = 12$. Now, multiply 12 by 20 to get the answer as 240.

○

Let's try one more.

18. A given trapezoid has a height of 8 and base lengths of 10 and 12. What is the area of the figure?

A 80

B 88

C 96

D 176

Here's How to Crack It

Remember to use the right formula! This question mentions a trapezoid, so make sure you use the formula for area of a trapezoid. A trapezoid's area is $\dfrac{\left(b_1 + b_2\right) \times h}{2}$, so in this case, it is $\dfrac{\left(10 + 12\right) \times 8}{2}$. This gives $\dfrac{22 \times 8}{2}$, which is (B). Don't forget about the $\dfrac{1}{2}$ factor; (D) is there if you forget it!

Word Problems

Not all geometry questions involving shapes will be given as the ones above. Sometimes, the questions will be long wordy word problems that involve quite a bit more reading. When dealing with such problems, make sure you read carefully and that any images you draw fit the criteria and descriptions mentioned in the passage.

Let's try one.

19. A dairy farmer is sick of unruly kids coming in and tipping over his cows, so he decides to put up a fence. The cows are all kept in a rectangular area with a length of 40 yards and a width of 50 yards. How much fencing will the farmer need in order to keep his cows safe?

A 90 yards

B 180 yards

C 200 yards

D 2,000 yards

Here's How to Crack It

Since the question asks about fencing, it is asking for perimeter. The fencing needed would be 2(40 yards) + 2(50 yards) = 80 yards + 100 yards = 180 yards. Notice (A) is half of this in case you forget there are four sides rather than two, and (D) is actually the area of the space since it is 40 × 50. Whenever a question mentions fencing though, it is asking about area around a figure, not the space it takes up.

Let's try one involving a different shape now.

---

20. **Zoey is growing lavender and chives in a garden, separated by a diagonal fence from the northwest corner to the southeast corner. The garden measures 6 meters on both its sides. What is the area covered by the lavender plants?**

A 9 m²

B 18 m²

C 24 m

D 36 m²

Here's How to Crack It

Since the question is asking about area covered and not perimeter, the correct unit will be in m², eliminating (C). The area of the entire garden would be 6 m × 6 m = 36 m²—but that doesn't answer the question, so (D) is eliminated. The question asks only about the area covered by lavender plants, which the question specifies is only one-half of the total space. Therefore, the area covered by lavender would be 36 m²/2, or 18 m², (B). Choice (A) is obtained if the length of 6 is cut in half in both directions, rather than the total space cut in half. Also, (C) is actually the perimeter of the garden rather than the area. Be careful when working with word problems and make sure you always answer exactly what the question asked!

Now let's try one more that doesn't give a true shape—that is, unless you look at the big picture.

21. Lily lives 40 meters north and 43 meters east of the bookstore. James lives 60 meters south and 32 meters west of the bookstore. How far do Lily and James live from one another?

  A 75 meters

  B 100 meters

  C 125 meters

  D 175 meters

Here's How to Crack It

Start by drawing a representation of what the question says. Lily is 40 meters north and 43 meters east from the bookstore, whereas James is 60 meters south and 32 meters west. That would give us an image something like the following:

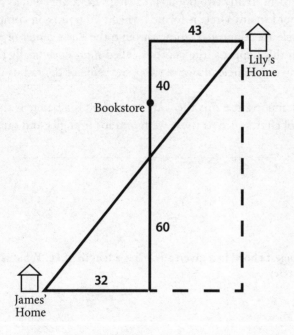

Notice what shape gets formed when drawing a diagonal connecting Lily and James' residences—it's a right triangle, so let's pull out the Pythagorean theorem. The total horizontal distance between the two is 75 meters, and the vertical distance is 100 meters. This means the distance between their homes is c in the expression $a^2 + b^2 = c^2$; plug in the numbers 75 and 100 to calculate the answer. Since $(75)^2 + (100)^2 = c^2$, $c = \sqrt{75^2 + 100^2}$, which is 125.

That should do it for now with straight-edged figures. Let's turn our attention to a more well-rounded shape—the circle.

PLANE GEOMETRY II

Circles

Let's say you and a group of friends all stand the same distance from a given point. If this happened, a certain shape would start to develop. This shape is called a **circle**, which is the term for the shape formed when connecting all points that are the exact same distance from a given point. The point from which the lines are connected is then called the **center** of the circle.

Diameter and Radius

The distance all points are from the center is called the **radius**, which connects any point on the circle to the center of the circle. Furthermore, all radii in a given circle are congruent. If any two points on a circle are connected, a **chord** is formed. The longest chord in any circle is formed when two points on completely opposite ends of the circle are connected, going through the exact center of the circle in the process. When this happens, the chord is called more specifically a **diameter**; the diameter of any given circle is always twice the value of the radius in the circle.

The two most important terms there are radius and diameter, as those are used to find qualities of circles such as those we found for triangles and quadrilaterals.

22. **The longest chord in a given circle has a length of 16. What is the radius of that circle?**

    A   2

    B   4

    C   8

    D   16

Here's How to Crack It

The longest chord in a circle is its diameter, so this question is just telling us that the diameter of the circle is 16. Since the diameter is twice the value of the radius, the radius of the circle would be half of 16, which is 8, (C). Remember the relationship carefully; if you accidentally took the square root of 16 rather than half of it, you would get (B).

The Nature and Definition of Pi

Circles are strange in that you can't find their area by multiplying their length and width. This is because they have no true straight-edged sides like the other figures we've seen so far. The closest thing they have is a diameter, but multiplying that by itself would net a square's area, not a circle's. This poses quite a conundrum, since knowing the amount of space a circle takes up is just as important as doing the same for straight-edged figures.

To solve this dilemma, a long time ago, someone decided that the way to calculate such quantities was dependent on a certain constant. This constant was the ratio of the total perimeter of a circle to its diameter. The quotient of any circle's perimeter and its diameter is about the same—3.141592653589793238462...

Actually, that's not even the end of it. No one has yet been able to calculate the ratio to an end; therefore, we typically just round the number to 3.14 or 3.142 when calculating. Also, rather than writing such a long and never-ending number, it was assigned the symbol of the Greek letter "pi," written π.

---

23. **Which of the following is the closest approximation to the value of π?**

    A 3

    B $\dfrac{25}{8}$

    C $\dfrac{13}{4}$

    D $\dfrac{22}{7}$

Here's How to Crack It

Go to the calculator; this would definitely be a calculator problem. Plug each of those values into the calculator and see which gives you the closest value to π. The closest representation of the value of π here would be (D).

Knowing the value of π is all well and good, but most of the time you will need to use that number to answer other questions besides how close a fraction is to the value of π. Let's start talking about one of those topics next.

Circumference of Circles

The perimeter of a circle gets a special name. The total length around the circle is called its **circumference**; notice the word "circle" is practically inside the term itself!

To find the circumference, the relationship that created π is used. Remember, π is the ratio of the circle's perimeter, or circumference, and its diameter. Since $\pi = C/d$, we can solve for the circumference to get $C = \pi d$.

24. The line AB crosses through the center of circle O, as shown below. Given A and B are on the circle, and $AB = 10$, what is the circumference of circle O?

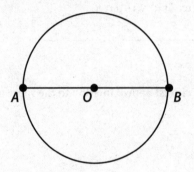

A 5

B 10

C 5π

D 10π

Here's How to Crack It

Since AB is given as a line that crosses through the center of the circle and that A and B are on the circle, AB is a diameter of the circle. Circumference then can be calculated using the formula $C = \pi d$ with $d = 10$. This gives a circumference of 10π, (D). If the radius is used accidentally, (C) is obtained; if the diameter is not multiplied by π, (B) is lying in wait.

Now, say rather than a diameter, the question gave the radius. Could the circumference be found?

The answer to that question becomes clear when the relationship between radius and diameter is considered. Since the diameter is just twice the value of the radius, the circumference could also be calculated using the radius and the formula

$C = 2\pi r$, where r is the radius. This simply takes into account that $d = 2r$ and substitutes that into the typical circumference formula.

25. **A given circle has a radius of 25. What would be the circumference of the circle?**

   A 25π

   B 50π

   C 100π

   D 125π

Here's How to Crack It

The radius is half the diameter; therefore, to calculate the circumference, that number must be doubled and multiplied by π. The circle has a radius of 25; since $C = 2\pi r$, $C = (2)(\pi)(25) = 50\pi$. Choice (D) actually is a different quality of a circle, and (A) is obtained if the number is simply multiplied by π.

What about when going the other way—how could radius be found from a given circumference? Let's give that a try.

26. **Circle A has a circumference of 16π. What would be the radius of circle A?**

   A 2

   B 4

   C 8

   D 16

Here's How to Crack It

Since the circle has a circumference of 16π and $C = 2\pi r$, $16\pi = 2\pi r$. Solving for r gives 8 as the radius. Be very careful when working this problem; the diameter would be 16, which is (D). Also, if instead of taking half of 16 the square root is taken, the answer would be 4, which is (B).

Not all questions about circumference will be quite as straightforward as those, though. Let's try one with some more steps to solving it, since algebra comes into play.

---

27. **Given the circle with center _C_ below, what would be the circumference of the circle?**

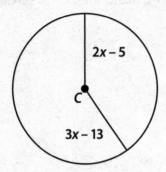

A 8π

B 11π

C 16π

D 22π

Here's How to Crack It

First, since all radii are congruent, $2x - 5 = 3x - 13$. Solving for x gives a value of 8 for x; however, that is not the radius. Find the radius by plugging in 8 to either of the expressions; $2(8) - 5 = 3(8) - 13 = 11$. This gives a radius of 11. Since the circumference is $2\pi r$, it would be $2\pi(11)$; this gives 22π, (D). Notice that missing a step could cause quite a problem; using the value of x as the radius gives a circumference of (C).

Area of Circles

The area of circles also requires knowledge of the value of π to solve. Area of a circle, or the space taken up by a circle, is equal to the product of the square of the radius and π.

> *Area* of a circle = πr^2

28. A circle has a radius of 7. What would be its area?

    A 7π

    B 14π

    C 49π

    D 289π

Here's How to Crack It

Just go ahead and use the formula. Since $A = \pi r^2$, plug in the known value of r and solve for A. This would give a value of 49π for the area, so the answer is (C). Choice (B) is the circumference—be careful to answer exactly what the question asks!

29. The area of circle A is 196π. What would be the length of AB?

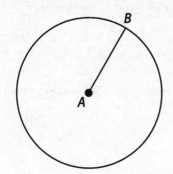

    A   14

    B   28

    C   98

    D   196

Here's How to Crack It

Use the area formula again. This time, though, the area is known; therefore, plug in the known area as A. This gives $196\pi = \pi r^2$. Since the square root of 196 is 14, that must be the radius. On the other hand, (B) was the diameter, and (C) would be the radius if the circumference was 196π (rather than the area).

Just like with circumference, we technically could write this formula using diameter as opposed to radius. However, due to the squaring factor, it's generally easier just to cut the diameter in half first and to find the radius than worry about another formula.

---

30. A given circular painting takes up a total of 144π in^2 on the wall. What would be the diameter of the painting?

    A   12 inches

    B   16 inches

    C   24 inches

    D   72 inches

Here's How to Crack It

Since the painting takes up an area of 144π inches, the area formula would assist here once more. As $A = \pi r^2$, the radius can be calculated as 12—but notice, this question did not ask about radius. Since the question asked about diameter, this number should be doubled to find the diameter, which is 24 inches.

Now let's try a question that utilizes both area and circumference.

---

31. Line *CD* in circle *B* below has a length of 10. What would be the ratio of the area to the circumference of circle *B*?

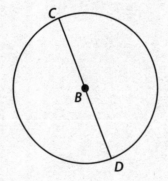

    A   1:4

    B   2:5

    C   5:2

    D   4:1

Here's How to Crack It

First, determine what *CD* is with relation to the circle. Since the line *CD* has both a start and end point on the circle and goes through the circle's center, it is the diameter of the circle; therefore, the circumference of the circle would be found using $C = \pi d$, which gives 10π. Since the diameter is 10, the radius would be 5; therefore, the area of the circle could be found from that. Since $A = \pi r^2$, the area of the circle would be $A = \pi(5)^2$, which gives 25π. The question asked for the ratio of the area to the circumference, which would be $25\pi{:}10\pi$, reducing to 5:2, (C). Notice another answer lies in wait if the order is backwards, so be careful!

Arcs and Interior Angles

A full circle is not always given. Sometimes, an **arc** is given instead; an arc is a piece of the circumference, and its length corresponds to what fraction of a circle it is. The total degrees in any circle is 360°; therefore, an angle measuring 90° would correspond to $\dfrac{90}{360} = \dfrac{1}{4}$ of a circle. Likewise, an angle measuring 60° would correspond to $\dfrac{60}{360} = \dfrac{1}{6}$ of a circle.

The central angle matters when attempting to determine area of a wedge or the length of an arc of a circle. Arc length is related to that angle proportionally; therefore, the given relationship becomes very useful.

$$\frac{central\ angle}{360°} = \frac{arc\ length}{\pi d} = \frac{area\ of\ wedge}{\pi r^2}$$

32. Points *G* and *H* lie on circle *F* shown. If *GFH* is 40° and the length of *FH* is 9, what would be the measure of arc *GH*?

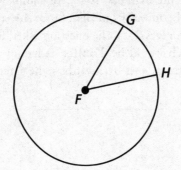

A π

B 2π

C 9π

D 18π

Here's How to Crack It

Since the points are on the circle and make a 40° angle, we can use the proportions to find the arc length. Because $\dfrac{40}{360} = \dfrac{\text{arc}}{\text{circumference}}$, the ratio of the arc to the total circumference must be $\dfrac{1}{9}$. The radius is given as 9, so the circumference can be found using $C = 2\pi r$. The circumference will be $2(\pi)(9)$, which is 18π; $\dfrac{1}{9}$ of this is 2π, so that must be the arc length, (B).

Word Problems

Before moving on to other topics, let's give a few problems a try that involve more real-world scenarios.

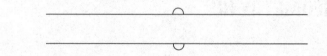

33. **Each of four tires on a car has a radius of 15 inches. How many revolutions would the tires make when travelling a total of 1,200 feet?**

    A $\dfrac{800}{\pi}$ revolutions

    B $\dfrac{480}{\pi}$ revolutions

    C $\dfrac{400}{\pi}$ revolutions

    D $\dfrac{240}{\pi}$ revolutions

Here's How to Crack It

Each revolution would be equal to the length of the circumference of a tire. Since the tire has a radius of 15 inches, it has a circumference of $2(\pi)(15) = 30\pi$ inches. Notice, however, the question mentions *feet*; therefore, we should convert this to feet. Since 12 inches = 1 foot, 30π inches will be $30\pi/12$ feet, or 2.5π feet. The revolutions could be then calculated by dividing the total distance by the amount per revolution; this would give $1,200/2.5\pi$, or $480/\pi$ revolutions, (B). If you forget to convert the units, you'd get (C)—so be careful!

34. **Two friends play a prank on a third friend and put him just inside a circular pen during the night. The third friend awakens the next day blindfolded, and he stumbles twelve feet west before hitting the boundary of the pen. He then turns due north and manages to find an exit after travelling five feet north. What is the area of the pen?**

    A $\dfrac{169\pi}{4}$

    B $\dfrac{169\pi}{2}$

    C 169π

    D 338π

Here's How to Crack It

Drawing a picture would be helpful here. The pen is circular and the friend starts by travelling 12 feet west, then 5 feet north. Therefore, the situation would look something like the following:

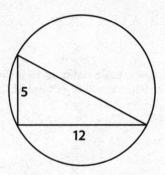

Notice that connecting the starting point with the ending point creates a right triangle; not even just any right triangle, but one of the three classic ones! The triangle would be a 5-12-13, so the diameter is 13. This means the radius would be half 13, or $\frac{13}{2}$. Area is equivalent to πr^2, or $\pi \left(\frac{13}{2}\right)^2$. This gives $\frac{169\pi}{4}$ as the answer, (A).

PLANE GEOMETRY III

Similar Figures

Ever see two shapes that look almost the same except for their size? For example, famous paintings are often recreated as photographs or portraits to hang on a wall, but are not the size of the original.

Similar figures exist when two shapes are the same, but have different sizes. The angle measures and proportions of side lengths are identical in such cases. Based on these parameters, two specific shapes are always similar: circles and squares. Any two circles and any two squares are similar to one another because they would by default have the same angle measures and overall shape, but different sizes.

On the other hand, rectangles and triangles are often, but not always, similar to one another. For example, consider the 3-4-5 and 6-8-10 right triangles. Both triangles have the same angle measures, but different side lengths that are proportional to one another, as $\frac{3}{6} = \frac{4}{8} = \frac{5}{10}$. Therefore, a 3-4-5 and 6-8-10 triangle would be similar figures.

35. **Triangles *ABC* and *XYZ* are similar. Given the lengths of sides shown, what is the length of *XY*?**

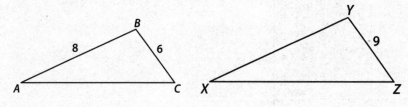

A 8

B 11

C 12

D 15

Here's How to Crack It

Since the two triangles are similar, a proportion can be used to solve this question. Sides *BC* and *YZ* correlate to one another, as do sides *AB* and *XY*. Set up the proportion as large/small = large/small; for example, $\frac{9}{6} = \frac{x}{8}$. Cross-multiplying and solving for *x* gives a result of 12, so the unknown side must be 12 units, (C).

Which angles are equal?
What sides therefore must
be proportional?

36. **What is the length of side *FH*?**

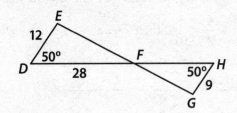

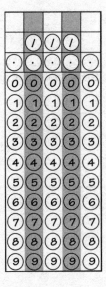

Here's How to Crack It

This time the similar triangles may not be as easy to see. Notice that angles *D* and *H* are the same; also, angles *DFE* and *GFH* are equivalent because they are vertical angles. Angles *E* and *G* must also therefore be equal, and the two triangles are similar, and a proportion can solve this question. Sides *DE* and *HG* are opposite equal angles, as are sides *DF* and *FH*. This means $\frac{12}{9} = \frac{28}{x}$. Cross-multiply and solve; the value of *x* will be 21.

Combined Figures

Other times on the TASC test, figures will be combined to form odd shapes. When the original shapes are considered instead, such figures become not as bad as they originally were.

Is there a formula for the area of this shape? What line would separate this image into more manageable shapes?

---

37. **What is the area of the figure shown?**

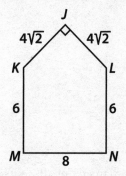

A 16

B $20 + 8\sqrt{2}$

C 48

D 64

Here's How to Crack It

Draw a line connecting points K and L. This would form a rectangle and an isosceles right triangle; to find the area of the whole figure, therefore, the two areas should be added. Since the rectangle $KMNL$ would have an area of $6 \times 8 = 48$ and the triangle would have an area of $\left(\frac{1}{2}\right)\left(4\sqrt{2}\right)\left(4\sqrt{2}\right) = 16$, the area of the whole figure would be $48 + 16 = 64$.

---

38. A circle and a square overlap to form the shape shown. If the given line, which is a diameter of the circle, has a length of 10, what would be the perimeter of the figure?

A 20 + 5π

B 20 + 10π

C 40 + 5π

D 40 + 10π

Here's How to Crack It

First, focus on the circular piece. The circle has a diameter of 10, so its circumference would be found using $C = \pi d$. Since $d = 10$, the circumference is 10π. However, only two corners—so two-fourths, or $\frac{1}{2}$—are actually used as a boundary. Therefore, the arched pieces would be 5π. Now, focus on the straight-edged pieces. The perimeter of the entire square, were it there, would be $4 \times 10 = 40$; however, again only half of that is shown (the upper left and bottom right quarters). Therefore, the straight-edged pieces would be half of the perimeter, or 20. The sum would be $20 + 5\pi$, so the answer would be (A).

Shaded Regions

On the TASC test, sometimes images will be partially shaded or unshaded. Such questions could ask to determine the fraction shaded or unshaded or the perimeter or area of a shaded region.

Let's give each type of question a try.

---

39. If the radius of the smaller circle is $\frac{2}{3}$ the radius of the larger circle, what fraction of the larger circle would be shaded?

Here's How to Crack It

Plug in numbers; for example, say the radius of the larger circle is 3 and the radius of the smaller is 2. The area of the large circle would be equal to πr^2, or 9π; the smaller circle would have an area of $\pi(2^2)$, or 4π. Therefore, $\frac{4\pi}{9\pi}$, or $\frac{4}{9}$, is shaded.

---

40. A circle is inscribed in an equilateral triangle. If the radius of the circle is 1, what is the area of the shaded region?

A $\pi - 4.5$

B $\pi - 3\sqrt{3}$

C $4.5 - \pi$

D $3\sqrt{3} - \pi$

Here's How to Crack It

First, use some POE. Since the circle has a radius of 1, the area of the circle is π; for this reason, the area inside the triangle but outside the square (as shaded) would be the area of the triangle minus the area of the circle. The answer must be some number minus π, then; eliminate (A) and (B). Now, draw in two more radii, connecting the center of the circle to the tangent points on each the left and right sides. Doing so forms a special right triangle—the 30-60-90 triangle, as shown.

All 30-60-90 triangles have a special relationship among their sides—they are in a ratio of s, $s\sqrt{3}$, and $2s$. The side opposite the 30° angle is a radius, so its length is 1; therefore, the side opposite the 60° angle is $\sqrt{3}$, and the side inside the triangle is 2. Therefore, the total height of the triangle is 3 and the total length of the sides is $2\sqrt{3}$. The area of a triangle is $\left(\dfrac{1}{2}\right)(base)(height)$, so it would be $\left(\dfrac{1}{2}\right)(2\sqrt{3})(3)$, or $3\sqrt{3}$. The area inside the triangle but outside the circle is therefore $3\sqrt{3} - \pi$, (D).

Word Problems

Let's try a few word problems involving similar figures, combined regions, and shaded regions.

---

41. A painter wants to create a smaller version of his most famous painting, as he has heard not many people will buy it at its current size. The original painting is triangular with a height of 8 feet and a base length of 10 feet; however, most people have requested a version that at most is 3 feet in height. How many *inches* should the base of his recreation be?

    A   45

    B   28.8

    C   3.75

    D   2.4

Here's How to Crack It

First, draw up the proportion that would represent this information, such as $\dfrac{3\text{ ft}}{8\text{ ft}} = \dfrac{x\text{ ft}}{10\text{ ft}}$. This would give a value for x of 3.75—but that is in *feet*, and the question asked about *inches*. Therefore, the number of feet needs to be multiplied by 12 to convert it into inches, which gives (A). Choice (C) is the number of feet, not inches, and both (B) and (D) can be obtained if the proportion is set up incorrectly, relating the base of one to the height of the other for example. Be careful to set up accurate proportions when working with similar figures.

---

42. A target for archery practice is designed as shown. If the diameter of the full target is 20 inches and the radius of each inner ring is 3 inches less than the radius of the ring outside it, what fraction of the circle would be shaded?

A $\dfrac{33}{50}$

B $\dfrac{1}{2}$

C $\dfrac{17}{50}$

D $\dfrac{15}{49}$

Here's How to Crack It

The diameter of the largest region is 20 inches; therefore, the radius of the largest region is 10 inches. The radius of the entire target therefore would be found using $A = \pi r^2$, in this case, that would give 100π. The radius of the next innermost target would be 7 inches, for an area of 49π. Working closer to the inside, the next innermost circle would have a radius of 4 inches, for an area of 16π. Finally, the bulls-eye in the center would have a radius of 1 inch, for an area of π inches. To then find the answer to the question of what fraction is shaded, the sum of the shaded pieces would be divided by the area of the target itself. The first shaded ring from the center would have an area of $16\pi - \pi$, or 15π. The outer ring would have an area of $100\pi - 49\pi$, or 51π. The total shaded area then would be $51\pi + 15\pi$, or 66π; dividing this by the 100π area of the full target would give $\dfrac{33}{50}$ as the answer, (A).

3-D GEOMETRY

Volume

Since real life is in three dimensions, it should be no surprise that 3-D figures can show up as well. Let's take a quick look at each of the types of 3-D figures you would be most likely to see.

When geometric figures enter the third dimension, the quantities of area and perimeter become much less useful. In three dimensions, the area formula expands to encompass the dimension of depth; this quality, the amount of space an object takes up, would be its **volume**. Volume is similar to the area of a 2-D figure in that it encompasses not just the outer boundary, but the entire region that is covered by it. For example, a box that has a base of 4 m^2 and a height of 3 m would take up a total of 12 m^3. Notice that in three dimensions, the volume will end up being a cubic unit of measure.

Surface Area

Much as how volume is similar to the area formula for two dimensions, **surface area** can be thought of as the similar quantity to perimeter. Whereas perimeter is the total boundary around an object, surface area is the total area of the faces that comprise an object—in other words, the area that creates the boundary for the three-dimensional figure. It is a squared unit of measure because it is the sum of areas, which are squared units of measure.

Rectangular Prisms

First and foremost, start with the most basic—a box, formally called a "rectangular prism." A rectangular prism is essentially a rectangle that has the added depth dimension, and its formulas for area and surface area show as much.

Volume of a rectangular prism = $l \times w \times h$. Surface area = $2lw + 2wh + 2lw$.

43. A rectangular prism has a length of 3, a width of 5, and a height of 9. What would be the volume of the prism?

Here's How to Crack It
Volume of a rectangular prism is determined by finding the product of the length, width, and height (depth). A length of 3, width of 5, and height of 9 have a volume therefore of $3 \times 5 \times 9$, which is 135.

Cubes

A **cube** is a special type of rectangular prism in which all sides are equal. Essentially, a cube is the square of the 3-D world. Its formulas for surface area and volume are therefore simpler; since all its sides are the same, the variable s is used to refer to any one edge.

Volume of a cube = s^3. Surface area = $6s^2$.

44. A cube has a surface area of 96. What would be its edge length?

A 4

B 5

C 6

D 7

Here's How to Crack It

Since the surface area is equal to $6s^2$, the side can be calculated by dividing 96 by 6 and then taking the square root. This gives an answer of 4, (A).

Cylinders

Cylinders are the most common type of 3-D figure that involves circles. **Cylinders** are formed when a circle has the added dimension of depth, and look something like this:

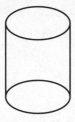

Since a cylinder is a circle with the dimension of a depth or height, the volume is simply the product of the base's area and the height mentioned. The surface area though can be tougher; therefore, think about how a cylinder is formed.

First off, a cylinder has a top and a bottom that are both circles; therefore, the sum of the areas of the circles would give the surface area of the top and bottom, which would yield $2\pi r^2$. But what about the piece connecting the two circles?

Take a sheet of paper and roll it so the edges across from one another are connected. See how the cylinder gets formed? In actuality, a cylinder can be formed by a rectangle that is just rolled. Notice also that the height of the paper is one dimension, whereas the length of the paper becomes the other; therefore, the circumference of the circle is actually the other important piece of information. The area of the rolled sheet of paper would be the product of the circumference and height, or $2\pi rh$.

The volume of a cylinder is $\pi r^2 h$. The surface area is $2\pi r^2 + 2\pi rh$.

45. **A given cylinder has a base diameter of 8 and height of 10. What would be the cylinder's surface area?**

   A 112π

   B 160π

   C 288π

   D 640π

Here's How to Crack It

First, remember that the surface area formula utilizes radius and not diameter. Therefore, take half the diameter to get the radius as 4. Now, plug in the known numbers to the formula for surface area, $2\pi r^2 + 2\pi rh$. Doing so would yield $2\pi(4)^2 + 2\pi(4)(10)$; this math gives 112π, (A). Watch your math; (B) is the volume, and (C) and (D) are obtained using the diameter in the formulas rather than the radius as needed.

Word Problems for Volume and Surface Area

Okay, so now let's try a few more word problem examples.

---

46. While wrapping Christmas gifts, Joy starts to run low on wrapping paper. All she has left is an odd t-shaped piece as shown. She plans to fold the sides up and the longer edge around so she can wrap a box-shaped object. What is the greatest volume that could be covered using the piece of paper shown?

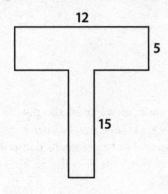

A 80 in³

B 100 in³

C 120 in³

D 140 in³

Here's How to Crack It

The side of 12 will be folded into 3, so each edge that direction will be 4 units long. The other direction will be folded to wrap around the object, so the dimensions of those boxes will be 4 × 5. The total figure will, in the end, look like this:

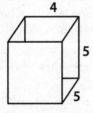

Since volume is the product of the length, width, and height, this box would have a volume of 4 × 5 × 5, which is 100, (B).

---

47. A cylindrical water pipe 10 feet long has a uniform diameter of 6 inches. How much water could be in the pipe at any one time?

A 30π

B 60π

C 90π

D 360π

Here's How to Crack It

Since the pipe is a cylinder and the amount of water in the pipe is asked, the answer will be the volume of the pipe as that is how much water it can hold. The pipe has a length of 10 inches and a diameter of 6; therefore, its radius is 3, and the volume formula can be used. Volume of a cylinder is given by $\pi r^2 h$, so the volume here would be $\pi(3)^2(10)$. That gives 90π, (C).

COORDINATE GEOMETRY

The *x* and *y* Axes

Sometimes information will be presented that refers to the coordinate plane. The coordinate plane is essentially the combination of two number lines—one horizontal and one vertical. Placing values onto a coordinate plane allows for determination of effects of one variable on another, which is why such graphical representations are used often in the sciences. Therefore, coordinate planes allow for information to be presented in two dimensions, rather than just one.

There are different areas of a coordinate plane. The horizontal axis is called the **x-axis,** and the vertical axis is called the **y-axis.** The point at which the two axes meet is called the **origin,** and is considered to be the point (0, 0)—where both *x* and *y* are 0. The grid shown is an example of such a coordinate plane, often called specifically the "Cartesian coordinate system" to differentiate this more basic plane from the other such planes.

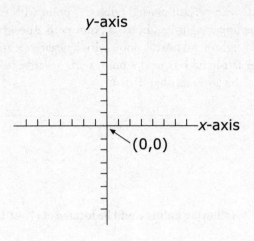

Plotting Points

A coordinate plane with nothing on it would not be very helpful. Points are plotted on a coordinate plane by first matching the x coordinate to the correct value on the horizontal (x-) axis. The second number is the y value; the point is moved that many units up or down on the vertical axis. For example, consider the point (3, 4).

Start at the origin. The x-value given is 3; therefore, this would be represented as 3 units to the right. The y-value is given as 4, so this is represented by 4 units up. This would give the point as shown below.

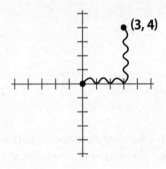

A positive x-coordinate moves right; a negative x-coordinate moves left. A positive y-coordinate moves up; a negative y-coordinate moves down.

Notice some trends with certain plotted points. A point with two positive coordinates will be in the upper right-hand box; a point with a positive *x* and negative *y* will be in the lower right-hand box. A point with a negative *x* and positive *y* will be found in the upper left-hand box, and a point with negative values for both *x* and *y* will be located in the lower left-hand area.

48.   **Which of the following points could be located at (7, −2)?**

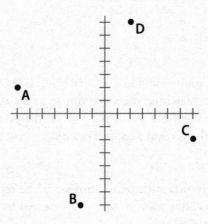

A   A
B   B
C   C
D   D

Here's How to Crack It

Since the point has a positive *x*-coordinate and negative *y*-coordinate, it should be in the lower right-hand box. The only one located near there is point C, so the answer is (C). Watch the signs and the order of the coordinates carefully; remember, all points are given as (*x*, *y*). Therefore, the *x* here was 7 and the *y* was −2.

Slope and *y*-Intercept

On a graph that forms a line, two quantities are very useful to determine: slope and *y*-intercept. The **slope** of a line is the ratio of how much the value of *y* changes as the value of *x* changes, whereas the *y*-intercept is the point at which a line crosses the a line crosses the *y*-axis and the value of *x* = 0. The *y*-intercept is often determinable just by looking at a graph, whereas the slope requires more careful calculation.

$$\text{Slope} = \frac{y_2 - y_1}{x_2 - x_1}, \text{ where } (x_1, y_1) \text{ and } (x_2, y_2) \text{ are two points on the line.}$$

49. **Which of the following pairs of points would be on a line with a slope of 3?**

   A   (0, 4) and (2, 9)

   B   (1, –6) and (–2, 3)

   C   (–5, –2) and (–4, –6)

   D   (–4, –2) and (–1, 7)

Here's How to Crack It

Calculate the slope of the line linking each pair of points using the slope formula. The only pair that will give a slope of 3 is (D), which will yield $\frac{7-(-2)}{(-1)-(-4)} = \frac{9}{3}$, or 3. Another useful tidbit of information regards slopes themselves: Positive slopes will move upward, toward the upper right-hand corner of the plane, whereas negative slopes will move downward, toward the lower right-hand corner.

50.   **What would be the *y*-intercept of the line shown?**

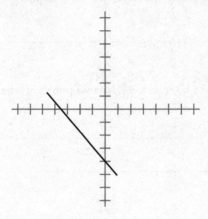

A   −4
B   −1
C   1
D   4

Here's How to Crack It

The *y*-intercept is the point at which a line crosses the *y*-axis, or where *x* = 0. Notice that the point at which the line crosses the *y*-axis here is on the bottom half of the plane; therefore, the *y*-intercept will be negative, eliminating (C) and (D). Count down; the line crosses the axis when *y* = −4, so that is the *y*-intercept, (A).

Equation of a Line

The slope and y-intercept of a line together can be used to explain a relationship between an original value, x, and output value, y. These together form the equation of a line, which is often written in what is called **slope-intercept form**. This form shows the relationship between x and y as a function of the input value x.

Slope-intercept form of a line is given by $y = mx + b$, where m is the slope, b is the y-intercept, and (x, y) is a point on the line.

For example, consider the four lines shown below. Each is plotted, so the importance of the sign for both the slope and y-intercept can be clearly seen.

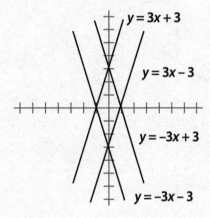

Notice that positive slopes move upward and negative downward, but if the slope itself is the same, the lines look identical. Likewise, notice positive versus negative effects for the y-intercept.

51. Which of the following lines could have the equation $y = \dfrac{2}{3}x - 4$?

A

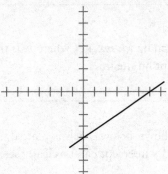

B

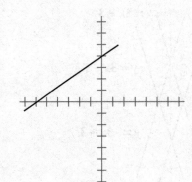

C

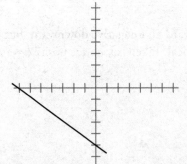

D

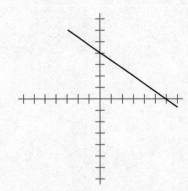

Here's How to Crack It

Since the line has a positive slope and a negative *y*-intercept, it should be a line sloping upward that crosses the *y*-axis on the bottom half of the image. The only answer that shows such a relationship is shown in (A); (B) has a positive *y*-intercept, and (C) and (D) have negative slopes.

52. **What could be the equation of a line crossing through (0, –2) and (4, 6)?**

    A $y = 2x + 2$

    B $y = 2x - 2$

    C $y = -2x - 2$

    D $y = -2x + 2$

Here's How to Crack It

If the point crosses through (0, –2), its *y*-intercept is –2. This eliminates (A) and

(D), which have positive *y*-intercepts. Now, calculate the slope using the slope for-

mula; since $\dfrac{6 - (-2)}{4 - 0} = 2$, the slope is 2. Therefore, this line would be $y = 2x - 2$, (B).

Systems of Equations on a Graph

Another use of the coordinate plane will appear when a system of equations is given. When provided with a system of equations, there are two ways to solve for the answer: to use algebra or to use a graph. Using a graph can often at least help you to ballpark some answers out of contention for being in the wrong area of the graph, or could even give the answer if the graph is done well enough.

53. At which point do the equations $y = 4x - 9$ and $y = -\dfrac{1}{3}x + 4$ intersect?

A (−3, 5)

B (1, −5)

C (3, 3)

D (6, 2)

Here's How to Crack It

Plot the lines. Doing so would give a graph something like what is shown here. Notice the point of intersection is in the upper right area of the plane; this eliminates (A) and (B). Looking carefully at the graph, the two lines seem to cross closer to (3, 3) than to (6, 2), therefore, the answer is (C). Testing it could help too; plug in (*x, y*) = (3, 3) and both statements will be true, again proving (C) as the correct answer.

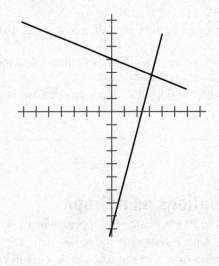

Word Problems

54. A certain state has a population density of 150 people per square mile. If there are 100 more people than the average population density living in the state capital, which is one square mile in size, which of the below equations would represent the total population y of the state with x square miles?

A $y = 150x + 100$

B $y = 150x - 100$

C $y = -150x + 100$

D $y = -150x - 100$

Here's How to Crack It

Since the population density is 150 people per square mile, the slope of people/miles is 150. This eliminates (C) and (D), which would represent negative people. Since one city in the state has 100 extra people, that needs to be added as the starting number of people, and is essentially the y-intercept; this leaves only (A) as a possibility. Choice (B), on the other hand, removes 100 people from the group, which would go against the information provided.

55. A company that makes various souvenirs averages a cost of production per item of $1.25. The company also tracks its revenue, and knows that its total revenue after selling x items is given by $y = 2.5x - 80$. How many items must the company sell in order for its revenue to exceed its cost of production?

A 16

B 32

C 48

D 64

Here's How to Crack It

It may not say outright, but this question involves a system of equations. There are two equations given here: cost and revenue. The cost per item is simply given by the line $y = 1.25x$, since each item costs 1.25 to make. The revenue was given as $2.5x - 80$. Plot both of those, and you will get a graph something like the following, in which each unit on the graph is equivalent to 10 items made/sold. Notice that only the right-hand area is important here, since there can't be negative items made/sold. The two lines cross one another somewhere around 65 items, so only (D) makes sense; all the other answers here are too small.

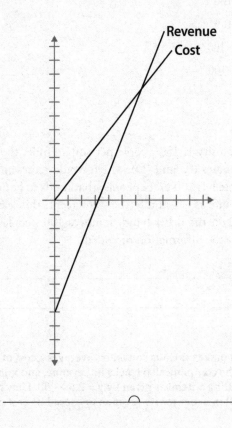

Geometry Drill

Your turn! Give the following questions a try. Remember, don't use a calculator when attempting the questions with the "no-calculator" icon. To check your answers, register your book at **PrincetonReview.com/cracking** and download the Chapter Drill Answers and Explanations supplement.

1. A quadrilateral has two sets of parallel sides. Though not all four sides are equivalent, there are two equal pairs—the top and bottom have sides of length 3, and the sides have a length of 4. If the diagonal of the figure is 5 units, what would be the most accurate description of the type of quadrilateral this is?

    A Rectangle

    B Rhombus

    C Square

    D Trapezoid

2. A circle has an area of 121π. What would be the circumference of the circle?

    A 11

    B 22

    C 11π

    D 22π

3. Harry lives seven blocks north and twenty-four blocks east of Guinevere. However, a shortcut is available to take him directly from his home to Guinevere's home. What is the distance, in blocks, of the shortcut?

    A $\sqrt{527}$

    B 25

    C 30

    D 31

4. Triangles *ABC* and *DEF* are similar. What is the length of *EF*?

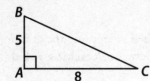

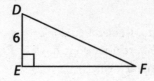

5. A town's population can be given by the equation $y = 2{,}500x - 3{,}000$, where x is the number of square miles the town covers. If the town covers a total of 168 square miles, what is its population, in thousands?

   A   417

   B   423

   C   429

   D   436

6. Ice has a density of 0.917 g/cm³. If a cube of ice measures 1.25 cm on each of its sides, approximately what would be the mass of the ice? (Density = mass/volume)

   A   1.43 g

   B   1.70 g

   C   1.79 g

   D   2.12 g

7. A cylindrical barrel has a 20-inch diameter and 40-inch height. What would the volume of the soda contained in the cylindrical barrel be?

   A $4{,}000\pi$ in³

   B   16,000 in³

   C   32,000 in³

   D $16{,}000\pi$ in³

8. A rectangular aquarium tank measures 4 feet in length by 1.25 feet in width and has a height of h inches. If the aquarium holds 30 ft³ when it is $\dfrac{3}{4}$ full, what would be the value of h?

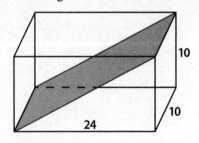

9. A ballet dancer is attempting to execute a perfect pirouette (a full turn on one foot). She knows that when she performs this move, her knee comes out 18 inches from the center of her body. What would be the area, in feet, of the space she would require, given that she needs at least a 2 foot buffer on all sides of her body while performing the move?

A $\dfrac{9\pi}{4} + 4$

B $\dfrac{49\pi}{4}$

C 324π

D 400π

10. An inclined plane is being placed in a rectangular box, as shown. The inclined plane will run from the top side of one edge of the box to the bottom corner across from it. If the box measures 24 feet in width by 10 feet in length and has a height of 10 feet, what would be the area of the inclined plane in the box?

10

10

24

A 168 ft²

B 175 ft²

C 240 ft²

D 260 ft²

11. A circle is inscribed in a square. If the diagonal of the square has a length of $12\sqrt{2}$, what is the area of the circle?

A   36

B   36π

C   144

D   144π

12. What could be the equation of the line shown?

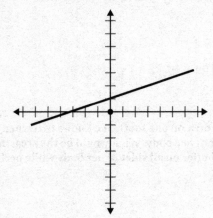

A $y = \dfrac{1}{4}x - 1$

B $y = \dfrac{1}{4}x + 1$

C $y = 4x - 1$

D $y = 4x + 1$

Chapter 18
Trigonometry

In this chapter, we'll guide you through the key topics related to trigonometry on the TASC Mathematics test. We will discuss trig identities and terms, the unit circle, quadrants, and the connection to the Pythagorean theorem. Following the content lessons, we'll give you some practice questions.

TRIGONOMETRY AND THE TASC TEST

Trigonometry is a topic that scares a lot of people. However, there are two bits of good news. First, trigonometry is not heavily emphasized on the TASC test, so if you have only limited time for preparation, do not prioritize this chapter. Second, what is tested from trigonometry doesn't go beyond the trigonometric identities provided on your mathematical reference sheet. Even though these identities may look very confusing at first, they're not that complicated if you understand what all the terms mean.

Trig Identities and Terms

Trigonometry is based on right triangles, so let's look at one.

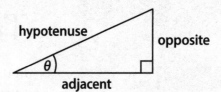

Notice that one of the angles is marked with the symbol θ. θ is a Greek letter pronounced "theta." It's a variable that is commonly used for angles. It's really no different from any other variable (such as x or y) other than the fact that, by convention, θ is commonly used for angle measures.

In the diagram above, the three sides of the triangle are labeled based on their relationships with the angle marked with θ. The side labeled **opposite** is the side that is not used form the angle marked θ. It is called the "opposite" because you can draw a straight line from the angle marked with θ that will intersect that side. The side labeled **hypotenuse** is the side that is opposite the right angle. The side labeled **adjacent** is the side that is used to form the angle marked with θ but that is not the hypotenuse. It's called "adjacent" because it is next to the angle. These labels are important because they are used to define the three main trigonometric functions: sine, cosine, and tangent. These are defined by these three trigonometric identities:

$$\sin\theta = \frac{opp}{hyp}$$

$$\cos\theta = \frac{adj}{hyp}$$

$$\tan\theta = \frac{opp}{adj}$$

The **sine** of the angle, abbreviated "sin," is equal to the length of the opposite side divided by the length of the hypotenuse. The **cosine** of the angle, abbreviated "cos," is equal to the length of the adjacent side divided by the length of the hypotenuse. The **tangent** of the angle, abbreviated "tan," is equal to the length of the opposite side divided by the length of the adjacent side. The important thing to understand is that for a given angle in a right triangle, the ratios between the sides will always be the same no matter how large or small the triangle is. Therefore, the sine, cosine, or tangent of any given angle is a **constant**. Let's look at an example.

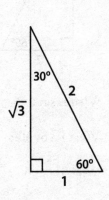

What is sin 30°? _____   What is sin 60°? _____

What is cos 30°? _____   What is cos 60°? _____

What is tan 30°? _____   What is tan 60°? _____

Here's How to Crack It

First, let's look at the 30° angle. The opposite side is 1, the adjacent side is $\sqrt{3}$, and the hypotenuse is 2. Therefore, $\sin 30 = \dfrac{opp}{hyp} = \dfrac{1}{2}$, $\cos 30 = \dfrac{adj}{hyp} = \dfrac{\sqrt{3}}{2}$, and $\tan 30 = \dfrac{opp}{adj} = \dfrac{1}{\sqrt{3}}$. Now, let's look at the 60° angle. This time, the opposite side is $\sqrt{3}$, the adjacent side is 1, and the hypotenuse is 2. Therefore, $\sin 60 = \dfrac{opp}{hyp} = \dfrac{\sqrt{3}}{2}$, $\cos 60 = \dfrac{adj}{hyp} = \dfrac{1}{2}$, and $\tan 60 = \dfrac{opp}{adj} = \dfrac{\sqrt{3}}{1} = \sqrt{3}$.

Now let's look at a larger version of this same triangle.

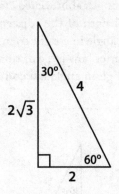

What is sin 30°? _____   What is sin 60°? _____

What is cos 30°? _____   What is cos 60°? _____

What is tan 30°? _____   What is tan 60°? _____

Here's How to Crack It

Even though it's a larger triangle, the angles are the same. Remember from the previous chapter that when the angles of two figures are the same, they are similar, so the sides are still in the same ratio. Therefore,

$$\sin 30 = \frac{opp}{hyp} = \frac{2}{4} = \frac{1}{2}, \ \cos 30 = \frac{adj}{hyp} = \frac{2\sqrt{3}}{4} = \frac{\sqrt{3}}{2}, \tan 30 = \frac{opp}{adj} = \frac{2}{2\sqrt{3}} = \frac{1}{\sqrt{3}},$$

$$\sin 60 = \frac{opp}{hyp} = \frac{2\sqrt{3}}{4} = \frac{\sqrt{3}}{2}, \cos 60 = \frac{adj}{hyp} = \frac{2}{4} = \frac{1}{2}, \text{ and}$$

$$\tan 30 = \frac{opp}{adj} = \frac{2\sqrt{3}}{2} = \sqrt{3}.$$

Thus, the sine, cosine, and tangent of any angle are the same, no matter what triangle they are in.

Another trigonometric identity provided is the identity $sin^2\theta + cos^2\theta = 1$. What do those weird symbols sin^2 and cos^2 mean? These just mean "the square of sine" and "the square of cosine," respectively, so $sin^2\theta$ is just shorthand notation for $(sin\ \theta)^2$, and $cos^2\theta$ is just shorthand notation for $(cos\ \theta)^2$. The important thing to note is that the inequality, $sin^2\theta + cos^2\theta = 1$, is true for *any* value of θ. Let's try this using our two examples from above.

$$\sin^2(30°) + \cos^2(30°) = \left(\frac{1}{2}\right)^2 + \left(\frac{\sqrt{3}}{2}\right)^2 = \frac{1}{4} + \frac{3}{4} = \frac{4}{4} = 1$$

Similarly,

$$\sin^2(60°) + \cos^2(60°) = \left(\frac{\sqrt{3}}{2}\right)^2 + \left(\frac{1}{2}\right)^2 = \frac{3}{4} + \frac{1}{4} = \frac{4}{4} = 1$$

Let's look at another example.

───────────○───────────

1. If $\sin^2\theta + \cos^2\theta + \tan^2\theta = 1.25$, what is the value of $\tan\theta$?

   A 1.00

   B 0.75

   C 0.50

   D 0.25

Here's How to Crack It

The question tells you that $\sin^2\theta + \cos^2\theta + \tan^2\theta = 1.25$. Because of the identity, you also know that $\sin^2\theta + \cos^2\theta = 1$. Substitute this into the equation from the question to get $1 + \tan^2\theta = 1.25$. Subtract 1 from both sides to get $\tan^2\theta = 0.25$. The question asks for $\tan\theta$ not $\tan^2\theta$, so take to square root of both sides to get $\tan\theta = 0.5$, so (C) is correct.

───────────○───────────

The Unit Circle

Remember the coordinate plane from Chapter 17? The coordinate plane can be used to help clarify certain aspects of trigonometry. Start with a circle with center at the origin as below.

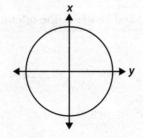

Since trigonometry is all about right triangles, draw a right triangle, using the *x*-axis as the base. Label the angle with vertex at the origin as θ, and label the vertex of the triangle that intersects the circle as (*x, y*).

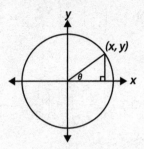

What do you know about this triangle? Start with the side opposite the angle marked θ. This side goes from the point (*x, y*) to the *x*-axis and is perpendicular to the *x*-axis, so its length is equal to the change in *y*-coordinate, which is *y*. Now, look at the side adjacent to the angle marked θ. This side is on the *x*-axis, so its length is equal to the change in *x*-coordinate, which is *x*. Finally, look at the hypotenuse. The hypotenuse is a radius of the unit circle. With that in mind, what are the sine, cosine, and tangent of θ? Using the identities to define these values,

$$\sin \theta = \frac{opp}{hyp} = \frac{y}{r}, \cos \theta = \frac{adj}{hyp} = \frac{x}{r}, \text{ and } \tan \theta = \frac{opp}{adj} = \frac{y}{x}.$$

Let's look at an example.

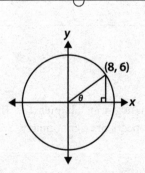

The circle above has radius 10 and center at the origin. The right triangle is at the point (8, 6).

sin θ = _____   cos θ = _____   tan θ = _____

Here's How to Crack It

Since $\sin \theta = \dfrac{y}{r}$, $\sin \theta = \dfrac{6}{10} = 0.6$. Since $\cos \theta = \dfrac{x}{r}$, $\cos \theta = \dfrac{8}{10} = 0.8$. Finally, since $\tan \theta = \dfrac{y}{x}$, $\tan \theta = \dfrac{6}{8} = 0.75$.

As convenient as this circle is, another circle is even more convenient: one in which the radius is 1. This circle is called the **unit circle**. If the radius is 1, the hypotenuse is 1, and the denominators of these fractions go away. When you use the unit circle, the same identities apply: $\sin \theta = \dfrac{opp}{hyp} = \dfrac{y}{r}$, $\cos \theta = \dfrac{adj}{hyp} = \dfrac{x}{r}$, and $\tan \theta = \dfrac{opp}{adj} = \dfrac{y}{x}$. However, since $r = 1$ in the unit circle, the identities for sine and cosine simplify to $\sin \theta = y$ and $\cos \theta = x$. Therefore, for any point on the unit circle, the coordinates are equivalent to $(\cos \theta, \sin \theta)$, where θ is the measure of the angle formed by positive x-axis and the radius at that point.

Let's look at an example using the unit circle.

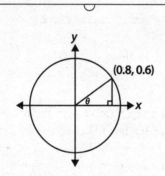

The circle above has center at the origin and radius 1.

$\sin \theta = $ _____ $\qquad\qquad\qquad$ $\cos \theta = $ _____

Here's How to Crack It

Since the radius is 1, this circle is the unit circle. Therefore, $\sin \theta = y = 0.6$ and $\cos \theta = x = 0.8$.

Note the answer to the above example is the same as the one on the previous example. This is because the above triangle is a similar triangle to the one in the previous example scaled down by a factor of ten. Remember that corresponding angles in similar triangles are equal. As discussed in the previous section, any angle of a given measure will have a same sine and cosine regardless of the size of the triangle. This is why the unit circle is so much more convenient. It yields the same results, and you won't have to worry about fractions.

The unit circle can even be applied beyond the acute angles normally used in trigonometry. For acute angles, the sine and cosine will always be between 0 and 1. However, when all angles are considered, these values can be from –1 to 1, inclusive. Start with the points at which the unit circle intersects with the *x*- and *y*-axes. For the point on the positive *x*-axis, the angle is 0° and the coordinates are (1, 0). Therefore, cos 0° = 1 and sin 0° = θ. For the point on the positive *y*-axis, the angle is 90° and the coordinates are (0, 1). Therefore, cos 90° = 0 and sin 90° = 1. For the point on the negative *x*-axis, the angle is 180° and the coordinates are (–1, 0). Therefore, cos 180° = –1 and sin 180° = θ. For the point on the negative *y*-axis, the angle is 270° and the coordinates are (0, –1). Therefore, cos 270° = 0 and sin 270° = –1.

The unit circle can be helpful for other angles, as well. To see how, think in terms of how the *x*- and *y*-axes divide the coordinate plane into sections called **quadrants**.

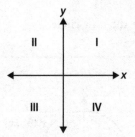

Quadrant I is the one on the top right. To get the other quadrants, continue in a counterclockwise direction. Quadrant II is on the top left, Quadrant III is on the bottom left, and Quadrant IV is on the bottom right. Why do the quadrants matter? The quadrant can be used to determine the sign of the *x*- and *y*-coordinates. In Quadrant I, the *x*- and *y*-coordinates are both positive. In Quadrant II, the *x*-coordinate is negative, but the *y*-coordinate is positive. In Quadrant III, the *x*- and *y*-coordinates are both negative. In Quadrant IV, the *x*-coordinate is positive, but the *y*-coordinate is negative.

Bringing this back to the unit circle, since the *x*- and *y*-coordinates are equivalent to the cosine and sine of the angle, respectively, the quadrants can be used to determine the sign of these values. If the angle is between 0 and 90 degrees, then the coordinate is in Quadrant I, so both the sine and the cosine of the angle are positive. If the angle is between 90° and 180°, then the coordinate is in Quadrant II, so sine of the angle is positive, but the cosine is negative. If the angle is between 180° and 270°, then the coordinate is in Quadrant III, so both the sine and the cosine of the angle is negative. If the angle is between 270° and 360°, then the coordinate is in Quadrant IV, so cosine of the angle is positive, but the sine is negative.

Let's look at an example.

Circle the negative values below.

sin 230°	cos 230°
sin 110°	cos 110°
sin 340°	cos 340°

Here's How to Crack It

Start with the 230° angle. This angle is between 180° and 270°, so it is in Quadrant III. Therefore, sin θ and cos θ are both negative, so circle both. Now, look at the 110° angle. It is between 90° and 180°, so it is in Quadrant II. Therefore, sin θ is positive and cos θ is negative. Circle cos 110° but not sin 110°. Finally look at the 340° angle. Since 340° is between 270° and 360°, it is in Quadrant IV, so sin θ is negative and cos θ is positive. Circle sin 340° but not cos 340°.

Connection to Pythagorean Theorem

Remember this from Chapter 17?

Pythagorean theorem

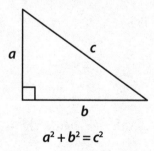

$$a^2 + b^2 = c^2$$

This is closely related to trigonometry, since both involve the study of right triangles.

For example, recall this diagram from earlier in the chapter.

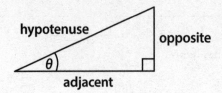

The opposite and adjacent sides represent the two legs of the right triangle (i.e., *a* and *b*), while the hypotenuse represents *c*. Since $a^2 + b^2 = c^2$, $O^2 + A^2 = H^2$. Look at the example below.

2.   **Consider this diagram.**

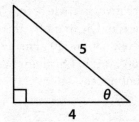

In the diagram above, what is the value of *sin θ*?

A $\dfrac{1}{5}$

B $\dfrac{3}{5}$

C $\dfrac{4}{5}$

D $\dfrac{5}{4}$

Here's How to Crack It

Remember that $\sin\theta = \dfrac{O}{H}$. Although figure shows the hypotenuse is 5, the opposite side is not given. However, the adjacent side is. Use the modified version of the Pythagorean theorem: $O^2 + A^2 = H^2$. Plug in $A = 4$ and $H = 5$ to get $O^2 + 4^2 = 5^2$. Square 4 and 5 to get $O^2 + 16 = 25$. Subtract 16 from both sides to get $O^2 = 9$. Take the square root of both sides to get $O = 3$. Therefore, $\sin\theta = \dfrac{O}{H} = \dfrac{3}{5}$, which is (B).

Remember the identity *sin²θ + cos²θ* = 1. This is really the Pythagorean theorem in disguise. Since $\sin\theta = \dfrac{O}{H}$ and $\cos\theta = \dfrac{A}{H}$, $\sin^2\theta = \dfrac{O^2}{H^2}$ and $\cos^2\theta = \dfrac{A^2}{H^2}$.

Therefore, $\sin^2\theta + \cos^2\theta = \dfrac{O^2}{H^2} + \dfrac{A^2}{H^2} = \dfrac{O^2 + A^2}{H^2}$. Since $O^2 + A^2 = H^2$,

$\dfrac{O^2 + A^2}{H^2} = \dfrac{H^2}{H^2} = 1$. Look at the example from before.

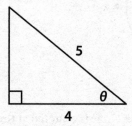

We know from the previous example that $\sin\theta = \dfrac{3}{5}$. We also know that $\cos\theta = \dfrac{A}{H} = \dfrac{4}{5}$. Therefore, $\sin^2\theta + \cos^2\theta = \dfrac{3^2}{5^2} + \dfrac{4^2}{5^2} = \dfrac{9}{25} + \dfrac{16}{25} = \dfrac{25}{25} = 1$.

We can also apply the Pythagorean theorem to the unit circle. Let's look at an example.

3. **Look at the figure below.**

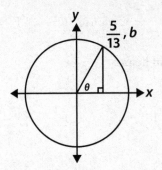

In the figure above, the circle is centered at the origin and has a radius of 1. What is the value of *sin θ*?

A $\dfrac{5}{13}$

B $\dfrac{7}{13}$

C $\dfrac{12}{13}$

D $\dfrac{12}{5}$

Here's How to Crack It

The *x*-coordinate of the point above is $\dfrac{5}{13}$. Since this circle is the unit circle, this means that $\cos \theta = \dfrac{5}{13}$. However, the question asks for sin θ, which is *b*. To get *b*, use the fact that $\left(\dfrac{5}{13}\right)^2 + b^2 = 1$. Square $\dfrac{5}{13}$ to get $\dfrac{25}{169} + b^2 = 1$. Subtract $\dfrac{25}{169}$ from both sides to get $b^2 = \dfrac{144}{169}$. Take the square root of both sides to get $b = \dfrac{12}{13}$.

Trigonometry Drill

Try the following questions. To check your answers, register your book at **PrincetonReview.com/cracking** and download the Chapter Drill Answers and Explanations supplement.

1. **Consider this figure.**

    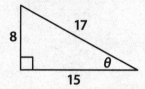

    In the figure above, what is *tan θ*?

    A $\dfrac{8}{17}$

    B $\dfrac{8}{15}$

    C $\dfrac{15}{17}$

    D $\dfrac{15}{8}$

2. **Consider this figure.**

    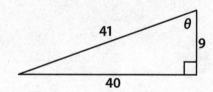

    In the figure above, what is the value of *cos θ*?

    A $\dfrac{9}{41}$

    B $\dfrac{9}{40}$

    C $\dfrac{40}{41}$

    D $\dfrac{40}{9}$

3. Consider this figure.

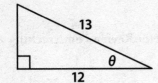

In the figure above, what is the value of *sin θ*?

A $\dfrac{12}{13}$

B $\dfrac{5}{13}$

C $\dfrac{1}{12}$

D $\dfrac{1}{13}$

4. Consider this figure.

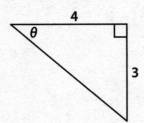

In the figure above, what is the value of *cos θ*?

A $\dfrac{3}{7}$

B $\dfrac{4}{7}$

C $\dfrac{3}{5}$

D $\dfrac{4}{5}$

5. If a right triangle has sides 9, 12, and 15, what is the sine of the smallest angle?

A $\dfrac{3}{5}$

B $\dfrac{3}{4}$

C $\dfrac{4}{5}$

D $\dfrac{4}{3}$

6. Consider this figure.

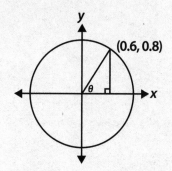

In the figure above, the circle with center at the origin has a radius of 1. What is the value of *sin θ*?

A 0.60

B 0.75

C 0.80

D 1.33

7. Consider this figure.

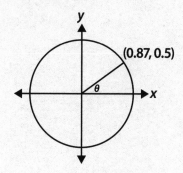

In the unit circle above, what is the value of *cos θ*?

A 0.50

B 0.57

C 0.87

D 1.73

8. Consider this figure.

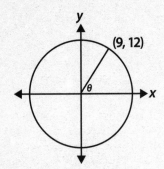

In the figure above, what is the value of *tan θ*?

A $\dfrac{3}{5}$

B $\dfrac{3}{4}$

C $\dfrac{4}{5}$

D $\dfrac{4}{3}$

9. Consider this figure.

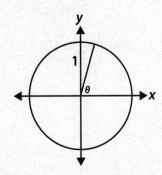

In the figure above *cos θ* = 0.36. If the radius of the circle were to double, what would be the *cos θ*?

A 1.00

B 0.72

C 0.36

D 0.18

10. If a point on the unit circle has an *x*-coordinate of $\frac{8}{17}$, what is the value of the *y*-coordinate?

A $\frac{5}{17}$

B $\frac{8}{17}$

C $\frac{9}{17}$

D $\frac{15}{17}$

11. If $\theta = 240°$, which of following is true?

A $sin\ \theta$ and $cos\ \theta$ are both negative.

B $sin\ \theta$ is negative but $cos\ \theta$ is positive.

C $sin\ \theta$ is positive but $cos\ \theta$ is negative.

D $sin\ \theta$ and $cos\ \theta$ are both positive.

12. If $sin\ \theta$ is positive, which of the following must be true?

A $\theta < 180°$

B $\theta > 180°$

C $cos\ \theta$ is positive

D $cos\ \theta$ is negative

Part V
Social Studies

Chapter 19
Social Studies
Overview

In this chapter, we will provide an overview of the Social Studies portion of the TASC test. In the following chapters, we will explore the specific content areas of this sub-test in more detail.

ABOUT THE SOCIAL STUDIES TEST

According to the test makers, the Social Studies portion of the TASC test is intended to evaluate test takers' understanding of the basic principles of geography, history, economics, civics, and government. In order to do well on the TASC Social Studies test, you will need to familiarize yourself with the structure and content of the exam and do a lot of practice questions. Unfortunately, the TASC Social Studies test is not simply a reading test that happens to be about Social Studies topics, and as such, you will have to do more than just interpret the information on the page in front of you. The Social Studies test requires you to have a thorough knowledge of high school-level Social Studies topics. By the time you're done reading the Social Studies chapters of this book, you should be feeling confident about the material and ready to try some practice tests. The end of each chapter within the Social Studies portion of the book has drills specific to the topic covered in that particular chapter.

To score well on the test, you first need to know what to expect on test day. First, there are two versions of the TASC Social Studies test: a computer-based version and a paper-based version. On the English and Spanish versions of the TASC Social Studies test you'll have 75 and 80 minutes, respectively, to complete the following:

Check out our supplementary tutorials on the constructed-response and tech-enhanced items when you register your book at **PrincetonReview.com/ cracking!**

Computer-Based	Paper-Based
48 Multiple-Choice Questions	49 Multiple-Choice Questions
1 Constructed-Response Item	1 Constructed-Response Item
1 Technology-Enhanced Item	

The questions on this test will be accompanied by eight types of stimuli in the form of charts, graphs, maps, tables, figures, or written passages. In order to achieve success on this section of the TASC test, you need to have basic knowledge of the topics tested on the TASC Social Studies test as well as reading comprehension skills.

According to the TASC test creators, questions will test your understanding of what you read (comprehension), your use of information in a concrete situation (application), your exploration of relationships among ideas (analysis), and your judgment of the soundness or accuracy of historical information or methods (evaluation).

WHAT IS SOCIAL STUDIES?

Broadly speaking, Social Studies is an integrated field of study that combines elements of the social sciences and the humanities. Social Studies can help one not only to understand history and the functioning of societies, but also to make good and well-informed decisions as citizens in a complex and interdependent world.

Most of the content that shows up on the TASC test is based upon written documents. When considering written documents, whether they relate to history, the functioning of government, or economic topics, it is important to consider a few basic questions:

- What was the context (historical, political, or cultural environment) in which the document was authored? What else was going on around the author at the time this was written?
- How does this author's perspective affect what he or she wrote and why? What is the author's position in society (gender, age, educational level, political or religious belief system)? How do these attributes inform what the author writes?
- When was the document written? Who was the intended audience, and what was the author trying to express?

CONTENT OF THE SOCIAL STUDIES TEST

Here are the topics as outlined by the TASC test makers:

U.S. History	25%
World History	15%
Civics and Government	25%
Geography	15%
Economics	20%

Some questions on the Social Studies test will require you to have general knowledge of the topics being tested. Depending on the question, you will need to have a basic knowledge of some of the key terms and concepts within the Social Studies realm. In some particularly annoying questions, you will need to know names and dates (or at least time periods). Other questions require less background knowledge, and you may be able to figure out the correct answer by interpreting a graph or photo.

The topics listed above are not very specific, but don't worry. Even though it may seem intimidating to acquaint yourself with all of the topics covered in a high school history or government class, the content review chapters that follow will give you all of the background knowledge that you will need to ace this test.

Chapter 20
Geography

In this chapter, we'll guide you through the key topics related to Geography on the Social Studies portion of the TASC test. We will focus on three broad categories: Environments, Human Impact, and Maps. Following the content lessons, we'll give you some practice questions.

GEOGRAPHY

Geography is the study of the physical features of the earth and the ways in which these features affect the people who live on the earth. When most people think about geography, they think only of surface terrain, but the study of geography also includes the natural resources underneath the surface of the earth and the climates of, and atmosphere above, the various regions of the world.

ENVIRONMENTS

In Social Studies, both physical and human dimensions characterize environments. The TASC test will require you to understand the basics of what makes different regions distinct and how the activities of humans both affect and are affected by environments.

The Physical Environment

Physical Environment is a broad category that encompasses living and non-living things in some particular region of the world. Physical environment includes the features of a region's landscape (mountains, rivers, forests, and other similar features), climate, natural resources, species diversity, soil, and many other elements. Naturally, all of these features have an impact upon the people who live in a particular region.

In order to understand the importance of physical environment, consider the earliest human populations: Our nomadic ancestors hadn't yet built cities, and they didn't yet know how to farm. Their sole focus in life was to satisfy their most basic needs: shelter and food. Because they didn't have any advanced tools and hadn't yet developed anything as sophisticated as farming, the best way for them to get shelter was to find it, and the best way to get food was to follow it. These populations were known as **foraging societies**.

This was the **Paleolithic Period**, and it was marked mostly by the use of stone tools. You won't be asked a lot of questions about nomadic societies or early human **civilizations** on the TASC test. However, you do need to understand why the development of more stable civilizations (which you will be asked a lot of questions about) was so significant, so it helps to think about how the earliest humans interacted with their environments.

Pastoral societies were characterized by the domestication of animals. These societies were often found in mountainous regions and in areas with insufficient rainfall to support other forms of settlement. Many of these societies used small-scale agriculture to supplement the main food supply of animal products (usually milk or eggs, which were much easier to produce and store than meat). Stratification and social status, which were limited in foraging societies, were based on the size of one's herd in pastoral societies. But as in foraging societies, people in

When historians talk about a "civilization," they are typically referring to a complex society that is characterized by urban development, social systems and institutions, and symbolic communication (oral or written).

pastoral societies had few personal possessions. Even though they had domesticated animals (as opposed to having to hunt for animals), they didn't settle down in towns because they had to continually search for new grazing areas and water for the herds.

As pastoral societies increasingly domesticated more and more animals, they also began to experiment with securing a more dependable food supply through the cultivation of plants. This was a revolutionary development that led to **agricultural societies**.

When people figured out how to cultivate plants, they could stay in the same place, as long as there was good soil and a stable source of water. Because they also knew how to domesticate animals and use simple tools, they could rely on a relatively varied and constant supply of food, and this encouraged them to stay in the same place for longer periods of time. Staying in the same place changed things dramatically, because people in a community stayed within close proximity of each other, which added to their sense of unity and helped them build and sustain cultural traditions. What's more, unlike nomadic societies, agricultural communities were not just collections of people, but people tied to a particular piece of land. In other words, they began to think of property in terms of ownership.

The Human Environment

Imagine two people who grow only enough food for themselves. They both have to farm all day every day. There's little time left to do anything else. Now imagine that one person farms enough food for two people. The second person can do something else, say, make tools, dig an irrigation ditch, or study to become a philosopher or religious leader. Now imagine that one person can farm enough food for five people, or ten people, or a hundred people. Now the other ninety-nine people can build towns, organize armies, develop a system of writing, create art, experiment, and discover new technologies. In other words, individual labor becomes specialized. Each person can get really good at doing a particular task because he or she no longer has to worry about where the next meal is coming from.

As agricultural societies became more complex, organized economies, governmental structures, and religious organizations began to emerge to keep things as predictable and orderly as possible. Suddenly, there was society, or the beginnings of what we'd call a civilization. With the invention of irrigation techniques, lands that previously couldn't be farmed could be used for additional surpluses. This would lead to more growth and complexity, which would lead to more agricultural advancements, which would lead to more growth and complexity, and so on.

Geography and Culture

Most of the world's early great civilizations were located in river valleys. Think about it. Rivers provided a regular supply of water, which is, of course, necessary for survival. Also important is that the lowlands around rivers tend to be covered with soil that is loaded with nutrients, which are deposited when the river recedes after floods to nourish the soil. The river itself may be home to animals and plants could also provide food for people. Rivers were also a vital means of transportation.

When we talk about civilizations, we're talking about large areas of land with large populations and distinct, organized cultures, as opposed to the smaller farming communities that characterized earlier time periods. Pay attention to the social, political, and economic developments of the civilizations in this section: These developments are what made them civilizations in the first place. A piece of advice: Do not assume that a central authority headed all civilizations. Many early civilizations, in fact, were composed of loosely connected city-states, which were made up of an urban center and the agricultural land around it under its control. These city-states were sometimes combined into one because they shared common cultural characteristics, but they were also independent of each other in many ways and often competed with each other. This is true in modern times as well, of course. When we speak of Western civilization, for example, we mean a whole host of countries that have similar characteristics and cultures but that are distinct from one another and, often, compete with one another.

HUMAN IMPACT

Now that we've covered some of the basics about environments, let's look at the human impact on these environments (and vice versa) in more depth.

Migrations

Throughout history, humankind has moved from one area to another in search of trade, food, adventure, and freedom. This dispersal of a population into new areas around the world is known as a **diaspora**. The early settlers came to America to escape persecution in Europe. These were the first of a long line of immigrants who found a new beginning in our country. The United States is sometimes called a "melting pot" because of the rich brew of different cultures that has helped form the American culture. In melting pots such as the United States, cultural diversity can lead to the spread of practices beyond the original culture. This phenomenon is called **cultural diffusion**. For instance, the popularity of Mexican food is not unique to Mexican Americans. Rather, it has diffused into mainstream American cultures, while undergoing some changes. Groups also practice **assimilation** as they sacrifice some of their cultural identity in order to fit into a new culture.

Why do people migrate? People migrate for the same reason animals do: to find food and a hospitable environment in which to live. In early human history, nomadic peoples by definition were migratory, moving from place to place with the seasons to follow food sources. Agricultural peoples also migrated, following the seasons and therefore agricultural cycles. To maintain a stable home, people also migrated to avoid natural disasters or climatic changes that permanently change the environment, making it too hot and dry (the Sahara Desert's expansion), too cold (Ice Ages), or too wet (flooding cycles of major rivers such as the Yellow River in China).

Migration isn't always solely the result of random environmental change. Over-population of a particular area can exhaust the food supply, forcing people to move elsewhere, often displacing a smaller or weaker population in the process. Massive migrations of people from Ireland during the famines of the mid-nineteenth century were caused by a mix of politics, destructive farming methods, and an unpleasant fungus that wiped out the populace's main source of food. The Jewish diaspora, the slave trade, and the waves of immigrants coming from Europe to the Americas in the late nineteenth and early twentieth centuries are examples of more modern-day migrations caused by people rather than nature.

Consider a case study: Beginning around 1500 B.C.E., farmers in the Niger and Benue River valleys in West Africa began migrating south and east, taking with them their languages (from the Bantu family of languages) and their knowledge of agriculture and metallurgy. These migrations, usually referred to as the Bantu migrations, continued over the course of the next 2,000 years. Bantu speakers gradually moved into areas formerly occupied by nomads. Some of the nomads simply moved on, and some of them adopted the more sedentary culture of the Bantu.

It is generally believed that the migration was spurred by climatic changes, which made the area now known as the Sahara Desert too dry to live in. People moved south out of the Sahara into the Bantu's homeland, which in turn caused them to move to the forests of Central Africa and then eventually beyond the forests to the east and south. However, not all Bantu-speakers moved away. Further north in the upper Niger River valley can be found the remains of Jenne-Jeno, believed to be the first city in sub-Saharan Africa. Beginning as a small fishing settlement around 250 B.C.E. and reaching urban size in 400 C.E., Jenne-Jeno is unusual because although it reached urban density, its architecture suggests that it was not a hierarchically organized society. Instead, archeologists believe that it was a unique form of urbanism comprising a collection of individual communities. It just goes to show that not all human societies have followed the same path toward sophistication, and that urbanization doesn't necessarily mean centralization.

Wars over Territory

Territoriality is the expression of political control over space. The concept of the state implies that the government controls land and the people who live there. **Citizenship** is the legal identity of a person based on the state where he or she was born or where he or she was naturalized as an immigrant. Keep in mind that when citizens go outside their state's political borders, they retain their citizen status and thus become an extension of their state (unless they apply for new citizenship as immigrants). This is why we strictly define the state as a population represented by a single government, without mentioning territory. However, don't forget that

Here is a quick guide to commonly used historical abbreviations:

B.C.E. = "Before the Common Era" (this refers to the same time period as B.C., "Before Christ")

C.E. = "Common Era" (this refers to the same time period as A.D., "anno Domini")

space matters; as it's not much of a state if it has no land, which can happen in the case of a government in exile, such as the Dutch or Polish governments during World War II.

Throughout human history, countless wars have been fought over territory. Often these wars have arisen due to conflicts over natural resources, such as water or minerals, but territorial wars have just as often arisen due to religious or cultural conflicts or simply as a result of imperialistic ambitions. Let's consider the example of Russia between the fifteenth and eighteenth centuries.

When the Turks conquered Constantinople and the Byzantine Empire fell, the center of Orthodox Christianity moved northward to Moscow. At around the same time, Russian leaders were overthrowing the Mongols in central Asia. In 1480, Ivan III of Moscow refused to pay tribute to the Mongols and declared Russia free of Mongol rule. He, and later his grandson Ivan IV, established absolute rule in Russia, uniting it and expanding it ever eastward. They recruited peasants and offered them freedom from their feudal lords if they agreed to settle in new lands to the east. The catch was that these peasants had to conquer the land themselves! Known as Cossacks, these peasant-soldiers expanded Russian territories in the sixteenth through the eighteenth centuries well into Siberia and southward to the Caspian Sea.

At around this same time, Peter the Great, who ruled from 1682 through 1725, came to power. He was convinced he needed to westernize Russia. He built Russia's first navy and founded St. Petersburg on the Baltic Sea as his new capital. The "window to the west," St. Petersburg became the home to hundreds of western European engineers, scientists, architects, and artists who were recruited specifically to westernize Russia. Under Catherine the Great, who ruled from 1762 until 1796, more enlightened policies of education and western culture were implemented. Still, Russia suffered because Catherine fiercely enforced repressive serfdom and limited the growth of the merchant class. Catherine continued the aggressive westward territorial expansion, gaining ground in Poland and, most significantly, territory on the Black Sea. This advance ensured Russia's access to the Mediterranean to its south and west.

In addition to wars and other subsequent border changes, there are a few other ways in which state territory can change shape. **Decolonization** after World War II, for example, significantly reduced the area and number of territorial and colonial holdings of the European powers and the United States. Although most areas were granted independence, some colonial holdings were **incorporated** and residents integrated with full citizen status. Examples include Hawaii, Alaska, and the French departments of Guadeloupe, Martinique, Reunion, and French Guyana. Residents of these places have full voting rights, pay taxes, and receive benefits just like the other citizens of the United States and France.

Annexation is another term used to describe the addition of territory as a result of a land **purchase** or when a territorial claim is extended through **incorporation**. The United States originally purchased Alaska from the Russian Empire in 1867 for $7,000,000 in gold and it became a full state in 1948. The U.S. Virgin Islands resulted from a cash sale of St. Thomas, St. John, and St. Croix by a financially strapped Danish government in 1917 (during World War I).

Trade

Trade, which is simply another way of describing the transfer of ownership of goods or services between different people, has been a crucial component of human societies for thousands of years. Before the development of currency, the most common type of trade was **barter**, or the exchange of one type of goods or services for another type of goods or services. For example, person A might be a wheat farmer who could exchange some of his wheat for some milk from person B, who has a herd of dairy cows. In modern times, of course, most trade involves the exchange of money (either physical or in the form of credit).

There have been many important trade routes throughout human history, and business along these trade routes has helped not only to spread goods and services, but also languages, religions, cultural practices, and disease. Consider, by way of example, one of the most well-known trade routes of ancient and medieval times: the Silk Road. This vast network consisted of approximately 4,000 miles of interconnected roads on which people and goods could travel from eastern Asia all the way to western Europe. The economic activity that occurred along the Silk Road was an important factor in the development of many major world civilizations, not least of which was the Chinese.

The name "Silk Road" comes from one of the earliest and most lucrative forms of trade between China and places to the west, namely trade in luxurious silk fabric.

Human Influence on the Environment

There's no question that the Agricultural Revolution had an impact on the environment. Farming villages began to dramatically change the lay of the land by diverting water, clearing land for farming, and creating farmland where none previously existed. As villages grew into more permanent towns and cities, roads were built to link them, further altering the landscape. Stones were unearthed and cut to build increasingly large buildings and monuments. All of this activity led to a world in which land and resources were continually being reconfigured to fit the needs of growing, geographically stable populations.

What's more, the impact on the animal kingdom was equally momentous. With the development of large-scale agriculture, animals began to be used not only as a source of food and clothing, but also as a direct source of agricultural labor. For example, oxen were used to pull plows on ever-expanding farmland. This enabled farmers to increase the size of their fields dramatically because they no longer had to turn the soil by hand.

If there had been a stock market for new technologies in the Neolithic Era, it would have attracted many investors. During this period, hard stones such as granite were sharpened and formed into farming tools such as hoes and plows. Pottery was made to use for cooking. Weaving was invented to shape baskets and nets; more complex and comfortable clothing was designed. Eventually, wheels were invented for use on carts, and sails for use on boats. The list goes on and on. But perhaps one of the most significant advances of the Neolithic Era was the knowledge of how to use metals. This greatly advanced the development of not only tools, but also weapons. When people figured out how to combine copper with tin to create an even harder metal, bronze, the building of civilizations was well on its way.

Industrialization

Farming tools, metallurgy, and the ability to manipulate the environment cause humans to transition from nomadic hunters and gatherers to builders of civilizations and empires. In order to farm successfully, people need tools, a way to transport what they've grown, and a place to store their surplus. Thus, the most important technologies developed by early civilizations included farming tools: ploughs, hoes, rakes, the wheel (and therefore the cart), and finally, pottery in which to store surplus for the off-season. While effective tools can be made out of bone and stone, they last longer and work more efficiently if they're made of metal. Copper was the first metal used, and other metallurgical techniques developed from there. From such primitive techniques developed more complex technologies that benefitted society in greater ways. The earliest public works projects focused on irrigation—often simple dikes and canals to capture floodwater and precious fertile silt. As cities grew, populations needed steady water supplies and a fairly reliable plumbing and sewage system. The large cities of the Indus River Valley (around 2500 B.C.E.), had elaborate public and private sewers, and similar systems were built much later in the Roman Empire. The most visible technological achievements were massive architectural monuments built by all civilizations—pyramids, ziggurats, walls, temples, aqueducts, coliseums, theaters, and stadiums, and roads. These structures were used to assert the authority of leaders, to facilitate the functioning of the state, and to keep the populace healthy, employed, and entertained. A stable supply of food allowed people to develop specialized skills and crafts beyond the basic needs of their neighbors. Although a lot of the trade in early societies tended to be smaller luxury items—silk, cotton and wool, semi-precious gems, and jewelry—heavier goods including olive oil and spices were also traded.

Now let's move forward several thousand years. The Industrial Revolution, which began in the mid-eighteenth century in Britain and spread rapidly through the nineteenth century, is inseparable from the Age of Imperialism, which reached its peak in the late nineteenth and early twentieth centuries. Industrial technology had two enormous consequences: (1) Countries with industrial technology by definition had advanced military weapons and capacity, and were therefore easily able to conquer people who did not have this technology; (2) To succeed, factories needed access to raw materials to make finished products, and then markets to sell those finished products.

The Industrial Revolution began in Britain, helping to propel the country to its undisputed ranking as the most powerful in the nineteenth century. But Britain wasn't the only country that industrialized. The revolution spread through much of Europe, especially Belgium, France, and Germany, as well as to Japan and ultimately to the country that would eclipse Britain as the most industrialized—the United States. Still, since most of the developments occurred in Britain first, and since the social consequences that occurred in Britain are representative of those that occurred elsewhere, this section will focus heavily on the revolution in Britain.

Hopefully you remember that early civilizations came about, in part, because of an Agricultural Revolution that resulted in food surpluses. This freed some of the population from farming, and those people then went about the business of building the civilization. In the eighteenth century, agricultural output increased dramatically once again. This time, it allowed not just some people, but as much as half of the population to leave the farms and head toward the cities, where jobs in the new industrial economy were becoming available. Keep in mind that agricultural techniques had been slowly improving throughout history. Since so many developments happened so quickly in the eighteenth century, this period was considered a revolution.

Agricultural output increased for a whole host of reasons. Potatoes, corn, and other high-yield crops were introduced to Europe from the colonies in the New World. Farmers began using more advanced farming methods and technology and increased their crop yields. Through a process known simply as enclosure, public lands that were shared during the Middle Ages were enclosed by fences, which allowed for private farming and private gain.

But what really cranked up the efficiency and productivity of the farms was the introduction of new technologies. New machines for plowing, seeding, and reaping, along with the development of chemical fertilizers, allowed farmers to greatly increase the amount of land they could farm, while decreasing the number of people needed to do it. Urbanization was a natural outgrowth of the increased efficiencies in farming and agriculture. In short, cities grew. In 1800, there were only 20 cities in Europe with a population of more than 100,000. By 1900, 150 cities had similar populations, and the largest, London, had a population of more than 6 million. Cities developed in areas where resources such as coal, iron, water, and railroads were available for manufacturing. The more factories that developed in favorable locations, the larger cities would grow. In 1800, along with London, the Chinese cities of Beijing (Peking) and Canton ranked in the top three, but just 100 years later, nine of the ten largest cities in the world were in Europe or the United States.

Prior to the Industrial Revolution, most Europeans worked on farms, at home, or in small shops. Even after Britain started importing huge amounts of cotton from its American colonies, most of the cotton was woven into cloth in homes or small shops as part of an inefficient, highly labor-intensive arrangement known as the domestic system. Middlemen would drop off wool or cotton at homes where women would make cloth, which would then be picked up again by the middlemen, who would sell the cloth to buyers. All of this was done one person at a time. However, a series of technological advancements in the eighteenth century changed all this. In 1733, John Kay invented the flying shuttle, which sped up the weaving process. In 1764, John Hargreaves invented the spinning jenny, which was capable of spinning vast amounts of thread. When waterpower was added to these processes, fabric-weaving was taken out of the homes and was centralized at sites where waterpower was abundant. In 1793, when Eli Whitney invented the cotton gin, thereby allowing massive amounts of cotton to be quickly processed in the Americas and exported to Europe, the textile industry was taken out of the homes and into the mills entirely.

Although industrialization hit the textile industry first, it spread well beyond into other industries. One of the most significant developments was the invention of the steam engine, which actually took the work of several people to perfect. In the early 1700s, Thomas Newcomer developed an inefficient engine, but in 1769, James Watt dramatically improved it. The steam engine was revolutionary because steam could be used to generate power not only for industry but also for transportation. In 1807, Robert Fulton built the first steamship, and in the 1820s, George Stephenson built the first steam-powered locomotive. In the hands of a huge, imperial power like Britain, steamships and locomotives would go a long way toward empire building and global trade. Because Britain had vast amounts of coal, and because the steam engine was powered by coal, Britain industrialized very quickly.

The Industrial Revolution permitted the creation of thousands of new products from clothing to toys to weapons. These products were produced efficiently and inexpensively in factories. Under Eli Whitney's system of interchangeable parts, machines and their parts were produced uniformly so that they could be easily replaced when something broke down. Later, Henry Ford's use of the assembly line meant that each factory worker added only one part to a finished product, one after another after another. These were incredibly important developments in manufacturing, and they made the factory system wildly profitable, but they came with social costs. Man wasn't merely working with machines; he was becoming one. Individuality had no place in a system where consistency of function was held in such high esteem. The factories were manned by thousands of workers, and the system was efficient and inexpensive primarily because those workers were way overworked, extremely underpaid, and regularly put in harm's way without any accompanying insurance or protection. In the early years of the Industrial Revolution, 16-hour workdays were not uncommon. Children as young as six worked next to machines. Women worked long hours at factories, while still having to fulfill their traditional roles as caretakers for their husbands, children, and homes.

This was a huge change from rural life. Whereas the farms exposed people to fresh air and sunshine, the factories exposed workers to air pollution and hazardous machinery. The farms provided seasonal adjustments to the work pattern, while the factories spit out the same products day after day, all year long.

Climate Change

A final topic, and one that is often mentioned in the news these days, is **climate change**. Scientists largely agree that climate change is affected by human activity and it is obvious that climate change has many implications for the places and ways in which humans live. Broadly speaking, climate change refers to long-term changes in weather patterns and conditions. Scientists work to understand past and future climatic patterns by examining such things as geological records, glaciers, sea levels, and sediment layers.

In the past, the earth has experienced both **global cooling** and **global warming**. Scientists warn that the earth is currently in an irreversible pattern of global warming: Temperatures, on average, have risen over the past century, and are predicted to continue in that same direction over the next century. The rise in average global temperatures has led to both minor and major weather events: Many regions have experienced an increase in rain, floods, and droughts, while other regions have experienced more severe heat waves than ever before. As the ice caps at the north and south poles and glaciers in places such as Greenland have melted, ocean levels have risen, affecting coastal communities and low-lying areas.

MAPS

On the Social Studies section of the TASC test, you will find a mixture of different question formats. Some of these will simply involve text, but others will contain photographs, tables, charts, and maps. Let's look more closely at the map format, as it may not be very familiar.

Maps and Atlases

A **globe** is a three-dimensional representation of the earth. On the TASC test, you may see two-dimensional drawings of a globe such as the one below:

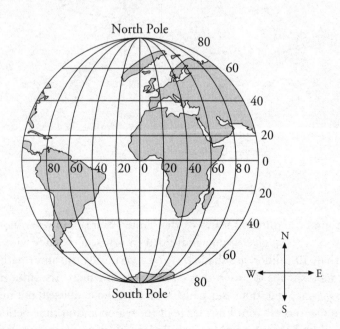

Map Lines
horizontal lines = latitude
vertical lines = longitude

In this figure, you can see about half of the earth's surface. You are looking at Africa in the middle of the globe. Above Africa, you can see most of Europe. At the bottom left of the globe, you can see most of South America. The line running horizontally across the center of the globe is called the equator. This line, like all the lines on this map, is imaginary. If you go to the equator, you will not, of course, find a line drawn all the way around the globe. The part of the earth above the equator is called the Northern Hemisphere. The part below is called the Southern Hemisphere. The horizontal lines above and below the equator are called lines of latitude. Any point on the equator has a latitude of 0 degrees. A point 20 degrees above the equator would be called 20 degrees north. The vertical lines running along the globe are called lines of longitude. A longitude of 0 degrees describes an imaginary line that runs right through Greenwich, England, dividing the globe into the Eastern and Western Hemispheres. Using a combination of latitude and longitude, you can locate the position of any point on the earth.

A **map** is a drawing of a smaller part of the globe. An atlas, on the other hand, is a collection of maps (usually of the earth or some particular region of the earth). Both maps and atlases commonly indicate geographical features or political boundaries, and often provide additional information about societies, economics, populations, and other characteristics. Below, you can see one of the TASC test's favorites: a map of the United States:

☐ population more than 10 million
(Source: U.S. Bureau of Census)

This map shows the different states of the United States. However, note that on this map, you are also given some additional information. States with a population more than 10 million are shaded. Almost certainly, this information will be necessary to answer the question that comes with this map. The information you need to answer map questions is usually located on the map itself, but may also require you to incorporate your knowledge of the region and/or time period in question. You will find that some maps include information on the population living in the area, others will show climate patterns, and others will give topographical information, such as how far the land is above sea level. As with almost all maps, north is at the top of the page, which means that south is at the bottom, west is toward the left, and east is toward the right.

Political Maps

A **political map** is a particular kind of map that shows up frequently on the TASC test. Simply put, this type of map indicates governmental boundaries, whether on the international, national, provincial, state, or county level. Let's look at an example:

As you can probably tell, the map above shows the political boundaries of modern Europe and a small sliver of North Africa. Each country is separated from its neighbors by a solid black line or by the geographical boundaries of a body of water, such as the Mediterranean Sea.

This map, unlike the map of the United States in the previous section, contains a **map scale**, which describes the ratio of distance on a map and distance in the real world in absolute terms. Map scales can be expressed in a couple of ways. Linear map scale expresses distance on the map surface. It can either be found in the legend or in a corner of the map, like so:

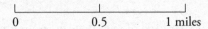

The ratio scale of the math will also be expressed on the map legend. This shows the mathematical relationship between the distance on the map compared to the real distance on the earth's surface. It will appear as a 1 separated by a colon from a much larger number, like so:

$$1:24,000$$

In this case, 1 inch on the map equals 24,000 inches on the earth's surface, or about two-thirds of a mile. This is the map scale used on topographic maps produced by the United States Geological Survey (USGS). This map scale can also be expressed as the mathematical ratio $\dfrac{1}{24,000}$.

A large-scale map is one with a ratio that is a comparatively large real number. A small-scale map is one with a ratio that is a comparatively small real number. Consider the amount of area and level of detail expressed depending upon the type of map scale.

Geography Drill

Now that you've learned all about geography, let's try some practice questions. To check your answers, register your book at **PrincetonReview.com/cracking** and download the Chapter Drill Answers and Explanations supplement.

1.   **Look at the map. Then answer the question.**

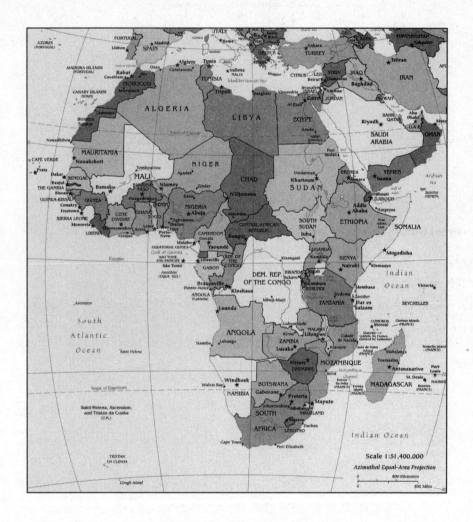

    The country in Africa that can have trade ports on two oceans is

A   Chad

B   Algeria

C   South Africa

D   Tanzania

2.   Look at the globe. Then answer the question.

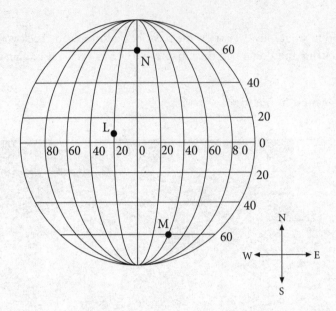

It can be inferred from the diagram above that which of the following statements is likely to be true:

A   Point M is warmer than Point L

B   Point N is warmer than Point M

C   Point N is warmer than Point L

D   Point L is warmer than Point N

3. Look at the map. Then answer the question.

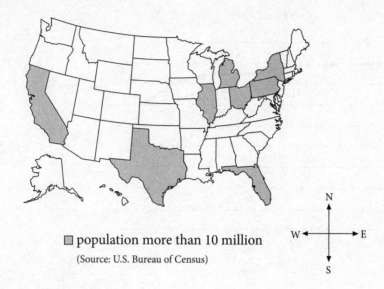

population more than 10 million
(Source: U.S. Bureau of Census)

N
W ← → E
S

According to the map above, the biggest concentration of states with large populations can be found in which region of the United States?

A the central region

B the southwestern region

C the northwestern region

D the northeastern region

4. Look at the graph. Then answer the question.

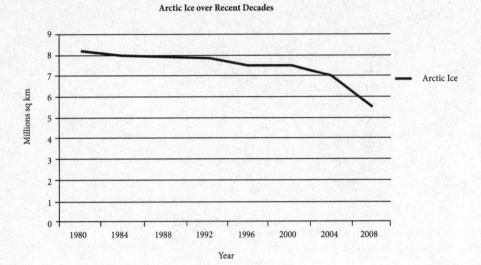

Arctic Ice over Recent Decades

In which set of years was the most significant change in Arctic ice recorded?

A 2004–2008

B 1996–2000

C 1988–1992

D 1980–1984

5. Read the excerpt from a letter written in 1818 by an Irish immigrant to the United States. Then answer the question.

> One thing I think is certain is that if the emigrants knew beforehand what they have to suffer for about the first six months after leaving home in every respect they would never come here. However, an enterprising man, desirous of advancing himself in the world will despise everything for coming to this free country, where a man is allowed to…act and speak as he likes, abuse public men in their office to their faces, wear your hat in court and smoke a cigar while speaking to the judge as familiarly as if he was a common mechanic, hundreds go unpunished for crimes for which they would be surely hung in Ireland; in fact, they are so tender of life in this country that a person should have a very great interest to get himself hanged for anything!

What does the author of this letter indicate was a primary reason for his emigration?

A freedom of religion

B freedom of speech

C freedom of privacy

D freedom to work

6. **Look at the map. Then answer the question.**

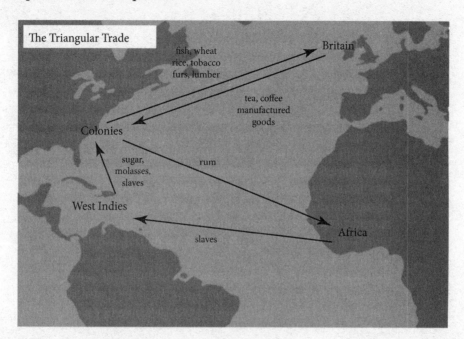

The Triangular Trade

fish, wheat rice, tobacco furs, lumber

Britain

tea, coffee manufactured goods

Colonies

sugar, molasses, slaves

rum

West Indies

Africa

slaves

According to the map above, one of the colonies' major exports was

A tobacco

B manufactured goods

C slaves

D sugar

Chapter 21
U.S. History I

In this chapter, we'll guide you through the key topics related to the early years of American history on the Social Studies portion of the TASC test (more recent American history will be covered in Chapter 22). We will focus here on two broad categories: the period up to and including the Revolutionary War, and the period between the Revolutionary War and the beginning of the twentieth century. Following the content lessons, we'll give you some practice questions.

EARLY EXPLORATION TO THE REVOLUTIONARY WAR

Contrary to popular belief, the United States of America was not born on July 4, 1776, with the signing of the Declaration of Independence. It did not spring up instantaneously, as if American colonists woke up one morning and decided that they were no longer British citizens. The War for Independence (1775–1783) was the end result of a long process of gradual independence. Indeed, after living for 150 years in the Americas (thousands of miles away from Europe), many colonists began to develop the characteristics that would go on to define the nation: a strong, independent work ethic, a keen eye for business opportunities, and, above all, a belief in divinely ordained human rights. Chapters 21 and 22 offer a brief introduction to the major eras in American history. The TASC test covers a fairly wide range of time, so prepping for this test can seem quite daunting. Begin by studying the early exploration of North America in the fifteenth century; then turn to the colonial period in the 1700s, with the establishment of the first English colony at Jamestown, Virginia. Then continue through the span of the 1800s and 1900s, with their social upheavals and ideological swings, up to history you will remember happening within your lifetime. Along the way you will learn about Jeffersonian versus Jacksonian Democracy, the bloody clash between the North and South, Westward Expansion, the Industrial Revolution, two World Wars, the Great Depression, the Cold War, and finally 9/11 and a few major topics in current events.

Exploring the New World

Christopher Columbus arrived in the New World in 1492. He was not the first European to reach North America—the Norse had arrived in modern Canada around 1000—but his arrival marked the beginning of the Contact Period, during which Europe sustained contact with the Americas and introduced a widespread exchange of plants, animals, foods, communicable diseases, and ideas in the **Columbian Exchange**. Unlike Leif Eriksson, Bjarni Herjolfsson, and other Norse explorers, the better-remembered Columbus arrived at a time when Europe had the resources and technology to establish **colonies** far from home. (A *colony* is a territory settled and controlled by a foreign power.) When Columbus returned to Spain and reported the existence of a rich new world with easy-to-subjugate natives, he opened the door to a long period of European expansion and colonialism.

During the next century, Spain was *the* colonial power in the Americas. The Spanish founded a number of coastal towns in Central and South America and in the West Indies, where the **conquistadors** collected and exported as much of the area's wealth as they could. Under Spain's **encomienda** system, the crown granted colonists authority over a specified number of natives; the colonist was obliged to protect those natives and convert them to Catholicism, and in exchange, the colonist was entitled to those natives' labor for such enterprises as sugar harvesting and silver mining. If this sounds like a form of slavery, that's because it was.

Spanish and Portuguese colonization of North America was also marked by liberal mixing of cultures, leading to a racial caste system, with Europeans at the top of the hierarchy, followed by **Mestizos** (those of mixed European and Native blood), **Zambos** (those of mixed African and Native American heritage), and pure-blooded Africans at the bottom of the ladder. Meanwhile, the strength of Spain's navy, the **Spanish Armada**, kept other European powers from establishing much of a foothold in the New World. In 1588 the English navy defeated the Armada, and consequently, French and English colonization of North America became much easier.

Once Spain had colonized much of modern-day South America and the southern tier of North America, other European nations were inspired to try their hands at New World exploration. They were motivated by a variety of factors: the desire for wealth and resources, clerical fervor to make new Christian converts, and the race to play a dominant role in geopolitics. The vast expanses of largely undeveloped North America and the fertile soils in many regions of this new land, opened up virtually endless potential for agricultural profits and mineral extraction. Concurrently, improvements in navigation, such as the invention of the **sextant** in the early 1700s, made sailing across the Atlantic Ocean safer and more efficient.

Intercontinental trade became more organized with the creation of **joint stock companies**, corporate businesses with shareholders whose mission was to settle and develop lands in North America. The most famous ones were the British East India Company, the Dutch East India Company, and, later, the **Virginia Company** which settled **Jamestown**.

Much of early American history revolves around the conflict between Native Americans and European settlers. Europeans were generally victorious. Why? One seemingly obvious answer is that the Europeans had more advanced technology, but this wasn't actually a major factor. In fact, in many ways, the Native Americans' technology was superior: Their canoes were far better at navigating North American rivers than any European ship, and their moccasins offered better footing than clumsy European boots. The most important factor, by a wide margin, was disease. Native Americans had never been exposed to European microbes and had never developed immunities to them. Epidemics, such as **smallpox**, devastated Native American settlements, sometimes killing 95% of the population years before Europeans themselves arrived to mop up the few survivors.

Increased trade and development in the New World also led to increased conflict and prejudice. Europeans now debated how Native Americans should be treated. Spanish and Portuguese thinkers, such as **Juan de Sepúlveda** and **Bartolomé de Las Casas,** proposed wildly different approaches to the treatment of Native populations, ranging from peace and tolerance to dominance and enslavement. The belief in European superiority was nearly universal.

Some American Indians resisted European influence, while others accepted it. Intermarriage was common between Spanish and French settlers and the natives in their colonized territories (though rare among English and Dutch settlers). Many Indians converted to Christianity. Spain was particularly successful in converting much of Meso-America to Catholicism through the **Spanish mission system**. Explorers, such as **Juan de Oñate,** swept through the American Southwest, determined to create Christian converts by any means necessary—including violence.

As colonization spread, the use of African slaves purchased from African traders from their home continent became more common. Much of the Caribbean and Brazil became permanent settlements for plantations and their slaves. Africans adapted to their new environment by blending the language and religion of their masters with the preserved traditions of their ancestors. Religions such as **voodoo** are a blend of Christianity and tribal animism. Slaves sang African songs in the fields as they worked and created art reminiscent of their homeland. Some, such as the **Maroon** people, even managed to escape slavery and form cultural enclaves. Slave uprisings were not uncommon, most notably the Haitian Revolution.

Unlike other European colonizers, the English sent large numbers of men and women to the agriculturally fertile areas of the East. Despite our vision of the perfect Thanksgiving table, relationships with local Indians were strained, at best. English intermarriage with Indians and Africans was rare, so no new ethnic groups emerged, and social classes remained rigid and hierarchical.

Settling the Thirteen Colonies

A good general guide for remembering which colonies were established for what reasons: The northern colonies were mostly established for religious reasons, whereas the southern colonies were mostly established for commercial gain.

England's first attempt to settle North America came a year prior to its victory over Spain, in 1587, when **Sir Walter Raleigh** sponsored a settlement on Roanoke Island (now part of North Carolina). By 1590 the colony had disappeared, which is why it came to be known as the **Lost Colony**. The English did not try again until 1607, when they settled **Jamestown**. Jamestown was funded by a **joint-stock company**, a group of investors who bought the right to establish New World plantations from the king. The company was called the **Virginia Company**—named for Elizabeth I, known as the Virgin Queen— from which the area around Jamestown took its name. The settlers, many of them English gentlemen, were ill-suited to the many adjustments life in the New World required of them, and they were much more interested in searching for gold than in planting crops. (The only "gold" to be found in Virginia was iron pyrite, aka "fool's gold," which the ignorant aristocrats blithely gathered up.) Within three months more than half the original settlers were dead of starvation or disease, and Jamestown survived only because ships kept arriving from England with new colonists. **Captain John Smith** decreed that "he who will not work shall not eat," and things improved for a time, but after Smith was injured in a gunpowder explosion and sailed back to England, the Indians of the **Powhatan Confederacy** stopped supplying Jamestown with food. Things got so bad during the winter of 1609–1610 that it became known as "the **starving time**": Nearly 90 percent of Jamestown's 500 residents perished, with some resorting to cannibalism. The survivors actually abandoned the colony, but before they could get more than a few miles downriver, they ran into an English ship containing supplies and new settlers.

One of the survivors, **John Rolfe,** was notable in two ways. First, he married Powhatan's daughter **Pocahontas**, briefly easing the tension between the natives and the English settlers. Second, he pioneered the practice of growing **tobacco**, which had long been cultivated by Native Americans, as a cash crop to be exported back to England. The English public was soon hooked, so to speak, and the success of tobacco considerably brightened the prospects for English settlement in Virginia.

Because the crop requires vast acreage and depletes the soil (and so requires farmers to constantly seek new fields), the prominent role of tobacco in Virginia's economy resulted in rapid expansion. The introduction of tobacco would also lead to the development of plantation slavery. As new settlements sprang up around Jamestown, the entire area came to be known as the **Chesapeake** (named after the bay). That area today comprises Virginia and Maryland.

Many who migrated to the Chesapeake did so for financial reasons. Overpopulation in England had led to widespread famine, disease, and poverty. Chances for improving one's lot during these years were minimal. Thus, many were attracted to the New World by the opportunity provided by **indentured servitude**. In return for free passage, indentured servants typically promised seven years' labor, after which they would receive their freedom. Throughout much of the seventeenth century, indentured servants also received a small piece of property with their freedom, thus enabling them (1) to survive and (2) to vote. As in Europe, the right to vote was tied to the ownership of property, and indentured servitude in America opened a path to land ownership that was not available to most working class men in populous Europe. However, indenture was extremely difficult, and nearly half of all indentured servants—most of whom were young, reasonably healthy men—did not survive their term of service. Still, indenture was common. More than 75 percent of the 130,000 Englishmen who migrated to the Chesapeake during the seventeenth century were indentured servants.

In 1618 the Virginia Company introduced the **headright system** as a means of attracting new settlers to the region and to address the labor shortage created by the emergence of tobacco farming, which required a large number of workers. A "headright" was a tract of land, usually about 50 acres, that was granted to colonists and potential settlers. Men already settled in Virginia were granted two headrights, totaling about 100 acres of land, while new settlers to Virginia were granted one headright. Wealthy investors could accumulate land by paying the passage of indentured servants and gaining a headright for each servant they sponsored. The headright system became the basis for an emerging aristocracy in colonial Virginia (where land was still the basis of wealth and political power) and was one of the factors that hindered the development of democracy in the region. Furthermore, it must be noted that these land grants infringed upon the rights of Native Americans, whose values regarding the environment and property ownership were vastly different from the values of the Europeans who settled in this region. In 1619 Virginia established the **House of Burgesses**, in which any property-holding, white male could vote. All decisions made by the House of Burgesses, however, had to be approved by the Virginia Company. That year also marks the introduction of **slavery** to the English colonies.

At first glance, the French colonization of North America appears to have much in common with Spanish and English colonization. While the English had founded a permanent settlement at Jamestown in 1607, the French colonized what is today Quebec City in 1608. Like the Spanish missionaries, the French Jesuit priests were trying to convert native peoples to Roman Catholicism, but they were much more likely to spread diseases, such as smallpox, than to convert large numbers to Christianity. Like colonists from other European countries, the French were exploring as much land as they could, hoping to find natural resources, such as gold, as well as a shortcut to Asia.

Unlike the Spanish and English, however, the French colonists had a much lighter impact on the native peoples. Few French settlers came to North America, and those who did tended to be single men, some of whom intermarried with women native to the area. They also tended to stay on the move, especially if they were *coureurs du bois* ("runners in the woods") who helped trade for the furs that became the rage in Europe. True, the French ultimately did play a significant role in the French and Indian War from 1754–1763; however, their chances of shaping the region soon known as British North America were slim from the outset and faded dramatically with the **Edict of Nantes** in 1598. This edict provided for religious tolerance of the **Huguenots** (the French Protestants), who might otherwise have fled their mother country just as the Puritans would flee England during the 1600s.

The four main colonizing powers in North America interacted with the native inhabitants very differently:

- **Spain** tended to conquer and enslave the native inhabitants of the regions it colonized. The Spanish also made great efforts to convert Native Americans to Catholicism. Spanish colonists were overwhelmingly male, and many had children with native women, leading to settlements populated largely by mestizos, people of mixed Spanish and Native American ancestry.
- **France** had significantly friendlier relations with indigenous tribes, tending to ally with them and adopt native practices. The French had little choice in this: French settlements were so sparsely populated that taking on the natives head-on would have been very risky.
- **The Netherlands** attempted to build a great trading empire, and while it achieved great success elsewhere in the world, its settlements on the North American continent, which were essentially glorified trading posts, soon fell to the English. This doesn't mean they were unimportant: One of the Dutch settlements was New Amsterdam, later renamed New York City.
- **England** differed significantly from the three other powers in that the other three all depended on Native Americans in different ways: as slave labor, as allies, or as trading partners. English colonies, by contrast, attempted to exclude Native Americans as much as possible. The English flooded to the New World in great numbers, with entire families arriving in many of the colonies rather than just young men, and intermixing between settlers and natives was rare. Instead, when English colonies grew to the point that conflict with nearby tribes became inevitable, the English launched **wars of extermination**. For instance, the Powhatan Confederacy was destroyed by English "Indian fighters" in the 1640s.

Several colonies were proprietorships; that is, they were owned by one person, who usually received the land as a gift from the king. **Connecticut** was one such colony, receiving its charter in 1635 and producing the **Fundamental Orders**, usually considered the first written constitution in British North America. **Maryland** was another, granted to Cecilius Calvert, Lord Baltimore. Calvert hoped to create a haven colony for Catholics, who faced religious persecution in Protestant England, but he also hoped to make a profit growing tobacco. In order to populate the colony's land more quickly, Calvert offered religious tolerance for all Christians, and Protestants soon outnumbered Catholics, recreating England's old tension between the faiths. After a Protestant uprising in England against a Catholic-sympathizing king, Maryland's government passed the **Act of Toleration** in 1649 to protect the religious freedom of most Christians, but the law was not enough to keep the situation in Maryland from devolving into bloody religious civil war for much of the rest of the century.

New York was also a royal gift, this time to James, the king's brother. The Dutch Republic was the largest commercial power during the seventeenth century and, as such, was an economic rival of the British. The Dutch had established an initial settlement in 1614 near present-day Albany, which they called New Netherland, and a fort at the mouth of the Hudson River in 1626. This fort would become New Amsterdam and is today New York City. In 1664 Charles II of England waged a war against the Dutch Republic and sent a naval force to capture New Netherland. Already weakened by previous clashes with local Native Americans, the Dutch governor, Peter Stuyvesant, along with 400 civilians, surrendered peacefully. Charles II's brother, James, became the Duke of York, and when James became king in 1685, he proclaimed New York a royal colony. The Dutch were allowed to remain in the colony on generous terms, and they made up a large segment of New York's population for many years. Charles II also gave **New Jersey** to a couple of friends, who in turn sold it off to investors, many of whom were Quakers.

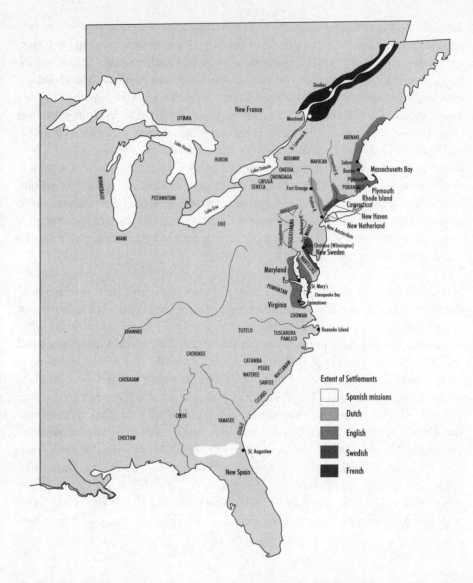

Ultimately, the Quakers received their own colony. William Penn, a Quaker, was a close friend of King Charles II, and Charles granted Penn what became **Pennsylvania**. Charles, like most Anglicans, perceived the egalitarian Quakers as dangerous radicals, but the two men's friendship (and Charles's desire to export the Quakers to someplace far from England) prevailed. Penn established liberal policies toward religious freedom and civil liberties in his colony. That, the area's natural bounty, and Penn's recruitment of settlers through advertising, made Pennsylvania one of the fastest growing of the early colonies. He also attempted to treat Native Americans more fairly than did other colonies and had mixed results. His attitude attracted many tribes to the area but also attracted many European settlers who bullied tribes off of their land. An illustrative story: Penn made a treaty with the Delawares to take only as much land as could be walked by a man in three days. Penn then set off on a leisurely stroll, surveyed his land, and kept his end of the bargain. His son, however, renegotiating the treaty, hired three marathon runners for the same task, thereby claiming considerably more land.

Carolina was also a proprietary colony, but in 1729 it officially split into **North Carolina**, settled by Virginians as a Virginia-like colony, and **South Carolina**, settled by the descendants of Englishmen who had colonized Barbados. Barbados's primary export was sugar, and its plantations were worked by slaves. Although slavery had existed in Virginia since 1619, the settlers from Barbados were the first Englishmen in the New World who had seen widespread slavery at work. Their arrival truly marked the beginning of the slave era in the colonies.

Eventually, most of the **proprietary** colonies were converted to **royal** colonies; that is, their ownership was taken over by the king, who could then exert greater control over their governments. By the time of the Revolution, only Connecticut, Rhode Island, Pennsylvania, and Maryland were *not* royal colonies.

The French and Indian War

British treatment of the colonies during the period preceding the **French and Indian War** (also called the **Seven Years' War**) is often described as **salutary neglect** or **benign neglect**. Although England regulated trade and government in its colonies, it interfered in colonial affairs as little as possible. Because of the distance, England set up absentee customs officials and the colonies were left to self-govern, for the most part. England occasionally turned its back to the colonies' violations of trade restrictions. Thus, the colonies developed a large degree of autonomy, which helped fuel revolutionary sentiments when the monarchy later attempted to gain greater control of the New World. During this century, the colonies "grew up," developing fledgling economies. The beginnings of an American culture—as opposed to a transplanted English culture—took root.

The Seven Years' War (1754–1763), despite its name, actually lasted for nine years. It is also called the **French and Indian War**, which is almost equally confusing because the French and Indians fought on the same side, not against each other. The Seven Years' War was the British name for the war. The colonists called it the "French and Indian War" because that's whom they were fighting. It was actually one of several "wars for empire" fought between the British and the French, and the Americans got stuck in the middle. This was arguably the first world war.

The war was the inevitable result of colonial expansion. (It was also caused by a number of inter-European power struggles, which is how Spain, Austria, Sweden, Prussia, and others got involved, but that is on the European history test, so you can worry about it some other time.) As English settlers moved into the Ohio Valley, the French tried to stop them by building fortified outposts at strategic entry spots. The French were trying to protect their profitable fur trade and their control of the region. A colonial contingent led by **George Washington** attacked a French outpost and lost badly. Washington surrendered and was allowed to return to Virginia, where he was welcomed as a hero. Other skirmishes and battles ensued, and in 1756, England officially declared war on France. Most Native Americans in the region, choosing the lesser of two evils, allied themselves with the French who had traditionally had the best relations with Native Americans of any of the European powers and whom, based on Washington's performance, they expected to win the war. The war dragged on for years before the English finally gained the upper hand. When the war was over, England was the undisputed colonial power of the continent. The treaty gave England control of Canada and almost everything east of the Mississippi Valley. The French kept only two sugar islands, underscoring the impact of mercantilism since the French prioritized two small but highly profitable islands over the large landmass of Canada.

During the Seven Years' War, many Americans served in the English army and, for the first time, came into prolonged contact with English soldiers. The English did not make a good impression, both in how they treated their own soldiers and in how the soldiers behaved themselves. These contacts sowed the first seeds of **anti-British sentiment** in the colonies, particularly in New England, where much of the fighting took place and where most of the colonial soldiers came from.

The English victory spelled trouble for Native Americans, who had previously been able to use French and English disputes to their own advantage. They negotiated their allegiances in return for land, goods, and the right to be left alone. The Native Americans particularly disliked the English, however, because English expansionism was more disruptive to their way of life. The French had sent few colonists, and many of those colonists were fur trappers who did not settle anywhere permanently. In the aftermath of the war, the English raised the price of goods sold to the Native Americans (they now had a monopoly, after all) and ceased paying rent on their western forts. In response, Ottawa war chief **Pontiac** rallied a group of tribes in the Ohio Valley and attacked colonial outposts. The attacks and resultant wars are known as **Pontiac's Rebellion** (or **Pontiac's Uprising**). In response to Pontiac's Rebellion, the **Paxton Boys**, a group of Scots-Irish frontiersmen in Pennsylvania murdered several in the Susquehanook tribe.

In response to the initial attacks, the British government issued the **Proclamation of 1763**, forbidding settlement west of the rivers running through the Appalachians. The proclamation came too late. Settlers had already moved west of the line. The proclamation did have one effect, however. It agitated colonial settlers, who regarded it as unwarranted British interference in colonial affairs.

Pontiac's Rebellion was, in part, a response to the colonists expanding into the Ohio River Valley and encroaching on the Native Americans' lands. (Recall similar events such as the Pequot War and Bacon's Rebellion.) The British were forced to quell this rebellion at great cost in addition to the costs of fighting the French. They used germ warfare, in the form of smallpox-infected blankets, to help defeat the Ottawa. The resulting Proclamation of 1763 is significant for a number of reasons. 1763 is often viewed as a turning point in British-colonial relations in that it marks the end of salutary neglect. The Proclamation of 1763 may be viewed as the first in a new series of restrictions imposed on the colonists by the British Parliament, and in that way, it marks the first step on the "road to revolution." Furthermore, it established a pattern of demarcating "Indian Territory," a pattern that would be adopted and pursued by the United States government long after the colonists gained their independence.

Pre-Revolutionary Events and People

One result of the Seven Years' War was that in financing the war the British government had run up a huge debt. The new king, **George III**, and his prime minister, **George Grenville**, felt that the colonists should help pay that debt. After all, they reasoned, the colonies had been beneficiaries of the war; furthermore, their tax burden was relatively light compared to that of taxpayers in England, even on the same goods. Meanwhile, the colonists felt that they had provided so many soldiers that they had fulfilled their obligation.

Accordingly, Parliament imposed new regulations and taxes on the colonists. The first was the **Sugar Act** of 1764, which established a number of new duties and which also contained provisions aimed at deterring molasses smugglers. Although Parliament had previously passed other acts aimed at controlling colonial trade and manufacturing, there was little colonial resistance prior to the decade leading up to the Revolutionary War. There were benefits to being part of the vast British Empire and most Americans accepted regulations of trade such as the **Navigation Acts** as part of **mercantilism**. Furthermore, although laws such as the Molasses Act of 1733 were on the books, smuggling was common practice and little revenue from taxes was actually collected. Some historians have gone so far as to suggest that Parliament never intended the Molasses Act to raise revenue but merely to function as a protective tariff aimed against French imports. Parliament was quite shrewd in passing the Sugar Act of 1764 in that this new act actually *lowered* the duty on molasses coming into the colonies from the West Indies. What angered the colonists the most was that this new regulation was to be more strictly enforced: Duties were to be collected. It became more difficult for colonial shippers to avoid committing even minor violations of the Sugar Act. Furthermore, violators were to be arrested and tried in vice-admiralty courts, courts in which a single judge issued a verdict without the deliberation of a jury. It was this last provision of the Sugar Act that suggested to some colonists that Parliament was overstepping its authority and violating their rights as Englishmen.

Another Parliamentary act, the **Currency Act**, forbade the colonies to issue paper money. Collectively, the Sugar Act, Currency Act, and Proclamation of 1763 caused a great deal of discontent in the colonies, whose residents bristled at what they correctly viewed as British attempts to exert greater control. These acts signaled a clear end to Britain's long-standing policy of salutary neglect. That these acts came during a postwar economic depression further aggravated the situation. Colonial protest to these acts, however, was uncoordinated and ineffective.

That all changed when Parliament passed the **Stamp Act** the following year, 1765. The Stamp Act included a number of provocative elements. First, it was a tax specifically aimed at raising revenue, thus awakening the colonists to the likelihood that even more taxes could follow. The Stamp Act demonstrated that the colonies' tradition of self-taxation was surely being unjustly taken by Parliament, much to the dismay of many colonists. Second, it was a broad-based tax, covering all legal documents and licenses. Not only did it affect almost everyone, but it particularly affected a group that was literate, persuasive, and argumentative—namely, lawyers. Third, it was a tax on goods produced within the colonies.

Two Types of Laws
One way to think of the unpopular laws imposed on the colonies in the years leading up to the Revolution is to divide them up into two types: restriction laws and taxation laws.

Restriction:
- Navigation Acts
- Proclamation Act
- Currency Acts
- Tea Act
- Intolerable Acts

Taxation:
- Navigation Acts (yes, this one was a double whammy!)
- Sugar Act
- Stamp Act
- Declaratory Act
- Townshend Acts

Reaction to the Stamp Act built on previous grievances and, consequently, was more forceful than any protest preceding it. A pamphlet by James Otis, called *The Rights of the British Colonies Asserted and Proved*, laid out the colonists' argument against the taxes and became a bestseller of its day. Otis put forward the "No taxation without representation" argument that later became a rallying cry of the Revolution. Because the colonists did not elect members to Parliament, he argued, they were not obliged to pay taxes (following the accepted precept that no Englishman could be compelled to pay taxes without his consent). Otis did *not* advocate secession; rather, he argued for either representation in Parliament or a greater degree of self-government for the colonies. Neither the British nor the colonists had much interest in creating a colonial delegation to Parliament. The British scoffed at the notion, arguing that the colonists were already represented in Parliament. Their argument was rooted in the theory of **virtual representation**, which stated that members of Parliament represented all British subjects regardless of who elected them. The colonists, for their part, knew that their representation would be too small to protect their interests and so never pushed the issue. What they wanted, and what the British were refusing to give them, was the right to determine their own taxes.

Opponents of the Stamp Act united in the various colonies. In Virginia, Patrick Henry drafted the Virginia Stamp Act Resolves, protesting the tax and asserting the colonists' right to a large measure of self-government. (The Virginia legislature removed Henry's most radical propositions before passing the resolves.) In Boston, mobs burned the customs officers in effigy, tore down a customs house, and nearly destroyed the governor's mansion. Protest groups formed throughout the colonies, calling themselves **Sons of Liberty**. The opposition was so effective that, by the time the law was supposed to take effect, not one of the Crown's appointed duty collectors was willing to perform his job. In 1766 Parliament repealed the Stamp Act. Just as important, George III replaced Prime Minister Grenville, whom the colonists now loathed, with Lord Rockingham, who had opposed the Stamp Act. Rockingham oversaw the repeal but also linked it to the passage of the Declaratory Act, which asserted the British government's right to tax and legislate in all cases anywhere in the colonies. Thus, although the colonists had won the battle over the stamp tax, they had not yet gained any ground in the war of principles over Parliament's powers in the colonies.

Rockingham remained prime minister for only two years. His replacement was William Pitt. Pitt, however, was ill, and the dominant figure in colonial affairs came to be the minister of the exchequer, Charles Townshend. Townshend drafted the eponymous **Townshend Acts**. The Townshend Acts, like the Stamp Act, contained several antagonistic measures. First, they taxed goods imported directly from Britain—the first such tax in the colonies. Mercantilism approved of duties on imports from other European nations but not on British imports. Second, some of the tax collected was set aside for the payment of tax collectors, meaning that colonial assemblies could no longer withhold government officials' wages in order to get their way. Third, the Townshend Acts created even more vice-admiralty courts and several new government offices to enforce the Crown's will in the colonies. Fourth, they suspended the New York legislature because it had refused to comply with a law requiring the colonists to supply British troops.

Last, these acts instituted *writs of assistance*, licenses that gave the British the power to search any place they suspected of hiding smuggled goods.

The colonists got better at protesting with each new tax, and their reaction to the Townshend Acts was their strongest yet. The Massachusetts Assembly sent a letter (called the **Massachusetts Circular Letter**, written by Samuel Adams in 1768) to all other assemblies asking that they protest the new measures in unison. The British fanned the flames of protest by ordering the assemblies *not* to discuss the Massachusetts letter, virtually guaranteeing it to be all anyone *would* talk about. Governors of colonies where legislatures discussed the letter dissolved those legislatures, which, of course, further infuriated colonists. The colonists held numerous rallies and organized boycotts, and for the first time they sought the support of "commoners" (previously such protests were confined largely to the aristocratic classes), making their rallies larger and much more intimidating. The boycotts were most successful because they affected British merchants, who then joined the protest. Colonial women were essential in the effort to replace British imports with "American" (New England) products. After two years, Parliament repealed the Townshend duties, although not the other statutes of the Townshend Acts, and not the duty on tea.

The Quartering Act of 1765 stationed large numbers of troops in America and made the colonists responsible for the cost of feeding and housing them. Even after the Townsend duties were repealed, the soldiers remained—particularly in Boston. Officially sent to keep the peace, these soldiers in fact heightened tensions. For one thing, the detachment was huge—4,000 men in a city of only 16,000. To make matters worse, the soldiers sought off-hour employment and so competed with colonists for jobs. Numerous confrontations resulted, with the most famous on March 5, 1770, when a mob pelted a group of soldiers with rock-filled snowballs. The soldiers fired on the crowd, killing five—hence, the **Boston Massacre**. The propaganda campaign that followed suggested that the soldiers had shot into a crowd of innocent bystanders. Interestingly, John Adams defended the soldiers in court, helping to establish a tradition of giving a fair trial to all who are accused.

Oddly enough, for the next two years, nothing major happened. The Boston Massacre shocked both sides into de-escalating their rhetoric, and an uneasy status quo fell into place during this period. Colonial newspapers discussed ways in which the relationship between the mother country and the colonies might be altered so as to satisfy both sides, but still, nobody except a very few radicals suggested independence. Things picked up in 1772 when the British implemented the part of the Townshend Acts that provided for colonial administrators to be paid from customs revenues (and not by the colonial legislatures). The colonists responded cautiously, setting up groups called **Committees of Correspondence** throughout the colonies to trade ideas and inform one another of the political mood. The committees also worked to convince more citizens to take an active interest in the conflict. Writers such as **Mercy Otis Warren**, a friend of Abigail Adams and Martha Washington, published pamphlets calling for Revolution. ***Letters From a Farmer in Pennsylvania*** were a series of essays written by John Dickinson, uniting the colonists against the Townsend Acts.

Not long after, the British granted the foundering East India Tea Company a monopoly on the tea trade in the colonies as well as a portion of new duties to be collected on tea sales. The result was cheaper tea for the colonists, but the colonists saw a more important issue: Parliament was once again imposing new taxes on them. In Boston, the colonists refused to allow the ships to unload their cargo, and the governor refused to allow them to leave the harbor. On December 16, 1773, a group of Sons of Liberty, poorly disguised as Mohawks, boarded a ship and dumped its cargo into Boston Harbor. It took them three hours to jettison the approximately £10,000 worth of tea. The incident is known as the **Boston Tea Party.**

The English responded with a number of punitive measures, known collectively as the **Coercive Acts** (also called the **Intolerable Acts**). One measure closed Boston Harbor to all but essential trade (food and firewood) and declared that it would remain closed until the tea was paid for. Several measures tightened English control over the Massachusetts government and its courts, and a new, stricter Quartering Act put British soldiers in civilian homes. The Coercive Acts convinced many colonists that their days of semi-autonomy were over and that the future held even further encroachments on their liberties by the Crown. To make matters worse, at the same time Parliament passed the Coercive Acts, it also passed the **Quebec Act**, which, to the colonists' chagrin, (1) granted greater liberties to Catholics, whom the Protestant colonial majority distrusted, and (2) extended the boundaries of the Quebec Territory, thus further impeding westward expansion.

The colonists met to discuss their grievances. All colonies except Georgia sent delegates to the **First Continental Congress,** which convened in late 1774. All perspectives were represented—Pennsylvania's delegation included conservatives such as Joseph Galloway, while Virginia sent two radicals, Richard Henry Lee and **Patrick Henry.** The goals of the meeting were to enumerate American grievances, to develop a strategy for addressing those grievances, and to formulate a colonial position on the proper relationship between the royal government and the colonial governments. The Congress came up with a list of those laws the colonists wanted repealed and agreed to impose a boycott on British goods until their grievances were redressed. The delegates also agreed to form a **Continental Association**, with towns setting up committees of observation to enforce the boycott; in time, these committees became their towns' de facto governments. Perhaps most important, the Congress formulated a limited set of parameters within which it considered Parliamentary interference in colonial affairs justified; all other spheres, the delegates agreed, should be left to the colonists themselves. This position represented a major break with British tradition and, accordingly, a major step toward independence.

Throughout the winter of 1774 and the spring of 1775, the committees of observation expanded their powers. In many colonies they supplanted the British-sanctioned assemblies. They led acts of insubordination by collecting taxes, disrupting court sessions, and, most ominously, organizing militias and stockpiling weapons. As John Adams would later comment about the period, "The Revolution was effected before the war commenced. The Revolution was in the minds and hearts of the people…This radical change in the principles, opinions, sentiments, and affections of the people was the real American Revolution."

The British underestimated the strength of the growing pro-revolutionary movement. Government officials mistakenly believed that if they arrested the ringleaders and confiscated their arsenals, violence could be averted. To that end, the English dispatched troops to confiscate weapons in Concord, Massachusetts, in April 1775. The troops had to first pass through Lexington, where they confronted a small colonial militia, called **minutemen** because they reputedly could be ready to fight on a minute's notice. Someone, probably one of the minutemen, fired a shot, which drew British return fire. When the **Battle of Lexington** was over, the minutemen had suffered eighteen casualties, including eight dead. The British proceeded to **Concord**, where a much larger contingent of minutemen awaited them. The Massachusetts militia inflicted numerous casualties on the British **redcoats** and forced them to retreat. That a contingent of colonial farmers could repel the army of the world's largest empire was monumental, which is why the **Battle of Concord** is sometimes referred to as "the shot heard 'round the world." The two opponents dug in around Boston, but during the next year only one major battle was fought. The two sides regrouped and planned their next moves.

For the colonists, the period provided time to rally citizens to the cause of independence. Not all were convinced. Among those remaining loyal to the Crown—such people were called **Loyalists**—were government officials, devout Anglicans (members of the Church of England), merchants dependent on trade with England, and many religious and ethnic minorities who feared persecution at the hands of the rebels. Many slaves believed their chances for liberty were better with the British than with the colonists, a belief strengthened when the royal governor of Virginia offered to free those slaves who escaped and joined the British army. The pre-Revolutionary War era saw an increase in the number of slave insurrections, dampening some Southerners' enthusiasm for revolution. The **patriots** were mostly white Protestant property holders and gentry, as well as urban artisans, especially in New England, where Puritans had long shown antagonism toward Anglicans. Much of the rest of the population just hoped the whole thing would blow over. The Quakers of Pennsylvania, for example, were pacifists and so wanted to avoid war.

The **Second Continental Congress** convened during this period, just weeks after the battles of Lexington and Concord. Throughout the summer, the Congress prepared for war by establishing a **Continental Army**, printing money, and creating government offices to supervise policy. The Congress chose **George Washington** to lead the army because he was both well-liked and a Southerner (thus bolstering support in an area with many loyalists).

Not all delegates thought that war was inevitable, and many followed John Dickinson, who was pushing for reconciliation with Britain using the **Olive Branch Petition**. Adopted by the Continental Congress on July 5, 1775, following the skirmish at Breed's Hill, often known as Bunker Hill, the Olive Branch petition was a last-ditch attempt to avoid armed conflict. King George III, however, was hardly interested in the proposal since he considered the colonists to be in open rebellion given their boycotts, attacks on royal officials, and resistance at Lexington and Concord. Still, it is worth noting that just one year before the adoption of the Declaration of Independence, the colonial leaders were trying to reconcile with the mother country.

Chronology of Events Leading to Revolutionary War	
1763	–French and Indian War ends –Pontiac's Rebellion –Proclamation of 1763
1764	–Sugar Act –Currency Act
1765	–Stamp Act –Stamp Act crisis –Sons of Liberty formed
1766	–Grenville replaced by Rockingham as prime minister –Stamp Act repealed –Declaratory Act
1767	–Townshend Acts
1770	–Townshend duties repealed (except tea tax) –Boston Massacre
1772	–parts of Townshend Acts implemented –Committees of Correspondence formed
1773	–British give the Dutch East India Tea Company monopoly on tea in colonies –Boston Tea Party
1774	–Coercive ("Intolerable") Acts –Quebec Act –First Continental Congress meets –Continental Association forms
1775	–Battles of Lexington and Concord –Second Continental Congress meets
1776	–Declaration of Independence

The Declaration of Independence

The rebels were still looking for the masterpiece of propaganda that would rally colonists to their cause. They got it in *Common Sense*, a pamphlet published in January of 1776 by an English printer named **Thomas Paine**. Paine not only advocated colonial independence, he also argued for the merits of republicanism over monarchy. The pamphlet was an even bigger success than James Otis's *The Rights of the British Colonies Asserted and Proved*. Though literacy rates in New England were somewhat higher, thanks to the Puritan legacy of teaching children to read the Bible, most of the nation's two million inhabitants could not read. Nevertheless, Paine's pamphlet sold more than 100,000 copies in its first three months alone, the proportional equivalent of selling 13 million downloads today. The secret to Paine's success was that *Common Sense* stated the argument for independence in plainspoken language accessible to colonists who couldn't always keep up with the lofty Enlightenment-speak of the Founding Fathers. It helped swing considerable support to the patriot cause among people who had worried about the wisdom of attacking the powerful mother country.

In June, the Congress was looking for a rousing statement of its ideals, and it commissioned **Thomas Jefferson** to write the **Declaration of Independence.** He did not let them down. The Declaration not only enumerated the colonies' grievances against the Crown, but it also articulated the principle of individual liberty and the government's fundamental responsibility to serve the people. Despite its obvious flaws—most especially that it pertained only to white, propertied men—it remains a work of enormous power. With the document's signing on July 4, 1776, the Revolutionary War became a war for independence.

After several years of fighting, the British surrendered at Yorktown in October of 1781. You should remember a few other facts about the war. The Continental Army (as opposed to local militias) had trouble recruiting good soldiers. Eventually, the Congress recruited blacks, and up to 5,000 fought on the side of the rebels (in return, most of those who had been slaves were granted their freedom). The **Franco-American Alliance**, negotiated by **Ben Franklin** in 1778, brought the French into the war on the side of the colonists, after the battle of Saratoga. This was hardly surprising given the lingering resentment of the French toward the English after the French and Indian War. It would be three years before French troops landed in America, but the alliance buoyed American morale, and with the help of militia units, especially in the South, the colonists kept up a war of attrition until support could arrive from France. By then, much like the United States in Vietnam almost two centuries later, the British found themselves outlasted and forced to abandon an unpopular war on foreign soil. The **Treaty of Paris**, signed at the end of 1783, granted the United States independence and generous territorial rights. (This Treaty of Paris is not to be confused with the Treaty of Paris that ended the French and Indian War or the Treaty of Paris that ended the Spanish-American War in 1898. Paris was all the rage as a treaty name, apparently.)

Neither the Declaration of Independence, with its bold statement that "all men are created equal," nor the revolution with its republican ideology, abolished slavery. These events also did not bring about a more egalitarian society. Like blacks, many women played a significant role in the Revolutionary War, either as "camp followers" or by maintaining households and businesses while the men were off fighting the Revolution. It would take another war to end slavery (the Civil War) and centuries of hard work toward progress to help bring about greater political and economic equality for women.

George Washington Versus Volunteer Militias

George Washington was one of the wealthiest men in America, and to a great extent his involvement with the independence movement grew out of his dissatisfaction with the mercantile system, which he felt was keeping him from expanding his fortune as much as he might have liked. The tobacco he sent to Britain never fetched the price he wanted, and the goods he received in return were too expensive and of shoddy quality. He wanted relief from British taxes and the freedom to sell to and buy from whomever he liked. The American Revolution was fueled in large part by libertarian sentiments such as these.

But after becoming commander of the Continental Army, Washington found that libertarian ideals sound terrific when you're a rich planter trying to fill your coffers, but don't work so well when you're trying to build a country or win a war. Washington pressed for a professional standing army, and demanded that the states raise money to pay the troops, but the libertarian-dominated Continental Congress replied that those ideas were precisely what they were fighting against and that Washington would have to make do with volunteers who paid their own way.

Revolution

The colonies did not wait to win their independence from England before setting up their own governments. As soon as the Declaration of Independence was signed, states began writing their own constitutions. In 1777 the Continental Congress sent the **Articles of Confederation**, the first national constitution, to the colonies for ratification. The colonists intentionally created little to no central government since they were afraid of ridding themselves of Britain's imperial rule only to create their own tyrannical government. The articles contained several major limitations, as the country would soon learn. For one, it did not give the national government the power to tax or to regulate trade. Furthermore, amendments to the articles required the unanimous consent of all the states, creating a situation in which one state could hold the others hostage to its demands. The Articles of Confederation were clearly more concerned with prohibiting the government from gaining too much power than with empowering it to function effectively.

With the end of the war, the colonies had other issues to confront as well. The decrease in England's power in the region opened a new era of relations with Native Americans. This new era was even more contentious than the previous one because a number of tribes had allied themselves with the Crown. Second-class citizens and noncitizens—namely, women and blacks—had made sacrifices in the fight for liberation, and some expected at least a degree of compensation. Abigail Adams wrote a famous letter to her husband pleading the case for women's rights in the new government; she reminded John to "remember the ladies and be more generous and favorable to them than your ancestors." The number of free blacks in the colonies grew during and after the war, but their increased presence among free whites was also accompanied by a growth of racist publications and legislation. Such conditions led to the early "ghettoization" of blacks and, for similar reasons, other minorities.

The problems with the Articles of Confederation became apparent early on. The wartime government, unable to levy taxes, tried to finance the war by printing more money, which led, naturally, to wild inflation. After the war, the British pursued punitive trade policies against the colonies, denying them access to West Indian markets and dumping goods on American markets. The government, unable to impose tariffs, was helpless. A protective tariff would impose duties on imported goods; the additional cost would be added to the selling price, thereby raising the cost of foreign products. By making domestic products cheaper than imports, most tariffs protected American manufacturers. Having just fought a war in part caused by taxes imposed by a central authority, the newly independent Americans were reluctant to give this power to their new federal government. In fact, the first protective tariff in United States history wasn't passed until 1816. The issue of the tariff exposed another source of tension within the new country—economic sectionalism—a major conflict that eventually led the new nation to civil war and continues to play a role in **partisan politics** to this very day.

Furthermore, when state governments dragged their heels in compensating loyalists for lost property, the British refused to abandon military posts in the States, claiming that they were remaining to protect the loyalists' rights. The government,

No Partying
The Framers of the Constitution disliked political parties and hoped to prevent them.

again, was powerless to expel them. Perhaps the rudest awakening came in the form of **Shays's Rebellion**. Lasting from August 1786 to January 1787, it started when an army of 1,500 farmers from western Massachusetts marched on Springfield to protest a number of unfair policies, both economic and political. They were armed and very angry, and they gave the elite class the wake-up call that the revolution might not be over yet. As with the earlier **Bacon's Rebellion** and later **Whiskey Rebellion**, this rebellion revealed lingering resentment on the part of the backcountry farmers toward the coastal elite. One thing that especially worried the wealthy, though, was that the Articles of Confederation had created a national government that was essentially powerless to stop such rebellions.

The government under the Articles was not totally without its successes, though. Its greatest achievements were the adoption of ordinances governing the sale of government land to settlers. Best known is the **Northwest Ordinance of 1787**, which also contained a bill of rights guaranteeing trial by jury, freedom of religion, and freedom from excessive punishment. It abolished slavery in the Northwest territories (northwest of the Ohio River and east of the Mississippi River, up to the Canadian border), and it also set specific regulations concerning the conditions under which territories could apply for statehood. Thus, the ordinance is seen as a forerunner to the Bill of Rights and other progressive government policies. It was not so enlightened about Native Americans, however; in fact, it essentially claimed their land without their consent. War ensued, and peace did not come until 1795 when the United States gained a military advantage over the Miami Confederacy, its chief Native-American opponent in the area. The Northwest Ordinance remained important long after the Northwest territories were settled because of its pertinence to the statehood process and to the issue of slavery.

FROM REVOLUTION TO THE BEGINNING OF THE TWENTIETH CENTURY

The Constitution

By 1787 it was clear that the federal government lacked sufficient authority under the Articles of Confederation. **Alexander Hamilton** was especially concerned that there was no uniform commercial policy and feared for the survival of the new republic. Hamilton convened what came to be known as the **Annapolis Convention**, but only five delegates showed up! Subsequently, Congress consented to a "meeting in Philadelphia" the following May for the sole purpose of "revising the Articles of Confederation." This meeting would eventually become the now-famous Constitutional Convention, comprising delegates from all states except Rhode Island, which met throughout the long, hot summer of 1787.

Much has been written about the framers of the Constitution. There were fifty-five delegates: all men, all white, many of whom were wealthy lawyers or landowners, many of whom owned slaves. They came from many different ideological backgrounds, from those who felt the Articles needed only slight adjustments to those who wanted to tear them down and start from scratch. **The New Jersey Plan** called for modifications, and it also called for equal representation from each state. **The Virginia Plan**, largely the brainchild of James Madison, called for an entirely new government based on the principle of **checks and balances** and for the number of representatives for each state to be based upon the population of the state, giving some states an advantage.

The convention lasted for four months, over the course of which the delegates hammered out a bundle of compromises, including the **Great Compromise** (also known as the **Connecticut Compromise**), which blended the Virginia Plan and the New Jersey plan to have a bicameral legislature, and the **Constitution**. This bicameral legislature included a lower house (the House of Representatives) elected by the people and the upper house (the Senate) elected by the state legislatures. (Direct election of senators, believe it or not, is a twentieth-century innovation.) The president and vice president were to be elected by the electoral college, not the citizens themselves.

The Constitution also laid out a method for counting slaves among the populations of Southern states for "proportional" representation in Congress, even though those slaves would not be citizens. This became known as the Three-Fifths Compromise, because each slave counted as three-fifths of a person. It also established three branches of government—the **executive**, **legislative**, and **judicial**—with the power of checks and balances on each other. Only 3 of the 42 delegates who remained in Philadelphia to the end refused to sign the finished document (two because it did not include a bill of rights).

Ratification of the Constitution was by no means guaranteed. Opposition forces portrayed the federal government under the Constitution as an all-powerful beast. These opponents, known as **Anti-Federalists**, tended to come from the backcountry and were particularly appalled by the absence of a bill of rights. Their position rang true in many of the state legislatures where the Constitution's fate lay, and some held out for the promise of the immediate addition of the **Bill of Rights** upon ratification. The **Federalist** position was forcefully and persuasively argued in **the Federalist Papers**, anonymously authored by **James Madison**, **Alexander Hamilton**, and **John Jay**. The Federalist Papers were published in a New York newspaper and were later widely circulated. They were critical in swaying opinion in New York, a large and therefore politically important state. (Virginia, Pennsylvania, and Massachusetts were the other powerhouses of the era.) The **Constitution** went into effect in 1789; the **Bill of Rights** was added in 1791.

Westward Expansion

One of the most significant events of the post-Revolution period in U.S. history was President Thomas Jefferson's purchase of the **Louisiana Territory** from the French government in 1803. When Spain gave New Orleans to the French in 1802, the government realized that a potentially troublesome situation was developing. The

Only three times (so far) has the popular vote in a presidential election failed to match the electoral outcome: in the Hayes-Tilden election of 1876, the Harrison-Cleveland election of 1888, and the Bush-Gore election of 2000.

The Federalist Papers
After the Constitutional Convention ended, Alexander Hamilton, James Madison, and John Jay wrote a series of newspaper articles supporting the Constitution. The articles were designed to persuade the states of the wisdom of a strong central government combined with autonomous political power retained by the states. Today, these essays are the primary source for understanding the original intent of the framers of the Constitution.

French, they knew, were more likely to take advantage of New Orleans' strategic location at the mouth of the Mississippi, almost certainly meaning that American trade along the river would be restricted. In hopes of averting that situation, Jefferson sent James Monroe to France. Monroe's mandate was to buy New Orleans for $2 million. Monroe arrived at just the right time. Napoleon was gearing up for war in Europe, and a violent slave revolt in Haiti against the French further convinced him to abandon French interests in the New World. The French offered to sell Monroe the whole Louisiana territory for $15 million.

Thomas Jefferson was now faced with a dilemma. As secretary of state under Washington, he had argued for a strict interpretation of the Constitution, thus limiting the power of the federal government to those powers specifically stated in the Constitution. Nowhere did the Constitution authorize the president to purchase land, yet clearly Jefferson could not pass up this opportunity to double the size of the United States. Ultimately, Jefferson resolved the issue by claiming his presidential power to negotiate treaties with foreign nations. His decision to purchase Louisiana without Congressional approval was not unanimously applauded: Some Federalists derided the deal as too expensive (though the land was three cents per acre). Some Republicans, led by John Randolph of Virginia, criticized Jefferson for violating Republican principles.

The Bill of Rights in a Nutshell

1. Freedom of religion, speech, press, assembly, and petition
2. Right to bear arms in order to maintain a well-regulated militia
3. No quartering of soldiers in private homes
4. Freedom from unreasonable search and seizure
5. Right to due process of law, freedom from self-incrimination, double jeopardy (being tried twice for the same crime)
6. Rights of accused persons; for example, the right to a speedy and public trial
7. Right of trial by jury in civil cases
8. Freedom from excessive bail and from cruel and unusual punishment
9. Rights not listed are kept by the people
10. Powers not listed are kept by the states or the people

Jefferson sent explorers, among them **Lewis and Clark**, to investigate the western territories, including much of what was included in the Louisiana territory. All returned with favorable reports, causing many pioneers to turn their attentions westward in search of land, riches, and economic opportunities. Those early explorers also reported back to Jefferson on the presence of British and French forts that still dotted the territory, garrisoned with foreign troops that had been (deliberately?) slow to withdraw after the regime changes of the previous half-century.

"The American continents, by the free and independent condition which they have assumed and maintain, are henceforth not to be considered as subjects for future colonization by any European powers."

— President James Monroe, declaring what came to be known as the Monroe Doctrine

Jefferson's second term as president was less successful, and the nation underwent a period of significant turbulence prior to and during the **War of 1812**. The postwar period ushered in a new wave of westward expansion. **John Quincy Adams**, son of former president John Adams, deftly negotiated a number of treaties that fixed U.S. borders and opened new territories. The United States acquired Florida from the Spanish by the Adams-Onis Treaty in 1819. Adams also had to handle international tensions caused by a series of revolutions in Central America and South America, as the inhabitants of those regions won their independence from Spain. Ultimately, events compelled Monroe and Adams to recognize the new nations. At the same time, they decided that America should assert its authority over the Western Hemisphere. The result was the **Monroe Doctrine**, a policy of mutual noninterference. You stay out of the Americas, Monroe told Europe, and we'll stay out of your squabbles. The Monroe Doctrine also claimed America's right to intervene anywhere in its own hemisphere, if it felt its security was threatened. No European country tried to intercede in the Americas following Monroe's declaration, and so the Monroe Doctrine *appeared* to work. No one, however, was afraid of the American military; Spain, France, and others stayed out of the Western Hemisphere because the powerful British navy made sure they did.

The Louisiana Purchase removed one major obstacle to U.S. western settlement, and the resolution of the War of 1812 removed another by depriving Native Americans of a powerful ally in Great Britain. By 1820 the United States had settled the region east of the Mississippi River and was quickly expanding west. Americans began to believe that they had a God-given right to the Western territories, an idea that came to be known as America's **Manifest Destiny**. Some took the idea of Manifest Destiny to its logical conclusion and argued that Canada, Mexico, and even all of the land in the Americas eventually would be annexed by the United States.

Western settlement was dangerous. The terrain and climate could be cold and unforgiving, and these settlers from the East were moving into areas that rightfully belonged to Native Americans and Mexicans, none of whom were about to cede their homes without a fight.

Texas presents a good case in point. When Mexico declared its independence from Spain in 1821, the new country included what is now Texas and much of the Southwest, including California. The Mexican government established liberal land policies to entice settlers, and tens of thousands of Americans (many of them cattle ranchers) flooded the region. In return for land, the settlers were supposed to become Mexican citizens, but they rarely did. Instead, they ignored Mexican law, including—and especially—the one prohibiting slavery. When Mexico attempted to regain control of the area, the settlers rebelled and declared independence from Mexico. It was during this period that the famous battle at the **Alamo** was fought (1836). For a while Texas was an independent country, called the **Republic of Texas.** The existence of slavery in the area guaranteed a Congressional battle over statehood, and Texas was not admitted to the Union until 1845.

Farther west and north, settlers were also pouring into the **Oregon Territory**. During the early 1840s, thousands of settlers traveled to the Willamette Valley, braving a six-month journey on the Oregon Trail. Again, the Americans were not the first ones in; not only was there a large Native American population, but the British were also there, claiming the territory for Canada. The Russians also staked a claim, and both the British and the Americans saw them as a threat. The Polk administration eventually settled the territorial dispute by signing a treaty with England.

By the late 1840s, though, those heading along the Oregon Trail had a new destination—**California**. In 1848 the discovery of gold in the California mountains set off the **Gold Rush**, attracting more than 100,000 people to the Golden State in just two years. Most of these people did not strike it rich, but they settled the area after discovering that it was very hospitable to agriculture. Its access to the Pacific Ocean allowed major cities such as San Francisco to develop as important trade centers.

Slavery

As mentioned in the discussion of early American colonization above, the extensive use of African slaves in the American colonies began when colonists from the Caribbean settled the Carolinas. Until then, indentured servants and, in some situations, enslaved Native Americans had mostly satisfied labor requirements in the colonies. As tobacco-growing and, in South Carolina, rice-growing operations expanded, more laborers were needed than indenture could provide. Events such as Bacon's Rebellion had also shown landowners that it was not in their best interest to have an abundance of landless, young, white males in their colonies either.

Enslaving Native Americans was difficult; they knew the land, so they could easily escape and subsequently were difficult to find. In some Native American tribes, cultivation was considered women's work, so gender was another obstacle to enslaving the natives. And as noted, Europeans brought diseases that often decimated the Native Americans, wiping out 85 to 95 percent of the native population. Southern landowners turned increasingly to African slaves for labor. Unlike Native Americans, African slaves did not know the land, so they were less likely to escape. Removed from their homelands and communities, and often unable to communicate with one another because they were from different regions of Africa, black slaves initially proved easier to control than Native Americans. The dark skin of the West Africans who made up the bulk of the enslaved population made it easier to identify slaves on sight, and the English colonists came to associate dark skin with inferiority, rationalizing Africans' enslavement.

The majority of the slave trade, right up to the Revolution, was directed toward the Caribbean and South America. Still, during that period more than 500,000 slaves were brought to the English colonies (of the over 10 million brought to the New World). By 1790 nearly 750,000 blacks were enslaved in England's North American colonies.

The shipping route that brought the slaves to the Americas was called the **Middle Passage** because it was the middle leg of the **triangular trade route** among the colonies, Europe, and Africa. Conditions for the Africans aboard were brutally inhumane, so intolerable that some committed suicide by throwing themselves overboard. Many died of sickness, and others died during insurrections. It was not unusual for one-fifth of the Africans to die on board. Most, however, reached the New World, where conditions were only slightly better. Mounting criticism (primarily in the North) of the horrors of the Middle Passage led Congress to end American participation in the Atlantic slave trade on January 1, 1808. Slavery itself would not end in the United States until 1865.

Slavery flourished in the South. Because of the nature of the land and the short growing season, the Chesapeake and the Carolinas farmed labor-intensive crops such as **tobacco**, **rice**, and **indigo**, and plantation owners there bought slaves for this arduous work. Slaves' treatment at the hands of their owners was often vicious and at times sadistic. While slavery never really took hold in the North the same way it did in the South, slaves were used on farms in New York, New Jersey, and Pennsylvania, in shipping operations in Massachusetts and Rhode Island, and as domestic servants in urban households, particularly in New York City. Although northern states would take steps to phase out slavery following the Revolution, there were still slaves in New Jersey at the outbreak of the Civil War. In both regions, only the very wealthy owned slaves. The vast majority of people remained at a subsistence level.

The new period of westward expansion in the nineteenth century resulted in a national debate over slavery, as would every period of expansion to follow until the Civil War resolved the slavery question. In 1820 the Union consisted of 22 states. Eleven allowed slavery; eleven prohibited it. Missouri was the first state to be carved out of the Louisiana Purchase, and its application for statehood threatened the balance, particularly in the U.S. Senate. Henry Clay brokered the **Missouri Compromise**, which (1) admitted Missouri as a slave state, (2) carved a piece out of Massachusetts—Maine—and admitted Maine as a free state, (3) drew a line along the 36°30′ parallel across the Louisiana Territory, and (4) established the southern border of Missouri as the northernmost point at which slavery would then be allowed in the western territories of the United States, except of course for Missouri itself, which in a way violated the Missouri Compromise since it was north of the line. The compromise was the first in a series of measures forestalling the Civil War. It also split the powerful Democratic-Republican coalition, ending its 20-year control of national politics.

Slavery grew to be an ever more controversial issue during the time of Jacksonian Democracy (ca. 1828–1854). As the Northern abolition movement grew stronger, the South experienced several slave revolts, which resulted in the use of more brutal disciplinary measures by slaveholders. The most famous of the insurrections was **Nat Turner's Rebellion**. Turner, a well-read preacher, had a vision, and he took this vision as a sign from God that a black liberation movement would succeed. As a result, he rallied a gang that proceeded to kill and then mutilate the corpses of 60 whites. In retaliation, 200 slaves were executed, some with no connection at all to the rebellion. Fearful that other slaves would hear of and emulate Turner's exploits, Southern states passed a series of restrictive laws, known as **black codes**, prohibiting blacks from congregating and learning to read. Other state laws even prevented whites from questioning the legitimacy of slavery. After Turner's Rebellion, Virginia's House of Burgesses debated ending bondage but did not pass a law.

Before the 1830s, few whites fought aggressively for the liberation of the slaves. The Quakers believed slavery to be morally wrong and argued for its end. Most other antislavery whites, though, sought gradual abolition, coupled with colonization, a movement to return blacks to Africa. For example, the **American Colonization Society**, established in 1816, sought to repatriate slaves to the newly-formed country of Liberia in Africa. Many politicians supported the cause, including Henry Clay. The religious and moral fervor that accompanied the Second Great Awakening, however, persuaded more and more whites, particularly Northerners, that slavery was a great evil. As in other reform movements, women played a prominent role.

White abolitionists divided into two groups. Moderates wanted emancipation to take place slowly and with the cooperation of slave owners. **Immediatists**, as their name implies, wanted emancipation at once. Most prominent among white immediatists was **William Lloyd Garrison,** who began publishing a popular abolitionist newspaper called the *Liberator* in 1831 and helped found the **American Anti-slavery Society** in 1833. His early subscribers were mostly free blacks, but as time passed, his paper caught on with white abolitionists as well.

Garrison fought against slavery and against moderates as well, decrying their plans for black resettlement in Africa as racist and immoral. Garrison's persistence and powerful writing style helped force the slavery issue to the forefront. His message, as you may imagine, did not go over well everywhere; some Southern states banned the newspaper, and others prohibited *anyone* from discussing emancipation. When congressional debate over slavery became too heated, Congress adopted a **gag rule** that automatically suppressed discussion of the issue. It also prevented Congress from enacting any new legislation pertaining to slavery. The rule, which lasted from 1836 to 1844, along with Southern restrictions on free speech, outraged many Northerners and convinced them to join the abolition movement.

The abolition movement existed prior to 1830, but it had been primarily supported by free blacks such as **David Walker**. Abolition associations formed in every large black community to assist fugitive slaves and publicize the struggle against slavery; these groups met at a national convention every year after 1830 to coordinate strategies. In the 1840s, **Frederick Douglass** began publishing his influential newspaper *The North Star*. Douglass, an escaped slave, gained fame as a gifted writer and eloquent advocate of freedom and equality; his *Narrative of the Life of Frederick Douglass* is one of the great American autobiographies. Other prominent black abolitionists included **Harriet Tubman**, who escaped slavery and then returned south repeatedly to help more than 300 slaves escape via the **underground railroad** (a network of hiding places and "safe" trails); and **Sojourner Truth**, a charismatic speaker who campaigned for emancipation and women's rights.

Abolitionists' determination and the South's inflexibility pushed the issue of slavery into the political spotlight. Westward expansion, and the question of whether slavery would be allowed in the new territories, forced the issue further. Together, they set in motion the events that led up to the Civil War.

The Civil War

For many people of the era, the Civil War was not solely (or even explicitly) about slavery. It is worth noting that Missouri, Kentucky, Maryland, and Delaware, the Border States, were slave states that fought for the Union. Except for active abolitionists, most Northerners believed they were fighting to preserve the Union. Most Southerners described their cause as fighting for their states' rights to govern themselves. But slavery was the issue that had caused the argument over states' rights to escalate to war. Lincoln's views on slavery evolved throughout the 1850s and the Civil War, but as late as 1862, Lincoln stated, "If I could save the Union without freeing any slaves I would do it, and if I could save the union by freeing all the slaves I would do it…. What I do about slavery, and the colored race, I do because I believe it helps to save the Union."

The Civil War took place not only on the battlefields but also in political, economic, and social realms. Although you do not need to know the military details of any specific battles for the TASC test, you should know the political or diplomatic consequences of battles like Gettysburg or Antietam, and you do need to know how political, social, and economic conditions influenced the outcome of the war.

Ironically, as the Southern states fought to maintain the right to govern themselves locally, the Confederate government brought them under greater central control than they had ever experienced. Jefferson Davis, the leader of the Confederacy, understood the North's considerable advantages in population, transportation, and economics, and he knew that the weak, poorly organized state governments of the South could not mount an effective defense. Davis took control of the Southern economy, imposing taxes and using the revenues to spur industrial and urban growth; he took control of the railroads and commercial shipping; and he created a large government bureaucracy to oversee economic developments. Davis, in short, forced the South to compensate quickly for what it had lost when it cut itself off from Northern commerce. When Southerners opposed his moves, he declared martial law and suspended the writ of *habeas corpus*, a traditional protection against improper imprisonment, in order to maintain control. Lincoln was upsetting Northerners with some of the exact same steps, but the use of the presidential power chafed especially badly in the Confederacy, where many believed they had seceded precisely to avoid the federal government commanding too much power.

Davis had some success in modernizing the Southern economy, but the Confederacy lagged too far behind in industrialization to catch up to the Union. Rapid economic growth, furthermore, brought with it rapid **inflation**. Prices rose so quickly that paychecks and payments for crops became worthless almost as soon as they were made, plunging many Southerners into poverty. In 1862 the Confederacy imposed **conscription** (a military draft), requiring many small farmers to serve in the Confederate Army. This act caused even greater poverty in the country, as many families could not adequately tend their farms without their men.

Confederate conscription also created class conflict. The government allowed the wealthy to hire surrogates to perform military service in their place and exempted anyone who owned more than twenty slaves from military service (on the grounds that the large plantations these men ran fed the Confederacy and its army). In effect, the wealthy did not have to serve, while the poor had no choice. As a result, **class tensions** increased, leading ultimately to widespread desertions from the Confederate Army. Toward the end of the war, it also led many Southerners in small towns to ignore the government and try to carry on as if there was no war. Many resisted when asked to feed, clothe, or house passing troops.

The Northern economy received a boost from the war as the demand for war-related goods, such as uniforms and weapons, spurred manufacturing. The loss of Southern markets harmed the economy at first, but soon the war economy brought about a boom period. A number of entrepreneurs became extremely wealthy; many succumbed to the temptations of greed, overcharging the government for services and products (**war profiteering**). Some sold the Union government worthless, shoddy food and clothing, while government bureaucrats looked the other way for the price of a bribe. Corruption was fairly widespread, eventually prompting a yearlong congressional investigation.

Like the South, the North experienced a period of accelerated inflation, although Northern inflation was nowhere as extreme as its Southern counterpart. (In the North, prices rose between 10 and 20 percent annually; in the South, the inflation rate was well over 300 percent.) Workers, worried about job security in the face of mechanization and the decreasing value of their wages, formed **unions**. Businesses, in return, blacklisted union members, forced new employees to sign contracts in which they promised not to join unions, and used violence to break strikes. The Republican Party, then (as now) believing that government should help businesses but regulate them as little as possible, supported business in its opposition to unions.

Lincoln, like Davis, oversaw a tremendous increase in the power of the central government during the war. He implemented economic development programs without waiting for congressional approval, championed numerous government loans and grants to businesses, and raised tariffs to protect Union trade. He also suspended the writ of *habeas corpus* in the border states, to make it easier to arrest secessionists, especially in Maryland. During the war, Lincoln initiated the printing of a **national currency**. Lincoln's able treasury secretary, Salmon P. Chase, issued **greenbacks**, government-issued paper money that was a precursor to modern currency.

As previously stated, neither the Union nor the Confederacy initially declared the Civil War to be a war about slavery. The Constitution protected slavery where it already existed, so many opponents (including Republicans) were opposed to the *extension* of slavery into the new territories. As a presidential candidate, Lincoln had argued for gradual emancipation, compensation to slaveholders for liberated slaves, and the colonization of freed slaves somewhere outside the United States, perhaps in Africa. When the Union dissolved and the South left Congress, Lincoln was faced with a legislature much more progressive in its thoughts on slavery than he was. The **Radical Republican** wing of Congress wanted immediate emancipation. To that end, the radicals introduced the **confiscation acts** in Congress. The first (1861) gave the government the right to seize any slaves used for "insurrectionary purposes." The second (1862) was much wider in scope, allowing the government to liberate any slave owned by someone who supported the rebellion, even if that support was limited to paying taxes to the Confederate government. The second confiscation act, in effect, gave the Union the right to liberate all slaves. This act had little effect, however, because Lincoln refused to enforce it.

Soon after, however, Lincoln took his first cautious steps toward emancipation. The primary reason was pretty simple: Slaves indirectly supported the Southern war effort. They grew the crops and cooked the meals that kept the rebel troops fed. Therefore any strategy the Union army adopted had to include capturing slaves as a key element. But what to do with them once they were captured? Lock them up somewhere and return them to their owners after the war? They had to be freed, or the government of the United States would become the world's biggest slaveholder. And there were other advantages of making the freedom of the slaves one of the side effects of Union victory. One was that it kept Britain and France out of the war. Jefferson Davis had hoped that these countries would support the Confederacy in order to keep receiving shipments of Southern cotton, but once Lincoln made it explicit that Union victory would mean freedom for the slaves, European governments dared not attempt to come to the aid of the rebels for fear of being quickly toppled by an outraged public. Another advantage was that emancipation would provide a new source of troops for the Union side: "The bare sight of fifty thousand armed and drilled black soldiers on the banks of the Mississippi would end the rebellion at once," Lincoln mused. But he dared not make this move until after a Northern victory, lest it appear like a desperate response to the defeats skilled Southern generals were inflicting upon the Union. The moment came in September 1862, with the Union victory at Antietam.

In the aftermath of the battle, Lincoln issued the **Emancipation Proclamation**. Note that the Emancipation Proclamation, for all intents and purposes, actually freed no slaves. Instead, it stated that on January 1, 1863, the government would liberate all slaves residing in those states still "in rebellion." Throughout the war, Lincoln refused to acknowledge secession and insisted on referring to the Confederate states as "those states in rebellion." The Proclamation did not liberate the slaves in the border states such as Maryland, nor did it liberate slaves in Southern counties already under the control of the Union Army. Again, legally, Lincoln had no power to abolish slavery in areas governed by the U.S. Constitution. Abolitionists complained that the Proclamation liberated slaves only where the Union had no power to enforce emancipation and maintained slavery precisely where it could liberate the slaves. The Proclamation also allowed Southern states to rejoin the Union *without* giving up slavery. On the positive side, the Emancipation Proclamation finally declared that the Civil War was, for the Union, a war against slavery, and thus changed the purpose of the war, much as the Declaration of Independence had changed the purpose of the Revolutionary War.

Not until two years later, while campaigning for reelection, did Lincoln give his support to complete emancipation. Just before the Republican convention, Lincoln lobbied for a party platform that called for a constitutional amendment prohibiting slavery; the result was the **Thirteenth Amendment**. After his reelection, Lincoln considered allowing defeated Southern states to reenter the Union and to vote on the Thirteenth Amendment. He tried to negotiate a settlement with Southern leaders along those lines at the **Hampton Roads Conference**. Lincoln also offered a five-year delay on implementing the amendment if it passed, as well as $400 million in compensation to slave owners. Jefferson Davis's commitment to complete Southern independence scuttled any chance of compromise.

As the 1864 presidential election approached, popular opinion in both the North and South favored an end to the war. Lincoln's opponent, General George McClellan, campaigned on a peace platform. In the South, citizens openly defied the civil authority.

It should be reemphasized that less than one percent of the Southern population owned more than 100 slaves, and as the war dragged on, many small, non-slave-holding farmers resented the Confederacy and the war, which they now believed was being waged merely to protect the planter aristocracy's lifestyle. In the North, some "War Democrats" conceded that the war was necessary to preserve the Union. Others, called the **Copperheads**, accused Lincoln of instigating a national social revolution and criticized his administration's policies as a thinly disguised attempt to destroy the South. Nowhere, however, was opposition to the war more violent than in New York City, where racial, ethnic, and class antagonisms exploded into draft riots in July of 1863. Irish immigrants, mostly the poor working-class who were already victims of **nativism**, resented being drafted into a war being fought to end slavery. Many immigrants feared that once freed, former slaves would migrate into Northern cities and compete with them for low-paying labor jobs. And yet, both sides fought on.

Just when a stalemate might have forced an end to the war, things began improving for the North. Victories throughout the summer of 1864 played a large part in helping Lincoln gain reelection. By the early spring of 1865, a Union victory was virtually assured, and the government established the **Freedman's Bureau** to help newly liberated blacks establish a place in postwar society. The Bureau helped with immediate problems of survival (food, housing) and developed social institutions, such as schools. Some historians see the Freedman's Bureau as the first federal, social welfare program in U.S. history. In April 1865 the Confederate leaders surrendered. John Wilkes Booth assassinated Lincoln just five days later, with devastating consequences for the reunited nation.

The Civil War was fought at enormous cost. More than 3 million men fought in the war, and of them, more than 500,000 died. At least as many were seriously wounded. Both governments ran up huge debts during the war, and much of the South was ravaged by Union soldiers. During **Sherman's March** from Atlanta to the sea in the fall of 1864, the Union Army burned everything in its wake (to destroy Confederate morale and deplete the South's material resources), foreshadowing the wide-scale warfare of the twentieth century. From a political perspective, the war permanently expanded the role of government. On both sides government grew rapidly to manage the economy and the war.

Reconstruction

At war's end, three major questions faced the reunited nation. First, under what conditions would the Southern states be readmitted to the Union? Second, what would be the status of blacks in the postwar nation? Black leaders hoped that their service in the military would earn blacks equal rights. The newly liberated slaves, called freedmen, were primarily interested in the chance to earn wages and own property. And third, what should be done with the rebels?

Reconstruction may be seen as both a time period and a process. As a time period, Reconstruction usually refers to the years between 1865 and 1877, that is, from the end of the Civil War until the end of military reconstruction when the Union army withdrew from the South. The *process* of reconstruction, however, was complicated and complex, and some argue it continues to this day. Reconstruction involved readmitting the Southern states that had seceded from the Union; physically reconstructing and rebuilding Southern towns, cities, and property that had been destroyed during the war; and finally, integrating newly freed blacks into American society. It is this last process that has proven to be most difficult.

The process of reconstruction had begun even before the Civil War ended, although not without controversy. As president of the United States and commander-in-chief of the armed forces, Lincoln had claimed that he had the authority to determine the conditions under which the Southern states might be readmitted to the Union. Lincoln had no intention of punishing the South and wanted to end the war and reunite the nation quickly and painlessly, as his immortal words from his second inaugural address indicate: "With malice toward none, with charity for all, with firmness in the right, as God gives us to see the right, let us strive on to finish the work we are in, to bind up the nation's wounds, to care for him who shall have borne the battle and for his widow and his orphan, to do all which may achieve and cherish a just and lasting peace among ourselves and with all nations."

Lincoln's plan is usually referred to as the **Ten-Percent Plan** and simply required that 10 percent of those voters who had voted in the 1860 election swear an oath of allegiance to the Union and accept emancipation through the Thirteenth Amendment. These men would then reorganize their state government and reapply for admission into the Union. Congress had another vision, however. It viewed the Southern states as "conquered territory" and as such, **Radical Republicans** in Congress argued, were under the jurisdiction of Congress, not the president. Most Republicans agreed that Lincoln's plan was too lenient and enacted the **Wade-Davis Bill** in July of 1864. This act provided that former Confederate states be ruled by a military governor and required 50 percent of the electorate to swear an oath of allegiance to the United States. A state convention would then be organized to repeal their ordinance of secession and abolish slavery within their state.

It should be noted that neither Lincoln's Ten-Percent Plan nor the Wade-Davis Bill made any provisions for black suffrage. Lincoln pocket-vetoed the Wade-Davis Bill, effectively destroying it. (A pocket veto can occur only at the end of a congressional session. If the president does not sign a bill within 10 days and Congress adjourns within those 10 days, the bill dies and must be reintroduced when Congress reconvenes. Unlike a regular veto, which requires the president to explain his objections to a bill and can subsequently be overridden, a pocket veto does not need to be explained nor is it subject to another congressional vote. It cannot be overridden.) Lincoln was assassinated the following year.

With Lincoln's assassination, Vice President Andrew Johnson assumed the presidency. Johnson, a Southern Democrat, had opposed secession and strongly supported Lincoln during his first term. In return, Lincoln rewarded Johnson with the vice presidency. When the war ended, Congress was in recess and would not reconvene for eight months. That left the early stages of Reconstruction entirely in Johnson's hands.

Johnson had lifted himself from poverty and held no great love for the South's elite planters, and at first he seemed intent on taking power away from the old aristocracy and giving it to the yeomen. **Johnson's Reconstruction Plan**, which was based on a plan approved by Lincoln, called for the creation of provisional military governments to run the states until they were readmitted to the Union. It also required all Southern citizens to swear a **loyalty oath** before receiving amnesty for the rebellion. However, it barred many of the former Southern elite (including plantation owners, Confederate officers, and government officials) from taking that vow, thus prohibiting their participation in the new governments. According to this plan, the provisional governments would hold state constitutional conventions, at which time the states would have to write new constitutions eliminating slavery and renouncing secession. Johnson did not require the states to enfranchise blacks by giving them the vote.

The plan did not work, mostly because Johnson pardoned many of the Southern elite who were supposed to have been excluded from the reunification process. After the states drafted new constitutions and elected new governments, former Confederate officials were again in positions of great power. Furthermore, many of their new constitutions were only slight revisions of previous constitutions. Southern legislators also passed new black codes limiting freedman's rights to assemble and travel, instituting curfews, and requiring blacks to carry special passes. In the most egregious instances, state legislatures simply took their old slave codes and replaced the word slaves with freedmen. When Congress reconvened in December 1865, the new Southern senators included the vice president of the Confederacy and other Confederate officials. Northern congressmen were not pleased. Invoking its constitutional right to examine the credentials of new members, Congress voted not to seat the new Southern delegations. Next, it set about examining Johnson's Reconstruction plan.

Congress was divided among conservative Republicans, who generally agreed with Johnson's plan; moderates, who were a large enough contingent to swing a vote in one or the other direction; and Radical Republicans. The Radical Republicans wanted to extend democracy in the South. Following the Civil War, most important political positions were held by appointees; very few officials were directly elected. (Of course, women could not vote and black men could vote only in a few northern states at this time.) The most radical among the Radical Republicans advocated a reconstruction program that punished the South for seceding. Historians of the time suggested that revenge was the real motivation behind the passage of the Thirteenth Amendment, although contemporary historians have dismissed this idea. Under General Sherman's Special Field Order No. 15, land seized from the Confederates was to be redistributed among the new freedmen, but President

Andrew Johnson rescinded Sherman's order, and the idea of giving freedmen "40 acres and a mule" never regained much ground.

All Republicans agreed that Johnson's Reconstruction needed some modification, but Johnson refused to compromise. Instead, he declared Reconstruction over and done with, vetoing a compromise package that would have extended the life of the Freedman's Bureau and enforced a uniform civil rights code on the South. Congress overrode Johnson's vetoes, which only increased tension between the two branches of the federal government.

In response, the radicals drew up the plan that came to be known as Congressional Reconstruction. Its first component was the Fourteenth Amendment to the Constitution. The amendment (1) stated that if you are born in the United States, you are a citizen of the United States and you are a citizen of the state where you reside; (2) prohibited states from depriving any citizen of "life, liberty, or property without due process of law"; (3) prevented states from denying any citizen "equal protection of the law"; (4) gave states the choice either to give freedmen the right to vote or to stop counting them among their voting population for the purpose of congressional apportionment; (5) barred prominent Confederates from holding political office; and (6) excused the Confederacy's war debt.

The first three points remain the most significant, to this very day, and are the basis for most lawsuits involving discrimination and civil rights. In fact, through a series of cases over the years, most of the first ten amendments have been extended to the states through the due process clause of the Fourteenth Amendment. It is helpful to remember that the Bill of Rights protects the individual from the federal government, while the Fourteenth Amendment protects you from the state government. The Fourteenth Amendment was intended to clarify the status of newly freed slaves, address the issue of citizenship raised by the Dred Scott decision, and limit the effects of the black codes. The radicals hoped to force states to either extend suffrage to black men or lose power in Congress. In the **Swing Around the Circle** public speaking tour, Johnson campaigned against the amendment and lost. In the congressional election of 1866, the North voted for a Congress more heavily weighted toward the radical end of the political spectrum.

The new Congress quickly passed the **Military Reconstruction Act of 1867**. It imposed martial law on the South; it also called for new state constitutional conventions and forced the states to allow blacks to vote for convention delegates. The act also required each state to ratify the Fourteenth Amendment and to send its new constitution to Congress for approval. Aware that Johnson would oppose the new Reconstruction, Congress then passed a number of laws designed to limit the president's power. As expected, Johnson did everything in his power to counteract the congressional plan. The conflict reached its climax when the House Judiciary Committee initiated **impeachment proceedings** against Johnson, ostensibly for violating the Tenure of Office Act (which stated that the president had to secure the consent of the Senate before removing his appointees once they'd been approved by that body; Johnson had fired Secretary of War Edwin Stanton, a Radical Republican) but really because he was getting in the way of Reconstruction. Johnson was acquitted by one vote in the Senate, but the trial rendered Johnson politically impotent, and he served the last few months of his presidency with no hope of re-election.

With a new president, **Ulysses S. Grant**, in office, Congress forged ahead in its efforts to remake the South. The **Fifteenth Amendment**, proposed in 1869, finally required states to enfranchise black men. (Women's suffrage would have to wait another half-century.) Ironically, the Fifteenth Amendment passed only because Southern states were required to ratify it as a condition of reentry into the Union; a number of Northern states opposed the amendment.

Reconstruction had its share of successes while the North occupied the South. New state constitutions officially allowed all Southern men to vote (previous constitutions had required voters to own property) and replaced many appointed government positions with elected positions. New Southern governments, directed mostly by transplanted Northern Republicans, blacks, and Southern moderates, created public schools and those social institutions such as orphanages popularized in the North during the reform movement of the 1830s. The new governments also stimulated industrial and rail development in the South through loans, grants, and tax exemptions. The fact that blacks were serving in Southern governments represented a huge step forward, given the seemingly insurmountable restrictions placed on blacks only a few years earlier, though it would prove to be only a temporary victory.

However, ultimately, Reconstruction failed. Although government industrialization plans helped rebuild the Southern economy, these plans also cost a lot of money. High tax rates turned public opinion, already antagonistic to Reconstruction, even more hostile. Opponents waged a propaganda war against Reconstruction, calling Southerners who cooperated **scalawags** and Northerners who ran the programs **carpetbaggers**. (The name came from the suitcases they carried, implying they had come to the South merely to stuff their bags with ill-gotten wealth.) Many who participated in Reconstruction were indeed corrupt, selling their votes for money and favors.

It should be noted that Northerners were just as guilty as Southerners of corruption. The period following the Civil War is also known as **The Gilded Age**, to suggest the tarnish that lay beneath the layer of gold. Political scandal was not new at the time, and in fact, Grant's administration was wracked with political scandals and intrigue; Grant himself was supposedly innocent and oblivious to the goings on in his administration. Grant had no political experience when he became president; in fact, he was elected because he was a popular war hero, not an experienced political leader. Like Jackson, Grant appointed his friends and supporters to governmental positions, not necessarily those men most qualified, let alone those with the most integrity.

At the end of the Civil War, the former slaves were thrust into an ambiguous state of freedom. Most reacted cautiously, remaining on plantations as sharecroppers where they had been relatively well treated but fleeing from those with cruel overseers. Many set out in search of family members from whom they had been separated. The Freedman's Bureau helped them find new jobs and housing and provided money and food to those in need. The Freedman's Bureau also helped establish schools at all levels for blacks, among them Fisk University and Howard University. Unfortunately, the Freedman's Bureau was terribly underfunded and had little impact once military reconstruction came to an end.

When it became evident that the government would not redistribute land, blacks looked for other ways to work their own farms. The Freedman's Bureau attempted to establish a system in which blacks contracted their labor to whites, but the system failed. Instead, blacks preferred **sharecropping**, in which they traded a portion of their crop in return for the right to work someone else's land. The system worked at first, but unscrupulous landowners eventually used the system as a means of keeping poor farmers in a state of near slavery and debt. Abuses of the sharecropping system grew more widespread at the end of Reconstruction, at which point no court would fairly try the case of a sharecropper against a landowner. Sharecropping existed well into the middle of the twentieth century and actually included more whites than blacks.

Disenchantment with white society led many freedmen to found communities as far removed from the sphere of whites as possible. Black churches continued to serve as another means by which the black community could bond and gain further autonomy. When Reconstruction ended, many blacks anticipated the fate that awaited them in the South and left. The **Great Migration** into Northern cities like Chicago and Detroit would not take place, however, until World War I.

Robber Barons

Remember our discussion of the Industrial Revolution in the previous chapter? As more and faster machines became available to manufacturers, businessmen in the eighteenth and early nineteenth centuries discovered that their cost per unit decreased as the number of units they produced increased. The more raw product they bought, the cheaper the suppliers' asking price. The closer to capacity they kept their new, faster machines running, the less the cost of labor and electricity per product. The lower their costs, the cheaper they could sell their products. The cheaper the product, the more they sold. That, simply put, is the concept of **economies of scale**.

The downside of this new business practice was that it required employees to work as efficiently, and repetitively, as machines. **Assembly line production** had begun to take hold when Eli Whitney developed interchangeable parts, but it reached a whole new level in Ford's plants in the early twentieth century. This type of production required workers to perform a single task over and over, often (before labor reform) for 12 to 14 hours a day. Factories were dangerous; machine malfunctions and human error typically resulted in more than 500,000 injuries to workers per year.

The overriding concern for businessmen, however, was that profits continued to increase by huge margins. Although government made some efforts to regulate this rapid growth, these were tentative. Furthermore, the government remained uncertain as to how to enforce regulations, and widespread corruption existed among those bureaucrats charged with enforcing the regulations. Finally, the courts of the era (especially the Supreme Court) were extremely pro-business. With almost no restraint, businesses such as railroad companies followed the path that led to greater economies of scale, which meant larger and larger businesses. This was known as **corporate consolidation**. Not surprisingly, the people known as the "captains of industry" to their fans (and the "robber barons" to others), who owned and controlled the new manufacturing enterprises, became extremely rich and powerful during this period.

One new form of business organization was called a **holding company**. A holding company owned enough stock in various companies to have a controlling interest in the production of raw material, the means of transporting that material to a factory, the factory itself, and the distribution network for selling the product. The logical conclusion is a **monopoly**, or complete control of an entire industry. One holding company, for example, gained control of 98 percent of the sugar refining plants in the United States. While the company did not control the entire sugar industry, it did control one very important aspect of it.

The most common forms of business consolidation at the end of the nineteenth century were **horizontal** and **vertical integration**. One is legal; one is not; both were practiced by "captains of industry" during the Gilded Age. For all intents and purposes, horizontal integration created monopolies within a particular industry, the best-known example being Standard Oil, created by John D. Rockefeller. In horizontal integration, several smaller companies within the same industry are combined to form one, larger company, either by being bought out legally or by being destroyed through ruthless business practices such as cutthroat competition or pooling agreements. Many of these business practices are illegal today because of antitrust legislation passed at the turn of the last century. Vertical integration remains legal, however, provided the company does not become either a trust or a holding company, but rather allows other companies in the same industry to survive and compete in the marketplace. In vertical integration, one company buys out all the factors of production, from raw materials to finished product. For example, Swift Premium might control the stockyards, the slaughterhouse, and the processing and packaging plants but still compete with Oscar Mayer or Hebrew National.

Business 101
A *trust* is the collective control of an industry by a small group of separate corporations working together. A *monopoly* is the control of an entire industry by a single corporation. Microsoft is one modern corporation that has dealt with accusations of operating a monopolistic enterprise.

Numerous problems arose because of this consolidation of power. First, rapid growth required lots of money. Businessmen borrowed huge sums, and when their businesses occasionally failed, bank failures could result. During the last quarter of the nineteenth century, the United States endured one major financial panic per decade. Although irresponsible investors caused the panics, the lower classes suffered the most, as jobs and money became scarce. Second, monopolies created a class of extremely powerful men whose interests clashed with those of the rest of society. As these businessmen grew more powerful, public resentment increased, and the government responded with laws to restrict monopolies (which the courts, in turn, weakened). The back-and-forth battle among the public, the government, and the courts is best exemplified by the Sherman Antitrust Act of 1890. Public pressure led to the passage of this law forbidding any "combination…or conspiracy in the restraint of trade."

Unfortunately, the wording of the Sherman Antitrust Act was ambiguous enough to allow the pro-business Supreme Court at the time to interpret the law as it saw fit. For example, in 1895 the Court ruled that E. C. Knight, a company that controlled 98 percent of the sugar refining plants in the United States, did not violate the Sherman Antitrust Act because local manufacturing was not subject to congressional regulation of interstate commerce. On the other hand, labor unions were often found to be "in restraint of free trade" and declared illegal. This loophole was closed during Wilson's administration in 1914 with the passage of the Clayton Antitrust Act, which made allowances for collective bargaining.

Another response to public pressure for reform came from industrialists themselves. Steel mogul **Andrew Carnegie** promoted a philosophy based on the work of Charles Darwin. Using Darwin's theory of evolution as an analogy, Carnegie argued that in business, as in nature, unrestricted competition allowed only the "fittest" to survive. This theory was called **Social Darwinism**. Aside from the fact that Carnegie's analogy to Darwin's theory was at best dubious, it also lacked consistency; while Carnegie argued against government regulation, he supported all types of government assistance to business (in the form of tax abatements, grants, tariffs, and so on). Carnegie further argued that the concentration of wealth among a few was the natural and most efficient result of capitalism. Carnegie also asserted that great wealth brought with it social responsibility. Dubbing his belief the **Gospel of Wealth**, he advocated philanthropy, as by building libraries and museums or funding medical research, but not charity. Some of his peers were as generous; others were not.

Populism

Alongside industrialization and the growing influence of the "robber barons" in the eighteenth and early nineteenth centuries, another movement was brewing in the United States: **Populism**. In the period after the Civil War, production on all fronts—industrial and agricultural—increased. Greater supply accordingly led to a drop in prices. For many farmers, lower prices meant trouble, as they were locked into long-term debts with fixed payments. Looking for a solution to their problem, farmers came to support a more generous money supply. An increase in available money, they correctly figured, would make payments easier. It would also cause inflation, which would make the farmers' debts (held by Northern banks) worth less. Not surprisingly, the banks opposed the plan, preferring for the country to use only gold to back its money supply.

The farmers' plan called for the liberal use of silver coins, and because silver was mined in the West, this plan had the added support of Western miners along with that of Midwestern and Southern farmers. Thus, the issue had a regional component. Because it pitted poor farmers against wealthy bankers, it also had elements of class strife. Although a complicated matter, the money issue was potentially explosive.

The "silver versus gold" debate provided an issue around which farmers could organize. They did just that. First came the **Grange Movement**, which, founded in 1867, boasted more than a million members by 1875. The Grangers started out as cooperatives, with the purpose of allowing farmers to buy machinery and sell crops as a group and, therefore, reap the benefits of economies of scale. Soon, the Grangers endorsed political candidates and lobbied for legislation. The Grangers ultimately died out due to lack of money, but they were replaced by **Farmers' Alliances**. The Farmers' Alliances were even more successful than the Grange movement, and they soon grew into a political party called the **People's Party**, the political arm of the **Populist** movement.

The People's Party held a convention in 1892. (The platform it drew up presented many of the ideas that would later be championed by the Progressives.) Aside from supporting the generous coinage of silver, the Populists called for government ownership of railroads and telegraphs, a graduated income tax, direct election of U.S. senators, and shorter workdays. Although their 1892 presidential candidate, James Weaver, came in third, he won more than 1 million votes, awakening Washington to the growing Populist movement.

As Cleveland took office in 1893, the country entered a four-year financial crisis. Hard economic times made Populist goals more popular, particularly the call for easy money. (Most people at the time, after all, had no money at all.) Times got so bad that even more progressive (some would say radical) movements gained popularity; in 1894 the **Socialists**, led by **Eugene V. Debs**, gained support. By 1896 the Populists were poised for power. They backed Democratic candidate **William Jennings Bryan** against Republican nominee **William McKinley**, and Bryan ran on a strictly Populist platform; he based his campaign on the call for **free silver**. He is probably best remembered for his "Cross of Gold" speech (a typical multiple-choice question). He argued that an easy money supply, though inflationary, would loosen the control that Northern banking interests held over the country. He lost the campaign; this, coupled with an improved economy, ended the Populist movement.

U.S. History I Drill

Now that you've learned all about the early years of American history, let's try some practice questions. To check your answers, register your book at **PrincetonReview.com/cracking** and download the Chapter Drill Answers and Explanations supplement.

1. Read the quotation from *Plessy v. Ferguson* (1896). Then answer the question.

> Laws permitting, and even requiring, their separation in places where they are liable to be brought into contact do not necessarily imply the inferiority of either race to the other, and have been generally, if not universally, recognized as within the competency of State Legislatures in the exercise of their police power. The most common instance of this is connected with the establishment of separate schools for white and colored children, which has been held to be a valid exercise of legislative power.

The above quote best exemplifies which of the following ideas?

   A civil rights and racial equality

   B separation of powers

   C racism

   D separate but equal

2. Which one of the following statements about the Spanish conquest of the Americas is most accurate?

   A African slavery was a direct result of Spanish settlements in Florida.

   B Early native civilizations in Mexico introduced Spanish explorers to cattle ranching and wheat cultivation.

   C Christopher Columbus was not the first European to have explored North America.

   D Due to racial prejudice, Spanish explorers shunned intermarriage with native people.

3. The Puritans believed that the freedom to practice religion should be extended to

   A Puritans only

   B all Protestants only

   C all Christians only

   D all Christians and Jews only

4. A major weakness of the Articles of Confederation was that they

   A created a too-powerful chief executive

   B did not include a mechanism for their own amendment

   C made it too difficult for the government to raise money through taxes and duties

   D denied the federal government the power to mediate disputes between states

5. **Read the quotation from John L. O'Sullivan's "The Great Nation of Futurity" (1839). Then answer the question.**

> The far-reaching, the boundless future will be the era of American greatness. In its magnificent domain of space and time, the nation of many nations is destined to manifest to mankind the excellence of divine principles; to establish on earth the noblest temple ever dedicated to the worship of the Most High—the Sacred and the True. Its floor shall be a hemisphere—its roof the firmament of the star-studded heavens, and its congregation a Union of many Republics, comprising hundreds of happy millions, calling, owning no man master, but governed by God's natural and moral law of equality, the law of brotherhood—of "peace and good will amongst men."

Which of the following best states the principle described above?

A Colonists were destined to leave the British Empire because of the distance between the New World and England.

B Women are biologically predestined to lives of child rearing and domestic labor.

C America's expansion to the West Coast was inevitable and divinely sanctioned.

D The abolition of slavery in the United States was certain to come about because slavery was immoral.

6. **By what means did the United States take possession of the Oregon Territory?**

A The United States was granted the territory in a postwar treaty with France.

B The United States bought it from the Native Americans who lived there.

C U.S. settlers were the first to arrive in the region; they claimed it for their country.

D Great Britain ceded it to the United States as part of a negotiated treaty.

7. **Read the quotation by Frederick Douglass (1857). Then answer the question.**

> In one view the slaveholders have a decided advantage over all opposition. It is well to notice this advantage—the advantage of complete organization. They are organized; and yet were not at the pains of creating their organizations. The State governments, where the system of slavery exists, are complete slavery organizations. The church organizations in those States are equally at the service of slavery; while the Federal Government, with its army and navy, from the chief magistracy in Washington, to the Supreme Court, and thence to the chief marshalship at New York, is pledged to support, defend, and propagate the crying curse of human bondage. The pen, the purse, and the sword, are united against the simple truth, preached by humble men in obscure places.

Which of the following groups would be most likely to support the perspective of Frederick Douglass illustrated in the quote above?

A Southern Democrats in the 1880s

B Western ranchers in the 1850s

C Southern farmers in the 1830s

D Northern Republicans in the 1860s

8. **Which of the following was most directly a cause of the success of the Populist party?**

 A Western farmers and ranchers favored conservation and organized to promote the National Parks system.

 B The growth of corporate power and banking interests inspired rural activists to lobby for political reform.

 C Western farmers resisted the mechanization of agriculture and resented government interference in rural affairs.

 D After the Civil War, westward migration slowed, causing a long-term recession in many Western territories.

Chapter 22
U.S. History II

In this chapter, we'll guide you through the key topics related to the more recent years of American history on the Social Studies portion of the TASC test. We will focus here on two broad categories: the early twentieth century, including the two major world wars, and the period from the end of World War II to the present day. Following the content lessons, we'll give you some practice questions.

THE EARLY TWENTIETH CENTURY

By the early twentieth century, the Populist movement that we discussed in the previous chapter had largely dissipated, but not before raising the possibility of reform through government. The Populists' successes in both local and national elections encouraged others to seek change through political action. Building on Populism's achievements and adopting some of its goals (e.g., direct election of senators, opposition to monopolies), the **Progressives** came to dominate the first two decades of twentieth-century American politics. While the Populists were mainly aggrieved farmers who advocated radical reforms, the Progressives were urban, middle-class reformers who wanted to increase the role of government in reform while maintaining a capitalist economy.

One of the reasons Populism failed is that its constituents were mostly poor farmers whose daily struggle to make a living made political activity difficult. The **Progressives** achieved greater success in part because theirs was an urban, middle-class movement. Its proponents started with more economic and political clout than the Populists. Furthermore, Progressives could devote more time to the causes they championed. Also, because many Progressives were Northern and middle class, the Progressive movement did not intensify regional and class differences, as the Populist movement had.

The roots of Progressivism lay in the growing number of associations and organizations at the turn of the century. The National Woman Suffrage Association, the American Bar Association, and the National Municipal League are some of the many groups that rallied citizens around a cause or profession. Most of these groups' members were educated and middle class; the blatant corruption they saw in business and politics offended their senses of decency, as did the terrible plight of the urban poor.

Over the course of two decades, Progressives achieved great successes on both the local and national levels. They campaigned to change public attitudes toward education and government regulation in much the same way reformers of the previous century had campaigned for public enlightenment on the plight of orphans, prostitutes, and the mentally infirm.

Double Duty

William Howard Taft is the only former President to also serve on the Supreme Court of the United States. He was the tenth Chief Justice, from 1921 to 1930.

The most prominent Progressive leader was President **Theodore Roosevelt**. McKinley was a conservative president, and Roosevelt was expected to emulate his policies, though rumors had begun to circulate that Roosevelt harbored progressive sympathies. After he convincingly won the 1904 election on the strength of his handling of Latin American affairs, Roosevelt began boldly enacting a progressive agenda. He was the first to successfully use the **Sherman Antitrust Act** against monopolies, and he did so repeatedly during his term, earning the nickname "the Trustbuster." Among Roosevelt's other progressive achievements were tightening food and drug regulations, creating national parks, and broadening the government's power to protect land from overdevelopment. (Roosevelt, an avid outdoorsman, was a particularly impassioned conservationist.) Presidents Taft and Wilson continued to promote Progressive ideals. **William Howard Taft** spearheaded the drive for two constitutional amendments, one that instituted a national income tax (the Sixteenth Amendment) and another that allowed for the direct election of senators (the Seventeenth Amendment). He pursued monopolies even more aggressively than Roosevelt. On the foreign policy front, Taft is best known for **dollar diplomacy,** the attempt to secure favorable relationships with Latin American and East Asian countries by providing monetary loans.

The Progressive Era is a turning point in American history because it marks the ever-increasing involvement of the federal government in our daily lives. It's no coincidence that Prohibition took effect during this era. The third Progressive president was Woodrow Wilson, a Democrat who had to distinguish himself from Teddy Roosevelt, who ran for reelection (after Taft's one term) on the Bull Moose ticket in 1912. While Roosevelt's policies are often referred to as New Nationalism, Wilson referred to his ideas and policies as New Freedom. Thomas Jefferson had suggested limiting the power of the federal government in order to protect individual liberty, but Wilson now argued that the federal government had to assume greater control over business to protect man's freedom. For Roosevelt there were "good trusts and bad trusts." For Wilson trusts were monopolies, which violated freedom for workers and consumers. Wilson was committed to restoring competition through greater government regulation of the economy and lowering the tariff.

Progressivism lasted until the end of World War I, at which point the nation, weary from war and from the devastating **Spanish Flu** outbreak of 1918, stepped back from its moral crusade. The war had torn apart the Progressive coalition; pacifist Progressives opposed the war while others supported it. A **Red Scare**, heightened by the Russian Revolution (more on this in Chapter 23), further split the Progressive coalition by dividing the leftists from the moderates. Moreover, the Progressive movement had achieved many of its goals, and as it did, it lost the support of those interest groups whose ends had been met. Some say that the Progressive movement was brought to an end, at least in part, by its own success.

The United States as a World Power

Roosevelt differed from his predecessor on domestic policy, but he concurred with his foreign policy. Roosevelt was, if anything, an even more devout imperialist than McKinley had been. In 1903 the Roosevelt administration strong-armed Cuba into accepting the **Platt Amendment**, which essentially committed Cuba to American control. Under Platt's stipulations, Cuba could not make a treaty with another nation without U.S. approval, and the United States had the right to intervene in Cuba's affairs if domestic order dissolved. A number of invasions and occupations by the Marine Corps resulted. For ten of the years between 1906 and 1922, the American military occupied Cuba, arousing anti-American sentiments on the island.

Roosevelt's actions were equally interventionist throughout Central America. During his administration, the country set its sights on building a canal through the Central American isthmus; a canal would greatly shorten the sea trip from the East Coast to California. Congress approved a plan for a canal through **Panama**, at the time a province of Colombia. Because Colombia asked for more than the government was willing to spend, the United States encouraged Panamanian rebels to revolt and then supported the revolution. Not surprisingly, the new Panamanian government gave the United States a *much* better deal. Because American commercial interests were so closely tied to the canal's successful operation, the United States military became a fixed presence throughout the region. During the next twenty years, troops intervened repeatedly, claiming that Latin American domestic instability constituted a threat to American security. This assertion came to be known as the **Roosevelt Corollary to the Monroe Doctrine** and is often referred to as the Big Stick Policy.

American foreign policy continued to adhere to the Monroe Doctrine, which asserted America's right to assume the role of an international police force and intervene anywhere in the Western Hemisphere where it felt its national security was at stake. It also stated that the United States wanted no part of Europe's internal disputes. American commitment to that aspect of the Monroe Doctrine would soon be tested, as Europe started down the path leading to **World War I**. Complicating matters was the fact that the United States and England were quickly forming a close alliance. To America's benefit, England had not opposed its many forays into Central American politics, although it could have. The British were not merely being friendly; they were trying to line up the United States as a potential ally in their ongoing rivalry with Germany, the other great European power of the era.

World War I

Fortunately, you do not need to know the tangled series of events that led Europe into war in 1914. You do, however, have to know about the United States' initial efforts to stay out of the war and the events that ultimately drew it into the conflict. Woodrow Wilson won the election of 1912, a three-way race in which the third-party candidate, Theodore Roosevelt, outpolled Taft, the Republican incumbent. Wilson entered office with less than a commanding mandate—only 40 percent of the electorate voted for him. However, with regard to the simmering European conflict, he and the electorate were of the same mind: The United States should stay out of it.

When war broke out in Europe in August 1914, Wilson immediately declared the U.S. policy of **neutrality**. Neutrality called for America to treat all the belligerents fairly and without favoritism. It was Wilson's hope that the United States would help settle the conflict and emerge as the world's arbiter. However, the neutrality policy posed several immediate problems, owing to America's close relationship with England and relatively distant relationship with Germany and Austria-Hungary. A number of Wilson's advisors openly favored the Allies (led by the British).

The situation quickly grew more complicated. England's strategic location and superior navy allowed it to impose an effective **blockade** on shipments headed for Germany, particularly those coming from the United States. Protests proved futile; the British government impounded and confiscated American ships. They then paid for the cargo, reducing the pressure that American merchants would otherwise have put on the U.S. government to take action against the blockade.

Germany attempted to counter the blockade with **submarines**, or **U-boats**. According to contemporaneous international law, an attacker had to warn civilian ships before attacking. Submarines could not do this because doing so would eliminate their main advantage. Furthermore, when the Germans attacked civilian ships, it was usually because those ships were carrying military supplies. The Germans announced that they would attack any such ship, but that did not satisfy Wilson, who believed that the Germans should adhere to the strict letter of international law. Thus, when the German submarines sank the passenger ship *Lusitania* in 1915 (killing 1,198 passengers, including 128 Americans), the action provoked the condemnation of both the government and much of the public. That the *Lusitania* was carrying tons of ammunition to the British was a fact that received much less public attention than did the loss of 1,198 innocent lives.

The sinking of the Lusitania, and the bad publicity it generated, led the Germans to cease submarine warfare for a while. Britain made steady gains, however, and as the U-boats were Germany's most effective weapon, the Germans resumed their use. In 1916, while Wilson was campaigning for reelection on the slogan "He kept us out of war," Germany sank another passenger liner, the *Arabic*. In response, Wilson, while still maintaining neutrality, asked Congress to put the military into a state of preparedness for war, just in case. While most Americans wanted to stay out of the war, popular support for entry was beginning to grow.

Then, in early 1917, the British intercepted a telegram from German Foreign Minister Zimmermann. The telegram, imaginatively called the **Zimmermann telegram**, outlined a German plan to keep the United States out of the European war. The telegram stated that *if* Mexico were to declare war on the United States, Germany would provide Mexico help in regaining the lands lost in the Mexican War. The telegram also suggested that Germany would help Japan if they, too, wanted to go to war against America. Published in newspapers around the country, the telegram convinced many Americans that Germany was trying to take over the world. Although the public was by no means universally behind the idea of war, the balance had shifted enough so that within a month, America would declare war on Germany.

As is often the case during wartime, the government's power expanded greatly during the three years America was involved in World War I. The government took control of the telephone, telegraph, and rail industries, and a massive bureaucracy arose to handle these new responsibilities. The **War Industry Board (WIB),** created to coordinate all facets of industrial and agricultural production, sought to guarantee that not only the United States but also the rest of the Allies would be well supplied. (European production had been drastically cut by the war.) The WIB had mixed success; like most large bureaucracies, it was slow and inefficient.

The government also curtailed individual civil liberties during the war. In response to the still-sizable opposition to U.S. involvement, Congress passed the **Espionage Act** in 1917 and the **Sedition Act** in 1918. The Espionage Act prohibited anyone from using the U.S. mail system to interfere with the war effort or with the draft that had been instituted under the **Selective Service Act of 1917** upon America's entry into the war. The Sedition Act made it illegal to try to prevent the sale of war bonds or to speak disparagingly of the government, the flag, the military, or the Constitution. Like the Alien and Sedition Acts in the late 1790s, both laws violated the spirit of the First Amendment but were worded vaguely, giving the courts great leeway in their interpretation.

American participation in the war tipped the balance in the Allies' favor, and two years after America's entry, the Germans were ready to negotiate a peace treaty. Wilson wanted the war treaty to be guided by his **Fourteen Points**, his plan for world peace delivered to Congress in January of 1918, before the end of the war. The Fourteen Points called for free trade through lower tariffs and freedom of the seas; a reduction of arms supplies on all sides; and the promotion of self-determination, both in Europe and overseas—in other words, the end of colonialism. The plan also called for the creation of the **League of Nations**, a mechanism for international cooperation much like today's United Nations. Wilson's Fourteen Points served as a basis for initial negotiations, but the negotiations soon took a different direction.

The European Allies wanted a peace settlement that punished Germany, and ultimately they got it. Under the **Treaty of Versailles**, Germany was forced to cede German and colonial territories to the Allies, to disarm, to pay huge reparations, and to admit total fault for the war, despite other nations' roles in starting it. Most historians agree that by leaving Germany humiliated and in economic ruin, the Treaty of Versailles helped to set the stage for World War II. Although much of Wilson's plan was discarded, the Treaty of Versailles did create the League of Nations. Wilson hoped that the League would ultimately remedy the peace settlement's many flaws, but when he returned home, a rude surprise awaited him. According to the Constitution, the president has the power to negotiate treaties with foreign nations, but these treaties are subject to Senate ratification. This illustrates the principles of **separation of powers** and **checks and balances**.

At the center of the conflict was the debate over the League of Nations, particularly Article X of the League's covenant, which many people believed curtailed America's ability to act independently in foreign affairs, specifically Congress's power to declare war. The Senate split into three groups: Democrats, who sided with Wilson and were willing to accept America's entrance into the League of Nations; a group of Republicans who were totally opposed to the League and were known as the Irreconcilables; and the Reservationists, a group of Republicans led by **Henry Cabot Lodge**, Chairman of the Senate Foreign Relations Committee and Wilson's political nemesis and intellectual rival.

Much has been made of Wilson's stubbornness and inability to compromise, and in particular, his refusal to accept what were known as the Lodge Reservations. Ultimately, the Democrats and Irreconcilables joined forces and defeated the treaty, which had been amended to include the changes suggested by Henry Cabot Lodge and the Reservationists. Thus, the United States was not a signatory of the

Treaty of Versailles, nor did it ever join the League of Nations, an international organization envisioned by an American President to maintain world peace. Weary of war, America was receding into a period of isolationism. The public wanted less interaction with Europe, not more, as the League would have required. Wilson tried to muster popular support for the treaty. However, while campaigning, Wilson suffered a major stroke, thereby ending whatever chance the treaty may have had for ratification. Many people wonder whether the League of Nations would have been more successful in preventing World War II had the United States been a member.

The Great Depression

After World War I the American economy went through a brief slump and then started to grow rapidly. By 1922 America was hitting new peaks of prosperity every day. The invention of a practical electric motor was largely responsible for the economic boom; like computers in the 1990s, electric motors became essential to work and home environments, driving industrial machines and household appliances. With the new prosperity, other industries arose to serve the growing middle class in its search for the trappings of affluence.

As the age of progressive reform ended, many Americans became more comfortable with the idea of large, successful businesses. Some of these businesses, such as department stores, offered both convenience and reasonable prices. Others, such as the automobile industry, offered products that made life more convenient and conferred status on their owners.

The government, which had worked closely with business leaders as part of the war effort, also grew to be more **pro-business** during the era. Government regulatory agencies (such as the Federal Trade Commission) more often assisted business than regulated it. Labor unions fell further out of public favor, particularly when they struck against industries necessary to keeping industrial America running smoothly. Unions striking for higher wages and safer work conditions in the steel, coal, and railroad industries were suppressed by federal troops. The Supreme Court overturned a minimum wage law for women and nullified child labor restrictions.

All three of the era's presidents—**Warren Harding**, **Calvin Coolidge**, and **Herbert Hoover**—pursued pro-business policies and surrounded themselves with like-minded advisors. Like Grant, Harding had the misfortune of surrounding himself with corrupt advisors; several of his cabinet members wound up in prison. The most infamous incident of his administration was the **Teapot Dome Scandal**, in which oil companies bribed the secretary of the interior in order to drill on public lands. Conservative on economic issues, Harding proved more liberal than his predecessor Wilson on issues of civil liberty. He supported anti-lynching laws and tried to help farmers (who were benefiting less from the new economy than were middle-class city dwellers) by providing more money for farm loans. Harding died in office, and Coolidge, his vice president, assumed the presidency. When Coolidge ran for the presidency in 1924, he turned the election into a debate on the economy by running on the slogan "Coolidge prosperity." Coolidge won easily and, following his mandate, continued Harding's conservative economic policies. He also pushed for lower income-tax rates. We will discuss Hoover's presidency later, when we discuss the causes of the Great Depression.

The pro-business atmosphere of the era led to a temporary decline in the popularity of labor unions; membership levels dropped throughout the decade. Also contributing to this drop were the efforts of businesses to woo workers with pension plans, opportunities for profit sharing, and company parties and other events designed to foster a communal spirit at work. Businessmen hoped that, if they offered some such benefits, they could dissuade workers from organizing and demanding even more. Such practices were often referred to as **welfare capitalism**.

In 1928 the Republicans nominated **Herbert Hoover**. Like Coolidge, Hoover was able to parlay a strong economy into an easy victory. During his campaign, Hoover predicted that the day would soon come when no American would live in poverty. He turned out to be very wrong.

In October 1929 the bottom fell out of the stock market, and this was one of the reasons for the Great Depression, but not the main reason. Prices dropped, and no matter how far they dropped, nobody wanted to buy. Hoover and his advisers underestimated the damage that the stock market crash would eventually cause. Convinced that the economy was sound, Hoover reassured the public that only stock traders would be hurt because of their irresponsible speculation. (Traders had been allowed to buy on margin, which meant that they might have to put up only 10 or 20 percent of the cost of each stock, allowing them to borrow against future profits that might or might not materialize. Margin buying is a destabilizing practice that was made illegal soon after the crash.) Unfortunately, among those speculators were huge banks and corporations, which suddenly found themselves on the verge of bankruptcy and unable to pay employees or guarantee bank deposits.

Other factors contributed to plunging the nation into a deep depression. Immediately following World War I, the carnage of the conflict, along with Germany's disastrous attempts to satisfy its reparations obligations under the Treaty of Versailles, had put Europe's economy, and much of the rest of the world's, into a depression. Domestically, though, manufacturers and farmers had been overproducing for years, creating large inventories. This led factories to lay off workers and made the farmers' crops worth much less on the market. Furthermore, production of new consumer goods was outstripping the public's ability to buy them. Supply so exceeded demand for so many goods, that this might be the main underlying cause for the Great Depression, ultimately leading to deflation, unemployment, and business failures. Finally, government laxity in regulating large businesses had led to the concentration of wealth and power in the hands of a very few businessmen. When their businesses failed, many people were thrown out of work.

The Depression had a calamitous effect on tens of millions of Americans. People lost their jobs as their employers went bankrupt or, to avoid bankruptcy, laid off the majority of workers. People lost their life savings as thousands of banks failed, and many lost their homes when they could not keep up with mortgage payments. The homeless built shantytowns, sarcastically called **Hoovervilles**. In rural areas farmers struggled to survive as produce prices dropped more than 50 percent. Furthermore, a prolonged drought afflicted the Great Plains area of the Midwest, turning the region into a giant **Dust Bowl**. The situation encouraged agrarian unrest; farmers fought evictions and foreclosures by attacking those who tried to enforce them. Farmers also conspired to keep prices at farm auctions low and then returned the auctioned property to its original owner. In addition, they formed the **Farmers' Holiday Association**, which organized demonstrations and threatened a nationwide walkout by farmers in order to raise prices.

At first Hoover opposed any federal relief efforts because he believed they violated the American ideal of "rugged individualism," but as the Depression worsened, he initiated a few farm assistance programs and campaigned for federal works projects (such as the Hoover Dam and the Grand Coulee Dam) that would create jobs. He hoped that raising tariffs would help American business, but the **Hawley-Smoot Tariff** actually worsened the economy. The Hawley-Smoot Tariff was the highest protective tariff in U.S. history, and it was enacted during one of the worst economic depressions ever.

Hoover's most embarrassing moment came in 1932 when Congress considered early payment of benefits to World War I veterans. Tens of thousands of impoverished veterans and their families, calling themselves the **Bonus Expeditionary Force (BEF),** came to Washington to lobby for the bill. When the bill was narrowly defeated, many refused to leave. They squatted in empty government offices or built shanties and stayed through the summer. In July Hoover ordered the Army to expel them, which Douglas MacArthur chose to do with excessive force. Employing the cavalry and attacking with tear gas, Army forces drove the veterans from D.C. and then burned their makeshift homes. One hundred people died during the attack, including two babies who suffocated from exposure to tear gas.

News of the Army attack on the BEF killed any chance Hoover had for re-election, partly because he had taken the heat for MacArthur's actions. Nonetheless, by the summer of 1932, he had already secured the Republican nomination. He ran a campaign stressing his traditional conservative values. (His main concession was to accept the repeal of Prohibition; Hoover had opposed repeal during his first term.) His opponent, New York Governor **Franklin D. Roosevelt**, argued for a more interventionist government. Roosevelt also promised relief payments to the unemployed, which Hoover had opposed throughout his term. Roosevelt won the election easily.

FDR may have been elected to four terms as president, but his last two victories were not without controversy. So much so that, in 1951, the Twenty-second Amendment set a limit of two terms for all future presidents.

World War II

In his inaugural address, Roosevelt declared war on the Depression, and he asked the country to grant him the same broad powers that presidents exercise during wars against foreign nations. He also tried to rally the public's confidence. In the most famous line of the speech, Roosevelt declared, "The only thing we have to fear is fear itself—nameless, unreasoning, unjustified fear." Both a powerful presidency and the people's confidence in Roosevelt played a large part in the implementation of his sweeping reforms, called the **New Deal**.

In the decade that followed World War I, American foreign policy objectives were aimed primarily at promoting and maintaining peace and have been described as "independent internationalism" rather than "isolationism." The **Washington Conference** (1921–1922) gathered eight of the world's great powers; the resulting treaty set limits on stockpiling armaments and reaffirmed the Open Door Policy toward China. In 1928, a total of 62 nations signed the **Kellogg-Briand Pact**, which condemned war as a means of foreign policy. Although it contained no enforcement clauses, the Kellogg-Briand Pact was widely considered a good first step toward a postwar age.

All the while, Roosevelt poured money into the military—just in case. As it became more apparent that Europe was headed for war, Roosevelt lobbied for a repeal of the arms embargo stated in the first **Neutrality Act** (1935) so that America could help arm the Allies (primarily England, France, and, later, the Soviet Union). From the outset of the war until America's entry in 1941, Roosevelt angled the country toward participation, particularly when Poland fell to German troops and other countries followed in rapid succession. In 1940 Hitler invaded France, and a German takeover of both France and England appeared a real possibility. The chance that America might soon enter the war convinced Roosevelt to run for an unprecedented third term. Again, he won convincingly.

Within the limits allowed by the neutrality acts that had been passed as a way to keep the United States out of foreign wars, Roosevelt worked to assist the Allies. He found creative ways to supply them with extra weapons and ships; he appointed pro-Ally Republicans to head the Department of War and the Navy; and he instituted the nation's first peacetime military draft. It becomes increasingly difficult to describe U.S. foreign policy as isolationist by the 1940s. In 1941 Roosevelt forced the **Lend-Lease Act** through Congress, which permitted the United States to "lend" armaments to England, which no longer had money to buy the tools of war. Roosevelt sent American ships into the war zone to protect Lend-Lease shipments, an act which could easily have provoked a German attack.

"Yesterday, December 7, 1941—a date which will live in infamy—the United States of America was suddenly and deliberately attacked by naval and air forces of the Empire of Japan."

—President Franklin Delano Roosevelt, 1941

Given all this activity in the European theater, it seems odd that America's entry to the war came not in Europe but in Asia. Japan entered into an alliance (called the **Tripartite Pact**) with Italy and Germany in 1940. By 1941 France had fallen to Germany, and the British were too busy fighting Hitler to block Japanese expansion, which had continued south into French Indochina (modern-day Vietnam, Cambodia, and Laos). The United States responded to Japanese aggression by cutting off trade to Japan, which was dependent on foreign imports. The embargo included oil, which Japan needed to fuel its war machine. Despite peace talks in November of 1941 between the United States and Japan to avoid war, the United States had broken Japan's secret communication codes and knew that Japan was planning an attack but did not know the location. The Japanese attacked **Pearl Harbor**, Hawaii, on December 7, and U.S. participation in the war began.

Complicated military strategy and the outcome of key battles played a big part in World War II. Fortunately, you do not have to know much about them for the TASC test; nor do you need to know about the many truly unspeakable horrors the Nazis perpetrated on Europe's Jews, gypsies, homosexuals, and dissidents. You should know about the various wartime conferences, however, when the Allies met to discuss military strategy and the eventual postwar situation. It was no secret that the Grand Alliance between the Soviet Union and the West was tenuous at best, held together by the thread of a common enemy but threatened by Stalin's impatience at the Allies' delay in opening a "second front" while the Soviets bore the brunt of the Nazi onslaught.

The first meeting of the **big three** (Roosevelt, Churchill, and Stalin) took place in the Iranian capital of Tehran in November of 1943. It was here that they planned the Normandy invasion, **D-Day**, and agreed to divide a defeated Germany into occupation zones after the war. Stalin also agreed to enter the war against Japan once Hitler had been defeated. The Allies fought the Germans primarily in the Soviet Union and in the Mediterranean until early 1944, when Allied forces invaded occupied France (on D-Day). The Soviet Union paid a huge price in human and material loss for this strategy and after the war sought to recoup its losses by occupying Eastern Europe. In the Pacific, both sides incurred huge numbers of casualties. The Allies eventually won a war of attrition against the Germans, and the Americans accelerated victory in the East by dropping two atomic bombs on Japan.

As the war neared its end in Europe, the apparent victors—the Allies—met to discuss the fate of postwar Europe. In February of 1945, the Allied leaders met at **Yalta** and in effect redrew the world map. By this time the Soviet army occupied parts of Eastern Europe, a result of the campaign to drive the German army out of the Soviet Union.

Stalin wanted to create a "buffer zone" between the Soviet Union and Western Europe; he wanted to surround himself with nations that were "friendly" toward the government in Moscow. Because of the presence of the Red Army, Stalin was given a free hand in Eastern Europe, a decision the other Allies would later regret, with the promise to hold "free and unfettered elections" after the war. Despite this promise, Soviet tanks rolled into Romania three weeks after Yalta, thus beginning the establishment of Soviet **satellites** and the descent of the **Iron Curtain**. (The Iron Curtain was a metaphor coined by Winston Churchill in 1946 to describe the symbolic division of Eastern and Western Europe, thus the origins of the Cold War following World War II.)

The Allies agreed on a number of issues concerning borders and postwar settlements. They also agreed that once the war in Europe ended, the USSR would declare war on Japan. Toward the end of the war, the Allies agreed to help create the **United Nations** to mediate future international disputes. The Allies met again at **Potsdam** to decide how to implement the agreements of Yalta. This time, **Harry S. Truman** represented the United States, as Roosevelt had died in April. Things did not go as well at Potsdam; with the war's end closer and the Nazis no longer a

The United Nations
Woodrow Wilson's dream of an international body to legislate diplomatic differences emerged after World War II as the United Nations. Founded in 1945, the United Nations originally began with 51 member countries whose guiding principles were international law and security, economic development, and social equity. It was created in the hopes that an international adjudicating body would prevent the world from ever seeing another world war. The five permanent members of the Security Council are those countries (or their successor states) that came out of World War II as its most powerful victors: the United States, the People's Republic of China, Russia, France, and the United Kingdom.

As of 2011, there were 193 member countries.

threat, the differences between the United States and the Soviet Union were growing more pronounced.

Some argue that American-Soviet animosity prompted Truman's decision to use the **atomic bomb** against the Japanese. (By this argument, America feared Soviet entry into the Asian war where the Soviets might then attempt to expand their influence, as they were doing in Eastern Europe. Along the same line of reasoning, one could assert that the United States wanted to put on a massive display of power to intimidate the Soviets.) However, the manner in which the war in the Pacific had been fought to that point also supported Truman's decision. The Japanese had fought tenaciously and remained powerful despite the long war; casualty estimates of an American invasion of Japan ran upward of 500,000. Some military leaders estimated that such an invasion would not subdue Japan for years. In August the United States dropped two atomic bombs, first on **Hiroshima** and then three days later on **Nagasaki**. The Japanese surrendered soon after.

POST-WORLD WAR II

The end of World War II raised two major issues. The first concerned the survival of the combatants; with the exception of the United States, the nations involved in World War II had all seen fighting within their borders, and the destruction had been immense. The second issue involved the shape of the new world and what new political alliances would be formed. This question would become the major source of contention between the world's two leading political-economic systems, capitalism and communism.

The stakes in this power struggle, called the **Cold War** (because there was no actual combat as there is in a "hot war"), were high. Though the major powers (the United States and Soviet Union) didn't enter into combat in the Cold War, the United States did fight hot "proxy" wars in Korea and Vietnam during this time. The American economy was growing more dependent on exports; American industry also needed to import metals, a process requiring (1) open trade and (2) friendly relations with those nations that provided those metals. In addition, with many postwar economies in shambles, competition for the few reasonably healthy economies grew fiercer. Finally, those countries that were strongest before the war—Germany, Japan, and Great Britain—had either been defeated or seen their influence abroad greatly reduced. The United States and the Soviet Union emerged as the two new superpowers. Although they were allies during World War II, the war's end exposed the countries' many ideological differences, and they soon became enemies.

The Cold War

The differences between Soviet and American goals were apparent even before the war was over, but became even clearer when the Soviets refused to recognize Poland's conservative government-in-exile. (The Polish government had moved to

England to escape the Nazis; this government was backed by the United States.) A communist government took over Poland. Within two years pro-Soviet communist coups had also taken place in Hungary and Czechoslovakia. The propaganda in the United States and USSR during this period reached a fever pitch. In each country the other was portrayed as trying to take over the world for its own sinister purposes.

Then, in 1947, communist insurgents threatened to take over both Greece and Turkey, but England could no longer prop up these nations. In a speech before Congress in which he asked for $400 million in aid to the two countries, Truman asserted, "I believe it must be the policy of the United States to support free peoples who are resisting attempted subjugation by armed minorities or outside pressures." This statement, called the **Truman Doctrine,** became the cornerstone of a larger policy, articulated by George Kennan, called **containment.** The idea of containment came from what is known as the **Long Telegram**, which Kennan sent to Washington from his duty station in Germany, in 1946. This policy said that the United States would not instigate a war with the Soviet Union, but it would come to the defense of countries in danger of Soviet takeover. The policy aimed to prevent the spread of communism and encourage the Soviets to abandon their aggressive strategies.

Meanwhile, the United States used a tried-and-true method to shore up its alliances—it gave away money. The **Marshall Plan**, named for Secretary of State George Marshall, sent more than $12 billion to Europe to help rebuild its cities and economy. In return for that money, of course, countries were expected to become American allies. Although the Marshall Plan was offered to Eastern Europe and the Soviet Union, no countries in the Soviet sphere participated in the program, as Stalin viewed the initiative as further evidence of U.S. imperialism. The United States also formed a mutual defense alliance with Canada and a number of countries in Western Europe called the **North Atlantic Treaty Organization** (**NATO**) in 1949. Truman did not have an easy time convincing Congress that NATO was necessary; remember, from the time of Washington's Farewell Address, American sentiment has strongly favored avoiding all foreign entanglements.

The crisis in **Berlin** the previous year, however, helped convince Congress to support NATO. The crisis represented a culmination of events after World War II. In 1945 Germany had been divided into four sectors, with England, France, the United States, and the USSR each controlling one. Berlin, though deep in Soviet territory, had been similarly divided. Upon learning that the three Western Allies planned to merge their sectors into one country and to bring that country into the Western economy, the Soviets responded by imposing a **blockade** on Berlin. Truman refused to surrender the city, however, and ordered airlifts to keep that portion under Western control supplied with food and fuel. The blockade continued for close to a year, by which point the blockade became such a political liability that the Soviets gave it up. Don't confuse the **Berlin Blockade** with the **Berlin Wall**. The Berlin Blockade occurred when the Soviets closed off access to the city during the Truman administration in 1948, while the Soviets erected the Berlin Wall in 1961 during the Kennedy administration (1961–1963) to divide the city between the East and the West. Constructed of concrete and barbed wire, the wall separated the Soviet sector of Berlin from West Berlin and became a symbol of the Cold War. The wall was finally dismantled in 1989.

As if Truman didn't have enough headaches in Europe, he also had to deal with Asia. Two issues dominated U.S. policy in the region: the **reconstruction of Japan** and the **Chinese Revolution**. After the war the United States occupied Japan, and its colonial possessions were divided up. The United States took control of the Pacific Islands and the southern half of Korea, while the USSR took control of the northern half of Korea. Under the command of General Douglas MacArthur, Japan wrote a democratic constitution, demilitarized, and started a remarkable economic revival. The United States was not as successful in China, where it chose to side with Chiang Kai-shek's Nationalist government against **Mao Zedong**'s Communist insurgents, during China's 20-year civil war. Despite massive American military aid, the Communists overthrew the Nationalists, whose government was exiled to Taiwan. For decades the United States refused to recognize the legitimacy of Mao's regime, creating another international "hot spot" for Americans. Truman also chose to aid the French during the Vietnamese war for independence in Indochina, although most Americans were not aware of this at the time.

All this conflict with communists resurrected anti-communist paranoia at home, just as anti-communism had swept America during the Red Scare after World War I. In 1947 Truman ordered investigations of 3 million federal employees in a search for "security risks." Those found to have a potential Achilles' heel—either previous association with "known communists" or a "moral" weakness such as alcoholism or homosexuality (which, the government reasoned, made them easy targets for blackmail)—were dismissed without a hearing. In 1949 former State Department official **Alger Hiss** was found guilty of consorting with a communist spy (Richard Nixon was the congressman mostly responsible for Hiss's downfall). Americans began to passionately fear the "enemy within." Even the Screen Actors Guild, then headed by Ronald Reagan, attempted to discover and purge its own communists.

It was this atmosphere that allowed a demagogic senator named **Joseph McCarthy** to rise from near anonymity to national fame. In 1950 McCarthy claimed to have a list of more than 200 known communists working for the State Department. He subsequently changed that number several times, which should have clued people in to the fact that he was not entirely truthful. Unchallenged, McCarthy went on to lead a campaign of innuendo that ruined the lives of thousands of innocent people. Without ever uncovering a single communist, McCarthy held years of hearings with regard to subversion, not just in the government, but in education and the entertainment industry as well. Those subpoenaed were often forced to confess to previous associations with communists and name others with similar associations. Industries created lists of those tainted by these charges, called **blacklists**, which prevented the accused from working, just as blacklists had been used against union organizers at the turn of the last century. McCarthy's downfall came in 1954, during the Eisenhower administration, when he accused the Army of harboring communists. He had finally chosen too powerful a target. The Army fought back hard, and with help from **Edward R.**

Murrow's television show, in the **Army-McCarthy hearings**, McCarthy was made to look foolish. The public turned its back on him, and the era of **McCarthyism** ended, but public distrust and fear of communism remained.

There are a number of terms associated with the Cold War policy of President **Dwight D. Eisenhower** (served 1953–1961) and Secretary of State **John Foster Dulles** that you may see on the TASC test. The administration continued to follow the policy of containment but called it **liberation** to make it sound more intimidating. It carried the threat that the United States would eventually free Eastern Europe from Soviet control. Dulles coined the phrase **massive retaliation** to describe the nuclear attack that the United States would launch if the Soviets tried anything too daring. **Deterrence** described how Soviet fear of massive retaliation would prevent their challenging the United States and led to an arms race. Deterrence suggested that the mere knowledge of **mutually assured destruction (MAD)** prevented both nations from deploying nuclear weapons. Dulles allowed confrontations with the Soviet Union to escalate toward war, an approach called **brinksmanship**. Finally, the Eisenhower administration argued that the spread of communism had to be checked in Southeast Asia. If South Vietnam fell to communism, the nations surrounding it would fall quickly like dominoes; hence, the **domino theory**.

Cold War tensions remained high throughout the decade. Eisenhower had hoped that the death of **Joseph Stalin** in 1953 might improve American-Soviet relations. Initially, the new Soviet leader **Nikita Khrushchev** offered hope. Khrushchev denounced Stalin's totalitarianism and called for "peaceful coexistence" among nations with different economic philosophies. Some Soviet client states took Khrushchev's pronouncements as a sign of weakness; rebellions occurred in Poland and Hungary. When the Soviets crushed the uprisings, U.S.-Soviet relations returned to where they were during the Stalin era. Soviet advances in nuclear arms development (the USSR exploded its first hydrogen bomb a year after the United States blew up its first H-bomb) and space flight (the USSR launched the first satellite, *Sputnik*, into space, motivating the United States to quickly create and fund the **National Aeronautics and Space Administration**, or **NASA**) further heightened anxieties.

In his final days in office, Eisenhower warned the nation to beware of a new coalition that had grown up around the Cold War, which he called the military-industrial complex. The combination of military might and the highly profitable arms industries, he cautioned, created a powerful alliance whose interests did not correspond to those of the general public. In retrospect, many would later argue that in his final statement, Eisenhower had identified those who would later be responsible for the escalation of the **Vietnam War**.

The Vietnam War

Like Truman and Eisenhower, Kennedy perceived the Soviet Union and communism as the major threats to the security of the United States and its way of life. Every major foreign policy issue and event of his administration related primarily to these Cold War concerns.

The Domino Theory

"You have broader considerations that might follow what you might call the 'falling domino principle.' You have a row of dominoes set up. You knock over the first one, and what will happen to the last one is that it will go over very quickly."

–President Harry S. Truman, 1954

Although the Vietnam War lasted more than 12 years and cost the lives of more than 50,000 American soldiers, Congress never officially declared war.

Two major events during Kennedy's first year in office heightened American-Soviet tensions. The first involved **Cuba**, where a U.S.-friendly dictatorship had been overthrown by communist insurgents led by **Fidel Castro**. When Castro took control of the country in 1959, American businesses owned more than 3 million acres of prime Cuban farmland and also controlled the country's electricity and telephone service. Because so many Cubans lived in poverty, Cuban resentment of American wealth was strong, so little popular resistance occurred when Castro seized and nationalized some American property. The United States, however, was not pleased. When Castro signed a trade treaty with the Soviet Union later that year, Eisenhower imposed a partial trade embargo on Cuba. In the final days of his presidency, Eisenhower broke diplomatic relations with Cuba, and Cuba turned to the Soviet Union for financial and military aid.

Taking office in 1961, President Kennedy inherited the Cuban issue. Looking to solve the dilemma, the CIA presented the ill-fated plan for the **Bay of Pigs invasion** to the new president. The plan involved sending Cuban exiles, whom the CIA had been training since Castro's takeover, to invade Cuba. According to the strategy, the army of exiles would win a few battles, and then the Cuban people would rise up in support, overthrow Castro, and replace his government with one more acceptable to the United States. Kennedy approved the plan but did not provide adequate American military support, and the United States launched the invasion in April 1961. The invasion failed, the Cuban people did not rise up in support, and within two days Kennedy had a full-fledged disaster on his hands. Not only had he failed to achieve his goal, but he had also antagonized the Soviets and their allies in the process. His failure also diminished America's stature with its allies.

In 1962 the United States and the Soviet Union came the closest they had yet to a military (and perhaps nuclear) confrontation. The focus of the conflict was once again Cuba. In October, American spy planes detected missile sites in Cuba. Kennedy immediately decided that those missiles had to be removed at any cost; he further decided on a policy of brinksmanship to confront the **Cuban missile crisis**. He imposed a naval quarantine on Cuba to prevent any further weapons shipments from reaching the island, and then went on national television and demanded that the Soviets withdraw their missiles.

By refusing to negotiate secretly, Kennedy backed the Soviets into a corner; if they removed the missiles, their international stature would be diminished, especially since the quarantine was effectively a blockade, which diplomats defined as an act of war on the part of the United States. Therefore, in return, the Soviets demanded that the United States promise never again to invade Cuba and that the United States remove its missiles from Turkey (which is as close to the USSR as Cuba is to the United States). When Kennedy rejected the second condition, he gambled that the Soviets would not attack in response. Fortunately, behind-the-scenes negotiations defused the crisis, and the Soviets agreed to accept America's promise not to invade Cuba as a pretext for withdrawing the missiles. In return, the United States secretly agreed to remove its missiles from Turkey a few months later, thus making it look like the United States had won.

The greatest theater for American Cold War policy during this era, however, was **Vietnam**. From the Truman administration until the fall of Soviet Communism in 1991, U.S. foreign policy leaders asserted an American right to intervene anywhere in the world to stop the spread of communism and to protect American interests. Nowhere did that policy fail more miserably than in Vietnam, where the United States maintained an economic and military presence for almost 25 years. The Vietnam War divided America as no war before had.

The United States did not recognize Vietnamese independence or the legitimacy of its leader Ho Chi Minh's government, in part because of America's alliance with France (which wanted its colony back), and in part because Ho was a communist. Instead, the United States recognized the government of Bao Dai, the Vietnamese emperor whom the French had installed in the South, which France still controlled. Subsequently, Vietnam fought a war for independence against the French from 1946 until 1954, when the French were defeated. Although Ho appealed to President Truman for assistance on several occasions, Truman never responded. Ho hoped the United States would honor its commitment to the principle of self-determination and empathize with the Vietnamese rather than support the colonial power. Truman continued to aid the French. The United States financed more than 80 percent of France's war effort in Indochina, a fact few Americans knew then or know now.

In 1954 all of the involved parties met in Geneva, Switzerland, and drew up the **Geneva Accords**, which divided Vietnam at the 17th parallel, with Communist forces controlling North Vietnam and (so-called) democratic forces controlling the South. It was agreed that this division was to be temporary and that elections would be held in two years to reunite the country and determine who would rule a unified Vietnam. The elections never took place, however. The United States, certain that Ho Chi Minh would win an election, sabotaged the peace agreement. First, the United States made an alliance with another South Vietnamese leader named **Ngo Dinh Diem** and helped him oust Bao Dai (whom the United States felt was too weak to control the country). Then, the CIA organized commando raids across the border in North Vietnam to provoke a Communist response (which the South Vietnamese could then denounce). Diem pronounced South Vietnam an autonomous country and refused to participate in the agreed-upon national election. The United States rallied Britain, France, Thailand, Pakistan, the Philippines, New Zealand, and Australia to form the NATO-like **Southeast Asian Treaty Organization (SEATO)** to provide for South Vietnam's defense against Communist takeover.

Unfortunately, the situation continued its downward spiral. Diem, it turned out, was a vicious leader. He took despotic control of South Vietnam, imprisoning political enemies, persecuting Buddhist monks, and closing newspapers that criticized his government. As a result, many South Vietnamese citizens joined the North Vietnamese side. These communist South Vietnamese insurgents were called the **Vietcong**. Rather than cut its losses, the United States continued to support Diem and the South Vietnamese economically. Committed to the policy of containment and intent on nation building, President Kennedy increased America's involvement in Vietnam by sending in military advisors known as the

Green Berets. Finally, in 1963 the CIA helped the South Vietnamese military stage a coup to overthrow Diem's government. During the coup, Diem and his brother were killed and Kennedy was appalled by the outcome. A few weeks later, Kennedy was assassinated, and Lyndon Johnson (president from 1963–1969) took control of America's war efforts.

Upon taking office, Johnson had the opportunity to withdraw American forces in a way that would not have embarrassed his administration. The United Nations, backed by France and the Vietcong, would have intervened and set up a coalition government to rule South Vietnam. Kennedy's advisers, however, convinced Johnson that U.S. forces could overwhelm any opposition in the region. He remained committed to using those forces to achieve "total victory."

In 1964 the United States supported a second coup in South Vietnam; apparently, the United States was not terribly selective as to who ran the country, so long as it was not the Communists. (The United States followed a similar pattern in Latin America.) The U.S. Army also started bombing the neighboring country of Laos, through which the North Vietnamese were shipping weapons to the Vietcong. Then, in August of the same year, reports stated that the North Vietnamese had fired on two American destroyer ships in the **Gulf of Tonkin**. (However, the North Vietnamese attack was never confirmed.) Johnson used the event to get Congress to pass the **Gulf of Tonkin Resolution**, which allowed the president to take any measures he deemed necessary to protect American interests in the region. The Tonkin Gulf resolution gave Johnson carte blanche to escalate U.S. participation in the war. It also is the closest Congress ever came to an official declaration of war in Vietnam. Thus, the first ground troops began to arrive in the early months of 1965.

Soon, Johnson had flooded the region with American troops. He also authorized massive Air Force bombing raids into North Vietnam. Throughout Johnson's administration, the United States essentially took over the war effort from the South Vietnamese; hence, the **Americanization** of the Vietnam War. As the war ground on and the draft claimed more young Americans, opposition to the war grew. Protest rallies grew larger and more frequent, and more and more young men either ignored their draft notices or fled to a foreign country (more than 30,000 went to Canada) to avoid military service.

Johnson's advisers continued to assure him that the war was "winnable" until January 1968, when the North Vietnamese launched the **Tet Offensive** (named after the Vietnamese holiday celebrating the New Year). In conjunction with the Vietcong, the North Vietnamese inflicted tremendous damage on American forces and nearly captured the American embassy in the South Vietnamese capital of Saigon. Though the North Vietnamese and Vietcong forces were, in the end, decisively driven back, the severity of the strikes was an ugly shock for the American people, who had been assured by the Johnson administration that the United States was winning the war. This would be a major turning point in the war, as most Americans had been confident their superior technology could easily defeat the underdeveloped Third World nation. The Tet Offensive was a highly calculated series of attacks carried out around the country, demonstrating that American military experts had vastly underestimated the sophistication of Vietnamese strategy. That the North Vietnamese and Vietcong could launch such a large-scale offensive and nearly succeed in taking the American embassy made the American public come to believe it was being lied to and that perhaps this war was not winnable.

President Nixon (served 1969–1974) entered office promising to end American involvement in Vietnam by turning the war over to the South Vietnamese, a process he called **Vietnamization**. He soon began withdrawing troops; however, he also increased the number and intensity of air strikes. Like his predecessors, Nixon was a veteran cold warrior who believed that the United States could, and must, win in Vietnam. He ordered bombing raids and ground troops into Cambodia, in hopes of rooting out Vietcong strongholds and weapons supplies. American involvement in Vietnam dragged on until 1973, when Secretary of State **Henry Kissinger** completed negotiations for a peace treaty with the North Vietnamese.

The Nixon years added two new terms to the vocabulary of foreign policy. Together, Nixon and Kissinger formulated an approach called **détente**, a policy of "openness" that called for countries to respect each other's differences and cooperate more closely. Détente ushered in a brief period of relaxed tensions between the two superpowers but ended when the Soviet Union invaded Afghanistan in 1979. The **Nixon Doctrine** announced that the United States would withdraw from many of its overseas troop commitments, relying instead on alliances with local governments to check the spread of communism.

Civil Rights

Although the **Thirteenth**, **Fourteenth**, and **Fifteenth Amendments** abolished slavery, extended citizenship to former slaves, and gave African American men the right to vote, respectively, the second half of the nineteenth century was far from idyllic for African Americans. As **Reconstruction** came to an end, many parts of the United States, especially the south, returned to governing systems based on white supremacy. **Racial segregation** (division on the basis of race) was legalized under **Jim Crow laws**, which restricted African Americans to the rear of streetcars and busses, to separate public drinking fountains and toilets, to separate schools and hospitals, and even to separate cemeteries. In addition to being separated from other races, African American men were being denied the right to vote through the use of poll taxes, literacy tests, and intimidation and acts of violence. The Supreme Court upheld these laws in the famous case, *Plessy v. Ferguson*. In its decision, the Supreme Court held that laws requiring **separate but equal** facilities were constitutional.

Despite the lack of support from the Supreme Court, many strong African American leaders emerged during the Progressive Era. The **National Association for the Advancement of Colored People (NAACP)** and the **National Urban League** were multiracial groups founded to combat racial discrimination and pursue political, educational, social, and economic equality for all people. While most African Americans were in favor of racial equality, they were split as to how this could best be achieved. **Booker T. Washington**, an educator who founded the **Tuskegee**

Institute, an all-black vocational school, advocated that rather than fight for political rights, African Americans should strive for economic equality through job training and hard work. Washington presented these views at the **Atlanta Exposition** in 1895 in a speech known as the **Atlanta Compromise**. Whites welcomed Washington's views as they advised African Americans to work quietly rather than to agitate openly for equality. In sharp contrast to Booker T. Washington, **W.E.B. DuBois**, who helped found the NAACP, argued that African Americans should aggressively pursue political, social, and economic rights. Du Bois believed that a **Talented Tenth** of the African American population should assume roles of academic and community leadership, advancing the race through intellect and skill. **Marcus Garvey**, a Jamaican immigrant and founder of the **UNIA (Universal Negro Improvement Association)**, believed that blacks should separate from corrupt white society. Garvey promoted black owned businesses and founded the **Black Star Line** to help blacks emigrate to Africa through his **Back to Africa** movement. Although he was the most extreme of the three African American leaders, Garvey still attracted a large following among African Americans.

The decade following World War II brought general affluence and an improved standard of living for most Americans. Also, when soldiers returned from World War II, they and their spouses again began making babies, lots of babies. The explosive increase in the birthrate in the postwar period was known as the **baby boom**, the demographic implications of which are still felt today in the United States.

Nonetheless, many groups of Americans remained economically disenfranchised and failed to enjoy the same improved standard of living enjoyed by other Americans. This was especially true of black Americans. These differences worsened with the growth of suburbs, as white Americans left the cities for less congested, greener areas. As they left in what came to be known as **white flight,** they took their buying power (and tax payments) with them. Blacks and other minority groups that remained came to make up increasingly larger proportions of the cities' populations. This physical separation of the racial groups, accompanied by relatively stagnant income levels for African Americans, contributed to some of the tensions that would erupt in the 1960s.

"We conclude that in the field of public education the doctrine of 'separate but equal' has no place. Separate educational facilities are inherently unequal."

–Chief Justice Earl Warren, who wrote the unanimous opinion in the case of *Brown v. Board of Education of Topeka* .

Indeed, in the South, these physical separations had been enshrined in law for decades. But during this period, these laws came into serious question. *Brown v. Board of Education of Topeka* (1954) was a landmark Supreme Court decision that helped open the door for civil rights progress. Under the 1896 Supreme Court ruling *Plessy v. Ferguson*, public schools and other institutions were legally segregated under the "separate but equal" doctrine. In reality, the white schools and facilities far surpassed the quality of those for African Americans. In the 1954 decision, the Supreme Court unanimously reversed this decision and declared this policy unconstitutional. **Chief Justice Earl Warren** wrote in the majority opinion that "separate educational facilities are inherently unequal" and ordered that all public schools desegregate. This ruling helped to unify the black community, which began to organize openly against the segregation that was so tightly woven into the fabric of southern society.

The **Montgomery Bus Boycott** of 1955 was sparked when **Rosa Parks**, a black woman, refused to give up her seat on a bus to a white man. Her subsequent arrest was the last straw for many residents of Montgomery, who were upset by the city's unfair public transportation policies. The black community united under the leadership of a young preacher and civil rights leader named **Martin Luther King Jr. (MLK)**, and refused to ride the buses. The boycott continued for over a year until the Supreme Court handed down its decision that segregated seating was, in fact, unconstitutional.

Many white Southerners were angered by this upsetting of their racially stratified society. A widely publicized incident illustrating the discord that resulted, took place in **Little Rock, Arkansas**, in 1957, as the city's board of education selected nine black students to enroll at the previously all-white Central High School. The governor of the state ordered the Arkansas National Guard to bar the students from the building. President Eisenhower declared the governor's action to be in violation of federal law. When the governor withdrew the National Guard, an angry white mob sought to block the students from entering the school. In order to end the stand-off, Eisenhower federalized the Arkansas National Guard and sent additional **federal troops** to protect the black students; the soldiers remained through the entire school year. Outside of his actions in Little Rock, Eisenhower also supported the **Civil Rights Acts of 1957 and 1960**, which sought to remove the voting barriers that many Southern states had put into place and also to help minimize the **violence** that had been directed toward African Americans (e.g., the bombing of black churches and schools) in many places across the South.

In the 1950s, progress had been made in confirming and strengthening some civil rights for African Americans, but starting in the early 1960s, the pace of progress quickened. African Americans became more forceful in claiming their rights and denouncing their "second-class citizen" status. Under the leadership of Martin Luther King Jr., protesters embraced the tactic of nonviolent resistance to achieve their goals. They engaged in several types of demonstrations. **Sit-ins** involved blacks going into "whites only" restaurants and other establishments, sitting down, and refusing to leave, even as service was denied them. On **Freedom Rides**, African Americans and their white supporters rode interstate buses to test the interstate desegregation legislation passed in the 1950s. Freedom riders encountered hostility and violence as the buses rode into "whites only" bus terminals. Eventually, the government explicitly ordered that interstate buses be desegregated, and airplanes and trains voluntarily followed suit. Another form of demonstration was the mass demonstration or **march**; the most famous example of this was the **March on Washington, D.C.** to make clear the scale of support for civil rights legislation that had been advanced by Kennedy. The assembled group was the largest ever in the nation's capital, and it held that record for more than 20 years. During this protest, Martin Luther King Jr. gave his historic **"I Have a Dream"** speech from the steps of the Lincoln memorial.

After an extended delay due to the actions of Southern Congressmen, the **Civil Rights Act of 1964** was passed and signed into law by President Johnson. It mandated new, stronger voting protections for African Americans and prohibited discrimination in public accommodations, housing, and employment based on a

"I have a dream that one day this nation will rise up and live out the true meaning of its creed: 'We hold these truths to be self-evident; that all men are created equal.'"

–Martin Luther King Jr., from his "I Have a Dream" speech, given during the March on Washington in 1963

person's race, color, religion, or gender. The strength of the law was tested the next year in **Selma, Alabama**, a city that had a large population of African Americans, of whom only a few were registered to vote. The local police violently suppressed groups demonstrating for their voting rights and prevented them from registering.

Martin Luther King, Jr., and other members of his **Southern Christian Leadership Council (SCLC)**, became involved and organized a march from Selma to the state capitol in Montgomery. Although King and his supporters advocated nonviolence, many of those who opposed them, including the local police forces, were openly and frequently violent. The first attempt to march on Montgomery was aborted because of brutal retaliation on the marchers by police and an angry mob. The incident came to be known as **Bloody Sunday**. In another infamous incident in **Birmingham, Alabama**, police used fire hoses, nightsticks, cattle prods, and dogs to disband nonviolent protesters. The incidents were televised, offering the opportunity for many Americans to see for the first time the face of violent racial hatred. It helped generate much sympathy and support for the civil rights movement among white Americans, and was a turning point in the legislative effort to pass new civil rights measures in Congress.

The onslaught of violence endured by African American protesters spurred division within the ranks of the civil rights movement about how best to respond to it. The NAACP and Martin Luther King Jr. continued to advocate nonviolent protest, but more militant African American groups felt those who insisted on nonviolence were sending young marchers into harm's way unduly. Malcolm X, who acted as the chief spokesman for the Nation of Islam (sometimes referred to as the Black Muslims), favored total separation of the races, although he eventually broke with the Nation of Islam and rethought his separatist views toward the end of his short life. CORE (Congress on Racial Equality) and SNCC (Student Nonviolent Coordinating Committee) represented those who had come to advocate more forceful self-protection, as did the Black Panthers, one of the best-known groups of the period. Across this militant front, the term **Black Power** was often used, not only in reference to the idea that African Americans should arm themselves for an "imminent" revolution against the white power structure, but in reference to the empowerment that they believed came from self-pride.

Tragically, both men were felled by assassins' bullets; Malcolm X was shot in New York City in 1965 and Martin Luther King Jr. was shot in Memphis, Tennessee, in 1968.

Women's Rights

The early nineteenth century saw the beginnings of true social reform in the United States, and much of the impulse to improve the lives of others came from citizens' religious convictions. In fact, early social reform movements grew out of the Second Great Awakening, which, like the first, was a period of religious revival, mainly among Methodists, Presbyterians, and Baptists. The Second Great Awakening began in the "burned-over district" of western New York and then spread throughout the country, sparking an intense period of evangelicalism in the South and West. The burned-over district was a place so heavily evangelized, so burned over by the metaphorical fires of religious revival, that there were no more people left to convert. Evangelist **Charles G. Finney**, known as the "Father of Modern Revivalism," founded numerous churches in places where previously there had been only occasional religious meetings (called **revivals**, or camp meetings). A few reform societies sprang up in the South and West, but in the Northeast, the Second Great Awakening gave birth to numerous societies dedicated to the task of saving humanity from its own worst impulses. Much of the language of reform had a religious tone. For example, drinking and poverty were considered social evils.

Important Civil Rights Legislation
The key pieces of civil rights legislation in the twentieth century:

- *Brown v. Board of Education* (1954)—Declared the previous policy of segregation of schools and other public institutions unconstitutional

- *Civil Rights Act of 1964*—Strengthened voting legislation and outlawed discrimination based on a person's race, color, religion, or gender

- *Twenty-fourth Amendment* (1964)—Prohibited the use of poll taxes to deny people the right to vote

- *Voting Rights Act of 1965*—Specifically prohibited the use of discriminatory practices such as literacy tests that had been used to deny blacks the right to vote in some states

Usually, the most active members of reform groups were women, particularly those of the middle and upper classes. **Temperance societies**, some of which tried to encourage people to sign the pledge not to drink and some of which sought outright prohibition of liquor, formed and remained powerful until the adoption of the Eighteenth Amendment in 1919 provided for nationwide prohibition. (Not coincidentally, prohibition finally succeeded at the same time it became evident to politicians that women would soon gain the right to vote.) These groups battled other vices as well, particularly **gambling**. By 1860 every state in the Union had outlawed **lotteries**, and many had prohibited other forms of gambling. Many Northern states also prohibited the manufacture or purchase of alcoholic beverages during this period. A group called **The Female Moral Reform Society** led the battle against **prostitution** in the cities, focusing not only on eliminating the profession but also on rehabilitating those women involved in it.

Charitable middle-class organizations, usually run by women, also made efforts at urban reform. These groups lobbied local governments for building-safety codes, better sanitation, and public schools. Frustrated by government's slow pace, their members also founded and lived in settlement houses in poor neighborhoods.

These houses became community centers, providing schooling, childcare, and cultural activities. In Chicago, for example, Jane Addams founded Hull House to provide such services as English lessons for immigrants, day care for children of working mothers, childcare classes for parents, and playgrounds for children. Addams also campaigned for increased government services in the slums. She was awarded the Nobel Peace Prize for her life's work in 1931.

The Slow March of Progress
Although a constitutional amendment extending voting rights to women was sent to Congress in the 1880s, the Nineteenth Amendment wasn't ratified until 1920.

It was also during the nineteenth century that **women's suffrage** became an important political issue. **Susan B. Anthony** led the fight, convincing Congress to introduce a suffrage amendment to the Constitution. The bill was introduced every year and rarely got out of committee, but the fight had begun in earnest. Meanwhile, organizations such as the **American Suffrage Association** fought for women's suffrage amendments to state constitutions. By 1890 they had achieved some partial successes, gaining the vote on school issues. The adamant, conservative opposition that women's rights advocates faced gave birth to the **feminist** movement. One early advocate, **Margaret Sanger**, faced wide opposition for promoting the use of contraceptives (illegal in most places). The movement's greatest success was in winning women the right to vote, granted by the **Nineteenth Amendment** in 1920.

Treaties in American History
Landmark treaties have defined the closure of American wars.

- Treaty of Paris (1763)—Ended the French and Indian War and marked the beginning of British dominance in North America

- Treaty of Paris (1783)—Ended the American Revolution by guaranteeing American independence

- Treaty of Ghent (1814)—Ended the War of 1812, essentially declaring it a stalemate

- Treaty of Guadalupe-Hidalgo (1848)—Ended the Mexican-American War; United States gained California, Utah, Nevada, and parts of other states

- Treaty of Versailles (1919)—Ended World War I and required that Germany pay extensive war reparations (fines) to certain Allies

- Paris Peace Accords (1973)—Ended the Vietnam War; the United States declared neither victory nor defeat

In the twentieth century, World War I also presented new opportunities for women. Although the number of women in the workforce did not increase greatly during the war, women's means of employment did change. Many women quit domestic work and started working in factories; at one point, 20 percent of factory-floor manufacturing jobs were held by women. These workplace advances largely ended with the end of the war, as veterans returned home and reclaimed their jobs.

Despite the persistence of traditional roles for women, a new image of American women emerged and became a symbol of the Roaring Twenties—the **flapper**. World War I, the allure of the "big city," the right to vote, and new attitudes brought about by the ideas of Sigmund Freud (whose ideas were just beginning to circulate in the United States during the 1920s) opened up a whole new world for this new generation of emancipated women. They discarded the corset, layers of petticoats and long, dark dresses worn by their Victorian grandmothers, in favor of waistless dresses worn above the knee (shocking!), flesh-colored silk stockings (brought back from Paris), cute little hats, strings of long beads, a wrist full of bracelets, and ruby-red lips. Many flappers risked ruining their reputation by smoking cigarettes; drinking in public (despite Prohibition); and dancing the tango, the lindy, and the shimmy.

World War II affected almost every aspect of daily life at home and abroad. It created both new opportunities and new tensions within American society. More than a million African Americans served in the U.S. military during World War II, but they lived and worked in segregated units. The U.S. army was not desegregated until after the war, during the Truman administration in 1948. A popular image, familiar to most Americans, is that of Rosie the Riveter. Originally featured on a poster of the era, Rosie came to symbolize the millions of women who worked in war-related industrial jobs during World War II. Unfortunately for the cause of feminism, most women were expected to take off the coveralls and put the apron back on when the soldiers returned home.

Later in the twentieth century, President Kennedy's civil rights agenda produced varied results. Kennedy supported **women's rights**, establishing a presidential commission that in 1963 recommended removing all obstacles to women's participation in all facets of society. Congress enacted the **Equal Pay Act** in 1963, which required that men and women receive equal pay for equal work. Unfortunately, employers continue to get around this federal law by simply changing job titles.

Most left-leaning groups of the mid-twentieth century, while passionate about eradicating racism and poverty, were male-dominated and insensitive to the cause of women's rights. Women became frustrated with being treated as second-class citizens and started their own political groups. In 1963 Betty Friedan's book *The Feminine Mystique* openly challenged many people's assumptions about women's place in society. Friedan identified "The problem that has no name" and is credited with restarting the women's movement, a movement that had faded once women's suffrage was achieved with the Nineteenth Amendment in 1920. She was also one of the founders of **NOW**, the **National Organization for Women**, formed in 1966 to fight for legislative changes, including the ill-fated **Equal Rights Amendment** (ERA) to the Constitution. The modern movement for gay rights also began to solidify in the 1960s, with the first Gay Pride parades occurring on the anniversary of the **Stonewall** riots, an event at which gays fought back against the police in New York City.

Feminists fought against discrimination in hiring, pay, college admissions, and financial aid. They also fought for control of reproductive rights, a battle that reached the Supreme Court in the 1973 case *Roe v. Wade*, which enabled women to obtain abortions in all 50 states within the first trimester. Many states argued that they had an obligation to protect "life," as stipulated in the Fourteenth Amendment, and quickly passed state laws prohibiting a woman from having an abortion after the first three months of her pregnancy. Although there is no specific mention of a constitutional right to privacy, the Supreme Court had established this important precedent in 1965 in the case *Griswold v. Connecticut. Roe v. Wade* remains a controversial decision and continues to play a central role in American politics and society.

The Fall of the USSR

One of the most significant global changes that occurred in the late twentieth century was the fall of the Soviet Union and the demise of communism in eastern Europe. Within the Soviet Union, significant developments followed the death of Stalin in 1953. The winner of the power struggle for his replacement was Nikita Khrushchev (1894–1971), who, in a significant reversal from the previous regime, did not execute the losers in this political contest. At the Communist Party's twentieth national congress in 1956, Khrushchev, standing before a secret session, made a speech in which he attacked the many crimes of Stalin. Khrushchev claimed that Stalin's government had deviated from the political program of Marxist-Leninism, rather than being a natural outgrowth of it, and that the only reforms that would be acceptable would be those that stayed within the guidelines offered by Marxist-Leninism. Although Khrushchev made a successful visit to the United States in 1959, tensions between the two nations were heightened in the following year when the Soviet Union shot down an American U-2 spy plane over Russia. By October 1962, the two nuclear superpowers nearly went to war when the Soviets placed missiles in Cuba. President Kennedy's skillful handling of the crisis, however, allowed both nations to avoid the specter of a nuclear nightmare.

The relative liberalization of the Khrushchev years came to an end with his forced retirement in 1964. His successor, Leonid Brezhnev (1906–1982), did not reinstate the terror of the Stalin years, but he did seek to once again strengthen the role of the party bureaucracy and the KGB (the USSR's main security agency), and encouraged the further clampdown on reform in the satellite states.

The Warsaw Pact: Members Only
Soviet Union
East Germany
Poland
Czechoslovakia
Hungary
Romania
Bulgaria
Albania

By 1968, disaffection with this step backward led to the emergence of a reform movement in Czechoslovakia. The goal of this "Prague Spring" was to bring about a more humanistic socialism within certain limits, such as keeping the nation within the Soviet Bloc. Brezhnev still saw this as a threat to the entire Warsaw Pact and initiated what became known as the **Brezhnev Doctrine,** declaring that the Soviet Union would support with all the means at its disposal (including military intervention) any established communist state in Eastern Europe that was threatened by internal strife. The reform movement was crushed and its leader, Alexander Dubček, was replaced by someone more to Brezhnev's liking.

The most significant challenge to the Brezhnev Doctrine came in Poland, a land whose people were deeply stirred when in 1978 Karol Wojtyla, a Polish Cardinal, was elected Pope John Paul II. Two years later, led by Lech Walesa, an electrician, a massive strike took place at the Lenin shipyard in Gdansk, where workers demanded the right to form an independent trade union. Solidarity, as the new union was called, survived the declaration of martial law and being outlawed by going underground, in part with the aid of the Catholic Church. By 1989, the Polish economy was in such a shambles that the government was forced to negotiate with Walesa and his union. Surprisingly, the negotiations resulted in the promise for multiparty elections, which, when they took place in that same year, resulted in the defeat of all Communist candidates.

When the reform-minded Mikhail Gorbachev (b. 1931) took charge of the Kremlin, he indicated his opposition to the Brezhnev Doctrine. With reform looming overhead, 1989 proved to be one of the most remarkable years of the century, as Communist-led regimes peacefully collapsed in Hungary, Czechoslovakia, Bulgaria, and Albania. In East Germany, the collapse of the regime in that same year was followed in 1990 by the reunification of East and West Germany and the destruction of the Berlin Wall. Romania proved to be an exception to this peaceful transformation, as the violent dictator Nicolae Ceausescu (1918–1989) desperately tried to hold on to power. In the end, his government collapsed, and he and his wife, Elena, were executed on Christmas Day 1989.

As their satellite states underwent a complete political transformation, people within the Soviet Union expressed their desire for change. Disasters like the Soviet invasion of Afghanistan and the nuclear accident at Chernobyl revealed the deplorable state of affairs within the nation. Gorbachev wanted to limit the extent of this change; he accepted the need for **glasnost**, or openness in debate, as well as **perestroika**, an economic restructuring of the state, but he was no democrat and still wanted to see the Communist Party lead these reforms. Events, however, went beyond his control, and in 1990, the government was forced to allow the political participation of non-Communist parties. Nationalist movements throughout the Soviet Union also popped up, beginning with the declaration of independence by Lithuania, followed by the insistence of the Russian Republic, another Soviet state, that its laws superseded those of the Soviet Union.

By the end of 1990, Gorbachev appointed some hard-liners to government positions to make the prospect of future reform far less likely. Instead, the whole system collapsed. In part, this was the result of the rivalry between Gorbachev and Boris Yeltsin (1931–2007), who served as chairman of the Russian Parliament. In August 1991, hard-line communists decided that Gorbachev's policies were threatening the existence of the Communist Party and staged a coup while Gorbachev was on vacation, placing him under arrest in his Crimean home. This turned out to be the last gasp of the Soviet Union, as Yeltsin bravely defied the plotters when he stood on a tank outside the parliament building and led the resistance. The coup failed and with it any hope of preserving Communist control. One by one, the assorted republics left the Soviet Union, and by the end of 1991, the Soviet Union was dissolved; soon after, Gorbachev resigned.

9/11, Terrorism, and Wars in the Middle East

The TASC Social Studies section does not focus very heavily on events of the late twentieth century leading up to the present time. There are, however, a few important things with which you should be familiar.

On **September 11, 2001**, four commercial airliners were hijacked and used as weapons of destruction. Two planes were flown into the **World Trade Center** in New York City, exploding and causing the towers' collapse; another plane was flown into the **Pentagon** in Washington, D.C., causing extensive damage; and a fourth plane crashed in a field near Shanksville, Pennsylvania, the hijacking thwarted by crew and passengers who perhaps prevented its striking some other terrorist target. More than 2,800 people were killed in the tragedy. The attacks, attributed to Saudi-born **Osama bin Laden** and a radical Muslim terrorist group named **al Qaeda**, shocked the United States and the world. President Bush responded by launching a **War on Terror** which included, but was not limited to, a war in Afghanistan against the **Taliban**, a group that supported and harbored anti-American terrorists, including Osama bin Laden and other members of al Qaeda.

Following the attacks, there was increased security nationwide in an effort to protect citizens against terrorism, prompting concerns over potential violations to **civil liberties** as well as **racial and ethnic profiling**. Also during Bush's first term, the United States **invaded Iraq**. The invasion of Iraq, which removed Saddam Hussein from power, was publically justified prior to the war on the basis of Iraq possessing an arsenal of weapons of mass destruction that threatened both Saddam's neighbors and, through his connections to terrorism, the United States. The invasion and subsequent **occupation of Iraq** became mired in controversy, as Saddam's weapons of mass destruction were never found, and as an increasingly violent sectarian feud destabilized the fledgling postwar Iraqi democracy and cost the lives of American service members and Iraqi civilians caught in the cross-fire.

The **economic crisis of late 2008**, fueled by a collapse in the housing and housing credit market, has caused many people to reevaluate the economic and social reforms and policies enacted not just during George W. Bush's and Bill Clinton's presidencies, but during the first President Bush and Reagan years, as well. The economic crisis, along with America's War on Terror, became major campaign issues in 2008, when the United States elected its first African-American president, **Barack Obama**. During his first term in office, Obama signed into a law a bill rolling back the Bush tax cuts, the **Tax Relief**, **Unemployment Insurance Reauthorization**, **and Job Creation Act** of 2010, and ended the military's **Don't Ask, Don't Tell** policy, which banned homosexuals from serving openly in the armed forces. He also enacted a sweeping healthcare reform bill, the **Patient Protection and Affordable Care Act** or **Affordable Care Act**, often referred to as **Obamacare**. The controversial legislation is one of the most hotly debated issues in American politics in decades. In foreign policy matters, Obama ordered the final withdrawal of American troops from Iraq and the military action that led to the death of Osama Bin Laden in Abbottabad, Pakistan.

We can't say how historians will evaluate the late twentieth and early twenty-first centuries in light of terrorism, globalization, and the worldwide financial crisis and its aftermath, but it's probably safe to say that the United States will still play a significant—but possibly significantly different—role in the increasingly interconnected and interdependent global community.

U.S. History II Drill

Now try some practice questions. To check your answers, register your book at **PrincetonReview.com/cracking** and download the Chapter Drill Answers and Explanations supplement.

1.   **Prior to the administration of Theodore Roosevelt, the Sherman Antitrust Act had been used primarily to**

   A   dismantle corporate monopolies

   B   suppress trade unions

   C   impose import tariffs

   D   enforce civil rights in the South

2.   **Which of the following best summarizes the contents of the Zimmermann telegram, which was intercepted in 1917?**

   A   Germany offered Mexico a chance to regain the land it had lost in the Mexican Cession if Mexico attacked the United States and helped prevent the United States from assisting the Allies.

   B   A British spy alerted the world to the existence of mass extermination camps in German-held territories.

   C   The United States assured the British that it would join the war in Europe if the war were to continue for another year.

   D   The owner of the Boston Red Sox revealed a plan to sell star player Babe Ruth to the New York Yankees for a large amount of cash.

3.   **Wilson's Fourteen Points plan for peace after World War I included all of the following <u>except</u>**

   A   promotion of universal self-determination

   B   lower tariffs to promote free trade

   C   repayment of all Allied war expenses by Germany

   D   across-the-board arms reductions

4.   **President Theodore Roosevelt's "Big Stick" policy in Latin America was best characterized by his**

   A   repudiation of the Monroe Doctrine

   B   belief that European nations had the right to protect their economic interests in any remaining colonies throughout the region

   C   recognition of the sovereignty of newly independent nations in the Western hemisphere

   D   belief that the United States had an obligation to protect security and stability by assuming a protective role throughout the Western hemisphere

5.   **Which of the following best accounts for the success of labor unions?**

   A   Throughout the early 1900s, Congress promoted the interests of labor unions over captains of industry.

   B   Immigrants helped to promote a more diverse workforce less reliant on child labor.

   C   Sharecroppers in the South largely voted for Democrats who championed labor causes.

   D   Locally and nationally, organizations such as the American Federation of Labor negotiated directly with corporations to effect change in the workplace.

6. All of the following are social movements inspired by the civil rights movement <u>except</u>

A women's rights

B gay and lesbian rights

C states' rights

D Native American rights

7. Desegregation of schools was, in part, a response to unfulfilled promises from which of the following initiatives?

A The Great Society

B The Square Deal

C The New Deal

D Reconstruction

8. Which of the following best characterizes the policy of détente?

A direct confrontation

B covert sabotage

C decolonization

D mutual coexistence

Chapter 23
World History

In this chapter, we'll guide you through the key topics related to world history on the Social Studies portion of the TASC test. We will focus here on three broad categories: early civilizations, Europe prior to the twentieth century, and the twentieth century up to the present day. Some twentieth-century topics, such as the Industrial Revolution, the two world wars, and the Cold War, are covered in detail in Chapter 21 and Chapter 22. As such, only brief summaries will be provided here and you should review the previous chapters for more thorough coverage. Following the content lessons, we'll give you some practice questions.

EARLY CIVILIZATIONS

The TASC test places relatively low emphasis on humanity's prehistory and the important early civilizations. Nevertheless, it is very useful to have a basic sense of where our modern world came from, along with an understanding of the major belief systems of the ancient world.

"Prehistory" refers to the period of human history before the advent of the written word.

Civilization did not arise instantaneously once people settled down and planted things. People did not even start to form societies in only one place. Civilization arose in a number of places—not all at the exact same time, but with some common characteristics and patterns of development. Among these patterns are settled agriculture, some type of formal political organization, a shared religious/ philosophical code, the development of writing, the creation of more diverse labor and social class divisions, advancements in metallurgy and architecture, and the pursuit of knowledge and artistic creativity.

The most vital of these characteristics was settled agriculture, as it provided the food stocks necessary for the building of cities—the breeding grounds for human creativity. Not surprisingly, then, ancient history was dominated by civilizations that arose in fertile river valleys on different continents. Despite their extremely intermittent contact, these ancient societies—in India, China, Africa, Egypt, and Mesopotamia—share most of the characteristics of civilization. Only one group of major ancient civilizations—those of Central America—developed according to a different pattern. Although less well-known, civilizations of North America, South America, and New Guinea tended to develop separately from the river-valley pattern.

Mesopotamia

Ancient **Mesopotamia**, nestled between the Tigris and Euphrates rivers, is often called the cradle of human civilization. Mesopotamia, which literally means "the land between the rivers," is a great case study for us to see how the earliest human societies developed into outright civilizations. The Sumerians, who settled southern Mesopotamia sometime around 3500 B.C.E., were the first people of the Fertile Crescent to be considered a civilization. We know from personal names recorded on inscriptions dating back to around 3000 B.C.E. that the Sumerians spoke an early form of **Semitic**, a language group that also includes Hebrew, Aramaic, and Arabic.

In this context, "Semitic" is a linguistic rather than an ethnographic term.

The Sumerians had many firsts: They developed the first written language, they invented the wheel, they invented the way we tell time, they may have written the first novel, and they probably invented beer. Perhaps the Sumerians' greatest achievement, however, and the one that led to these other inventions, was the development of settled agriculture. How, exactly, did these Mesopotamian peoples accomplish such a feat? **Irrigation**. By building complex networks of canals, drainage ditches, dikes, and dams, they were able to move water from the large rivers and their tributaries to the surrounding countryside.

Settled agriculture resulted in a vastly greater population, which in turn energized the development and organization of political structures, a defining characteristic of civilization. Settled agriculture required people to work together in large groups, both for building irrigation networks and for harvesting crops, shearing animals, and other tasks. Population sizes larger than in any previous human experience required new ways for people to relate to one another, so that strangers without family ties would live peacefully instead of trying to kill one another on sight. In most societies, this mutual tolerance first developed under a powerful chieftain or strongman, who was able to intimidate others into behaving peaceably.

While the earliest years of the Sumerian civilization were probably characterized by small village settlements, as these villages grew larger they would have morphed into larger communities (city-states) with leadership structures that developed out of the village council model. In Sumeria, these early leaders eventually became powerful kings who first ruled individual city-states and then came to rule over many city-states. Although these early kings were powerful, they shared their power with the temple priests, who together ruled on behalf of their city-state's patron god.

The stable food source supplied by settled agriculture made the first cities possible. Although not large by today's standards, the largest Sumerian cities reached as many as 100,000 residents (however, the norm of the time was cities of only a few thousand residents). Cities this large could not be supported without a constant, stable food supply. Fortunately, the Sumerians were able to grow more food than the farmers themselves needed.

The ability to create a food surplus freed around 10 percent of the population to pursue other interests such as governing, writing, reading, building, buying, and selling. Such large groups of people living together also meant reaching a critical mass of human creativity for the development and spread of new ideas. This stability, together with the freedom to do something other than spend all day in the fields, made cities and civilization possible.

Cities were the centers not only of power and religion, but also of the trading of goods and ideas. At the center of Sumerian cities were the great **ziggurats**, large, sloping step-pyramid temples that symbolized the power of the kings, the priests, and the gods. Each city-state probably had at least one temple complex dedicated to a single deity or multiple deities that were thought to preside over the wellbeing of the community. As such, the priests in charge of these temples wielded enormous power: The temples owned land, so the priests were powerful in economics and politics as well as religion.

Knowledge and creativity flourished in the Sumerian cities of Uruk, Lagash, Ur, Nippur,

Systems of Writing

Logographic: A single character represents a complete unit of meaning, often a complete grammatical word. Ancient Egyptian hieroglyphs and Chinese are examples of logographic systems.

Alphabetic: A single letter represents a sound, or part of a syllable. English is included here, as are the other European languages.

Syllabic: A single character represents a syllable or group of sounds. Cuneiform and the writing systems of many Native American languages are syllabic.

and Eridu. Sumerian society was the first to develop writing, possibly as early as 3300 B.C.E. Starting with pictograms (a type of writing that conveys meaning through the images' resemblance to physical objects), the Sumerians eventually developed the **cuneiform** script, which became the standard alphabet across much of the region as Sumerian culture spread as a result of trade and conquest. It is important to note that cuneiform is not a language, but rather a writing style that was used by people who spoke Sumerian, Akkadian, Hittite, and Persian, among other languages.

While only a small percentage of the population would have been able to read and write, the development of cuneiform writing served to create entirely new categories of workers: scribes, teachers, and students. Writing allowed leaders to document laws, merchants to record their sales, and poets to transcribe the stories that had been passed down through the generations. The oldest known examples of cuneiform writing document economic transactions, but the Sumerians wrote other types of texts as well. Some of the many pieces of writing that archaeologists have found concern politics, religion, philosophy, and science.

Beyond their agricultural and literary achievements, the ancient Mesopotamian civilizations developed other important technologies. There is evidence to indicate that they used wheeled carts and sleds (pulled by animals), and some pretty sophisticated engineering must have been involved in building the great ziggurats. In warfare, horse-drawn chariots were widely used, and Mesopotamian armies used siege machinery to encircle and attack their enemies' fortified cities.

The Sumerians were skilled in astronomy and math as well. Have you ever wondered why we use units of 60 to count time? This system comes from ancient Mesopotamia, where mathematicians used a base-60 number system to account for fractions and percentages (as opposed to the base-10 number system that we use for most things today).

Egypt

We cannot review ancient Egypt without talking about the importance of the Nile River to the development of Egyptian civilization. Unlike the unpredictable nature of the Tigris and Euphrates rivers, the Nile flooded regularly every year, providing natural irrigation and vital silt for the nourishment of crops. In this sense at least, settled agriculture was easier in Egypt than in ancient Mesopotamia. The Nile was also an oasis of civilization surrounded by natural geographic barriers. To the west and east, vast and inhospitable deserts bordered the Nile Valley.

To the south, a series of cataracts, or large waterfalls, prevented any invaders from readily sailing down the Nile into Egyptian territory. And finally to the north, Egypt was bordered by the Mediterranean Sea, a natural barrier in the infancy of ocean travel. Although Egypt was relatively close to ancient Mesopotamia, its culture developed rather independently, and somewhat differently, because of the natural barriers of water and desert.

Historians have identified roughly thirty dynasties in early Egyptian civilization, so the details can get a bit overwhelming. We'll focus on just a few of the most important political developments. The Nile flows from south to north, so the northern delta region is lower in elevation than the southern region. The study of ancient Egypt generally begins with the unification of Upper (southern) and Lower (delta region) Egypt, possibly under the rule of a king named Narmer, or Menes, around 3100 B.C.E. This time period is often referred to as the Early Dynastic period.

After this era, the history of ancient Egypt is divided into three "kingdoms"—Old, Middle, and New—with three intermediate periods of instability falling in between. Egypt's unification likely occurred over a period of decades, if not centuries, as leaders of local **nomes** (local units of administration) consolidated their power over more and more towns and cropland up and down the Nile. **Hieroglyphic writing**, too, developed during this same general time period. Unlike Sumerian cuneiform writing, hieroglyphs were pictures that resembled physical objects or animals but symbolized words or syllables. During its early stages, hieroglyphic writing was used primarily by the priestly class.

The great power of the Pharaohs during the Old Kingdom period (2700–2200 B.C.E.) is best symbolized by the building of the **Great Pyramids** of Giza. The Great Pyramid of Khufu, the largest of the three Great Pyramids and built around 2500 B.C.E., remained the tallest human-built structure in the world for nearly 4,500 years until the construction of the Eiffel Tower in 1889 C.E. Until relatively recently, historians believed that only slaves could have built the Great Pyramids, yet recent excavations of worker villages near the site have suggested that the pyramid builders were not only working voluntarily, but were also quite well cared for. Only a king, and only a government of great power and influence, could have assembled the tens of thousands of workers needed to build the Great Pyramids. After the fall of the Old Kingdom, no pyramids approaching the size of the Giza Pyramids were ever built again.

So why did the Egyptians expend so much energy constructing the pyramids? They believed that there existed a cosmic order characterized by renewal (a mirror of the natural world and the consistent patterns of the Nile's rise and fall). Because the Pharaohs were associated with this cycle of renewal and because they were thought to be so vital to the proper functioning of the world, the Egyptians went to great length to make sure that their leaders' bodies and spirits were prepared for the afterlife. The famous Book of the Dead, which archaeologists have found in many royal tombs, contains magical spells and ritual instructions that were intended to guide the spirit in the afterlife.

Egyptians also took great care to preserve the physical bodies of the deceased, and not just for royals. The wealthy were able to have their bodies preserved using the most advanced techniques of mummification, in which the vital organs were removed from the cadaver and preserved in stone jars. The body was then desiccated (dried out) using salts and chemicals, and wrapped in linen before being placed in coffins and buried inside tombs. The pyramids, the most recognizable burial places, were the tombs for the Pharaohs and their wives, but other wealthy people had less elaborate tombs constructed for their burials as well. Common people did what they could afford to preserve their bodies for the afterlife, but often had to make do with simpler mud brick tombs or pit graves.

The story of ancient Egypt is another example of the emergence of civilization—of how humans developed government, language, and shared religious philosophy, and built timeless works of art and architecture. Because of the way Egyptians practiced mummification, they developed a fairly advanced knowledge of anatomy. The pyramids and other monumental structures required expertise in engineering and construction techniques. In other realms, the Egyptians made advances in mathematics and astronomy.

Like all ancient civilizations, Egyptian society came to an end under the pressures of time and outside domination. Although its culture died out nearly 2,000 years ago, one example of how Egypt's culture still influences our modern time is the Washington Monument in the American capital—it's an Egyptian obelisk.

Greece

The early Greek societies were not good candidates for imperial glory. Their cities were rather small compared to those in ancient Mesopotamia because of the lack of major river systems and arable land suitable for large-scale agriculture. Therefore, the character of early Greek society was the city-state, or **polis**. As the population of Greece grew, the poleis (plural of polis) didn't get much larger; the Greeks merely built more and more cities, eventually moving beyond the Greek mainland to colonize the shores of western Anatolia (modern-day Turkey) as well as the coasts of eastern Italy and Sicily.

Most of the Greek city-states consisted of only a few thousand inhabitants; a few, such as Athens, were larger, ranging into the tens or hundreds of thousands. Many had common characteristics, such as a hilltop **acropolis** (literally, "top of the city") with temples and administrative buildings, an **agora** (gathering place for trade and other activities), and fortified walls surrounding the center of the urban area. People lived outside the city walls as well, but came inside for protection when necessary.

The city-states of ancient Greece were relatively independent and fought each other frequently. Instead of relying upon a professional standing army, the Greeks practiced a type of warfare that involved farmer-warriors who were called up or conscripted during times of conflict but otherwise lived and worked with their families. Because so many of the warriors had responsibilities to take care of on their lands, military campaigns often took place during times of the year when there were fewer agricultural tasks to attend to.

One might assume that these geographically diverse city-states would become culturally diverse as well. However, this did not happen. The Greek city-states remained culturally unified by the Greek language and by shared events such as the Olympic games, as well as by their shared history as recorded in such literary masterpieces as *The Iliad* and *The Odyssey*. The Greek city-states did, however, differ greatly from one another politically, which allowed for a great variety of political structures, from good old-fashioned kingship to the purest form of democracy the world has ever seen.

Athens itself went through this great variety in political structures. As Greece emerged from the dark ages, Athens was ruled by a series of kings, many of whom were considered **tyrants** (tyrant comes from the Greek *turannos*, meaning "one absolute ruler"). The move toward less autocratic rule began under the reign of Solon, who ruled beginning c. 590 B.C.E. His greatest achievement was writing a constitution, which created the **Council of Four Hundred**, allowed all free men to vote, and canceled all public and private debts. However, after Solon left Athens for travels around the Mediterranean, Athens again succumbed to tyrannical rule. Things had deteriorated so badly in Athens that by 510 B.C.E., a group of Athenians called upon Sparta, considered by many in Greece at the time as the unofficial military of Peloponnesus (the large, southernmost peninsula in Greece), to come in and restore order.

After the Spartans restored order in Athens, a reformer in the mold of Solon, named Cleisthenes, came to power. By 508 B.C.E., he had established citizenship based on geography, rather than on social rank or nobility, and he subsequently created ten voting districts throughout Athens and its countryside, from each of which fifty citizens were selected by lottery to the new Council of Five Hundred for one-year terms. All free male citizens (the poor were still excluded) of Athens were expected to participate in a popular assembly on almost a weekly basis. Six thousand Athenians were needed to achieve a **quorum** (minimum number for conducting business) during the assembly meetings. Although the Council guided the discussions of the assembly meetings, the power resided with the people, and, thus, **demokratia** (demos, people; kratos, power), or **democracy**, was born.

It is important to note that while Greece was indeed the birthplace of democracy, it hardly resembled the democracies of the modern era. Only free adult males of pure Athenian lineage were eligible to participate in this "people power," and since that eligibility excluded women, children, slaves, and foreigners, probably only about 10% of the Athenian population could actually participate in assembly meetings.

It is impossible for historians to know the exact numbers, but it has been estimated that approximately one-third of the Greek population in classical antiquity were slaves. Unlike slavery in the United States prior to the Civil War, slavery in ancient Greece was not racially based. Most slaves were foreigners (i.e. foreign to the city-state in which they were enslaved), but were not necessarily ethnically different from their masters. Slaves participated in all sorts of activities, but most of them worked in households performing menial tasks.

The status of women in ancient Greece varied widely. In Sparta, for example, it seems that women were more independent than elsewhere in Greece (indeed, Sparta was criticized by Athenian men for allowing its women to participate in public activities to a degree unheard of in Athens). Generally speaking, Greek

Ostracism had a special meaning in ancient Athens. Athenian citizens would occasionally hold popular votes to banish individuals deemed dangerous to the state by writing those individuals' names on pottery shards (or "ostraka").

women were expected first and foremost to be wives and mothers, and to run the household with the assistance of their domestic slaves. Slave women, on the other hand, had no rights, and could be used sexually by their masters (as could male slaves).

The Greeks were polytheistic people whose deities were both male and female. Some of these deities were associated with nature, such as Poseidon (lord of the sea), while others were idealized versions of heroic humans (such as Apollo). Religious ritual in ancient Greece was an important part of private family life as well as public ceremonial life. The temples, which were thought to be the residences of the gods on earth, were the primary location in which religious rituals took place. Chief among these rituals was sacrifice, ranging from simple gifts of wine or bread to more elaborate (and bloody) slaughtering of animals.

In addition to the religious activities of the temples, the Greeks sought advice and prophecies from oracles, which were sacred places at which the gods were believed to communicate directly with humans. The most famous of these is the **Oracle at Delphi**, where, according to myth, Zeus declared the center of the earth was located. At the Temple of Apollo at Delphi, the Greeks kept an eternal flame burning continuously. So important was the oracle that Greek rulers almost always consulted it before undertaking wars, founding new city-states or colonies, and other major endeavors.

Finally, we cannot move on to the Romans without saying a brief word about the Greek intellectual tradition. **Philosophy**, literally "love of wisdom," has long been associated with ancient Greece. The Sophists were among the earliest teachers of wisdom; wise men who often traveled itinerantly and taught public speaking and logic in the agoras, the Sophists helped to develop the nascent Greek discipline of **rhetoric** (persuasive speaking that has applications in philosophy, politics, and law).

It was during the golden age of Athens that philosophers such as **Socrates**, **Plato**, and **Aristotle** made their greatest impact. Socrates, who lived approximately 470 to 399 B.C.E., was an innovator in the sense that he shifted philosophical inquiry from the natural world to questions of ethics. As a teacher, Socrates had a number of young disciples with whom he would converse and debate. Unfortunately, Socrates, who was critical of the status quo, angered quite a few Athenian elites, who eventually put him on trial for "corrupting the youth" and had him executed. One of Socrates' students, Plato, founded a philosophical academy outside of Athens in which young men could come to receive the ancient equivalent of a college education. Plato wrote all sorts of treatises, most of which take the form of "dialogues" between Socrates and others (some of which may have been imagined and some of which may have been based on oral traditions).

Another important classical philosopher was Aristotle, who lived approximately 384 to 322 B.C.E. A former student at Plato's academy, Aristotle founded his own philosophical school (called the Lyceum) and lectured and wrote on a huge number of topics, ranging from politics and law to ethics to physics and astronomy. Aristotle, in fact, was so well regarded that Philip of Macedon hired him to be the private tutor to his son, Alexander the Great.

Rome

The ancient Romans traced their mythological history all the way back to Aeneas, one of the few survivors of the Trojan War. Aeneas is said to have escaped the Greek siege of Troy with a band of survivors who then sailed across the Mediterranean to land on the Italian peninsula. Through some creative mythology, including help from Mars, the god of war, the bloodline of Aeneas was passed down to two brothers, Romulus and Remus. According to Roman legend, the rule of Romulus was followed by six kings, many of whom are believed to be Etruscan, a people who lived along the western coast of Italy north of Rome. It is likely the early Romans incorporated much of Etruscan culture into their own, including language (Latin), mythology, art, and architecture. The last of the Etruscan kings, Tarquinius Superbus, was a tyrant who was expelled from the city in a Roman rebellion. After the expulsion of the last Etruscan king, Romans vowed never to allow Rome to be ruled by a tyrant again.

After the expulsion of Tarquinius Superbus, the Romans established a **republican** form of government in 509 B.C.E. in order to limit the possibility that any one man could become supreme ruler. They divided the power of the state among different branches of government, most notably the Senate, run by the patrician upper classes, and the popular assemblies, run by the plebian common classes (the upper classes, it must be noted, wielded most of the power in this arrangement). The Romans also instituted yearly term limits and dual office holders as further checks on personal power. The highest of these office holders were the consuls, all of whom held the highest civil and military authority of the government. The Senate, however, remained the primary legislative and deliberative body of the Roman government, as it was dominated by the wealthiest and most notable of Roman families.

Rome, however, would be nothing without its armies. Although the republic would provide for stable government, Rome's armies would provide the conquests for the fledgling power of the Mediterranean. Over the 250 years following the formation of the republic, Rome conquered the entire Italian peninsula using a generous helping of "big stick" diplomacy. Basically, the young republic's neighbors knew they were little match for Rome's increasingly powerful armies, and many simply formed alliances with Rome without offering a fight. By 264 B.C.E., Rome dominated the entire Italian peninsula and increasingly threatened its neighbors across the Mediterranean.

Although Rome looked unbeatable after defeating Carthage and subduing Greece, all was not well on the home front. Centuries of war had placed an unbearable burden upon the common people, whose farms were nearly ruined while Rome's citizen-soldiers were off fighting. This "agrarian crisis" sparked a political clash that ended in the assassinations of high-level magistrates in the government. The Roman republic was trading debate for violence and murder, and by 100 B.C.E., the once stable state was now in full-fledged crisis.

As the republic weakened, a series of military generals began to assert their power in Roman politics. The most famous of these generals was **Julius Caesar**, who made a name for himself by conquering Gaul (modern-day France), and adding to the Roman Empire's possessions, as well as by invading Britain. Upon returning to Italy from his conquests in 49 B.C.E., Caesar refused to give up authority over his army (which was customary for a returning general) and decided instead on civil war.

By 45 B.C.E., Caesar was victorious and declared himself dictator for life. His leadership, however, was short-lived; a group of senators led by Brutus and Cassius killed him on the Ides (15th) of March in 44 B.C.E. The senators who killed Caesar believed they were fulfilling the vow made by their ancestors never to allow a tyrant to rule over Rome.

Caesar's death destabilized the republic even more, leading it back into civil war for the next thirteen years. The planners of Caesar's assassination were not particularly prepared for Caesar's adopted son, **Octavian**, to avenge his father's death. Octavian and his allies pursued his political rivals Mark Antony and Brutus, defeating Brutus in battle and driving Antony to suicide.

Octavian, however, was an unlikely candidate to bring stability back to Rome. He was adopted, had plenty of potential enemies, was an inexperienced general, and by all accounts, not a particularly healthy man. But he was a political genius. Rather than claim for himself the position of dictator for life, as did Caesar, he called himself **princeps**, "first citizen," meaning first among equals. This gesture signified to Romans, especially those who made up the Senate, that Octavian was more interested in healing Rome than claiming power for himself. In return, in 38 B.C.E., the Senate granted Octavian the honorific title of imperator, or emperor, and in 27 B.C.E. they added the title **Augustus** as a mark of their respect. Augustus, as he was henceforth known, created a new government, replacing the republic of old with an imperial government that placed the emperor and the elite Senate as the seats of power.

Although far less representative than the republic, this system of government provided enough stability to launch Rome into its greatest era of peace and prosperity, the **Pax Romana** (Roman peace); this period lasted from the ascendancy of Augustus in 27 B.C.E. to the death of Marcus Aurelius in 180 C.E.

The empire reached its zenith during the Pax Romana in 138 C.E. under the reign of Hadrian, whose wall in Britain (near the border between England and Scotland) marked the northernmost reach of the empire. But following the death of Marcus Aurelius in 180 C.E., Rome once again fell into an era of civil unrest and instability. In order to overcome a century of instability, the emperor Diocletian, who came to power in 284 C.E., created the tetrarchy, or "rule of four." In doing so Diocletian broke the empire into two pieces—the Roman-dominated west and the Greek-dominated east—with each piece to be ruled by an emperor and a second-in-command. If the emperor, or Augustus, of either the east or the west were to die, the second-in-command, or Caesar, would step in. Diocletian thought the empire's division and planned succession would make it easier to manage a large empire, but it may have actually hastened its fall.

Constantine, Diocletian's successor, instituted even more dramatic changes to the empire. Unlike Diocletian, who actively persecuted Christians, Constantine passed the Edict of Milan in 313 C.E., granting official toleration to Christians throughout the empire. Furthermore, Constantine, a Christian convert himself, promoted Christianity above all other religions by funding church-building programs throughout Rome, Jerusalem, and his new capital city, Constantinople. Constantinople (modern-day Istanbul), built upon the old city of Byzantium, continued a shift of political power and influence toward the eastern, Greek-dominated portion of the Roman Empire.

Although ruled politically by Rome, the eastern empire was dominated by Greek language and culture a legacy of Alexander the Great's conquests several centuries earlier). Yet Christianity came to dominate both the eastern and western part of the empire. In 300 C.E., Christianity could be found only in the major metropolitan areas of the empire. By 600 C.E., however, Christianity was dominant throughout the entire lands of the empire including Spain, North Africa, Egypt, and even Mesopotamia.

As Christianity's power and influence was rising throughout the empire, the power of the Roman state and of the Roman emperors was waning. In 380 C.E., emperor Theodosius required that all Romans believe as the archbishop of Rome, or the Pope, believed. The power of the Christian church became evident in 452 C.E. when it was Pope Leo I, not the emperor, who convinced Attila the Hun to withdraw his invading forces from Rome. Finally, in 476 C.E., an invading Germanic king deposed the last emperor of the western empire, Romulus Augustulus.

Although the eastern part of the empire lived on as the Byzantine Empire, most historians consider 476 the official end of the Roman Empire. Many factors contributed to the fall of Rome: political instability, strains on the military, invasions from Germanic barbarians, the rise of Christianity, economic struggles, and the sheer bureaucratic difficulty of managing a geographically expansive, culturally diverse empire. But even though the Roman state ended in 476, the Romanization of Europe had already taken place. The Germanic tribes who inherited control of Western Europe from Rome wanted to be Roman. The Latin language formed the basis of many regional languages throughout Europe as well. And although republican government remained dormant for nearly 1,800 years, the Roman ideas of representative rule and balance of power were resurrected during the Enlightenment of the eighteenth century.

Judaism

We have already explored a little bit about Christianity's relationship with the Roman Empire. However, we need to take a step backward and discover where Christianity came from: **Judaism**.

The three great monotheistic religions of the world are Judaism, Christianity, and Islam. These three are typically grouped together because they are bound by two broadly unifying themes. First, they promote the worship of a single god—the

Blah Blah
The word barbarian comes from the ancient Greek word barbaros, meaning a "non-Greek," or one who speaks a language one doesn't understand. The word is onomatopoeic: "Bar-bar" is the sound that people speaking unintelligibly make, similar to "blah-blah" in English.

same god, in fact; second, all three can trace their theological histories back to the **patriarch** (meaning "father") **Abraham**. Although they share some of the same traits, the histories of these great religions differ tremendously. In the next few sections we'll look at a very brief history of Judaism, Christianity, and Islam from their births through around the twelfth century C.E.

The earliest years of Judaism remain somewhat obscure to historians. Theologically, of course, Jews trace their ancestry back to the mythical Adam and Eve, but the oldest texts that we know about date to around 1200 B.C.E. As was the case in many ancient societies, the Jews transmitted stories about their own history and traditions orally over a period of several hundred years before formally writing anything down, and as such it is somewhat difficult to use texts such as the Hebrew Bible to reconstruct the exact history of any given time period.

The uniqueness of Abraham's story was his claim that the Hebrew God, declaring himself the one and only God, creator of the earth, revealed himself directly to Abraham. Scholars disagree about the exact timeline of events, so while some consider Judaism the first monotheistic religion, others think Zoroastrianism claims the title. In any event, Abraham's declaration of monotheistic faith had the effect of asserting that everyone else's gods were false gods, which certainly didn't win him many friends.

According to the biblical account, King David successfully united the Jews and moved his administrative capital to Jerusalem, where remains of his building achievements can still be seen today. Legend holds that David brought the Ark of the Covenant to Jerusalem and thus the city became extremely important both politically and religiously in the history of Judaism. Indeed, it was David's son, King Solomon, who commissioned the building of the First Temple in Jerusalem around 960 B.C.E. During Solomon's time, Israel actively traded with its neighbors and its leaders amassed a fair amount of wealth.

Nearly all of what we know about the ancient Jewish peoples comes from Hebrew scripture with little other historical corroboration. But what we do learn from historical evidence is that the ancient Jews, like most Mesopotamian peoples, were conquered many times over. Ancient Assyrian records from Nineveh confirm some stories of the Old Testament, including the Assyrian destruction of ancient Israel (one of two ancient Jewish kingdoms, the other being Judah) and siege of Jerusalem in 722 B.C.E.

The Babylonian king Nebuchadnezzar conquered Judah, the kingdom that survived the Assyrian onslaught, in 586 B.C.E. Nebuchadnezzar destroyed the temple of Jerusalem, the center of Jewish worship, and exiled the Jewish ruling classes, taking them back to Babylon. This period of exile is known as the Babylonian Captivity and marks the beginning of the Jewish **Diaspora**, meaning "scattering" or "spreading out."

Many historians believe that it was during this period of Jewish history that the Hebrew scriptures (Old Testament) were written down for the first time in order to preserve Jewish tradition during a time of imprisonment away from their homeland. Other changes occurred as a result of the Babylonian Captivity as well: Since the Jews could not physically go to Jerusalem to conduct their religious rituals, they began to meet in synagogues, gathering places in which the community could worship and participate in educational activities. Other markers of Jewish communal identity were strengthened and developed during this time period, including the importance of the Sabbath (day of rest), dietary guidelines, and the concept of ritual purity.

The Babylonian captivity lasted less than fifty years, because the Jews were released from their long-distance imprisonment when the Persian Empire conquered the Babylonians in 539 B.C.E. After being freed by the Persians, most of the exiled Jews returned to Jerusalem and gradually rebuilt their temple and the kingdom, naming their new kingdom Judea. Alexander the Great disrupted Independent Jewish rule yet again in 333 B.C.E., when his army rolled through Judea to claim it as a part of Alexander's great empire.

After about 250 years of Hellenistic rule, a Jewish revolt briefly regained Hebrew rule over Judea. The leaders of this revolt were the Maccabees, military rulers of the Hasmonean Dynasty. This victory in 165 B.C.E. is celebrated today as the Jewish holiday of Hanukkah. In addition to reducing the influence of Hellenistic culture among the Jews, the Hasmoneans expanded the boundaries of Judea by conquering neighboring provinces.

After a hundred years, however, Judea lost its independence as it was brought under the control of Rome in 63 B.C.E. The Romans ruled over the Jews through a series of governors, whom the Jews considered merely puppet-kings. The Romans initially tolerated the Jews and gave them a somewhat special status because of their "ancient" religion; they didn't require the Jews to worship Roman gods. Growing tired of Roman rule, the Jews attempted the First Revolt, from 66 to 73 C.E. The result was disastrous for the Jews. The Romans reacted by laying siege to Jerusalem, destroying the temple, and overtaking the last Jewish holdouts in the Masada fortress.

The Romans then exiled many Jews from Judea and turned it into a true Roman colony ruled by Romans, who worshiped the Roman pantheon of gods. Even after this defeat, the Jewish peoples attempted another fight to gain independence in Judea by launching a Second Revolt from 115–117 C.E. The Second Revolt ended in failure just as the First Revolt had; the Romans destroyed Jerusalem and banished Jews from returning to their homeland. From 132–135 C.E. there was a Third Revolt, but this too was a failure. Following these revolts, more Jews lived outside ancient Palestine than within. This Jewish diaspora spread across the Mediterranean and the Near East, forming close-knit Jewish communities throughout the lands of the Roman Empire and beyond.

Living outside of their homeland was a challenge for the Jewish people of the diaspora. However, the discrimination and persecution they faced from the communities to which they moved helped the Jews maintain their cultural and religious identity. Often unwilling to assimilate Jews into their own cultures and forcing them to live in separate communities, their new homelands encouraged the Jews to rely upon themselves for their success and survival. This "otherness" felt by the Jews throughout history contributed to the Zionist, or return to the homeland, movement of the late nineteenth century and the creation of the modern state of Israel in the middle of the twentieth century.

The irony of the history of the Jewish people is their impact relative to the size of their population. The introduction of monotheism to the ancient world changed the course of history. Christianity, also a monotheistic religion, itself began as a Jewish sect. And even Islam traces its history to the Jewish patriarch Abraham.

Christianity

Christianity adopted the Hebrew Bible as its own Old Testament and therefore shares the same religious history as Judaism, including a lineage from the Hebrew patriarch, Abraham. In fact, in the early years of the Jesus movement, it is somewhat difficult to distinguish Judaism from Christianity. Jesus's disciples and most of the earliest believers in Jesus were Jewish, and it was not until some years after Jesus's death that the religion began to spread among the Gentiles (non-Jews).

Christianity begins, of course, with Jesus, who was born around 4 B.C.E. in the town of Bethlehem (near Jerusalem) and grew up in the town of Nazareth in Galilee (northern Israel). We know very little about the historical Jesus, just as we know little about early Judaism. In fact, all of what we know about him comes from Christian scripture, particularly the four gospels of the New Testament, which were written decades after Jesus's death in c. 30 C.E. Although born a Jew, Jesus's teachings differed from the Jewish norms of the times. He rejected both Jewish dietary laws and the dominant role of the Jewish priesthood.

Most in the Jewish community, particularly those in the elite Jewish priesthood, did not recognize Jesus as an authority figure, but as Jesus continued his teachings, both he and his followers left behind a growing rank of converts and a fledgling organizational structure that would eventually turn into the Christian church. While the Jesus movement did not attract too much notice during Jesus's own lifetime, it eventually spread throughout the Mediterranean region and beyond. As Jesus's message and congregation spread, both Jewish leaders and the Romans became increasingly suspicious of his growing influence. According to Christian scripture, the authorities seized Jesus, held a mock trial under the Roman prefect Pontius Pilate, and executed Jesus by crucifixion. Christianity, like many Jewish sects of the day, could have ended with Jesus's death, but it was with Jesus's death that Christianity began to evolve from an obscure sect into a religion that would come to dominate the Roman Empire and beyond.

Even by 100 C.E., Christianity was not guaranteed any measure of future success. Christians were regularly persecuted throughout the Roman Empire during the 300 years following the death of Jesus. There are complex reasons for this persecution, but at least in part it was due to the Christians' refusal to worship the emperors as the Roman imperial cult required. It is important to note, however, that despite the many literary accounts of martyrdom in early Christianity, most persecutions were short-lasting and localized.

The reality of persecution certainly played a huge role in the development of Christian communal identity and brought Christians closer together. In one well-known event, the Emperor Nero infamously scapegoated Christians in 64 C.E. for a great fire in Rome by burning them at the stake and using them as fodder for the lions in sporting events (allegedly, anyway). Although not every Roman emperor chose to persecute Christians as vehemently as did Nero, for a while Christians were regular targets of the Roman political leadership.

Despite this hostility, Christianity took root among the common people of the empire. Rome's native religion, largely borrowed from the Greeks, was primarily the domain of the Roman elite, and only the wealthiest of Romans participated in major religious rituals of the state religion. Therefore, most commoners felt rather distanced from the complex Roman pantheon of gods and goddesses. For the common folk left out of Roman religion, Christianity presented a welcoming and desirable message. Many of the earliest Christians, furthermore, were slaves and women, who may have found Christianity's emphasis on the equality of all believers somewhat liberating.

Christianity offered a belief in a single, benevolent God and an eternal afterlife. The stories of Jesus gave ordinary Romans a personality with whom they could make an emotional connection. Furthermore, the teachings of Christianity required a stricter moral code than that of Roman traditional religion, which was enticing to those living in the turbulent provinces of the Roman Empire. In sum, Christianity offered what Roman religion did not: a better way of living during this life and the next.

Islam

The origins of the Islamic faith are traced back to the life of **Muhammad** (570–632 C.E.), an Arab merchant. Muhammad was evidently born in Mecca, was married to several wives, and had numerous children. According to Islamic teachings, in 610, Muhammad was meditating in a cave in the mountains outside of Mecca when he heard the voice of the angel Gabriel commanding him to recite and memorize the word of God. This was the first of many such visitations during which Gabriel recited the word of God to Muhammad, who subsequently related these revelations to his close friends and family orally and later dictated what he had learned to scribes who wrote it down in Arabic (which is why Muslims believe that Arabic is the "language of God").

After his death, Muhammad's followers gathered all the known writings and transcriptions of these visitations to create the **Qur'an** ("recitations"). The word **Islam** means "submission," and Muslims are "those who submit" to the word of God as embodied in the text of the Qur'an. Among other beliefs, one core tenet of Islam is that Muhammad was the final messenger from God to the people of earth (although Muslims also believe in many of the Jewish and Christian prophets, including Jesus, who is discussed in many sections of the Qur'an). Another distinguishing characteristic of Islam is the belief that Muslims are descended not from Abraham's son Isaac, as were the Jews, but from Ishmael, Abraham's other son.

The Qur'an and the hadith (accounts of Muhammad's saying and actions) are the basis of Islamic Law, the **shari'a**, which is practiced by **qadis**, Islamic judges. In early Islam, the governing and religious leaders worked more closely together, but over time the scope of power of the political rulers and religious leaders became more separate and a true Islamic Empire was born.

The **Five Pillars of Islam** are the five basic tenets of the faith, combining individual spiritual responsibility, social justice, and worship of one God. First is the belief that "There is no god but God, and Muhammad is his Prophet." Second, Muslims are required to pray five times a day in the direction of Mecca and, if possible, also in a group service at midday on Friday. Third, believers must care for those less fortunate in their communities in the form of charity to the poor, orphans, or others who are in need. Fourth, believers must fast during daylight throughout the month of Ramadan. Finally, Muslims should complete the **hajj**, the pilgrimage to Mecca, at least once during their lifetime if they are physically and financially capable of doing so.

After his first visitations, Muhammad did not find many other followers outside his close family circle: His first wife Khadija, a wealthy widow, and his cousin Ali were among his first followers. Unpopular in Mecca, Muhammad fled to Medina, an agricultural center several hundred miles north of Mecca, in 622. This decamping to Medina is known as the **hijra**, the "migration" or "flight." Muhammad's removal to Medina marks the beginning of the Muslim calendar; therefore, Year 1 in the Muslim calendar corresponds to 622 in the Christian calendar. In Medina, Muhammad built up a community of believers, or **umma**. This marked a major shift for the Arabs, who traditionally defined community around kinship rather than faith. In Medina, Muhammad became a leader and saw some of his teachings made into law. In their efforts to spread the faith, followers of Islam clashed with surrounding tribes and those of other faiths. Eventually Muhammad and his followers took over the town of Mecca, site of the Ka'aba, an ancient site of religious worship. The Ka'aba was stripped of its idols and was converted to a Muslim shrine, and remains a major site of pilgrimage today. The Ka'aba, now considered the house of God on earth, became the focal point of Muslim religious devotion, and it is in the direction of Mecca that Muslims face when they pray.

Muhammad died in 632. Leadership of the umma was given over to Abu Bakr, Muhammad's father-in-law by his second wife, Aisha. Abu Bakr became **caliph**, ruler of the Muslim community (khalifah in Arabic means "successor"). Under Abu Bakr, Islam spread via warfare across the Arab peninsula. Islamic armies fought and defeated Byzantine and Persian Sassanid troops, spreading further until they reached beyond the Arab peninsula into Asia Minor and North Africa, but they didn't yet get past the Byzantines holding their ground at the Anatolian peninsula. Islamic forces saw many victories: Damascus, Jerusalem, and the Persian Sassanid Empire's capital at Ctesiphon all fell to Muslim invaders. In short, Islam spread rapidly and widely, stretching from the Indus River in the east to the northwest coast of Africa by the late eighth century.

A Sixth Pillar?

The jihad, or sacred struggle, is another important tenet of Islamic belief. Jihad in times of war could be physical or military combat to expand dar al-Islam, the "abode of Islam," which could mean either territory ruled by Muslims or wherever Islam is practiced. However, in daily life, the greater jihad is simply a personal spiritual call to live righteously and struggle for self-perfection.

By 700 C.E., only 70 years after the death of Muhammad, Islam, under the Umayyad dynasty, had spread to North Africa and much of the eastern Mediterranean, completely isolating Christian Europe from Asia and the Near East. Furthermore, Islam had even penetrated into Europe itself through the Iberian Peninsula (modern-day Spain and Portugal), moving well into modern-day France. The Muslim invaders were stopped, however, by the Frankish-Carolingian ruler, Charles Martel ("The Hammer"), who defeated them in western central France at the Battle of Tours in 732 C.E. Over the next 700 years, Spanish Christians fought to drive the Muslims from the Iberian Peninsula and from Europe, a struggle known as the **reconquista**. Furthermore, Charlemagne, Martel's grandson, fought to solidify Christian orthodoxy (along Frankish lines) over much of Western Europe.

Different sects developed among Muslims, mainly as a result of problems with the succession of caliphs. The third caliph Uthman was assassinated, and Ali, son-in-law of Muhammad, became the fourth caliph, although he was not the popular choice of the umma. Backers of Ali—the Shi'at Ali, or **Shi'ites**—felt that caliphs must be of Muhammad's family. On the other hand, those who supported the first three caliphs (the "Rightly Guided Caliphs") became known as **Sunni**, who believed that he whom the umma named caliph is rightfully its leader.

In the early development of Islam, Shi'ites were more concerned with spiritual purity of the faith than were the Sunnis, and fought to have their **imams**, or religious leaders, become caliphs. All eleven of the eventual Shi'ite imams died, and the twelfth (and last) disappeared, taking the bloodline of Muhammad with him. The ancient split between Sunni and Shi'ite Muslims over the caliphate still exists today, although this rivalry is now often about how the umma should be ruled and the place of the imams in governance. The majority of Muslims in the world today are Sunni Muslims, although Shi'ite Muslims are a majority in Iraq, Iran, and Azerbaijan.

EUROPE PRE-TWENTIETH CENTURY

The Middle Ages

Developments in Europe and points east became quite complicated during the **Middle Ages**, which is the period after the fall of Rome and before the Renaissance. As you might recall from earlier in this chapter, the Roman Empire, and eventually Christianity, was divided into two factions that split, reconnected, and then split again. Ultimately, the eastern Roman Empire, centered in Constantinople, became the highly centralized government known as the **Byzantine Empire**; whereas, in the west, the empire collapsed entirely, although the religion retained a strong foothold. The important point to remember about all this is that even though both segments of the empire followed Christianity, they practiced different forms of the religion; moreover, their populations competed for supremacy.

The best place to begin a discussion of political developments in western Europe in the Middle Ages is with the **Franks**. After the classical Roman Empire fell apart, due in part to invasions from Germanic tribes, these tribes settled throughout western Europe. Most of the tribes converted to Christianity relatively quickly, though politically they continued to run their own shows. That meant they came into regular conflict with each other, and they formed alliances and expanded, sometimes enough to be considered kingdoms. The most significant of these early kingdoms was the Franks.

The Franks were a Germanic tribe that united under the leadership of King Clovis in the late fifth century. He built a rather large empire that stretched from present-day Germany through Belgium and into France. He converted to Catholicism and established his capital in Paris. After he died, his empire was divided among his sons, after which it declined in influence.

Nevertheless, the empire did help the various peoples of western Europe solidify under a common culture, which made it easier for them to unify against Muslim invasions, which in the eighth century took over parts of Spain and Italy. Charles Martel led the revolt against the advancing Muslim armies and in 732 defeated them at the Battle of Tours.

Martel then used his position as a political and military leader under the declining Frankish **Merovingian Dynasty** to put his sons forth as successors, thus founding the **Carolingian Dynasty**. Martel had worked during his tenure to reunite the region under his control, and when his son Pepin the Short (there were several Pepins in Frankish history) ascended to the throne in 752 C.E., he chose to have his succession certified by the pope, a significant step that sent the clear signal that an empire's legitimacy rested on the Catholic Church's approval.

In the centuries following the breakup of the Roman Empire, no true empire existed in western Europe. The Franks had built a large kingdom, but it could hardly be considered an empire by historical standards. It would be Pepin's son, Charles (747–814 C.E.), who would revitalize the concept of the empire in western Europe. Like his father, Charles was crowned by the pope in 800 and became known as Charlemagne ("Charles the Great").

The empire Charlemagne built would come to be called the Holy Roman Empire upon the coronation of Otto the Great in 962. It's important to point out that this empire had little in common with the original Roman Empire, other than the fact that power was once again centralized and Rome began to think of itself again as a world center. The size of the Holy Roman Empire, in comparison to its namesake, was relatively small. It included northern Italy, Germany, Belgium, and France. Nevertheless, it marked the beginning of western European ambition in terms of empire-building, especially among those in the church.

Under Charlemagne, a strong focus was placed on the arts and education, but not surprisingly with a much more religious bent—much of this effort centered in the monasteries under the direction of the church. And though Charlemagne was very powerful, his rule was not absolute. Society was structured around feudalism.

Charlemagne had overall control of the empire, but the local lords held power over the local territories, answering to Charlemagne only on an as-needed basis. And because Charlemagne did not levy taxes, he failed to build a strong and united empire. After his death, and the death of his son Louis, the empire was divided among his three grandsons according to the Treaty of Verdun in 843.

During this time, western Europe continued to be attacked by powerful invaders, notably the Vikings from Scandinavia and the Magyars from Hungary. Although the Vikings were not the only raiders, they were perhaps the most successful. Beginning around 800, they used their highly maneuverable, multi-oared boats to raid well beyond their borders—on the open seas, up and down the North Atlantic coast, and along the inland rivers.

Remarkably, however, in spite of their various victories, the Vikings, too, were converted to Christianity. This continued in a pattern of invading tribes assimilating to a common civilization in western Europe because of religion, not political power. Catholicism became institutionalized at every level of life. By the middle of the Middle Ages, the Catholic Church had become the most powerful institution in western Europe and one of the most powerful institutions in the world.

Feudalism, the name of the European social, economic, and political system of the Middle Ages, had a strict hierarchy. At the top was a king, who had power over an entire territory called his kingdom. Beneath him were the nobles, who in exchange for military service and loyalty to the king were granted power over sections of the kingdom. The nobles, in turn, divided their lands into smaller sections under the control of lesser lords called vassals. The vassals could also split their lands into smaller pieces and give custody of them to subordinate vassals, who could divide their lands into even smaller pieces in the custody of even more subordinate vassals, and so on. Below the vassals were peasants, who worked the land. For this system to work, everyone had to fulfill obligations to others at different levels in the hierarchy: to serve in the military, produce food, or serve those who were at a higher level.

The estates that were granted to the vassals were called fiefs, and these later became known as manors. The lord and the peasants lived on the manor. The peasants worked the land on behalf of the lord, and in exchange the lord gave the peasants protection and a place to live. Many of the manors were remarkably self-sufficient. Everything that was needed to live was produced on them. Food was harvested, clothing and shoes were made, and so on. Advances made in the science of agriculture during this time helped the manors to succeed.

Peasants (called serfs) in the feudal social system, whether male or female, had few rights. As manorial life evolved, an increasing number of peasants became tied to the land quite literally: They couldn't leave the manor without permission from their lord. Peasants were not quite slaves, but not free either. Ironically, however, it was this "imprisonment" on the land that led to the serfs becoming highly skilled workers. In short, they learned how to do whatever it took to make the manor on which they worked self-sufficient.

Black Death
One of the most well-known features of the Middle Ages was the prevalence of disease. Historians and scientists believe the Black Death was most likely bubonic plague, caused by a bacterium named Yersinia pestis, which was spread by fleas that lived on the rats that were everywhere in the Middle Ages. By the time the first plague pandemic died out (yes, this was the first of many) it had killed as many as 75 million people worldwide!

As many of the serfs became skilled in trades other than farming, and Europe slowly but surely started trading with the rest of the world, some of these skilled craftspeople began to earn extra income. Over time, this chipped away at the rigid social stratification of the manor system. When banking began in Europe, towns and cities started to gain momentum. The result was the emergence of a **middle class**, made up of urban craftsmen and merchants. Their success lured more people into towns, in the hopes of making more money or learning new skills. By the eleventh century, western Europe was re-engaging with the world.

The Magna Carta

Since the time of William the Conqueror, England had followed a tradition of a strong monarchy. But during the rule of King John, powerful English nobles rebelled and forced him to sign the **Magna Carta** (1215 C.E.). This document reinstated the feudal rights of the nobles, but also extended the rule of law to other people in the country, namely the growing burgher class. This laid the foundation for the Parliament. Initially, an assembly was established made up of nobles who were responsible for representing the views of different parts of England on law-making and taxation issues. After a trial period, the Parliament was established. Later, it was divided into two branches: the House of Lords (nobles and clergy) and the House of Commons (knights and wealthy burghers). The House of Lords presided over legal issues and advised the king; the House of Commons was concerned with issues of trade and taxation. The result was that England established its identity pretty early on.

The Renaissance

The Intellectual Renaissance: Europe's Oldest Universities

Bologna, Italy—1088
Paris, France—1150
Oxford, England—1167
Cambridge, England—1209
Salamanca, Spain—1218
Padua, Italy—1222
Siena, Italy—1240
Charles University, Prague, Czech Republic—1348
Jagiellonian University, Krakow, Poland—1364
Vienna, Austria—1365

The **Renaissance** is a period of flourishing artistic and intellectual developments that took place roughly between the fourteenth and seventeenth centuries. It has no defined starting point and developed in different places at different times. However, the basic ideas of the Renaissance were articulated in the writings of Francesco **Petrarch** (1304–1374), who considered the Roman Empire to be the high point of human civilization, and everything after the fall of the empire in the west to be a period of social deterioration that he termed the **Dark Ages**. Only by returning to the learning of the great Greek and Roman thinkers could humanity redeem itself. Therefore, the Renaissance was metaphysically a rebirth of European thought through the rediscovery of ancient manuscripts of the Greeks and Romans. Access to the intellectual wealth of antiquity was made possible by Islamic scholars who had translated the teachings of ancient thinkers after the Muslims conquered the homeland of ancient Greece.

Philosophically, the Renaissance centered on the ideas of **humanism**, which placed man himself—rather than god—at the center of study and inquiry. In medieval Europe, thoughts of salvation and the afterlife so dominated personal priorities that life on Earth was, for many, something to be suffered through on the way to heaven rather than lived through as a pursuit of its own. As Europeans rediscovered ancient texts, they were struck with the degree that humanity—personal accomplishment and personal happiness—formed the central core of so much of the literature and philosophy of the ancient writers. The emphasis began to shift fulfillment in the afterlife to participating in the here-and-now. As a consequence, people began to shift their focus to life on Earth and to celebrating human achievements in the scholarly, artistic, and political realms.

Humanism, however, was not necessarily in conflict with an active spiritual life. **Desiderius Erasmus** (1466–1536) and **Sir Thomas More** (1478–1535) were just two of the notable humanist philosophers of this era, promoting ideas of equality and tolerance. Erasmus, of the Netherlands, (known as the "Prince of the Humanists"), along with being one of the most well-known learned men of the times who counseled kings and popes, was also a priest. His works focused on both ecclesiastic and humanist subjects, and he promoted religious toleration as the best pathway to truth. Sir Thomas More, of England, wrote *Utopia*, which described an ideal society, in which everyone shared the wealth, and everyone's needs were met. Erasmus and More were Christian Humanists, meaning that they expressed moral guidelines in the Christian tradition, which they believed people should follow as they pursued their own personal goals. However not all Humanist writers at this time adopted the moralistic approach in their work. The political writings of **Niccolo Machiavelli** were born from his humanist emphasis on human behavior and the nature of virtue, though they were more cynical than the Roman principles that underlay humanism. Secular education also gained prominence in the Renaissance; many of the world's greatest universities were founded in this period. Education became a means not only to be a man of God, but also to develop the skills and knowledge needed to serve the state; leaders could be made, not just born, a significant change in thought.

The great city-states of Italy and mercantile centers of northern Europe hosted an enormous outpouring of artistic creation, fueled by the wealth of merchants who commissioned some of the greatest art of the era. In Italy, where powerful families in city-states such as Florence, Venice, and Milan became rich on trade, art was financed on a scale not seen since the classical civilizations of Greece and Rome. The Medici family in Florence, for example, not only ruled the great city and beyond but turned it into a showcase of architecture and beauty by acting as patron for some of the greatest artists of the time. And Renaissance art is a Who's Who of great artists: in southern Europe were Michelangelo, Fillipo Brunelleschi, Leonardo Da Vinci, Donatello, and Tommaso Masaccio; in northern Europe were Jan and Hubert van Eyck and Albrecht Dürer. Unlike medieval paintings, which depicted humans as flat, stiff, and out of proportion with their surroundings, paintings of the Renaissance demonstrated the application of humanist ideals learned from the ancients. Careful use of light and shadow made figures appear full and real.

In essence, the Renaissance (along with the university system and theology more generally) set the stage for the next great period in European history, the Reformation. It did so by encouraging the spread of secular thought as well as more critical approaches to Christian thought not mediated by the Catholic Church in Rome. The idea that the health of society rested not just on the graces of God, but also in the actions of men toward other men, shifted the paradigm of power in ways that would soon prove to be truly revolutionary.

The Reformation

The origins of the Reformation era lay in a broad dissatisfaction with the Catholic Church. Three large groups had a bone to pick with the Church:

1. The lower classes/peasants, who saw the Church as being made up of large landholders who were in cahoots with the ruling elites, who all were generally abusive to the masses. Baptists and Mennonites arose out of this class.

2. The budding middle class, who felt that the Church was working with the aristocrats in order to protect aristocratic privilege and economic supremacy. The middle class wanted a bigger piece of the pie, economically speaking, and felt the Church was hindering this. Calvinist (Switzerland), Puritan (England), and Huguenot (France) sects, as well as the Dutch Reformed Church, resulted from this class.

3. Kings and other nobility who fought with the Church regarding taxes, legal jurisdiction, and political power and influence. The Middle Ages had already set the stage for a clash between secular rulers and the Church, so it isn't surprising that many rulers supported the Protestant cause as a way to curb the Church's influence in their own lands. The Anglican Church (England) and Lutherans (Germany) are two sects that had aristocratic foundations.

You may recognize these as the middle class plus the two medieval classes of society that were not the Church: In short, this list includes pretty much everyone. However, the Reformation was obviously not just about economics and power; it was a religious movement that sought to curb the excesses of the Church and correct Church doctrine. Protestants believed not only that Church leaders had become abusive and oppressive, but also that the Catholic leaders were wrong in the way they interpreted Christian doctrine—a hugely important issue. An error in doctrine could impede one's salvation.

Martin Luther (1438–1546) was the catalyst for the Reformation, a devout Catholic priest who at first tried to reform the Catholic Church from within. He was particularly against selling indulgences, a process by which a wealthy penitent could pay money to the Church in exchange for the expiation of sins. When his complaints were ignored, Luther nailed his **Ninety-Five Theses** to the door of the Castle Church in Wittenburg, a traditional way to open up discussion on theology at the time. The Church was extremely displeased, to put it mildly: Pope Leo X, with the support of Holy Roman Emperor Charles V, had Luther excommunicated at the Diet of Worms in 1521. But Luther soon found himself under the protection of German princes who agreed with him (and who—coincidentally, of course—opposed the authority of the Holy Roman Emperor), and he eventually produced a translation of the New Testament in German, the first step to allowing people to read the Bible for themselves.

The Power of the Press

Before the invention of the printing press and the spread of books in vernacular (spoken) languages in Europe, most people didn't know how to read. Reading material existed mostly in the form of Latin manuscripts, handwritten documents produced in monasteries, usually on religious topics. So not only was there not much to read, few knew how to read Latin.

Luther's ideas (eventually published as the Augsburg Confession) formed the core of Protestantism, a word which came to mean anyone who protested against the Catholic Church. Luther wanted to break the Church's monopoly on the interpretation of the Bible, believing that individuals needed only to learn from the Bible directly to find the path to salvation; the cycle of sin, confession, and penance—and the clergy who facilitated that cycle—was in Luther's view largely unnecessary. Luther's ideas were dangerous because he undermined the Church's justifications for its existence in a way that had never before been so fully articulated. As his ideas spread, the clergy lost their unique power over interpreting doctrine, and instead city councils and other town leaders became more central to running local churches. Revolts spread in the 1520s, as literal-minded reformers from the lower classes challenged the tax system and other rules that weren't in the Bible. These reforms went in directions Luther had not intended: He was opposed to the idea of the liberation of the peasants and of increased political rights for non-aristocrats, as were most of the princes who supported him. But although he started the changes, he was personally powerless to stop them (aside from encouraging the nobility to be brutal in putting down peasant revolts).

Luther's ideas sparked the Reformation, but soon other theologians added their own unique contributions to the mix. Few Protestant thinkers were more influential to early American history than **John Calvin** (1509–1564), who preached a more severe brand of Protestantism. Calvin believed that only certain people were born into salvation, and these "elect" had a responsibility to lead others in creating just, well-ordered societies and to accumulate wealth, a further sign of God's favor. Those who were poor were poor exactly because they were not among the elect. Calvin's ideas were at the heart of the Reformed (Calvinist) church, which first grew in influence in Geneva, Switzerland, but developed followers in the Netherlands and France as well as the New World, forming the basis of many communities in the New England colonies.

As Reformation ideas spread, Europe soon found itself divided between Catholic and Protestant beliefs. Although Holy Roman Emperor Charles V had issued an imperial edict that no one harbor Luther, various princes ignored the edict, using the Protestant threat as leverage against the Church to have their own complaint heard. In other places, secular leaders took advantage of the Church's weakness to seize Church land for themselves. The Church, meanwhile, was occupied not only with the proliferation of Protestants, but more importantly, with the invasions of the Turks, who had taken Constantinople in 1453 and attacked Vienna in 1529 under the leadership of Suleiman. Once the Turkish threat was under control, the Church could return to the Protestant claims.

Warfare between Protestant and Catholic forces worsened in the 1540s and 1550s, ending with the Peace of Augsburg in 1555, which proclaimed the principle of *cuius regio eius religio* (whose realm, his religion), according to which a prince could accept either the Protestant or Catholic faith according to his conscience, and the citizens of his territory would have to follow his lead. As Protestantism spread across Europe, Catholic rulers sought to stem the tide and reclaim Protestant lands for Catholicism, even though Augsburg protected the right of Protestant rulers within the Holy Roman Empire to maintain their faith. Charles V soon abdicated the Holy Roman throne, exhausted from the battles over land, politics, and faith.

The Reformation developed differently in different regions, each focusing on one aspect of reform more than another. In England, the Reformation instituted more political and monarchical changes and facilitated the rise of the Anglican Church. In France, Calvinists focused more on the behavior of the clergy. In Scandinavian countries, Lutheranism became the dominant religion, championed by kings who had long desired a break from Rome.

The Enlightenment

The revolutions that changed the political face of monarchic Europe in the seventeenth and eighteenth centuries didn't come out of nowhere. They were the natural progression of political, economic, and philosophical development, and were particularly influenced by the ideas of **Enlightenment** thinkers. The Enlightenment signaled a shift toward secular ideas, a trend that had begun with the Reformation. The Enlightenment continued the development of ideas that supported secular power at the expense of ecclesiastical power and the rights of the individual over those of the aristocracy. This mindset is a logical extension of the Reformation idea of individual salvation, which is the heart of Protestant belief and in agreement with the individualistic ethos of the classical world.

Authority came to mean something very different than it had previously; it didn't just come from God via the Church anymore. Laws governing human conduct weren't dictated by the spiritual teachings of the Church or the self-serving mandates of the aristocrats; they could be derived from human reason. This in turn meant that man had natural rights, unalienable and universal, that should guide both individual and state conduct. Englishman **Thomas Hobbes** (1588–1679) was the most influential spokesman for the idea that a king's power to rule came not from God, but from the will of the people.

"To understand political power aright, and derive from it its original, we must consider what estate all men are naturally in, and that is, a state of perfect freedom to order their actions, and dispose of their possessions and persons as they think fit, within the bounds of the law of Nature, without asking leave or depending upon the will of any other man."

–John Locke, Second Treatise of Government, 1690

Enlightenment ideas influenced nearly every facet of life: government, economics, education, and culture. In England, political liberalism promoted the right to life, liberty, and property most importantly. Property was significant because it was believed that citizens gave the government authority to control society in return for protection of citizens' property rights, an idea developed by Englishman **John Locke** (1632–1704). This is called the **social contract**. Also, according to English law, a citizen is defined as someone who owns property—so property ownership, especially land ownership, was very important. English liberalism also calls for minimal government intervention into the economic and social lives of its citizens; the state's power is restricted to establishing boundaries that allow people to express their natural rights without infringing on the rights of others.

In France, the birthplace of the Enlightenment, arose the *philosophes*, writers and social critics who championed the idea that human reason should be the basis for solving the problems of society and creating a social order that benefited nearly everyone. Human progress could happen only with the constant development and expansion of knowledge, a theme that encouraged the support of scientific study and the spread of education to those beyond the nobility. The greatest Enlightenment thinkers all shared this belief in the power of knowledge and the perfectibility of human society through the political application of human reason: Montesquieu, Condorcet, Diderot, Rousseau, and Voltaire are among the most influential of the era. However, the Enlightenment ideas did not necessarily mean the end of monarchies; the idea of the enlightened despot—one who was autocratic but was supported by the people—was popular at the time. Democracy was an idea that did not really take off until the eighteenth century.

European Exploration

Exploration before the late fifteenth century was largely limited to land travel. To be sure, ships were used on the Mediterranean and Indian Ocean trade routes for centuries, but they were linked up to land routes through Persia, Arabia, northern Africa, or central Asia on the Silk Road. Eager to eliminate Muslim middlemen and discover more efficient trade routes to Asia, the Portuguese and their Iberian rivals, the Spanish, set out to sea. Advances in navigation, shipbuilding, and the development of gunpowder weapons allowed for increased sea travel. These "floating empires of the wind" soon controlled major shipping routes in the Indian Ocean, Indonesia, and the Atlantic Ocean.

The increase in European trade encouraged by the formation of the Hanseatic League and the Crusades spawned a search for new, efficient trade routes on the seas. Portugal led the way because it was strategically situated near the coast of Africa, had long-standing trade relations with Muslim nations, and, most important of all, was led by a royal family that supported exploration (King John I of Portugal's most famous son was Prince Henry the Navigator). In 1488, Portugal financed a voyage by Bartholomew Dias who rounded the tip of Africa (which became known as the Cape of Good Hope). In 1497, Vasco da Gama rounded the Cape of Good Hope, explored the east African kingdoms, and then went all the way to India, where he established trade relations.

Shortly thereafter, Spain, which had recently been unified under Isabella and Ferdinand, wanted in on the action. As you well know, in 1492 Christopher Columbus convinced them to finance a voyage to reach the east by going west. While those who were educated understood that the earth was a sphere, few people understood how large it was. Despite the fact that some scholars had accurately estimated the earth's size, most people, including Columbus, thought it was smaller. As a result, Columbus thought that China and India were located where the American continents are. He sailed, found Cuba and the islands that came to be known as the West Indies, and the exploration of the Americas was underway.

By 1494, Portugal and Spain were already fighting over land in the newly found Americas. To resolve their differences, the two countries drew up the Treaty of Tordesillas, which established a line of demarcation on a longitudinal (north-south) line that runs through the western Atlantic Ocean. They agreed that everything to the east of the line belonged to Portugal; everything to the west belonged to Spain. The western side was enormous (they had no idea how enormous at the time) so Spain became a mega-power quickly. Brazil happened to lie to the east of the line, which is why modern-day Brazilians speak Portuguese instead of Spanish.

Soon, England, the Netherlands, and France launched their own expeditions. These seafaring nations competed with each other by rapidly acquiring colonies and conquering new lands. The cost and risk associated with these explorations made it necessary for explorers to rely on the backing of strong and wealthy states. In addition, merchants wanted protection for their trade routes, which could also be acquired through allegiance to a particular sovereignty. Colonialism and the expansion of the trade routes contributed to the rise in nationalism and the development of strong monarchies.

Colonization

The trading, empire building, and conquest of the Age of Exploration was made possible by new financing schemes that now form the basis of our modern economies. Though many elements had to come together at once for the new economy to work, timing was on the side of the Europeans, and everything fell into place. First, the church gave in to state interests by revising its strict ban on what are now standard business practices, like lending money and charging interest on loans. Once banking became respectable, a new business structure emerged: the **joint-stock company**, an organization created to pool the resources of many merchants, thereby distributing the costs and risks of colonization and reducing the danger for individual investors. Investors bought shares, or stock, in the company. If the company made money, each investor would receive a profit proportional to his or her initial investment. Because huge new ships were able to carry unprecedented cargoes, and because the goods were often outright stolen from their native countries, successful voyages reaped huge profits. A substantial middle class of merchants continued to develop, which in turn attracted more investors, and the modern-day concept of a stock market was well under way.

These corporations later secured royal charters for colonies, like the Jamestown colony in Virginia, and funded them for business purposes. Even when they didn't establish colonies, monarchies granted monopolies to trade routes. The Muscovy Company of England monopolized trade routes to Russia, for example. The Dutch East India Company controlled routes to the Spice Islands (modern-day Indonesia). Increased trade led to an early theory of macroeconomics for the nations of Europe. Under the theory of **mercantilism**, a country actively sought to trade, but tried not to import more than it exported; that is, it attempted to create a favorable balance of trade. Trade deficits forced dependencies on other countries, and therefore implied weakness. Of course, one country's surplus had to be met with another country's deficit. To resolve this dilemma, European countries were feverish to colonize. Colonies gave the mother country raw resources (not considered imports because the mother country "owned" them), while creating new markets for processed exports. To further aid the effort, monarchies promoted domestic industry and placed tariffs on imports from competing empires. As you'll see in the next chapter, once the Industrial Revolution was under way, mercantilism really took off.

It shouldn't be surprising that mercantilism fostered resentment in colonies. The colonial resources were shipped back to Europe while the colonists were forced to pay for products from Europe. Add taxes, and you've got major resentment. You already know that the American Revolution was in part due to colonial fury over this arrangement. One by one, beginning with America, European colonies revolted against the abuses by the unforgiving mercantilist economies of the European powers.

The Age of Revolutions

In the late seventeenth and for much of the eighteenth century, political revolutions in Europe and its holdings continued the trends seen in previous centuries. Revolutionaries rejected the divine rights of kings and fought for increased secular power at great cost to church power. By doing so, political revolutionaries put more power in the hands of the common people (non-aristocracy) and solidified the nation-state as the form of government in ascendance.

In the late 1600s there was great unrest in England regarding the religious tolerance of King James II of England, a Catholic with close ties to France. Those higher up in the political spheres of England were concerned over these troubling facts, and their concern turned to outright alarm when the King issued a male heir, redirecting the line of succession from Mary, the wife of William of Orange and a Protestant. With the support of many from both parties of Parliaments, the Whigs and the Tories, William built political and financial support in order to overthrow the king and assume the throne in 1688.

This revolution, although short and relatively light on bloodshed, had a lasting, and a very detrimental effect, on Catholicism in England. The chance of Catholicism being re-established in any meaningful way in England, at least compared to its past dominance, was completely destroyed. Not only were the future hopes of Catholic growth in the country thwarted, but the immediate effects for practicing English Catholics were severe; they were denied the right to vote or to sit in Parliament (a restriction which lasted for more than a century), they were ineligible to obtain commissions in the army, and the monarchy was restricted from either the practice of Catholicism or marriage to a Catholic.

In 1789, King Louis XVI called the Estates General, a council of representatives of three sectors of French society, to discuss the severe economic crisis that France had found itself in as a result of war and taxation issues. The Estates General consisted of the bourgeoisie, or urban professional and merchant classes (which led the Third Estate—a group consisting of all commoners) with support from some members of the clergy, the nobility (the Second Estate), and the Church (the First Estate). However, it wasn't just the king who wanted something out of the meeting; the nobility wanted to use the Estates General to create a constitutional government. The Third Estate, however, felt that the nobles were about as bad as the king and the Church. When excluded from the meetings, the Third Estate met on its own and declared itself the National Assembly speaking for the people of France. The National Assembly took an oath not to dissolve until a constitution had been written, an event known as the Tennis Court Oath, named after the site where the Assembly convened.

Under pressure, the king ceded power to the National Assembly. The National Assembly then abolished feudalism, noble privilege, and tithes paid to the Church, and issued the Declaration of the Rights of Man and the Citizen, which proclaimed the equality of all men in the eyes of the law and the power of the law above any other power. Basic freedoms of religion, speech, thought, and due process under the law were guaranteed to all. The National Assembly eventually produced a constitution in 1791, establishing a constitutional monarchy. However, things devolved from there. The Assembly was disbanded, and a new National Convention based on universal male suffrage was elected. The Convention soon voted to execute the king, an event that began the **Second Revolution**. The aristocracy was actively persecuted as part of a campaign of widespread violence now known as **The Reign of Terror**. France was already involved in battles with neighboring countries that both harbored French nobles, and had their own interest in taking advantage of internal conflict to attack France.

"My principle is:
France first...."

—Napoleon Bonaparte

Napoleon Bonaparte was a general brought in by the Convention to protect it, but Napoleon had other plans. Staging a coup d'état, he proclaimed himself First Consul of the Convention and essentially became the head of the government in 1799. The Napoleonic Wars pitted France against a coalition by Austria, Britain (which dominated shipping at the time), and Russia, which supported Britain. Having beaten almost all of his continental opponents, Napoleon lost to Britain at sea at the Battle of Trafalgar in 1805, preventing an invasion of England. Also, his invasion of Russia in 1812 was a disaster, costing hundreds of thousands of French soldiers' lives. In France's colonies, Saint-Domingue/Haiti, under the leadership of Pierre Toussaint L'Ouverture, revolted against its colonial oppressors and, after a decade of bloodshed, gained its independence in 1804, the first successful slave revolt in history. Napoleon eventually was deposed and exiled, and Louis XVIII was installed as king.

THE TWENTIETH CENTURY AND BEYOND

Several topics related to the twentieth century and beyond have been covered in previous chapters. Here, we will take a quick look at a few topics that we skipped earlier.

The Russian Revolution

We briefly touched on the **Russian Revolution** in Chapter 22, but let's go into a bit more depth on this important development in Russian history that had a much broader global impact. By the time Nicholas II reigned (1894–1917), revolution was in the wind. The Socialists began to organize. Nicholas tried to rally Russians around the flag by going to war with Japan over Manchuria in 1904, but the Russians suffered a humiliating defeat. On a Sunday in 1905, moderates marched on the czar's palace in a peaceful protest, an attempt to encourage him to enact Enlightened reforms, but Nicholas felt threatened and ordered his troops to fire on the protestors. The day has since been known as Bloody Sunday.

For the next decade, resentment among the working classes festered. In 1906, the czar attempted to enact legislative reforms by appointing a Prime Minister, Peter Stolypin, and by creating the Duma, a body intended to represent the Russian people, but every time the Duma was critical of the czar, he immediately disbanded it. In the end, the attempts at reform were too little, too late. The Romanov Dynasty would soon come to an end.

The Russian Revolution occurred even before World War I had ended. Russia entered the war with the world's largest army, though not the world's most powerful one, because the nation was not nearly as industrialized as its Western neighbors. Very quickly, the army began to suffer large-scale losses and found itself short on food, munitions, and good leadership. In February 1917, in the face of rising casualties and food shortages, Czar Nicholas was forced to abdicate his throne. The Romanov Dynasty came to an end. Under Alexander Kerensky, a provisional government was established. It was ineffectual, in part because it shared power with the local councils, called soviets, which represented the interests of workers, peasants, and soldiers. Although the provisional government affirmed natural rights (such as the equality of citizens and the principle of religious toleration—changes that were inconceivable under the czar), it wanted to continue war against Germany in the hope that Russia could then secure its borders and become a liberal democracy. But the working classes, represented by the soviets, were desperate to end the suffering from the war. The idealism of the provisional officials caused them to badly miscalculate the depths of hostility the Russian people felt for the czar's war.

By 1918, the soviets rallied behind the socialist party, now called the Bolsheviks. Amid this turmoil, Vladimir Lenin, the Marxist leader of the party, mobilized the support of the workers and soldiers. He issued his April Theses, which demanded peace, land for peasants, and power to the soviets. Within six months, the Bolsheviks took command of the government. Under his vision of mass socialization,

Lenin rigidly set about nationalizing the assets and industries of Russia. In March 1918, the soviets signed an armistice with Germany, the Treaty of Brest-Litovsk, which ceded a huge piece of western Russia to Germany, so Russia dropped out of World War I. It therefore wasn't part of the negotiations during the Treaty of Versailles.

In the Baltic republics of what would soon be called the Soviet Union, and in the Ukraine, Siberia, and other parts of the former Russian Empire, counterrevolutionary revolts broke out. The Bolsheviks faced nonstop skirmishes between 1918 and 1921. To put down these struggles, the Bolsheviks created the Red Army, a military force under the command of Leon Trotsky. By 1918, the Red Army was a sizeable force, and with the support of the peasants, it defeated the counterrevolutionaries. But the counterrevolution had two lasting implications. First, the prolonged civil war deepened the distrust between the new Marxist state and its Western neighbors, who had supported the counterrevolutionaries. And second, the Bolsheviks now had a very powerful army, the Red Army, at its disposal.

The impact of the Russian Revolution was vast. Russia was the first of many countries to adopt a communist government, and as such ushered in a new era of global affairs in which people began to think differently about economics, politics, and the role of government in society. The strength of communism ultimately did not last, but the clashes between capitalists and socialists in the twentieth century were widespread, and thus the Russian Revolution cannot be ignored.

The USSR

Once the Soviets removed themselves from World War I, they concentrated on their own domestic problems. Lenin first instituted the New Economic Policy (NEP) in the early 1920s, which had some capitalistic aspects, such as allowing farmers to sell portions of their grain for their own profit. The plan was successful in agriculture, but Lenin didn't live long enough to chaperone its expansion into other parts of the Soviet economy. When Lenin died, the leadership of the Communist Party shifted to Joseph Stalin.

Stalin believed the NEP was ridiculously slow, so he discarded it. Instead, he imposed his Five Year Plans, which called for expedient agricultural production by ruthlessly taking over private farms and combining them into state-owned enterprises, a process known as collectivization. The plans also advocated for the construction of large, nationalized factories. This process was achieved in the name of communism, but it was really totalitarianism. The people didn't share in the power or the profits, and had no choices regarding participation. Untold numbers died fighting to protect their farms. Even more died in famines that resulted when Stalin usurped crops to feed government workers at the expense of the farmers themselves.

Stalin's plans successfully industrialized the **USSR** (Union of Soviet Socialist Republics), the formal name for the Soviet Union, and improved economic conditions for the country as a whole, but Stalin relied on terror tactics, such as a secret police force, bogus trials, and assassinations. These murders peaked between 1936 and 1938. Collectively, they are sometimes referred to as the **Great Purge** because the government systematically killed so many of its enemies. Stalin also established labor camps to punish anyone who opposed him. It's hard to know for sure how many Soviet citizens were imprisoned or killed during the 1930s, especially because so many died of famines during the collectivization process, but historians agree that millions of Soviets were slaughtered under Stalin's direction.

Fascism

Between the First and Second World Wars, fascist parties emerged across Europe. They did not possess identical sets of beliefs, but they held a few important ideas in common. The main idea of fascism was to destroy the will of the individual in favor of "the people." Fascists wanted a unified society (as did the communists), but they weren't concerned with eliminating private property or class distinctions (the principal aim of communists). Instead, fascists pushed for another identity, one rooted in extreme nationalism, which often relied on racial identity.

Italy was the first state to have a fascist government. The founder and leader was **Benito Mussolini**, who created the National Fascist Party in 1919. The Party paid squads, known as **Blackshirts**, to fight socialist and communist organizations, an action that won over the loyalty of both factory owners and landowners. By 1921, the party seated its first members in the Italian parliament.

Although the fascists held only a few seats in the legislature, Mussolini demanded that King Victor Emmanuel III name him and several other fascists to cabinet posts. To rally support, Mussolini organized his paramilitary thugs to march to Rome and possibly attempt to seize power. If the king had declared martial law and brought in the army, most believe that the fascists would have scattered. However, the king was a timid man—facing economically troubling times—who was not unsympathetic to the fascist program. So, he named Mussolini prime minister, and the fascist march on Rome turned into a celebration.

As the postwar economy failed to improve, Italy was demoralized. Mussolini faced very little opposition to his consolidation of political power. He dabbled as a parliamentary leader for several months before completely taking over Parliament in 1922. He then implemented a number of constitutional changes to ensure that democracy no longer limited his actions, and, by 1926, Italy was transformed into a totalitarian fascist regime. To rally the people in a nationalistic cause, Italy started to focus on expansion, specifically in North Africa.

Immediately following the end of World War I, a revolt occurred in Germany when the emperor abdicated. Germany might well have become socialist at this point. Workers' and soldiers' councils (not unlike Russian soviets) formed in cities like Berlin. Yet, because the middle class in Germany was quite conservative and a large number of Germans had been relatively prosperous before the war, a socialist or communist system was rejected in favor of a fairly conservative democratic republic, called the **Weimar Republic**.

At the same time, Germany was in economic crisis, and Mussolini's success influenced Germany in many ways. The National Socialist Party (Nazis) rose to power in the 1920s, ushered in by the worldwide depression. As Germany's economy collapsed under the harsh reparations dictated by the Treaty of Versailles and the faltering world economy, German people increasingly rejected the solutions of the Weimar Republic's elected body, the Reichstag.

During this period **Adolf Hitler** rose to power as head of the Nazi Party. Like Mussolini's fascism, Hitler's Nazism inspired extreme nationalism and the dreams of renewed greatness for a depressed and divided country. But Hitler's philosophies differed from Mussolini's in their emphasis on the superiority of one race over others. Well versed in social Darwinism, Hitler was convinced that the Aryan race was the most highly evolved race, and that inferior races, such as Slavs and Jews, had "corrupted" the German race. He argued that Jews should be deported (later that changed to "eliminated") and that Germans should take over Europe.

The Nazi Party gained political power in the 1920s with Hitler as its guide, or **führer**. At first, the Nazis received votes democratically and participated in the Reichstag. In the early 1930s, as the Great Depression devastated the German economy, Hitler received increasing support. In the election of 1930, the Nazi Party increased its seats in Parliament tenfold. By 1932, the Nazis dominated German government and many who disagreed with Hitler still backed him, thinking he was the country's only hope. In 1933, Hitler became chancellor, or leader of the Reichstag. He then seized control of the government, known under his fascist rule as the Third Reich, and set his eyes on conquering Europe.

In 1933, Hitler began to rebuild the German military. This was a clear violation of the Treaty of Versailles—which was specifically intended to limit future German aggression—but the other nations of Europe, especially Britain and France, chose not to object, fearing another war. Later that year, Germany again snubbed world opinion by withdrawing from the League of Nations.

Meanwhile, Spain, which had established a parliamentary democracy in 1931, was falling apart following the fall of the Spanish monarchy. In the summer of 1936, a group of army officers under the leadership of General **Francisco Franco** took control of large parts of Spain. Democratic loyalists organized to defend the state, and a brutal and divisive civil war ensued. Germany and Italy supported Franco's troops, called **nationalists**. Although Franco was not a fascist, the Germans and Italians believed that the defeat of democracy in Spain was a step in the right direction.

France and Great Britain, still scarred from the loss of life and money in the Great War, adopted a nonintervention policy and refused to aid the supporters of the Spanish democracy. By 1939, Franco's troops captured Madrid and installed a dictatorship in Spain that managed to stay neutral throughout the war that soon erupted in Europe. The message was clear: Germany and Italy were more than willing to exercise their influence and support antidemocratic uprisings. All of these fascist movements influenced the shape of Europe and helped to create the divisions and alliances that arose during World War II, discussed in depth in Chapter 22.

The European Union

The end of the Cold War removed the last obstacles to true global interaction and trade. Currencies were no longer tied to old alliances, and new business opportunities emerged. This deregulation, along with the development of systems of instantaneous communication such as the Internet, resulted in globally integrated financial networks. Commercial interdependence intensified in the 1980s as eastern Asia began to flex its industrial and commercial muscles.

Competition further drove global developments, and regional trading blocks were created such as North American Free Trade Agreement (NAFTA) in the early 1990s. The European Economic Community (EEC), originally formed in 1957, transformed into the modern European Union (EU) tied to a single currency, the euro. The ease with which goods and ideas are transported across the world has resulted in cultures being more homogenous and integrated. This does not mean that local culture is lost, but it does mean that one can satisfy a craving for a Starbucks latte inside Beijing's Forbidden City. It also means almost instantaneous access to a wider range of music, art, literature, and information. Much of this is facilitated by the spread of English as the language of business and communication across the globe. This began in the eighteenth century with the far-flung colonies of the British Empire and continued with the emergence of the United States as a global power after World War II.

The European Union or EU was formed to give the United States some economic competition by banding Europe together in a single market. The real impetus to expand the powers of the EU came in the early 1990s when the collapse of the Soviet Union simultaneously opened Europe and left the United States unchallenged as the world's superpower. In 1989, the EU had 12 members; by 2011, it had 27, of which 10 were former Soviet satellite nations. The EU has three branches: executive, legislative, and judicial. Elections are held throughout Europe every five years. The formation of a monetary union, the Eurozone, in 1999, led all but three nations (the United Kingdom, Sweden, and Denmark) to adopt a unified currency, the euro, in 2002.

While economic integration initially seemed relatively easy and produced a few boom years, in the crisis of the late 2000s (which began slightly earlier in Europe than in the United States), it became clear that stronger economies such as Germany's had borne the freight of weaker, over-extended economies such as Greece's, and by 2010, economic collapse in states such as Greece, Ireland, and Portugal threatened to destabilize the entire Eurozone. This has provoked sharp debates about economic integration that have now piled onto existing concerns about political and judicial integration, putting national interests and questions of sovereignty at stake.

The Middle East and OPEC

After the fall of the Ottoman Empire and the creation of the modern nation of Turkey at the close of World War I, the Middle East, which was largely comprised of old Ottoman lands, was temporarily put under the control of the League of Nations. As if the two European powerhouses didn't already control enough of the world, France was put in charge of Syria and Lebanon, while Britain got Palestine, Jordan, and Iraq. Persia (Iran) was already carved up into spheres of influence between Britain and Russia during the nineteenth century. As for Arabia, it united as a Saudi kingdom immediately following the fall of the Ottoman Empire. The Middle East during the twentieth century is complicated stuff, but a good chunk of the essential information involves the creation of the modern nation of Israel, so that's where we'll start.

If you remember from our discussion of Judaism earlier in the chapter, the Hebrews (Jews) occupied lands in Palestine at the time of the ancient Roman Empire. While a few Jews managed to stay in the region, most bolted for Europe or other areas as Palestine became increasingly entrenched in Islam. All the while, however, many Jews had wanted to return to what they believed was the "promised land." But in the meantime, generation after generation of Muslim Palestinians had made that land home.

During World War I, **Zionists** (Jewish nationalists) living in Britain convinced Arthur Balfour, Britain's foreign secretary, that a Jewish homeland in Palestine was both desirable and just. He issued what became known as the **Balfour Declaration** of 1917, which explicitly stated the right for a home in Palestine for the Jewish people, but he also stated that it should in no way displace the Palestinians who currently lived there. As history would have it, Britain gained control of Palestine in 1920 as a mandate from the League of Nations—which meant that it was to govern on behalf of the League of Nations—and was therefore in a position to make good on its declaration.

But the declaration was messy because it essentially provided that the Palestinians and Jews were to divide land that they both claimed. Not long after, many Jews, mainly Russian Jews fleeing violent, anti-Semitic mobs (**pogroms**), began streaming into Palestine. As their numbers grew, the Palestinians started to get uneasy. In the 1930s, huge numbers of Jews flooded the region to escape Germany as Hitler came to power. By the beginning of World War II, nearly 500,000 Jews had emigrated to Palestine. While Palestinians still outnumbered Jews, the Jewish population was now large enough to pull some serious weight, especially because money was pouring into the region from Jewish communities worldwide.

In 1948, the United Nations (which had replaced the ineffectual League of Nations) officially created two Palestines, one for Jews and the other for Muslims (Palestinians). As soon as David Ben-Gurion, the first prime minister of Israel, announced the official creation of the Jewish homeland on May 14, 1948, Muslims from six Arab countries attacked Israel in what became known as the 1948 Arab-Israeli War. But the Israelis shocked and awed them with their quick organization and military capability. Within months, the Israelis controlled most of Palestine, including the Palestinian parts, while Jordan held the remaining portions (the West Bank). Suddenly, Palestinians were without a home. They had no land to call their own.

As Jews flocked to Israel from all over the world, Israel and Arab countries continued to have skirmishes. In 1967, the amazingly short Six-Day War resulted in total victory for the Israelis, who took control of the West Bank from Jordan, the Sinai Peninsula and Gaza Strip from Egypt, and the Golan Heights from Syria. With the West Bank came control of the city of Jerusalem, Judaism's historical homeland. However, Muslims throughout the region resented Israeli control of the Dome of the Rock, a revered Islamic shrine dating back to the Abbasid caliphate which is also the site of the Temple Mount, an important Jewish historical site. The territorial gains resulted in new waves of Palestinian refugees to Jerusalem. In 1977, Israeli Prime Minister Menachem Begin and Egyptian President Anwar Sadat signed the **Camp David Accords**, an agreement that did not mention Golan Heights, Syria, or Lebanon, but which led to Israel pulling out of the Sinai and Egypt becoming the only Arab country yet to recognize Israel's right to exist. This was a huge blow to the Palestinians and other Arab nations. Sadat was assassinated and the lands gained in the Six-Day War remain some of the most contested in the region.

In the years since, the Israelis and the Palestinians have been fighting over the Israeli occupation of the West Bank, Golan Heights, and Gaza Strip. The Palestine Liberation Organization (PLO), a group dedicated to reclaiming the land and establishing a Palestinian state, has so far been unsuccessful in negotiating a homeland. The efforts are complicated by the **intifada** (uprising), an on-again off-again movement that sometimes uses terrorism against Israeli citizens in an attempt to either destroy Israel or force it into withdrawal from the occupied territories.

In 2000, a new intifada reignited violence between Palestinians and the occupying Israeli forces. As suicide bombings became more frequent, newly elected Israeli prime minister Ariel Sharon approved the construction of a wall to be built between the Palestinian West Bank and Israel in order to protect Israelis against suicide attacks. Often compared to the Berlin Wall, Israel's protective wall has been criticized by some in the international community for employing such a draconian measure to fight terrorist attacks. Many in Israel, meanwhile, have pointed to the wall as a successful way to prevent needless violence and terrorism.

Not limiting itself to criticism, however, in 2003 the international community, led by the United States, the European Union, the UN and Russia, proposed a **Roadmap to Peace**, which outlined a set of goals to achieve peace in the region. Progress on the Roadmap remained stalled until the death of Palestinian president (and former PLO leader) **Yassir Arafat** in November 2004. Arafat had been consistently blamed by Israel and the United States for blocking such progress. Following his January 2005 election, Palestinian president Mahmoud Abbas quickly signed a cease-fire with Israel that effectively ended the intifada that began in 2000.

Under a **disengagement plan** adopted by the Israeli government, all Israeli settlers were supposed to have vacated the Gaza Strip by August 2005. Residents of the settlements who did not leave were forcibly removed by the Israeli army, a military action which greatly divided the Israeli public. Additional settlements were disbanded in the West Bank as part of the same plan. It is likely, however, that lasting peace will remain elusive until the Israelis and Palestinians can reach agreement on issues such as movement into and outside of the Palestinian Authority-controlled territories, the disarmament of militant groups, and the potential independence of a Palestinian state.

The situation is made even more complicated by limited financial stability and political divisions among Palestinians. The governing Palestinian Authority is divided into two factions: **Fatah**, a branch of the former Palestinian Liberation Organization, and **Hamas**. Translating to "Islamic Resistance Movement," Hamas was founded as an offshoot of the Muslim Brotherhood in 1987. Because of its open willingness to support terrorist tactics, Hamas is frequently the target of Israeli military attacks.

Despite similar goals for a Palestinian state, Hamas and Fatah are deeply divided, and violent clashes occur with increasing frequency. After the creation of a unity government in 2006, Hamas led a coup in 2007 which concluded with a Hamas-imposed government in the Gaza Strip and a Fatah-run West Bank. Further complicating governance, in retaliation, President Mahmoud Abbas (Fatah) named Salam Fayyad prime minister. Hamas contends that Fayyad's appointment is illegitimate, as he was not voted into office. Israel's current government, led by Prime Minister Benjamin Netanyahu, and the United States show willingness to work with Fatah; the United States and a number of European countries list Hamas as a terrorist organization and so do not negotiate with that party.

Israel's border with Lebanon and Syria is another hotspot. **Hezbollah**, a militant Shia group backed by Syria and Iran, operates in the region. In 2006, Israel launched a major offensive against Hezbollah after two Israeli soldiers were captured in Israeli territory. These new hostilities threatened the stability of a country which had been the scene of intense fighting between Syrian, Israeli, and PLO forces throughout the 1980s and 1990s. Syria is widely seen to have a controlling hand in Lebanese politics. In 2005, when Prime Minister Rafiq Hariri was assassinated, fingers quickly pointed to Hezbollah and Syrian sources.

In Iran, Reza Shah Pahlavi rose to power in 1925 by ousting the then-ruling shah, who had allowed Persia to fall under European spheres of influence. Taking a stance similar to the Japanese during the Meiji Restoration, Reza Shah decided that the best way to beat the Westernizers was to join them. Iran (formerly Persia) modernized slowly at first, but once the Europeans left after World War II, the Westernization efforts gained momentum, and in the 1960s, the shah instituted land reform and education reform, and increased the rights of women, including the right to vote. Women also pursued higher education and careers, and began to adopt Western dress. All of this infuriated many Islamic fundamentalists who wanted to make the teachings of the Qur'an the law of the land. Believing that the influence of the West was too strong, they sought to reverse the economic and social changes. Others believed that the shah was not reforming enough, especially with regard to the political system, which lacked significant democratic changes.

The shah reacted violently against dissent from both sides, pressing forward with his own mix of social and economic reform even in the face of strong public opposition. When President Carter of the United States visited Iran to congratulate it on its programs of modernization and Westernization, the Islamic fundamentalists had had enough. In 1979, the shah was ousted from power during the **Iranian Revolution**, which sent Iran back to a theocracy led by Ayatollah ("Mirror of God") Khomeini. Iran is primarily Shia, and the ayatollah is the Shi'ite caliph (this was important during the Iran-Iraq war, as Iraq was ruled by Sunni Muslims). Immediately, modernization and Westernization programs were reversed, women were required to wear traditional Islamic clothing and to return to their traditional roles, and the Qu'ran became the basis of the legal system.

In 1980, soon after the revolution, Iraq invaded Iran following a series of border disputes between the two countries. Iran's position was further complicated by Iraqi leader Saddam Hussein's quiet support from the United States, which was still quite furious over Iran's taking of U.S. hostages during the revolution. Even with some U.S. support, the Iran-Iraq War turned into an eight-year war of attrition with neither side gaining much ground until a cease-fire was signed in 1988. Since the Ayatollah Khomeini's death in 1989 (watch out—he was succeeded by the differently spelled Ayatollah Khamenei!), Iran has been characterized by a power struggle between powerful Islamic fundamentalist clerics and an increasingly vocal reform-minded and somewhat pro-Western minority. Most recently however, Iran has caused international concern (particularly in the United States) by pushing ahead with efforts to develop what they deemed "peaceful" nuclear technologies, claiming they have a right as an independent nation to develop such technology as they see fit. Along with the International Atomic Energy Agency and the European Union, the United States is currently calling on Iran to sign an international agreement limiting or even eliminating its nuclear programs.

From 2005 until 2013, Tehran's ultra-conservative mayor Mahmoud Ahmadinejad was president of Iran. He was succeeded by the more politically moderate leader Hassan Rouhani. The American-led war in Iraq that began in 2003, the relationship of Iran and Iraq's Shia populations, and Iran's development of weapons programs and nuclear research have only complicated matters further.

The Industrial Revolution was a huge bonanza for the Middle East. That's because they'd been sitting on over two-thirds of the world's known oil reserves since the beginning of civilization. Prior to the Industrial Revolution, it was goo. After the Industrial Revolution, it was fuel. As multinational corporations rushed to the Middle East throughout the twentieth century to obtain drilling and production rights, Middle Eastern governments such as those of Saudi Arabia, Kuwait, Iran, and Iraq started to earn billions of dollars annually. But the oil also meant that the rest of the world had become very, very interested in the Middle East, because oil allowed the West to do one of its favorite things: drive. This world interest sometimes led to intervention and war.

Once the oil-producing nations of the Middle East realized how much power they wielded, they organized. In 1960, the region united with a few other oil-exporting nations, such as Venezuela, to form a petroleum cartel known as **OPEC** (Organization of Petroleum Exporting Countries). With three-quarters of the world's petroleum reserves, OPEC members collectively cut supply dramatically in the 1970s, sending the price of oil through the roof. Billions of extra dollars flowed into OPEC member nations' coffers. Nations like Saudi Arabia used the extra money to modernize their infrastructures, and spent billions on attempts to improve their agricultural sectors. Since the 1970s, OPEC hasn't been able to keep its members in line, and is therefore a much less powerful organization, but the individual members who make up the organization continue to wield huge power over the world economy.

World History Drill

Now try some practice questions. To check your answers, register your book at **PrincetonReview.com/cracking** and download the Chapter Drill Answers and Explanations supplement.

1. **The movement to industrialize Russia was most dependent on**

   A   emancipating serfs to provide a substantial labor pool for industry

   B   becoming more active in colonizing other lands to obtain raw materials and develop new markets

   C   importing coal and other fuel sources plus the equipment necessary to build manufacturing factories

   D   developing a capitalistic system with laissez-faire and free market economic policies

2. **During the latter half of the twentieth century, wealth and prosperity began to emerge in the Middle East. This was largely due to which of the following?**

   A   an Industrial Revolution in the region

   B   political reform among the Middle Eastern states

   C   large-scale production of oil and petroleum products

   D   religious reform among the Middle Eastern states

3. **The Magna Carta**

   A   created a system of common law in Anglo-Saxon England

   B   established a Model Parliament with advisory powers

   C   eliminated heredity as a requirement to hold the throne

   D   did little to stop the growth of centralized government in England

4. **Which of these factors played the greatest role in European interest in South Africa in the late 1800s?**

   A   the need for additional sources of African slaves

   B   the desire for new markets for European goods

   C   the discovery of precious metal resources

   D   political turmoil along northern European trade routes

5. **Which of the following is a major difference between the classic periods in Rome and the Islamic civilizations?**

   A   While Roman society had strict social class delineations and little mobility, Islam was egalitarian with few barriers to social mobility.

   B   The Islamic civilization was more dependent on agriculture and therefore more susceptible to fluctuations in food supply.

   C   While the Roman Empire fell as a result of internal warfare over succession to the throne, Islamic dynasties faced few internal divisions.

   D   Islamic scientific thought and art forms borrowed heavily from Hellenistic sources, while Rome's scientific, philosophical, and artistic advancements were unique to its culture.

6. **The most direct result of the Protestant Reformation was**

   A Christianity spread into the Ottoman Empire and Southeast Asia

   B the printing press was invented

   C interest in the arts and scientific inquiry increased

   D literacy rates across Europe rose

7. **The split between Sunni and Shi'a Muslims occurred as a result of**

   A divergent interpretations of religious texts

   B conflict over the translation of liturgy into native languages

   C disagreement over leadership succession issues

   D a rift between more fundamentalist and more liberal branches of Islam

8. **The reasons for intense imperialism among European nations included all of the following <u>except</u>**

   A industrialization generated demand for new sources of raw materials

   B the military need to establish strategic bases around the world

   C a belief in the racial superiority of Europeans

   D population decline in European nations required new sources of labor

Chapter 24
Economics

In this chapter, we'll guide you through the key topics related to economics on the Social Studies portion of the TASC test. We will focus here on two categories: broad economic concepts and macroeconomics. Following the content lessons, we'll give you some practice questions.

BASIC ECONOMIC CONCEPTS

While economic questions are not as prevalent on the TASC test as those involving U.S. and World History, it is important to be familiar with some fundamental concepts relating to economics.

Positive economics describes the way things are, whereas **normative economics** addresses the way things should be. For example, "The unemployment rate hit a three-year high," is a positive statement, while "The Fed should lower the federal funds rate," is a normative statement.

Economics is the study of how to allocate scarce resources among competing ends. Although some think economics is only about business and money, in truth, the field is as broad as the list of scarce resources, and deals with everything from air to concert tickets. Few things have an infinite supply or zero demand, meaning that the need to make choices in response to scarcity—economics—can apply to almost everything and everyone. Economists are currently studying war, crime, endangered species, marriage, systems of government, child care, legal rules, death, birth . . . the sky's the limit.

Scarcity occurs because our unlimited desire for goods and services exceeds our limited ability to produce them due to constraints on time and **resources**. The resources used in the production process are sometimes called **inputs**, or **factors of production**. They include

- **labor**—the physical and mental effort of people
- **human capital**—knowledge and skills acquired through training and experience
- **entrepreneurship**—the ability to identify opportunities and organize production, and the willingness to accept risk in the pursuit of rewards
- **natural resources / land**—either term can refer to any productive resource existing in nature, including wild plants, mineral deposits, wind, and water
- **capital**—manufactured goods that can be used in the production process, including tools, equipment, buildings, and machinery

Energy and technology are also important contributors to the production process but they can be treated as by-products of the five factors of production listed above.

Consider the factors of production needed for a bagel shop. The shop building, mixers, and ovens are examples of capital. Natural resources, including land and rain, will help provide the wheat for the dough. Labor will form the dough into bagels, place them into the ovens, and sell them. The bagel chef uses her skill and experience—human capital—to make the bagels smooth on the outside and soft on the inside. How did this shop come about? An entrepreneur risked a large amount of money and poured his ideas and organizational talents into the success of the shop. Thus, our bagel shop requires all five factors of production. In contrast, a soda-pop machine is an example of a capital-intensive business that requires little beyond canned drinks and the machine itself to produce soft drink sales.

When people have different abilities, having them specialize in what they are relatively good at enhances productivity. This is more efficient than having each person contribute equally to every task. It is better for LeBron James to be a fulltime basketball player and Brad Pitt to be a full-time actor than to have them both divide their time equally between the court and the stage. Even if every person were identical, efficiency would be improved by a division of necessary tasks among those carrying out the tasks. This is because such a **division of labor** permits people to develop expertise in the task(s) that they concentrate on—practice improves performance. If different members of your family specialize in shopping, car repair, cooking, or childcare, your family exhibits a division of labor not unlike what occurs in businesses and governmental agencies.

Supply and Demand

In a capitalist economy, prices are determined by **supply and demand**. Supply is the amount of goods and services available at a particular time. Demand is the consumers' need for those goods and services. For example, a sneaker company might produce 200,000 pairs of sneakers. This is its supply. The public might end up buying 150,000 pairs. This is the demand for this particular product. If supply and demand are equal, then the price will remain the same. However, if there is more supply than demand, then prices fall. For example, because there was a surplus of 50,000 pairs of sneakers that were not sold, the company is going to have to reduce its price to make the public want to buy them.

However, if there is more demand than supply, then prices rise. For example, if these sneakers become very popular, then there will be a shortage, and the sneaker company may charge more for the sneakers because they are scarce.

These forces work on a global scale, which is why the prices of oil, gold, and shares of stock in different companies go up and down every day in reaction to the supply and demand of the market (we will discuss markets in more detail below).

If an economy is functioning properly, there is an ever-increasing demand for goods and services that is met by an ever-increasing supply. However, if there is too much demand and not enough supply, then **inflation** can result. Inflation is a general rise in prices. A little inflation is to be expected, but too much can start a spiraling effect in which prices rise so rapidly that a country's currency loses it value. During the 1930s in Germany, it was not uncommon to see people bringing wheelbarrows full of money to the store to pay for their groceries.

The concept of supply and demand is one of the most fundamental tenets of economics. Basically, the price of a good is determined by the *supply* of the good (how much there is of it) and the *demand* in the market for that good. The higher the price, the higher the quantity supplied, because obviously a producer wants to sell a lot of high-priced items. But if the price gets too high, demand for the item will fall. The market aims for equilibrium: the price at which there is exactly enough supply of an item to meet consumers' demand for it.

Vocabulary

recession—a period during which employment and economic activity decline

depression—a longer period of drastic declines in the economy and employment

import—to buy goods from another country and bring them back to your own country for consumption

export—to sell goods to another country for consumption in that country

When there is too little demand and too much supply, then **deflation** can result. Most of the countries of the world experienced deflation during the Great Depression.

MICROECONOMICS

Broadly speaking, **microeconomics** refers to the branch of economics that is focused upon the allocation of resources as it relates to individuals and small organizations. Microeconomics is concerned with the various ways in which people's and institutions' behavior and decisions affect supply and demand, the flow of goods and services, and markets.

Capital is the primary catalyst for industrial production. Both material wealth and the ability to produce wealth are known as capital (hence the term capitalism). In many industries, the most important form of capital is **human labor**—the people who produce a given product.

Another factor in production is the concept of **incentives**. Incentives are anything that motivates or discourages economic behavior. For example, if a company receives tax breaks for hiring more employees, then it has an incentive to increase its labor force, thus increasing production. Other incentives occur at the consumer level. If a company wants to encourage people to purchase its product, it may create an incentive by lowering the price.

A further factor of production is **opportunity cost**. Opportunity cost is the foregone option when a more advantageous option is chosen. For instance a person may choose to purchase Brand X or Brand Y. If she chooses Brand X, then Brand Y is the opportunity cost. In matters of production, opportunity costs can come in the form of materials used, the decision to hire more or fewer workers, the price set for a product, and other decisions related to economic behavior. The ability of a company in a particular country to produce its product at a lower opportunity cost than a company in another country is referred to as a comparative advantage.

A **market** is a system in which goods, services, and capital are exchanged. If one company controls an entire industry or becomes the only company to make a certain product, that company is said to have a monopoly. In the United States, this is illegal. If the government believes that one company is gaining control of an industry, it will institute an antitrust court action to force that company to let other companies into the field. An example of this was the antitrust action that forced AT&T to break up into smaller independent telephone companies. The case against Microsoft was another antitrust action.

Because all countries lack some natural resources, each country trades certain goods and services in exchange for other goods and services that it needs. This is known as **international trade**. If a country buys more goods from foreign countries than it sells, it has a balance of payments **deficit**. If it sells more than it buys, it has a balance of payments **surplus**.

MACROECONOMICS

Macroeconomics is the branch of economics that deals with the whole economy and issues that affect most of society. These issues include inflation, unemployment, gross domestic product, national income, interest rates, exchange rates, and so on.

A country's annual **Gross Domestic Product (GDP)** is the total value of all final goods and services produced in a year within that country. The expression "final goods and services" indicates that to avoid double counting, GDP does not include the value of intermediate goods like lumber and steel that go into the production of other goods like homes and cars, or the repurchase of used goods, which were included in GDP in the year in which they were first produced. Also excluded from the calculation of GDP are financial transactions such as the buying and selling of stocks and bonds, since there is no productive activity associated with them to measure. Public and private transfer payments also are not considered in GDP, nor are underground economic activities (both legal and illegal) and home production. The media is prone to use changes in GDP as indicators of societal well-being. Although an increase in this measure might reflect an increase in the standard of living, GDP also increases with expenditures on natural disasters, deadly epidemics, war, crime, and other detriments to society. Unless "bads" such as these are subtracted, be cautious in interpreting changes in GDP.

National income is the sum of income earned by the factors of production owned by a country's citizens. It includes wages, salaries, and fringe benefits paid for labor services, rent paid for the use of land and buildings, interest paid for the use of money, and profits received for the use of capital resources. **Personal income** is the money income received by households before personal income taxes are subtracted, and **disposable income** is personal income minus personal income taxes.

The labor force includes employed and unemployed adults. To be considered unemployed, a labor force participant must be willing and able to work, and must have made an effort to seek work in the past four weeks. The labor force participation rate is the number of people in the labor force divided by the working-age population. The unemployment rate is the number of unemployed workers divided by the number in the labor force, and then multiplied by 100 to get the percentage. The various categories of unemployment are defined below.

Discouraged workers are those who are willing and able to work, but become so frustrated in their attempts to find work that they stop trying. Because they are not making an effort to find a job at least once every four weeks, discouraged workers are not counted among the unemployed in official statistics, and are a reason why the unemployment rates might understate the true unemployment problem. On the other hand, dishonest workers bias the unemployment figures upward. These individuals claim to be unemployed in order to receive unemployment benefits when, in fact, they do not want a job or are working for cash in an unreported job.

The natural rate of unemployment, about 5 percent in the United States, is the typical rate of unemployment in a normally functioning economy and is often thought of as the sum of frictional and structural unemployment. Full employment is not 100 percent employment, but the level of employment that corresponds with the natural rate of unemployment. With full employment there is no cyclical unemployment.

Taxes

A **tax** is a financial charge imposed upon an individual by a government (local, state, or federal) for the purpose of funding that government's various programs or expenditures. Common types of taxes include **income tax** (a percentage of what an individual or company earns), **capital gains tax** (a percentage of what an individual earns through stocks, bonds, and the like), **property tax** (a percentage of the value of an individual's home or a business's real estate), and **sales tax** (a percentage of the price that a consumer pays for certain goods or services).

The United States government and those of many other countries levy from citizens what is known as a **progressive income tax**. A progressive tax increases tax rates for people with higher incomes. Those citizens at the poverty level, for example, may pay few or no taxes. Middle-class citizens may be taxed at a 15 percent rate, while the wealthy are taxed at two or three times that rate. The goal of a progressive tax is to allow those with greater need to keep more of what they earn while taking more from those who can best afford it. We will discuss taxes in more detail when we discuss the government's role in the U.S. economy below.

Capitalism and Mixed Economies

Capitalism is a system in which the means of production and development are privately owned and traded. The concept of pure capitalism was first described in 1776 by Scottish economist Adam Smith, in a book called *The Wealth of Nations*. Smith advocated a laissez-faire (from the French "to let alone") economic system in which the government does not interfere with the free market at all, allowing the interplay of supply and demand to determine prices. In later years, other economists, such as John Maynard Keynes, argued that in the real world, governments must use a combination of tax and spending programs to stabilize a capitalist-based economy.

Capitalist free-market systems in which both government and private industry play a role are called **mixed economies**. Mixed free-market systems are characterized by both private and public (government) ownership of the means of production and distribution of goods and services. The price of goods and services is determined by the free-market interplay of supply and demand. The profits after taxes are kept by the owners.

Free-market economic systems are plagued by periods of prosperity followed by periods of economic contraction (decreased activity, economic downturn). Because the United States has a mixed free-market system, the major problem for policy makers is how to maintain prosperity and economic growth while reducing the impact of the inevitable economic contraction. In capitalist systems, the basic question is to what extent the government should intervene.

Laissez-faire economists believe that the government should never become involved in economic issues. They believe that the narrow pursuit of individual profit serves the broader interest of society. Central to laissez-faire economics is the belief that free markets are governed by the laws of nature and government should not interfere with those laws. In vogue with rugged individualists in the nineteenth century, laissez-faire economics disappeared as a viable government policy option during the Great Depression of the 1930s.

Government's Role in the U.S. Economy

Of all the issues that face politicians, the economy is often the most important. Success or failure usually rests with the person the public perceives as responsible for the condition of the economy; and whether it is true, the electorate usually holds the president responsible. In 1992 the economy was in recession and George H. W. Bush was blamed. In 1996 the economy was booming, and Clinton was given credit and reelected.

Because of the importance of the economy in the eyes of the voters, it is in a politician's self-interest to make policies that will increase people's standard of living. The electorate looks to Washington to achieve this objective. For the policy maker, the vexing question is how to achieve it.

Sound economic policy that achieves prosperity is probably the most elusive of all policies. There are many elements to the problem: inflation, deflation, interest rates, the supply of money in circulation, the profitability of corporations, foreign competition, international agreements, and consumer confidence, just to name a few. Complicating the problem are the various economic theories that drive policy decisions, and the various government agencies and institutions that make decisions affecting economic conditions.

Perhaps the most influential economist of the twentieth century was John Maynard Keynes, an interventionist. **Keynesian economics**, on which FDR's New Deal was based, holds that the government can smooth out business cycles by influencing the amount of income individuals and businesses can spend on goods and services.

Fiscal policy refers to the government action of either lowering or raising taxes, which results in more or less consumer spending or enacting of government spending programs, such as building highways or hospitals. Keynesians believe that during economic downturns the government should spend money on projects to inject money into the economy. They are less worried about government deficit spending than about keeping the economy prosperous. A prosperous economy means a larger tax base, which will eventually correct deficit spending. In effect, the Keynesian school believes that when the economy is good, surplus taxes (money left over from tax revenues) should be saved to pay for the government spending that must take place during an economic downturn. Using this school of thought, the policy alternatives are obvious, but questions still remain: Should there be tax cuts? If so, how much, and who should get them? How much spending should the government engage in? How much deficit spending (funds raised by borrowing rather than taxation) should be allowed? The answers to these questions are extremely difficult, with major political consequences.

In the 1980s, the Reagan-Bush administration became the champion of the **supply-side** school of economic thought. The supply-siders take issue with supporters of Keynesian economics. Inflation is caused by too many dollars chasing too few goods. If the supply of goods is raised, the cost of the goods will decline. According to this theory, supply-siders argue that the government should cut taxes and spending on domestic programs to stimulate greater production.

Going along with supply-side theory, Congress in the 1980s enacted extensive tax cuts and reductions to social welfare programs, a policy later dubbed "Reaganomics." Inflation was brought under control, but huge yearly budget deficits, caused in part by a defense buildup, created a four-trillion-dollar debt. In the 1990s, budget surpluses began to shrink the deficit but these gains were reversed as a result of policies enacted during the Bush and Obama administrations, particularly during the Great Recession. Tax cuts followed by rising costs associated with the War on Terrorism, the invasion and occupation of Afghanistan and Iraq, and government stimulus programs have resulted in record budget deficits. The most recent estimates of the **Congressional Budget Office (CBO)** have warned against increasingly large budget deficits. In 2010, a $1.5 trillion deficit in the federal budget stoked political controversy and contributed to historic Republican gains in both houses of Congress in the 2010 mid-term elections. The next year, congressional Republicans forced a showdown over plans to increase the federal debt ceiling, generating concern over the United States' international credit rating.

Monetary policy refers to the process by which the government controls the supply of money in circulation and the supply of credit through the actions of the **Federal Reserve Board** (the Fed). The Fed can increase the amount of money in circulation by lowering interest rates. Rate reductions make borrowing money less expensive because interest on the money is low. This action usually inflates (expands) the economy, resulting in higher prices and wages. If the Fed raises interest rates, the impact on the economy will be deflationary, resulting in either more stable or lower prices or wages.

Some economists believe that government should intervene only to manipulate the money supply, an idea championed by Milton Friedman. These monetarists believe that the money supply should be increased at a constant rate to accommodate economic growth. Monetarists do not believe that interest rate changes and manipulation of tax rates have much of an impact on economic conditions. In the 1990s, the U.S. economy expanded without tax cuts, creating record employment levels with little inflation. Many gave the credit to the monetary policy of Alan Greenspan and the Federal Reserve.

Budgets

In the United States, as everywhere in the world, budgets are a crucial component of economic policy. Loosely speaking, **budgets** refer to estimates of incomes and expenses for a given period of time.

In the United States government, the Director of the **Office of Management and Budget (OMB)** is responsible for initiating the budget process. The director meets with the president to discuss his policy initiatives. The state of the economy is discussed, centering on government revenue projections, which is the predicted income from taxes. Based on the president's priorities, some executive departments will receive more money than others.

The OMB then writes the president's budget and submits it to Congress. Upon its arrival the budget is sent to three committees. **The House Ways and Means Committee** deals with the taxing aspects of the budget. Authorization committees in both houses decide what programs Congress wants to fund. **Appropriations committees** in both houses then decide how much money to spend for those programs that have been authorized.

The budget process is complicated, politically divisive, and, in recent years, nearly impossible to conclude. The president's projected revenues and expenditures often conflict with those of Congress. Congress often simply does not trust the president's numbers, and conversely, the president does not trust Congress's. These yearly budget problems forced passage of the **Budget Reform Act of 1974**, which created the **Congressional Budget Office**, with budget committees in both the House and Senate. The congressional committees set their own revenue and spending levels. Negotiations then take place among the White House and the two houses of Congress in an effort to get one budget acceptable to everyone. Failure to achieve a budget by the beginning of the fiscal year could mean shutting down the government and sending employees home. When this occurs, budget stop-gap bills are passed to temporarily appropriate money to keep the government operating.

The **Budget Enforcement Act of 1990** was an effort to streamline the budget process and make it easier to arrive at a compromise budget. The law categorizes government expenditures as either mandatory or discretionary spending. Mandatory spending is required by law, to fund programs such as the **entitlement programs**, Social Security, Medicare, veterans' pensions, and payment on the national debt. Discretionary spending programs are not required by law and include defense, education, highways, research grants, and all government operations. **Discretionary programs** are the primary targets for making cuts to balance the budget.

Socialism and Communism

Some countries have installed economies based on central planning—in other words, government ownership of a country's resources and government control of its economic activities. **Communism**, as it was practiced in the former Soviet Union, is an example of such an economy. All the means of production in the Soviet Union were owned by the state, which decided what would be produced and when. **Socialism** is also an example of an economy based at least in part on central planning. In a socialist country, many of the largest industries (such as the transportation industry or the steel industry) are owned and operated by the government, as is a comprehensive system of public welfare.

"Let the ruling classes tremble at a Communist Revolution. The proletarians have nothing to lose but their chains. They have a world to win. Working-men of all countries, unite!"

–Karl Marx, The Communist Manifesto, 1848

Under Communism, **Karl Marx**'s political-economic theories attempted to right the wrongs of feudalism and inequalities of capitalism in free-market democracies. One of the main goals of **Marxism** was to create a class-free society where there were no inequalities in terms of wealth or power. To do this, the state would own all land and industry, the government would direct economic productivity, and everyone regardless of labor position would earn the same amount of money.

The key to this working was the planned economy, which did not rely on supply and demand like capitalism. The central government would calculate the economic needs of the state, its industries, and people. Then the government would set quotas for each individual operational unit of agricultural or manufacturing production to meet these needs. Theoretically, the productivity of the economy would result in a collective wealth that would be shared equally across the population. It's a utopian ideal that the system should create a harmonious peaceful social existence, but Communism in practice failed to reproduce Marx's utopia.

You may have heard the statement, "A good idea in theory but not in practice." This is true for Communism. Marx died in 1883 and the first Communist country, the Union of Soviet Socialist Republics (USSR or Soviet Union), was established in 1917, with the fall of the czar's absolute monarchy in Russia. This time gap is significant. Had Marx seen how his ideas were put into practice, he'd have "blown a fuse," "had a cow," "had kittens"—pick your own analogy. On an essay you could describe him as upset or disapproving.

There were a number of unintended consequences to the Russian revolution, including a protracted and bloody civil war, human rights violations, murders on the part of the Communist government, and forced resettlement of over a million citizens. Despite all this, Soviet Communism emerged functioning under Marx's basic principles. Under Stalin, the USSR developed **Five-Year Plans,** which were comprehensive long-term economic plans that dictated all production in minute detail. In the 1930s, when the rest of the world was suffering through the poverty of the Great Depression, the Soviets were doing comparatively well.

However, fifty years later the USSR was falling apart. The **devolution** of the Soviet system was due in part to several political-economic problems in the USSR. One thing that would have caught Marx's eye was that, in reality, **three classes of Soviet citizens** emerged early in the Soviet Union. Most were workers, as Marx had envisioned his **proletariat.** However, to achieve an important position in Soviet society, like government officials, professors, or factory managers, you had to join the **Communist Party**. Party members made up of about 6 percent of the USSR population and enjoyed many perks such as special stores, nicer homes, and personal cars. Likewise, a **military officer class** emerged that had a similarly high quality of life in comparison to the regular working class.

Working-class people were resentful. But what could they do? Heavy-handed secret police and laws that made public protest punishable by hard labor in prison camps (known as **gulags**) kept open criticism to a minimum. Creative, inventive, and industrious people stagnated. Another reason for this was that there was a **lack of incentive** in the system that would motivate people to have better lives. It didn't matter if you were a brain surgeon or a garbage man; you got the same monthly pay. Sure, there are some perks to being a doctor, but were these enough to struggle through examinations and years of training with no financial reward? This was a problem.

The lack of incentive also affected economic productivity. Neither farms nor factories had any reason to produce more food or products than what was stipulated in government quotas. This resulted in a **lack of surplus**, leaving many stores with few items on the shelf and lines of people waiting to receive rations for food and clothing.

These problems have also plagued other communist countries, and now only two cases of Soviet-style Communism remain: Cuba and North Korea. Despite the historic restoration of diplomatic relations between Cuba and the United States in 2014, Cuban president Raul Castro continues to declare Cuba a communist state.

The positive things that came out of Communism were mainly in the realm of infrastructure and social welfare. Health care is a good example. Prior to Communism in the Soviet Union, China, and Cuba, there had been almost no health care available to the common people. Socialism meant that everyone had a right to health care, and early on hospitals, clinics, and rural travelling doctor programs were established. Similarly, infrastructure programs for public schools, free universities, drinking water, care for the elderly, and public transit were built to improve the efficiency and quality of life in Communist society. It may not look glamorous today, but it successfully replaced the utter poverty that existed under the former feudal and corrupt capitalist societies in these countries.

These socialist successes impacted the non-Communist world as well during the latter twentieth century. Government leadership and control of health care, education, and pensions are Marxist-socialist ideals which have since been incorporated in Western free-market democracies such as Canada and Great Britain.

Categorizing Governments and Economies

We can categorize countries in terms of their level of economic development. We use the following terms to compare development level verbally and to acknowledge the patterns of **uneven development** in the world economy. Some categories are better descriptors than others and some countries aren't categorized as easily as others. Make sure to use terms appropriately.

The First World and Third World categories are two of the most commonly used. However, there are related characterizations at second, fourth, and fifth levels:

First World: **Industrialized** and **service-based economies** that have free markets, a high level of productivity value per person and thus, a high quality of life. In addition to the United States and Canada, there are the European Union countries, Norway, Switzerland, Iceland, Israel, Australia, New Zealand, Japan, South Korea, Singapore, Taiwan, and Middle-Eastern oil states Saudi Arabia, Kuwait, United Arab Emirates, Oman, and Bahrain.

Borderline First World economies might include Argentina, Chile, South Africa, and some island nations like Trinidad and the Seychelles. These have productivity statistics that are higher than the Third World, but not quite at First World levels yet. You might be tempted to call them Second World, but that term has a very different meaning.

Second World: Describes the **Communist** countries of which only two "hard line" Communist states remain today: Cuba and North Korea. These states still have centrally planned economies. The term is occasionally used to designate "former Communist" states that are still **restructuring** their economy to free-market systems like the former Soviet Union and Eastern European states, although many have joined the EU. It can also describe China and Vietnam, which are newly industrialized countries still controlled by Communist parties but that have adapted **free-market reforms** to their economies.

Third World: Countries with mainly **agricultural** and **resource-based economies** that have low levels of per-person productivity and a low quality of life. These **underdeveloped states** are found across Latin America, the Caribbean, Africa, and the Asian countries not listed above. Some Third World states have made a distinct economic shift toward industrialization and urbanization (see newly industrialized countries or NICs, below), while others remain firmly in a rural, agricultural category. Examples of the poorest Third World states are Haiti, Niger, Malawi, Tanzania, Madagascar, Nepal, and the former USSR countries Kyrgyzstan and Tajikistan.

Fourth World: Third World states that have experienced some sort of **economic crisis** that has immobilized the national economy. Crises can include a crash of the country's banking system, devaluation of a country's currency, a failed government taxation system, or events that shut down the economy such as warfare and natural disasters.

Fifth World: Third World states that both lack a functioning economy (like Fourth World states) and have no formal national government.

More developed countries (MDCs) and **less developed countries (LDCs)** are terms used to describe the relative economic differences between states. First and Second World countries generally tend to fit in the MDC category, while Third, Fourth, and Fifth World are LDCs—even if they are **NICs (Newly Industrialized Countries)**.

Newly industrialized countries (NICs) are Third World states that have economies that have made a distinct shift away from agriculture and toward manufacturing as the focus of economic development and production. Industrialization is a long-term process that can last decades in larger countries. NICs are in a constant process of building **infrastructure** (roads, ports, power plants, water systems, railways), which facilitate the construction and operation of factories.

Two characteristics of NICs link back to your knowledge of population and migration. First, NICs have **rapid population growth** and are usually on the border of stage two and stage three of the demographic transition model. Several of the more advanced NICs like Brazil, Mexico, and India are well into early stage three. China, due to its one-child policy, appears to be the most advanced in terms of demographic transition, but in fact it should be economically categorized with the other NICs. Secondly, NICs experience **rapid rural-to-urban migration** as their economies industrialize and, as a result, urbanize.

International Trade

The United States is by far the richest nation in the world. The output of the economy of the state of California alone ranks among the top ten nations in the world. The economic outputs of each of the three cities of Los Angeles, Chicago, and New York rank among the output of the top twenty nations. For better or for worse, the United States is the largest producer and consumer of products.

Foreign nations depend on the United States as a market for their products, as we depend on them for ours. The ratio of imported products to exported products is called the **balance of trade**. **Trade deficits** occur when imports exceed exports. Trade deficits cause wealth to flow from a nation. When nations face trade deficits, they often place restrictions on imported goods. The nation facing the restrictions can take retaliation by imposing high import taxes or unfair regulations on products, effectively keeping out foreign goods. Trade wars can result, stopping trade between countries. Trade surpluses are the result of more money flowing into a country than out. The oil-producing nations have huge amounts of money flowing into their treasuries and therefore have large trade surpluses when prices are high. In an effort to promote trade, the United States signed the General Agreement on Tariffs and Trade (GATT), which evolved into the **World Trade Organization (WTO)**. The 125 members of the WTO account for 97 percent of the world's trade. The organization works to lower tariffs and quotas and reduce unfair trade practices.

In an effort to promote free trade between the United States, Canada, and Mexico, the three nations signed the **North American Free Trade Agreement (NAFTA)** in 1994, effectively removing import tariffs from one another's products. As an economic policy, NAFTA is controversial. It is opposed by U.S. industrial labor unions who fear that jobs will be lost to cheap Mexican labor. Others fear that the industrial capacity of the United States will be damaged because factories will move to Mexico where environmental laws are not strictly enforced. NAFTA supporters claim it will improve the U.S. economy and will also create jobs in Mexico, resulting in less illegal immigration. Supporters also claim that a richer Mexico will purchase more American products. NAFTA has proven to be something of a mixed blessing. Its passage has led to cheaper labor (in Mexico) for many U.S. companies and an increase in trade between the two countries. Nevertheless, many American jobs have undeniably been sent south of the border, and many Mexican farmers are losing their land in a futile attempt to compete with American agribusinesses.

Economics Drill

Now try some practice questions. To check your answers, register your book at **PrincetonReview.com/cracking** and download the Chapter Drill Answers and Explanations supplement.

1. Ben creates a company that sells and repairs musical instruments. When the economy experiences a recession and Ben's business slows down, he realizes that he cannot continue selling musical instruments. He decides to move into a smaller building with cheaper rent and continue his business by doing only musical instrument repairs. Which of the following represents Ben's opportunity costs after the recession occurred?

   A selling musical instruments

   B a smaller building

   C cheaper rent

   D musical instrument repairs

2. Look at the graph summarizing Country X's international trade. Then answer the question.

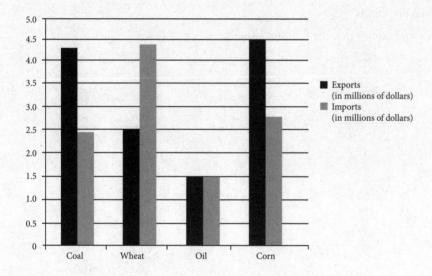

   According to the graph above, for which product does country X have a balance of payment deficit?

   A coal

   B wheat

   C oil

   D corn

3. Read the following excerpt from a radio address given by President Franklin Roosevelt in 1933. Then answer the question.

> Two months ago we were facing serious problems. The country was dying by inches. It was dying because trade and commerce had declined to dangerously low levels; prices for basic commodities were such as to destroy the value of the assets of national institutions such as banks, savings banks, insurance companies, and others… The legislation which has been passed or is in the process of enactment can properly be considered as part of a well-grounded plan.
>
> First, we are given opportunity of employment to one-quarter of a million of the unemployed, especially the young men who have dependents, into forestry and flood prevention work. This is a big task because it means feeding, clothing, and caring for nearly twice as many men as we have in the regular army itself. In creating this civilian conservation corps we are killing two birds with one stone. We are clearly enhancing the value of our natural resources and second, we are relieving an appreciable amount of actual distress.

According to the speech above, Franklin Roosevelt combatted the economic crisis by

A cutting taxes to save federal money

B saving banks to protect America's credit

C selling neutral resources to stabilize funds

D allowing the government to spend money in order to invest in workers

4. Look at the graph. Then answer the question.

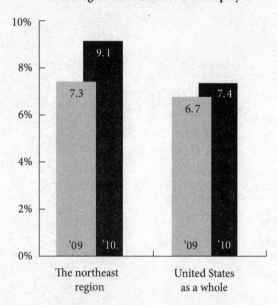

Percentage of the Labor Force Unemployed

An evaluation of the graph above would show that the overall economy of the United States in 2010 probably performed

A worse than it did in 2009

B worse than it did in the northeast region

C better than the economies of other nations

D better than it did in 2009

5. The Office of Management and Budget (OMB) is in charge of

A assessing the nation's economic health

B writing the national budget to reflect the interests of Congress

C planning out the national budget for the president

D providing long-term and highly theoretical economic advice

6. Which of the following is an example of a policy that a believer in laissez-faire economics might support?

A giving the Environmental Protection Agency greater power to fine factories that contribute to global warming

B increasing taxes across higher income groups to aid the poor

C creation of a law that protects unions and grants them collective bargaining rights

D the implementation of a flat tax

Chapter 25
Civics

In this chapter, we'll guide you through the key topics related to civics on the Social Studies portion of the TASC test. We will focus here on two categories: types of governments in general and the United States government specifically. Following the content lessons, we'll give you some practice questions.

ESSENTIALS

In previous chapters, we discussed the processes by which agricultural societies made significant advancements during the Neolithic age. As human populations increased and people lived in larger and larger social groups, there arose a need for institutions and governmental structures. Governments originally arose for a variety of reasons, including the need for protection and the need for law and order among people living in fixed groups.

The Nature of Government

The term *nation* is used loosely in normal conversation. A **nation**, in its most basic definition, is a population represented by a singular culture. Another term for nation would be a *culture group*. What defines a nation is a common identity, which is a complex of genetic heritage and political allegiance embodied in the term *ethnicity*. Ethnic groups often claim a single identifiable lineage or heritage, which all members tend to identify with as a common social bond. Keep in mind that several ethnicities can exist within the same linguistic region. Likewise, within a single ethnicity more than one language can be used, such as the French Canadians, South Asian Indians, or Belgians. Not all nations have a representative state, as a state in its most simple form is a population represented by a single **government**.

There are a number of political geography terms such as nation and state that we use in everyday speech as synonyms. However, the technical definitions of these terms have specific and important meaning in the geography of politics. Here's how to keep them straight:

> **Country:** an identifiable land area
>
> **Nation:** a population with a single culture
>
> **State:** a population under a single government
>
> **Nation-state:** a single culture under a single government

A nation is the same as a **culture group**. "State" implies that there is a **sovereign territory**. Sovereignty generally means that a state is fully independent from outside control, holds territory, and that it has **international recognition** from other states or the United Nations.

The United States and most other sovereign states are **multi-national states** made up of a number of different nations represented by the multitude of culture groups who have migrated and intermixed around the world. Multinational, sometimes called **multiethnic states,** are most common in the Americas, where there are no nation-states.

There are a number of nation-states in which one culture group is represented by a singular government. Many are smaller states or island countries. Although no nation-state is truly made up of only one cultural group, places such as **Japan, Iceland, Tonga, Ireland, Portugal**, and **Lesotho** are places that have not seen permanent invasion or mass immigration from other culture groups in their histories.

The term *nation-state* is also applied, theoretically, to multinational states where the state has come to represent a singular and contemporary culture, as opposed to the ancient cultures from which the population originates. One could argue that there is an identifiable American culture in the United States, or a unique Brazilian culture in Brazil. In both of these cases, the new political nation is the result of the blending of several culture groups together along with the idea of political nationalism.

Nationalism can derive from an existing culture group that desires political representation or independence, or from a political state that bonds and unifies culture groups. Politicians use nationalism as motivation to support the state and oppose foreign or other political influences. Individuals tend to take pride in their nationalist identities, even though they or their neighbors may be from a mix of different ethnic backgrounds.

Although many culture groups are politically represented or are part of larger political entities, there are some **stateless nations,** where a culture group is not included or allowed share in the state political process. Here are a few examples:

- **Kurds** are an ethnic group spread across northern Iraq, western Iran, eastern Syria, and southeastern Turkey. A semi-autonomous Kurdistan has existed in Iraq since the U.S.-led invasion in 2003. However, full independence is limited geopolitically due to Turkish government resistance to their sovereignty, based upon Kurdish Marxist rebels, the PKK, who have been fighting in Turkey for several decades. Since the start of the Syrian Civil War, Kurds have taken territory and started a semi-autonomous government.
- **Basques** are an ethnic group in northern Spain and southwestern France who do not have Celtic or Latin cultural or language roots. In fact, their people's origin is poorly understood by historians. Spain has granted limited autonomy to the Basque region around the city of Bilbao, but many Basque nationalists seek full independence and statehood. A militant group, ETA, has used terror tactics to fight against Spanish rule.
- **Hmong** (pronounced "mung") are mountain peoples who have existed in rural highlands isolated from others in Laos, Vietnam, Thailand, and southern China. However, their alliance with the United States against the Communists during the Vietnam War caused many families to leave their traditional homeland. Today many Hmong have resettled in the upper Midwestern states of Wisconsin and Minnesota. Hmong immigrants are featured in the 2008 film Gran Torino.

Federal states and **confederations** are a common approach to government. The United States, Australia, Canada, Germany, Brazil, Russia, and Mexico are all confederations of several smaller states or provinces under a federal government. Like an umbrella, the federal state provides military protection, administers foreign diplomacy, and regulates trade as well as a number of internal administrative (executive branch), legislative, and judicial services across the country. The states each have their own governments, legislatures, regulations and services. The overlapping roles in the administration may seem redundant, but each has its own division of responsibilities. For instance, the federal government regulates interstate trade, whereas states can make rules about the sale of goods within each state.

At the other end of the international scale, **microstates** are sovereign states that despite their very small size still hold the same position of much larger states like the United States or Canada. Many are island states, ports, or city-states, or they sit landlocked with no access to the sea. The Vatican City is also a sovereign microstate but is not a member of the UN. It is not a nation-state despite the common religion of its residents, who are mostly clergy drawn from around the world and a small Ethiopian boy's school.

Supranationalism is the concept of two or more sovereign states aligned together for a common purpose. A number of **supranational organizations** have been formed for the purposes of trade alliances, military cooperation, and diplomacy. The largest of these is the **United Nations** (193 member states) whose purpose is primarily diplomatic. The UN also provides a number of services internationally through its World Health Organization (WHO), Food and Agriculture Organization (FAO), Development Program (UNDP), International Children's Education Fund (UNICEF), peacekeeping forces, and other smaller directorates such as the UN High Commissariat for Refugees (UNHCR). Each of these units is an important supranational organization in its own right.

Another important supranational organization with several purposes is the **European Union** (EU). In 2013, the EU grew to 28 member states with a small number of applicant states awaiting membership. The EU was named in 1991 under the Treaty of Maastricht, which expanded the organization's role beyond trade relations. Prior to that, the European Coal and Steel Community (created in 1957) helped strengthen steel production between Italy, France, Luxembourg, Belgium, and the Netherlands. The success of this limited free-trade network encouraged the development of the European Economic Community, "the Common Market" or EEC. By 1973, the EEC eliminated all tariffs on trade goods between its 12 Western European member states.

Today, the EU acts like a federal government for Europe but lacks some of the administrative aspects of other confederations like the United States. The modern EU serves five main purposes:

- **Free-trade union:** No taxes or tariffs are charged on goods and services that cross the internal borders of the EU. By eliminating these fees, European businesses can save money and be more economically competitive with the United States and Japan.

- **Open-border policy:** Between EU member states there are no longer any border control stations for immigration or customs inspections. People and commercial vehicles cross internal EU borders without stopping. This began with the Schengen plan in 1985 when West Germany, France, Belgium, Luxembourg, and the Netherlands opened their borders to one another. Workers can now take jobs in other EU states without applying for work permits (some professions may be protected from this).

- **Monetary union:** In 2000, the first EU members began converting to the Euro and phasing out their old forms of money. This eliminated the costs of currency exchange fees. Only 12 members retained their own currencies. The United Kingdom kept the British pound due to its high value—converting to the less valuable Euro would have cause significant financial problems in the United Kingdom. New member states have to meet strict EU economic regulations before they can join the monetary union. However, the world financial crisis of 2008 revealed some weaknesses of the Euro as indebted countries were unable to devalue the Euro as they'd been able to with national currencies. Countries like Greece, Ireland, and Portugal received bailouts as part of the Eurozone crisis. These events have forced countries to question the desirability of using the Euro currency.

- **Judicial union:** The European Court of Justice in Luxembourg provides a legal venue for cases between litigants in separate EU member states. With the increase in cross-border trade and labor, there were bound to be lawsuits and contract issues that would require the EU's decisions. In addition, a European Court of Human Rights has been established to preserve civil rights regardless of their member states' local laws.

- **Legislative and regulatory bodies:** The 785-seat EU Parliament was established to propose and approve laws within the union. The European Commission is a separate council with one seat for each member state. Each year the presidency shifts to one member state, allowing it to set the year's policy agenda. The European Commission also acts as the executive branch of the union to enact programs and enforce regulations set by the EU Parliament and Council. The EU Commission president is appointed by the European Council.

Territoriality is the expression of political control over space. The concept of the state implies that the government controls land and the people who live there. **Citizenship** is the legal identity of a person based on the state where he or she was born or where he or she was naturalized as an immigrant. Keep in mind that when citizens go outside their state's political borders, they retain their citizen status and thus become an extension of their state (unless they apply for new citizenship as immigrants). This is why we strictly define the state as a population represented by a single government, without mentioning territory. However, don't forget that space matters; as it's not much of a state if it has no land, which can happen in the case of a government in exile, such as the Dutch or Polish governments during World War II.

We can't forget that each state has to have a capital city. Why? There will always need to be a **seat of government** where political power is centered. In a way, political power is a form of currency just like money. And just as market areas need financial centers of exchange, politicians need a place to have organized exchanges of power. Occasionally they make laws and have elections, as well. Federal states can have several scales of capitals, just as they have several scales of sub-state units. Most countries have one national capital, but some have more than one. Often this is done to share power across different regions of the country. Occasionally countries change the location of their capital. Sometimes this is due to a shift in political power or can be due to congestion in the old capital. Some new capitals are often **planned capital cities,** which are located in places where cities did not previously exist.

Types of Governments

Feudal political economies, which were very common across the globe during the medieval period, operated with the vast majority of land and wealth being controlled by an **aristocracy**—a **peerage** of lords, earls, marquis, barons, dukes, princes, kings, and queens. Conversely, the vast majority of the population, as peasants, commoners, serfs, or slaves, were poor farmers and laborers who worked the land controlled by aristocrats. Peasants paid rents and had their harvests taxed for the right to live on and work the land.

Feudal states tended to have **absolute monarchy.** This is where the supreme aristocrat, a king, prince, or duke, is both **head of state** and **head of government,** and therefore does not share power with anyone. Like medieval-style feudalism, the concept of absolute monarchy has diminished over time and mostly exists in the Islamic world. Only a few absolute monarchies exist today:

> Saudi Arabia
> Brunei
> Morocco (limited power-sharing)
> Emirates within the United Arab Emirates

You may have learned that a few countries in the Middle East are **theocracies**, where religious leaders hold the senior positions of governance. In fact, only Iran has a supreme religious council that serves as the **head of state** and can overrule the elected parliament and president. Some but not all Middle-Eastern states are **republics or monarchies** that abide by *Sharia,* or Islamic law, based on the Koran and Haddith. A few absolute monarchies (that unlike constitutional monarchies have no elected parliament) have all-powerful kings and large aristocracies, who in turn enforce religious standards on the populace.

Other states in the region are more **secular**, meaning the state is not directly governed in a religious manner and instead often utilize French or British legal tradition and government structure. Even in these states, the influence of religion on government policy remains, and tension between the secular government and religious activists can cause difficulty or violent conflict.

Here are a few Middle-Eastern examples of each case:

> Theocracy: Iran, formerly Afghanistan under the Taliban
> *Sharia* States: Saudi Arabia, Kuwait, Yemen
> Secular States: Jordan, Turkey

Revolutions and wars from the late 1700s to the 1900s forced many feudal states to accept some form of democracy. Events such as the French Revolution of 1789 inspired many monarchs to accept power-sharing with commoners to avoid losing control of their states. Under **constitutional monarchy,** the supreme aristocrat remains **head of state,** but the leader of the elected parliament is the **head of government,** with integrated legislative and executive powers. In most cases this is a **prime minister** or **premier**, who appoints senior members of parliament to be ministers or secretaries of executive-branch departments.

In most constitutional monarchies, the monarch retains the power to dismiss parliament; appoints judges, ambassadors, and other officials; is commander and chief of the military; and retains significant land holdings and estates. However, the monarch's political power is mostly diminished to a symbolic role, and he or she holds a small but important position in dictating policy and proposing laws.

Here are some examples of constitutional monarchies:

Great Britain	Thailand
Belgium	Luxembourg
The Netherlands	Kuwait
Japan	Jordan
Norway	Bahrain
Denmark	Monaco
Sweden	Cambodia
Spain	

Let's consider the example of the British aristocracy and government as an in-depth illustration of these principles. The current form of constitutional monarchy in Great Britain has been in place since the Magna Carta was signed in 1215. Feudalism has reigned throughout, but in the Magna Carta there was some degree of power-sharing with the aristocracy and later with commoners voting in elections (1689).

Today, feudal rents to local aristocrats are still technically paid in a number of rural areas of the United Kingdom, although many are symbolic and small fees. A majority of Britons live in urban areas and are not subject to these fees. Many rural farms are now owned privately, though some may still be required to pay feudal rents.

The British aristocracy's structure and role has also been modified in recent years. Traditionally, aristocratic peers sat in the **House of Lords,** the upper house of parliament, which also serves as the supreme court. The House of Lords numbers more than 760 members. When the king or queen elevated someone to the peerage, a new seat was added. Eventually, they had too many members. Beginning in 1999, Queen Elizabeth II reformed the house with two types of members. Hereditary peers, who at death pass their title and seat to their firstborn son, were reduced in number, and life peers, mainly senior public servants who were rewarded with a title, kept their title and seat for their lifetime only.

Since the late 1600s, the power has steadily increased in the **House of Commons**, the lower house of parliament. The Commons has 650 seats apportioned to local districts across the U.K.; Scotland, Wales, and Northern Ireland also have regional parliaments of their own. The Prime Minister (PM) is head of government, but is also a member of parliament (MP). Generally the PM is the political leader of the party with the most MPs. Other senior MPs from this **ruling party** serve as ministers of the executive branch of government. This is another example of how parliamentary democracy integrates the three branches of government.

Most but not all member states of the **Commonwealth of Nations** (independent former parts of the British Empire) retain the British monarch as their head of state. These commonwealth countries have their own parliaments and prime ministers as head of government. Each also has a royally appointed governor-general as the crown representative in the country. The governor-general's role, like the monarch's, is mostly a symbolic and ceremonial position. These countries are nonetheless considered independent sovereign states. Yet they do retain some minor political link to the U.K.—most provide military support to the U.K. in times of war. The following countries claim the British monarch as head of state:

Canada	Papua New Guinea
Jamaica	Belize
Dominica	Guyana
St. Vincent and the Grenadines	Bahamas
New Zealand	Antigua and Barbuda
Australia	Grenada
Fiji	

India, Pakistan, Sri Lanka, Nigeria, and Kenya are a few of the commonwealth members that do *not* claim the British monarch as head of state. However, all commonwealth nations have parliamentary governments, which integrate executive, legislative, and judicial powers, like that of Great Britain. In addition, the Commonwealth of Nations is an important supranational organization that provides special trade, education services, government funding, and preferred immigration status between member governments and citizens.

Former colonies that are now dependent territories (not sovereign states) of the U.K. are not Commonwealth members and are still controlled from London with limited local governance; these include Anguilla, Cayman Islands, Turks and Caicos, British Virgin Islands, Bermuda, Montserrat, the Falkland Islands, St. Helena, Ascension Island, and Gibraltar.

Generally, countries with elected representative parliamentary systems such as the United States, the United Kingdom, commonwealth countries, and other constitutional monarchies or republics are classified as **free-market democracies**. Internal to a state, this system generally relies upon balancing the relationship between the elected representative government, its citizens, and business interests. In most cases, there is a variable system of regulation and taxation by the state. As a result, the marketplace is not totally free, as it would be in a completely unregulated laissez-faire economic system, but it's close enough.

Government regulatory influence of the private lives of its citizens and practices of businesses is usually limited to areas concerning public safety and economic protections. The point of democracy is that people have a say in who makes the rules and thus have some influence over the rule-making process.

France, Germany, Italy, and many former colonial states are technically republics, under the broader category of free-market democracy. Some republics, such as France, are centrally governed from a single capital. Others, such as Germany or the United States, are confederations that apportion some government power of legislation and administration to their component states or provinces (*Lander* in Germany). The main thing to keep in mind is that republics are free of aristocracy or monarchal control. The governments are fully under the control of the "common" people, as opposed to hereditary monarchy.

Unlike parliamentary systems that assign legislative, executive, and judicial power to the same people, republics generally have a **separation of powers.** Here, the executive, legislative, and judicial branches of government are held by separate groups of people that keep each other in check. This may seem less efficient, but it reduces the potential for corruption of the whole government. If one branch's leadership fails or its practices are called into question, the other branches can act to correct problems or replace leadership if necessary.

This is not to say that republics are perfect systems, as you might feel if you read too much Plato. The written **constitutions** of these governments need to be flexible enough to allow governments to deal with political and other crises when they occur. The United States has had two constitutions, the former being the Articles of Confederation, which did not work out. The French have had five different types of government since the revolution, and the current government system in France is known as the "Fifth Republic." There is no perfect constitution, but a constitution can be refined over time by the addition of amendments. Another problem is that wealthy businesspeople and corporations have replaced the aristocracy in terms of the control of money, land, and resources. Their personal and corporate **political influence** overshadows that of many thousands of private citizens. The purchase of political favoritism to influence the setting of regulations is a constant problem in republics, as it is in other democracies, especially within the legislative branch. This has created uneven power relations in free-market democracies.

Another type of separation that is sometimes employed to blunt the power of the executive branch is to have separate presidents and prime ministers (or chancellors in Germany). In the United States, Mexico, and Argentina, the president is both head of state and head of government. In most other republics there is executive separation. Depending on the country, this can be done in a couple of ways. In France, the president is head of government and the prime minister is head of state, but it's the opposite in Italy.

THE U.S. GOVERNMENT

You will need to know about global governmental systems on the TASC test, but most questions related to civics will ask specifically about the government of the United States.

Ideas Underlying U.S. Government

The Framers of the Constitution lived in a unique time when new ideas on how government should be organized and run challenged conventional wisdom regarding the roles of people and their governments. The Enlightenment was an eighteenth-century philosophical movement that began in Western Europe with roots in the Scientific Revolution. The focus was on the use of reason rather than tradition to solve social dilemmas.

The following Enlightenment philosophers contributed directly to the formation of thought that led to the creation of the American Constitution and government.

- **Thomas Hobbes:** Hobbes's famous work *Leviathan* (1660) argued that if humans were left to their own devices, chaos and violence would ensue. In a state of nature, life would be "solitary, poor, nasty, brutish, and short." He argued that the best way to protect life was to give total power to an absolute monarch.
- **John Locke:** While Hobbes was concerned primarily with the protection of life, Locke went further and argued in his *Second Treatise on Civil Government* (1690) that liberty and property also needed to be respected. According to Locke, life, liberty, and property were natural rights granted by God; it was the duty of all governments to respect and protect these rights. If the government did not, Locke contended, the citizens have the right of revolution.
- **Charles de Montesquieu:** Montesquieu was a French philosopher who greatly influenced the founders. His *De l'Esprit des Lois* (*The Spirit of the Laws,* 1748) advocated for the separation of power into three branches of government.
- **Jean Jacques Rousseau:** Rousseau argued that the only good government was one that was freely formed with the consent of the people (1762). This consent was shown in a powerful "social contract," which was an agreement among people.

The first government of the newly born United States of America was formed under the Articles of Confederation, the predecessor to the Constitution. These Articles were informally followed from 1776 to 1781 when they were ratified and so named. The government under the Articles achieved some notable accomplishments, including the following:

- It negotiated the treaty that ended the Revolutionary War (on favorable terms for the United States' victorious army).
- It established the Northwest Ordinance, creating methods by which new states would enter the Union.
- It set the precedent of federalism, whereby the states and central government shared governing responsibilities.

However, the Articles of Confederation had insurmountable weaknesses that placed the newly independent states at risk. By 1787, trade between the states was in decline, the value of money was dropping, potential threats from foreign enemies were growing, and there was the real threat of social disorder from groups within the country. The inability of the state of Massachusetts to effectively deal with Shays' Rebellion, a six-month rebellion in which more than 1,000 armed farmers attacked a federal arsenal to protest the foreclosure of farms in the western part of the state, was a major concern at the Constitutional Convention. The nation's leaders began to see the necessity of a stronger central government, as **Shays' Rebellion** frightened the statesmen and exposed the weakness of the Articles of Confederation.

The federal government under the Articles

- could not draft soldiers
- was completely dependent on the state legislatures for revenue—the federal government was not permitted to tax citizens
- could not pay off the Revolutionary War debt
- could not control interstate trade
- had no Supreme Court to interpret law
- had no executive branch to enforce national law
- had no national currency
- had no control over import and export taxes imposed between states
- needed unanimity to amend the Articles
- needed approval from 9 out of 13 states to pass legislation (69% majority)

These deficiencies of the Articles of Confederation were the direct causes for calling a convention. But amending the articles became so difficult that James Madison did not have difficulty persuading the other delegates that a complete rewrite was necessary. The result was the **Constitution,** and the convention came to be known as the **Constitutional Convention**.

When the Framers of the Constitution met in Philadelphia in 1787, they were divided over their views of the appropriate power and responsibilities of government. Some saw the current government, formed under the Articles of Confederation, as weak and ineffective, while others believed that changes to the Articles would be infringements on the responsibilities of state governments and intrusions into the lives of citizens. Some historians (such as Charles Beard) see the convention as an elitist conspiracy to protect the wealth of the rich, while others see the convention as a meeting of political pragmatists who knew that by protecting everyone's property and rights, they could best protect their own. Today, the generally accepted view is that the Framers were pragmatists.

The delegates agreed that a stronger central government was necessary but were fearful of the corrupting influences of power. How to control the federal legislature was a central theme at the convention. The large states seized the agenda at the beginning of the convention and proposed the **Virginia Plan**, a recipe for a strong government with each state represented proportionately to its population. The small states worried that a government dominated by the large states would be overly strong, so they proposed the **New Jersey Plan**, under which each state would be represented equally. The **Great** (or **Connecticut**) **Compromise** created the solution: a **bicameral** (two-house) **legislature** with a House of Representatives, based on population, and a Senate, with equal representation for all states. Another major conflict arose over the representation of slaves. (Remember that slaves could not vote then.) Northerners felt that slaves should not be counted when determining each state's number of electoral votes, while Southerners disagreed. The "solution" was the infamous Three-Fifths Compromise, in which the decision was made that slaves would count as three-fifths of a person when apportioning votes.

Under the Articles of Confederation there was no executive authority to enforce laws. The Framers of the Constitution corrected that problem by addressing the issue of a chief executive, or president. Under the Constitution, the executive is the enforcer of law and a second check on the power of the legislature. Before bills become law, they require presidential approval, and the president has the power to veto acts of the legislature. However, presidential power is not absolute. Congress can override a presidential veto if two-thirds of both houses of the legislature vote to do so.

In order to arbitrate disputes between the Congress and the president, between states, and between the states and the central government, the Framers created the Supreme Court. Despite all of the compromises that were reached at the convention, acceptance of the Constitution was by no means assured. It had to be submitted to the states for ratification. Supporters and opponents of the Constitution broke into two camps, Federalists and Anti-Federalists. Alexander Hamilton, James Madison, and John Jay wrote a series of newspaper articles supporting the Constitution, collectively known as *The Federalist Papers*. These essays are the primary source for understanding the original intent of the Framers. They were designed to persuade the states of the wisdom of a strong central government coupled with autonomous political power retained by the states.

The Anti-Federalists opposed the creation of a stronger national government, arguing that a Constitution would threaten citizens' personal liberties and effectively make the president a king. Keep in mind that only 12 years prior, these

"Bicameral legislature" means a legislature that is divided into two houses. The system began in England in the 1600s with the two houses of Parliament: the House of Commons and the House of Lords. (Funnily, the House of Lords has no real power in British government now.)

people had declared independence from Britain, and many were fearful that a large government with a Constitution would recreate that same state of tyrannical control from which they had just escaped. The opposition to the Constitution centered on the lack of a **Bill of Rights** that would protect the rights of individuals from government infringement. Once the Federalists guaranteed that a Bill of Rights would be added to the Constitution immediately after ratification, opposition diminished, and the Constitution became the foundation of American government.

The Structure of American Government

The Constitution is vague and skeletal in form, containing only about 5,000 words. It was intended to be a blueprint for the structure of government and a guide for guaranteeing the rights of citizens. It was written to allow change, anticipating unknown needs of future generations, through amendments that require widespread support. The branches of government have all grown and evolved since the ratification of the Constitution.

- The **necessary and proper** clause of the Constitution (Article I, Section 8) allows Congress to "make all laws" that appear "necessary and proper" to implement its delegated powers. This is also called the **elastic clause**. For example, there is nothing in the Constitution that creates the Federal Reserve System, which is the central bank for the United States. Neither is there any mention of a cabinet in the executive branch. The Federal District Courts and the Courts of Appeals were both created by congressional elaboration.

- Executive power has expanded through the use of **presidential practice**. **Executive orders**, which have the same effect as law, bypass Congress in policy making and are not mentioned in the Constitution. Presidents use them as part of the enforcement duties of the executive branch. **Executive agreements** between heads of countries have many of the same elements as treaties. These agreements bypass the ratification power of the Senate but are not mentioned in the Constitution. An extreme example of an executive order is Executive Order 9066, in which Franklin D. Roosevelt ordered people removed from a military zone. It was no coincidence that these people were Japanese American and German American. This order paved the way for all Japanese Americans on the West Coast to be sent to internment camps for the duration of World War II. Thousands of German Americans and Italian Americans were also sent to internment camps under executive order.

- When the Supreme Court decided the case of *Marbury v. Madison* in 1803, it drastically increased its own power by granting itself the ability to overturn laws passed by the legislature, also known as **judicial review**.

A more recent example of executive orders is the set of immigration orders enacted by President Obama in November, 2014. These orders are intended to expand protections for some categories of undocumented immigrants (children who arrived before age 16 and lived in the United States continuously for 5 years, and parents of U.S. citizens), punish immigrants who don't pass background checks, and reform visa programs.

- Finally, custom and usage have changed the system to meet differing needs. The political party system, with its organization, technology, and fund-raising capabilities, was created from custom and usage. The rules used in Congress were also created from custom and usage. Central to the Constitution is the idea that the United States government is a federal government. As we discussed earlier in the chapter, the term **federalism** describes a system of government under which the national government and local governments (state governments, in the case of the United States) share powers. Under federalism, some government powers belong exclusively to the national government, some exclusively to the states, and some are shared by the two. Those powers that belong to the national government only are called **delegated**, **expressed**, or **enumerated** powers. Among them are
  - printing money
  - regulating interstate and international trade
  - making treaties and conducting foreign policy
  - declaring war

Powers that belong exclusively to the states are called **reserved powers**. According to the Tenth Amendment, these powers include any that the Constitution neither specifically grants to the national government nor denies to the state governments. These powers are not listed in the Constitution; in fact, they are made up of all powers not mentioned in the Constitution. They include

- the power to issue licenses
- the regulation of intrastate (within the states) businesses
- the responsibility to run and pay for federal elections

Some powers are shared by the federal and state governments. These are called **concurrent powers**. Among them are the powers to

- collect taxes
- build roads
- operate courts of law
- borrow money

The Constitution specifies which powers are denied to the national government and which powers are denied to the states.

The Constitution also obliges the federal government to guarantee the states a republican form of government and protection against foreign invasion and domestic rebellion. The federal government must also prevent the states from subdividing or combining to form new states without congressional consent. The states, in turn, are required by the Constitution to accept the court judgments, licenses, contracts, and other civil acts of all the other states; this obligation is contained in the **full faith and credit** clause. The states may not refuse police protection or access to their courts to a U.S. citizen just because that person lives in a different state; this provision appears in the **privileges and immunities clause**. Finally, the states usually must return fugitives to the states from which they have fled; this process is called **extradition**.

The supremacy clause of the Constitution requires conflicts between federal law and state law to be resolved in favor of federal law. State laws that violate the Constitution, federal laws, or international treaties can be invalidated through the **supremacy clause**.

The nature of federalism has changed over time. For the first part of the nation's history, the federal and state governments remained separate and independent. The relationship between the national and state governments during this period is called **dual federalism**. What little contact most Americans had with government occurred on the state level, as the national government concerned itself primarily with international trade; the construction of roads, harbors, and railways; and the distribution of public land in the West.

As with all parts of the Constitution, the definition of federalism is in the eye of the beholder. Ideological **States' Righters** define federalism as a relationship in which the states retain most of the political power. **Nationalists** often see the federal government as being supreme in all matters and ultimately in control.

Most federal government programs, such as those to aid the poor, clean the environment, improve education, and protect the handicapped, are administered through the states. The federal government pays for these programs through grants-in-aid, which are outright gifts of money to the states. Nationalists prefer to tie strings to the grants, ensuring that the federal government maintains control over the money. States' Righters want no strings attached, leaving decisions about how the grant money is to be used to state and local governments, who they believe know best how to use it.

Nationalists like **categorical grants**, aid with strict provisions from the federal government on how it may be spent. States' Righters like **block grants**, which permit the state to experiment and use the money as they see fit. In the final analysis, however, the federal government can use a number of techniques, including direct orders and preemption, to force the states to abide by federal law. The federal government can also use a crossover sanction, which requires a state to do something before a grant will be awarded. An example would be to raise the drinking age to 21 before federal highway money to build state roads is released.

Categorical Grants
Examples of categorical grants include Head Start, Medicaid, and the Food Stamp Program.

Separation of Powers

The Framers of the Constitution decided that no one faction of the government should be able to acquire too much power. To prevent this, they borrowed the concept of the **separation of powers** from the French political philosopher **Charles de Montesquieu**. The Framers delegated different but equally important tasks to the three branches of government. The **legislative branch** (Congress) makes the laws; the **executive branch**, led by the president, enforces the laws; and the **judicial branch** interprets the laws.

Separation of powers also prevents a person from serving in more than one branch of the government at the same time. A congressperson (legislative branch), for example, may not also be a judge (judicial branch), nor a cabinet member (executive branch). If a congressperson were appointed to one of these positions, he or she would first have to resign his or her seat in Congress.

The system of checks and balances is another constitutional safeguard designed to prevent any one branch of government from becoming dominant. The system of checks and balances requires the different branches of government to share power and cooperate with one another to accomplish anything of importance.

- Nomination of federal judges, cabinet officials, and ambassadors. The president chooses nominees for these positions. However, the president's nominees must be approved by the Senate.
- Negotiation of treaties. The president is empowered to negotiate treaties. No treaty can go into effect, however, until it is approved by two-thirds of the Senate.
- Enactment of legislation. Only Congress may pass laws. However, the president has the power to veto, or reject, legislation. The president's veto power encourages the legislature to consider the president's position on a law, and to negotiate with the president to prevent a veto. Congress can also check the president's veto by overriding the veto, but to do so it must pass the same law with a two-thirds majority in both houses (a congressional override is difficult, but not impossible). If Congress succeeds in overriding the president's veto, the legislation becomes law regardless of the president's position. Finally, the courts may determine the constitutionality of the law. Thus, the courts have the power to overturn laws passed by Congress and approved by the president (only on constitutional grounds, however; judges may not overturn laws simply because they don't like them).

The Bill of Rights

One reason that the Constitution has lasted more than 200 years is that it is flexible. Many of its provisions require interpretation, allowing the document to become more conservative or progressive as the times warrant. Furthermore, the Constitution can be changed through **amendments** (the addition of provisions to the document).

To amend the Constitution, a proposed amendment must be introduced to both houses of Congress and approved by a two-thirds majority in each. The amendment is then passed on to each of the fifty state legislatures. Three-fourths of the state legislatures must **ratify** (approve) the amendment for it to become part of the Constitution. The states themselves are allowed to determine how many votes are required to ratify an amendment. Most states require a simple majority of their legislatures, but seven states require either three-fifths or two-thirds majorities. Also, rather than use the state legislatures, Congress can mandate that each state use a **ratifying convention**, with delegates expressly elected to vote on the proposed amendment. This method was once used to ratify the Twenty-First Amendment, which ended Prohibition in 1933.

The Constitution allows for a second means of amendment. Two-thirds of the state legislatures could petition Congress to call a **constitutional convention**. Because no constitutional convention has ever taken place, nobody knows for certain how extensively conventioneers would be allowed to alter the Constitution. Could they rewrite it entirely, or would they be restricted to amendments mentioned specifically in their petitions for a convention? Fear that a constitutional convention could attempt drastic alterations has persuaded many state legislators to oppose any call for a convention. There are ongoing movements in many states to call a constitutional convention to add a balanced budget amendment to the Constitution. While about 30 state legislatures have approved a convention, the movement has not yet met the bar of 34 states required to call the convention.

The first ten amendments were added to the Constitution within three years of its ratification. These amendments are known collectively as the **Bill of Rights**. Originally written by James Madison, many provisions of the Bill of Rights have been expanded and clarified over the years.

The First Amendment

Supreme Court Justice Benjamin Cardozo (1932–1937) said that the First Amendment of the Bill of Rights contains "the fundamental principles of liberty and justice which lie at the base of all of our civil and political institutions."

- Freedom of religion. The government may not interfere with an individual's right to practice his or her faith as described in the free exercise clause. Furthermore, as stated in the establishment clause, Congress may not establish an official church of the United States nor give a particular faith or sect preferential treatment over others. This constitutional provision is usually referred to as the separation of church and state.
- Freedom of speech and freedom of the press. Congress may not pass a law that prevents citizens from expressing their opinions, either in speech or in writing. Nevertheless, the Supreme Court has placed some limits on these freedoms. Speech or writing intended to incite violence or used to intentionally slander or libel is not protected. Justice Oliver Wendell Holmes articulated the clear and present danger test, in which the government has the right to interfere in free speech if it poses a threat to others, in the case of *Schenck v. United States* (1917). Nevertheless, criticism of the government and its politics is protected. When it comes to censoring the press, there are few instances in which the government can use prior restraint—crossing out sections of an article before publication. These strong protections for the press were established in the case of *Near v. Minnesota* (1973).

- Freedom of assembly and freedom to petition the government. The Constitution protects the people's rights to assemble peacefully, to hold demonstrations, and to ask the government for changes in policy. Rallies and demonstrations that encourage or incite violence and those that do not seek official sanction to trespass on public property are not protected.

The Second Amendment

The Second Amendment to the Constitution, which protects the citizens' right to bear arms, has led to a debate over whether the Constitution protects citizens' rights to bear arms under all circumstances, or only when those citizens serve in "well-regulated militias."

The Third Amendment

The most antiquated of all the amendments, though not at the time of its creation, the Third Amendment forbids the quartering of soldiers and the direct public support of armed forces. It was a direct reaction to the British practice of using civilian support to conduct military operations. Still, it later had importance as it became part of the foundation of the right to privacy as established in the case of *Griswold v. Connecticut* (1965).

The Fourth Amendment

The Fourth Amendment places restrictions on government agencies regarding criminal or civil procedural investigations and does much to protect an individual's "person, house, papers, and effects against unreasonable searches and seizures." This amendment was most dramatically reviewed in the twentieth century, as evidenced in *Mapp v. Ohio* (1961). Questions regarding the use of probable cause, traffic-stop and stop-and-frisk searches, and the use of search warrants have led to challenges regarding the interpretation of the exclusionary rule regarding evidence seized without proper procedures. In its original form, the exclusionary rule holds that all evidence unlawfully gathered must be excluded from judicial proceedings.

The Fifth Amendment

The Fifth Amendment does the most to protect an individual from the broad powers of the federal government. It provides a guarantee of a grand jury when a suspect is held for a capital or other "infamous" crime. It eliminates the possibility of a person being maliciously prosecuted for the same crime again and again by prohibiting double jeopardy. It establishes the right of the government to seize property for public use under the auspices of eminent domain but only if such seizure can be "justly compensated." Nor may defendants be forced to testify against themselves if on trial, thus prohibiting self-incrimination (commonly known as "pleading the fifth"). The most significant attribute of the Fifth Amendment is its mandate that the federal government not deprive an individual of "life, liberty, or property by any level unless due process of law is applied."

The Miranda rights, which you may be familiar with ("You have the right to remain silent..."), help to maintain both the Fifth and Sixth Amendments. They remind the accused that they do not have to incriminate themselves (Fifth) and that they are guaranteed the right to representation (Sixth).

The Sixth Amendment

This amendment allows persons accused of a crime to be prosecuted by an impartial jury in a "speedy" public trial. Individuals have the right to be informed of their charges, to confront witnesses, to subpoena witnesses for their defense, and to have a lawyer for their defense. The sixth amendment forms the basis for habeas corpus, which protects against unlawful imprisonment and ensures that a person cannot be held indefinitely without being formally charged before a judge or in a court, or without a legal reason to extend his or her detention.

The Seventh Amendment

Although statutory, or written, law has come to replace or supersede common law, which is law based on past court decisions, the Seventh Amendment allows for trial by jury in common-law cases.

The Eighth Amendment

The Eighth Amendment prohibits excessive bail in federal cases. Yet its most significant challenges have arisen from the clause that prohibits "cruel and unusual punishment." Capital punishment is one of the most contentious issues of the modern day. At issue is whether it constitutes "cruel and unusual punishment." Federal and state Supreme Courts have taken different positions on this debate.

The Ninth Amendment

The Ninth Amendment reaffirms the principles of a limited federal government. "The enumeration in the Constitution, of certain rights, shall not be construed to deny or disparage others retained by the people" means that rights not specifically mentioned in the Constitution are still protected—everyone has the right to brush their hair, for example—even though that right is mentioned nowhere in the Bill of Rights. Although somewhat vague in its premise, the Ninth Amendment has led to the implied right to privacy and other questions regarding individual rights not identified or even understood at the time of the creation of the Constitution.

The Tenth Amendment

The Tenth Amendment defines the relationship between the states and the national government under the concept of federalism. It states that when powers are not defined or delegated by the Constitution, the states have reserved power to make their own individual judgments—so long as they do not infringe with the explicit rules of the Constitution and the federal government. State issues such as death penalty, speed limit, and drinking age are within the jurisdiction of the states to decide so long as they do not contradict the Constitution.

Selected Other Amendments

There are 27 amendments total, so we don't have time to discuss each of them in detail. A few particularly important ones are the Civil War amendments and the amendments related to suffrage and prohibition.

The Thirteenth Amendment (1865)

This amendment prohibited the institution of slavery except as punishment for a convicted crime, and was a direct result of the Union victory in the Civil War.

The Fourteenth Amendment (1868)

Remember, the Bill of Rights did not originally apply to state law. After the Civil War, Northerners pushed for a constitutional amendment that would prevent the South from denying equal rights to the newly freed slaves. The Fourteenth Amendment was designed to accomplish this purpose, stating that "No state shall make or enforce any law which shall abridge the privileges or immunities of citizens of the United States; nor shall any state deprive any person of life, liberty, or property, without due process of law; nor deny to any person within its jurisdiction the equal protection of the laws."

The Fourteenth Amendment expanded the right to due process to all Americans; however, it did not immediately apply the protections of the Bill of Rights to all state laws. Instead, the Supreme Court has used the "due process" and "equal protection" clauses to extend most of the Bill of Rights protections but has done so on a case-by-case basis. This process of incorporating some of the Bill of Rights protections to state law is called selective incorporation.

The Fifteenth Amendment (1870)

The Fifteenth Amendment granted voting rights to males of all races, and was originally designed to extend voting rights to newly freed male slaves. Ultimately, the Supreme Court and southern states later narrowed, and in some cases eliminated, the provisions of this amendment during the late nineteenth and early twentieth century. Voter rights were only later made secure by the passage of the Twenty-Fourth Amendment and the Voting Rights Act of 1965.

The Eighteenth Amendment (1920)

Known as the Prohibition amendment, this amendment prohibited the manufacture, sale, and transportation of alcohol in or out of the United States.

The Nineteenth Amendment (1920)

This amendment granted voting rights to all American women.

The Twenty-First Amendment (1933)

Prohibition had largely led to the rise of organized crime and widespread law-breaking. The Twenty-First Amendment recognized the failure of this government experiment and repealed prohibition, allowing for the legalization of the sale of alcohol.

Contemporary Political Ideas as They Affect Citizenship

The ways in which contemporary political ideas affect citizens and their lives are often referred to as **public policy**. The process of public policy making consists of first deciding what the problem is and then deciding how to solve it. Policy making can have the following three purposes:

- solving a social problem, such as high crime rates, high unemployment, poverty among the aged, or teenage drinking
- countering threats, such as terrorism or war
- pursuing an objective, such as building a highway, exploring outer space, or finding a cure for cancer or AIDS

Policy can be achieved by prohibiting certain kinds of behavior, such as polygamy, murder, rape, and robbery. It can also be achieved by protecting certain activities. Granting patents and copyrights to individuals for their intellectual property, protecting the environment, and setting rules for workplace safety are all examples. Policy can promote some social activity; giving tax deductions for donations to charities is an example. Policy can be achieved by providing direct benefits to citizens. These benefits may include building roads, libraries, or hospitals. Benefits can also take the form of individual government subsidies, student loans, and pensions for the elderly.

Policy making can be frustrating because it often depends on public opinion, which can be fickle and unpredictable. The issue-attention cycle requires policy makers to act quickly, before the public becomes bored and loses interest. Public complaints over high energy prices can cause a flurry of policy making. But when prices go down, the public forgets about it until the next time.

Policy making often involves trade-offs between competing goods. To find additional energy resources may require access to pristine wildlife reserves. The risks to wildlife and the environment may be too high of a price to pay for the additional energy. Conservation, smaller cars, and alternative energy sources may be better solutions, but each will have its supporters and opponents.

Because policy making can have unforeseen results and can touch off bitter disputes, legislators often use incrementalism—the slow, step-by-step approach to making policy—or legislators may decide to use the policy of inaction, because taking no action is one way of making policy. Conflicts over health care reform and Social Security entitlements can result in simply maintaining the status quo.

While economic policy is contentious, domestic policy is sometimes even more so because it gets to the very essence of the purposes of government. Liberals believe government has an obligation to provide for social welfare, to help the needy. Conservatives believe social-welfare programs are encroachments on individual liberties and responsibilities. They think these programs turn the government into an instrument used to create a permanent class of the underprivileged, dependent upon government handouts. Somewhere in between are the moderates who believe government should provide opportunities and limited help during difficult times.

The twentieth century has seen a dramatic change in the way society perceives the role of government in providing for the basic needs of people. Before the Great Depression, there were no government programs to help people who suffered from the hardships of old age, disabilities, unemployment, and poverty. So many people needed help in the 1930s that the government enacted programs to create jobs, provide housing, and feed the hungry. Later on, the Great Society programs of the Johnson administration expanded government welfare programs, but because of the expense and questions about their effectiveness, many of the Great Society programs were eliminated or scaled back during and after the Reagan administration.

Social Security is an entitlement program mandated by law. The government must pay benefits to all people who meet the requirements of the program. Changing the law would require congressional action. Because the largest voting block of the electorate is made up of those nearing or at retirement age, there is little chance of major changes to the system, even though some experts warn that the Social Security trust fund will go bankrupt in the near future. Currently, entitlement programs account for the largest expense in the federal budget.

In its original form Social Security provided benefits only to retired persons beginning at age 65. The program has now been expanded to include four categories of persons:

- Retired workers and their survivors who are presently age 65 and older receive monthly payments from the Social Security trust fund. To help maintain a recipient's standard of living, recipients are entitled to a **COLA** (cost of living adjustment) if the inflation rate exceeds 3 percent. COLAs put a strain on the ability of the trust fund to meet its obligations. Changes in the demographic composition of society are also putting a strain on the system. Society is aging, and the ratio of workers to retirees is declining. Because Social Security is a pay-as-you-go system, the money that is now paid into the system pays the present beneficiaries. As the ratio of workers to retirees continues to decline, workers will be faced with higher taxes to maintain the income of those who are retired.
- Insurance for the disabled provides monthly payments to those citizens who are permanently and totally disabled. This category includes the learning disabled and those dependent on drugs and alcohol.

- **Medicare** provides government assistance to people older than 65 for health care. For those retirees who pay an additional tax on their social security benefit, Medicare Part B will pay approximately 80 percent of their doctor's bills. The high and rising cost of health care has led some to question the solvency of this program, but recent reports note that it is more than able to cover 100% of its costs through at least 2030.
- **Medicaid** provides medical and health-related services for low-income parents, children, seniors, and people with disabilities. It is jointly funded by the states and federal government and is managed and run by the individual states.
- Temporary unemployment insurance for those out of work provides a weekly benefit, for a limited time. Each state government administers its own unemployment insurance program. Both the federal and state governments pay into a trust fund to provide the benefit. While states have traditionally set their own rules on the amount and duration of benefits, Congress has responded at the federal level to the recession that began in 2009 by helping states offer up to 99 weeks of benefits to the unemployed, significantly more than the previous standard of 26 weeks. In 2012, however, Congress imposed additional restrictions on those extended federal benefits, including a measure to gradually decrease the limit to 73 weeks. With the unemployment rate below 6% at the beginning of 2015, the extension of benefits continues to decrease.

No matter how well intentioned the government has been, and no matter how much money has been spent, poverty has remained a perpetual problem for policy makers at both the state and federal levels. The first federal welfare programs were established by the Social Security Act in the 1930s. The largest and most controversial became known as Aid to Families with Dependent Children (AFDC).

All social welfare programs are designed to help targeted groups. Public assistance programs, known as welfare, target families whose total income falls below the federally determined minimum amount required to provide for the basic needs of a family. The present amount is approximately $17,000 for a family of four. The larger the family, the more income is required and the more money is paid out. Critics claimed that welfare was an incentive for families to have more children. Further complicating matters were complaints from recipients about a system that was degrading because investigators, looking for welfare cheaters, were invading their privacy.

In addition to AFDC, the federal government has established **supplemental public assistance** programs (known as SSI) to help the disabled and the aged who are living at or near the poverty level. To improve the diet and increase the buying power of the poor, the federal government also provides **food stamps**. Recipients use government-provided debit cards to help pay for food. Both SSI and the food-stamp program are federal programs administered through local and state agencies.

In an effort to reduce the number of people living on public assistance, the **Welfare Reform Act** was passed in 1996. Under the new law, social welfare programs are funded by both the state and federal governments, with the federal government contributing the greatest share in the form of block grants. Block grants are important because they allow states to experiment with new types of programs designed to get people off welfare and into work programs. The administration of programs (the distribution of cash payments) and the incentives for finding work and providing job training are left to the states. The intent of the law is to reduce the welfare rolls and force people to find work. This is accomplished by

- abolishing Aid to Families with Dependent Children (AFDC), which has affected 22 percent of the families in the United States with children and replacing it with Temporary Assistance for Needy Families (TANF)
- requiring adults to find work within two years or be cut off
- placing a lifetime limit of five years for welfare eligibility, although it is possible to get a waiver if a recipient is actively seeking work
- prohibiting illegal immigrants from receiving assistance

The political debate over public assistance centers on two issues: Who pays how much, and what is the fair standard to be used for the recipient? Both Democrats and Republicans have tried to reduce these programs. Cutting them, however, places more people at risk, reducing food stamp programs and school lunch programs, causing increased hunger. To make matters more complicated, the Welfare Reform Act moved millions off the welfare rolls of the states as it coincided with a boom in unemployment.

One of the most vexing problems for policy makers is what to do about the high cost of health care. Americans spend more than 17 percent of the nation's gross **domestic product**, or **GDP** (the total of goods and services produced in a year), on health care. The United States has the most expensive health care system in the world and is the only fully industrialized nation without a national health care program. High costs have not guaranteed any longer life expectancy, nor better treatment than that found in other industrialized nations. Instead of a national program run by the government, most Americans have relied on various types of insurance programs to pay for health care costs. The premiums for these health care programs are paid by workers and employers. For many reasons, but primarily because of cost, 15.4 percent of the population was without health insurance in 2010.

As with other government programs, the electorate is divided on how to solve the two issues of universal health care and the burden of health care costs. Voters seem to want increased coverage but there is little evidence to indicate they are willing to pay for it. The only taxes the American electorate seems willing to pay are the so-called "sin taxes"—still fairly unpopular in some circles—on alcohol and tobacco products, which will not generate enough revenues to provide increased coverage. Proposals for "anti-obesity" taxes on sugary drinks and sodas have been met with mixed reactions from the public. Another basic issue for which there is no consensus is whether health benefits should be a government or privately administered program. With little public consensus, over the past two decades, reform has been extremely contentious.

An ill-fated attempt at health care reform was made in the first Clinton administration. The proposed policy called for universal coverage and strict cost controls. The policy would have required increased taxes coupled with cost-cutting limits on the types of medical procedures allowable. The lack of public consensus killed the proposal within a year.

The debate over health care continued during the 2000 presidential election. Both candidates agreed that something had to be done about both escalating costs and the increasing numbers of uninsured. The Democrats promoted a policy of a government-paid prescription drug program for senior citizens. The Republicans promoted a prescription-drug program run by insurance providers, but again there was no consensus.

The most significant health-care legislation in American history was signed into law by President Obama on March 23, 2010. The **Patient Protection and Affordable Health Care Act**, popularly known as **Obamacare**, was passed over the course of several months and it generated significant political debate and controversy. The law was celebrated by most Democrats, who touted it as the much-needed solution to the long-term flaws in the American health-care system. Republicans and some independent voters criticized the law, claiming it was an expensive intrusion of the federal government into the public sector. The debate lasted until the midterm elections in November of 2010, when Republicans gained a large number of congressional seats partly as a result of voter discontent with the law.

Civics Drill

Now try some practice questions. To check your answers, register your book at **PrincetonReview.com/cracking** and download the Chapter Drill Answers and Explanations supplement.

1. **Look at the chart describing the United States' constitutional amendment process. Then answer the question.**

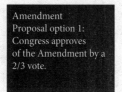

Amendment Proposal option 1: Congress approves of the Amendment by a 2/3 vote.		Amendment Proposal option 2: 2/3 of the states' legislatures request Congress to establish a national convention.	
Ratification option 1: The legislatures in 3/4 of the states ratify the amendment.	Ratification option 2: 3/4 of states ratify the amendment in state conventions.	Ratification option 1: The legislatures in 3/4 of the states ratify the amendment.	Ratification option 2: 3/4 of states ratify the amendment in state conventions.

According to the passage above, it is <u>not</u> possible for an amendment to be passed without the input of

A the president

B the state legislatures

C Congress

D state conventions

2. **The Constitution as ratified in 1788 most clearly reflects the Framers' commitment to**

A the idea of direct democracy

B the principle of limited government

C the abolition of slavery

D protecting the rights of the accused

3. **American foreign policy is directed primarily by the**

A House of Representatives

B Senate

C president

D Supreme Court

4. Which of the following describe limitations that may constitutionally be placed on freedom of speech and freedom of the press?

    I.   Under no circumstances may the government limit speech or censor the press.

    II.   The government may censor the press in the interest of national and military security.

    III. The government may outlaw obscene publications.

    IV. The government may prevent individuals from engaging in "offensive" speech.

A   I only

B   II only

C   II and III only

D   III and IV only

5. Of the following, American federalism is most clearly exemplified by the

A   system of checks and balances among the three branches of the national government

B   process by which international treaties are completed

C   special constitutional status of Washington, D.C.

D   Tenth Amendment to the Constitution

6. All of the following are specifically mentioned in the Constitution <u>except</u>

A   judicial review

B   the national census

C   rules of impeachment

D   the State of the Union address

7. The Constitution, as originally ratified, addressed all of the following weaknesses of the Articles of Confederation <u>except</u> the

A   lack of a chief executive office

B   national government's inability to levy taxes effectively

C   insufficiency of the government's power to raise an army

D   omission of a universal suffrage clause

8. The largest portion of the federal budget covers the costs of

A   national defense

B   the Department of Energy

C   interest on the national debt

D   entitlement programs

Part VI
Science

Chapter 26
Science Overview

In this chapter, we will provide an overview of the Science portion of the TASC test. In the following chapters, we will explore the specific content areas of this subtest in more detail.

If you find that the idea of spending an hour and a half answering science questions sends you into a cold sweat, have no fear! You may find that you can answer some of the questions in the Science test simply by reading the short passages, charts, and graphs that the test provides, or by using scientific thinking. Of course, other questions will require you to have a foundation of scientific knowledge, but in the chapters that follow we'll address the topics that the TASC test covers, so that you'll be well prepared by the time that test day arrives.

ABOUT THE SCIENCE TEST

To score well on the test, you first need to know what to expect on test day. First, there are two versions of the TASC Science Test: a computer-based version and a paper-based version. On the English and Spanish versions of the TASC Science test you'll have 85 and 90 minutes, respectively, to complete the following:

Computer-Based	Paper-Based
48 Multiple-Choice Questions	49 Multiple-Choice Questions
1 Constructed-Response Item	1 Constructed-Response Item
1 Technology-Enhanced Item	

Remember to check online for our supplementary tutorials on the constructed-response and technology-enhanced items.

The questions on this test will be accompanied by eight types of stimuli in the form of charts, graphs, maps, tables, figures, or written passages. In order to achieve success on this section of the TASC test, you need to have some basic scientific knowledge. However, you must also be able to effectively read and interpret scientific data.

According to the TASC test creators, questions will test your understanding of what you read (comprehension), your use of information in a concrete situation (application), your exploration of relationships among ideas (analysis), and your judgment of the soundness or accuracy of scientific information or methods (evaluation).

What's on the Science Test?

Here are the topics as outlined by the TASC test makers:

Life Science	36%
Physical Sciences	36%
Earth and Space Sciences	28%

If this list seems slightly vague, have no fear. While trying to acquaint yourself with all of the topics covered in a high school biology class might take a long time, you don't need an in-depth knowledge of all of those topics in order to ace the

Science test. In the chapters that follow, you'll discover just exactly what information you will need.

While some questions won't require you to have any particular knowledge of biology, earth science, physics, or chemistry, others will require you to have some general knowledge of these topics, including knowledge of their specialized vocabularies. As you read, you'll discover just exactly what basic knowledge of these subjects that you'll need. You may even find that science is more fascinating than you imagined, and may want to learn more about these topics!

WHAT IS SCIENCE?

At multiple points in your educational career you've been exposed to science. But, what *is* science? **Science** is knowledge about the natural world that is based on facts learned through observation and experimentation. The field of science is constantly expanding as we learn more about the biological and physical aspects of our universe. Accordingly, science is a process; i.e., there is no end point. As long as we have questions about our world, scientific investigations will be conducted. The **scientific method** is the widely adopted process for conducting effective scientific investigations.

Scientific Method

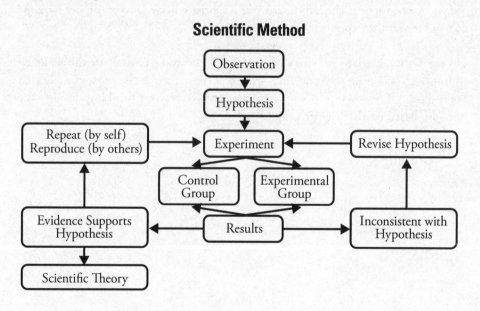

The Scientific Method

How did scientists learn anything about biology, the solar system, or the movement of continents in the first place? In each case, a scientist first came up with a hypothesis to explain an observable event, or **observation**, that was not yet understood. A **hypothesis** is simply a possible explanation of an event or a phenomenon. Once she has her hypothesis, the scientist performs **experiments** to see whether

The Scientific Method Quiz

Q: If you were testing the effectiveness of a cream that's supposed to grow hair on men's heads, which of the following would be a good control group?

1) a group of bald women

2) a group of men with full heads of hair who are also given the cream

3) a group of bald men who are given a harmless cream that has no effect

Turn the page for the answer.

the hypothesis is correct. These experiments must be carefully designed to make sure that the information they provide is accurate and that each experiment tests only one phenomenon, or **variable**, at a time. Sometimes the scientist will use what is called a control group. A **control group** is a group of test subjects that are not subjected to the phenomenon being tested, while an **experimental group** is a group of test subjects that are subjected to the phenomenon being tested. By controlling for both internal and external factors, you are establishing a controlled sample that reduces the potential of encountering issues with **validity**, or logic, and **reliability**, or reproducibility. Often, an experiment will be repeated many times to make sure that the same results occur. Only after other scientists have conducted the same experiments and obtained the same results is a hypothesis accepted as **theory**. And even then, scientists continue to re-examine their own thinking and the thinking of their predecessors. Sometimes accepted facts turn out to be wrong.

Consider a scientist who hypothesizes that human cells act abnormally when exposed to microwaves, the variable in this scenario. The scientist would have a group of cells exposed to microwaves, the experimental group, and a group of cells that are not exposed to microwaves, the control group. The scientist will watch both groups closely, collecting data that she can then analyze to conclude whether her hypothesis is correct. If the data supports her hypothesis, and others can replicate the experiment's results, the hypothesis will become scientific theory. If the data does not support the hypothesis, the scientist will need to revise her hypothesis and repeat the experimental process.

On the TASC Science test, you will occasionally be asked to evaluate the accuracy of information or the relevance of a method. These can be the most complicated questions on the test—and they almost always involve your thinking through the question based on the scientific method.

Chapter 27
Life Science

In this chapter, we'll guide you through the key topics related to Life Science on the Science portion of the TASC test. We will focus on three broad categories: Organisms and Cells, Life and Ecosystems, and Heredity and Evolution. Following the content lessons, we'll give you some practice questions.

ORGANISMS AND CELLS

When we look at flowers, kittens, or human beings, we tend to see singular entities. What we don't see are the millions of cells that make up each living organism; the human body, for example, is composed of over 100 trillion cells! All living organisms are composed of one or more cells. Those made of a single cell are referred to as **unicellular** organisms, while those composed of more than one cell are referred to as **multicellular** organisms.

While cells are extremely small, cells are extremely complex. Cells are able to acquire and use energy, reproduce and pass along genetic information, and maintain homeostasis; all of these capabilities will be addressed in more detail later in this chapter.

Before we dive into our cellular journey, let's consider the three tenets of **cell theory**:

1. All organisms are either unicellular or multicellular.
2. Cells are the basic units of structure and function in living things.
3. All new cells are created from existing cells.

Cell Structure

There are two main types of cells: **prokaryotic cells** and **eukaryotic cells**. Prokaryotic cells lack defined structure and are typically found in unicellular organisms. Conversely, eukaryotic cells are highly structured, work together, and are generally found in multicellular organisms.

While there are multiple types of specialized cells within this world, there are certain structural components that are present in all cells. The cell membrane is a selectively permeable, flexible barrier of **phospholipids** that separates the inside of the cell from the external environment. The primary function of the cell membrane, also known as the **lipid bilayer**, is to control the movement of materials, such as food, water, and waste, between the interior and exterior of the cell.

One way that materials cross the cell membrane is via **passive transport**, which does not require cells to expend energy. Have you ever sprayed air freshener in a room? If so, you will recall that the scent spread throughout the air until it was evenly dispersed. This process, in which particles spread from an area of greater concentration to an area of lesser concentration, is **diffusion**. When molecules of water diffuse across a membrane, the process is called **osmosis**. Passive transport can also take place through **facilitated diffusion**, during which **carrier proteins** embedded in the cell membrane transport substances across the membrane itself.

Passive Transport Quiz

Q: Which of the following is not a type of passive transport?

A Osmosis
B Diffusion
C Endocytosis
D Facilitated Diffusion

Turn the page for the answer.

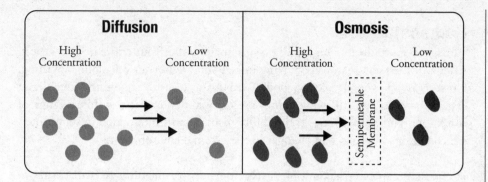

Diffusion

High Concentration   Low Concentration

Osmosis

High Concentration   Low Concentration

Semipermeable Membrane

Not all substances are able to cross the cell membrane through passive transport and the cell must expend energy, a process referred to as **active transport**. Sometimes a substance needs to move from an area of low concentration to one of high concentration. In order to facilitate such movement, substances can travel across the lipid bilayer via carrier proteins that function as pumps. One type of active transport involves the use of the cell membrane's **sodium-potassium pumps**, which carry sodium ions out of a cell and potassium ions into a cell. At times, a cell may need to absorb a substance that is too large to pass through the cell membrane via **endocytosis**. In this scenario, the cell membrane extends outward and engulfs the particle. When the particle is surrounded and the edges of the membrane connect, a **vesicle** is formed. The vesicle then travels through the cell and reopens when it reaches its destination. Conversely, the process of removing large molecules, such as waste particles, occurs through **exocytosis**. In exocytosis, a vesicle forms around particles, travels to the membrane, and forces the particles out of the cell. In essence, exocytosis is the reverse process of endocytosis.

Endocytosis

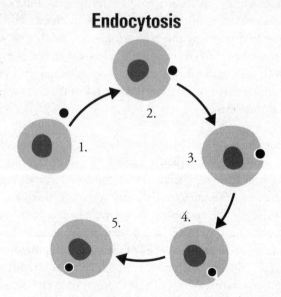

Homeostasis

When you go to sleep at night, it's easy to imagine that your entire body is at rest. After all, when you rest, you are lying in bed and are not actively doing anything. However, while you sleep, your body is adjusting to both changing internal and external conditions. All living things are capable of surviving within a range of conditions, and **homeostasis** is the ability of an organism to maintain stable internal conditions, regardless of changes in the external environment.

Homeostasis operates at multiple levels in an organism, from cells to tissues to organs to organ systems to the organism itself. At a cellular level, cells are able to regulate the materials that both enter and leave through the cell membrane, thus ensuring internal stability of each cell. Organs also maintain stability by reproducing to replace old or damaged cells. For example, your body is continually replacing the skin cells that are washed off when you shower. If your skin cells did not reproduce, you would have no skin and, in turn, no protection from the elements. Your entire body also works together to maintain homeostasis. Consider walking outside in the 105° heat of the Texas summer. Since your normal body temperature is 98.6° F, the extra heat will cause you to sweat as your body attempts to adjust to the external environment and stay cool. Without balanced conditions within your cells, organs, systems, and body, your body is unable to function properly.

Organelles

As noted, all cells have a cell membrane. Unlike prokaryotes, which simply house a single molecule of DNA, eukaryotes have a number of cellular components. One of the key components of a eukaryotic cell is the **nucleus**, which both controls the cell's activities and contains the cell's genetic material. The substance that is between the nucleus and the cell membrane is known as the **cytoplasm**, which is composed of water, salts, and other particles. Not only does the cytoplasm contain the **organelles**, which perform cellular functions, but it also consists of stabilizing fibers called the **cytoskeleton**.

A cell can be thought of as a self-contained factory: Each organelle has a specific function and all cells work together to ensure the cell performs properly. **Ribosomes,** the most prevalent organelle, are responsible for creating proteins based upon instructions from the nucleus; the ribosomes can be thought of as the factory workers of the cell. The **endoplasmic reticulum** can be thought of as a series of conveyor belts; it is a system of folded membranes that transports substances throughout the cell. There are two types of endoplasmic reticulum: rough, which has ribosomes attached to it, and smooth, which composes lipids and decomposes waste. The **Golgi apparatus**, which can be thought of as the distribution center of the cell, is responsible for sorting, modifying, and packing substances into vesicles. The **mitochondria**, or the power plants of the cell, are responsible for releasing the energy that is used for the cell's development and movement. It should also be noted that much of the cellular respiration process takes place in the mitochondria; the mitochondria process nutrients to create energy for the cell. In order to acquire such energy, however, **lysosomes** must utilize enzymes to digest food into usable particles of nutrients. Lysosomes are also responsible for decomposing old organelles and certain waste particles; they can be thought of as the cleaning crew. The storage units of the cell are known as the **vacuoles,** which are sacs that can contain water, protein, salt, and other materials.

Two organelles that are unique to plant cells are **cell walls** and **chloroplasts.** The cell wall forms around the cell membrane of a plant cell, protecting the cell from damage, providing a distinct shape, and connecting the cell to surrounding cells. Through the process of photosynthesis, chloroplasts make energy in the form of carbohydrates.

Cell Quiz
Q: Which organelle plays a pivotal role in cellular respiration?

A Nucleus
B Cell Wall
C Ribosomes
D Mitochondria

Turn page for the answer.

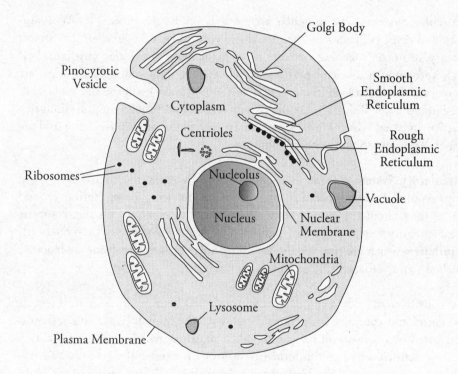

Organs and Organ Systems

As you've no doubt noticed, a single cell is extraordinarily complex. Consider the fact that the human body has over 100 types of specialized cells, each of which performs a specific function. However, cells are not free agents. Groups of cells are known as **tissues,** of which there are four types: epithelial, nervous, connective, and muscle. When two or more tissues work together to carry out a task, it is an **organ**. And, every organ belongs to at least one **organ system**. An organ system is a set of organs that cooperate to carry out the **essential functions of life,** such as breathing and moving.

While you won't need to know the nitty-gritty details about every human organ system for the TASC test, you should familiarize yourself with the basic function of each system.

Cell Quiz
A: Cellular respiration takes place in the mitochondria, or the power houses of the cell.

Integumentary System—The integumentary system is composed of your skin, hair, and nails. Not only does this system protect the body from injury and infection, but it also is helps maintain the body's temperature.

Skeletal System—The skeletal system performs a number of important functions in the human body. Not only does the skeletal system support and protect the body and its organs, but it also is responsible for producing blood cells and aiding in movement. The major structures of the skeletal system are **bones**, **ligaments**, which connect bones together, and **joints**, which are the meeting places of two bones that allow movement.

Muscular System—The muscular system aids bodily movement, provides support, and consists of muscles that are either **voluntary**, or controllable, or **involuntary**, or uncontrollable. There are three main types of muscles: **cardiac, skeletal,** and **smooth.** Skeletal muscles, which are the only voluntary muscles, are attached to bones and aid in movement. Smooth muscles comprise the majority of the human body, lining the insides of our organs and functioning involuntarily. Cardiac muscles, which are also involuntary, are found only in the heart and are responsible for keeping the heart pumping.

Circulatory System—Through a series of **blood vessels,** the circulatory system helps regulate body temperature and transports nutrients, gases, hormones, and wastes throughout the human body. The network of blood vessels that comprise the circulatory system consists of **arteries**, which carry blood away from the heart, **capillaries**, which are tiny vessels that allow substances to pass from the blood to the body, and **veins**, which carry blood to the heart.

Nervous System—The nervous system uses both chemical and electrical signals to control and coordinate functions throughout the human body. This system is comprised of a network of nerve cells called **neurons**, which receive information in their **dendrites** and send information from their **axons**. The nervous system is divided into two parts: the **central nervous system**, which consists of the brain and spinal cord, and the **peripheral nervous system**. The peripheral nervous system contains **sensory neurons** that send information from organs and **motor neurons** that send commands to organs.

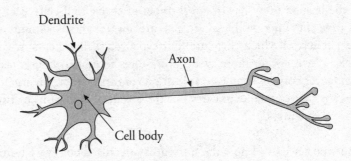

Respiratory System—Without the respiratory system, you would be unable to breathe. Through the process of **cellular respiration**, carbon dioxide travels through the bloodstream to the **lungs**, where it is exchanged for oxygen.

Digestive System—The digestive system plays a major role in absorbing food's nutrients in the process called **digestion**. Digestion begins when food enters the mouth, is broken down by enzymes in **saliva**, and travels from the esophagus to the stomach, wherein large particles are dissolved with the stomach's gastric juices. From here, particles enter the small intestine, wherein excretions from the pancreas, liver, and gallbladder complete the digestion of proteins, fats, and carbohydrates. After the nutrients have been removed, the remaining material travels through the large intestine and exits through the anus in the form of feces.

Excretory System—The excretory system is responsible for removing wastes, other than feces, from the human body. The lungs, skin, and kidneys are organs that play a primary role in blood purification and regulating the concentration of bodily fluids.

Endocrine System—The endocrine system plays a major role in maintaining the stability of the human body and regulating other organ systems through **hormones**. Produced in **endocrine glands**, such as the hypothalamus and pituitary glands, hormones are chemical messages secreted by cells to maintain homeostasis.

Reproductive System—In order for sexual reproduction to take place, the male gamete, **sperm,** must combine with the female gamete, the **egg**, to form a **zygote**, or fertilized egg. The reproductive system for men primarily consists of the testes, which produce sperm, and the penis, which ejects the sperm into the female's reproductive system. In the female reproductive system, an **ovum**, or mature egg, is released from the **ovaries** in a monthly cycle called **ovulation**. Upon release, the ovum travels through the **fallopian tubes** towards the **uterus**, where it waits to be fertilized by the male's sperm. If the ovum is not fertilized within a couple of days, it dies. If the ovum is fertilized, the egg attaches itself to the uterus' lining, and, roughly nine months later, a baby passes through the **vagina**.

Immune System—The purpose of the immune system is to defend the body against **pathogens** that can cause both infections and diseases. In order to combat invading pathogens, the body has a set of **nonspecific defenses** that target all invaders. Nonspecific defenses include the body's skin, enzymes, and mucous membranes, which can trap and prevent pathogens from entering the body. However, such defenses are not always adequate. If a pathogen makes it past the nonspecific defenses, the body's **inflammatory response** is activated, during which blood flow to the infected area increases and **white blood cells** attack the pathogen.

DNA and RNA

In the 1950s, James Watson and Francis Crick were able to determine that **deoxyribonucleic acid (DNA)** has a double helix structure comprised of **nucleotides**. Each nucleotide consists of a phosphate group and a five-carbon sugar molecule, and a nitrogen-containing base. Except for the nitrogen-containing base, which can be **adenine, thymine, cytosine,** or **guanine,** the nucleotides are identical. It should be noted that adenine pairs only with thymine, and cytosine pairs only with guanine. The DNA molecule is arranged so that the phosphate group and sugar form the sides of the DNA ladder, while the bases make up the rungs. The two strands of the DNA are complementary—you'll note that if the left strand has a base of adenine, the respective base on the right strand will be thymine. An organism's genetic code is determined by the way in which these nucleotides are arranged in a strand of DNA.

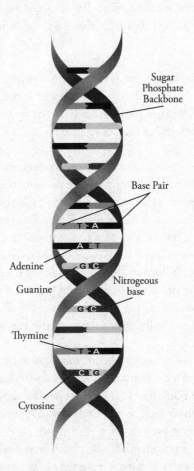

In order to pass genetic code to offspring, DNA can replicate itself. Through the process of **DNA replication**, the double helix unzips itself down the middle. Once separated, **DNA polymerase** enzymes move along the individual strands, adding nucleotides to the exposed nitrogen bases. Once complete, there are two completed DNA molecules. Now, like most processes, DNA replication is subject to errors, which cause **mutations**.

Since you have a basic understanding of DNA and its replication process, let's talk about **ribonucleic acid (RNA)**, which uses instructions received from DNA in the cell's nucleus to synthesize proteins in the cell's cytoplasm. Despite having similar structures, there are three main differences between DNA and RNA: RNA has only one strand of nucleotides, RNA's sugar is ribose, and RNA contains the base of **uracil** instead of thymine.

In order to synthesize proteins, RNA must participate in the processes of **transcription**, during which protein-making instructions are transferred from a gene to a molecule of RNA, and **translation**, during which the sequence of nucleotides in RNA are converted into a sequence of amino acids to form proteins.

Both DNA and RNA are, in structure and function, quite complex. However, if you know the basics about DNA and RNA, you will be able to successfully answer any TASC questions you encounter!

LIFE AND ECOSYSTEMS

If you were to look outside, you'd be observing millions of living organisms, some you can see and others that are only visible with a microscope. But, where did all this life come from? In fact, how did *you* come to exist? And, come to think of it, how do you manage to stay alive on a daily basis? While nobody knows *exactly* how life came to exist on Earth, many scientists believe that the Big Bang theory accurately describes the formation of the universe we know. (For more information on the Big Bang theory, refer to the Earth and Space Sciences section of this book.) Throughout this chapter, we are going to discuss the early forms of life, the processes of photosynthesis and cellular respiration that keep us alive, and the interactions that take place between organisms on Earth.

Early Forms of Life

During the Pre-Cambrian period, when Earth initially took a solid form, no organism was able to survive because it had an atmosphere that was extremely poisonous. In fact, Earth's early atmosphere likely mirrored Jupiter's current atmosphere, which contains helium, hydrogen, methane, and ammonia gasses, making it unsuitable for life. However, scientists believe that the constant bombardment of space matter, coupled with the continuous volcanic explosions on Earth, allowed compounds such as water vapor, carbon dioxide, carbon monoxide, and nitrogen to form. Once Earth began to cool, 4.1 billion years ago, its crust hardened and clouds formed, releasing vast amounts of rainwater that led to our oceans.

During the Archean Period, which occurred between 3.8 and 2.5 billion years ago, Earth's landmasses began to form and the first life-forms, in the form of bacteria, appeared. It should be noted that the first bacteria were pretty hardcore; after all, they were able to survive in the highly toxic atmosphere that existed. Towards the end of the Archean Period, and the beginning of the Proterozoic Period, oxygen-forming photosynthesis first occurred. The oldest recovered fossils have shown that a type of blue-green algae was the first organism to actively obtain energy via the process of photosynthesis.

It was because of these photosynthesizing bacteria that oxygen accumulated on Earth, setting the stage for an explosion of life during the Cambrian Period, which began approximately 525 million years ago. During this period, the majority of the plant and animal groups were formed. Over the next 498 million years, Earth's species were faced with numerous trials and tribulations that led to massive extinctions of many early species. However, the stage had been set for life on Earth, and roughly 2.2 million years ago the first modern humans arose.

Photosynthesis

All right. We've established that the majority of species on Earth require oxygen to survive, which was first provided by photosynthesizing organisms. But, what is photosynthesis? Well, the processes of photosynthesis and cellular respiration are extremely complicated. Thankfully, for the TASC Science test, you don't need to know the intricate details. However, you should have a general understanding of the reactions and their importance to living organisms.

Photosynthesis, which occurs in the leaves of plants, is the process by which light energy is converted to chemical energy. Plants take carbon dioxide, water, and energy from the sun and produce glucose. The chemical reaction of photosynthesis is represented as

$$6CO_2 + 6H_2O \xrightarrow{\text{Sunlight}} C_6H_{12}O_6 + 6O_2$$

There are two stages in photosynthesis: the **light reaction** (also called the light-dependent reaction) and the **dark reaction** (also called the light-independent reaction). The whole process begins when the photons of sunlight strike a leaf, activating chlorophyll and exciting electrons. The activated chlorophyll molecule then passes these excited electrons down to a series of electron carriers, ultimately producing ATP and NADPH. The whole point of the light reaction is to produce two things: (1) energy in the form of **adenosine triphosphate (ATP)** and (2) electron carriers, specifically **NADPH**. Both of these products, along with carbon dioxide, are then used in the dark reaction (light-independent) to make carbohydrates, or sugar.

Photosynthesis

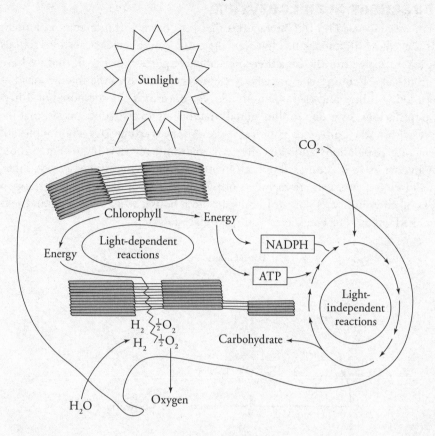

Cellular Respiration

All organisms perform **cellular respiration** in order to produce energy, in the form of ATP, for survival. Cellular respiration occurs when a sugar is combined with oxygen and water to produce carbon dioxide, water, and energy, in the form of ATP. The chemical reaction of cellular respiration is

$$C_6H_{12}O_6 + 6O_2 \rightarrow 6CO_2 + 6H_2O + ATP$$

We can break cellular respiration down to two different approaches: aerobic respiration or anaerobic respiration. If ATP is made in the presence of oxygen, we call it **aerobic respiration**. There are four stages in aerobic respiration: glycolysis, formation of acetyl CoA, the Krebs cycle, and oxidative phosphorylation. If oxygen isn't present, we call it **anaerobic respiration**.

So, maybe you've noticed that the products of photosynthesis are the reactants in cellular respiration. This is because these processes are closely linked. Let's put it real-world terms. When we breathe, we expel carbon dioxide and take in oxygen. Where do we get this oxygen? Well, the plants use our expelled carbon dioxide and produce oxygen. The oxygen we need to survive! Photosynthesis and cellular respiration are two processes in a cycle of amazingness that allows us to live.

Interactions in an Ecosystem

So far, we've focused on the interactions that take place within plant and human cells that allow life on earth. However, there are a number of other interactions that take place within the **biosphere**, or habitable portion of Earth, that we have yet to discuss. **Ecology** is a branch of science that examines the interactions between living things and their environment. A **community** is composed of different **populations**, or groups of individuals that belong to the same species, that interact within the same geographical area. An **ecosystem** is a community of interacting populations and their physical environment. It is important to note that an ecosystem is composed of both living and non-living things. For example, you and Fluffy, your cat, are members of two different populations, but belong to the same community. If you and Fluffy live in a house, which is abiotic and self-contained, it could be considered your personal ecosystem.

Food Chain Quiz

Q: Which of the following is not a producer?

A Cactus
B Pea Plant
C Wombat
D Sunflower

Turn the page for the answer.

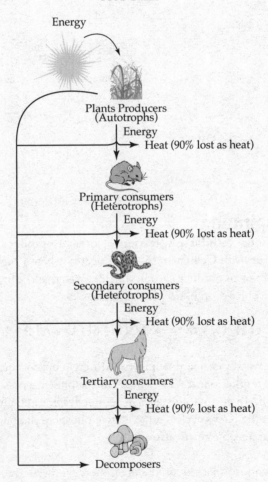

Food Chain

Each organism has its own **niche**—its position or function in a community. Because every species occupies a niche, it's going to have an effect on all the other organisms. These connections are shown in the **food chain**, which describes the way different organisms depend on one another for food. There are basically four levels, sometimes called **trophic levels**, to the food chain: producers, primary consumers, secondary consumers, and tertiary consumers. By using water and gases that exist in the atmosphere and the sun's energy, **producers**, or **autotrophs**, make their own food through photosynthesis. Producers make up the first trophic level and make up 99% of the living earth! **Consumers**, or **heterotrophs**, are incapable of photosynthesis and must find energy sources in the outside world. **Primary consumers**, which make up the second trophic level, are herbivores that directly feed on producers. **Secondary consumers**, which occupy the third trophic level, eat both producers and primary consumers. Secondary consumers are either omnivores or carnivores. The fourth trophic level is composed of **tertiary consumers**, who eat all of the aforementioned. You should also know that **decomposers** are bacteria or fungi that break down dead plant or animal matter, making organic nutrients available to the ecosystem, and **detrivores** are organisms that feed on the remains left by decomposers.

In a food chain, only about 10 percent of the energy is transferred from one level to the next—this is called **The 10% Rule**. The other 90 percent is used for things like respiration, digestion, running away from predators—in other words, it's used to power the organism doing the eating! The producers have the most energy in an ecosystem, the primary consumers have less energy than producers, the secondary consumers have less energy than the primary consumers, and the tertiary consumers will have the least energy of all. (For the sake of simplicity, and because they contribute to all trophic levels, decomposers and detrivores are not usually a part of the energy pyramid.) The energy flow, biomass, and numbers of members within an ecosystem can be represented in an **energy pyramid**. Organisms that are "higher up" on the pyramid have less biomass and energy, and smaller population sizes.

Energy Pyramid

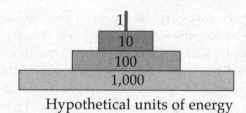

Hypothetical units of energy

Note that 90% of energy is lost
at each step

As you're probably already aware, food chains are an oversimplified way of demonstrating the myriad feeding relationships that exist in ecosystems. Because there are so many different types of species of plants and animals in ecosystems, their relationships in real-world ecosystems are much more complicated than can be depicted in a single food chain. Therefore, we use a **food web** in order to represent feeding relationships in ecosystems more realistically. Note that the arrows in a food web move from the provider of food to the organism that eats the food; e.g., in the provided food web, grass provides nutrition for the cricket, the cricket provides nutrition for the mouse, and the mouse provides nutrition for the fox.

Food Web

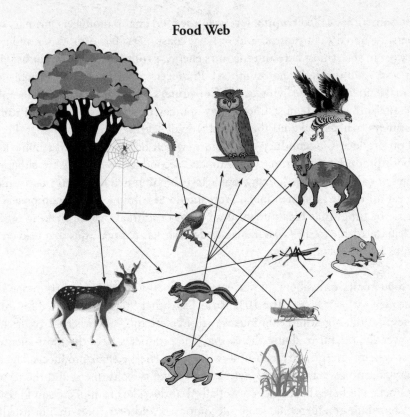

Food Chain Quiz
A: Wombat

A producer is an organism that converts energy from the sun to make food. Cacti, pea plants, and sunflowers all produce food through photosynthesis.

Populations

Luckily, the TASC test won't require you to be an expert on how populations affect ecosystems. However, you should know the general ideas of population dispersion, carrying capacity, growth, and decline.

Two important characteristics of populations are the density of the population and how the population is dispersed. **Population density** refers to the number of individuals of a population that inhabit a certain unit of land or water area. An example of population density would be the number of squirrels that inhabit a particular forest. **Population dispersion** refers to how individuals of a population are spaced within a region. An example of population dispersion would be how the squirrels are spread out in the forest. There are three main types of population dispersion: random, clumping, and uniform. **Random dispersion** occurs when the position of each individual is not determined or influenced by other members of the population; this type of dispersion is uncommon. **Clumping** occurs when members of a population occupy the same region; this is the most common type of dispersion. For example, fish clump together, swimming in schools to avoid predation. **Uniform dispersion** occurs when members of the population are evenly spread throughout the ecosystem; this type of dispersion is often the result of competition for resources in an ecosystem.

The **biotic potential** of a population is the amount that the population would grow if there were unlimited resources in its environment. This is not a practical model for population growth simply because in reality the amount of resources in the environments of populations is limited. In every ecosystem, members of a population compete for space, light, air, water, and food. The **carrying capacity** (K) of a particular region is defined as the maximum population size that can sustainably be supported by the available resources in the region. Since different species have different requirements for life, geographic regions have different carrying capacities for populations of different species. For example, in a given area, you would expect the population size of bacteria to be quite a bit larger than the population of zebras. This is because individual bacteria are much smaller than individual zebras; thus, each bacterium requires fewer resources to live than each zebra.

So, how does population growth work in the real world? In reality, after an initial burst in population growth, the growth rate generally drops; when modeled, this population growth curve resembles a flattened S. The **logistic growth model** basically says that when populations are well below the size dictated by the carrying capacity of the region they live in, they will grow exponentially, but as they approach the carrying capacity, their growth rate will decrease and the size of the population will eventually become stable. This logistic growth is shown in the accompanied graph.

Logistic Growth Model

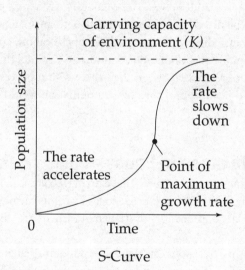

S-Curve

We can predict long-term population growth rates using a model called the Rule of 70. The **Rule of 70** says that the time it takes for a population to double can be approximated by dividing 70 by the current growth rate of the population. For example, if the growth rate of a population is 5 percent, then the population will double in 14 years ($\frac{70}{5}$ percent = 14 years). The Rule of 70 can be used to estimate the number of years for any variable to double, the doubling time.

Rule of 70 Quiz

Q: If the growth rate of a population is 20%, how long will it take the population to double in size?

Turn the page for the answer.

Not surprisingly, the rates of growth and decline of a population depend on the species that makes up the population. Species can be divided into two groups based on their reproductive strategies: the *r*-selected pattern or the K-selected pattern. **r-selected** organisms reproduce early in life and often, and have a high capacity for reproductive growth. In these species, little or no care is given to the offspring, but due to the sheer numbers of offspring in the population, enough of the offspring will survive to enable the population to continue. Some examples of *r*-selected species are bacteria, algae, and protozoa. On the other hand, **K-selected** organisms reproduce later in life, produce fewer offspring, and devote significant time and energy to the nurturing of their offspring. For these species, it is important to preserve as many members of the offspring as possible *because* they produce so few; parents have a tremendous investment in each individual offspring. Some examples of K-selected species are humans, lions, and cows.

When we observe populations in their natural habitats there are two distinct patterns that occur: the boom-and-bust cycle and the predator-prey cycle. The **boom-and-bust cycle** is very common among *r*-organisms. In this type of cycle there is a rapid increase in the population and then an equally rapid drop off. These rapid changes may be linked to predictable cycles in the environment, such as temperature or nutrient availability. When the conditions are good for growth, the population increases rapidly. When the population's conditions worsen, its numbers rapidly decline. The **predator-prey cycle** is exemplified by the relationship between rabbits, the prey, and wolves, the predators. In a year of relatively high rainfall, rabbits have plenty of food, which enables them to reproduce very successfully. In turn, because the coyote is a predator of the rabbit, coyotes would also have plenty of food, and their populations would also rise rapidly. However, if the rainfall is below average a few years later, then there would be less grass; the population of rabbits would decline, and the coyote population would decline in turn.

The Effect of Humans in Ecosystems

Unfortunately, humans have disturbed the existing ecological balance, and the results are far-reaching. Soils have been eroded and various forms of pollution have increased. The potential consequences on the environment are summarized below.

Acid rain—The burning of fossil fuels produces pollutants such as sulfur dioxide and nitrogen dioxide. When these compounds react with droplets of atmospheric water in clouds they form sulfuric and nitric acids, respectively. The rain that falls from these clouds is weakly acid and is called acid rain. Acid rain lowers the pH of aquatic ecosystems and soil, which damages water systems, plants, and soil. For example, the change in soil pH causes calcium and other nutrients to leach out, which damages plant roots and stunts their growth. Furthermore, useful microorganisms that release nutrients from decaying organic matter into the soil are also killed, resulting in less nutrients being available for the plants. Low pH also kills fish, especially those that have just hatched.

Greenhouse effect—The increasing atmospheric concentrations of carbon dioxide through the burning of fossil fuels and forests have contributed to the warming of the earth. Higher temperatures may cause the polar ice caps to melt and flooding to occur. Other potential effects of global warming include changes in precipitation patterns, changes in plant and animal populations, and detrimental changes in agriculture.

Ozone depletion—Pollution has also led to the depletion of the atmospheric ozone layer by such chemicals as chlorofluorocarbons (CFCs), which are used in aerosol cans. Ozone (O_3) forms when UV radiation reacts with O_2. Ozone protects the earth's surface from excessive ultraviolet radiation. Its loss could have major genetic effects and could increase the incidence of cancer.

Desertification—When overgrazed by animals, land turns grasslands into deserts and reduces the available habitats for organisms.

Deforestation—When forests are cleared, erosion, floods, and changes in weather patterns can occur.

Pollution—Another environmental concern is the toxic chemicals in our environment. One example is DDT, a pesticide used to control insects. DDT was overused at one time and later found to damage plants and animals worldwide. DDT is particularly harmful because it resists chemical breakdown and today it can still be found in the tissues of nearly every living organism. The danger with toxins such as DDT is that as each trophic level consumes DDT, the substance becomes more concentrated by a process called **biomagnification**.

Reduction in biodiversity—As different habitats have been destroyed, many plants and animals have become extinct. Some of these plants could have provided us with medicines and products that may have been beneficial.

HEREDITY AND EVOLUTION

You've undoubtedly been in a situation where you've had to adapt to less than favorable circumstances. For example, imagine that you are in a room that is freezing cold. Since the human body is unable to withstand freezing conditions, you would need to adapt to the circumstances. Maybe you would turn off the air conditioning, put on a sweater, or simply leave the room. Regardless of how you fix the situation, you would need to do something in order to survive. When you put on a sweater, however, you've simply put a band-aid on the problem; you're no longer cold, but you haven't actually altered yourself in any way.

In biology, an **adaptation** is a feature produced for natural selection for its current function, and can be psychological, biological, or anatomical in nature. To be considered an adaptation, a feature must be heritable, functional, increase the evolutionary fitness of the organism. Furthermore, the trait must have arisen when the current function of the adaptation arose. For example, birds have feathers, which are heritable, functional features that increase the evolutionary fitness of the species. However, feathers did *not* form in conjunction with the act of flying; fossils of dinosaurs with feathers, which pre-date flying animals, have been found. Therefore, feathers were not an adaptation for flight, even though feathers can currently serve that function.

So, how are these super-helpful features passed on to offspring? And, how do species manage to change over time and adapt to changing circumstances? Well, it all begins with the chromosome.

Chromosomes

Perhaps people tell you that you have your mother's smile or your father's eyes. It's true! Your parents passed along these traits through **chromosomes**, structures that hold the DNA of a cell. Situated in the nucleus of a cell, chromosomes consist of DNA wrapped around proteins called **histones**. **Genes** are sections of chromosomes that control the inheritance of a particular trait. Chromosomes direct and control all the processes necessary for life, including passing themselves and their information to future generations.

Each human chromosome pair consists of one chromosome from the father and another from the mother; this is why you resemble, at least to some extent, both your father and mother. Human cells have 23 pairs of chromosomes, or 46 chromosomes total. Of those 23 pairs, one pair is made up of **sex chromosomes**; males have one X and one Y sex chromosome, while females have two X sex chromosomes. The remaining 22 pairs of chromosomes are called **autosomes**, and each autosome pair is a **homologous pair**, or a pair of chromosomes, one from the father and one from the mother, with the same structure.

Mitosis

As you read this sentence, some of your cells are dying. Don't worry; your dead cells are continually being replaced through the process of **cell division**. So, we said that chromosomes pass genetic traits to future generations…but how do they do it? Well, every cell has a life cycle, known as the **cell cycle**, which consists of two stages: interphase and mitosis.

Interphase is the initial, and longest, segment of a cell's life cycle that is the time between cell divisions. During interphase, the chromosomes are not visible. Rather, the genetic material is scattered throughout the nucleus and is called **chromatin**. Interphase can be broken down into three phases: the G1 phase, during which the enzymes for replication are produced, the S phase, during which the cell replicates the chromosomes in its nucleus, and the G2 phase, during which the cell grows rapidly, synthesizes proteins, and readies itself for **mitosis**, the second segment of a cell's life cycle when the cell divides.

Mitosis, shown below, has four stages: prophase, metaphase, anaphase, and telophase. In **prophase**, the nucleolus of the cell disappears and the chromosomes thicken, coiling and becoming visible. During prophase, cylindrical bodies called **centrioles** start to move away from each other, toward opposite ends of the cell. The centrioles will spin out a system of microtubules known as the **spindle fibers**. These spindle fibers will attach to a structure on each chromatid called a **kinetochore**, which is part of the centromere. During **metaphase**, the chromosomes begin to line up along the **metaphase plate** of the cell, because the spindle fibers are attached to the kinetochore of each chromatid. During **anaphase**, the sister chromatids of each chromosome separate at the centromere and migrate to opposite poles. The chromatids are pulled apart by the microtubules, which begin to shorten. Each half of a pair of sister chromatids now moves to opposite poles of the cell and non-kinetochore microtubules elongate the cell. During **telophase**, nuclear membrane forms around each set of chromosomes and the nucleoli reappear. The cytoplasm splits through a process called **cytokinesis** and the cell then divides along the **cleavage furrow**, forming two, distinct **daughter cells**. Each daughter cell is an exact replica of the original cell and, once replicated, enters interphase.

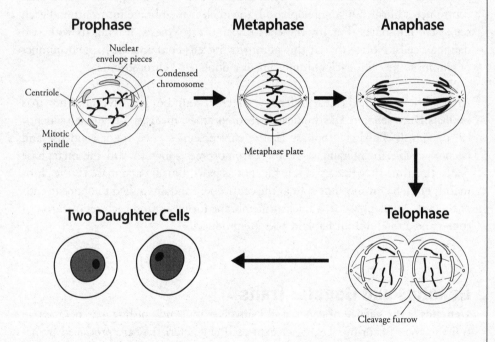

Meiosis

Although most cells in the human body are **diploid**, or filled with pairs of chromosomes, there are **haploid** cells, which are unpaired and called sex cells, or **gametes**. To preserve the diploid number of chromosomes in an organism, each parent must contribute only half of its chromosomes. This is the point of meiosis. **Meiosis** is the production of gametes. Since sexually reproducing organisms need only haploid cells for reproduction, meiosis is limited to sex cells in special sex organs called **gonads**. In males, the gonads are the **testes**, while in females they are the **ovaries**. The special cells in these organs—also known as germ cells—produce haploid cells (n), which then combine to restore the diploid (2n) number during fertilization. Meiosis is also known as **gametogenesis**. If sperm cells are produced, then meiosis is called **spermatogenesis**. During spermatogenesis, four sperm cells are produced for each diploid cell. If an egg cell or an ovum is produced, this process is called **oogenesis**. Oogenesis produces only one ovum, not four.

Meiosis I consists of four stages: prophase I, metaphase I, anaphase I, and telophase I. Prophase I is a little more complicated than regular prophase. As in mitosis, the nuclear membrane disappears, the chromosomes become visible, and the centrioles move to opposite poles of the nucleus. Then, during an event known as **synapsis**, the chromosomes meet up with their counterparts to form a **tetrad**, or group of four chromatids. After synapsis, "pieces" of chromosomes are exchanged between the homologous partners, a process known as **crossing-over**. By the end of prophase I, the chromosomes will have exchanged regions containing several alleles, or different forms of the same gene. During metaphase I, the chromosome pairs—now called tetrads—line up at the metaphase plate. During anaphase I, one of each pair of chromosomes within a tetrad separates and moves to opposite poles. The chromosomes do not separate at the centromere, separating with their centromeres intact. During telophase I, the nuclear membrane forms around each set of chromosomes. Finally, the cells undergo cytokinesis, leaving us with two daughter cells. Notice that at this point the nucleus contains the haploid number of chromosomes, but each chromosome is a duplicated chromosome.

After a brief period, the cell undergoes a second round of cell division, known as **meiosis II**, to separate the duplicated chromosomes; meiosis II is virtually identical to mitosis. During prophase II, the chromosomes once again condense and become visible. In metaphase II, the chromosomes move toward the metaphase plate. This time they line up single file, not as pairs. During anaphase II, the chromatids of each chromosome split at the centromere and are pulled to opposite ends of the cell. At telophase II, a nuclear membrane forms around each set of chromosomes and a total of four haploid cells are produced

Genetics and Genetic Traits

Genetics is the science of genes, and it involves the study of how parents pass on traits to their offspring. **Traits**, or expressed characteristics, are produced by hereditary factors known as genes. As previously noted, a gene is a segment of a chromosome, and a chromosome has many genes, each controlling the inheritance of a particular trait. For example, in cats, there's a gene on the chromosome that codes for fur length. The position of a gene on a chromosome is called a **locus**.

A person's **genotype** is the genetic code that he or she carries, and it provides information about particular traits. **Phenotypes** are the physical expressions of those traits. For example, your hair color, which is an expression of instructions carried in your genetic code, is a phenotype. Phenotypes often depend upon genotype, but they can also result from environmental factors.

Alleles

If genes are instructions for traits, **alleles** are versions of the instructions for traits. For example, you might have an allele for attached earlobes, or you might have an allele for detached earlobes. Each allele is a different form of the same gene. An allele can be **dominant** or **recessive**. In simple cases, an organism can express contrasting conditions. For example, a cat can have short or long hair. The convention is to assign one of two letters for the two different alleles. The dominant allele receives a capital letter and the recessive allele receives a lowercase of the same letter. For instance, we might give the dominant allele for short-haired in cats an "H" for short-haired; in turn, the recessive allele would be "h."

When an organism has two identical alleles for a given trait, the organism is **homozygous**. For instance, SS and ss both represent homozygous organisms. SS is homozygous dominant and ss is homozygous recessive. If an organism has two different alleles for a given trait, Ss, the organism is **heterozygous**.

Mendelian Inheritance

Back in the nineteenth century, a monk named Gregor Mendel became interested in genetics. One of Mendel's hobbies was to study the effects of cross-breeding on different strains of pea plants. Mendel worked exclusively with true-breeder pea plants. This means the plants he used were genetically pure and consistently produced the same traits. For example, tall plants always produced tall plants; short plants always produced short plants. Mendel crossed two true-breeding plants with contrasting traits: tall pea plants and short pea plants. This type of cross is called a **monohybrid cross**, which means that only one trait is being studied. In this case, the trait was height. Let's take a closer look at monohybrid crosses.

Punnett Squares

A simple way to represent a monohybrid cross is to set up a **Punnett square**. Punnett squares are used to predict the results of a cross. Let's construct a Punnett square for the cross between Mendel's tall and short pea plants. Let's first designate the alleles for each plant. As we saw earlier, we can use the letter "T" for the tall, dominant allele and "t" for the short, recessive allele. Since one parent was a pure, tall pea plant, we'll give it two dominant alleles (TT homozygous dominant). The other parent was a pure, short pea plant, so we'll give it two recessive alleles (tt homozygous recessive). Let's put the alleles for one of the parents across the top of the box, and the alleles for the other parent along the side of the box.

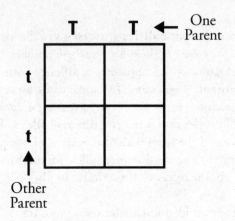

Now you can fill in the four boxes by matching the letters.

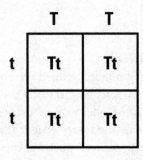

Each offspring received one allele from each parent. They all received one T and one t allele, and all the offspring have genotypes Tt! Our parents had duplicate copies of single alleles, TT and tt, respectively. We could therefore refer to them as homozygous. The offspring, on the other hand, are heterozygous: They possess one copy of each allele.

Mendel's Laws

Through his pea plant experiments, Mendel came up with three principles of genetics: the law of dominance, the law of segregation, and the law of independent assortment.

- **The Law of Dominance** states that one trait masks the effects of another trait. For example, the dominant allele T overpowers the recessive allele t in pea plants with Tt genotypes.
- **The Law of Segregation** states that alleles can segregate and recombine. Consider the cross of two heterozygous pea plants, Tt crossed with Tt, which results in offspring having TT, Tt, Tt, and tt genotypes. While the parents are both tall pea plants, there is a 3:1 **phenotypic ratio** of tall to short pea plants, but a 1:2:1 **genotypic ratio**, among the offspring. This is why two brown-eyed parents can have a blue-eyed child.

Inheritance Quiz

Q: The trait for blue eyes is a recessive trait, only expressed in organisms that have two recessive alleles. What percent of offspring from a pairing of two heterozygous parents would have blue eyes?

Turn the page for the answer.

- **The Law of Independent Assortment** states that traits can segregate and recombine independently of other traits. For example, if you are looking at pea height, which can be tall or short, and color, which can be green or yellow, the traits could combine as TG, Tg, tG, or tg.

Mutation and Variation

Sometimes, a set of chromosomes has an extra or a missing chromosome. This occurs because of **non-disjunction**—the chromosomes failed to separate properly during meiosis. This error, which produces the wrong number of chromosomes in a cell, results in severe genetic defects. For example, humans typically have 23 pairs of chromosomes, but individuals with **Down syndrome** have three—instead of two—copies of the 21st chromosome. Chromosomal abnormalities also occur if one or more segments of a chromosome break. For example, **translocation** is a mutation that occurs during meiosis when a chromosome breaks and the segment moves to another chromosome. Luckily, damaged chromosomes can usually be repaired with special repair enzymes.

Variation, which is due to random mutation, exists within the genes of every population or species, and is the driving force of evolution. When it comes to genetic variation, meiosis is a big plus. The more variation there is in a population, the more likely it is that some members of the population will survive extreme changes in the environment. Meiosis is far more likely to produce these sorts of variations than is mitosis, and therefore confers selective advantage on sexually reproducing organisms.

Evolution

While you don't need to be an evolutionary expert on the Science TASC test, you should be familiar with how species evolve over time. A **species** is defined as a group of organisms that are capable of breeding with one another, but incapable of breeding with other species. Charles Darwin first published the **theory of evolution**, which states that species change slowly in response to factors in their environment. For example, if Earth's climate started to get colder, dogs that happened to have thicker, warmer fur would tend to survive better than members of their species with thinner fur, thus allowing the **survival of the fittest**. The surviving dogs would pass on the thicker fur gene to their puppies, and so this trait would gradually become a dominant characteristic of their species. This process in which traits that help an organism survive gradually triumph over traits that don't is called **natural selection**.

The other way evolution operates is genetic drift. **Genetic drift** is the accumulation of changes in the frequency of alleles over time due to sampling errors—changes that occur as a result of random chance. For example, in a population of owls there may be an equal chance of a newly born owlet having long talons or short talons, but due to random breeding variances a slightly larger number of long-taloned owlets are born. Over many generations, this slight variance can

Darwin's Diary
In 1859, Charles Darwin published his book, *On the Origin of Species*. Not only did this text detail his thoughts on natural selection, but it also contained a plethora of information from his journey to Brazil, Chile, Australia, the Falkland Islands, and the Galapagos Islands. Darwin's work provided so much evidence for the theory of evolution that it became a landmark work in the field of evolutionary biology.

develop into a larger trend, until the majority of owls in that population have long talons. These breeding variances could be a result of a chance event—such as an earthquake that drastically reduces the size of the nesting population one year. Small populations are more sensitive to the effects of genetic drift than large, diverse populations.

Common Ancestry

Darwin theorized that all species on Earth descended from one or two very simple organisms that gradually evolved into different kinds of more complex organisms. Thus, according to Darwin, human beings are thought to have evolved from simple sea creatures that gradually changed over millions of years into a common ape-like ancestor that in turn gradually evolved into Homo sapiens.

Phylogenetic Tree

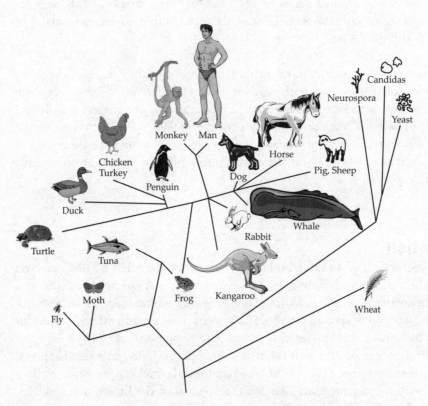

A **phylogenetic tree** is used to model evolution. Phylogenetic trees can be very broad, like the one shown, which encompasses many types of species, or they can be very specific, and describe the evolutionary relationships that exist between two species.

Inheritance Quiz

A: The cross between two heterozygous individuals, Bb, would result in offspring with the alleles BB, Bb, Bb, and bb. Since blue eyes are expressed in only individuals who are homozygous recessive, bb, 25% of the offspring would have blue eyes.

Life Science Drill

Now try some practice questions. To check your answers, register your book at **PrincetonReview.com/cracking** and download the Chapter Drill Answers and Explanations supplement.

Directions Use the following information to help answer questions 1 through 3.

1. In kittens, the gene for pointy ears is dominant (E) and the gene for floppy ears is recessive (e). Kittens will express the pointy ear trait if the kitten is pure or has a hybrid of alleles. In order for floppy ears to be expressed on a kitten, the kitten must be pure for the recessive gene. Below is a Punnett Square of a cross between two parents.

	e
?	Ee
Ee	ee

(left column header: ____, row label: e)

What genotype should replace the "?" in the Punnett Square?

A EE

B Ee

C eE

D ee

2. The genotypic ratio of this Punnett Square is best expressed as

A 3:1

B 1:4

C 4:1

D 1:2:1

3. What is the probability that an offspring will have pointy ears?

A 25%

B 50%

C 75%

D 100%

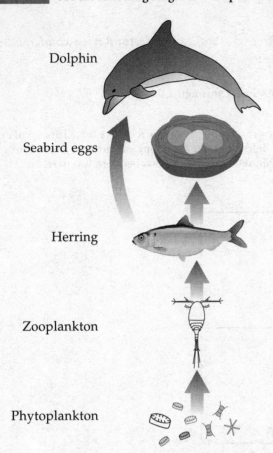

Dolphin

Seabird eggs

Herring

Zooplankton

Phytoplankton

4. Which term best describes the image provided?

A energy pyramid

B food chain

C phylogenetic tree

D evolution

5. Which term best describes the phytoplankton in the image provided?

A detrivore

B decomposer

C producer

D consumer

6. According to the energy pyramid for food chains, approximately what percentage of energy stored in the herring would be transferred to the dolphin?

A 100%

B 90%

C 50%

D 10%

7. Which of the following sequences of DNA base pairs will pair with the DNA sequence ATTGGCTAG?

   A TAACCGATC

   B CGGTTAGCT

   C GATCGGTTA

   D TUUCCGUTC

8. Which of the following body systems plays a role in movement?

   A digestive system

   B muscular system

   C endocrine system

   D reproductive system

9. Jimmy goes running on a warm summer day. As he runs, his body sweats in an attempt to cool down his core body temperature. This maintenance mechanism of the body is referred to as

   A circulation

   B purification

   C homeostasis

   D mutualism

10. The initial, and longest, phase of the cell life cycle is called

    A interphase

    B prophase

    C metaphase

    D anaphase

Chapter 28
Earth and Space Science

In this chapter, we'll guide you through the key topics related to Earth and Space Science on the Science portion of the TASC test. We will focus on three broad categories: the Universe and Solar System, the Earth, and Humans and the Earth. Following the content lessons, we'll give you some practice questions.

THE UNIVERSE AND SOLAR SYSTEM

Astronomy is the study of the universe beyond the earth. Astronomers study the moon, planets, solar system, galaxy, and everything farther away. Astronomy is one of the oldest branches of science, dating back to ancient times. In fact, some scientists theorize that the pyramids in Egypt were actually used for astronomical purposes. Thankfully, the questions on the TASC test won't require you to know everything about the deepest reaches of space, but you should know the basics of the universe.

Big Bang Theory

Where did we come from? How did the universe come into being? These and many similar questions continue to boggle even the greatest scientists. The origin of our universe has been, and continues to be, one of the most studied concepts in science. The fact is that we do not know how the universe was formed. However, there are a number of theories.

One of the most widely accepted, but also the most misunderstood, scientific theories is the Big Bang Theory. First of all, let's clear up a major misconception about this theory: It does not state that there was a big explosion that led to the current universe. In short, the **Big Bang theory** proposes that approximately 13.8 billion years ago the universe began as a small **singularity**, an area thought to exist at the core of black holes that are infinitely dense, that inflated, expanded, and cooled to form the solar system.

Let's put that in some more straightforward terms. Scientists believe that a huge cloud of dust and gas was at the center of a black hole. Since **black holes** are places of intense gravitational pressure, the cloud collapsed under the weight of this pressure, forming a star at the center, and began spinning in a circle. As this cloud continued to spin, it collected more dust and gas, becoming massive. Simultaneously, smaller clouds of dust and gas were forming and collapsing. Eventually, the large star ignited, becoming the sun, and the smaller clouds became the planets and other celestial bodies. Once the sun was ablaze, it began to produce strong solar winds that blew the remaining gas and dust out of our solar system. Since there was no more matter for the celestial bodies to collect, they stopped growing; this is why the planets closer to the sun are smaller—they had less time to gather mass before the sun blew the matter away.

So, what evidence is there that supports the Big Bang theory? In 1929, Edward Hubble observed that galaxies are moving away from us, or expanding, at speeds proportional to their distance—a phenomenon known as **Hubble's Law**. If the universe is continually expanding, it must have started at some point. This discovery supports the idea that the universe was, at one time, smaller and continues to expand. In fact, according to the Big Bang theory, the universe is expanding as you read this sentence!

Big Bang Bonanza!
So, how did scientists figure out that the universe began 13.8 billion years ago? Well, by measuring the composition of matter and energy density of the universe, scientists could determine how fast the universe expanded in the past. This enabled them to calculate the time in between the Big Bang and the current universe. Cool, right?

More evidence supporting the Big Bang theory was discovered by radioastronomers Arno Penzias and Robert Wilson. Penzias and Wilson proposed the idea that if the universe was initially extremely hot, there should be some remnant of that heat in the universe. In 1965, Penzias and Wilson found a −455° F **Cosmic Background Radiation** that saturates the universe. Many scientists view this background heat as the greatest evidence for the Big Bang theory.

Scientists have determined that elements were created in one of two ways during the Big Bang. Light elements, such as hydrogen, helium, and deuterium, are thought to have been created within the first few minutes of the big bang, while heavier elements are thought to have been formed at a much later time due to the initially inhospitable conditions; this theory is known as the theory of **nucleosynthesis**. Based on this theory, hydrogen and helium comprise approximately 75% and 25% of the universe's mass, while other elements comprise less than .01% of the universe's mass. To date, observations have supported this theory; in fact, no observations have been made where helium exists in quantities of less than 23%, lending support for the Big Bang theory.

Remember, this is an area of science that is not well understood. While you won't be expected to have all the answers about the origin of the universe on the TASC test, you should be familiar with the Big Bang theory and the current evidence that supports it.

The Solar System

The **solar system** is the collection of planets and their moons that orbit around the sun, as well as smaller celestial bodies such as asteroids, meteoroids, and comets. Our solar system was formed roughly 4.6 billion years ago. All solar systems are made up of a sun and the objects that revolve around the sun. For a long time, scientists believed that the earth was the center of the solar system. However, all that changed in the sixteenth century when **Nicolas Copernicus** introduced the idea of a **heliocentric**, or sun-centered, model of the solar system.

Located closest to the sun, the **terrestrial planets**, those that have solid surfaces, are Mercury, Venus, Earth, and Mars. Located farthest from the sun are Jupiter, Saturn, Uranus, and Neptune. Our solar system is located in the **Orion Arm** of the **Milky War Galaxy**. While we don't know for certain, there are likely billions of other solar systems in our galaxy and billions of galaxies in the universe. Which, of course, is why we continue to look for life elsewhere in the universe!

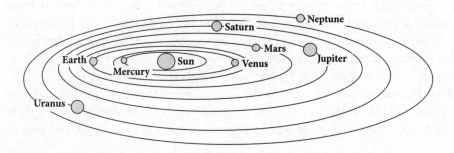

Heliocentric Model of Our Solar System

The solar system also contains millions of smaller objects. The **Kuiper Belt** is a disk-shaped region past the orbit of Neptune that is thought to be the source of short-period comets; this is also where most of the known dwarf planets exist. **Asteroids** are large pieces of rock that orbit the sun, just as the planets do. Most asteroids are located between Mars and Jupiter in an area that is called the **asteroid belt. Meteoroids** are small pieces of rock and metal. When a meteoroid enters the earth's atmosphere, it is called a **meteor.** Usually, the meteor will burn up when passing through the atmosphere. However, on rare occasions meteors hit the earth and are then called **meteorites. Comets** are made up of rock, dust, methane, and ice. Like asteroids, comets orbit the sun.

The Sun

Without the sun, there would be no life on Earth. As shown in the heliocentric model of our solar system, the sun is the center of the solar system. There are two major facts you should know about the sun: The sun is extremely hot and extremely large. The **corona**, or outer layer of the sun, averages 2,000,000° C, while the **core**, or center of the sun, averages 15,000,000° C. The sun is also huge, having a size that is roughly 109 times larger than the earth. The sun is so big, in fact, that it accounts for 99% of the total mass of the solar system! Because of its size, the sun's gravitational pull forces other planets to orbit around it.

Planets and Moons

The definition of a planet has stirred up much controversy and undergone numerous changes since the Greeks coined it back in the day. The debate surrounding the definition of a planet came to a head in 2005, when astronomers discovered an object orbiting around Neptune that was larger than Pluto, an established planet at the time. The International Astronomical Union has since defined a **planet** as a celestial body that orbits the sun, is massive enough for its own gravity to make it round, and is the largest body around its orbital zone. (Under this new definition of a planet, Pluto was kicked out of the planetary ranks. Poor Pluto.)

The **inner planets** are those closest to the sun: Mercury, Venus, Earth, and Mars. The inner planets consist mainly of rock with metal cores and, notably, do not have rings. Earth and Mars are the only inner planets that have moons; Earth has one moon and Mars has two moons, Phobos and Deimos.

The **outer planets,** sometimes called the Jovian planets, are those farthest from the sun: Jupiter, Saturn, Uranus, and Neptune. The outer planets are the largest in the solar system, with Jupiter being the largest. Jupiter and Saturn are known as **gas giants** as they are primarily made up of gasses, not rock or solid matter. Conversely, Uranus and Neptune are known as **ice giants,** as they are primarily made of ice. Remember how we said that the sun's solar winds pushed the dust and gasses outwards? Well, the outer planets were able to pull a lot of objects into their orbits. Accordingly, all of the outer planets have many **moons**, or natural objects that revolve around a planet, with Saturn having 53 moons! Another characteristic of the outer planets is that they have rings; again, Saturn has the most rings. The rings that encircle the outer planets are primarily made of ice, but also have some trace bits of rocky material.

Stars and Nuclear Reactions

If you look in the sky on a clear night, you will see a myriad of stars. A **star** is a massive ball of gas, mainly hydrogen and helium, which is held together by its own gravity. Often, stars occur in groups of at least two stars that orbit around their center of mass; this is called a **binary star system**. Large groups of unorganized stars are known as **clusters**. Scientists categorize stars by color, which also indicates the star's size and heat intensity. The largest, hottest stars are blue, medium sized stars are yellow, and the smallest, coolest stars are red. The smaller stars are called **dwarfs**, while the larger stars are called **giants**.

Remember how we discussed the sun's formation in the section on the Big Bang theory? Well, the same process that formed the sun forms the stars. During the **birth** phase of a star, a large cloud of dust and gas, called a **nebula**, collapses under its own gravitational pressure. All the collapsing causes heat energy to build until the nuclei of the hydrogen and helium atoms fuse, which causes energy to be created via the process of **nuclear fusion**. The nuclear fusion reactions take place in the core of the star, and generate both light and heat energy. At this point, the star has entered the **main sequence** phase of its lifecycle, and will continue to glow until there is no more hydrogen in the star. Once the hydrogen in the star is gone, the outside of the star expands and it becomes a **red giant**. The changing composition of the star enables it to create iron that, inevitably, will cause the star to **collapse**. Upon collapse, most stars will become white dwarfs, which are remnants of collapsed stars, while a larger star may explode, creating a supernova. However, the exact fate of the collapsed star is dependent on its initial mass.

So, why don't we use nuclear fusion to power the earth? Unfortunately, we haven't really figured out how to control the process of nuclear fusion. Once we figure it out, however, we'll have a great source of renewable energy!

The Spectra of Light

As you'll read in the Physical Science chapter, humans can only see light that falls within a specific range of wavelengths and frequencies; this range is referred to as the **visible spectrum of light**. You should know that frequency and wavelength have an inverse relationship to one another; e.g., a high frequency wave has a short wavelength. Within the visible spectrum of light, **ultraviolet** light has the greatest frequency (roughly 750 Terahertz), while **infrared** light has the lowest frequency (approximately 380 Terahertz). If you've ever seen a rainbow, you've seen the whole spectrum in action.

Poor Pluto

In 2006, Pluto was reclassified from a planet to a dwarf planet. However, while many people believe Pluto was demoted because of its size, it was actually reclassified because it is not unique. Simply put, Pluto is the brightest member of the Kuiper Belt, a mass of objects that exist beyond Neptune.

To see a full-color version, visit **www.britannica.com/media/full/340440/91330**.

Visible Spectrum of Light

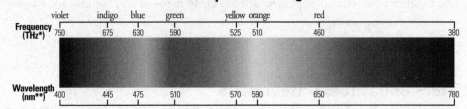

	violet	indigo	blue	green	yellow	orange	red	
Frequency (THz*)	750	675	630	590	525	510	460	380
Wavelength (nm)**	400	445	475	510	570	590	650	780

* In terahertz (THz); 1 THz = 1×10^{12} cycles per second
** In nanometers (nm); 1nm = 1×10^{-9} meter

Interestingly, the color that we see when we look at an object is the result of reflected light. Consider green grass. When you look at the grass, you will see the color green. However, the grass is actually absorbing every other color *except* green. The frequency of light that we recognize as green is simply reflecting off the grass. The colors black and white work differently; we see black when an object absorbs all the colors of light, while we see white when an object reflects all the colors of light. **Additive colors** red, blue, and green, are the primary colors of light. By combining the additive colors of light, any other color on the visible light spectrum can be created. Conversely, cyan, magenta, and yellow are known as **subtractive colors,** used to create new colors by filtering colors out of white light.

So, how does the frequency of a wave affect the color of the visible light? Well, that depends on whether the object exuding light is moving towards us or away from us. Let's consider a red star and a blue star. If you look at the visible light spectrum, you will see that blue light has high frequencies, while red light has the lowest frequencies. As the blue star travels towards Earth, the star's light waves are squished together, increasing the light's frequency, and making the light appear bluer; this effect is known as a **blue shift**. Conversely, as the red star travels away from earth, the light waves the star gives off are stretched out, decreasing the light's frequency, and making the light appear redder; this effect is known as a **red shift.**

The Red Shift and Blue Shift of Light

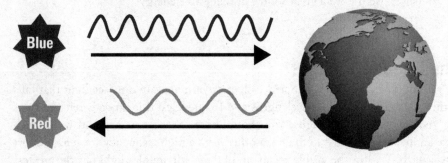

THE EARTH

The Age of the Earth

The first thing you should know about Earth is its history. Earth is thought to be between 4.5 and 4.8 billion years old. That amount of time is pretty inconceivable to humans, but the following geologic time scale will help you get a sense of the vast amount of time that has gone by since Earth was formed. You will not be responsible for memorizing all of the eons, eras, periods, and epochs for the TASC test, but you should be familiar with the major ones; they will come in handy.

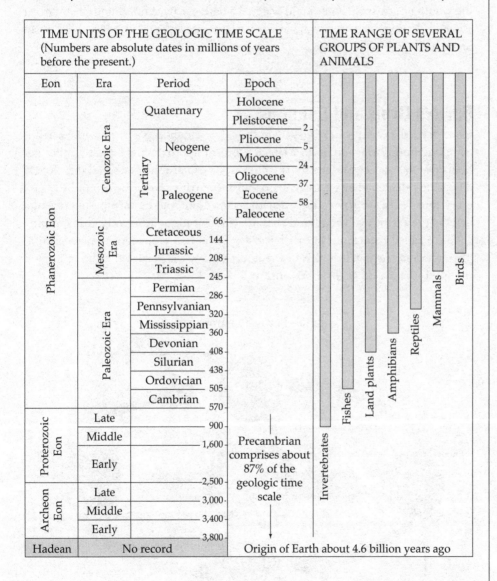

TIME UNITS OF THE GEOLOGIC TIME SCALE (Numbers are absolute dates in millions of years before the present.)

TIME RANGE OF SEVERAL GROUPS OF PLANTS AND ANIMALS

Eon	Era	Period		Epoch	
Phanerozoic Eon	Cenozoic Era	Quaternary		Holocene	
				Pleistocene	
		Tertiary	Neogene	Pliocene	2
				Miocene	5
					24
			Paleogene	Oligocene	37
				Eocene	58
				Paleocene	
	Mesozoic Era	Cretaceous			66
		Jurassic			144
		Triassic			208
	Paleozoic Era	Permian			245
		Pennsylvanian			286
		Mississippian			320
		Devonian			360
		Silurian			408
		Ordovician			438
		Cambrian			505
Proterozoic Eon	Late				570
	Middle				900
	Early				1,600
Archeon Eon	Late				2,500
	Middle				3,000
	Early				3,400
Hadean	No record				3,800

Precambrian comprises about 87% of the geologic time scale

Origin of Earth about 4.6 billion years ago

Invertebrates
Fishes
Land plants
Amphibians
Reptiles
Mammals
Birds

Why Life Developed on Earth

Truth be told, nobody really knows how or why life developed on Earth. However, scientists have discovered a number of interesting things about the origins of Earth. First, by studying the fossils found in ancient rocks, scientists have determined that life on earth began approximately 3.8 billion years ago. That means that, for nearly a billion years, nothing lived on Earth! So, what allowed life to form? Well, many scientists believe that life began in water that was either on the surface of the Earth or at the bottom of the oceans. Other scientists believe that comets and asteroids collided with Earth, depositing different elements. All scientists, however, agree that organic atoms combined and evolved, resulting in the modern Earth we know today. Furthermore, it is a widely accepted notion that life would not exist without liquid water. To date, we have not found life on other planets. However, scientists generally believe that any planet with liquid water can breed life.

Earth's Orbit and Seasons

Crazy fact: the earth is moving as you read this sentence. Right now, the earth is traveling around the sun at an average speed of approximately 65,865 miles per hour. Do you feel it? The earth's **revolution**, or trip around the sun, takes 365.35 days. The calendar that we use is based on the earth's revolution around the sun; every four years, we have a leap year to compensate for the missing quarter of a day. As the earth revolves around the sun, it is spinning on its **axis**; this spinning action is called **rotation**. On earth, it takes 24 hours, or one day, to make a complete rotation. As you'll notice in the figure below, the earth's revolution around the sun is the reason we have seasons.

Life on Other Planets?

Only one condition must be met for life to exist—there must be liquid water. To date, scientists have found only two places in the solar system with liquid water: Mars and Europa. Accordingly, there is a strong possibility that bacterial life could be present in these places. So, it's entirely possible that alien lifeforms exist… we just haven't made contact yet.

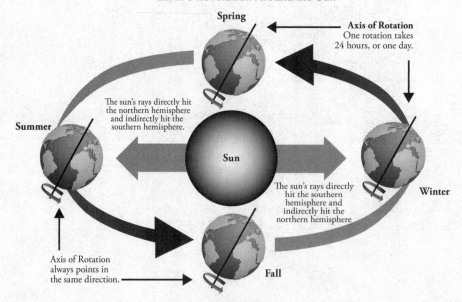

Earth's Revolution Around the Sun

Both the orbit of Earth around the Sun—and the fact that Earth is tilted on its axis by 23.5°—together create the seasons that we experience on Earth. When Earth is in the part of its orbit in which the Northern Hemisphere is tilted toward the sun, the northern half of the planet receives more direct sunlight for longer periods of time each day than does the Southern Hemisphere. This means that when the Northern Hemisphere is experiencing summer, the Southern Hemisphere is experiencing winter. Interestingly, because of the earth's tilt, the sun rises and sets just once a year at the North and South Poles. Approximately six months of the year at the poles are daytime, while the other six months are dark, and considered nighttime.

Climate

The earth's atmosphere has physical features that change day to day as well as patterns that are consistent over a space of many years. The day-to-day properties such as wind speed and direction, temperature, amount of sunlight, pressure, and humidity are referred to as **weather**. The patterns that are constant over many years (30 years or more) are referred to as **climate**. A region's weather and climate are the result of the rotation of the earth coupled with the sun's unequal warming of the earth. The two most important factors in describing climate are **average temperature and average precipitation amounts**.

The Structure of the Earth

Earth is made up of three concentric zones that are composed of either solid or liquid (molten) rock. The outermost layer of the earth is called the **lithosphere**. The lithosphere contains a rigid upper mantle and the **crust**, our solid, rocky surface of earth. The middle zone of the earth is called the **mantle**, which is primarily composed of solid rock. However, the mantle does have an area called the **asthenosphere**, which is slowly moving molten rock. The center of the earth is called the **core**. The earth's core has two parts: the inner core, which is solid due to tremendous pressure, and the outer core, which is semi-solid due to lower pressure.

Although it generally feels pretty solid underfoot, the earth is undergoing constant change. We have discovered that the **continents**—Antarctica, Africa, Asia, Australia, Europe, North America, and South America—are actually moving slowly on the face of the earth. This is called **continental drift**. Looking at the world map, you will notice that if you pushed the continent of Africa up against the continent of South America, you would have an almost perfect fit.

World Map

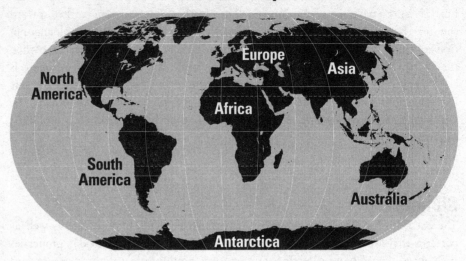

Plate Tectonics

Scientists theorize that during the Paleozoic and Mesozoic eras, the continents were joined together, forming a supercontinent known as **Pangaea**. (Fun fact: In ancient Greek, the word *pan* meant whole, while the word *gaia* meant land. Thus, Pangaea means whole land!) Roughly 200 million years ago, Pangaea began to break apart.

Today, it is believed that the earth's crust is composed of several large pieces—called **tectonic plates**—that move slowly over the mantle of the earth. Tectonic plates, which are made up of both mantle and crust, move independently of one another. The majority of the land of Earth sits above six giant plates, while the remainder of the plates lie under the ocean and continents.

The edges of the tectonic plates are known as **plate boundaries**, or **fault lines**, and when these boundaries interact, the friction between them causes earthquakes, volcanoes, and sea floor spreading. There are three types of plate boundary interactions that you should know for the TASC test. A **convergent boundary** occurs when two plates are pushed towards one another, and one of the plates is pushed deep into the mantle. Convergent boundary interactions often result in **subduction**, in which a heavy ocean plate is pushed below the other plate and melts as it encounters the hot mantle. Subduction results in the formation of mountain chains, like the Himalayas, the Alps, and the Appalachian Mountains. A **divergent boundary** occurs when two plates move away from each other, causing a gap to form that will be filled with magma. Once the magma in the gap cools, a new section of the earth's crust is formed. A **transform fault boundary** occurs when two plates slide from side to side relative to each other—like when you rub your hands back and forth.

Earth's Plates

Soil and Erosion

One very important, but often underappreciated, player in Earth's interdependent systems is soil. **Soil** plays an active role in the cycling of nutrients, and acts as a crucial link between the **abiotic** (the nonliving components of the world) and the **biotic** (the living components of the world). Let's take a moment to review the major characteristics of soil that you'll be expected to know on the TASC test.

Soils can be categorized into three groups: clay, silt, and sand. The category with the smallest particles is **clay**, which is extremely compact; clays easily adhere to each other and there is little room between particles for water. The next largest particle is **silt**, which is less compact and can hold more water than clay. **Sand** is the largest, coarsest type of soil, having particles that are too large to easily stick together; sand particles also have large pores, which allow them to hold more water than any other type of soil.

Another very important characteristic of soil types is soil **acidity** or **alkalinity**. The **pH** of a substance ranges from 0–14, with 0 indicating a highly alkaline substance, 7 indicating a neutral substance, and 14 indicating a highly acidic substance. Most soils fall into a pH range of about 4–8, meaning that most soils range in pH from being slightly acidic to neutral. Soil pH is important because it affects the solubility of nutrients; and this in turn determines the extent to which these nutrients are available for absorption by plant roots. If the soil in a region is too acidic or basic, certain soil nutrients will not be able to be used by the regional plants.

pH Quiz
Q: Which of the following tastes is associated with acidic food?

A Sour
B Salty
C Sweet
D Bitter

Turn the page for the answer.

So, where does all this soil come from? Well, soil is a combination of organic material and rock that has been broken down by chemical and biological weathering, processes known as **erosion**. There are three categories of erosion, or weathering, that you should know for the TASC test. **Physical weathering**, sometimes referred to as **mechanical weathering**, is any process that breaks rock down into smaller pieces without changing the chemistry of the rock; this is generally caused by wind and water. **Chemical weathering** occurs when water, atmospheric gases, and bedrock have chemical interactions; e.g., iron rusts when it comes into contact with water. **Biological weathering** takes place as the result of the activities of living organisms, such as tree roots growing and expanding through rocks.

While erosion is a continual and normal process, it can become a problem for humans when it removes valuable topsoil or deposits soil in undesirable places. Eroded topsoil usually ends up in bodies of water, posing a problem for both farmers, who need healthy soil for planting, and people who rely on bodies of water to be uncontaminated with soil runoff.

Landforms

Continental drift, movements of the tectonic plates, and erosion have all played an important role in shaping the different features, or **landforms**, on Earth's terrain. There are certain types of landforms you should be familiar with for the TASC test.

pH Quiz
A: Acidic foods, such as vinegar and lemon juice, taste sour because of their acidic nature.

- **Canyons** are narrow areas that lie between plateaus that are formed by the movements of rivers, erosion, and tectonic activity. One of the most well known canyons is the Grand Canyon in Arizona.
- **Deserts** are regions of dry, hot land that are covered in sand, receive little rainfall, and, in turn, have minimal vegetation. Deserts can be either hot, such as the Sahara Desert, or cold, such as Antarctica— yes, Antarctica is considered the largest cold desert in the world!
- **Hills** are masses of land that have rounded summits and rise above the surrounding area. They are shorter than mountains, usually standing fewer than 1,000 feet tall.
- **Islands** are landforms that are surrounded by water on all sides. Islands are formed as a result of volcanic activity, which pushes magma through the crust at a single point. A group of islands is called an archipelago.
- **Mountains** are the highest landforms on Earth's surface. Mountain peaks such as Mount Everest, the highest peak in the world, are formed when two tectonic plates move towards each other, squeezing the earth's surface upwards.
- **Plains** are areas of flat land at low elevations that are generally fertile regions, providing a great area for civilization. Coastal plains are those that meet the oceans or seas, while river plains, obviously, meet at rivers.

- **Plateaus** are large masses of land that rise above the surrounding area and have both flat tops and steep sides, called cliffs. A plateau is formed when magma is pushed towards the earth's surface, but is unable to break through the crust.
- **Valleys** are low-lying areas between hills or mountains. As water flows down hillsides and mountainsides, it erodes the rock and soil, carving the v-shaped grooves we know as valleys. Like the plains, valleys have access to water, making them a great place for civilizations such as the Indus Valley Civilization.

Water Cycle

Water surrounds us and, without it, our lives would cease to exist. The water that exists in the atmosphere is in a gaseous state, and when it condenses from the gaseous state to form a liquid or solid, it becomes dense enough to fall to the earth because of the pull of gravity. This process is known as **precipitation**. When precipitation falls onto the earth, it may travel below ground to become **groundwater**, or it may travel across the land's surface as **runoff** and enter a drainage system, such as a **stream** or **river**, that will eventually deposit it into a body of water such as a **lake** or an **ocean**. Lakes and oceans are reservoirs for water. In certain cold regions of Earth, water may also be trapped on the earth's surface as snow or ice; in these areas, the blocks of snow or ice are reservoirs.

Water is returned to the atmosphere from both the earth's surface and from living organisms in a process called **evaporation**. Because all living organisms are primarily made up of water, they act as exchange pools for water. Specifically, animals respire and release water vapor and additional gases to the atmosphere. In plants, the process of **transpiration** releases large amounts of water into the air. Finally, other major contributors to atmospheric water are the vast number of lakes and oceans on Earth's surface. Incredibly large amounts of water continually evaporate from their surfaces.

Take a look at the graphic on the next page, which depicts the water cycle. For the TASC test, you should have a general idea about how water cycles throughout the earth.

The Water Cycle

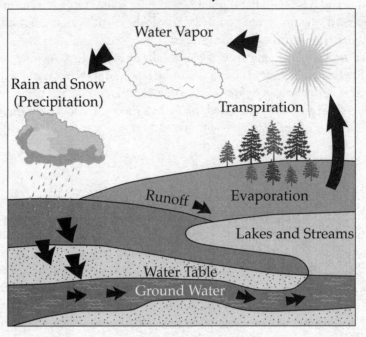

Carbon Cycle

Now let's talk about carbon. The key events in the carbon cycle are **respiration**, in which animals (and plants!) breathe in oxygen and give off carbon dioxide, and **photosynthesis**, in which plants take in carbon dioxide, water, and energy from the sun to produce carbohydrates. In other words, living things act as exchange pools for carbon.

When animal consumers eat plants, the carbon locked in the plant carbohydrates passes to other organisms and continues through the food chain (more on this later in the chapter). In turn, when organisms—both plants and animals—die, their bodies are decomposed through the actions of bacteria and fungi in the soil; this releases carbon dioxide back into the atmosphere.

One aspect of the carbon cycle that you should definitely be familiar with for the TASC test is this: When the bodies of once-living organisms are buried and subjected to conditions of extreme heat and extreme pressure, eventually this organic matter becomes oil, coal, and gas. Oil, coal, and natural gas are collectively known as fossil fuels, and when fossil fuels burn, or **combust**, carbon is released into the atmosphere. Finally, carbon is also released into the atmosphere through volcanic action.

There are three major reservoirs of carbon; the first is the world's oceans, because carbon dioxide is very soluble in water. The second large reservoir of carbon dioxide is Earth's rocks. Many types of rocks—called carbonate rocks—contain carbon, in the form of calcium carbonate. Finally, fossil fuels are a huge reservoir of carbon, as well.

Carbon Cycle Quiz

Q: Plants are primary consumers of carbon dioxide.

A) True
B) False

Turn the page for the answer.

The Carbon Cycle

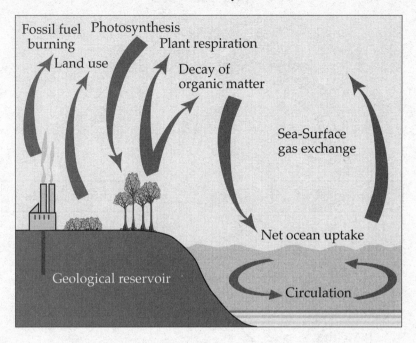

Rock Cycle

Rocks are everywhere—in the soil, our buildings, and the ore used in industry. So, where do all those rocks come from? The answer is: other rocks. The oldest rocks on Earth are 3.8 billion years old, while others are only a few million years old. This means that rocks have to be recycled. The process that does this is the rock cycle. In the rock cycle, time, pressure, and the earth's heat interact to create three basic types of rocks.

- **Igneous**—this type of rock results when rock is melted (by heat and pressure below the crust) into a liquid and then resolidifies. The molten rock (magma) comes to the surface of the earth, and when it emerges it is called lava; solid lava is igneous rock. An example of an igneous rock is basalt.
- **Sedimentary**—these rocks are formed as **sediment**, eroded rocks and the remains of plants and animals, builds up and is compressed. One place this can occur is at a subduction zone where ocean sediments are pushed deep into the earth and compressed by the weight of rock above it. An example of a sedimentary rock is limestone.
- **Metamorphic**—this type of rock is formed as a great deal of pressure and heat is applied to rock. This can happen as sedimentary rocks sink deeper into the earth and are heated by the high temperatures found in the earth's mantle. An example of a metamorphic rock is slate (it is product of metamorphosis of shale).

The following diagram illustrates the rock cycle. Make sure you are familiar with it before the TASC test!

The Rock Cycle

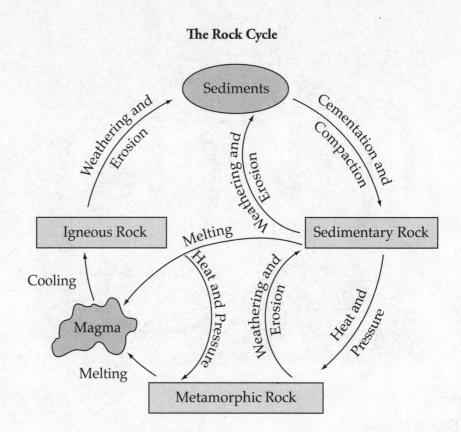

Carbon Cycle Quiz

A: True!

Plants are primary consumers of carbon dioxide, while animals are the primary producers of carbon dioxide.

HUMANS AND THE EARTH

Remember when we discussed energy? Well, we are going to revisit the sources of our energy. On a daily basis, you perform a multitude of tasks that require power; e.g., you may brush your teeth, make toast, drive a car, use electric light, or a host of other power-sucking tasks. So, where does all that power come from? And, more importantly, what happens if the sources of power run dry? In the following section we will talk about the resources that make it possible for us to perform a multitude of tasks on a daily basis.

Consumption of Resources

A large amount of energy is required to produce the power supplied throughout the world. In order to produce this energy, it is necessary to utilize a combination of human ingenuity and the earth's resources. A **resource** is defined as an available supply that can be drawn on as needed. There are two types of **natural resources:** renewable and nonrenewable.

Renewable resources are those that can be replenished or regenerated over the course of time by natural processes and can be replaced at a sustainable rate; i.e., the supply of the energy is able to meet the demand for energy. In the United

States, only eight percent of electricity is produced with five main renewable resources: biomass, hydroelectric, geothermal, wind, and solar. Worldwide, renewable resources provide approximately 10% of the world's energy consumption. As technology continues to improve, and the world becomes increasingly aware of the environmental hazards associated with fossil fuels, researchers project that renewable resources will provide 15% of the world's energy by 2040.

Conversely, **nonrenewable resources** are those that exist in a limited supply and cannot be naturally replaced on a level to meet its consumption; i.e., the demand exceeds the supply. Roughly 90% of the world's energy consumption comes from nonrenewable resources; clearly, this is problematic if we hope to sustain life on earth.

Renewable Resources

Biomass, or biofuels, is organic matter such as plants, animals, or waste products from organic sources that is burned in a biomass boiler to produce energy. Using biomass as an energy source is beneficial because it is low-cost, readily available and renewable, and better for the environment than fossil fuels. Biomass can also help reduce the amount of waste in landfills, as it relies on the burning of organic matter. The major downsides of biomass include the initial cost and large land mass required for installation of a biomass boiler.

Biomass Power Process

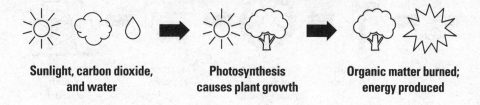

Sunlight, carbon dioxide, and water → Photosynthesis causes plant growth → Organic matter burned; energy produced

An increasingly researched renewable energy source is **geothermal energy,** which is produced by harnessing the earth's internal heat. (Fun fact: *Geo* means "from the earth," and *thermal* means "heat.") Geothermal energy is produced when heat, coming from steam or hot water reservoirs deep in the earth, is transferred through large pipes that drive an electrical generator. The benefits of geothermal energy are that it is reliable when installed, safe to use, and does not produce pollutants in the energy production process. Unfortunately, geothermal energy hasn't gained popularity, is expensive to install, and can potentially release toxic gas during the drilling process. Furthermore, the use of geothermal energy is limited by geography; if a location lacks a geothermal source, energy production cannot take place.

Geothermal Power Process

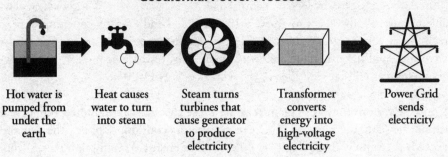

| Hot water is pumped from under the earth | Heat causes water to turn into steam | Steam turns turbines that cause generator to produce electricity | Transformer converts energy into high-voltage electricity | Power Grid sends electricity |

Hydroelectric power works via the systematic placement of river dams that spin turbines to produce electricity. The process involved in creating electricity from hydroelectric power is not unlike that of geothermal energy; instead of having water pumped from beneath the earth, however, water in a dam's reservoirs is responsible for spinning the turbines and generating electricity. Despite the fact that hydroelectric power does not generate any pollution and can be cost-effective, the usefulness of this resource is limited by geography. Hydroelectric power is practical only in areas that receive significant rainfall and are located near rivers. Environmentalists also note that hydroelectric dams require the diversion of waterways that leads to the disturbance, and often destruction, of habitats and ecosystems.

Wind Power Process

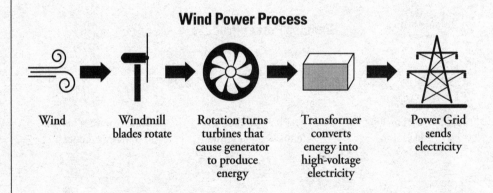

| Wind | Windmill blades rotate | Rotation turns turbines that cause generator to produce energy | Transformer converts energy into high-voltage electricity | Power Grid sends electricity |

With recent advents in technology, both **solar** and **wind power** have become increasingly accessible, affordable, and reliable. Perhaps one of the greatest benefits of both resources is that they are indefinitely renewable. Wind power produces electricity by erecting large windmills that harness wind that spin turbines. While wind power can provide energy for a reasonable cost, it has seen a slow adoption rate. Indeed, wind power is not always practical in a given environment, as large, unobstructed areas of land are needed for windmill placement. For wind power to work effectively, large windmills with turbines must be installed, which have been met with criticism for various reasons. One criticism is regarding the aesthetic nature of a windmill farm, which can stretch over vast swaths of land. Others note the deadliness of the wind turbines, which have been known to suck in and kill migrating birds.

Solar Power Process

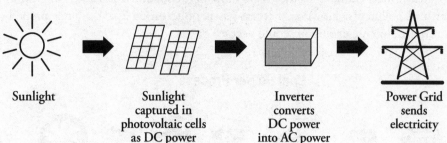

Sunlight → Sunlight captured in photovoltaic cells as DC power → Inverter converts DC power into AC power → Power Grid sends electricity

Solar power, however, has seen a rapid adoption rate, as individuals and corporations alike install **photovoltaic cells**, which transform the sun's light into DC power. DC power then travels to an inverter that converts the DC power into AC electricity to fuel your home. Two benefit of solar energy are that passive solar energy production produces no air pollutants and users can save significant amounts of money by receiving energy 'off the grid.' Unfortunately, the production of photovoltaic cells requires the use of fossil fuels, which have a detrimental impact environment, and the initial installation cost of a passive solar collection system is quite significant. Furthermore, areas that receive limited amounts of sunlight are not practical for solar energy systems. In summation, it should be noted that there is a huge benefit associated with the use of renewable resources: Compared to nonrenewable energy, renewable energy is significantly less harmful to the environment and is considered **green technology**.

Nonrenewable Resources

Despite the fact that **fossil fuels** are non-renewable and the cause of many environmental problems, such as pollution, acid rain, and ozone destruction, they remain the top energy choice for many countries. Fossil fuels, such as coal, oil, and natural gas, are the world's primary source of energy, comprising approximately 80% of the world's energy. Formed from fossilized remains of organic matter, fossil fuels are found deep within the earth. In order to locate fossil fuels, geologists dig **exploratory wells** to take samples from the earth and determine whether or not the area is a **proven reserve**, or a location known to house fossil fuel deposits.

One major fossil fuel is **coal**, a combustible black rock composed of fossilized organic plant matter. Coal is extracted from the earth via **underground mining**, during which coal miners to enter and manually retrieve coal from a series of underground tunnels. One major issue associated with coal mining is **subsidence**, which is the caving in of mine shafts. Many times throughout history, cave-ins have trapped men underground, in what would become their final resting place. Like other fossil fuels, coal releases harmful pollutants into the environment that destroy the ozone layer, pollutes the air with smog and smoke, and produces **acid mine drainage**, or highly acidic water that can damage the areas surrounding the mine. Comprised mainly of methane and pentane, **natural gas** can be found deep in the earth where it is stored in the space between rocks. Like oil extraction,

Resource Review

Q: Which of the following energy sources contributes the least to global warming?

A Coal
B Oil
C Wind
D Wood

Turn the page for the answer.

natural gas extraction occurs when gas is carried to the surface and harnessed to produce power. Unlike the other types of fossil fuels, natural gas does not produce harmful pollutants. However, natural gas is quite unstable and, if not properly controlled, intense explosions could occur.

Coal Power Process

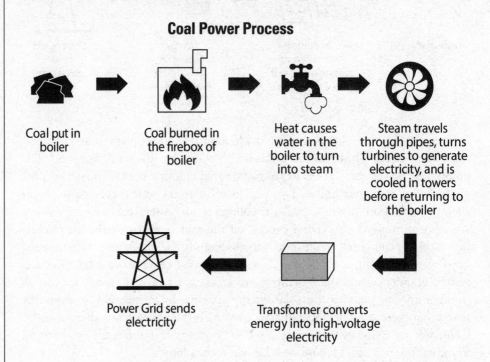

Coal put in boiler

Coal burned in the firebox of boiler

Heat causes water in the boiler to turn into steam

Steam travels through pipes, turns turbines to generate electricity, and is cooled in towers before returning to the boiler

Power Grid sends electricity

Transformer converts energy into high-voltage electricity

Another major nonrenewable resource is oil. Once a proven reserve has been tapped, oil is pumped up from the reserve to the surface. This form of oil is **crude oil**, which can vary greatly in viscosity, sulfur output, and color. There are four main modes of oil extraction: primary extraction, during which oil is easily pumped to the surface; pressure extraction, during which water and CO_2 push oil out of the reserve; steam and gas extraction; and, the newest mode, fracking, the process of injecting liquid at high pressure into the earth so existing fissures can be opened and oil can be extracted. The process of creating energy in an oil power station is not unlike that of a coal power plant. The major difference is the use of oil (obviously) instead of coal. Like coal, however, oil is burned to heat water that transforms into steam that turns the turbines and, eventually, creates electricity.

Another form of nonrenewable energy is **nuclear power**, which uses uranium in a process called **nuclear fission**, which occurs when an isotope of uranium 235 is split. Despite the low-cost associated with nuclear energy, there are many concerns with widespread use. Primarily, concerns regarding the radioactive waste produced by the fission process, coupled with the potential for tragic nuclear meltdowns as seen in Chernobyl, Ukraine and Fukushima, Japan, has slowed the adoption of nuclear power. In the future, nuclear power will likely involve **nuclear fusion**, which is the process of fusing two nuclei to create power.

Nuclear Power Process

Bundles of uranium rods are placed in water

→

Fuel rods heat water

→

Heat causes water in the boiler to turn into steam

→

Steam travels through pipes, turns turbines to generate electricity, and is cooled in towers before returning to the boiler

Power Grid sends electricity

←

Transformer converts energy into high-voltage electricity

↰

Sustainability

In order to be sustainable, an action must be able to continue indefinitely. From an environmental perspective, **sustainability** occurs when humans and nature exist in harmony, and when future generations have resources necessary for survival and well-being. Back in 1968, a man named Garret Hardin published a paper titled, "Tragedy of the Commons." In this paper, Hardin referenced the way resources were used in the 1880s; at this time, an open piece of land, called the commons, was used collectively by the townspeople for cattle grazing. Each member of the town would add cattle to the commons until the land was overgrazed. What's the problem with that? Well, as Hardin stated, "Each man is locked into a system that compels him to increase his herd without limit—in a world that is limited. Ruin is the destination toward which all men rush, each pursuing his own best interest in a society that believes in the freedom of the commons. Freedom in a commons brings ruin to all." In short, Hardin brings attention to the idea that people who use the earth's resources without limitations will lead to the eventual demise of the earth. Hopefully, this makes sense; after all, nonrenewable resources will, eventually, run out.

As our understanding of the nonrenewable nature of many of earth's resources has increased, so too has the push for resource conservation. **Conservation** is the management or regulation of a resource so that its use does not exceed the capacity of the resource to regenerate itself. Conversely, **preservation** is the maintenance of a species or ecosystem in order to ensure their perpetuation, with no concern as to their potential monetary value. Take note that resources are not limited to energy supplies, but also extend to plants and animals. For example, numerous laws have been passed, such as the **Wilderness Act** and the **Endangered Species**

Act, which restrict activities in U.S. National Parks and provide broad protection for species of fish, wildlife, and plants that are listed as threatened or endangered, respectively.

In order to determine whether or not a resource should be used, citizens, governments, and businesses engage in a process called **cost-benefit analysis.** Costs and benefits can be either tangible, or measurable, or intangible, or immeasurable. Consider a corporation interested in clearing a forest for wood. The benefits are jobs and lumber (both tangible), while the costs are the loss of beauty (intangible), decreased biodiversity, recreation space, and a decrease in carbon dioxide removal (the latter three are tangible costs).

Phew! We've conquered the amazing world of resources! Remember, for the TASC test, you just need to know the basics about renewable and nonrenewable resources and their respective costs and benefits. You should also have a general idea about sustainability and why it is important. Don't panic, however, you've got this!

Earth and Space Science Drill

Now try some practice questions. To check your answers, register your book at **PrincetonReview.com/cracking** and download the Chapter Drill Answers and Explanations supplement.

1. **Planets that are located closest to the sun and have solid surfaces, such as Mercury and Earth, are known as**

   A gas giants

   B heliocentric

   C terrestrial planets

   D ice giants

2. **Humans are only able to see light that falls within a specific range of wavelengths and frequencies, shown below.**

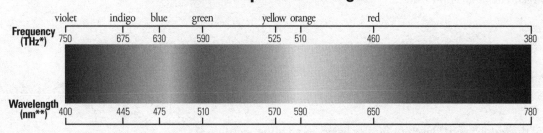

Visible Spectrum of Light

* In terahertz (THz); 1 THz = 1×10^{12} cycles per second
** In nanometers (nm); 1nm = 1×10^{-9} meter

   What is this range called?

   A ultraviolet light

   B visible spectrum of light

   C subtractive colors of light

   D additive colors of light

3. **Alex is looking up at the sky on a clear night. He notices that one star is particularly large and bright. According to the way stars are classified, this star's color is most likely**

   A blue

   B white

   C yellow

   D red

4. Acid rain, which typically has a pH of 5.5, is formed after the burning of fossil fuels releases compounds containing nitrogen and sulfur into the atmosphere. The higher acidity of soil and water affects many living organisms adversely. The table below shows the effects of pH on the size of adult fish.

pH of lake	Average length of fish (cm)	Average mass of fish (g)
7.5	30 cm	454 g
7.0	28 cm	450 g
6.5	29 cm	453 g
6.0	25 cm	401 g
5.5	20 cm	288 g
5.0	17 cm	127 g
4.5	No living fish	No living fish

Based on the table provided, which of the following best describes the relationship between the pH of the lake and the average mass of an adult fish?

A direct

B zero

C inverse

D constant

5. Which of the following pH levels indicate a basic, or alkaline, substance?

A 7.5

B 7.0

C 6.5

D 1.0

6. Which of the following processes likely contributed to the increased acidity of the lake?

A production of solar power

B tapping oil reserves

C constructing a dam

D burning coal

Use the following image to help answer questions 7 and 8.

7. The landform indicated by Label 1 would best be described as a

   A plain

   B plateau

   C desert

   D canyon

8. The landform indicated by Label 2 would best be described as a

   A hill

   B plateau

   C valley

   D canyon

9. Which of the following processes contributes to erosion?

   A physical weathering

   B chemical weathering

   C biological weathering

   D all of the above

10. From an environmental perspective, stewardship refers to the responsible use and protection of resources. Which of the following is an example of environmental stewardship?

    A cost-benefit analysis

    B conservation

    C consuming non-renewable resources

    D cross-cut agriculture

Chapter 29
Physical Science

In this chapter, we'll guide you through the key topics related to Physical Science on the Science portion of the TASC test. We will focus on five broad categories: Atoms and Molecules, Reactions, Forces, Energy and Heat, and Waves. Following the content lessons, we'll give you some practice questions.

ATOMS AND MOLECULES

Thankfully, you don't need to be an organic chemistry whiz to tackle the science section of the TASC test. However, you should have a general understanding of basic biological molecules and their purposes in life. In this section, we will cover the basics of organic chemistry and discuss the role of biological molecules.

Atoms

The book you are holding? It's made of atoms. Your pet cat, Moose? She's also made of atoms. **Atoms** are the fundamental units of all matter in the physical world, and a substance that is solely composed of a single type of atoms is known an **element**. In 530 B.C.E., Democritus proposed the idea of the atom, but it wasn't until the early 1800s that John Dalton established modern atomic theory. According to **atomic theory**, every element is composed of atoms, all atoms of an element are identical, and an atom's properties are dependent on its element. Like all matter, atoms cannot be created, destroyed, or split in a chemical reaction, an idea known as conservation of mass, which will be discussed later in this chapter. When atoms of different elements interact, compounds are formed; you should know, however, that the compounds have an identical number of atoms both prior and post reaction. For example, when two hydrogen atoms interact with one oxygen atom, water is formed, which is composed of two hydrogen atoms and one oxygen atom. All told there are 118 types of atoms, 92 of which are natural and 26 of which are man-made.

Recall that an atom's properties are dependent on its element. One characteristic that scientists were particularly interested in was the weight of an atom, or an atom's mass. Since atoms are super small and invisible, scientists are unable to simply plop them on the scale to find their weight to determine the number of atoms in a compound. Instead, a chemist named Amadeo Avogadro noticed that gases combined in distinct ratios when temperature and pressure was equal. In turn, the ratios of atomic masses could be determined by weighing the volume of the gases; e.g., if a liter of oxygen weighs 16 times more than a liter of hydrogen, the mass of an oxygen atom must be 16 times greater than the mass of a hydrogen atom. This observation led to **Avogadro's Law**, which states that equal volumes of any two gases at identical temperatures and pressures must hold an equal number of molecules. Based on Dalton's and Avogadro's work, the scientific unit known as a **mole** was established to determine the number of atoms in a substance. Because of its stability, availability, and adherence to Avogadro's law, scientists used carbon as the comparison factor when determining the atomic mass of each element. A single mole is equal to the number of particles found in 12 grams of carbon-12. Moles are particularly useful as they allow us to discuss the mass associated with even the tiniest particles. Indeed, the weight of an atom is expressed in **atomic mass units** (amus), which is equal to $\frac{1}{12}$ of a carbon-12 atom, and is approximately the sum of the protons and neutrons in the nucleus. Based on all of this science jazz, **Avogadro's number**, 6.022×10^{23}, was established to find the number of particles in a given substance. For example, if you have a mole of kittens, you have 6.022×10^{23} kittens; if you had a mole of feathers, you'd have 6.022×10^{23} feathers.

So, what does an atom look like? At the center of an atom is the nucleus, which is composed of **protons** and **neutrons**, and orbiting around the nucleus are **electrons**. What are protons, neutrons, and electrons? Keep reading to find out!

Structure of a Beryllium Atom

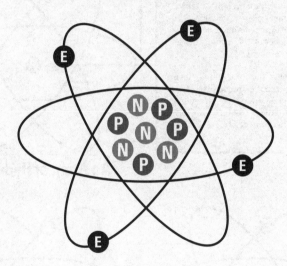

Protons, Neutrons, and Electrons

Every atom is composed of **subatomic particles** that are even tinier particles than atoms and, in turn, impossible to see with the naked eye. Like cells, atoms have a **nucleus**, which houses the protons and neutrons. **Neutrons** have no charge and are composed of even tinier particles called **quarks**, which can be classified as up, down, top, bottom, charm, and strange. Both an atom's mass and radioactivity are affected by the number of neutrons it has. Also located in the atom's nucleus are positively charged particles called **protons.** The majority of atoms have more than one proton, and there must be at least one neutron for every proton that exists; the exception to this rule is hydrogen, which has no neutrons and a single proton.

Negatively charged **electrons** are the smallest of the three subatomic particles that zoom around the nucleus in elliptical patterns called **orbitals**. Orbitals have associated energy levels, and are classified, in order from lowest to highest energy, as **p, s, d,** and **f orbitals.** Electrons found in the outermost energy level of an atom are known as **valence electrons.** In any given atom, the number of protons and electrons is the same; e.g., an atom of hydrogen has one proton and one electron, an atom of helium has two protons and two electrons, and an atom of beryllium has four protons and four electrons.

The **atomic number** of an atom is equal to the number of protons in an element's atom, and corresponds to an element's position on the periodic table. In order to find the **relative atomic mass** of an atom, you simply total the number of protons and neutrons. The more protons and neutrons present in an atom, the heavier the atom is. The relationship between protons, neutrons, electrons, and both atomic number and relative atomic mass are depicted below.

Atomic Attack!
Q: If calcium has 20 protons, what is its atomic number?

A 10
B 20
C 30
D 60

Turn the page for the answer.

Structure of a Beryllium Atom

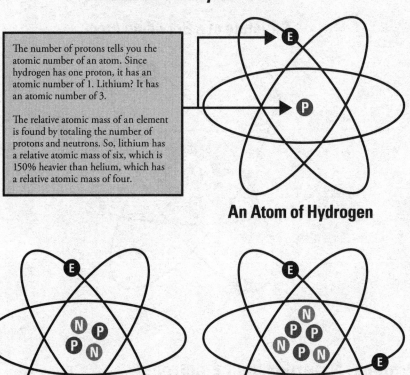

The number of protons tells you the atomic number of an atom. Since hydrogen has one proton, it has an atomic number of 1. Lithium? It has an atomic number of 3.

The relative atomic mass of an element is found by totaling the number of protons and neutrons. So, lithium has a relative atomic mass of six, which is 150% heavier than helium, which has a relative atomic mass of four.

An Atom of Hydrogen

An Atom of Helium

An Atom of Lithium

The Periodic Table

After all this information regarding atoms was discovered, scientists needed a way to organize everything. Accordingly, the **periodic table** was established as a way of listing elements according to their relative atomic structures. Elements are organized in rows according to their atomic number; these horizontal rows are called **periods** (which is where the name periodic table comes from!). The first period consists of only hydrogen and helium, whereas the sixth period has 32 elements.

In broad terms, the periodic table also groups elements as metals, non-metals, or metalloids, or elements that have characteristics of both metals and non-metals. The periodic table distinguishes elements even more by organizing them into one of 18 different **groups** based on the number of electrons an atom has in its outer shell. For example, the first column (with the exception of hydrogen) consists of reactive alkali metals that all have only one electron in their outer shells,, while the last column groups together the stable noble gases that have a full outer shell of electrons.

Each element is represented on the periodic table by a two-letter acronym; e.g., H represents helium, Na represents sodium, and Kr represents Krypton. The periods and groups shown on the periodic table help scientists predict how two or more elements will react to one another. Don't panic; you don't need to memorize the periodic table for the TASC test. Rather, you should just understand how the periodic table organizes our knowledge of the elements and is based on the structure of elements' atoms.

Visit **www.ptable.com** for an interactive, full-color periodic table.

PERIODIC TABLE OF THE ELEMENTS

1 IA																	18 VIIIA
1 **H** 1.008	2 IIA											13 IIIA	14 IVA	15 VA	16 VIA	17 VIIA	2 **He** 4.00
3 **Li** 6.94	4 **Be** 9.01											5 **B** 10.81	6 **C** 12.01	7 **N** 14.1	8 **O** 16.00	9 **F** 19.00	10 **Ne** 20.18
11 **Na** 22.99	12 **Mg** 24.30	3 IIIB	4 IVB	5 VB	6 VIB	7 VIIB	8	9 VIIIB	10	11 IB	12 IIB	13 **Al** 26.98	14 **Si** 28.09	15 **P** 30.97	16 **S** 32.06	17 **Cl** 35.45	18 **Ar** 39.95
19 **K** 39.10	20 **Ca** 40.08	21 **Sc** 44.96	22 **Ti** 47.90	23 **V** 50.94	24 **Cr** 52.00	25 **Mn** 59.94	26 **Fe** 55.85	27 **Co** 58.93	28 **Ni** 58.69	29 **Cu** 63.55	30 **Zn** 65.39	31 **Ga** 69.72	32 **Ge** 72.59	33 **As** 74.92	34 **Se** 78.96	35 **Br** 79.90	36 **Kr** 83.80
37 **Rb** 85.47	38 **Sr** 87.62	39 **Y** 88.91	40 **Zr** 91.22	41 **Nb** 92.91	42 **Mo** 95.94	43 **Tc** (98)	44 **Ru** 101.1	45 **Rh** 102.91	46 **Pd** 106.42	47 **Ag** 107.87	48 **Cd** 112.41	49 **In** 114.82	50 **Sn** 118.71	51 **Sb** 121.75	52 **Te** 127.60	53 **I** 126.91	54 **Xe** 131.29
55 **Cs** 132.91	56 **Ba** 137.33	57 ***La** 138.91	72 **Hf** 178.49	73 **Ta** 180.95	74 **W** 183.85	75 **Re** 186.21	76 **Os** 190.2	77 **Ir** 192.2	78 **Pt** 195.08	79 **Au** 196.97	80 **Hg** 200.59	81 **Tl** 204.38	82 **Pb** 207.2	83 **Bi** 208.98	84 **Po** (209)	85 **At** (210)	86 **Rn** (222)
87 **Fr** (223)	88 **Ra** 226.02	89 **†Ac** 227.03	104 **Rf** (261)	105 **Db** (262)	106 **Sg** (266)	107 **Bh** (264)	108 **Hs** (277)	109 **Mt** (268)	110 **Ds** (271)	111 **Rg** (272)							

	58 **Ce** 140.12	59 **Pr** 140.91	60 **Nd** 144.24	61 **Pm** (145)	62 **Sm** 150.4	63 **Eu** 151.97	64 **Gd** 157.25	65 **Tb** 158.93	66 **Dy** 162.50	67 **Ho** 164.93	68 **Er** 167.26	69 **Tm** 169.93	70 **Yb** 173.04	71 **Lu** 174.97
*Lanthanide Series														
†Actinide Series	90 **Th** 232.04	91 **Pa** 231.04	92 **U** 238.03	93 **X** (237)	94 **Pu** (244)	95 **Am** (243)	96 **Cm** (247)	97 **Bk** (247)	98 **Cf** (251)	99 **Es** (252)	100 **Fm** (257)	101 **Md** (258)	102 **No** (259)	103 **Lr** (262)

Molecules

Wow! Up until this point, we've focused on the atom, or the building blocks of matter. But what happens when two atoms decide to join together? Well, whenever two or more atoms connect, **molecules** are formed. A molecule of hydrogen, for example, consists of two hydrogen atoms that are bonded together.

Compounds are formed when atoms of different elements bond; e.g., water consists of two hydrogen atoms and one oxygen atom. Unlike atoms, there are countless types of molecules in this world. Think about it; how many different ways could you combine the elements of the periodic table? Many. In fact, the majority of Earth's substances are compounds, not elements.

Types of Bonds

Thus far, we've established that atoms combine to form molecules, but we have yet to discuss the bonding process. **Chemical bonding** takes place when one atom's outermost electrons interact with those of a different atom. These chemical reactions cause atoms to gain, share, or lose electrons in order to fill the outermost electron shell. There are two types of bonds that you should be familiar with for the TASC test: ionic bonds and covalent bonds.

Remember how we said that chemical reactions cause electrons to move around? Well, when atoms of metal elements lose electrons, they create positively charged **ions**. An **ionic compound** is a substance that consists of ions joined by **ionic bonds**, which are formed when an electron is transferred from the atom of one element to the atom of another element. The transfer of an electron leaves one atom with a positive charge and the other atom with a negative charge, causing them to attract and bond together.

Conversely, **covalent bonds** are formed when atoms share electrons in order to fill their outermost electron shells. Consider a fluoride atom that has seven valence electrons—two electrons short of having a full outer shell. By sharing a pair of electrons, two fluoride atoms would be able to have a full outer shell of electrons. Not only can covalent bonds occur between atoms of different elements, but atoms are also able to share more than one set of electrons. It's totally possible for atoms to form double and triple covalent bonds!

$$\mathbf{:\overset{\cdot\cdot}{\underset{\cdot\cdot}{F}}\cdot \ + \ \cdot\overset{\cdot\cdot}{\underset{\cdot\cdot}{F}}: \ = \ :\overset{\cdot\cdot}{\underset{\cdot\cdot}{F}}:\overset{\cdot\cdot}{\underset{\cdot\cdot}{F}}:}$$

REACTIONS

Reactions are happening in the world around you all the time. A **reaction** is simply an object's response to stimuli that leads to physical or chemical changes. A **physical change** may alter the form and properties of an object, but will not alter the object's chemical composition. Consider water. When water is placed in an environment less than 32° F, water freezes and turns to ice; the chemical composition of water, H_2O, remains stable throughout this physical change. If you take an ice cube and place it outside in the hot sun, the ice will melt and revert to liquid water. Again, a physical change may alter the form of a substance, but not its chemical composition.

Now, some reactions are far more interesting to observe than watching ice melt. A science project that most people have seen involves combining vinegar and baking soda. While both vinegar and baking soda individually are pretty boring to watch, combining the two substances initiates a **chemical reaction**, which occurs when **bonds** between atoms are broken to form new **molecules**, that visually results in a bubbling volcano of amazingness. This experiment also results in a **chemical change**, which occurs when the molecules of one or more substances react and transform into new substances with different properties. For example, when you combine vinegar and baking soda, you end up with sodium acetate, water, and carbon dioxide.

Chemical Equations

Sadly, scientists don't use pictures to depict chemical reactions. Instead, **chemical equations** are used to show the molecules that exist prior to and after a chemical reaction. While you won't need to be an organic chemistry wizard to ace the TASC test, you should understand a few basic concepts about chemical equations. First, the original substances are known as **reactants**, while the resulting substances are known as **products**. In the previous scenario, the reactants are vinegar and baking soda, and the products are sodium acetate, water, and carbon dioxide.

In chemical equations, symbols are used to represent molecules of an element. You don't need to memorize the every element on the periodic table, but you should know the symbols for a few elements. C represents carbon, H represents hydrogen, O represents oxygen, and Na represents sodium; you should probably also know that water is represented as H_2O. A coefficient in front of the molecule, such as $2H_2O$, indicates that there are two molecules; in this case, there are two water molecules. The subscript associated with a letter, the small 2 in H_2O, indicates the number of atoms; in this case, there are two hydrogen atoms in water.

Take a look at the chemical equation that represents the reaction between vinegar and baking soda.

$$CH_3COOH + NaHCO_3 \rightarrow NaC_2H3O_2 + H_2O + CO_2$$
Vinegar + Baking Soda → Sodium Acetate + Water + Carbon Dioxide

According to the equation above, a molecule of baking soda consists of one sodium atom, one hydrogen atom, one carbon atom, and three oxygen atoms.

Perhaps most importantly, chemical equations *must* be balanced. So, what does that mean? If you look at our chemical equation, you will note that there is one sodium atom on each side of the equation. In fact, there are equal amounts of each atom on both sides of the equation! Since matter is never destroyed in a chemical reaction, there must be an equal number of atoms on each side of a chemical equation.

Chemical Reactions
Chemical reactions can be classified as combinations, in which two or more substances form a single product, *decompositions*, in which one substance forms two or more products, displacements, in which an element reacts with a compound to form a new compound and single element, and exchanges, in which compounds switch partners.

Conservation of Mass and Energy

You've no doubt heard someone say that matter can neither be created nor destroyed; this is the **law of conservation of mass**. While physical changes may alter the way matter looks, and chemical reactions alter the molecular makeup of substances, neither change creates or destroys atoms. Regardless of the change, the absolute mass of the matter remains the same.

The concept of conservation of mass is exemplified in chemical equations. Recall that chemical equations must be balanced. Because matter cannot simply disappear, every atom present in the reactants must be present in the products. The law of conservation of mass is exemplified in our vinegar and baking soda reaction, in which there are an equal number of atoms both before and after the reaction.

The law of conservation of energy is often taught in conjunction with the law of conservation of mass. According to the **law of conservation of energy**, energy can neither be created nor destroyed in a closed system; rather, energy may change form or be transferred between objects. For example, when you use a toaster you transform electrical energy into heat energy. When you eat the toast, you are using kinetic energy to eat the toast that, in turn, transforms into chemical energy to fuel your body. In short, energy may change its state, but it cannot simply be made or unmade.

Radioactivity

As you know, atoms have a nucleus, composed of protons and neutrons, and electrons that orbit around it. Recall that an element's atom has equal numbers of protons and electrons, and it's atomic mass is based on the number of protons and neutrons. Sometimes, however, an atom can have an equal number of protons and electrons, but a different number of neutrons; these atoms are called **isotopes**. Neutrons have mass, but carry no electrical charge, so the mass of the element is changed, while chemistry of an element remains unchanged.

Every element has isotopes and, sometimes, these isotopes are unstable because of the number of neutrons in the nucleus. Unstable isotopes are known as **radioactive isotopes**, as they emit energy in the form of **radiation** as the nucleus decomposes. There are three primary types of radiation you should know.

- **Alpha**—When there is an excess number of protons in a nucleus, the element will emit radiation in the form of positively charged alpha particles. Alpha particles do not travel far, but alpha radiation is extremely harmful when inside the human body.
- **Beta**—When there is an excess number of neutrons in a nucleus, the element will emit radiation in the form of negatively charged beta particles. Beta particles can travel a bit farther than alpha particles, but like alpha particles, beta particles are harmful when in the human body.

- **Gamma**—When there is an excess amount of energy in the nucleus, the element emits gamma particles that have no overall charge. Gamma particles can travel much farther and are similar to X-rays.

So, how do we determine radioactive strength? Radioactivity is measured in **curies**, which indicates the number of atoms that spontaneously decay each second. This **radioactive decay** occurs at a predictable and constant rate known as a **half-life**. An isotope's half-life is the average time it takes for half the atoms to decay. For example, carbon-14, the isotope used in **carbon dating** to determine the age of fossils, has a half-life of 5,730 years. So, if you had a sample of carbon-14 with 100 atoms, you could expect 50 of those atoms to decay over 5,730 years. After 11,460 years, you could expect 25 of the 50 remaining atoms to decay, leaving you with 25 of the original 100 carbon-14 atoms.

Now, radiation can be both good and bad. For example, when the nuclear meltdown in Fukushima, Japan occurred, the volatile isotope uranium-238 emitted radiation capable of causing mutations and extreme bodily harm. However, radiation is also used in the medical field to take X-rays and kill cancer cells. Crazy, right? Don't get overwhelmed; just remember the basics and you'll be fine on the TASC test!

FORCES

Have you ever been in a car, and the car next to you began to go forward, but you felt as if you were moving *backwards*? Interestingly, in relation to the car next to you, you *were* moving backwards. This is because **motion** is a change in an object's position relative to time and a distinct reference point. Motion is a part of all matter in the universe and is affected by **forces**, which are push or pull factors that change an object's speed or direction. The amount of force an object has can be found with the following equation: *force = mass × acceleration*.

Speed and Momentum

Speed refers to how fast an object moves. When an object travels equal distances in equal amounts of time the object is traveling at a **constant speed**. In order to calculate the speed of an object, you will use the following equation: $speed = \dfrac{distance}{time}$. Related to speed is the concept of **momentum**, which can be thought of as the amount of motion an object has or the power behind an object. Consider a car and a truck that are traveling at the same speed and in the same direction. If the vehicles were asked to stop moving, it would be harder to stop the truck because it has greater momentum than the car. Indeed, heavier objects have more momentum than lighter objects. An object's momentum is dependent upon its mass and **velocity**, which refers to both the direction and speed of an object. Momentum can be calculated using the following equation: *momentum = mass × velocity.* If I say the word "accelerate," you may think of pushing the gas pedal down in a car to increase the speed. In physics, the meaning of **acceleration** is any change in velocity—i.e., either an increase or decrease in speed or a change in direction.

Work and Machines

When we think of work, we think of something we have to do and, usually, it requires us to expend some effort. If you have to mow the lawn, you use force to push the lawnmower forward across the grass—you are doing work. **Work**, therefore, occurs when a force moves an object in the direction of the force. Work is calculated using the following equation: *work = force × distance.* As you are probably aware, not all work is equal. After all, it would take a team of five people less time to mow a lawn than if you had to mow the same lawn by yourself. **Power** is the rate at which a certain amount of work is accomplished, and is calculated with the following equation: $power = \dfrac{work}{time}$. Power is measured in watts. One watt is the amount of power it takes to complete one joule of work in one second.

Compound Machines
When combined together, simple machines form compound machines. Take a look around you, and you will notice a bunch of compound machines. For example, scissors combine both wedges and levers to create a compound machine.

With all this work, wouldn't it be nice to catch a break? Thankfully, with the advent of machines, work *is* much easier than it was in the past. **Machines** are implements that make work easier by redirecting or multiplying forces. Just like work, not all machines are created equal. Machines that can complete work faster are said to have a **mechanical advantage**. The mechanical advantage of a simple machine is a ratio between the force put into the machine and the force put out by the machine.

There are *six* **simple machines** (machines that change the direction or magnitude of a force) that you should know for the TASC test. The **inclined plane** category of simple machines includes tools that both magnify and redirect force. An inclined plane can be thought of as a ramp, which requires less force to move an object than would be necessary with direct vertical movement. Historians often discuss the use of inclined planes in relation to the ancient pyramids in Egypt. Many researchers hypothesize that the Egyptians used a series of inclined planes to transport the giant stones that make up each pyramid. **Wedges** are inclined planes that redirect downward force into two forces pointing outward. **Screws** are spiral inclined planes that redirect a linear force into a rotational one, thus requiring less work. Levers and pulleys, which comprise the second category of simple machines, are tools in which the object and the force move in opposite directions. A **lever** consists of a long object, often a bar, and a **fulcrum**, or pivot point. When force is applied to one end of the bar, it pivots at the fulcrum, multiplying the force at the opposite end of the bar. There are three types of levers: first-class levers, such as a seesaw; second-class levers, such as a wheelbarrow; and third-class levers, exemplified by the act of hammering in a nail. Closely related to the lever is the **pulley**, which can be created by looping rope around two or more wheels to alter the direction of force, thus providing a mechanical advantage. The last simple machine is the **wheel and axle**, which consists of a wheel or lever connected to a shaft. When a small input of force is applied to the wheel, and the wheel is turned, the shaft turns as well, but with a larger, resulting output of force. Consider the steering wheel of a car; minor adjustments to the steering wheel result in much larger changes to the overall movement of the car.

Gravity

Everybody talks about gravity, but it is quite complex and rarely defined. For the TASC test, you should know that **gravity** is a force that attracts two objects toward each other. Gravity affects all matter, and the strength of the gravitational pull depends on both the mass of each object and the distance between them. Earth's gravitational force keeps the moon orbiting around it, just as the sun's gravitational pull keeps Earth and the other planets orbiting around it. Earth's gravitational force also keeps your feet anchored firmly to the ground.

You can't discuss gravity without mentioning both mass and weight. **Mass** is the absolute matter of an object; the mass of an object never changes, regardless of the object's location. Conversely, the **weight** of an object is the force of gravity on an object; the weight of an object changes according to the gravitational pull.

Newton's Laws

In the late 1600s, a scientist named Sir Isaac Newton developed three laws of motion that describe the relationships between objects, forces, and motion.

- **The First Law**—This law states that an object will remain at rest or continue moving at the same speed and in the same direction forever, unless some outside force intervenes. This is also called the law of **inertia**, which is an object's resistance to a change in motion. According to Newton, if you threw a ball, it would move forever, except that the forces of gravity and air resistance interfere.
- **The Second Law**—This law discusses how external forces affect the velocity of an object. Newton states that when an object accelerates because another force propels it, it will accelerate in proportion to that force. In other words, that ball will be propelled only as hard as you throw it in the first place.
- **The Third Law**—The third law states that for every action, there is an equal but opposite reaction. This law can be exemplified by air escaping from a balloon. As the air rushes out of the bottom of a balloon, the balloon is forced upwards.

Newton's Nuggets
Q: Which of Newton's laws states that the relationship between an object's mass (m), its acceleration (a), and the applied force (F) is $F = ma$?

A First
B Second
C Third

Turn the page for the answer.

Newton's Nuggets
A: Newton's second law
discusses how external
forces affect the velocity
of an object. In order to
calculate how acceleration
changes when different
forces are applied, use the
formula $F = ma$.

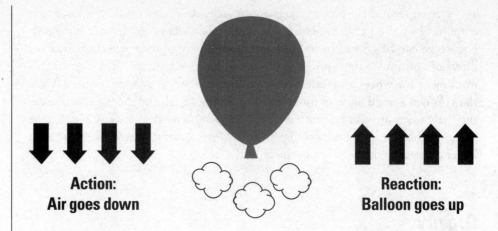

Action:
Air goes down

Reaction:
Balloon goes up

Magnetism and Electromagnetism

Remember those alphabet letters that magically stuck to the fridge but, no matter how hard you tried, would not stick to each other? Those letters were **magnets**, objects that have strong **magnetic fields** that **attract** or **repel** other objects. Magnets have both a **north pole** and a **south pole**, and like poles repel each other, while unlike poles attract one another. Fun fact: The earth acts like a huge magnet, having both north and south poles; this is why magnetic compasses allow us to navigate across the world.

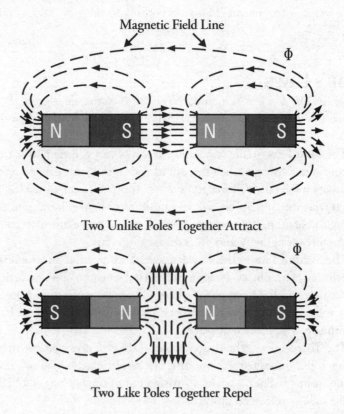

Two Unlike Poles Together Attract

Two Like Poles Together Repel

While all matter experiences **magnetism**, the force caused at a distance by a magnetic field, certain materials are more magnetic than others. For example, **permanent magnets** are made from highly magnetic materials, such as iron, and experience **ferromagnetism**, which is the only type of magnetism that humans can feel. Common permanent magnets are refrigerator magnets, bar magnets, and horseshoe magnets. Through the process of **magnetization**, you can create magnets from magnetic material; e.g., if you take a magnet and run it over an unmagnetized iron nail a few times, the nail will become magnetic.

Temporary magnets that function through the use of electricity are known as **electromagnets**. An electromagnet's strength is dependent on both the size of the electric current and the number of times the wire is coiled. Consider our iron nail. If you coiled wire around it and passed electricity through the wire to the nail, the nail would become a magnet. When the current is halted, the magnetism of the nail would disappear. A doorbell is a common example of an electromagnet; when you press the button an electrical current causes a magnet to temporarily hit a chime.

Magnet Mayhem
A permanent magnet is a material that continually keeps its magnetic properties, regardless of location. Horseshoe, bar, and refrigerator magnets are all examples of permanent magnets.

ENERGY AND HEAT

Kinetic and Potential Energy

No doubt you've been studying for the TASC test and thought to yourself, "I don't have the energy to study anymore." According to physics, you might be right. An object possesses **energy** if it has the ability to do work. So, if you don't have the energy to study, you don't have the ability to do work. Makes sense, right? All energy is either potential or kinetic. While **potential energy** cannot be observed, it is the amount of energy an object has due to its position or shape, which can be measured in terms of the amount of work an object *could* perform. Conversely, **kinetic energy** is directly related to motion, and can be thought of as the energy an object possesses because of its motion. Potential energy can be classified even further. **Gravitational potential energy** is energy that an object has due to its vertical or horizontal position in a gravitational field. The amount of gravitational potential energy an object has is dependent upon the mass of an object and its height in the environment. For example, if you were to hold a bowling ball a few inches from the ground, it would have less gravitational potential energy than would a bowling ball held a few feet from the ground. The second type of potential energy is **elastic potential energy**, which is the energy stored in elastic objects resulting from stretching and compressing. Elastic potential energy is based on both the mass and speed of an object. Consider the following. Imagine that you put a rock in a slingshot and pull back, increasing the tension of the slingshot. The further back you pull the slingshot, the more elastic potential energy the object acquires. When you release the slingshot, the elastic potential energy is converted into kinetic energy. An object's **mechanical energy** is the sum total of the object's gravitational potential energy, elastic potential energy, and kinetic energy. It is important to remember that energy can be transformed from one type to another. As already mentioned, an important physics principle is the **law of conservation of energy**, which states that energy cannot be created or destroyed. More information on the law of conservation of energy can be found in the Reactions section of this chapter.

Heat Energy

While an object can have mechanical energy, there are many other types of energy. Indeed, energy can come in many forms, such as light, sound, and electricity, but one important form of energy is heat. **Heat** is the energy transfer from the particles of one object to another because of the objects' different temperatures. It is important to note that energy will always move from a hotter object to a cooler object. An **exothermic reaction** occurs when heat is generated in a system and released to its surroundings, while an **endothermic reaction** is one that absorbs heat from its surroundings. Think about the last time you burned your tongue on a hot drink. You felt the burn as the energy transferred from the hotter liquid to your cooler mouth; this was an endothermic reaction, as your mouth absorbed the energy. The scale for measuring heat is **temperature**, or the kinetic energy of the molecules in an object, and is measured using either the **Celsius** or **Fahrenheit** scales. You should know that water freezes at 0° Celsius (32° Fahrenheit) and boils at 100° Celsius (212° Fahrenheit). Interestingly, the particles can stop moving altogether if the temperature is low enough—this point is referred to as **absolute zero** and is the basis of a third scale of measurement for temperature, the **Kelvin** scale. The amount of energy required to raise the temperature of 1kg (kilogram) of a substance by 1° C is referred to as **specific heat**.

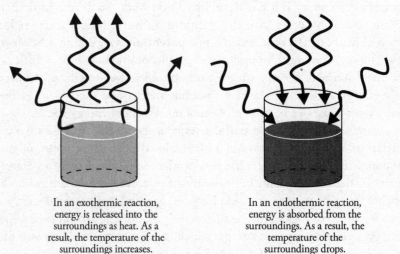

In an exothermic reaction, energy is released into the surroundings as heat. As a result, the temperature of the surroundings increases.

In an endothermic reaction, energy is absorbed from the surroundings. As a result, the temperature of the surroundings drops.

Conduction on a Smaller Scale

So, what happens during conduction? Well, as a molecule is heated, it begins to move rapidly, passing some of its heat energy to surrounding molecules. As the molecule continues to shake, heat is passed between molecules until evenly distributed.

Heat can also move through an object via either convection or conduction. **Convection** is a process that occurs in liquids and gasses when heated molecules carrying energy rise before eventually cooling and sinking, thus producing a continuous cycle of heat transfer; this cyclic process is known as a **convection**

current. Heat can also be transferred through **conduction**. Conduction is a process of heat energy transfer that occurs when particles are in direct contact and have different temperatures.

Great! You have now covered the material regarding kinetic, potential, and heat energy necessary to tackle those pesky TASC questions.

WAVES

Generally, when we hear the word *wave*, we either think of the ocean's waves on the beach or of moving our hand. You don't have to go to the beach to be surrounded by waves—they surround us all the time. We use microwaves to cook our food, light waves help us see, and sound waves cause vibrations in our eardrums that allow us to hear. In physics, and for the science portion of the TASC test, you should know that a **wave** is a disturbance that carries energy from one point to another through a **medium** or space. A medium is the matter that carries a wave between locations. As noted in the definition of wave, a wave is a disturbance. Usually, the disturbance is some sort of vibration that provides energy for the wave; for example, a plucked guitar string vibrates to cause sound waves and friction between tectonic plates can cause shock waves. It is important to remember that waves transfer energy, *not* matter.

For the TASC test, you should know that all waves can be categorized as either **electromagnetic** or **mechanical**. Electromagnetic waves, such as light, radio, and microwaves, can travel through empty space and do not require a medium to transfer energy. Conversely, mechanical waves, such as sound and water waves, require a medium to transfer their energy.

Mechanical waves can be further categorized based on the direction of the medium's particle motion in relation to the direction of the wave's motion. A **transverse wave** is one in which particle motion is perpendicular to the wave motion. As shown in Figure A, the direction of energy travel is at a right angle to the direction of the disturbance, or wave. Conversely, a **longitudinal wave** is a mechanical wave in which particle motion moves in the same direction as the wave motion. In a longitudinal wave, particles alternate between **compressions**, when particles are pushed together, and **rarefactions**, when particles are pulled apart.

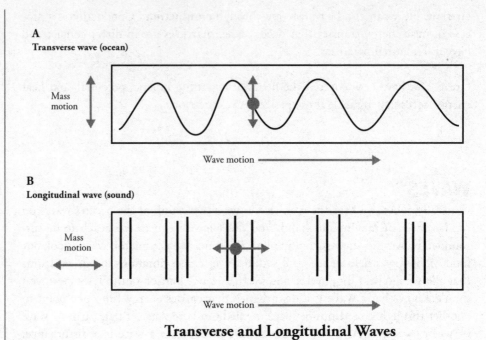

A
Transverse wave (ocean)

Mass motion

Wave motion

B
Longitudinal wave (sound)

Mass motion

Wave motion

Transverse and Longitudinal Waves

In a wave, the highest point is known as the **crest** and the lowest point is called the **trough**. The height of a wave, which is referred to as **amplitude**, is found by halving the vertical distance between the crest and the trough. As you notice in Figure A, a wave cycles, with each crest followed by a trough, when traveling from the origin to the final destination. A single **wavelength** is equal to the distance between two consecutive crests or troughs. The number of times a wave cycles in one second is referred to as **frequency**. Frequency is measured in **hertz**, or cycles per second. Related to frequency is the **period** of the wave, which is the time it takes for a single wave cycle, or the time between two consecutive crests of the wave. Waves that have a short period will have a high frequency, while waves that have a longer period will have a lower frequency.

Radiation

Radiation Exposure
So, how are people exposed to radiation in the United States? Well, according to the Environmental Protection Agency, Radon accounts for 55% of all radiation exposure, while natural sources account for another 26%. Medical X-rays? They only account for 11% of all radiation exposure.

Recall that, unlike mechanical waves, electromagnetic waves do not require a medium and travel through space. Electromagnetic waves are induced by disturbances, such as changes in magnetic and electric fields. Like transverse waves, charged particles move in a perpendicular direction to the direction of the wave's movement. The energy transferred through electromagnetic waves is referred to as **radiant energy**, or **radiation**.

The following electromagnetic waves are ordered from lowest to highest frequency: radio waves, microwaves, infrared waves, visible light, ultraviolet (UV) light, X-rays, and Gamma rays. Radio, micro, infrared rays, and visible light emit **nonionizing radiation**, due to their ability to ionize atoms and break chemical bonds, and are considered relatively harmless. After all, you are exposed to radio waves when you watch television, microwaves when you make popcorn, infrared light when you change the channel using a remote control, and visible light when you walk outside.

Conversely, **UV light**, **X-rays**, and **Gamma rays** emit **ionizing radiation** and can be considered harmful. You might be thinking, "Hey. Wait. I hear about the dangers of UV light all the time." Thankfully, the earth's atmosphere filters out the majority of the harmful rays associated with electromagnetic waves such as ultraviolet light. However, we are not fully protected—you can thank the ionizing, electromagnetic radiation associated with UV light for that sunburn you got at the beach last year. X-rays are commonly used for medical exams, during which special precautions are taken to protect reproductive organs from harmful ionizing radiation. The true danger of ionizing radiation can be seen in cancer treatments like radiation therapy, which uses X-rays and Gamma rays to kill cancer cells. While effective at killing cancer cells, radiation treatment can also damage and kill normal, healthy cells. Thus, treatment sessions are generally short and spread out over time.

Below is a table of the different types of waves and the way in which their energy is harnessed in everyday life. Don't panic—you don't need to memorize this information for the TASC test. Rather, just have a general idea of the way wave radiation is used.

Wave Type	Wavelength Size	Application
Radio Waves	Greater than 30 cm	Aircraft Navigation, TV, AM/FM Radio
Microwaves	30 cm–1 mm	Microwave Ovens, Mobile Phones
Infrared Waves	1mm–700 nm	Remote Controls, Toasters, Night Vision
Visible Light	700 nm–400 nm	Physical Therapy, Light Bulbs, Photography
Ultraviolet Light	400 nm–60 nm	Sanitation, Air Purification, Forgery Detection
X-Rays	60 nm–nm	Medical Examination, Cancer Treatment
Gamma Rays	0.1 nm–nm	Cancer Treatment, Food Irradiation

Light as a Wave

Throughout our discussion so far, we've been talking about light, but have yet to define it. **Light** is the visible form of electromagnetic radiation. People always talk about **the speed of light**, but few people know that light travels roughly 186,000 miles per second. (Fun fact: It takes approximately eight minutes for light to travel from the sun to the earth.) Light also travels in a perfectly straight line—until it encounters a new medium. For the TASC test, you should know that light is capable of diffraction, reflection, and refraction when it behaves like a wave.

Diffraction is a wave-like behavior of light that occurs when light waves bend around an obstacle while traveling through a medium. Diffraction can occur when light waves are forced to travel through a narrow opening or encounter an object. If you were to take a flashlight and point it against a wall, you will notice that the light spreads out from the main point of light; the light waves are hitting the wall and diffracting at different angles on your wall.

Reflection is a wave-like behavior of light that occurs when light waves encounter a new medium and bounce off the surface. The amount of light that is reflected, absorbed, or transmitted is dependent upon the reflectivity of the medium. Furthermore, the **angle of reflection** will equal the **angle of incidence** of the incoming light wave. What does that even mean?! Take a look at the diagram below to see a visual depiction. There are two main types of reflection you should understand. **Spectacular reflection** occurs when the rays of light reflect off a medium in a single direction; these reflections take place on smooth surfaces. Conversely, **diffuse reflection** occurs when the rays of light reflect off a medium in multiple directions; these reflections take place on rough surfaces.

Refraction is a wave-like behavior of light that occurs when light waves travel from one medium to another and change directions. You can test this yourself if you take your finger and stick it in a clear glass of water; your finger will look like it is disconnected and bent. Refraction in action! The **index of refraction** is used to measure the behavior of light in different mediums.

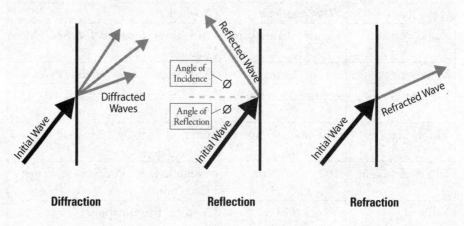

Doppler Effect

Have you ever noticed how the sound of a siren changes from a high to low pitch as it passes you? This is an example of the Doppler Effect, which is the apparent upward shift in frequency for observers towards whom the source is advancing and an apparent downward shift in frequency for observers from whom the source is withdrawing. Note, however, that this is a *perceived* effect, not an actual change in frequency.

Light as a Particle

You're now an expert on how light behaves like a wave, so let's delve into this particle business. You don't need to know everything in the world about the behavior of light as a particle (which is good, because this area of science is not well understood and quite contentious).

All light is composed of tiny particles of light called **photons**, which are particles of electromagnetic energy. Photons are **elementary particles**, or particles that are not composed of smaller particles, that are the basic unit of light. Photons are stable particles that have zero mass, no electric charge, and travel at the speed of light in empty space. Up until the late 1800s, scientists believed that light was composed of waves. End of story. Then, in 1900, a scientist named Max Planck came along and said something along the lines of, "Hey, guys. Photons carry energy and interact with matter. That's particle-like behavior." So, after Planck realized that photons carry energy, he did some research regarding the amount of energy that each light particle carries. And, thus, **Planck's constant**, a conversion factor between frequency and energy, was created.

According to the wave-theory of light, the intensity of the light should be proportional to the energy carried by the ejected electrons. However, Planck's research indicated that the wave-theory of light wasn't sufficient. After experimenting a while, Einstein found that when matter absorbs the energy of a photon, the matter can emit electrons, a particle-like behavior of photons known as the **photoelectric effect.** The photoelectric effect illustrates the idea that increasing the intensity of the light increases the number of ejected electrons, but does not affect their maximum kinetic energies. Based on the photoelectric effect, Einstein established that the relationship between a photon's energy and frequency is described by the equation $E = hv$, where E is energy, v is frequency (color of the light), and h is Planck's constant. In short, the photoelectric effect shows that the energy of the emitted electrons was independent of the intensity of the light, a characteristic of particles, not waves. For example, regardless of intensity, red light will not result in the ejection of electrons, green light will eject low-energy electrons, and blue light will emit high-energy electrons. It is because of the photoelectric effect that light is described as both a wave and a particle…and the reason quantum physics was born! Now you know everything about light that is needed to ace that portion of the TASC test!

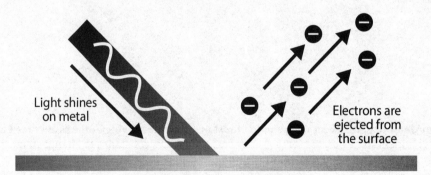

The Photoelectric Effect

Physical Science Drill

Now try some practice questions. To check your answers, register your book at **PrincetonReview.com/cracking** and download the Chapter Drill Answers and Explanations supplement.

1. Atoms are the basic building blocks of all matter. A substance that is composed of at least two different types of atoms is called a(n)

    A element

    B cation

    C compound

    D molecule

2. Atoms are composed of subatomic particles called protons, neutrons, and electrons. For example, an atom of hydrogen has one proton and one neutron, while an atom of helium has two protons, two neutrons, and two electrons. The number of protons in an element's atom corresponds to the atom's

    A relative atomic mass

    B atomic number

    C conductivity

    D atomic mass

3. Chemical bonding occurs between atoms when the outermost electrons of atoms interact. The following shows how two chlorine atoms share electrons to form a(n)

    $$:\ddot{\underset{..}{C}}l. + .\ddot{\underset{..}{C}}l: = :\ddot{\underset{..}{C}}l:\ddot{\underset{..}{C}}l:$$

    A covalent bond

    B metallic bond

    C ionic bond

    D basic bond

4. Newton's first law of motion states that an object will remain at rest or continue moving at the same speed and in the same direction forever, unless some outside force intervenes. An object's resistance to change in motion is known as

    A momentum

    B force

    C inertia

    D velocity

5. After eating a large breakfast, which provides his body with chemical energy, Norman goes outside to play catch with Joey. As Norman throws the ball towards Joey, the potential energy in the ball is transformed into

A   mechanical energy

B   kinetic energy

C   nonmechanical energy

D   heat energy

6. The law of conservation of energy states that

A   energy can be created, but it can never be destroyed

B   an object's kinetic energy is dependent on its mass and speed

C   matter can be created or destroyed

D   energy cannot be created or destroyed

7. A temporary magnet uses electricity to function. When electricity is passed through a current to a magnetic material, it becomes magnetized; when the electricity is turned off, the material demagnetizes. All of the following items use temporary magnets <u>except</u>

A   telephone

B   doorbell

C   refrigerator magnet

D   electrical motor

8. Two magnets are shown below.

According to the rules of magnetism, the two southern poles of these magnets will

A   repel each other

B   remain neutral

C   attract each other

D   demagnetize each other

9. Waves are disturbances that carry energy through a medium. The following shows two transverse waves, which are characterized by having particle motion that is perpendicular to the wave motion. As shown, the frequency of Wave A is greater than that of Wave B.

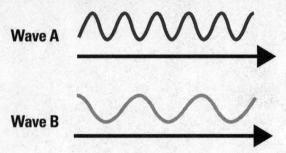

Wave A

Wave B

Which of the following is true regarding Waves A and B?

A The wavelength of Wave A is greater than that of Wave B.

B The wavelengths of Wave A and Wave B are equal.

C Nothing can be determined regarding the wavelengths of Waves A and B.

D The wavelength of Wave B is greater than that of Wave A.

10. How are a wave's frequency and wavelength related?

A inversely

B directly

C unrelated

D constant

Part VII
Practice Test

DIRECTIONS FOR THE PRACTICE TESTS

Now it's time to use the skills and knowledge you've cultivated. The questions in both the in-book and online practice tests are modeled closely on actual TASC test questions in terms of what content they cover, their levels of difficulty, and the formats you should expect to encounter (with the exception of the constructed-response and technology-enhanced questions). If you prefer NOT to write directly in this book, we have provided **two custom answer sheets**, one for each practice test, which you may download and print out when you register your book online.

Before you begin, make sure to have the following items on hand:

- Pencils with erasers

- A notepad for scratch paper—and for writing your responses to the Essay prompts.

- A Texas Instruments T1-30XS calculator, or any of the alternate scientific calculators mentioned at **TASCtest.com/tasc-test-calculators-for-test-takers.html**.

- The official Mathematics Formula Reference Sheet. You can download a PDF of it at **TASCtest.com/assets/mathrefsheet.pdf**.

- The official calculator reference sheet, which you can download here: **TASCtest.com/tasc-test-calculators-for-test-takers.html.**

- A clock or watch to help you keep track of time

To give yourself the closest possible experience of the actual testing conditions, we recommend taking each section of the test in one sitting. You may take a short break after each section and between the calculator and no-calculator parts of the Mathematics section.

After you've finished, check your answers and read through the explanations.

We also recommend downloading our scoring tables for both tests (available when you register your book). These tables won't provide exact TASC test scores, but they will give you an idea of your likelihood of passing the real TASC test based on the number of questions you answer correctly.

Good luck!

Chapter 30
Practice Test 1

You have 50 minutes to complete the Calculator Session of the Mathematics test.

 Calculator Session

1. The income a person makes in a week is given by $f(x) = \frac{1}{6}x + 300$ for $x > 0$, where x represents the total amount in sales an employee makes that week. If someone working there makes sales of \$3,000 the first week, \$900 the second week, and \$2,700 the third week, how much total would he make over the three-week span?

   A \$450

   B \$750

   C \$800

   D \$2,000

2. What is the ratio of the fifth term to the ninth term of a geometric sequence starting with 2 and with a common ratio of 4?

   A 1:4

   B 1:16

   C 1:64

   D 1:256

3. The function for a given parabola can be written as $f(x) = x^2 - 8x - 26$. Which of the following functions would produce the same parabola when graphed?

   A $f(x) = (x - 4)^2 + 10$

   B $f(x) = (x - 4)^2 - 42$

   C $f(x) = (x + 4)^2 + 10$

   D $f(x) = (x + 4)^2 + 42$

4. John deposits \$1,000 into a bank account and saves \$50 per month. Sam deposits \$250 into an account and saves \$125 per month. After how many months will Sam have more money in his account than John, assuming no interest is accrued and the monthly deposits are the only transactions made?

GO ▶

5. The likelihood a person is a fan of a given football team is inversely related to the distance the person lives from the team's stadium. If there is a 22% probability a person likes a team that plays 330 miles from the person's home, what is the approximate likelihood a person is a fan of a team that is located 781 miles away?

    A   6.7 %

    B   9.3%

    C   22%

    D   52.07%

6. Simplify the following:

    $(a - 3)^2 \le (a + 3)^2 + 16$?

    A $a \le \dfrac{-4}{3}$

    B $a \le \dfrac{-3}{4}$

    C $a \ge \dfrac{-3}{4}$

    D $a \ge \dfrac{-4}{3}$

7. An Italian kitchen receives 5,000 tomatoes per week from its supplier. The following chart shows the breakdown of what percent of the tomatoes are used for each recipe.

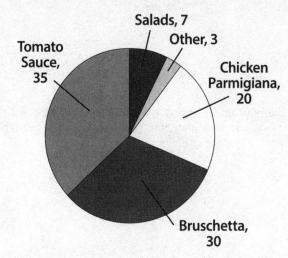

Salads, 7
Other, 3
Tomato Sauce, 35
Chicken Parmigiana, 20
Bruschetta, 30

Based on this pie chart, how many of the 5,000 tomatoes are <u>not</u> used in bruschetta or salads?

8. Given a block with a density of 10.5 g/cm³, what is the mass of the block, in kg, if it measures 15 cm by 20 cm by 10 cm?

A 3

B 31.5

C 3,000

D 31,500

GO ▶

9. Density of an object is given by the quotient of its mass and volume. If the density of a bowling ball is 1.61 g/cm³ and it has a radius of 9.8 cm, what is its mass in kg?

A 1.52 kg

B 3.94 kg

C 6.34 kg

D 15.78 kg

10. A frozen yogurt shop has 8 available flavors, 10 dry toppings such as sprinkles, and 5 "wet" toppings such as hot fudge. If a person chooses any two distinct flavors for a sundae, how many total sundaes would be available that have two flavors, one wet topping, and one dry topping?

A 1,400

B 2,800

C 4,200

D 8,400

11. What is the sum of the roots of the equation $6x^2 - 7x - 20$?

A $-\dfrac{10}{3}$

B $-\dfrac{4}{3}$

C $\dfrac{7}{6}$

D $\dfrac{5}{2}$

12. To calculate kinetic energy (KE), the equation $KE = \dfrac{1}{2} mv^2$ is used, where KE is in Joules, m is the mass of the object in kg and v is its velocity at a given point in meters per second. If 2,000 J of kinetic energy are produced by an object with a mass of 160 kg, what is the velocity of the object?

13. Each year, Jessica pays 22% of her $60,000 salary in taxes. Her rent costs 25% of the money she takes home after taxes. How much does Jess retain for her other expenses?

A $35,100

B $31,800

C $28,200

D $24,900

14. If $f(x) = x^2 + 3$ and $g(x) = f(x+3)$, what is $g(4)$?

A   –10

B   22

C   52

D   364

15. Which of these answers, if put into the blanks, would make the following a valid arithmetic sequence:
3, ___, ___, 81?

A   9, 27

B   27, 54

C   28, 54

D   29, 55

16. A player on a given team has a win percentage of 41.6%. If he has won 52 games, how many games has he played?

A   23

B   42

C   100

D   125

17. Matt drives 64 mph for 224 miles and enjoys an amusement park for seven hours before driving 50 mph for 75 miles to his hotel. How many hours does this take in total, from the time he leaves his house to the time he arrives at his hotel?

GO ▶

18. A six-pack holds six equal cylindrical cans, tightly packed in two rows of three cans so no space exists between them. If a box to hold the six-pack measures nine inches by six inches on its base and has a height of 5 inches, what is the combined volume of the six cans inside?

A $\dfrac{45\pi}{4}$

B $\dfrac{135\pi}{2}$

C 90π

D 135π

19. A tent is pitched outdoors. It will have a pyramidal top over a rectangular space below. The rectangular area covered by the tent is 22 feet by 24 feet, and the poles forming the corners of the tent are six feet high. If the center of the tent has a height of 8 feet from the ground, what is the volume of the space covered by the tent in cubic feet?

20. A billiard ball has a radius of $2\dfrac{1}{8}$ inches. The cue ball is a little smaller so the table can recognize it; the cue has a radius of only $1\dfrac{7}{8}$ inches. What is approximately the difference in volume between the standard balls and the cue ball?

A $\dfrac{1}{2}\pi$

B 2π

C 4π

D 8π

21. Solve for x in the following equation:

$$\sqrt[3]{(2x+5)^2} = 9$$

A 11

B 16

C 38

D 362

22. Evaluate $2c\left(4c-m\right)^{\frac{m}{c}}$ if $m = 15$ and $c = 5$.

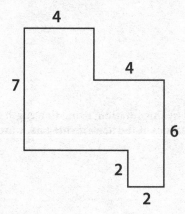

23. What is the area of the figure shown?

4

4

7

6

2

2

A 24

B 28

C 48

D 52

GO

24. Simplify $\sqrt[4]{625^2}$.

25. A pyramid with a rectangular base has edge lengths of 12 and 8 cm and a height of 20 cm. What is its volume?

A $\dfrac{1280}{3}$ cm^3

B 640 cm^3

C 960 cm^3

D 1920 cm^3

26. $\text{Log}_7 \, 343 =$

A 1

B 2

C 3

D 4

27. A flag is waved in a complete circle. The cylinder that would be formed by this rotation, using the length of the flag as its base and the width of the flag as its height, is 384π. Given the sides of the flag are integers, which of the following could be the dimensions of the flag?

A 6×8

B 7×9

C 8×10

D 9×11

You have 55 minutes to complete the Non-Calculator Session of the Mathematics test.

 Non-Calculator Session

28. The table shows how many pages are in each book of a series of seven books.

Book 1	Book 2	Book 3	Book 4	Book 5	Book 6	Book 7
223	251	317	636	766	607	607

What is the most reasonable estimate for the average number of pages per book?

A 460

B 485

C 510

D 535

29. Given a line crossing through the points $(11, y)$ and $(x, 4)$, what is the slope of the line?

A $\dfrac{y-4}{x-11}$

B $\dfrac{4-y}{11-x}$

C $\dfrac{-y-4}{x-11}$

D $\dfrac{y-4}{11-x}$

30. The provided box plot shows the results for a test in a college Linear Algebra course.

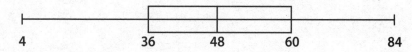

What is the range of scores students received on the test?

A 12

B 24

C 48

D 80

GO ▶

Mathematics

31. Set A consists of the first ten consecutive prime numbers, and set B consists of the odd numbers less than 20. If someone picks a number at random between 1 and 30, inclusive, what is the probability of picking a number that is in both sets A and B?

32. A square is inscribed in a circle. If the diameter of the circle is $\sqrt{50}$, what is the area of the square?

A 5

B 10

C 25

D 100

33. One mole of an ideal gas at standard temperature and pressure (STP) occupies .0224 m³. How many moles of an ideal gas would be present in a cylinder with radius of .5 m and height of 2 m if the gas is at STP?

A $\dfrac{0.0448}{\pi}$

B $\dfrac{2}{\pi}$

C $\dfrac{\pi}{2}$

D $\dfrac{\pi}{.0448}$

34. $9^2 - 3^0 - 4^3 = ?$

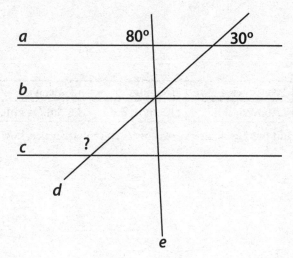

35. Consider parallel lines *a, b,* and *c,* which are intersected by transversals *d* and *e.*

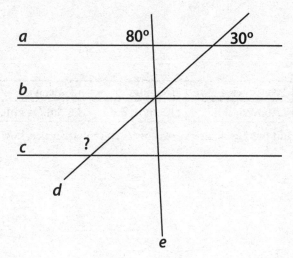

What would be the value of the indicated angle?

A   150°

B   110°

C   80°

D   30°

36. Consider this inequality.

$$(x + 3)(2x - 5)(x - 7) \leq 0$$

Which number line represents all possible solutions to the inequality?

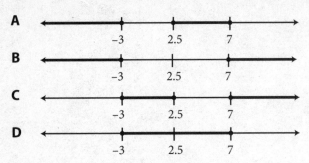

A

               −3   2.5   7

B

               −3   2.5   7

C

               −3   2.5   7

D

               −3   2.5   7

37. Four lines are graphed on a coordinate plane. The lines $y = \frac{1}{3}x + 4$, $y = \frac{1}{3}x - 1$, $y = -3x + 4$, and $y = -x + 6$, when connected, would form which shape?

A parallelogram

B rectangle

C square

D trapezoid

38. The table shows the population density of five cities.

New York Metro	San Francisco	Los Angeles	Honolulu	Chicago
30,000/sq mile	12,000/sq mile	12,000/sq mile	11,500/sq mile	8,500/sq mile

If the New York metro area covers 60 square miles and the Los Angeles area covers 100 square miles, how many people live in the two areas combined?

A 42,000

B 120,000

C 1,800,000

D 3,000,000

39. Solve for x in the following equation: $9(2x - 8) = 6x - 16$.

40. Which of the following could be the equation of a line parallel to the line $3x + 2y = 5$?

A $6x + 4y = 22$

B $9x + 6y = 15$

C $4x - 6y = 20$

D $-6x + 4y = 18$

41. A salesperson earns \$200 per week and an 8% commission on his sales. If he makes \$2,000 in sales, how much is his pay for that week?

A \$160

B \$200

C \$360

D \$1,800

42. Shelly lives 3 miles south and 5 miles west of the post office. Her boyfriend John lives 7 miles north and 11 miles east of the post office. How far do they live from one another?

A $\sqrt{52}$ miles

B $\sqrt{136}$ miles

C $\sqrt{272}$ miles

D $\sqrt{356}$ miles

GO ▶

43. A two-liter bottle of soda starts off full. Over the course of five days, the entire bottle is consumed slowly by a family. Which of the following functions would be an accurate way to describe how many <u>milliliters</u> of soda remain in the bottle $R(x)$, given that x is the number of <u>hours</u> that have passed since the bottle was opened and $0 \leq x \leq 120$?

A $R(x) = 2 - 5x$

B $R(x) = 2 - 120x$

C $R(x) = 2{,}000 - (50x/3)$

D $R(x) = 2{,}000 - 120x$

44. The total income for a car sales company on a given day is given by $I(s) = 2s - 1{,}000$, where s is the amount in sales made rounded to the nearest dollar. Some days are better than others; in fact, not every day is something sold. However, the sales at this company are never negative. What is the <u>best</u> domain for this function?

A   All integers

B   All real numbers

C   All positive numbers

D   Whole numbers

45. What are the real roots to the equation $2x^2 + 3x - 35$?

A $-5, -3.5$

B $-5, 3.5$

C $-3.5, 5$

D $3.5, 5$

46. If two more than half of a number is greater than one third the sum of that same number and 12, which inequality would represent the solutions for the unknown number n?

A $n < -12$

B $n > -12$

C $n < 12$

D $n > 12$

47. Baking a cake requires one box of cake mix, $1\frac{1}{4}$ cups of water, $\frac{1}{3}$ cup of oil, and 3 eggs. To bake a wedding cake, however, a baker needs two dozen eggs. How much water is needed to bake a wedding cake?

A   8 cups

B   10 cups

C   12 cups

D   14 cups

48. Stuart is half as old as Rachel. In 4 years, Rachel will be 10 years older than Stuart. How old is Stuart right now?

A 6

B 10

C 20

D 24

49. A class is composed of 36 people. What could be the ratio of boys to girls?

A 2:3

B 3:4

C 4:5

D 5:6

50. What is the inverse of $f(x)$ if $f(x) = \sqrt{3x+9}$?

A $f^{-1} = \dfrac{1}{3}x^2 - 3$

B $f^{-1} = \dfrac{1}{3}x^2 + 3$

C $f^{-1} = 3x^2 - 3$

D $f^{-1} = 3x^2 + 3$

GO ▶

51. Angle *ACB* is inscribed in circle *O* and measures 55°.

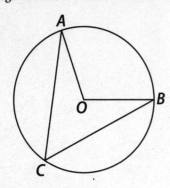

What is the measure of arc *AB* ?

52. Which of the following sets would have the smallest standard deviation?

A −1, 0, 1, 2, 3

B −2, 1, 3, 7, 9

C −3, 0, 6, 12, 19

D −4, −2, 1, 3, 5

53. The line graph provided shows the relationship between the number of seasons a television show has and the number of episodes it airs. Given this graph, what is the <u>best</u> estimate of the number of episodes a show would have if it ran for eleven seasons?

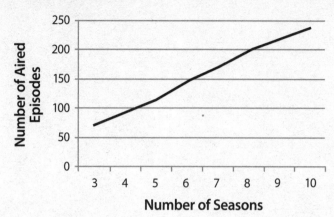

A 225

B 260

C 295

D 320

54. Which of the following is equivalent to $\left(\dfrac{125}{64}\right)^{\frac{-4}{3}}$?

A $\dfrac{256}{625}$

B $\dfrac{4}{5}$

C $\dfrac{5}{4}$

D $\dfrac{625}{256}$

GO ▶

THIS PAGE INTENTIONALLY LEFT BLANK.

You have 105 minutes to complete the Writing test.

Part 1: Language

Directions   For Numbers 1 through 4, read the question and choose the best answer.

1.   Read the sentences.

> The moment I had been anticipating finally came.
>
> On a seemingly routine Tuesday afternoon, I arrived home to my apartment.
>
> A round package was left by the delivery man casually leaning against the front screen door.

Which revision most clearly combines the three sentences?

A   The moment I had been anticipating finally came, when, while it was a seemingly routine Tuesday afternoon, I arrived home to my apartment and found a round package leaning against the front screen door that was left by the delivery man.

B   The moment I had been anticipating finally came on a seemingly routine Tuesday afternoon when I arrived home to a round package that was left by the delivery man at my apartment, casually leaning against the front screen door.

C   The moment I had been anticipating finally came on a seemingly routine Tuesday afternoon when I arrived home to my apartment, looked at the front screen door, and found a round package that had been left by the delivery man.

D   The moment I had been anticipating finally came, but on a seemingly routine Tuesday afternoon, I arrived home to my apartment and noticed a round package that had been left by the delivery man casually leaning against the front screen door.

2.   Which of these sentences includes a misspelled word?

A   Before he married my grandmother, my grandfather earned a living as a juggler.

B   He often performed at carnivals and circuses, juggling everything from oranges to bowling pins.

C   Tired of life on the road, Grandpa finally gave up the circus life to pursue a career in business.

D   It took him many years to aquire this skill.

3.   Read this sentence.

> There was a passion with which Gina read her poetry, but it was the having to project her voice loudly to the members of the audience—because of the largeness of the room—that tired her most by the end of the evening.

Which version of the sentence <u>best</u> expresses the idea precisely and concisely?

A   Gina and her poetry were tired by the end of the evening, having to project her voice to the large room.

B   Having to project her voice loudly, Gina's poetry tired her, but she was able to project her voice loudly to the members of the audience.

C   Though tired by the effort to project her voice loudly to the audience in the large room, Gina read her poetry with passion.

D   There was a passion and tiredness in how Gina read her poetry—because of the largeness of the room—and she was having to project her voice loudly.

GO

4. Read the paragraph.

> When I was a child, I used to spend summers at my aunt and uncle's cabin in the foothills of Tennessee. I can still remember the sound of birds singing and the smell of the roses growing in my aunt's garden. At night, my cousins and I would gather around the campfire to roast marshmallows, cook hot dogs, and listen to my uncle's ghost stories. Sometimes, too, Papa would pick up his guitar and play all of our familiar tunes.

Which sentence <u>best</u> concludes this paragraph?

A Many people have memories of Tennessee.

B My uncle was a coal-miner.

C We watched the sunrise, basking in the orange glow of morning.

D Those times are among the best memories of my life.

Directions Read the draft of an essay. Then do Numbers 5 through 7.

> (1) During World War II, the government made an effort to use of all of our national resources. (2) American industrial facilities were turned into war production factories, and the government targeted the female population as an essential source of labor. (3) Women worked in factories and shipyards as riveters, welders, and machinists making everything from uniforms to munishuns to airplanes. (4) The number of women in the workforce increased from 12 million in 1940 to 18 million in 1944. (5) By 1945, 36% of the laborers were women. (6) Women's increased presence in wartime workforces were not limited to factories and shipyards. (7) Thousands moved to Washington D.C. to fill government jobs exclusively held by men before the war. (8) Some women engaged in farm labor, and others joined the military as field nurses. (9) The shortage of men also led to openings in non-traditional fields, such as _____. (10) Since many players had been drafted into the armed services, Major League Baseball parks around the country were on the verge of collapse. (11) The All-American Girls Professional Baseball League was created in 1943 and offered a unique blend of baseball and softball suitable for female players.

5. The writer wishes to divide this essay into two paragraphs. Where is the most effective place to start the second paragraph?

A After Sentence 2

B After Sentence 3

C After Sentence 5

D After Sentence 9

6. Which would most logically complete the blank in Sentence 9?

A day-care

B baseball

C welding

D the military

7. In Sentence 3, which word is misspelled?

A "riveters"

B "welders"

C "machinists"

D "munishuns"

Directions For Numbers 8 through 16, read the question and choose the best answer.

8. Read the sentences.

(1) Sherwood Anderson's masterpiece, *Winesburg, Ohio,* was published in 1919.

(2) Something between a short-story collection and a novel, *Winesburg* is often considered one of the earliest examples of American Modernism.

(3) _____.

(4) Anderson was able to fuse his sense of the passing of the Industrial Age in America with a type of uniquely American expression.

Sentence 3 is missing. The author wishes to create a complete paragraph. Which answer would be the **best** sentence to add in the position of Sentence 3 to create coherence to the ideas presented?

A Anderson tirelessly continued his literary experimentation until his death in 1941.

B But it takes only a few pages of *Winesburg* to see that Anderson's literary genius is still very much with us today.

C In the contemporary popular imagination, Anderson's influence often appears to be diminishing.

D Sherwood Anderson was the first author to create a type of literature that was previously associated only with Europe.

9. Which of these sentences is punctuated correctly?

A Halley's is the only known comet that is clearly visible to the naked eye, and the only comet that may be observed twice in a human lifetime.

B Halley's is the only known comet that is clearly visible to the naked eye and the only comet, that may be observed twice in a human lifetime.

C Halley's is the only known comet that is clearly visible to the naked eye; and the only comet that may be observed twice in a human lifetime.

D Halley's is the only known comet that is clearly visible to the naked eye and the only comet that may be observed twice in a human lifetime.

10. Read the paragraph.

I do not remember how I came to like using a fountain pen. Friends view it as an odd habit of mine, since so few people use fountain pens today. I think my fondness for these old-fashioned implements comes down to the desire to proclaim what type of person I am.

Which sentence **best** concludes this paragraph?

A People who do not use fountain pens are foolish indeed.

B I am a good person, or so my mother tells me.

C I like to take my time in crafting my writing and appreciate the simplicity of a well-crafted tool.

D I have many odd habits.

GO ▶

11. **Which sentence includes a misspelled word?**

   A   Even if we are not supposed to judge a book by its cover, we very often judge a person by his or her clothing.

   B   A pair of jeans indicates to all that you are laid-back, just as a suit and tie tells the world you are serious and conservetive.

   C   A cowboy hat may indicate you are from Texas, while a beret suggests you are from France.

   D   We even use clothing as a kind of code for moral character, judging people who wear clothing that is too tight, too revealing, or dirty and tattered.

12. **Select the sentence that best uses grammar to express its ideas.**

   A   Deserving congratulations, I hugged my sister as she walked off the stage; her performance was magnificent!

   B   As she is deserving congratulations, I hugged my sister as she walked off the stage; her performance was magnificent!

   C   Because she deserved my congratulations, I hugged my sister as she walked off the stage—her performance was magnificent!

   D   To deserve congratulations, I hugged my sister as she walked off the stage—her performance was magnificent!

13. **Read the sentence.**

> When Bobby has exciting news for me, he can hardly keep it to himself, if the news has to be kept secret, I can't promise to stay quiet.

Which revision of the sentence best expresses the idea precisely and concisely?

   A   Whenever Bobby has an exciting secret, he can hardly keep it to himself; honestly, I can't promise to stay quiet either!

   B   I can't promise to stay quiet when Bobby has exciting news, but he can't keep it to himself.

   C   He can hardly keep the news to himself when I promise to stay quiet.

   D   Keeping it to himself, an exciting secret is hardly easy for me to keep quiet.

14. **Which of the following sentences is punctuated correctly?**

   A   I have always had a passion, for history.

   B   History helps me to think of my own life in the context of life-changing world events.

   C   In other words, history, helps me feel like a daring explorer in search of larger meaning.

   D   The real reason I like history however is that it allows me to escape away from everyday life.

15. **Read the paragraph.**

> One guitarist and saxophonist, Bruce Diamond, recorded nearly a hundred songs from his home in Lexington, Kentucky. Recently, hundreds of these rough recordings have been re-mastered. They have captured the attention of musicologists for a number of reasons.

Which sentence would best open the paragraph to introduce the topic?

   A   As soon as cassette recorders with built-in microphones became available in 1963, amateur songwriters were able to record songs that had been formerly undocumented.

   B   Many guitarists and saxophonists record their music on highly sophisticated equipment.

   C   Musicology is the study of the history of music.

   D   Which is easier to play—guitar or saxophone?

16. Read the sentence.

> While sources of music from major music towns like New Orleans, Detroit, and Nashville are _____, little is known about Lexington's music scene because the town lacks a real recording studio.

Choose the word that <u>best</u> provides a contrast to the remainder of the sentence.

A scarce

B high quality

C popular

D abundant

Directions Read the paragraph. Then do Numbers 17 through 19.

> (1) It is apparent to many art critics that Andy Warhol was influenced by many different popular designs of the day. (2) One of Warhol's prints is a reproduction of multiple campbell's soup cans. (3) Another print is a colorful portrait of Marilyn Monroe. (4) The themes used within each piece are seemingly random, and one is led to wonder what inspired them. (5) One art critic observed that Warhol found it convenient to exploit designs that were already in common use. (6) Even after his death, Warhol continues to be a household name in the American Art World. (7) Warhol himself spoke of every person experiencing "fifteen minutes of fame."

17. Which of the following sentences would be the most effective end to the paragraph?

A But that's not necessarily true.

B In Warhol's case, though, fame seems to be eternal.

C Fifteen minutes, though, may not be nearly long enough to create great art.

D Who's watching the clock?

18. Which revision most effectively combines the ideas of Sentences 2 and 3?

A One of Warhol's prints being a reproduction of multiple Campbell's soup cans, another being a colorful portrait of Marilyn Monroe.

B Although one of Warhol's prints is a reproduction of multiple Campbell's soup cans, another print is a colorful portrait of Marilyn Monroe.

C One of Warhol's prints is a reproduction of multiple Campbell's soup cans; in fact, another print is a colorful portrait of Marilyn Monroe.

D One of Warhol's prints is a reproduction of multiple Campbell's soup cans, while another is a colorful portrait of Marilyn Monroe.

19. Which two Sentences contain errors in capitalization?

A Sentences 1 and 2

B Sentences 2 and 4

C Sentences 2 and 6

D Sentences 3 and 5

GO ▶

Writing

Directions   For Numbers 20 through 25, read the question and choose the best answer.

20.   **Select the sentence that best uses grammar to express its ideas.**

A   Since it was originally an oral poem, *Beowulf*'s author is unknown in England and is now written in modern English for anyone to read.

B   Originally an anonymous English oral poem, *Beowulf* has now been translated into modern English and is available to readers everywhere.

C   After being translated into modern English, *Beowulf*'s author was unknown in England, but he is now read by everyone.

D   *Beowulf*, now having been translated into modern English, was once unknown in England.

21.   **Which of these sentences contains a misused word?**

A   When I left my home in rural Missouri to attend college in New York City, I didn't consider myself a veteran subway rider.

B   Luckily, I was able to overcome this fear by having my first trip by subway guided by a neighbor named Sasha.

C   He had grown up in Manhattan, so he was familiar with the dense, intricate subway routes.

D   Riding with Sasha effected my opinion of subways in a very positive way.

22.   **Read the sentence.**

Because of <u>her family's warnings,</u> Jenny was afraid to walk the streets of her neighborhood without a chaperone.

Choose the <u>best</u> version of the underlined portion:

A   her family's warnings,

B   her familys' warnings

C   her families' warnings

D   her families warnings,

23.   **Which of these sentences contains a grammatical error?**

A   My mother and my sister are going to the store because one of them wants to buy a new dress.

B   Either my mother or my sister is going to the store to buy a dress.

C   Neither my mother nor my sister are going to the store to buy a dress.

D   Both my mother and my sister are going to the store to buy dresses.

24.   **Read this sentence.**

The woman at the ticket booth at the movie theater took my money and slipped a ticket through a slot in the window.

Which of these is the most effective and accurate revision of the sentence?

A   At the ticket booth, the woman at the movie theater took my money and slipped a ticket through a slot in the window.

B   At the movie theater, the woman at the ticket booth window first took my money and then slipped a ticket through the slot.

C   The woman took my money, then slipped a ticket through the ticket booth window, at the movie theater.

D   Taking my money, the movie theater woman took my money at the ticket booth and slipped a ticket through a slot in the window.

25. Read the paragraph.

Black holes are possibly the most fascinating topic in contemporary astronomy. The concept of a black hole—a region of space with such intense gravitational pull that nothing can escape—is truly the stuff of science fiction. That is what Albert Einstein believed, at least.

Choose the concluding sentence that would most logically follow this paragraph.

A His general theory of relativity predicted their existence, but he was skeptical that his prediction was true.

B Most people don't believe in black holes, though.

C There are other fascinating topics in astronomy, too.

D He often read science fiction authors such as H.G. Wells.

Directions Read the paragraph. Then do Numbers 26 through 33.

(1) Drive through any suburb in the U.S. today, and it's hard to miss the bins, that have become companions to America's trashcans. (2) Recycling has <u>become</u> commonplace, as people recognize the need to care for the environment. (3) _____ most people's recycling consciousness <u>is extending</u> only as far as paper, bottles, and cans. (4) People seldom find themselves confronted with the growing phenomenon of e-waste. (5) Activists who track such waste estimate that users discarded nearly 2 million tons of TVs, VCRs, computers, cell phones, and other electronics in 2005. (6) Unless we can find a safe alternative, this e-waste may leak into the ground and poison the water with dangerous toxins. (7) Burning the waste also _____ contaminates the air.

26. Select the word for the blank in Sentence 3 that <u>best</u> clarifies the transition between ideas.

A While

B Yet

C Since

D Perhaps

27. Suppose the author wanted to create a new paragraph after Sentence 4 <u>and</u> wished to add a sentence. Which sentence would be the most effective to insert between Sentences 4 and 5?

A Many people are unfamiliar with the concept of e-waste.

B E-waste is created when people constantly upgrade to the most cutting-edge devices, sending their old devices to landfills.

C There are many environmental problems that confront us today.

D E-waste is a silly-sounding name.

28. Sentence 1 contains an error. Which of following <u>best</u> describes the error?

A There should be no comma after the word *today*.

B The phrase *in the U.S.* is unnecessary.

C There should be no comma after the word *bins*.

D *companions* is spelled incorrectly.

GO ▶

29. Which is the <u>best</u> version of the underlined word in Sentence 2?

   A   become

   B   became

   C   becoming

   D   becomes

30. Which is the <u>best</u> version of the underlined word in Sentence 3?

   A   is extending

   B   extended

   C   had extended

   D   extends

31. Which choice would most effectively emphasize a lack of awareness of this problem?

   A   People seldom find themselves confronted with the growing phenomenon of e-waste.

   B   Many in our communities simply don't realize the dangers of the growing phenomenon of e-waste.

   C   A majority of local governments are assiduously studying the growing phenomenon of e-waste.

   D   Little attention is paid by the people in our neighborhoods to the growing phenomenon of e-waste.

32. In Sentence 5, what word could <u>best</u> be used as a substitute for "users"?

   A   abusers

   B   computer specialists

   C   consumers

   D   governments

33. Select the correct word or phrase for the blank in Sentence 7.

   A   dangerous

   B   more dangerous

   C   most dangerous

   D   dangerously

Directions   For Numbers 34 and 35, read the question and choose the best answer.

34. **Which sentence contains a misspelled word?**

A   A growing number of states have adopted laws to prohibit cell phone use while driving.

B   Still, some people refuze to comply with the laws.

C   Some people insist upon text-messaging at stoplights or checking email on the highway.

D   Nevertheless, a growing number of us realize the danger of cell phone distraction and have gone hands-free while on the road.

35. **Which of these sentences is punctuated correctly?**

A   In 1867 on an unassuming farm in tiny Delta Louisiana, a daughter was born to former slaves Minerva and Owen Breedlove.

B   Little did anyone realize that Sarah Breedlove, orphaned at age six when her parents died, would grow up to become one of the most successful African American entrepreneurs in history.

C   At twenty Sarah Breedlove found herself widowed with an infant daughter A'Lelia.

D   Sarah packed up her few belongings and moved to St. Louis, hoping to take advantage of its' more numerous opportunities.

Directions   Read the sentence. Then do Numbers 36 and 37.

> coco chanel not only oversaw a vast financial empire but also become one of the best known women in the united states.

36. **Which of the words in the sentence above should be capitalized?**

A   Coco Chanel

B   Coco Chanel, Financial Empire

C   Coco Chanel, United States

D   Coco Chanel, Empire, United States

37. **Which of these words or phrases in the sentence above have been corrected to reflect correct hyphenation:**

A   "over-saw"

B   "vast-financial"

C   "best-known"

D   "best-known-women"

GO ▶

38. Read the sentences.

(1) He claimed that the secret design for the Eliminator had come to him in a dream.

(2) After months of success, he finally branded his contraption the Eliminator.

(3) Bob undertook countless journeys to sell his mousetrap door-to-door as well as at county fairs and flea markets.

(4) Bob invented an ingenious mousetrap, in part because, for years, he had suffered a mouse infestation in his attic.

The author wishes to create a paragraph with these sentences. Which of the following would arrange the sentences in the **best** order to create flow and coherence?

A   1, 2, 3, 4

B   2, 1, 3, 4

C   3, 4, 1, 2

D   4, 3, 2, 1

Directions   Read the paragraph. Then do Numbers 39 through 43.

> (1) At one time, there were relatively few beauty salons, so many women received beauty treatments at home. (2) In 1905 a woman named Sarah Walker decided to start a business. (3) She traveled her city selling beauty potions to housewives. (3) Sarah taught her methods to other women. (3) They were highly focused on making sales and became known as the "Walker Agents." (4) <u>Below</u> Sarah's supervision, these agents became familiar sights in their white shirts and black skirts. (5) Sarah called them "scalp specialists" and hair and beauty "culturists" using these terms to emphasize the professional nature of the treatments.

39. Where is the **best** place to insert a comma in Sentence 2?

A   After "1905"

B   After "a woman"

C   After "Sarah Walker"

D   No commas are necessary.

40. Suppose the author wishes to combine Sentences 3 and 4. Which of these would be the most accurate and effective combination?

A   Sarah taught her methods to other women, they focused on sales and became known as the "Walker Agents."

B   Sarah taught her methods to other women, who focused on sales and became known as the "Walker Agents."

C   Sarah taught her methods to other women, with whom focused on sales and became known as the "Walker Agents."

D   Sarah taught her methods to other women those focused on sales and became known as the "Walker Agents."

41. Which is the <u>best</u> version of the underlined word in Sentence 4?

   A Below

   B Above

   C As

   D Under

42. Which form of punctuation would be most appropriate after the word "culturists" in Sentence 5?

   A no punctuation

   B a semicolon (;)

   C a colon (:)

   D a comma (,)

43. Which sentence would be the most effective addition to the end of the paragraph?

   A In time, Sarah Walker became one of the most wealthy business women in America.

   B Many customers did not believe in beauty treatments, though.

   C It's a mystery how Walker's Agents were so successful.

   D White shirts and black skirts were fashionable at the time.

> **Directions**   **For Numbers 44 through 47, read the question and choose the best answer.**

44. Read the sentence.

> In 1859, Charles Darwin published *On the Origin of Species,* and in 1839 he traveled to the Galapagos Islands.

Which revision of the sentence <u>best</u> expresses the ideas clearly and precisely?

   A In 1859, Charles Darwin published *On the Origin of Species*, but in 1839 he traveled to the Galapagos Islands.

   B In 1859, Charles Darwin published *On the Origin of Species*, then in 1839 he traveled to the Galapagos Islands.

   C In 1839, Charles Darwin traveled to the Galapagos Islands; then, in 1859, he published *On Origin of Species.*

   D Charles Darwin traveled to the Galapagos Islands and published *On the Origin of Species* in both 1839 and 1859.

45. Read the paragraph.

> During the last eighteen years of his life, he gave away to charities, foundations, and universities about $350 million—almost 90 percent of his fortune. His 1889 article proclaiming "The Gospel of Wealth" called on the rich to use their wealth to improve society, and it stimulated a wave of philanthropy.

Which sentence would <u>best</u> open the paragraph to introduce the topic?

   A Andrew Carnegie was born in poverty in rural Scotland.

   B Andrew Carnegie was a wealthy industrialist.

   C Many people thought he was stingy, but this is not true.

   D Even now, America is known as a charitable nation.

GO ▶

46. **Which sentence is punctuated correctly?**

A Upon his death in 1865, President Abraham Lincoln—now often regarded as the greatest American president—was mourned by millions.

B Upon his death, in 1865, President Abraham Lincoln; now often regarded as the greatest American president—was mourned by millions.

C Upon his death in 1865 President Abraham Lincoln, now often regarded as the greatest American president was mourned by millions.

D Upon his death in 1865: President Abraham Lincoln—now often regarded as the greatest American president—was mourned by millions.

47. **Read the sentence.**

   As my mother and I finished our dinners, we were hardly saying a word.

   Which of the following alternatives to the sentence above would not be acceptable?

A While my mother and I finished dinner, we hardly said a word.

B My mother and I were almost finished eating, but we hardly said a word.

C My mother and I finished our dinners, however, we hardly said a word.

D As my mother and I were finishing our dinners, we were hardly saying a word.

> **Directions** **Read the paragraph. Then do Numbers 48 through 51.**

> (1) For the most part, it was a very ordinary birthday celebration. (2) _____ we had my favorite meal, lamb chops, my uncle made me his famous banana split sundae for dessert. (3) Banana splits are best with two scoops of chocolate ice cream, in my opinion. (4) Normally, my uncle would get very excited watching me eat dessert and have me make wishes for the coming year. (5) However, as our spoons clinked around mounds of ice cream and banana, his mood turned sad and soft-spoken. (6) I knew the source of our ten-tion: today was my eighteenth birthday and next month I'd be at boot camp.

48. **Should any additional words be added to the end of Sentence 1?**

A No, do not add any additional words.

B Add the phrase "just like always."

C Add the phrase "with nothing abnormal."

D Add the phrase "and traditional."

49. **Which word would most logically begin Sentence 2?**

A After

B Such as

C For example

D Including

50. **Is the colon (:) in Sentence 6 correct as written?**

A   Yes, do not change it.

B   No punctuation is necessary in Sentence 6.

C   No, replace it with a semicolon (;)

D   No, replace it with a comma (,)

51. **Which word in the above paragraph is misspelled?**

A   sundae

B   dessert

C   soft-spoken

D   tention

GO ▶

Writing

Part 2: Essay

There is an ongoing debate in the public domain about emissions trading. What are the implications for society of a "cap-and trade" policy? Does it promote good environmental practices or hinder them?

Weigh the claims on both sides, and then write an argumentative essay supporting either side of the debate in which you argue for or against emissions trading. Be sure to use information from both texts in your argumentative essay.

Before you begin planning and writing, read the two texts:

1. Indications that Cap-and-Trade Works

2. Criticisms of Cap-and-Trade

As you read the texts, think about what details from the texts you might use in your argumentative essay. You may take notes or highlight the details as you read.

After reading the texts, create a plan for your argumentative essay. Think about ideas, facts, definitions, details, and other information and examples you want to use. Think about how you will introduce your topic and what the main topic will be for each paragraph.

Now write your argumentative essay. Be sure to:

• Introduce your claim.

• Support your claim with logical reasoning and relevant evidence from the passages.

• Acknowledge and address alternate or opposing claims.

• Organize the reasons and evidence logically.

• Use words, phrases, and clauses to connect your ideas and to clarify the relationships among claims, counterclaims, reasons, and evidence.

• Establish and maintain a formal style.

• Provide a concluding statement or section that follows from and supports the argument presented.

Indications that Cap-and-Trade Works

1   "Cap-and-trade" is a market-based policy tool for controlling large amounts of harmful emissions, such as sulfur dioxide (SO_2) and nitrogen oxides (NO_x), from a group of sources. A cap-and-trade program from the Environmental Protection Agency (EPA) first sets an aggressive "cap," or maximum limit, on emissions. Businesses and industries covered by the program then receive authorizations to produce emissions in the form of emissions permits, with the total amount of permits limited by the cap. Each business or industry can develop its own strategy to comply with the overall reduction requirement, including the sale or purchase (the "trade") of permits, installation of pollution controls, and implementation of efficiency measures, among other options. Businesses and industries must also completely and accurately measure and report all emissions in a timely manner to guarantee that the overall cap is met.

2   Under the right circumstances, cap-and-trade programs have proven extremely effective, providing certainty in allocations, rules, and penalties; substantial emission reductions; cost-effective, flexible compliance choices for regulated sources; complete accountability, unprecedented data quality, and public access to program data and decisions; and minimized administrative costs for industry and government. EPA's cap-and-trade programs have the force of federal and state standards behind them, including national health-based air quality standards. This ensures that local public health needs are met in conjunction with achievement of regional or national emission reductions.

3   Examples of successful cap-and-trade programs include the nationwide Acid Rain Program (ARP) and the regional NO_x Budget Trading Program in the Northeast. Additionally, EPA issued the Clean Air Interstate Rule (CAIR) on March 10, 2005, to build on the success of these programs and achieve significant additional emission reductions.

4   The programs have had measurable results:

5   • Since the 1990s, SO_2 emissions have dropped 40%, and according to the Pacific Research Institute, acid rain levels have dropped 65% since 1976.

6   • NOx reductions due to the NO_x Budget Trading Program have led to improvements in ozone and particulate matter, saving an estimated 580 to 1,800 lives in 2008.

7   • Ozone season NO_x emissions decreased by 43 percent between 2003 and 2008, even while energy demand remained essentially the same during the same period.

8   • The EPA estimates that by 2010, the overall costs of complying with the program for businesses and consumers will be $1 billion to $2 billion a year, only one fourth of what was originally predicted.

9   Therefore, cap-and-trade has been proven to be effective in protecting human health and the environment. Successful cap-and- trade programs reward innovation, efficiency, and early action and provide strict environmental accountability without inhibiting economic growth.

Criticisms of Cap-and-Trade

1   Critics have several objections to cap-and-trade. Skeptical environmentalists have argued that reductions in emissions occurred due to broad trends unconnected to the program. For example, there were many other regulations that impacted emissions at the time the ARP was implemented. Therefore, the effectiveness of the emissions trading element of the ARP in reducing emissions has been questioned, since the EPA also used other regulations in conjunction with the ARP during the time period the emissions reduction took place.

2   "Carbon leakage" occurs when there is an increase in carbon dioxide emissions in one country as a result of an emissions reduction by a second country with a strict climate policy. If one country has a strict emissions policy that raises production costs, then production may move offshore to the cheaper country with lower standards, and global emissions will not be reduced. Furthermore, cheap "offset" carbon credits are frequently available from the less developed countries, where they may be generated by local polluters at the expense of local communities.

3   Regulatory agencies run the risk of issuing too many emission credits, which can result in a very low price on emission permits. This reduces the incentive for companies to cut back their emissions, since permits are cheap. On the other hand, issuing too few permits can result in an excessively high permit price. Another issue with cap-and-trade programs has been over-allocation, whereby the cap is high enough that sources of emissions do not need to reduce their emissions.

4   The price and supply of permits can result in perverse incentives. If, for example, polluting firms are given free emission permits, this may create a reason for them not to cut their emissions. A firm making large cuts in emissions could then be granted fewer emission permits in the future. This perverse incentive can be alleviated if permits are sold, rather than given, to polluters.

5   Some environmentalists argue that offsets for emission reductions are not a substitute for actual cuts in emissions, and that offsets are an excuse for business as usual, since expensive long-term changes will not be made if there is a cheaper source of carbon credits. Environmental protection will require more radical change than the modest changes driven by pollution trading schemes. These critics advocate solutions that leave most remaining fossil fuels underground.

You have 75 minutes to complete the Reading test.

Directions Read the text. Then do Numbers 1 through 6.

Excerpt from "George Eliot"

by Virginia Woolf

Note: This excerpt from an article first published in 1919 is about George Eliot, a nineteenth-century female writer who used a male pseudonym.

1   But is it upon the heroines that we would cast a final glance. "I have always been finding out my religion since I was a little girl," says Dorothea Casaubon. "I used to pray so much—now I hardly ever pray. I try not to have desires merely for myself." She is speaking for them all. That is their problem. They cannot live without religion, and they start out on the search for one when they are little girls. Each has the deep feminine passion for goodness, which makes the place where she stands in aspiration and agony the heart of the book—still and cloistered like a place of worship, but that she no longer knows to whom to pray. In learning they seek their goal; in the ordinary tasks of womanhood; in the wider service of their kind. They do not find what they seek, and we cannot wonder. The ancient consciousness of woman, charged with suffering and sensibility, and for so many ages dumb, seems in them to have brimmed and overflowed and uttered a demand for something—they scarcely know what—for something that is perhaps incompatible with the facts of human existence. George Eliot had far too strong an intelligence to tamper with those facts, and too broad a humour to mitigate the truth because it was a stern one. Save for the supreme courage of their endeavour, the struggle ends, for her heroines, in tragedy, or in a compromise that is even more melancholy. But their story is the incomplete version of the story that is George Eliot herself. For her, too, the burden and the complexity of womanhood were not enough; she must reach beyond the sanctuary and pluck for herself the strange bright fruits of art and knowledge. Clasping them as few women have ever clasped them, she would not renounce her own inheritance—the difference of view, the difference of standard—nor accept an inappropriate reward. Thus we behold her, a memorable figure, inordinately praised and shrinking from her fame, despondent, reserved, shuddering back into the arms of love as if there alone were satisfaction and, it might be, justification, at the same time reaching out with "a fastidious yet hungry ambition" for all that life could offer the free and inquiring mind and confronting her feminine aspirations with the real world of men. Triumphant was the issue for her, whatever it may have been for her creations, and as we recollect all that she dared and achieved, how with every obstacle against her—sex and health and convention—she sought more knowledge and more freedom till the body, weighted with its double burden, sank worn out, we must lay upon her grave whatever we have it in our power to bestow of laurel and rose.

1.   **Read the following sentence describing Eliot's heroines. Then answer the question.**

   Each has the deep feminine passion for goodness, which makes the place where she stands in aspiration and agony the heart of the book—still and cloistered like a place of worship, but that she no longer knows to whom to pray.

   Which of the following is the <u>best</u> explanation for what the author means when she says Eliot's heroines are "cloistered"?

   A   They are alone.

   B   They are in a monastery.

   C   They are imprisoned.

   D   They are lost in prayer.

GO

2. Read the following sentence from the excerpt. Then answer the question.

> The ancient consciousness of woman, charged with suffering and sensibility, and for so many ages dumb, seems in them to have brimmed and overflowed and uttered a demand for something—they scarcely know what—for something that is perhaps incompatible with the facts of human existence.

In this sentence, "the facts of human existence"

A restrict both men and women

B are only applicable to Eliot's heroines

C restrict women only

D are incompatible with any human aspirations

3. According to the passage, Eliot

A enjoyed excellent health

B suffered from her independence and knowledge

C was prevented from attaining fame by men

D was very unlike the heroines of her books

4. Read the following sentence from the passage.

> Clasping them as few women have ever clasped them, she would not renounce her own inheritance—the difference of view, the difference of standard—nor accept an inappropriate reward.

The "differences" mentioned in this sentence pertain to Eliot's

A profession

B class

C education

D gender

5. The author's attitude toward George Eliot is <u>best</u> described as one of

A idolatrous devotion

B profound admiration

C qualified enthusiasm

D reasoned objectivity

6. Read the following sentence, where the author describes Eliot.

> Thus we behold her, a memorable figure, inordinately praised and shrinking from her fame, despondent, reserved, shuddering back into the arms of love as if there alone were satisfaction and, it might be, justification, at the same time reaching out with "a fastidious yet hungry ambition" for all that life could offer the free and inquiring mind and confronting her feminine aspirations with the real world of men.

It is reasonable to assume that the quoted phrase, "a fastidious yet hungry ambition,"

A is spoken by one of Eliot's heroines

B comes from one of the author's own literary works

C is borrowed from one of Eliot's critics

D does not represent the author's point of view

Directions   Read the text. Then do Numbers 7 through 12.

Excerpt from "Niagara"

by Mark Twain

1   ...When you start out to "do" the Falls you first drive down about a mile, and pay a small sum for the privilege of looking down from a precipice into the narrowest part of the Niagara River.... You can descend a staircase here a hundred and fifty feet down, and stand at the edge of the water. After you have done it, you will wonder why you did it; but you will then be too late.

2   Then you drive over to Suspension Bridge, and divide your misery between the chances of smashing down two hundred feet into the river below, and the chances of having the railwaytrain overhead smashing down onto you....

3   When you have examined the stupendous Horseshoe Fall till you are satisfied you cannot improve on it, you return to America by the new Suspension Bridge, and follow up the bank to where they exhibit the Cave of the Winds.

4   Here I followed instructions, and divested myself of all my clothing, and put on a waterproof jacket and overalls. This costume is picturesque, but not beautiful. A guide, similarly dressed, led the way down a flight of winding stairs, which wound and wound, and still kept on winding long after the thing ceased to be a novelty, and then terminated long before it had begun to be a pleasure. We were then well down under the precipice, but still considerably above the level of the river.

5   We now began to creep along flimsy bridges of a single plank, our persons shielded from destruction by a crazy wooden railing, to which I clung with both hands—not because I was afraid, but because I wanted to. Presently the descent became steeper and the bridge flimsier, and sprays from the American Fall began to rain down on us in fast increasing sheets that soon became blinding, and after that our progress was mostly in the nature of groping. Now a furious wind began to rush out from behind the waterfall, which seemed determined to sweep us from the bridge, and scatter us on the rocks and among the torrents below. I remarked that I wanted to go home; but it was too late. We were almost under the monstrous wall of water thundering down from above, and speech was in vain in the midst of such a pitiless crash of sound.

6   In another moment the guide disappeared behind the deluge, and, bewildered by the thunder, driven helplessly by the wind, and smitten by the arrowy tempest of rain, I followed. All was darkness. Such a mad storming, roaring, and bellowing of warring wind and water never crazed my ears before. I bent my head, and seemed to receive the Atlantic on my back. The world seemed going to destruction. I could not see anything, the flood poured down savagely. I raised my head, with open mouth, and the most of the American cataract went down my throat. If I had sprung a leak now I had been lost. And at this moment I discovered that the bridge had ceased, and we must trust for a foothold to the slippery and precipitous rocks. I never was so scared before and survived it. But we got through at last, and emerged into the open day, where we could stand in front of the laced and frothy and seething world of descending water, and look at it. When I saw how much of it there was, and how fearfully in earnest it was, I was sorry I had gone behind it.

7.   **Read this sentence from the first paragraph of the excerpt.**

> **After you have done it, you will wonder why you did it; but you will then be too late.**

Which of the following best explains why the author chose to conclude the paragraph with this sentence?

   A   to show how important it is to arrive at the falls on time

   B   to offer advice to any readers who might consider visiting Niagara Falls

   C   to demonstrate the narrator's affinity with the reader

   D   to predict a tourist's feelings about the effort needed to view the site

GO ▶

8. **Which of the following quotations from the passage stands out in contrast to the author's attitude towards his subject?**

    A "... we got through at last, and emerged into the open day."

    B "... kept on winding long after the thing ceased to be a novelty, and then terminated long before it had begun to be a pleasure."

    C "...bewildered by the thunder, driven helplessly by the wind, and smitten by the arrowy tempest of rain, I followed…"

    D "...our persons shielded from destruction by a crazy wooden railing, to which I clung with both hands ..."

9. **During his excursion behind the falls, the narrator says he "remarked that I wanted to go home." How does this remark develop the character of the narrator?**

    A It reveals that he is homesick.

    B It shows that he is unhappy.

    C It reinforces how apprehensive he is.

    D It illustrates how childish he is.

10. **Read the following sentences from the passage.**

    Such a mad storming, roaring, and bellowing of warring wind and water never crazed my ears before. I bent my head, and seemed to receive the Atlantic on my back.

    This detailed description of the author's surroundings enhances the story by

    A revealing the author's predicament after falling into the Atlantic

    B further emphasizing the flimsy nature of the bridges the author must cross

    C showing the fury of the storm that catches the author off guard

    D using exaggeration to illustrate the volume of water the author experiences

11. **Read this sentence from the passage.**

    When I saw how much of it there was, and how fearfully in earnest it was, I was sorry I had gone behind it.

    Which definition best matches the use of the phrase "in earnest"?

    A serious

    B vigorous

    C sincere

    D ardent

12. **From the passage, which fact can the reader not infer about the Niagara Falls site?**

    A Part of it is located outside the United States.

    B The river into which it empties is far below the road.

    C The Cave of the Winds is on the same side of the river as Horseshoe Fall.

    D The Suspension Bridge runs between a railway track and the river.

Directions   Read the text. Then do Numbers 13 through 18.

The Mower to the Glowworms

by Andrew Marvell

Ye living lamps, by whose dear light
The nightingale does sit so late,
And studying all the summer night,
Her matchless songs does meditate;
Ye country comets, that portend
No war nor prince's funeral,
Shining unto no higher end
Than to presage the grass's fall;
Ye glowworms, whose officious flame
To wandering mowers shows the way,
That in the night have lost their aim,
And after foolish fires do stray;
Your courteous lights in vain you waste,
Since Juliana here is come,
For she my mind hath so displaced
That I shall never find my home.

---

13.   **Calling the glowworms "living lamps" serves to**

   A   reveal that the speaker isn't sure if the glowworms are real or if he is imagining them

   B   show how much the speaker admires and respects the glowworms

   C   suggest that the speaker sees the glowworms as existing solely for his benefit

   D   connect the natural and the mechanical worlds

14.   **"The Mower to the Glowworms" could most reasonably be considered**

   A   a celebration of glowworms

   B   an elaborate compliment to a woman

   C   a testament to the power of love at first sight

   D   an allegory about a divine presence in the world

15.   **In the context of the poem, the word "portend" means**

   A   "predict," and refers to the belief that the glowworms serve a divine purpose

   B   "predict," and alludes to the superstition that comets were omens of evil

   C   "forecast," and implies that the behavior of insects reveals the next day's weather

   D   "imitate," and suggests that motion of the glowworms reflects the cyclical flight of comets

GO ▶

16. The speaker implies that, without the glowworms, mowers who have "lost their aim" (line 11) would be likely to

   A   be led astray by other sources of light

   B   mow the wrong fields

   C   be unable to hear the nightingale's song

   D   never find their way home

17. Which of the following is the <u>best</u> paraphrase for the last line of the poem?

   A   I am blinded by my resentment toward Juliana.

   B   I will continue wandering forever.

   C   I will never be myself again.

   D   I will never go home without her.

18. The main verb in the sentence that states the overall theme of the poem is

   A   "sit"

   B   "waste"

   C   "come"

   D   "find"

Directions Read the text. Then do Numbers 19 through 26.

Excerpt from "On the Duty of Civil Disobedience"

by Henry David Thoreau

1　But, to speak practically and as a citizen, unlike those who call themselves no-government men, I ask for, not at once no government, but *at once* a better government. Let every man make known what kind of government would command his respect, and that will be one step toward obtaining it.

2　After all, the practical reason why, when the power is once in the hands of the people, a majority are permitted, and for a long period continue, to rule, is not because they are most likely to be in the right, nor because this seems fairest to the minority, but because they are physically the strongest. But a government in which the majority rule in all cases cannot be based on justice, even as far as men understand it. Can there not be a government in which majorities do not virtually decide right and wrong, but conscience? … Must the citizen ever for a moment, or in the least degree, resign his conscience to the legislator? Why has every man a conscience, then? I think that we should be men first, and subjects afterward. It is not desirable to cultivate a respect for the law, so much as for the right. The only obligation which I have a right to assume is to do at any time what I think right. It is truly enough said that a corporation has no conscience; but a corporation of conscientious men is a corporation with a conscience. Law never made men a whit more just; and, by means of their respect for it, even the well-disposed are daily made the agents of injustice. … Visit the Navy Yard, and behold a marine, such a man as an American government can make, or such as it can make a man with its black arts—a mere shadow and reminiscence of humanity, a man laid out alive and standing, and already, as one may say, buried under arms with funeral accompaniments, though it may be,—

3　"Not a drum was heard, not a funeral note,
　　As his corpse to the rampart we hurried;
　　Not a soldier discharged his farewell shot
　　O'er the grave where our hero we buried."

4　The mass of men serve the state thus, not as men mainly, but as machines, with their bodies. They are the standing army, and the militia, jailers, constables, posse comitatus, etc. In most cases there is no free exercise whatever of the judgment or of the moral sense; but they put themselves on a level with wood and earth and stones; and wooden men can perhaps be manufactured that will serve the purpose as well. Such command no more respect than men of straw or a lump of dirt. They have the same sort of worth only as horses and dogs. Yet such as these even are commonly esteemed good citizens.

19. **Which of the following most closely explains what the author believes is wrong with democracy as a system of government?**

　A When "power is once in the hands of the people," they forget the purpose for which they wanted power.

　B Majority rule divorces the law from justice.

　C A democracy eventually transforms itself into a dictatorship.

　D When a large group of people has power, that group will inevitably include some who do not have the intellectual capacity or skills required to govern.

GO ▶

20. According to the author, the purpose of the law is to

    A   create a population that can easily be ruled

    B   encourage citizens to act for the good of society instead of in their own self-interest

    C   destroy justice

    D   make men forsake what is right

21. Which of the following lines <u>best</u> sums up the author's main point in this excerpt?

    A   "The mass of men serve the state thus, not as men mainly, but as machines..."

    B   "The only obligation which I have a right to assume is to do at any time what I think right."

    C   "...there is no free exercise whatever of the judgment or of the moral sense..."

    D   "...a government in which the majority rule in all cases cannot be based on justice..."

22. From the passage, you can infer that the "better government" the author wants would be characterized chiefly by which of the following?

    A   concern for the minority

    B   processes that encourage and honor individual achievements

    C   law that delivers justice

    D   a state of chaos

23. In this excerpt, the author develops his argument against government by the majority

    A   by stating his position, elaborating on why he feels that way, and giving examples of how the current government creates the opposite to the type of person he is

    B   by stating his position, then supporting it with examples of the negative results of the type of government he criticizes

    C   by stating his position, describing negative aspects of the current government, then repeating that pattern

    D   by describing the current type of government, then explaining how it could be improved

24. The four-line verse insert primarily serves to

    A   strengthen the author's connection between good citizens and military personnel

    B   emphasize the author's point about citizens voluntarily relinquishing their humanity to the state without receiving any thanks for it

    C   heighten the contrast between a military hero and a citizen

    D   stress the absence of justice in the current government

25. The author refers to "horses and dogs"

    A   as an example of creatures who can be trained to do what their masters demand

    B   to demonstrate what the government wants to create of its citizens

    C   to illustrate what fate awaits citizens who don't respect the law

    D   as an example of beings who don't exercise their free will

26. In the title, the author calls civil disobedience a "duty." How does the passage support this concept?

A It explains that a democracy is incompatible with justice.

B It asserts that most people lose their humanity when they become citizens.

C It says that under the current government, the law triumphs over individual conscience.

D It describes an alternative, much better form of government which would result if the majority of citizens disobeyed the rules and regulations of the current government.

Directions   Read the text. Then do Numbers 27 through 32.

Excerpt from *Barchester Towers*

by Anthony Trollope

1   It is not my intention to breathe a word against Mrs Proudie, but still I cannot think that with all her virtues she adds much to her husband's happiness. The truth is that in matters domestic she rules supreme over her titular lord, and rules with a rod of iron. Nor is this all. Things domestic Dr Proudie might have abandoned to her, if not voluntarily, yet willingly. But Mrs Proudie is not satisfied with such home dominion, and stretches her power over all his movements, and will not even abstain from things spiritual. In fact, the bishop is henpecked.

2   The archdeacon's wife, in her happy home at Plumstead, knows how to assume the full privileges of her rank, and express her own mind in becoming tone and place. But Mrs Grantly's sway, if sway she has, is easy and beneficent. She never shames her husband; before the world she is a pattern of obedience; her voice is never loud, nor her looks sharp; doubtless she values power, and has not unsuccessfully striven to acquire it; but she knows what should be the limits of a woman's rule.

3   Not so Mrs Proudie. This lady is habitually authoritative to all, but to her poor husband she is despotic. Successful as has been his career in the eyes of the world, it would seem that in the eyes of his wife he is never right. All hope of defending himself has long passed from him; indeed, he rarely even attempts self-justification; and is aware that submission produces the nearest approach to peace which his own house can ever attain.

4   One other marked peculiarity in the character of the bishop's wife must be mentioned. Though not averse to the society and manners of the world, she is in her own way a religious woman; and the form in which this tendency shows itself is by a strict observance of Sabbatarian rule. Dissipation and low dresses during the week are, under her control, atoned for by three services, an evening sermon read by herself, and a perfect abstinence from any cheering employment on the Sunday. Unfortunately for those under her roof to whom the dissipation and low dresses are not extended, her servants namely and her husband, the compensating strictness of the Sabbath includes all. Woe betide the recreant housemaid who is found to have been listening to the honey of a sweetheart in the Regent's park, instead of the soul-stirring discourse of Mr Slope. Not only is she sent adrift, but she is so sent with a character, which leaves her little hope of a decent place. Woe betide the sixfoot hero who escorts Mrs Proudie to her pew in red plush breeches, if he slips away to the neighbouring beer-shop, instead of falling in the back seat appropriated to his use. Mrs Proudie has the eyes of Argus for such offenders. Occasional drunkenness in the week may be overlooked, for six feet on low wages are hardly to be procured if the morals are always kept at a high pitch, but not even for grandeur or economy will Mrs Proudie forgive a desecration of the Sabbath.

27.   **Mrs. Proudie's authoritarian character is shown most pointedly in which of the following phrases from the excerpt?**

   A   "not satisfied with such home dominion"

   B   "knows how to assume the full privileges of her rank"

   C   "submission produces the nearest approach to peace"

   D   "not even for grandeur or economy will Mrs. Proudie forgive a desecration of the Sabbath"

28. Read the following sentence from the excerpt. Then answer the question.

> Woe betide the recreant housemaid who is found to have been listening to the honey of a sweetheart in the Regent's park, instead of the soul-stirring discourse of Mr. Slope.

In context, the adjective "recreant" is <u>best</u> interpreted as meaning

A unfaithful and disloyal

B engaging in a pastime

C craven and cowardly

D depraved

29. The author includes the description of Mrs. Grantly in order to

A provide another example of the power of the religious elite

B imply specific faults in Mrs. Proudie

C suggest a rivalry between her and Mrs. Proudie

D describe the type of wife Dr. Proudie wishes he had

30. What is the effect of the repetition of the phrase "Woe betide…" in the final paragraph?

A It highlights the seriousness of the consequences of not following Mrs. Proudie's rules.

B It mocks the fate of the servants.

C It slows readers down, forcing them to read the section more carefully.

D It signals a change in the narrator's attitude.

31. How does the last paragraph in the excerpt contribute to the development of Mrs. Proudie's character?

A It suggests a cause of Mrs. Proudie's moral transformation.

B It illustrates how Mrs. Proudie's religious beliefs reflect her character.

C It exposes another undesirable aspect of her character.

D It explains why Mrs. Proudie has difficulty hiring household servants.

32. The style of the passage as a whole can <u>best</u> be described as

A emotional and subjective

B descriptive and metaphorical

C terse and epigrammatic

D witty and analytical

GO ▶

Directions   Read the text. Then do Numbers 33 through 38.

Excerpt from *Avalanche Handbook*

by the U.S. Department of Agriculture—Forest Service

Fracture Mechanics of Snow

1   The properties of steel, wood, ceramics, and other common materials have been worked out in the laboratory and in theory to an accuracy that permits confident engineering design. Snow has also been studied as a material. As would be expected, the higher its density, the more it behaves like other materials. In fact, many studies have been made of the suitability of high-density snow (more than 400 kg/m^3) as a construction material in polar regions.

2   Some studies have also been made of the lower density snow typical of alpine, seasonal snowpacks. It is fair to conclude from these tests that low-density snow is a complex and unique material. Unfortunately, its properties are so complex that it is hardly possible to predict confidently how it will behave on the mountainside. On the other hand, although many properties of low-density snow cannot be identified accurately, laboratory tests provide at least a broad picture of its behavior.

3   In the laboratory, when a compressive force is applied to a snow sample, the sample deforms considerably. The amount of deformation depends on the intensity of the force and the rate at which the force is applied. When the force is removed suddenly, the sample springs back slightly, but a large amount of permanent deformation remains in the sample. The important point is that in the deformation of snow under load there are both a springy or elastic component and a permanent deformation component. The elastic component represents energy that is stored and recovered, and the permanent deformation component represents energy that is unrecoverable or has been dissipated.

4   The recoverable component of the deformation is a consequence of the springiness or elastic nature of the grains and necks in the ice skeleton. The unrecoverable energy is lost in the sliding of grains and necks. Some energy is also lost through viscous like flow of the skeleton. Many other substances, which are classified as viscoelastic, have recoverable and unrecoverable components. Almost all solids have a viscoelastic response when deformed at temperatures near their melting point.

5   As mentioned earlier, the ice skeleton is highly compressible and can sustain large amounts of permanent deformation. If the load is applied slowly enough that deformation is slow, then, in principle, the sample can be compressed to a mass of solid ice. If the applied force is strong enough and pushes fast enough on the sample, then the snow cannot respond by gradual collapse, and brittle fracture occurs.

6   What causes brittle fracture in snow? The answer, which is of deep significance in avalanche stability evaluation, is that any snowmass, depending on its temperature and texture, has two limitations: (1) it can store only a limited amount of elastic strain energy, and (2) it can dissipate the extra energy at a limited rate.

7   During brittle fracture propagation, the energy of the system is quickly redistributed into fracture surfaces, kinetic motion, and heat. Fractures initiate at flaws or localized regions of stress concentration. Because of the random nature of the ice skeleton, any snowmass is bound to have a weakest site where fractures are most likely to originate. In the mountain snowpack, trees, rocks, ski tracks, etc. are regions of stress concentrations and likely spots for fracture initiation.

33. The passage implies that a group of back country skiers being dropped off by helicopter would most likely be safest from avalanche danger if

   A   they landed on high-density snow

   B   the helicopter landed first, then let the skiers get out slowly, one by one

   C   the skiers dropped from the hovering helicopter individually, some distance apart

   D   the temperature was extremely low

34. A substance is classified as "viscoelastic" if

   A   the energy created by placing it under load is all dissipated when the load is removed

   B   applying, then removing a load causes both a permanent deformation and a slight spring-back to the original shape

   C   energy is stored and recovered if force is applied to it

   D   a permanent deformation is created when it is placed under load

35. The author is likely writing for which of the following audiences?

   A   academics who plan to advance the study of snow's properties

   B   the general public

   C   professional avalanche rescue teams

   D   experienced back country skiers and mountaineers

36. In this excerpt, the writer's primary objective is to

   A   train the audience

   B   inspire the audience to investigate further

   C   provide information only

   D   teach readers how to do something

37. Some knowledge about the amount and rate of energy retention and dissipation in a snowmass would most likely be important to readers because

   A   it would alert them to the dangers traversing a vulnerable area with a group of snowmobiles

   B   it would discourage amateurs from entering back country areas

   C   it would encourage them to stay away from high-density snowpacks

   D   it would ensure that mountaineers only apply load very slowly

38. After reading this excerpt, which of the following is one question that this passage answers?

   A   How can I predict how low-density snow will behave on a mountainside?

   B   Is there an intermediate type of snow between high- and low-density?

   C   What visible clues could warn me to avoid an area?

   D   Who conducted these studies about the properties of snow, and when?

| Directions | Read the text. Then do Numbers 39 through 44.

Excerpt from "Clausewitz's Center of Gravity: Changing Our Warfighting Doctrine—Again!"

By Antulio J. Echevarria II

Note: Carl von Clausewitz (1780–1831) was a Prussian general and influential military theorist. In this excerpt, "Center of Gravity" is abbreviated as "CoG."

1   Clausewitz's original definition follows the physics analogy more closely than previous analyses of his work have appreciated. In fact, it is not a source of strength or a critical capability, but a focal point that is essentially effects-based, rather than capabilities-based. In modern elementary physics, which was about the state of the mechanical sciences in Clausewitz's day, a CoG represents the point where the forces of gravity converge within an object. Striking at the CoG with enough force will usually cause the object to lose its balance, or equilibrium, and fall. A CoG is, therefore, not a source of strength, but a factor of balance.

2   A closer look at the German text shows that Clausewitz never used the term "source" (Quelle). Moreover, the concept remains valid only where the enemy possesses sufficient "unity" or "interdependence" (Zusammenhang) to act as a single body. Before applying the concept in war planning, therefore, we must ask ourselves whether we can consider the enemy to act as a single entity. If so, we should look for connections among the various parts of an adversary, or adversaries, in order to determine what holds them together. This is the CoG.

3   Furthermore, Clausewitz's CoG focuses on achieving a specific effect, the collapse of the enemy. Hence, it is an effects-based approach, rather than a capabilities-based one and it resembles an emerging concept called Effects-Based Operations (EBO) more than it does the capabilities-based notion that underpins today's doctrine. Another important point is that Clausewitz did not distinguish between tactical, operational, or strategic CoGs. The CoG is defined by the entire system (or structure) of the enemy, not by a level of war. In addition, Clausewitz emphasized that we should look for CoGs only in wars designed to defeat the enemy completely. Only the vast amount of energy and other resources that go into wars aimed at achieving decisive victory can cause CoGs and their areas of influence to emerge.

Toward a Simple Method

4   However, getting the definition of a CoG correct is only half the battle. War planners need a practical method for determining what a specific adversary's CoG is. Such as:

5   Step 1: Determine whether identifying and attacking a CoG is appropriate for the type of war we are going to wage.

6   Step 2: Determine whether the adversary's whole structure or system is sufficiently connected to be treated as a single body.

7   Step 3: Determine what element has the necessary centripetal force to hold the system together.

Source: Strategic Studies Institute, U.S. Army War College

39. According to the author, what is wrong with the current interpretation of Clausewitz's Center of Gravity concept?

A It loses the clear lines that distinguish between strategic, operational, and tactical levels of conflict.

B It doesn't apply to small, autonomous groups operating outside a centralized command structure.

C It misdirects resources by aiming at the wrong thing.

D It doesn't allow for the state of physics in Clausewitz's day.

40. In which of the following conflict situations would Clausewitz's concept of Center of Gravity be <u>most</u> useful in gaining an advantage over an adversary?

A against an opponent that consists of several different groups pursuing a common goal

B in a conflict where the strategic mission and operational limits have been established, and planning is now taking place at the tactical level

C in a conflict where it's crucial to undermine an adversary's capabilities

D in a limited engagement where the goal is to stop the adversary from making further gains

41. According to the information in the excerpt, the author's primary purpose in writing this report was

A to stress that Clausewitz's concept concerns equilibrium, not strength

B to describe the types of conflicts in which Clausewitz's Center of Gravity concept applies

C to explain the connection between Clausewitz's thinking and physics

D to return readers to Clausewitz's original concept of Center of Gravity

42. What is one possible difficulty to which the author alludes in preserving the original meaning of Clausewitz's concept of Center of Gravity?

A Interpretations are relying on translations instead of the original German text.

B The nature of military conflict has changed since the early seventeenth century.

C Modern analysts don't understand the state of mechanical sciences in Clausewitz's era.

D Adversaries today are smaller and operate more as decentralized units than they did in Clausewitz's day.

43. Read the following sentence from the excerpt.

> Determine what element has the necessary centripetal force to hold the system together.

As it's used in the passage, "centripetal" refers to

A constrained

B towards the center

C a synonym for "centrifugal"

D strong

44. Where would Clausewitz's concept of Center of Gravity most probably <u>not</u> be applicable?

A during the third (of three) sets of a tennis match, where you and your opponent have each won one set

B in a dispute with your manager about whether you should receive a raise

C when you're complaining that your bank has been overcharging for your monthly checking account fee

D during a conflict with your neighbor about a large branch on your tree that he feels is dangerously overhanging his roof

GO

Directions   Read the text. Then do Numbers 45 through 49.

Excerpt from *A Doll's House*

by Henrik Ibsen

1   KROGSTAD: Tell me, Mrs Helmer, can you by any chance remember what day your father died?—on what day of the month, I mean.

2   NORA: Papa died on the 29th of September.

3   KROGSTAD: That is correct; I have ascertained it for myself. And, as that is so, there is a discrepancy [taking a paper from his pocket] which I cannot account for.

4   NORA: What discrepancy? I don't know--

5   KROGSTAD: The discrepancy consists, Mrs Helmer, in the fact that your father signed this bond three days after his death.

6   NORA: What do you mean? I don't understand--

7   KROGSTAD: Your father died on the 29th of September. But, look here; your father has dated his signature the 2nd of October. It is a discrepancy, isn't it? [NORA is silent.] Can you explain it to me? [NORA is still silent.] It is a remarkable thing, too, that the words "2nd of October," as well as the year, are not written in your father's handwriting but in one that I think I know. Well, of course it can be explained; your father may have forgotten to date his signature, and someone else may have dated it haphazard before they knew of his death. There is no harm in that. It all depends on the signature of the name; and that is genuine, I suppose, Mrs Helmer? It was your father himself who signed his name here?

8   NORA [after a short pause, throws her head up and looks defiantly at him]: No, it was not. It was I that wrote papa's name.

9   KROGSTAD: Are you aware that is a dangerous confession?

10   NORA: In what way? You shall have your money soon.

11   KROGSTAD: Let me ask you a question; why did you not send the paper to your father?

12   NORA: It was impossible; papa was so ill. If I had asked him for his signature, I should have had to tell him what the money was to be used for; and when he was so ill himself I couldn't tell him that my husband's life was in danger—it was impossible.

13   KROGSTAD: It would have been better for you if you had given up your trip abroad.

14   NORA: No, that was impossible. That trip was to save my husband's life; I couldn't give that up.

15   KROGSTAD: But did it never occur to you that you were committing a fraud on me?

16   NORA: I couldn't take that into account; I didn't trouble myself about you at all. I couldn't bear you, because you put so many heartless difficulties in my way, although you knew what a dangerous condition my husband was in.

17   KROGSTAD: Mrs Helmer, you evidently do not realise clearly what it is that you have been guilty of. But I can assure you that my one false step, which lost me all my reputation, was nothing more or nothing worse than what you have done.

45. Nora's initial relationships to the three men in the excerpt can <u>best</u> be described as

A victim to persecutor

B victim to persecutor and child to caregiver

C child to caregiver and caregiver to child

D caregiver to child and persecutor to victim

46. From the excerpt, you can infer that Nora believes that repaying Krogstad

A will absolve her of the crime of fraud

B will be difficult to do

C will be necessary before she can get another loan from him

D will restore her father's good name

47. What can you infer from this excerpt about the playwright's attitude towards the character Nora?

A He condemns her dishonesty in forging her father's signature, even though she did it to save her husband.

B He admires her.

C He doesn't think she's very bright because she dated the forged signature after her father's death.

D He feels sorry for her.

48. From the information in the passage, which of the following is the <u>most likely</u> reason that Nora would have needed her father's signature on the bond?

A because she was underage and not legally allowed to borrow money

B because Krogstad and Nora's father were old friends, so Krogstad felt more comfortable lending money to Nora's father than to Nora herself

C because Nora had previously failed to repay a loan, so Krogstad wanted her father's guarantee before he loaned her money again

D because only men were allowed to sign bonds

49. What can you infer from the excerpt about Nora's sense of duty?

A Her sense of duty as a citizen came first.

B She felt her first duty was to her husband.

C She felt no sense of duty to someone who had treated her badly.

D Her strongest sense of duty was to herself.

GO ▶

THIS PAGE INTENTIONALLY LEFT BLANK.

You have 85 minutes to complete the Science test.

1. What process is shown in the following reaction?

$$6CO_2 + 6H_2O \xrightarrow[\text{Sunlight}]{} C_6H_{12}O_6 + 6O_2$$

A cellular respiration

B burning of propane

C photosynthesis

D decomposition of water

2. In 1929, Edward Hubble found that galaxies are constantly expanding at speeds proportional to their distance. This observation, known as Hubble's Law, supports which of the following scientific theories?

A Cosmic Background Radiation Theory

B Big Bang Theory

C Theory of Nucleosynthesis

D Exponential Expansion Theory

3. Unlike plant cells, animal cells

A have cell walls

B are autotrophs

C have chloroplasts

D are consumers

GO ▶

4. The following chart depicts the dose response curve of *M. tuberculosis* to an antibiotic drug.

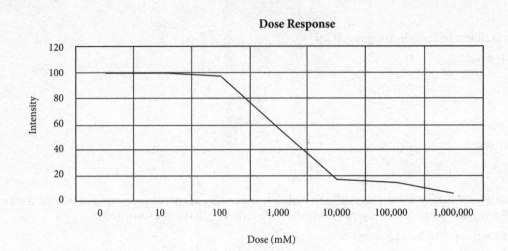

If an intensity score of 20 or less is considered acceptable, as the remaining bacteria can be eradicated by the host's immune response, what dose should the scientist recommend for patients?

A 100

B 1,000

C 10,000

D 1,000,000

Directions Use the following information to help answer questions 5 through 8.

> A molecule of DNA consists of two complementary strands: the sense strand and the antisense strand. The sense strand of a portion of DNA has the sequence TAGCCATTC.

5. Which of the following sequences represents the antisense strand of this DNA segment?

A TAGCCATTC

B CGATTGCCT

C ATCGGTAAG

D AUCGGUAAG

6. Unlike DNA, RNA

A consists of sugar called deoxyribose

B uses thymine as a nucleotide base

C forms a double-helix shape

D uses uracil as a nucleotide base.

7. Which of the following RNA sequences would be transcribed from the sense strand of this DNA segment?

A TAGCCTAAG

B AUCGGUAAG

C CGATTGCCT

D UACGGUAAG

8. All of the following are renewable forms of energy <u>except</u>

A nuclear

B geothermal

C solar

D biomass

9. Obsidian is a hard, dark glasslike rock that is formed by the rapid solidification of lava. Accordingly, obsidian is a(n)

A igneous rock

B sedimentary rock

C metamorphic rock

D fossilized rock

10. The graph below shows the population size of two different species, the Canadian lynx and the Arctic Hare, over a period of time.

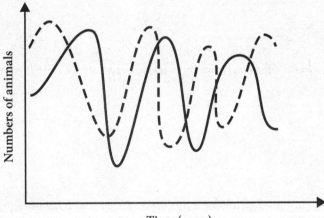

Which of the following does this graph depict?

A boom-bust cycle

B logistic growth model

C predator-prey cycle

D exponential growth model

GO ▶

11. Of the following types of radiant energy, which is most harmful to humans?

   A   radio waves

   B   infrared waves

   C   X-rays

   D   gamma rays

12. Eukaryotic cells contain organelles that perform specific functions to ensure the cell performs properly. Which organelle plays a pivotal role in cellular respiration?

   A   ribosomes

   B   endoplasmic reticulum

   C   Golgi apparatus

   D   mitochondria

Directions   Use the following information to help answer questions 13 through 15.

> In pigeons, the allele for black feathers (B) is dominant over the allele for white feathers (b). A homozygous dominant black-feathered pigeon (BB) mates with a homozygous recessive white-feathered pigeon (bb).

13. What percentage of the offspring would have white feathers?

   A   0%

   B   25%

   C   50%

   D   100%

14. What would the genotypic ratio be if one of the offspring from this mating bred with a heterozygous black-feathered pigeon (Bb)?

   A   3:1

   B   1:2:1

   C   1:1

   D   2:1:2

15. What would the phenotypic ratio be if one of the offspring from this mating bred with a heterozygous black-feathered pigeon (Bb)?

   A   3:1

   B   1:2:1

   C   1:1

   D   2:1:2

16. Which of the following substances are produced during the light reactions of photosynthesis?

A ATP and ADP

B ADP and NADPH

C ATP and NADPH

D ATP and NADH

Directions   Use the following information to help answer questions 17 and 18.

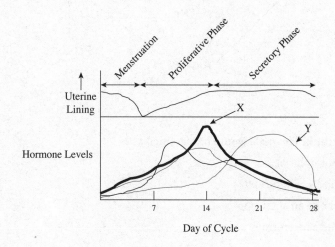

17. To which of the following bodily systems does the diagram refer?

A Muscular

B Digestive

C Reproductive

D Excretory

18. Based on the peak levels of hormone X, on what day of the cycle is ovulation most likely to occur?

A Day 10

B Day 14

C Day 21

D Day 24

19. A blue shift of the light from a star indicates that the star

A is moving away from Earth

B is anchored to the sun

C is moving towards Earth

D is about to collapse

GO ▶

Science

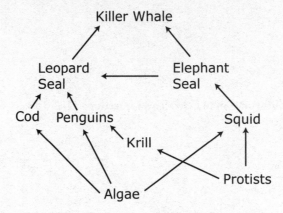

20. In the ecosystem above, the killer whale would be classified as a

   A producer and an autotroph

   B primary consumer and a heterotroph

   C secondary consumer and an autotroph

   D tertiary consumer and a heterotroph

21. If the population of krill were depleted, which of the following consumers would be most affected?

   A cod

   B squid

   C leopard seals

   D elephant seals

Directions Use the following information to help answer questions 22 through 24.

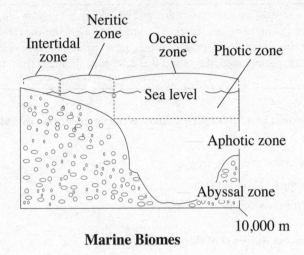

Marine Biomes

22. Algae that grow in this biome are examples of

    A *a*-selected organisms

    B K-selected organisms

    C P-selected organisms

    D *r*-selected organisms

23. Which of the following is the area of least productivity?

    A intertidal zone

    B oceanic zone

    C photic zone

    D aphotic zone

24. Organisms that live in the abyssal zone would need all of the following adaptations <u>except</u>

    A well-developed eyes

    B tolerance of cold temperatures

    C ability to utilize limited resources

    D ability to survive in areas with limited nutrients

GO ▶

Science

Directions Use the following information to help answer questions 25 and 26.

> A coal power plant was recently constructed on the outskirts of Ezraton, a small fishing town next to the river Schmeegen. Not only has the human population of Ezraton increased, but the ecosystem has also undergone major changes. After a couple of months, local fishermen note that the fish populations in the river Schmeegen have declined. After tests are conducted, it is found that acid mine drainage from the coal plant is running into the river Schmeegen.

25. **Which of the following would be an unexpected effect of the coal plant on this biome and the surrounding area?**

    A improved air quality in Ezraton

    B reduced biodiversity in the river Schmeegen

    C higher smoke and smog levels in Ezraton

    D increased acidity in the river Schmeegen

26. **Which of the following is the likely pH of the river Schmeegen?**

    A 5

    B 7

    C 8

    D 9

27. **Which chemical equation is incorrectly balanced?**

    A $4Al + 3O_2 \rightarrow 2Al_2O_3$

    B $2H_2S + SO_2 \rightarrow 3S + 2H_2O$

    C $3PbO + 2NH_3 \rightarrow 3Pb + 2N_2 + 3H_2O$

    D $2CH_3OH + 3O_2 \rightarrow 2CO_2 + 4H_2O$

28. The diagram below depicts the path of light as it travels through a piece of glass.

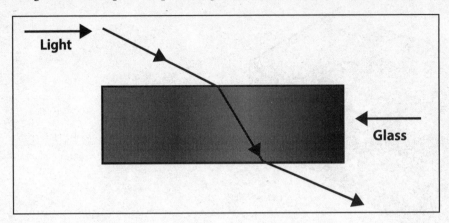

This behavior of light is known

A reflection

B refraction

C deflection

D diffraction

Directions Use the following information to help answer questions 29 through 31.

The transfer of heat occurs when particles move from an object with a high temperature to an object with a low temperature. On a cold day, Kristy and Eliz decide to build a campfire. After starting the fire, both girls felt much warmer than they did before the fire was made.

29. Which of the following occurred when Kristy and Eliz lit the campfire?

A Heat was absorbed in an endothermic reaction.

B Heat was released in an endothermic reaction.

C Heat was absorbed in an exothermic reaction.

D Heat was released in an exothermic reaction.

30. Based on the passage, which of the following is true?

A Via conduction, the girls absorbed heat from the campfire.

B Via convection, the girls absorbed heat from the campfire.

C Via conduction, the campfire absorbed heat from the girls.

D Via convection, the campfire absorbed heat from the girls.

31. Kristy takes a metal pole, places it in the fire, and burns her hand. All of the following occurred <u>except</u>

A conduction

B heat transfer

C convection

D exothermic reaction

GO ▶

32. The diagram below depicts a

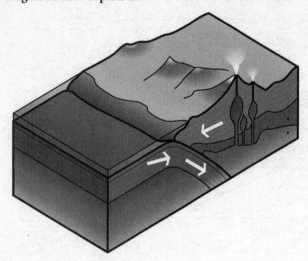

   A   convergent boundary

   B   divergent boundary

   C   transform fault boundary

   D   transport boundary

33.   **Covalent bonds**

   A   require at least one electron acceptor and one electron donor

   B   form when electrons are transferred between atoms

   C   are always polar

   D   form when valence electrons are shared between atoms

34. In the water cycle shown, which of the following processes does the letter A represent?

The Water Cycle

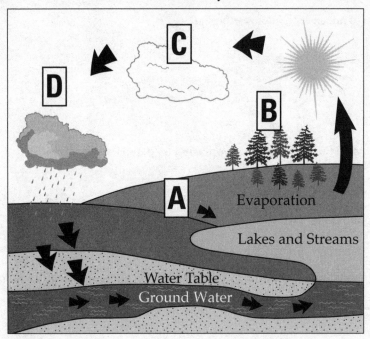

A transpiration

B evaporation

C runoff

D precipitation

35. Which of the following would happen if Austin were to break a bar magnet in half?

A The pieces would produce two electromagnetic fields.

B Both pieces of the bar magnet would be demagnetized.

C One piece would hold the north pole and one piece would hold the south pole.

D Two bar magnets would be created.

36. Which of the following is equal to the total number of protons and neutrons in an atom?

A atomic number

B relative atomic mass

C atomic charge

D atomic mass

37. Which of the following has the least momentum?

A a 10-kilogram cat moving 25 meters per second

B a 150-kilogram boat moving 10 meters per second

C a 70-kilogram girl moving 8 meters per second

D a 200-kilogram tiger moving 15 meters per second

GO ▶

Directions   Use the following information to help answer questions 38 through 40.

38.   The chart below describes the population of mice over a four-year period.

Year	Population Size
1	4
2	16
3	65
4	250

Assuming unlimited resources, what would be the approximate expected mouse population in year 5?

A   2,500

B   1,250

C   1,000

D   500

39.   If the current growth rate of the mouse population is 7 percent, how long will it take the mouse population to double in size?

A   7 years

B   10 years

C   20 years

D   70 years

40.   Which of the following <u>best</u> describes the role of mice in this ecosystem?

A   primary consumers

B   decomposers

C   tertiary consumers

D   producers

41.   The photoelectric effect shows that light

A   behaves as a wave

B   is reflective

C   behaves as a particle

D   is composed of quarks

42.   The human body uses hormones to cause the retention or excretion of fluid. When the body is lacking fluids, hormones signal the kidneys to decrease urine output and increase fluid retention. Conversely, if the body has too much fluid, hormones signal the kidneys to increase urine output and decrease fluid retention. This is an example of

A   the hydrologic cycle

B   homeostasis

C   cellular respiration

D   inflammatory response

43. The Big Bang theory proposes that, a few minutes after the Big Bang, light elements were formed through nucleosynthesis. Which of the following elements was <u>not</u> formed at this time?

A hydrogen

B helium

C deuterium

D uranium

44. The balanced equation below represents the oxidation process for propane.

$$C_3H_8 + 5O_2 \rightarrow 3CO_2 + 4H_2O$$

Which of the following describes the reaction shown above?

A Oxygen reacts with propane to create carbon dioxide and water.

B Oxygen and propane react to create water.

C Oxygen is converted into carbon dioxide.

D Propane is converted into water.

45. A particular UFO has a mass of 800 kilograms, and has alien technology that provides 32,000 newtons of thrust force. A second UFO has a mass of 1,400 kilograms, but has technology that provides exactly the same acceleration. What is the thrust force of the second UFO?

A 40 newtons

B 56 newtons

C 56,000 newtons

D 60,000 newtons

46. Mitosis is the second stage of a cell's life cycle, during which the cell divides.

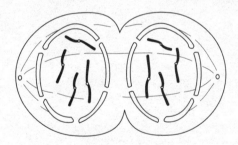

Which phase of mitosis is depicted in the image above?

A Prophase

B Metaphase

C Anaphase

D Telophase

47. During periods that are unfavorable for growth, some plants become dormant. Woody plants are protected during such periods by their bark. Perennial plants die above ground, but their roots remain alive. Annual plants die, but their seeds survive to continue the life of the species. Which of the following would most likely be a time of year during which plants might lie dormant?

A winter

B spring

C summer

D fall

Directions Use the following information to help answer questions 48 through 49.

> When humans come into contact with objects that inflict pain, they reflexively move away from those objects. Consider the example of a person who touches a hot stove. Provided that the individual has normal motor abilities and has not suffered nerve damage, he or she will almost instantly draw away from the stove.

48. Which of the following shows the process that occurs when an individual touches a hot object.

A Motor Neurons Excited → Muscle Cells Contract → Heat Detected → Spinal Interneurons Signaled→ Muscle Cells Signaled

B Heat Detected → Spinal Interneurons Signaled→ Muscle Cells Signaled→Motor Neurons Excited → Muscle Cells Contract

C Heat Detected → Spinal Interneurons Signaled → Motor Neurons Excited → Muscle Cells Signaled → Muscle Cells Contract

D Motor Neurons Excited → Spinal Interneurons Signaled→ Muscle Cells Contract → Muscle Cells Signaled→Heat Detected

49. All of the following organ systems are involved in this process <u>except</u>

A skeletal system

B muscular system

C nervous system

D digestive system

You have 75 minutes to complete the Social Studies test.

Directions Look at the timeline. Then answer questions 1 through 3.

1904	The National Child Labor Committee is formed to abolish all child labor.
1909	Ellen Key publishes *Century of the Child*, an influential American book about children's rights.
1921	Child Welfare League of America was founded by C. C. Carstens.
1938	President Franklin D. Roosevelt signed the Fair Labor Standards Act, which includes limits on many forms of child labor.
1944	The U.S. Supreme Court decision *Prince vs. Massachusetts* held that the government has broad authority to regulate the actions and treatment of children.

1. Which of the following beliefs was most likely the basis for the actions listed above?

    A Minors should judge the appropriateness of their own employment.

    B Employment of minors must be controlled to protect them from harm.

    C Minors should not be employed under any circumstances.

    D School children should focus on their studies and not be burdened with jobs.

2. Support for the passage of the Fair Labor Standards Act most likely came from

    A factory owners

    B child protection agencies

    C workers' unions

    D small companies

3. Child labor regulations could legally be used to deny a minor employment for all of the following reasons <u>except</u>

    A age

    B gender

    C hazard level

    D type of job

4. Read the quotation. Then answer the question.

    > As commanding general in the Civil War, he had defeated secession and destroyed slavery, secession's cause. As President during Reconstruction he had guided the South back into the Union. By the end of his public life the Union was more secure than at any previous time in the history of the nation. And no one had done more to produce the result than he.
    >
    > —H.W. Brands, *The Man Who Saved the Union*

    The above quotation is most likely referring to which American president?

    A Abraham Lincoln

    B Ulysses S. Grant

    C Jefferson Davis

    D Franklin D. Roosevelt

GO ▶

5. **Read the quotation. Then answer the question.**

> The old American Dream ... was the dream of the Puritans, of Benjamin Franklin's "Poor Richard"... of men and women content to accumulate their modest fortunes a little at a time, year by year by year. The new dream was the dream of instant wealth, won in a twinkling by audacity and good luck. [This] golden dream ... became a prominent part of the American psyche only after Sutter's Mill.
>
> —H.W. Brands

The historian quoted above is most likely referring to which major economic boom?

A the Industrial Revolution

B the Roaring Twenties

C the California Gold Rush

D the Baby Boom

Directions Read the excerpt from the First Amendment to the U.S. Constitution. Then answer questions 6 and 7.

> Congress shall make no law respecting an establishment of religion, or prohibiting the free exercise thereof; or abridging the freedom of speech, or of the press; or the right of the people peaceably to assemble, and to petition the Government...

6. **Which statement describes the primary purpose of the First Amendment?**

A The First Amendment protects the right to bear arms.

B The First Amendment increases the government's restriction of individual freedoms, such as the freedom of religion, of speech, and of the press.

C The First Amendment protects essential individual freedoms, such as the freedom of religion, of speech, and of the press.

D The First Amendment prohibits Congress from making laws.

7. **All of the following are guaranteed by the First Amendment <u>except</u>**

A the freedom to vote

B the freedom of petition

C the freedom of speech

D the freedom of the press

8. **Which of the following would <u>not</u> be found in a pure free market economy?**

A monopolies

B small businesses

C unemployed workers

D taxes and welfare benefits

9. Of the following groups, which would probably benefit the <u>least</u> from a transition from a pure free market economy to a socialist economy?

   A   government employees

   B   the unemployed

   C   small shop owners with small profits

   D   highly skilled labor

10. Automobiles in the early 20th century had all of the following characteristics <u>except</u>

    A   burned leaded gasoline, which resulted in air pollution

    B   a lack of seatbelts and other safety features

    C   heaviness due to a shortage of lightweight building materials

    D   the inability to burn fuels other than gasoline

11. After the Civil War, African Americans migrated to the North for all of the following reasons <u>except</u>

    A   to seek religious freedom

    B   to find employment in factories

    C   to escape poverty and racial discrimination

    D   to escape lynchings

12. All of the following are examples of plutocracy <u>except</u>

    A   Ancient Greece (2nd century B.C.E.)

    B   the Roman Empire (1st century C.E.)

    C   the Republic of Venice, Italy (12th century C.E.)

    D   Nazi Germany (20th century C.E.)

13. Which of the following is consistent with a monarchy?

    A   Citizens must abide by the decisions of the monarch in power.

    B   Monetary interests are valued above human interests.

    C   Leaders are determined by popular vote.

    D   A farmer is excluded from owning land.

GO ▶

14. **Read this quotation. Then answer the question.**

> The [oil monopoly] molds public opinion in a manner creating a complete misunderstanding of the petroleum situation and influences the judgment and acts of unknowing and unwise public officials to a point where they fall to these interests of monopoly as against the welfare of the people whom they are supposed to serve.
>
> —Andrew W. Mellon

Which of the following is an opinion most likely held by the speaker above?

A Those who profit from monopolies should not try to serve the public by running for office.

B The interests of the people are secondary to those of public officials.

C All should profit from the rewards gained by a monopoly.

D Public officials should value the interests of the people they serve over the interests of any one business.

15. **All of the following describe tasks for which the federal government is responsible <u>except</u>**

A declaration of War

B interstate Trade Regulation

C establishment of Post Offices

D adjudication of Divorce Settlements

16. **Which of the following economic or social factors <u>best</u> explains the geographical distribution of non-English-speaking children in the United States?**

A Income taxes are lower on the East and West coasts than in the middle of the country.

B Fewer children are born in states with cold climates.

C There are fewer opportunities to learn English the northern part of the United States.

D Recent immigrants to the United States have tended to settle in border and coastal states.

17. **Which factor would have the <u>least</u> effect upon the distribution of immigrants in the United States?**

A migration patterns

B climate

C job opportunities

D immigration laws

18. **Which generalization about immigration in the 20th century is most likely true?**

A Geographically, immigrants settled evenly across the United States.

B There were more Spanish-speaking immigrants in Arizona than in California.

C In Texas and California, more immigrant children were illiterate than were literate.

D There were fewer non-English speaking children in the northern middle portion of the United States than in other parts of the country.

19. Which of the following is an example of a state law that would be incompatible with the Constitution?

   A   a law that prohibits protests by a steelworkers' union

   B   a law that lowers the speed limit on a highway to 50 miles per hour

   C   a law that limits state senators to two six-year terms each

   D   legislation that requires reductions in emissions from factories

20. Which of the following is an example of a law compatible with the Constitution?

   A   legislation that prohibits the practice of certain religions

   B   a law that protects the rights of convicted criminals

   C   a law that suspends the right to trial by jury

   D   a law that prevents non-English speakers from voting

Directions   Look at the timeline. Then answer questions 21 through 25.

1945   Yalta Conference: The Allies of World War II (the USA, the USSR, Great Britain, and France) divide Germany into four occupation zones.

1947   Marshall Plan: A comprehensive program of economic assistance for the war-ravaged countries of Western Europe.

1948   Berlin Airlift: In response to Soviet Premier Joseph Stalin's attempt to block supplies to Berliners, France, Britain, and the United States launch the Berlin Airlift to supply the citizens of Berlin by air.

1949   North Atlantic Treaty Organization (NATO): Western nations unite in order to resist Communist expansion.

1955   Warsaw Pact: Soviet Union and Eastern European Communist nations unite to oppose NATO.

21. Why was the Berlin Airlift necessary?

   A   The Yalta Conference had impoverished the citizens of Berlin.

   B   The Marshall Plan had successfully assisted the citizens of Berlin to recover economically.

   C   The creation of the Warsaw Pact had prevented Berliners from accessing food supplies.

   D   The Soviets had closed supply routes to Berlin.

22. What event was a response to the formation of the North Atlantic Treaty Organization (NATO)?

   A   Communist countries united under the Warsaw Pact.

   B   Allies implemented the Berlin Airlift.

   C   Joseph Stalin blocked supplies to Berlin.

   D   Germany was divided into four occupation zones.

23. Which of these organizations was formed to prevent a common threat?

   A   NATO

   B   Yalta Conference

   C   Marshall Plan

   D   Berlin Airlift

GO ▶

24.   Which of these would be the <u>best</u> title for the above timeline?

    A   Timeline of Events Following World War I

    B   Timeline of Events Following World War II

    C   Timeline of Events Preceding the Korean War

    D   Timeline of Events Preceding the Vietnam War

25.   All of the following exemplify the policy of containment <u>except</u>

    A   the Truman Doctrine

    B   the Marshall Plan

    C   the creation of NATO

    D   the 1948 Berlin airlift

26.   If it is true that the purchase price of company stocks on the New York Stock Exchange is affected by many factors, which of the following can one conclude?

    A   The shares of two companies producing the same goods will have approximately the same price.

    B   The price of a stock increases as it attracts more amateur investors.

    C   It is possible to lose money by investing in a company that has been very profitable.

    D   An amateur stock investor will always earn less money than a professional.

27.   Which of the following is a characteristic of "laissez-faire" economics?

    A   deregulation

    B   labor laws

    C   building codes

    D   antitrust laws

28. Look at the photo. Then answer the question.

Source: Photofest Archives

The golden age of transatlantic passenger ships was quickly coming to an end in this photo taken of six ocean liners at dock in New York City circa 1953. Which of the following events was probably the most important reason for the end of the era of crossing the Atlantic by ship?

A A series of highly publicized liner accidents made the public too nervous to take ships.

B A major war made overseas travel impossible.

C The advent of passenger airlines cut down the time it took to get to Europe, leaving ships outmoded.

D The cost of travel by boat became prohibitively expensive.

29. The most important cash crop in seventeenth-century Virginia was

A tobacco

B corn

C wheat

D barley

30. Which of the following best describes the "muckrakers" of the Progressive era?

A politicians who slandered opponents in order to win elections

B state prisoners who, working in chain gangs, cleaned state roads

C journalists whose reports exposed corruption in government and business

D novelists who wrote historical fiction about the Civil War era

GO ▶

31. Read the following quotation. Then answer the question.

> In good time we are going to sweep into power in this nation and throughout the world. We are going to destroy all enslaving and degrading capitalist institutions and recreate them as free and humanizing institutions.

The statement above <u>best</u> represents the ideology of

A radical Republicans of the 1870s

B American socialists of the 1910s

C isolationists of the 1920s

D New Deal Democrats of the 1930s

32. The development of the Interstate Highway System was accompanied by a sizable population shift from

A western states to eastern states

B cities to suburbs

C rural areas to large urban centers

D single-family housing to apartment buildings

33. President Lyndon Johnson's social programs in the 1960s were known collectively as the

A American System

B New Deal

C New Frontier

D Great Society

34.   Look at the following cartoon. Then answer the question.

A MAN KNOWS A MAN

"Give me your hand, Comrade! We have each lost a Leg

for the good cause; but, thank God, we never lost Heart."

This cartoon from the Civil War era depicts two veterans of the Civil War greeting each other. What did the cartoonist mean to imply by the caption?

A   These two men were equals in each other's eyes.

B   These two soldiers who had lost their legs were not to be pitied because they were still men.

C   These soldiers had previously met.

D   Although they may have met before, these veterans had nothing in common.

35.   **What is a primary duty of the Legislative Branch of the federal government?**

A   To veto laws

B   To debate and vote on laws

C   To oversee the implementation of Supreme Court decisions

D   To nominate and appoint judges to the Supreme Court

GO ▶

Directions Read the quotation. Then answer questions 36 and 37.

> You seem to consider the judges as the ultimate arbiters of all constitutional questions; a very dangerous doctrine indeed, and one which would place us under the despotism of an oligarchy. Our judges are as honest as other men, and not more so. They have, with others, the same passions for party, for power, and the privilege of their corps.... Their power [is] the more dangerous as they are in office for life, and not responsible, as the other functionaries are, to the elective control.
>
> —Thomas Jefferson, in response to *Marbury vs. Madison*

36. What was Thomas Jefferson's opinion of *Marbury vs. Madison*?

A It balanced federal power by giving federal judges the right to override unjust laws.

B It conferred too much power to the Executive Branch.

C It made judges as honest as other men.

D It gave too much power to the Judicial Branch.

37. In context, what is the <u>best</u> substitute for the word "oligarchy"?

A tyranny

B democracy

C passion

D honesty

38. Which of the following statements about the authors of the Bill of Rights to the Constitution is most accurate?

A They were legal scholars.

B They believed that the government and the church should be united.

C They believed that the best type of government would have ultimate authority.

D They were wary of giving the government too much power over individual rights.

39. Read the excerpt from the Fourteenth Amendment to the U.S. Constitution. Then answer the question.

> No state shall make or enforce any law which shall abridge the privileges or immunities of citizens of the United States; nor shall any state deprive any person of life, liberty or property, without due process of law, nor deny to any person...equal protection under the law.

All of the following actions by a particular state would violate the Fourteenth Amendment <u>except</u>

A a zoning law prohibiting naturalized citizens from operating ethnic restaurants

B legislation requiring citizens to pay taxes regardless of their beliefs

C a bill requiring children of citizens of a particular ethnic origin to attend separate public schools

D sentencing a person accused of murder without a trial

40. Amelia Earhart is best known for which of the following accomplishments?

A the first female aviator to fly solo across the Atlantic Ocean

B the first female to serve on the Supreme Court

C the first female to run for national public office

D the first female to circumnavigate the world in an automobile

41. Look at the graph. Then answer the question.

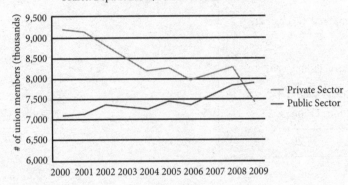

Union membership among public and
private sector workers
Source: Dept. of Labor, Bureau of Labor Statistics

All of the following are supported by the information in the graph <u>except</u>:

A There were about 7,500,000 public sector union members in 2007.

B There were about 9,000,000 private sector employees in 2002.

C There was an increase in both private and public sector union membership from 2006 to 2008.

D Combined union membership in both public and private sectors generally decreased from 2000 to 2009.

42.   Look at the chart. Then answer the question.

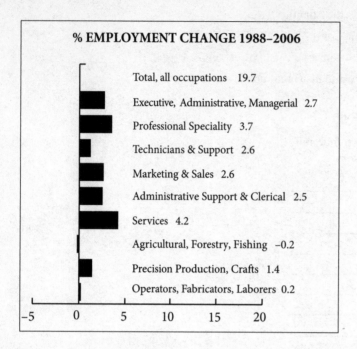

% EMPLOYMENT CHANGE 1988–2006

Total, all occupations   19.7

Executive, Administrative, Managerial   2.7

Professional Speciality   3.7

Technicians & Support   2.6

Marketing & Sales   2.6

Administrative Support & Clerical   2.5

Services   4.2

Agricultural, Forestry, Fishing   –0.2

Precision Production, Crafts   1.4

Operators, Fabricators, Laborers   0.2

The information in the chart supports the conclusion that from 1988 to 2006 there has been

A   an increase in agricultural jobs

B   more growth in administrative support jobs than in any other occupation

C   more growth in administrative support jobs than in services and technicians and support jobs combined

D   less growth in precision production than in professional specialties

43.   Which of the following statements about indentured servants in the seventeenth century is <u>not</u> correct?

A   Many Europeans were forced into indentured servitude.

B   The majority of British immigrants in the southern colonies were indentured servants.

C   Terms of indenture were usually seven years, after which indentured servants received their freedom and, often, a plot of land.

D   Indentured servants served under the exact same conditions as did African slaves.

44.   The system under which national and state governments share constitutional power is called

A   federalism

B   nationalism

C   idealism

D   autocracy

45. The majority of Japanese Americans imprisoned in internment camps during World War II

    A   were native-born Americans

    B   were employees of the Japanese government

    C   lived on Pacific islands

    D   had expressed their primary allegiance to Japan during the 1940 census

46. During World War II, the availability of consumer goods to civilians

    A   increased greatly, because the war invigorated the economy

    B   increased slightly, because some citizens were overseas serving in the armed forces

    C   decreased slightly, causing prices to rise; only the poor were substantially affected

    D   decreased greatly, to the point that the government had to ration most necessities

47. Read the quotation. Then answer the question.

> I have never been a quitter. To leave office before my term is completed is abhorrent to every instinct in my body, but as president I must put the interests of America first. America needs a full-time president and a full-time Congress, particularly at this time, with the problems we face at home and abroad. Therefore, I shall resign from the presidency, effective at noon tomorrow . . . .

The speech quoted above was delivered in which year?

    A   1944

    B   1954

    C   1964

    D   1974

GO ▶

48. Look at the chart. Then answer the question.

GDP per capita in Southeast Asia and Africa, 1970–1995

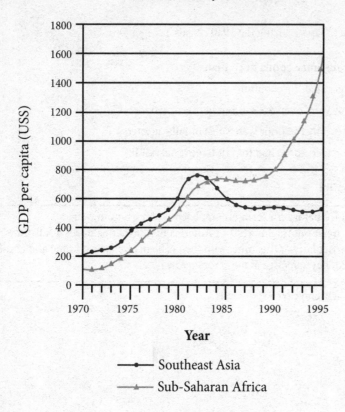

Based on this information, which statement is an <u>opinion</u>, rather than a fact, about the GDP per capita of these nations?

A The GDP per capita for Southeast Asia has increased substantially in recent years.

B The GDP per capita of Southeast Asia is now higher than that of Sub-Saharan Africa.

C Sub-Saharan Africa is in desperate need of foreign aid in order to sustain its economy.

D For many years, Southeast Asia and Sub-Saharan Africa had similar patterns of economic growth.

49. The idea that the United States was destined and divinely ordained by God to expand across the entire North American continent is called

A Manifest Destiny

B capitalism

C imperialism

D eminent domain

STOP

Chapter 31
Practice Test 1:
Answers and
Explanations

ANSWER KEY

Mathematics

Calculator Session

1. D
2. D
3. B
4. 11
5. B
6. D
7. 3,150
8. B
9. C
10. A
11. C
12. 5
13. A
14. C
15. D
16. D
17. 12
18. B
19. 3,520
20. C
21. A
22. 1,250
23. C
24. 25
25. B
26. C
27. A

Non-Calculator Session

28. B
29. D
30. D
31. $\frac{7}{30}$
32. C
33. D
34. 16
35. A
36. A
37. D
38. D
39. $\frac{56}{12}$
40. A
41. C
42. D
43. C
44. D
45. B
46. D
47. B
48. B
49. C
50. A
51. 110
52. A
53. B
54. A

Writing

Part 1: Language

1. C
2. D
3. C
4. D
5. C
6. B
7. D
8. D
9. A
10. C
11. B
12. C
13. A
14. B
15. A
16. D
17. B
18. D
19. C
20. B
21. D
22. A
23. C
24. B
25. A
26. B
27. B
28. C
29. A
30. D
31. B
32. C
33. D
34. B
35. B
36. C
37. C
38. D
39. A
40. B
41. D
42. D
43. A
44. C
45. B
46. A
47. C
48. A
49. A
50. A
51. D

Part 2—See Explanation

Reading

1. A
2. C
3. B
4. D
5. B
6. A
7. D
8. A
9. C
10. D
11. B
12. C
13. D
14. B
15. B
16. A
17. C
18. B
19. B
20. A
21. B
22. D
23. C
24. B
25. D
26. C
27. C
28. A
29. B
30. A
31. C
32. D
33. C
34. B
35. D
36. C
37. A
38. C
39. C
40. A
41. D
42. A
43. B
44. A
45. C
46. A
47. B
48. D
49. C

Science

1. C
2. B
3. D
4. C
5. C
6. D
7. B
8. A
9. A
10. C
11. D
12. D
13. A
14. B
15. A
16. C
17. C
18. B
19. C
20. D
21. C
22. D
23. D
24. A
25. A
26. A
27. C
28. B
29. D
30. B
31. C
32. A
33. D
34. C
35. D
36. B
37. A
38. C
39. B
40. A
41. C
42. B
43. D
44. A
45. C
46. D
47. A
48. C
49. D

Social Studies

1. B
2. B
3. B
4. B
5. C
6. C
7. A
8. D
9. D
10. D
11. A
12. D
13. A
14. D
15. D
16. D
17. B
18. D
19. A
20. B
21. D
22. A
23. A
24. B
25. D
26. C
27. A
28. C
29. A
30. C
31. B
32. B
33. D
34. A
35. B
36. D
37. A
38. D
39. B
40. A
41. B
42. D
43. D
44. A
45. A
46. D
47. D
48. C
49. A

MATHEMATICS

Calculator Session

1. **D** Read this question carefully. Three numbers need to be plugged into the equation and added together to find the answer. $\frac{1}{6}(3000) + 300 = 800$, $\frac{1}{6}(900) + 300 = 450$, and $\frac{1}{6}(2700) + 300 = 750$; since the question asks for the total amount made over the three weeks, add these numbers together to get the final answer. $800 + $450 + $750 = $2,000.

2. **D** The ratio of the fifth to the ninth term of a geometric sequence solely depends on the common ratio. Since the common ratio is 4, that means that from the fifth to ninth term, the value will quadruple a total of 4 times. Multiplying a number by 4 four times will give a multiple of 256. Alternatively, you could determine each of the terms—the fifth term will be 512 and the ninth 131,072. This reduces to 1:256.

3. **B** Since the two parabolas are equal, points that lie on the original parabola must also lie on the new one. For example, plug in $x = 0$. In the original function, $x = 0$ gives an $f(x)$ value of –26, so the equivalent form should do so as well. Plugging in $x = 0$ into the answer choices gives an $f(x)$ value of 26 for (A), –26 for (B), 6 for (C), and 58 for (D). Since the correct one should also have a value of –26, the answer must be (B). This can also be done by completing the square and manipulating the equation—but who wants to do so much work when plugging in can solve the question?

4. **11** First, write equations to represent the amount of money each of the two has in his account. John has $1,000 + 50m$, whereas Sam has $250 + 125m$. Solving for m gives that the number of months for the two to be equal is 10; therefore, since the question asks after how many months Sam will have <u>more</u>, we need to add one month for a total of 11 months.

5. **B** When two numbers are inversely proportional, one of them increases as the other decreases. Therefore, since the number of miles went up, the percent will definitely decrease. Furthermore, inverse proportionality means that the product of the two numbers will be consistent. 330 miles × 22% = 781 miles × x%; solving gives a percentage of 9.29%, which is closest to (B).

6. **D** Solve an inequality just as you would an equality, with one exception: If dividing or multiplying by a negative, remember to flip the sign. First, FOIL the squares; this gives $(a - 3)^2 = a^2 - 6a + 9$ and $(a + 3)^2 = a^2 + 6a + 9$. Rewriting the inequality gives $a^2 - 6a + 9 \leq a^2 + 6a + 9 + 16$, and simplifying and combining like terms, we are left with $-12a \leq 16$ or $a \geq -\frac{4}{3}$.

7. **3,150** Since 30% of the tomatoes are used for bruschetta and 7% are used for salads, that leaves 63% used for other things. Take 63% of 5,000; this will give 3,150.

8. **B** Remember to read carefully. The question asks about the mass in kg; therefore, at the end, the unit needs to be converted. First, find the volume of the object. Since it measures 15 cm by 20 cm by 10 cm, its volume is 15 cm × 20 cm × 10 cm or 3,000 cm³. Plug this number into the density equation to find the mass. 10.5 g/cm³ = mass/3,000 cm³. Mass = 10.5 g/cm³ × 3,000 cm³ = 31,500 g. Since there are 1,000 g in one kg, divide by 1,000 to find the answer.

9. **C** First, calculate the volume of the object. Since a bowling ball is a sphere, use the formula for volume of a sphere, which is $\frac{4}{3}\pi r^3$. A radius of 9.8 cm will give a volume of $(\frac{4}{3})\pi(9.8)^3$, which is approximately 3,940 cm³. Plugging this into the density equation gives 1.61 g/cm³ = mass/3,940 cm³, or a mass of 6,343 grams. Since the question asked for kilograms, don't forget to convert into proper units to get the answer.

10. **A** To calculate the number of options, create spaces to represent each unknown. In this case, that is two flavors: one wet topping and one dry topping. However, since the order in which the flavors are chosen would not change the sundae itself, don't forget to divide the final answer by 2 in order to compensate. Doing the math would give us $\frac{8 \times 7 \times 10 \times 5}{2}$, which is 1,400.

11. **C** Factor the quadratic first; this would give $(3x + 4)(2x - 5)$. This gives two roots of $-\frac{4}{3}$ and $\frac{5}{2}$, which have a sum of $\frac{7}{6}$. Weirdly enough, the sum of the roots of any quadratic is always equal to the opposite of the coefficient of the "x" term divided by the coefficient of the squared term; that route would also give $-(-\frac{7}{6})$, or $\frac{7}{6}$.

12. **5** Plug the numbers provided into the equation given. Since $KE = \frac{1}{2}mv^2$, 2,000 J $= \frac{1}{2}$ (160 kg)(v^2). Therefore, $2,000 = 80v^2$, and $25 = v^2$. That means 5 m/s = v.

13. **A** First, calculate how much of her salary Jessica takes home. Taking 22% of her salary gives $13,200 as the amount paid in taxes, and leaves her with $46,800. Do the same thing another time, but now with the percent that goes to rent; 25% of her $46,800 take-home pay, or $11,700, goes toward rent, leaving her with $31,500 remaining.

14. **C** Since this is a composite function, work from the outside in. The question asks for $g(4)$; therefore, plug 4 into the $g(x)$ function. That gives $g(4) = f(4+3)$, or $f(7)$. Then, plug the 7 into the $f(x)$ equation. That gives $f(7) = 7^2 + 3$, which is 52.

15. **D** An arithmetic sequence is always increased or decreased by a common value. Choice (A) would be the answer if the sequence were geometric, but not as an arithmetic sequence. Try the other answers and see which one increases by a constant value each time; (D) is the only one that works.

Alternatively, since the value increases by a total of 78 over three spaces, it must be increased by $\frac{78}{3}$, or 26, each time. The sequence starts at 3, so 3 + 26 = 29 as the second term, also giving (D).

16. **D** Since the player has a win percentage of 41.6%, and has won 52 games, an equation can be written to solve this. Since the question is essentially saying 41.6% of what is 52, this translates to $(\frac{41.6}{100})x = 52$. Solving for x gives 125.

17. **12** Determine how much time was spent driving each route. Since distance = rate × time, time is the distance divided by rate; this means Matt drove 224 miles at 64 mph on the way there, a total of 3.5 hours, and 75 miles at 50 mph on the way back for a time of 1.5 hours. He spent five hours driving and seven hours at the park for a total of 12 hours for the day.

18. **B** In order to calculate the volume occupied by all the cans, first the volume of one must be determined. To do so, the radius and height must be known; the height is given as 5 inches, and the radius can be determined using the dimensions of the box. Since there are two rows of three cans, the nine-inch side must have the three cans side-by-side, so each can has a diameter of 3 inches and therefore a radius of 1.5 inches. The volume of one can is then $\pi(1.5)^2(5)$, or $\frac{45\pi}{4}$. Multiply this by 6 to get the total volume all six cans occupy, and that gives a total of $\frac{135\pi}{2}$ as the volume.

19. **3,520** There are two spaces to find volumes for here. First, calculate the volume of the total area covered by the tent to the base of the tent itself. Since the space below the tent itself measures 22 by 24 feet and has a height of 6 feet, the total volume covered by that space is 22 ft × 24 ft × 6 ft for a total of 3,168 ft³. Then find the volume of the space within the tent itself. The height of the pyramidal top is only 2 feet, since the center is eight feet from the ground and the edges six feet from the ground. The other lengths of 22 and 24 feet are still the same, so reuse them in calculating volume. Volume of a pyramid is $\frac{1}{3}$ the product of the area of the base and the height, or in this case $(\frac{1}{3})(22 \text{ ft} \times 24 \text{ ft})(2 \text{ ft}) = 352$ ft³. Add the two volumes together to find the answer of 3,520 ft³.

20. **C** Find the volumes of the two spheres. Volume of a sphere is given by $\frac{4}{3}\pi r^3$, so first plug in $2\frac{1}{8}$ as the radius and then plug in $1\frac{7}{8}$ as the radius. The regular balls have a volume of 12.8π, and the cue has a volume of 8.8π, for a difference of 4π.

21. **A** Solving for x requires isolation of the variable, so work toward getting the variable on its own. First, cube both sides to get rid of the cube root; this gives $(2x + 5)^2 = 729$. From there, take the square root of both sides, which gives $2x + 5 = 27$. Subtract 5 from both sides to get $2x = 22$ and divide by 2 to get $x = 11$.

22. **1,250** When given an equation and values for the numbers, simply put the values into the expression provided. In this case, that means to substitute 15 wherever an "*m*" appears and a 5 wherever a "*c*" appears. This gives $2(5)\left[4(5)-(15)\right]^{\frac{15}{5}} = 10 \times 5^3 = 10 \times 125 = 1,250$.

23. **C** Break the image apart into smaller portions. Start with the left-most box; this box is given to have dimensions of 4 by 7, so the area of that box is 28. Then, look at the smallest box in the bottom right of the figure. That box is given as a 2 by 2 box, for a total area of 4. Using the total dimensions vertically on the right-hand side, the height of the remaining piece can be determined; the total length of that side is 6, but 2 of the 6 is taken by the bottom-most box. Therefore, the vertical length of the box remaining is 4, and the horizontal length given is 4. This is an area of 4 by 4, or 16, for a total area covered of 28 + 16 + 4, or 48.

24. **25** Simplify the expression by finding the fourth root of 625 and squaring the result. The same answer would be obtained by squaring 625 and then taking the fourth root, or even by simplifying the exponent itself first; the fourth root of a number squared is the same thing as taking the square root of the number itself, which also would be 25.

25. **B** Volume of a pyramid is equivalent to $\frac{1}{3}Bh$, where B is the area of the base and h is the height of the figure. In this case, the base is a rectangle, so its area is $l \times w$. The length and width were given as 12 and 8, so the area of the base is 96. Plugging that into the volume of a pyramid formula gives $\frac{1}{3}(96)(20)$, or 640 as the answer, (B).

26. **C** Remember that logarithms are just a weird way to write exponents. $\text{Log}_7 343$ means the same thing as $7^x = 343$. Plug in the answers and see which one works; since $7^3 = 343$, the answer is 3.

27. **A** Waving a flag in a circle would form a cylinder, which would have a volume in the form of $\pi r^2 h$. To save time, it is helpful to remember that the product of two odd numbers is always odd; therefore, the two answers featuring odd numbers only are eliminated. Pick one of the remaining options and give it a try; if the radius is 8 and the height 6, the correct volume would be obtained, giving the answer of (A).

Non-Calculator Session

28. **B** To do this without a calculator, estimate to see which answer is best. Round the numbers each to the nearest multiple of 25 for simplicity; for example, consider 223 as 225, 251 as 250, 317 as 325, 636 as 650; 766 as 775, and 607 as 600 for both times it appears. The sum is then 3,425, for about a 489 average. This is closest to the estimate of 485.

29. **D** Slope of a line is calculated by finding the change in y and dividing by the change in x. Use either point as the "starting"; just be consistent. Doing so gives either $\dfrac{y-4}{11-x}$ or $\dfrac{4-y}{x-11}$, or answer (D).

30. **D** The range of scores received is the difference between the highest and lowest scores received. Since the highest score was an 84 and the lowest a 4, this gives a difference and therefore a range of 80. Be sure to read the question carefully; answer (C), for example, is the median, not the range.

31. $\dfrac{7}{30}$ The first ten consecutive prime numbers are 2, 3, 5, 7, 11, 13, 17, 19, 23, and 29. The odd numbers less than 20 are 1, 3, 5, 7, 9, 11, 13, 15, 17, and 19. The elements in both sets are therefore 3, 5, 7, 11, 13, 17, and 19—a total of seven numbers. Since the question says the number is chosen from 1 to 30, inclusive, there are a total of 30 numbers available from which to choose, for a probability of 7 out of 30.

32. **C** The diameter of the circle, $\sqrt{50}$, can be rewritten another way—as $5\sqrt{2}$. If the diameter of the circle is $5\sqrt{2}$, the sides of the square are then 5 each, which means the area of the square is 25.

33. **D** First, find the volume of the cylinder. Since the volume of a cylinder is given by $\pi r^2 h$, the volume is $\pi(.5\text{ m})^2(2\text{ m})$, or $\dfrac{\pi}{2}$ m³. From there, a proportion can be set up to relate the volumes and moles, as in $\dfrac{0.0224\text{ m}^3}{1\text{ mol}} = \dfrac{\frac{\pi}{2}\text{ m}^3}{x\text{ mol}}$. Cross-multiplying and simplifying gives (D).

34. **16** Simplify one piece at a time. 9^2 is 81, 3^0 is 1, and 4^3 is 64. $81 - 1 - 64 = 16$.

35. **A** Focus on lines *a, c,* and *d*. Since *d* is a transversal that crosses over both *a* and *c*, all the small angles are the same and all the large angles are the same. The small angles are all 30°, so all the large ones are the supplement and are 150°. That gives the angle requested as 150°. In this question, the other provided angle of 80° is actually not needed.

36. **A** Notice all answers use the same numbers on the line but change the ranges of possible answers. Therefore, test out numbers that fall in each of the ranges listed. Test out 0 first; that does not work, eliminating (C) and (D). Since (A) and (B) both mention values less than −3, don't worry about testing that range; instead, test either a number between 2.5 and 7 or larger than 7. By testing a very large number, such as 100, it can be seen that the range larger than 7 does not work, leaving only (A).

37. **D** There are two ways to do this question—either recognize slopes of lines or draw the lines. Since two of the slopes are the same but have different *y*-intercepts, two of the lines are parallel. However, the other two lines are not parallel; therefore, all forms of parallelograms are eliminated, leaving (D). The following graph shows what these would look like plotted on a coordinate plane.

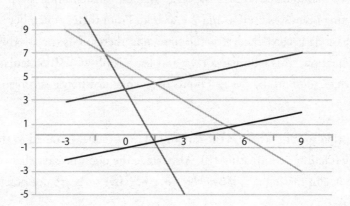

38. **D** Find the total population in each of the cities individually first. The New York metro area has 30,000 people per square mile times 60 square miles, for 1,800,000 people. Since that is already larger than answers (A) and (B), eliminate both. Since the population of Los Angeles must be added to that of New York, (C) will be too small. Therefore, the answer must be (D). Furthermore, the Los Angeles area has 12,000 people per square mile over 100 square miles, for 1,200,000 people. Added with those in New York, this does give a sum of 3,000,000 people.

39. $\dfrac{56}{12}$ First, distribute for the left half of the equation. $9(2x - 8)$ would become $18x - 72$, creating $18x - 72 = 6x - 16$. Isolate the *x* to solve by subtracting $6x$ from both sides and adding 72 to both sides. That gives $12x = 56$, so $x = \dfrac{56}{12}$. There's no need to reduce, either! If it fits, grid it!

40. **A** A line parallel to the provided line would have the same slope but a different *y*-intercept. Therefore, find the slope of each of the equations provided in the answer choices; this eliminates (C) and (D), which do not have the same slopes. Choice (B) is eliminated because it is the same exact line as the one provided, leaving only answer (A).

41. **C** First, calculate the commissions the salesperson would earn. 8% of $2,000 in sales gives $160. Since the salesperson also earns $200 a week as a base, add this to the $160 to get the answer as (C). POE is very helpful here also; since the salesperson earns $200 a week as a base, the answer cannot be (A) or (B).

42. **D** The information regarding how far the two live relative to the post office can be used to turn the directions into coordinates, with the post office as (0, 0). Three miles north and five miles west would be (–5, –3); seven miles north and eleven miles east would be (11, 7). Use the distance formula or draw a triangle to finish this problem; the total horizontal distance between the two is 16

miles, and the total vertical distance is 10. Using the Pythagorean theorem gives $\sqrt{16^2 + 10^2}$, or $\sqrt{356}$.

43. **C**   Since the numbers provided are in liters and the question asks about milliliters, the numbers in the problem will be manipulated to find the right answer. This eliminates (A) and (B), which would mean the starting point was 2 mL—not 2 L as told. From there, remember that 120 is not the rate of how fast the soda is consumed; it is the time, and therefore is the x term in the slope-intercept form of the equation. This eliminates (D), and leaves only (C). To calculate the slope itself, one could also divide 2,000 mL by the 120 hours over which the bottle is consumed; this gives 50/3 as the slope.

44. **D**   Since the question specifies that s is the amount of sales made, rounded to the nearest dollar, there cannot be any fractions, eliminating (B). Also, since the question says that some days no items are sold, s can be 0, eliminating (C). However, since negative sales are not possible, (A) is eliminated. This leaves (D).

45. **B**   To find the real roots of a quadratic, factor the quadratic. That, in this case, would give $(2x - 7)(x + 5)$, meaning the roots are $\frac{7}{2}$ and –5, for (B).

46. **D**   In order to solve this question, an equation would be needed. Translate the information provided —"two more than half of a number" would be $\frac{1}{2}x + 2$, and "one-third the sum of that same number and 12" would be $\frac{1}{3}(x + 12)$. Since the first piece is greater than the second, be sure to use the right symbol; the inequality is $\frac{1}{2}x + 2 > \frac{1}{3}(x + 12)$. Distribute the $\frac{1}{3}$; this gives $\frac{1}{3}x + 4$. Work on isolating the x to simplify the inequality. Starting with $\frac{1}{2}x + 2 > \frac{1}{3}x + 4$, subtract $\frac{1}{3}x$ and 2 from each side, giving $\frac{1}{6}x > 2$, so $x > 12$.

47. **B**   Set up a proportion to solve this question.

$$\frac{1\frac{1}{4} \text{ cup}}{3 \text{ eggs}} = \frac{x \text{ cups}}{24 \text{ eggs}}$$

Cross multiply and solve for x; doing so gives x is 10 cups.

48. **B**   Test out the answers or use algebra. Since Stuart is half as old as Rachel, $S = \frac{1}{2}R$; because in 4 years, Rachel will be 10 years older than Stuart, $R + 4 = 10 + (S + 4)$. Solve for S by substitution; $S = \frac{1}{2}R$, so $R = 2S$. Therefore, $2S + 4 = 10 + S + 4$; solve for S. Simplifying this expression first gives $2S + 4 = 14 + S$. Subtract 4 from each side and subtract S from each side, which gives $S = 10$.

49. **C**   The ratio of boys to girls must add up to a number that goes into 36 people; otherwise, there will somehow be partial people. Therefore, the answer is (C) because 4 + 5 = 9, which is the only factor of 36 of the answers listed.

50. **A**   Inverse functions are found by reversing the locations of the x and y and solving for y. In this case, because $f(x) = \sqrt{3x+9}$, or $y = \sqrt{3x+9}$, this would become $x = \sqrt{3y+9}$. To get rid of the square root symbol, both sides would be squared; this would give $x^2 = 3y + 9$. The number 9 would then be subtracted from both sides, leaving $x^2 - 9 = 3y$. Finally, both sides would be divided by 3, giving $\dfrac{x^2-9}{3}$. This can be rewritten as $\dfrac{1}{3}x^2 - 3$, so the answer is (A).

51. **110**   Look back at your math equations sheet if you need to; it shows there that the inscribed angle is always half that of the central angle and, therefore, arc length. Since the inscribed angle is 55°, the arc will be twice that—which is 110°.

52. **A**   The smallest standard deviation means the numbers will be the closest together. The closest together group of numbers is seen in (A), so that set will have the smallest standard deviation.

53. **B**   Continue the graph along the same general curve it seems to be following. At 10 seasons, it shows around 240 episodes, and at 9 seasons, it shows about 220; therefore, the answer should be around 260, so (B) is the best. Choice (A) is too small, and (C) and (D) would assume a very large jump from season 10 to 11.

54. **A**   The first step toward simplifying this expression is to flip the fraction. Since the exponent is negative, it can be made positive by flipping $\dfrac{125}{64}$ so it becomes $\dfrac{64}{125}$, but to the $\dfrac{4}{3}$ instead of $-\dfrac{4}{3}$. Take the cube root of both 64 and 125; that gives $\dfrac{4}{5}$. Finally, put both of those numbers to the fourth power, which would be the value as seen in (A). Remember to use POE here; even without knowing exactly what 4^4 or 5^4 is, the answer is (A) because (B) and (C) are eliminated when the fraction is $(\dfrac{4}{5})^4$ and the answer must be less than 1 because $\dfrac{4}{5}$ is less than 1.

WRITING

Part 1: Language

1. **C**   The key to this question is to make sure that various prepositional phrases are placed in an order to convey the most clear meaning. Choice (A) is wrong since "door" is placed next to the phrase about the "delivery man." The delivery man did not leave the door. Choice (B) is wrong, since it places "apartment" next to "casually leaning." Choice (D) is wrong, since it places "delivery man" next to "casually leaning" and uses the wrong conjunction: "but."

2. **D**   The correct spelling is "acquire," not "aquire."

3. **C**   Again, we must make sure that the correct words are placed next to each other in the sentence. Gina's poetry is not tired, so eliminate (A). Choice (B) contains a misplaced modifier, since "Gina's poetry" was not "projecting her voice loudly." Choice (D) is close, but it is unnecessary to use double dashes, and "having" is too wordy.

4. **D**   The theme of the paragraph is a narrator recalling fond memories of his summers in Tennessee. It is not about "many people" (A) or the uncle (B). Choice (C) cannot be right, since the campfire experience happens at night.

5. **C**   The first five sentences focus on women's participation in factory and shipyard work, while the remainder of the piece discusses less common occupations for women. Sentence 6 provides a good topic sentence for a second paragraph.

6. **B**   The rest of the essay is about the women's baseball league; therefore the best transition is (B). Choice (A) was a traditional job for women, (C) was mentioned previously, and (D) was never mentioned.

7. **D**   The correct spelling is "munitions," not "munishuns."

8. **D**   Sentence 2 tells us that Anderson is "often considered one of the earliest examples." This matches up with "first author." A mention of Anderson's death (A) would be more appropriate at the end of an essay or paragraph. Choice (C) is far too negative and does not agree with Sentence 4. Choice (B) starts with the word "But," but there is no contrast between this choice and Sentence 2.

9. **A**   Semicolons (;) are used only for two complete thoughts, so rule out (C). There is no natural pause after the word "comet," so rule out (B). Choices (A) and (D) are identical except for the comma after "eye." We do need this comma, since the sentence is two clauses joined together with a coordinating conjunction.

10. **C**   After Sentence 3, we would logically want to know why the author thinks that a fountain pen communicates "what type of person" she is. Choice (C) answers this question most effectively.

11. **B** The correct spelling is "conservative," not "conservetive."

12. **C** Again, you're being tested on misplaced modifiers. Rule out (A) because "I" am not "deserving congratulations," "my sister" is. "As she is" (B) and "To deserve" (D) are incorrect. (Note: It is often correct to start a sentence with "Because," if, in fact, there is a cause and effect relationship.)

13. **A** Beware of answers like (C) and (D) which leave out important details that affect the meaning of the sentence. The word "but" in (B) is inappropriate and may also change the meaning.

14. **B** Don't put a comma near a prepositional phrase unless that phrase is unnecessary to preserve the meaning of the sentence. Eliminate (A) and (C). Choice (D) is wrong, since we do need commas on both sides of the word "however."

15. **A** The paragraph is about music recording, so rule out (C) and (D). Since Diamond's recordings are "rough," eliminate (B).

16. **D** The word "While" tells us that this sentence will be changing direction. So, if "little is known" about Lexington's music scene, much must be known about the other cities listed. "Abundant" is the closest match.

17. **B** Sentence 6 tells us that "Warhol continues to be a household name." Choice (B) supports this idea, while (A) contradicts it. Choice (C) and (D) are much too literal.

18. **D** The two sentences are not conflicting, so eliminate (B). Choice (A) is much too wordy with the uses of "being." "In fact" is used to highlight a previous idea, so (C) is not quite right.

19. **C** "Campbell" is a surname/brand, so it must be capitalized. "Art World" need not be capitalized, since it is not a name, title, or place.

20. **B** Misplaced modifiers galore! "*Beowulf*'s author" was not "an oral poem," so rule out (A). Nor was he "translated into modern English," so rule out (C). "Now having been" is the wrong tense in (D) and perhaps leaves out some meaning.

21. **D** "Effected" means "executed, produced, or brought about." "Affected" means "made an impact on" and is therefore the correct word to use in this context.

22. **A** Since the sentence is referring to only a single family, eliminate (C) and (D). Between (A) and (B), remember that although a family includes many people, it is actually a singular noun, and its possessive should thus be punctuated as family's, as in (A).

23. **C** Notice that in this case we are looking for the *incorrect* sentence, not the correct one. This is testing you on the Either/or, Neither/nor rule of subject-verb agreement. In these cases, base the verb on the subject closest to the verb. "my sister is" (B) agrees. "my sister are" does not agree (C).

24. **B** The best answer will provide the most logical ordering of events. Choice (B) does this well by using the words "first" and "then."

25. **A** Why did Einstein believe that black holes were science fiction? Only (A) answers this question.

26. **B** Sentences 2 and 3 contain conflicting ideas. Eliminate (C) and (D). "While" could be used only if there was a second clause in the sentence.

27. **B** Choice (B) is best because it clearly explains why consumer products are being discarded at such a rapid rate.

28. **C** The clause "that have become companions to America's trashcans" is necessary information insofar as its omission would change the meaning of the sentence, so do not use a comma.

29. **A** Only (A) provides a form of the verb with a tense consistent with the preceding sentence. Since the word "has" is not underlined, you know that the underlined verb must be in the present perfect tense, as in "has become." The word "became" is not compatible with the word "has."

30. **D** The first sentence indicates that the passage is talking about the way things are today (and how they've progressed to this point from the way things were in the past). The most direct way to talk about what people think today would be to use present tense here: "extends."

31. **B** The question asked for an answer that emphasizes lack of awareness. Choices (A) and (D) say people don't often encounter or pay attention to the problem, not that they aren't aware of it. It's a small difference, but it's a difference that means you can cross these two choices out because (B) is better. Choice (C) refers to governments' attempts to study it, which means they are aware, so cross that one out, too. Only (B), which matches "realize" in the answer choice with "awareness" in the question, is consistent with what you are asked to emphasize.

32. **C** Since these "users" have purchased (and discarded) electronics, "consumers" is the closest match.

33. **D** Because the underlined word modifies the verb "contaminates," you need to choose an answer that provides an adverb, rather than an adjective. Adjectives modify nouns and pronouns; adverbs modify verbs, adjectives, and other adverbs. Choices (A), (B), and (C) provide adjectives and can therefore be eliminated. The proper adverb is "dangerously," which (D) provides.

34. **B** The correct spelling is "refuse," not "refuze."

35. **B** Always put commas after a modifier containing a date, such as "In 1867," (A). Same with ages, (C). Choice (D) is wrong since it uses an apostrophe with "its."

36. **C** Always capitalize names and places. The words in "financial empire" need not be capitalized, since they are not titles or names of any sort.

37. **C** "Best-known" is being used as an adjective and should thus be hyphenated.

38. **D**   4. "Bob invented…"   3. "Bob undertook…"   2. "After months of success…"

1. "He claimed…"

First, Bob must invent the machine. Then he can sell it. He named it only "after months of success." The "He claimed…" sentence must go last, since we need to introduce the name of the product with the "After months…" sentence.

39. **A**   Always put commas after a modifier containing a date.

40. **B**   Choice (A) is a type of run-on sentence sometimes called a comma splice, in which a comma separates two complete sentences or independent clauses. Choice (D) makes the same mistake as (A); (B) and (C) both rely on the second strategy, using pronouns to begin the second clause, so your goal is to decide which pronoun is right. The women are performing the action in the second clause, so you wouldn't use the object form "whom" but rather the subject form "who," (B).

41. **D**   This is an idiomatic expression; to get the right answer, you'll need to know what preposition is appropriate with "her supervision." The idiomatically correct preposition with supervise is "under," as in "under her supervision." Choice (D) works.

42. **D**   The sentence is composed of a complete idea and an incomplete idea, which need to be joined together with punctuation. A semicolon may be used only to separate two complete ideas, so eliminate (B). A colon in this situation would require a subject in the second idea in order to make sense. There is no subject, so eliminate (C). The phrase using these terms to emphasize…is not describing culturists; it's explaining why Walker employed those terms, so a comma is needed to make that clear—select (D).

43. **A**   Sentence 3 tells us that Walker's Agents were "highly focused on making sales," so (A) is most harmonious with this idea. Choices (B) and (C) are the opposite of what we want and (D) is irrelevant.

44. **C**   Pay attention to the dates! 1839 is *before* 1859, so rule out (B). The sentence is not changing direction, so rule out "but" in answer (A). Choice (D) creates the wrong meaning.

45. **B**   We need to know who this paragraph is about. Rule out (C) and (D). It would be nice to know how Andrew Carnegie got all this money. Choice (A) certainly does not answer this question.

46. **A**   The phrase "now often regarded as the greatest American president" adds an unnecessary fact to the sentence, so it must be surrounded by commas or dashes. Rule out (B) and (C). Choice (D) includes an unnecessary colon (:), so eliminate it.

47. **C**   Each answer choice ends with a complete idea or independent clause. Choices (A) and (D) begin with an incomplete idea and a comma, which are properly followed by a complete idea. Choice (B) is a complete idea followed by a comma and the coordinating conjunction "but," which is also properly followed by another complete idea. Choice (C), on the other hand, connects two complete ideas with a comma, which is incorrect.

48. **A** For questions like this, the shortest correct way of saying something is usually the best answer. If you are considering adding words, make sure they say something of added value. In this case, the original sentence indicates that this is an ordinary birthday. Choices (B), (C), and (D) are just different ways of redundantly restating that the occasion was typical. They add nothing to the original meaning of the sentence, which gives us no reason to prefer any of them to the original wording.

49. **A** People typically have dessert after dinner, so (A) makes the most sense. None of the other words would convey the meaning of a time shift.

50. **A** Colons (:) precede an explanation of "why" or "how." "I knew the source of our tension" is a complete thought, so this is the correct use of a colon.

51. **D** The correct spelling is "tension," not "tention."

Part 2: Essay

Use active reading to note each side's arguments and support. Your notes might look like the following.

Pro side

- Advantages to business (paragraph 2)
- Cost, accountability, flexibility (paragraph 2)
- Successful cap-and-trade programs (paragraph 3)
- SO_2 emissions drop 40%, ozone emissions drop 43% (bullet points)
- Saves lives (bullet points)
- In place since 1976 (bullet points)

Con side

- Other regulations may be responsible for good results (paragraph 1)
- Pollution will be moved offshore; offset carbon credits (paragraph 2)
- Permits will be cheap (paragraph 3)
- "perverse" incentives (paragraph 4)
- Discourages long-term solutions (paragraph 5)

Choosing Your Thesis: Both sides give several believable arguments. Remember that there is no "right" answer to whether cap-and-trade is favorable or not. You might have noticed, though, that the "Cap-and-Trade Works" article does provide more specific data to back up its claims. The essay need not reflect your "true" opinion on the issue; it is simply about analyzing the evidence that both authors use. Assuming that the statistics given on the "pro" side are accurate, they do seem to make a more compelling case. The "Criticisms of Cap-and-Trade" seem to be based more on hypothetical possibilities and the author does not cite any actual evidence of such events occurring in the past.

If you think you could make a better case for the critics, that would not be a wrong choice for a thesis. It could, however, be more challenging to debunk the statistics given by the "pro" side. Go with the easier task!

Organizing Your Argument: The critics of cap-and-trade don't directly address the statistical facts presented in the "pro" article. The critics present their own unique set of hypothetical objections. Be sure to address BOTH sides of the issue, acknowledging the critics' point of view, while explaining its flaws.

The two articles overlap in the discussion of cost. "Cap-and-Trade Works" presents lower costs as a benefit to businesses. The critics state that lower costs will actually undermine the purpose of cap-and-trade (paragraphs 3 and 5). Since both articles address this issue, you should definitely touch on it throughout your essay.

A good approach for this essay would be to discuss the evidence that proves your thesis first (cap-and-trade is good) and then point out that the critics do not provide compelling data and make numerous unsupported assumptions.

READING

1. **A** This question illustrates the importance of reading a couple of lines above and below the sentence given in the question stem. In that surrounding context, the author says that Eliot's heroines "cannot live without religion" and search for it from a young age, but they don't know "to whom to pray" and "do not find what they seek." Right away, that eliminates (D). Don't let the simile, "like a place of worship," mislead you. The "place where she stands" is spiritual, not physical, so (B) is gone, too. By checking the context and using Process of Elimination, you're now down to only two possible answers, (A) and (C), and you have a 50 percent chance of choosing the correct one. What about (C)? Their endless, fruitless search for religion can be seen as a type of spiritual imprisonment for Eliot's heroines. However, that inference would be extreme, and is not directly supported elsewhere in the passage. That makes (A) the best answer, and indeed, the spiritual quest is an intensely personal and individual one.

2. **C** In nineteenth-century England, when Eliot wrote, it was a man's world. However, you don't need to know that in order to find the correct answer. The author describes Eliot as "confronting her feminine aspirations with the real world of men." Women's aspirations are in conflict with the reality of men, so "the facts of human existence" at the time restrict only women. These "facts of human existence" aren't limited only to heroines in a book (B) and, in a man's world, they don't apply to men (A). Likewise, they don't apply to "any human aspirations" (D), which would include the aspirations of both men and women.

3. **B** At the end of the passage, Eliot's knowledge and freedom are described as a "double burden," indicating that she suffered as a result of them. The phrase "sank worn out," suggests that the burden led directly to Eliot's death. Clearly, she was not in good health, so (A) can be eliminated. Choice (C) is incorrect since Eliot was "praised and shrinking from her fame," so she was, in fact, not prevented from attaining fame. Choice (D) is also untrue, since the passage says that the story of Eliot's heroines "is the incomplete version of the story that is George Eliot herself."

4. **D**   Like men, Eliot sought and achieved a significant grasp of "art and knowledge," but she did not re-nounce the feminine qualities—the "inheritance" of her gender—that made her different from the men in whose world she lived. Her profession alone (A) doesn't explain differences in her point of view and standards, since there were many more male writers than female at the time. The passage does not describe her social class (B) or her education (C).

5. **B**   In the last line, the author says we should "bestow laurel and rose" upon George Eliot. This would have a positive connotation, so rule out the neutral "reasoned objectivity" (D). "Qualified" means "with some possible exceptions or reservations," so (C) is too negative. That leaves (A) and (B). Choice (B) is less extreme, so it is therefore the best answer.

6. **A**   The question boils down to this: Who is speaking in the quote? Let's use Process of Elimination and first search for the wrong answers in order to eliminate them. The author put the phrase in quotation marks to show that it is not hers; therefore (B) is incorrect. If the author borrowed it from one of Eliot's critics, she would need to cite the source somehow; therefore (C) does not seem plausible. From the context, it is clear that the phrase does represent the author's point of view; she is using it in her description of Eliot. So (D) can be eliminated. That leaves (A). The text centers on Eliot's relationship to her feminine protagonists, so it seems quite probable that the author would integrate a phrase from one of Eliot's heroines.

7. **D**   You'll need to reread the whole paragraph in order to consider the role the sentence plays in it. The paragraph relates how someone approaches the Falls: a short drive, a fee, a view from a distance, and then finally a torturous descent down a long staircase to get a closer look. Is it worth the effort? The last sentence sums up the author's opinion: As a tourist himself, he doesn't think it is. He is describing his own feelings as a tourist, and therefore predicting how other tourists will feel, mak-ing (D) the best answer. There is some merit to (B), since a current tourist's experience would serve as advice to future visitors. However, the sentence is not phrased as advice (for example, "learn from my experience and don't bother"). The author's use of the second person, "you," to address the reader makes (C) attractive. This direct address is only one aspect of what the author is saying, though. Finally, (A) is clearly wrong. Even though the author says "you will be too late," this refers to the effort already made, not to the arrival time at the falls.

8. **A**   This question requires that you first identify the author's attitude towards his subject, considering what is implied as well as what is stated directly. You also need to read the question stem care-fully to realize that you're looking for any quotation that *doesn't* support that attitude. Most of the passage highlights the dangers of the Falls and the narrator's discomfort while he is there. His negative attitude is revealed throughout the passage by the use of words like "precipice," "misery," and "flimsy," as well as the vivid description of the dangerous trip under the falls. Only (A) says anything positive about his visit—he survived the trip under the falls to reach the safety and light of open day. The other three choices all support the narrator's negative attitude towards the falls.

9. **C**   It's important to understand the context in order to interpret a quote like this one, since it could mean several different things. The sentence that precedes this statement describes the "furious wind" rushing from behind the waterfall, and says that wind "seemed determined to sweep us from the bridge, and scatter us on the rocks and among the torrents below." In this context, the remark about wanting to go home shows that the narrator wants to get out of a dangerous situation and reinforces how apprehensive he is. Nothing in the passage indicates that the narrator is constantly longing for home (A); only the danger of going behind the falls inspires the remark. Choice (B) is too vague—there are many reasons for being unhappy, so the narrator's remark in the midst of a dangerous situation doesn't necessarily reveal an unhappy attitude. The same could be said for (D)—a remark made out of fear in one dangerous situation doesn't necessarily point to a childish attitude.

10. **D**   The passage uses the phrase "storming, roaring, and bellowing of warring wind and water" to emphasize the intense pressure and strength of the waterfall. The narrator's statement that he "seemed to receive the Atlantic on my back" builds on this image by creating an exaggerated comparison to the Atlantic Ocean. Altogether, the sense is of an enormous, threatening amount of water. Since the narrator is at Niagara Falls, not the ocean, (A) is wrong because it takes the use of the word "Atlantic" too literally. Locating the quote and reading a couple of lines above and below will reveal the context and confirm that (B) is wrong—bridges are mentioned in the previous paragraph, while the quote describes the waterfall itself. Choice (C) again takes a word too literally (in this case, "storm"). The narrator exaggerates the experience of the waterfall by using words like "storming" and "Atlantic," to convey a sense of the intensity and amount of water pouring down.

11. **B**   Each of the answer options reflects a possible definition, so look closely at how the phrase is used in context. The "it" refers to the "seething world of descending water" in the previous sentence. So look for a word that would indicate "seething," which means "storming" or "furious." That type of movement of the water is "vigorous," so the closest choice is (B). "Serious" doesn't suggest the violence of the waterfall, so (A) is incorrect. A waterfall can't be "sincere" (which means true or heartfelt) or "ardent" (passionate or emotionally enthusiastic), so (C) and (D) are both wrong.

12. **C**   This question demonstrates the importance of reading the question stem carefully, so you don't miss the "*not*." Only one choice, (C), can*not* be inferred from the passage. The author had to cross the Suspension Bridge to reach the Cave of the Winds from Horseshoe Fall, so they are on different sides of the river. All of the other choices *can* be inferred from the passage. The author mentions returning to America after examining Horseshoe Fall, so part of the site is outside the United States (A). The author makes several references to how far he has to descend, so the river is far below the level of the road (B). On the Suspension Bridge, the author says he divides his misery "between the chances of smashing down two hundred feet into the river below, and the chances of having the railwaytrain overhead smashing down onto you," so the bridge does run between the railway track and the river (D).

13. **D** The best answer is (D). The glowworms are "living" (part of the natural world) and lamps are mechanical, man-made lights. The speaker addresses the glowworms directly throughout the poem; there is no suggestion that he wonders if he's only imagining them (A). Any admiration and respect is undercut in the last four lines, where the glowworms prove to be no match for Juliana (B). The glowworms help guide any of the "wandering mowers" (line 10), not just the speaker (C).

14. **B** The whole poem is stating that, although the glowworms shine powerful lights, they are nothing compared to Juliana, so (B) is the best answer. The poem simply describes some of the results of the glowworms' lights without going so far as to "celebrate" them (A). It does not mention love at first sight (C) and there is no evidence of religious allegory (D).

15. **B** The word "portend" means to predict. The poet is drawing attention to the glowworms' innocence to show that, unlike comets, they do not foretell negative events such as a war or a prince's funeral. They serve "no higher end" than predicting that the grass will fall to the mower (A). By using Process of Elimination to get rid of answers that are clearly wrong before you try to select the correct answer, you can eliminate (C) and (D) right away, since there is no mention of the weather (C) or of a comet's cyclical flight pattern (D).

16. **A** The speaker says that wandering mowers "after foolish fires do stray" meaning they are misled by the wrong sources of light. They are wandering "in the night," so it is unlikely they are still mowing fields (B). The poet establishes a connection between the glowworms and the nightingale, but not between the mowers and the nightingale (C). Although the speaker says he will never find his way home, it is not because there are no glowworms; it is because Juliana has "displaced" his mind so severely that he can't follow the glowworms' light (D).

17. **C** The best answer is (C)—the speaker's mind is so distracted by thoughts of Juliana that it will never go back to its original state. His tone is not necessarily resentful (A). Choice (B) is a tempting "decoy" answer. The speaker may well be wandering forever, unable to follow the guiding light of the glowworms. However, Juliana's effect on him is much broader than simply damaging his ability to follow the correct light; she has altered his mind. There is no suggestion that he refuses to go home without her. (D).

18. **B** The first 12 lines are all addressed to the glowworms and simply describe some of their functions (lighting the darkness for the nightingale and for lost mowers, and foreshadowing the falling grass that will be cut). Not until the last four lines does the reader get to the main-idea sentence ("Your courteous lights..."). Imagine these lines of poetry rewritten as a narrative sentence: "You [the glowworms] are wasting your light since Juliana entered my life, because she preoccupies my mind so much that I'll never find my way home, even with your light to guide me." The main verb in this sentence—the verb that belongs with the subject "you"—is "waste." The verb "sit" refers to the nightingales (A); "come" refers to Juliana (C), and "find" refers to the narrator, not the glowworms (D).

19. **B** Although majority rule demands "a respect for the law," the author asserts that "a government in which the majority rule in all cases cannot be based on justice." The author doesn't explain why "the people" wanted to hold power in the first place (A). He is criticizing a system in which the majority rules, which does not happen in a dictatorship (C). The author says the majority rules "because they are physically the strongest." He doesn't discuss differing levels of fitness to govern (D).

20. **A** This tricky question requires careful reading of the question stem. The *result* of respecting the law is that men abandon what is right (D). However, the question asks about the *purpose* of the law—what is it supposed to achieve?—and that answer is (A). Citizens who do not follow their own consciences (because they respect the law) are more easily ruled; they "serve the state...as machines." Choice (C) is likewise a result, not a purpose. Both options in (B) are incorrect—the law supports the government, not "the good of society," and people who respect it are abandoning their own consciences, not their own "self-interest."

21. **B** Three of these answers—(A), (C) and (D)—explain what the author believes is wrong with the government of the day and with what it demands of its citizens. His main point is summed up in (B). His only obligation is to serve his own conscience.

22. **D** The author suggests, "Let every man make known what kind of government would command his respect," and longs for "a government in which majorities do not virtually decide right and wrong, but conscience." A government formed from each individual's vision of what government should be, and which defines right and wrong according to each individual's conscience, would be chaotic, since no two people would likely agree completely. Each of the other three answers highlights only one aspect of the current government that the author says needs to be changed.

23. **C** The author says he wants a better government and then criticizes government by the majority; he says his only obligation is to follow his own conscience to what is right, and then criticizes the current government's law and the way the state turns citizens into unthinking machines. The structure is described in (C): position, criticism, position, criticism. Choice (A) ignores the criticism in the first few sentences of paragraph 2, while (B) ignores his restatement of his position in the middle of that paragraph. Choice (D) ignores the author's statement of his position at the beginning of the excerpt.

24. **B** You'll need to make an inference in order to answer this question, but it's a fairly easy one to make. If you were actively reading the passage—constantly asking "why is this here?" and "why did the author say it that way?" for instance—you should already have asked yourself this question. Why didn't the author simply describe a citizen as a "shadow...of humanity" who had already been buried with full military honors or perhaps buried unnoticed? The verse simply captures the "buried unnoticed" part of that description, and it's likely the author used it because it was well known to readers at the time. It would strengthen his point about how the good citizens who "serve the state...as machines" get no thanks or recognition for putting the government above their own individual humanity. The author does make a connection between good citizens and soldiers who automatically follow orders without a thought. However, the verse describes someone who gets no

recognition, not someone who blindly follows orders, so (A) can be eliminated. The author draws a comparison, not a contrast, between the military hero and a mindless good citizen (C). Although burying a war hero without honors could be seen as a lack of justice, the author doesn't directly blame the government. It's the citizens themselves who have voluntarily made themselves "a mere shadow ... of humanity" without demanding any recognition in return (D).

25. **D** Both (A) and (B) have some truth to them. However, the answer most directly supported in the passage is (D). Speaking of the "mass of men" who "serve the state...as machines," the author complains, "there is no free exercise whatever of the judgment or of the moral sense...They have the same sort of worth only as horses and dogs." There is no indication in the passage that the government plans a particular punishment for those who don't behave as it demands (C).

26. **C** The author asserts that "The only obligation which I have a right to assume is to do at any time what I think right." This obligation, or "duty," is to follow his own conscience, regardless of what the law says is right or wrong. When his conscience is in conflict with the law, his duty is civil disobedience—disobeying the law. Choice (A) is wrong because, while the author does say, "government in which the majority rule in all cases cannot be based on justice," he does not claim that people have a duty to restore justice, nor that disobeying the current government will automatically bring about that result. He complains that the "mass of men serve the state...not as men mainly, but as machines," but doesn't say they have a duty to regain their humanity (B). The author asks for "a better government"; however, he can't describe it yet because he first needs "every man" to "make known what kind of government would command his respect" (D).

27. **C** This is the best from among a set of close answers. It describes how thoroughly Mrs. Proudie's despotic behavior has cowed her husband in every single aspect of life. While tempting, (A) refers to only one facet of Mrs. Proudie's authoritarian character—its scope. Likewise, (D) covers only one facet—a particular behavior she demands from her servants and husband. Choice (B) refers to Mrs. Grantly, not to Mrs. Proudie.

28. **A** The maid has been unfaithful and disloyal to her employer by violating the standards Mrs. Proudie sets for her household servants. This answer also happens to match the dictionary definition for "recreant," which is fairly unusual in a question that asks how a word is used in the context of a passage. "Recreant" refers to the maid, not to the pastime in which she is engaging (B). The maid is certainly not displaying lack of courage (C) by defying Mrs. Proudie. Choice (D) is too extreme for simply "listening to the honey of a sweetheart in the Regent's park."

29. **B** The author sets up a series of virtues that Mrs. Grantly possesses (such as being obedient to her husband in public) and then, in the next paragraph, describes how Mrs. Proudie exhibits the opposite of every one. Choice (A) is incorrect because while Mrs. Grantly "doubtless ... values power," she doesn't display it in public and exercises it benevolently in her happy home. She is not an example of authoritarian power in the way Mrs. Proudie is. The author draws a contrast between the two women, but in the passage he does not suggest direct rivalry between them (C). Dr. Proudie

would quite possibly prefer a wife like Mrs. Grantly; however, the passage doesn't provide direct support for this assumption (D).

30. **A**   The repetition of "Woe betide" accentuates the serious consequences that await any servant, female or male, for any violation of Mrs. Proudie's rules. The maid will find herself unemployed (and unemployable), and the six-foot escort will likely suffer the same fate. The tone is serious, not mocking (B). The brief phrase occurs only twice—not enough to slow the reader down (C). The phrase is consistent with the narrator's attitude throughout the rest of the passage, so it doesn't signal a change (D).

31. **C**   The point of the paragraph is to illustrate Mrs. Proudie's hypocrisy by describing how she is given to "dissipation and low dresses" during the week, then atones for this pleasure-seeking behavior and lack of modesty on Sundays. Moreover, she demands the same atonement from her servants and husband, even though she does not allow them the same liberties during the week. Choice (A) might be tempting, but the paragraph does not explain the *cause* of Mrs. Proudie's transformation between pleasure-seeker and strict religious observer. It simply describes the transformation as evidence that "she is in her own way a religious woman." Her religious beliefs reflect only part of her character, so (B) can be eliminated. It's likely safe to infer that Mrs. Proudie might have difficulty hiring servants (D). However, the paragraph doesn't specifically support this inference.

32. **D**   The author analyzes Mrs. Proudie in an amusing way, mocking her cleverly by first pointing out her flaws in contrast to Mrs. Grantly (her social equivalent) and then by exposing her hypocrisy. Choices (A) and (B) fall into the half-right, half-wrong category, and half wrong is all wrong. Although the passage is certainly subjective, it is hardly emotional (A). The passage is certainly descriptive. However, the author doesn't make extensive use of metaphors (suggesting a similarity between two things by referring to one using a word or phrase that literally refers to another). Since the style lacks both terseness (brief, direct expression) and epigrams (concise, clever sayings), (C) should be an easy candidate for elimination.

33. **C**   Each of these answers could have some grain of truth to it. Your task is to find the "most likely" one, based only on the information given in the passage. Process of Elimination would toss out (B) first. The skiers' slow exit would reduce speed, one of the risk factors in causing a brittle fracture, but that precaution would be far outweighed by the force and speed of the helicopter landing. The correct answer, (C), minimizes both the amount and the speed of the force applied in one place. While the passage concedes that the behavior of high-density snow is more predictable because it behaves more like well-known materials, it does not claim that high-density snow is free of avalanche risk (A). The author allows for temperature as one factor influencing the ability of a snow-mass to store and dissipate energy, but doesn't specify the effects of low vs. high temperature, and says that texture is also a factor (D). This answer is plausible, but it's not the "most likely" because of the missing information in the passage.

34. **B**   The passage states that viscoelastic substances "have recoverable and unrecoverable components." The recoverable energy is evident in the way the substance springs back somewhat when a load is

removed suddenly, and the unrecoverable energy is evident in the permanent deformation that the force of the load causes. The dissipated energy in (A) refers only to the permanent deformation caused by the load, not to the elastic component. Choice (D) is wrong for the same reason. The stored and recovered energy in (C) refers only to the elastic component.

35. **D**   Since the passage doesn't give any information about the intended readers, you'll need to look for clues in the tone, the language, the level of detail, and the type of information covered. Those aspects will indicate what assumptions the writer is making about his readers' interests and existing level of knowledge. Academics would surely require more specific information about the studies and laboratory tests than the passage provides (A). The tone and language are not designed to engage someone with only a passing interest in the subject. They would likely cause a general reader to give up and move on to more interesting material (B). Choice (C) might be tempting, but one can infer that a rescue professional would probably already have the level of knowledge covered in this passage. In addition, professional rescuers would more likely need information pertaining to the aftermath of an avalanche than to the snow properties that might cause one. The passage is most suited to the audience described in (D)—experienced back country enthusiasts who are aware of the variety of snowpacks they might encounter and want to know more about the relationship between snowmass behavior and avalanches in order to increase their chances of avoiding one.

36. **C**   Throughout almost all of the excerpt, the writer provides information about the properties and behavior of snowmasses, and leaves it to readers to draw their own conclusions about how the facts apply to avalanches. He mentions "avalanche" only once, when he draws a connection between evaluating "avalanche stability" and understanding the cause of a "brittle fracture in snow." The passage does not attempt to train readers (A) or teach them how to do something (D). If training or education were the author's objective, he would have linked the facts and explanations in the excerpt to specific skills or actions. If the objective were to spur further investigation (B), the author would have directed readers to additional resources and perhaps mentioned current areas of study.

37. **A**   This information would warn conscientious back country riders that a force (such as a group of snowmobiles) that is strong enough and fast enough to exceed the limitations of the snowmass will result in a brittle fracture and the danger of an avalanche. The tone and language of the passage suggest that the author isn't writing for inexperienced amateurs (B). The caution applies to "the lower density snow typical of alpine, seasonal snowpacks," not to the high-density snow that behaves like a material (C). Choice (D) may not be practical or successful; the passage explains that a safe load and speed depend on the "temperature and texture" of the snowmass. In any case, an author cannot "ensure" that readers do anything.

38. **C**   The passage lists "trees, rocks, ski tracks" as examples of "a weakest site where fractures are most likely to originate," so the reader has an answer to visible clues that an area could be vulnerable. Readers would find the other three questions unanswered. The author says it's not possible to answer (A) because of the complex properties of low-density snow. He doesn't deal with an intermediate type of snow (B), and simply cites "laboratory tests" and "some studies" without giving specifics that would allow a reader to investigate further or judge the likely accuracy of the conclusions.

39. **C** Because of the current misinterpretation of Center of Gravity as "a source of strength or a critical capability," resources would be directed at destroying an adversary's main capability (such as air superiority in a military conflict, for instance). According to Clausewitz's original concept, resources should instead be directed at identifying what holds the various parts of the opponent's system together and striking that Center of Gravity with enough force to destroy the system's equilibrium. Air superiority would not be much of an advantage if the adversary couldn't coordinate the various components of its military system. The author states that, in its original form, the Center of Gravity "is defined by the entire system (or structure) of the enemy, not by a level of war," so Clausewitz didn't distinguish between the strategic, operational, and tactical levels either (A). No clear lines between the three have been lost in the current interpretation. Choice (B) is quite true; however, it has nothing to do with a current interpretation of Clausewitz's concept (as the question stem asks). In its original form, the Center of Gravity concept would not apply to small, autonomous groups either. The author complains that analysts don't give enough weight to how closely Clausewitz followed concepts of physics, not that they don't take account of the concepts of physics that were known in Clausewitz's era (D).

40. **A** Process of Elimination should have led you to discard (C) and (D). The passage specifies that Clausewitz's Center of Gravity "is not a ... critical capability, but a focal point that is essentially effects-based, rather than capabilities-based," so the concept is not designed to identify and undermine an opponent's capabilities (C). The author advises readers to "look for CoGs only in wars designed to defeat the enemy completely," suggesting the concept would not be helpful in a limited engagement scenario (D). It could be useful at a tactical level (B), since the "CoG is defined by the entire system (or structure) of the enemy, not by a level of war." However, the question stem asks where the Center of Gravity concept would be *most* useful, and the answer best supported by the passage is (A). The author explains that "the concept remains valid only where the enemy possesses sufficient 'unity' or 'interdependence'...to act as a single body," as different groups united in pursuing a common goal would do. The task would be to identify how the groups are held together and knock that united force off balance.

41. **D** Active reading—continually asking, "What is the author's main point? Why did he write this?" as you read through the passage—will lead you to the correct answer. The author's main point is that we've strayed away from the original meaning of Clausewitz's Center of Gravity concept, and therefore aren't applying it correctly. His purpose is to take readers back to the original concept (D). While (A), (B), and to a lesser extent, (C) are all facets of that purpose, each one on its own is too narrow. Each one is only a piece of the whole (D).

42. **A** Sometimes you'll end up having to choose the best-supported answer from the choices given, even though it may not be a terrific answer. This question is an example of that situation, and it tests your ability to make inferences from the information in the passage. In fact, the excerpt doesn't give a clear reason why the current interpretation of Clausewitz's Center of Gravity has veered away from the original concept. It gives only a hint when the author refers to the original German text, in which Clausewitz never used the German term for "source," while current interpretations

portray his Center of Gravity as a source of strength. The implication is that, if analysts went back to the original German text, they might see that Clausewitz wasn't defining the Center of Gravity as a source of anything. Choices (B) and (D) are quite true. However, they explain only why Clausewitz's original concept might not be as applicable today as it was in his time, not why the current interpretation has strayed from his original concept. The author doesn't claim that modern analysts don't understand mechanical sciences in Clausewitz's day (C). Choice (A) may not give a definitive reason, but it is the answer best supported by the passage.

43. **B** The passage states that "a CoG represents the point where the forces of gravity converge within an object." "Centripetal" force, therefore, refers to energy directed inward, toward the center of the object. Both "constrained" (A) and "strong" (D) are too general, since they don't necessarily imply a direction towards the interior of an object or system. "Centrifugal" (C) is the opposite; it refers to a force directed outward from the center.

44. **A** Answering this question requires you to make some inferences from the answer choices given. In the scenario described in (B), for instance, you need to consider the influences on your manager's decision about a raise. She is likely working within budget constraints imposed by *her* manager, within policies set by Human Resources, and in consideration of the performance of other members of her team. There you could have the interconnected grouping that Clausewitz sees as a complete system where a Center of Gravity forms. The situation is similar in (C), where there is likely a convergence of various bank policies and departments plus government banking regulators. Identifying the Center of Gravity within this interconnected system and knocking it off balance might result in a favorable response to your complaint. In the situation outlined in (D), your neighbor likely has allies from municipal bylaw enforcement and his insurance company, again operating as a united force. Choice (A) most clearly suggests a situation where Clausewitz's Center of Gravity concept would likely not apply. Two individuals are in conflict, and your opponent has already won one set. You need to limit her ability to make another gain, and exploit any weak spots in her capabilities in the game. The question stem asks for the *most probable* situation where the concept would not apply, and this scenario of limited engagement and a focus on capabilities would rule out Clausewitz's Center of Gravity as a means of gaining the advantage.

45. **C** Reading the question stem carefully will enable you to pick up two key concepts: You're looking for the "initial" character of the relationships, and looking for more than one. The passage says that Nora initially approached Krogstad for help (child to caregiver), and she needed the money in order to save her husband's life (caregiver to child), as listed in (C). Krogstad's accusation of fraud and veiled threat (that such an offense can lead to the complete loss of reputation) cast Nora as a victim and him as a persecutor (A), but that relationship is revealed later; it's not the initial relationship. Choices (B) and (D) contain the same incorrect "victim to persecutor" and "persecutor to victim" relationships, so they're also wrong—half wrong is all wrong.

46. **A** Nora asks how admitting she forged her father's signature on the bond is a dangerous confession, since Krogstad will have his money soon. The implication is that as long as she repays the debt, it doesn't matter that she committed fraud and she is absolved of the crime (A). Choices (B) and (C)

may well be true; however, there isn't enough information in the excerpt to support them. Nora says her father was so ill that she couldn't ask him to sign the bond or tell him about her husband's illness, so it's extremely unlikely she would have involved him in the fraud by telling him she was forging his signature. If he wasn't involved, his good name hasn't been damaged; therefore it doesn't need to be restored (D).

47. **B** This brief excerpt offers several clues that the playwright admires Nora. When she admits the fraud to Krogstad, she "throws her head up and looks defiantly at him," even though she could be getting herself into trouble with the admission. She is frank and brave when she tells this man who could now harm her, "I didn't trouble myself about you at all. I couldn't bear you, because you put so many heartless difficulties in my way." Her repeated assertions that doing anything else was "impossible" indicate Nora was strong enough to do what she had to do in order to save her husband and spare her father. From these clues, you can infer that the playwright doesn't condemn Nora's dishonesty (A). The post mortem date does indeed throw Nora's intelligence into some question, but the playwright doesn't draw any attention to that aspect of her action (C). The playwright's portrayal of her conversation with Krogstad doesn't suggest he feels sorry for her (D).

48. **D** This question provides a good reason for active reading—taking control of the passage—always questioning, inferring, predicting as you read instead of simply letting the passage feed you the literal words it contains. Nora's father's signature is at the heart of the dialogue, but the excerpt doesn't explain why she needed it. If you were actively reading the passage, though, that's a question you should have been asking. Approach this question by eliminating any answers that the passage does not support at all. The only interest Krogstad shows in the father's death is the date of it, so it doesn't seem they were old friends and (B) can be the first to go. There is no indication that Nora had borrowed from Krogstad before, and he does not seem like the type of person who would take a second risk, so (C) can go next. Choice (A) is possible, but rather unlikely since Nora is old enough to be married to a husband who is ill and to have a father who has died, so eliminate that one, too. The passage gives no information about whether (D) is true or not. The question only asks for the "most likely" reason, though, and (D) is the only choice left after eliminating those that the passage doesn't seem to support. If you noticed the date of this play (1879), then the reason given in (D) is plausible.

49. **C** When Krogstad asks if Nora realized she was defrauding him by forging her father's signature on the bond, Nora tells him, "I didn't trouble myself about you at all. I couldn't bear you, because you put so many heartless difficulties in my way." Clearly she felt no sense of duty to someone who had treated her badly. Since one obligation of the role of citizen is to obey society's laws, Nora's act of defrauding Krogstad eliminates (A). She did feel a duty to her husband (to enable him to take a life-saving trip). However, she was also trying to protect her dying father. It was "impossible" to cancel the trip, and "impossible" to tell her father why she needed the loan. So it's not accurate to infer that Nora felt her first duty was to her husband (B). She puts both her husband's and her father's welfare before her own, so (D) is wrong.

SCIENCE

1. **C** The process depicted by the reaction is photosynthesis. Note that photosynthesis requires carbon dioxide, water, and sunlight to produce sugar and oxygen.

2. **B** The Big Bang theory proposes that the universe started as a small singularity that inflated, expanded, and cooled to form our solar system. Hubble's discovery supports the idea that the universe was, at one time, smaller and continues to expand.

3. **D** Unlike plant cells, animal cells have neither chloroplasts nor cell walls. Plant cells are autotrophs that create energy through photosynthesis, while animal cells are incapable of photosynthesis and, therefore, are considered consumers.

4. **C** According to the information provided, an intensity score of 20 or less is considered acceptable. The intensity falls below 20 at the 10,000 mM point on the x-axis.

5. **C** The passage tells you that the sense and antisense strands are complimentary. Recall that DNA nucleotide bases have specific pairings; adenine and thymine bond together and cytosine and guanine bond together. Since the sense strand of this DNA sequence is TAGCCATTC, the antisense strand would be ATCGGTAAG.

6. **D** RNA is a single-stranded molecule that uses ribose as a sugar and uracil as a base. Conversely, DNA forms a double-helix shape and uses deoxyribose as a sugar and thymine as a nucleotide base.

7. **B** RNA does not use thymine as a base; rather, it uses a base called uracil. Accordingly, the transcription of the sense strand with the sequence TAGCCATTC would be RNA strand with the sequence AUCGGUAAG.

8. **A** Renewable resources are those that can be replenished or regenerated over the course of time by natural processes and can be replaced at a sustainable rate. Geothermal, biomass, and solar energy are all renewable resources. Nuclear energy, however, is a nonrenewable resource.

9. **A** Based on the description, obsidian is a hard, dark glasslike rock that is formed by the rapid solidification of lava. Igneous rocks, such as obsidian, are formed when magma erupts from Earth's surface as lava and solidifies.

10. **C** The graph that depicts the population size over time for both Canadian lynx and Arctic hare is the predator-prey cycle. The predator-prey cycle is exemplified by the relationship between prey and predator. In bountiful years, the hares reproduce very successfully. In turn, the lynx would also have plenty of food, and their population size would also rise rapidly. However, in years of scarcity, the population of hares would decline, and the lynx population would decline in turn.

11. **D** Both radio and infrared waves emit non-ionizing radiation and, therefore, are considered relatively harmless. Both X-rays and gamma rays emit ionizing radiation and can be harmful to humans. However, gamma rays emit higher doses of radiation than X-rays and, therefore, are the most harmful to humans.

12. **D** The mitochondria, commonly referred to as the power plants of the cell, play a pivotal role in cellular respiration. Mitochondria break down nutrients and create usable energy to fuel cellular activities.

13. **A** A monohybrid cross of a purebred black-feathered (BB) pigeon and a purebred white-feathered (bb) chicken would result in the following Punnet Square.

	B	**B**
b	Bb	Bb
b	Bb	Bb

Since the allele for black feathers (B) is dominant, and all of the offspring have the heterozygous genotype Bb, none of the offspring will have white feathers.

14. **B** In order to answer this question, you need to know that all of the offspring from the mating described would have the genotype Bb. The cross between two heterozygous genotypes would result in the following Punnet Square.

	B	**b**
B	BB	Bb
b	Bb	bb

A genotypic ratio is concerned with the genotypes of the offspring. When we cross two heterozygous pigeons, we end up with BB, Bb, Bb, and bb. Therefore, our genotypic ratio is 1:2:1.

15. **A** A phenotypic ratio is concerned with the phenotypes, or appearances, of the offspring. As shown in the explanation for question 14, when we cross two heterozygous pigeons, we end up with BB, Bb, Bb, and bb. Therefore, since we have three black-feathered pigeons and one white-feathered pigeon, our phenotypic ratio is 3:1.

16. **C** The light reactions of photosynthesis convert solar energy to usable energy in the form of ATP and NADPH. If it helps you remember, NAD***PH*** is associated with ***ph***otosynthesis.

17. **C** In order to answer this question, you need to refer to the diagram. The bottom of the diagram depicts the change in hormone levels over a 28-day cycle. The top of the diagram shows changes in the uterine lining through menstruation, proliferation, and secretion. Recall that the female reproductive system depends on a monthly cycle called ovulation, when an egg travels to the uterus. Thus, this diagram is depicting changes in the female reproductive system.

18. **B** The question tells us that hormone X is peaking during ovulation. According to the graph, hormone X peaks around Day 14 of the cycle.

19. **C** A blue shift of the light from a star indicates that the star is moving towards Earth; a red shift indicates that the star is moving away from Earth.

20. **D** An autotroph is capable of producing food via photosynthesis; therefore, a killer whale is not an autotroph and (A) and (C) can be eliminated. You are now left with two options: primary consumer and tertiary consumer. Recall that a primary consumer is an herbivore. Since killer whales eat other animals, the only possible answer is that the killer whale is a tertiary consumer and a heterotroph.

21. **C** Neither cod nor squid have a direct connection to the krill population. Penguins feed on both algae and krill. Therefore, were the krill population depleted, the penguin population would likely also be affected, which in turn would mean that the leopard seal population would likely be affected.

22. **D** *r*-selected organisms reproduce early in life and often, and have a high capacity for reproductive growth. In these species, little or no care is given to the offspring, but due to the sheer numbers of offspring in the population, enough of the offspring will survive to enable the population to continue. Some examples of *r*-selected species are bacteria, algae, and protozoa.

23. **D** The area of least productivity in the ocean is the area that does not receive any sunlight; i.e., photosynthesis cannot occur. The area without any sunlight is the aphotic zone.

24. **A** Since the abyssal zone is even further down in the ocean than the aphotic zone, it is not necessary that organisms have well-developed eyes. However, darkness, extreme cold, and low nutrient density are characteristics of the abyssal zone; i.e., organisms need to be tolerant of cold temperatures, and be able to survive off limited resources in areas of low nutrient density.

25. **A** Note that the question asks you to find an *unexpected* effect of the coal plant on Ezraton and the surrounding area. Higher smoke and smog levels, decreased biodiversity, and increased acidity (via acid mine drainage) are all expected effects of using coal power. It would be unlikely, however, for a coal plant to improve the air quality of the surrounding area.

26. **A** The passage states that the river Schmeegen has been tainted by acid mine drainage. Recall that a pH below 7 indicates acidity, a pH of 7 indicates neutrality, and a pH above 7 indicates alkalinity. The only acidic pH listed is 5 and, therefore, is the best answer.

27. **C** Recall that there must be the same number of atoms on each side of the equation. All of the equations are balanced except for $3PbO + 2NH_3 \rightarrow 3Pb + 2N_2 + 3H_2O$, which should *not* have nitrogen with a coefficient of 2. Instead, the equation should read $3PbO + 2NH_3 \rightarrow 3Pb + N_2 + 3H_2O$.

28. **B** Refraction is a wave-like behavior of light that occurs when light waves travel from one medium to another and change directions. Refraction is often called the bending of light; here, the light bends when it encounters the glass.

29. **D** An exothermic reaction occurs when heat is released in an energy transfer; these processes are accompanied by heat. Endothermic reactions require energy and absorb heat from the environment; these processes are accompanied by a loss of heat. When Kristy and Eliz started the fire, heat was released into the atmosphere; this was an exothermic reaction.

30. **B** Conduction occurs when objects are in direct contact with one another and there is no evidence that the girls touched the fire. Furthermore, the passage states that the girls became warmer. Therefore, via convection, the girls absorbed heat from the fire.

31. **C** Here, you need to determine what happens when Kristy burns her hand. Since she uses a metal pole that is in direct contact with the fire, heat is transferred by means of conduction. Thus, eliminate (A) and (B). Since an exothermic reaction occurs when heat is released to surrounding objects, which become warmer when they absorb the heat, the reaction is exothermic; heat from the fire was released and transferred to her hand. Thus, eliminate (D).

32. **A** A convergent boundary occurs when two plates are pushed towards one another, and one of the plates is pushed deep into the mantle. Convergent boundary interactions often result in subduction that results in the formation of mountain chains.

33. **D** Covalent bonds, which can be polar or non-polar, form when valence electrons are shared between atoms. Conversely, ionic bonds, which require at least one electron donor and one electron acceptor, form when electrons are transferred between atoms.

34. **C** The process represented by the letter A in the water cycle shown is that of runoff. When precipitation falls to the earth, it either travels below ground as groundwater or across the surface as runoff.

35. **D** Bar magnets are permanent magnets (those with electrons continually spinning around them creating magnetic force) that have north and south poles on opposite ends. If you were to split the bar magnet in half, you would simply redirect the electrons around the material, creating two smaller bar magnets.

36. **B** The relative atomic mass on an element is found by totaling the number of protons and neutrons in an atom. For example, beryllium has four protons, four neutrons, and a relative atomic mass of eight.

37. **A** Recall that *momentum* = *mass* × *velocity*. The cat has a momentum of 250 m/s, the boat has a momentum of 1,500 m/s, the girl has a momentum of 560 m/s, and the tiger has a momentum of 3,000 m/s. Therefore, the cat has the least momentum.

38. **C** If the resources are unlimited, the population would continue to grow at an exponential rate; e.g., there were 4 mice in the first year, there were 4^2 mice in the second year, there were 4^3 mice in the third year, there were 4^4 mice in the fourth year, and there would be 4^5, or approximately 1,024, mice in the fifth year. The best answer choice is 1,000.

39. **B** You can predict long-term population growth rates using a model called the Rule of 70, which states that the time it takes for a population to double can be approximated by dividing 70 by the current growth rate of the population. Here, the growth rate of a population is 7 percent, so the population will double in 10 years ($\frac{70}{7}$ = 10 years).

40. **A** Mice are not capable of photosynthesis and, therefore, are not producers. Furthermore, mice aren't decomposers; they aren't bacteria or fungi that break down and eat dead matter. Tertiary consumers are omnivores or carnivores that consume smaller animals, while primary consumers are herbivores that feed directly on producers. Mice are herbivores and, therefore, are primary consumers.

41. **C** The photoelectric effect shows that when light shines upon certain metals, photoelectrons are emitted. The ability of photons to carry energy shows that light can behave like a particle.

42. **B** Homeostasis is the ability of an organism to maintain stable internal conditions, regardless of changes in the external environment. In the passage provided, the body is maintaining stable internal conditions by regulating the amount of liquid present.

43. **D** Big Bang nucleosynthesis occurred within a few minutes of the start of the universe, and produced abundant amounts of lighter elements, such as hydrogen, helium, and deuterium. Conversely, uranium is the heaviest naturally occurring element, and would have been able to form only once the universe cooled and became more hospitable.

44. **A** On the left, the $5O_2$ term represents oxygen, so the C_3H_8 must represent propane. On the right, the $3CO_2$ represents carbon dioxide, and the $4H_2O$ term represents water. Since resulting substance is composed of both carbon dioxide and water, only (A) describes the reaction.

45. **C** Recall that *force = mass × acceleration*. Therefore, if a UFO has a mass of 800 kilograms, and has alien technology that provide a thrust force of 32,000 newtons, then the 32,000 newtons = 800 kilograms × acceleration, and 32,000 newtons/800 kilograms = 40 meters/second². The passage indicates that the second UFO experiences the same acceleration, so you know that force = 1,400 kilograms × 40 meters/second² = 56,000 newtons.

46. **D** The image shown depicts telophase, the final stage of mitosis. During telophase, nuclear membranes form around each set of chromosomes and the nucleoli reappear. The cytoplasm splits and a cleavage furrow forms, preparing to split into two, distinct daughter cells.

47. **A** The passage states that plants lie dormant during periods that are unfavorable for growth. Known for harsh and cold conditions, which are not conducive to plant growth, winter is the season least favorable for growth.

48. **C** In order to answer this question, you need to have a basic idea of how the nervous system communicates with the rest of the body. First, heat would be detected by nerves, which would signal the spinal interneurons. Next, motor neurons would be excited and signal muscle cells to move away from the hot item. Finally, as the person pulls away from the item, the muscle cells would contract.

49. **D** Motion involves both the muscular and skeletal systems, which provide support and allow both voluntary and involuntary movement. In order to move, however, the nervous system must send signals to cells throughout the body. While the digestive system plays an essential role is absorbing nutrients, it does not play a pivotal role in this scenario.

SOCIAL STUDIES

1. **B** Choice (A) says that it should be up to kids to decide when and whether they want to take a job—but that contradicts almost everything in the timeline, so you can eliminate this one. Choice (C) says kids can't work under any circumstances, which is rather extreme and violates common sense, so you can eliminate this one, too. Choice (D) is saying the same thing as (C) using different words. The correct answer, which sums up the reason for the need for regulations, is (B).

2. **B** Who would be likely to support regulations to protect children? Factory owners *may* be kind-hearted, but then again, there have been a lot of factory owners who have exploited child labor—so eliminate (A). Child protection agencies would seem very likely to protect children; let's hold onto (B) while we look at the other choices. Worker's unions might well also support regulations to protect children, so let's hold onto (C) as well. Small companies and agricultural workers *might* be kindhearted too, but we don't know that they will be, so eliminate (D). We have two choices left: (B) and (C). Only (B) is supported by the timeline. The correct answer is (B).

3. **B** This EXCEPT question is asking you to decide which answer choice can NOT be used to deny a child employment. Each of the choices is a legal reason to prevent children from working—except for one: (B), gender. Age (A) must be eliminated since the whole timeline is about "child" labor. As for (C), the actual phrase "hazard levels" is not in the timeline, but FDR sought to put "limits" on "many forms" of child labor. It makes sense that "children's rights" activists would want to protect children from hazards. This sentence also rules out (D).

4. **B** Franklin Delano Roosevelt was president well after the Civil War, so rule out (D). Choice (A) may be tempting if you read the quote too quickly, but Lincoln was not a Civil War general. Jefferson Davis (C) was never President of the United States, so rule out that one.

5. **C** If you remembered that Sutter's Mill is connected with the Gold Rush, then you can go straight for (C). Otherwise, use POE. The quote has nothing to do with giving birth to lots of babies, so rule out (D). Many captains of the Industrial Revolution did increase their wealth gradually, so rule out (A). Choice (B) is close, but has no connection to Sutter's Mill.

6. **C** The First Amendment protects five essential freedoms, three of which are listed in (C), the correct answer. The Second Amendment protects the right to bear arms (A). The Bill of Rights decreases government restriction of individual rights not increases as in (B). Choice (D) is obviously wrong: The primary role of Congress is to make laws.

7. **A** The First Amendment does not guarantee the right to vote. Rather it makes five guarantees: those listed in (B) through (D) and also the freedom of religion and assembly.

8. **D** This was a tough question, because it required you to know the definition of a "pure market economy." A pure market economy is one in which the forces of the market control what happens; in other words, there is no government control whatsoever. So which of the answer choices would NOT be found in a pure market economy? Monopolies (A) could occur in a pure market economy

because there would be no government rules to prevent them. Small businesses (B) would probably flourish—at least until monopolies put them out of business. There would certainly be unemployment (C) because the markets would hire people only when they needed them. The only things you would NOT find in a pure market economy, as unlikely as it seems, would be taxes and welfare (both of which are controlled by the government). The answer to this difficult question is (D).

9. **D** In a socialist economy, the goal is to distribute money equally among all the members of a society. So which of the groups in the answer choices would benefit the *least* from the switch to a socialist economy? Choices (B) and (C) would benefit quite a bit, because these are relatively poor people who would get a bigger slice of the pie than they have now. Eliminate (B) and (C). Between the two choices we have left, who benefits the *least*? The correct answer is (D), highly skilled labor, because presumably they were being well paid for their unique skills, and would lose money in the redistribution of wealth. Government employees (A) in socialist systems usually tend to gain power because they get to decide who receives the wealth.

10. **D** Early automobiles were quite primitive in the early twentieth century, but, interestingly, they did have the ability to run on pure grain alcohol (similar to ethanol).

11. **A** African Americans had their own churches after the Civil War, so they were not seeking religious freedom. They were, however, seeking economic opportunity (B) and fleeing the racial persecution persistent in the South. Choices (C) and (D) are both reasons that African Americans would have fled the South.

12. **D** The question is basically asking, "Which of the following is NOT an example of a plutocratic government?" In a plutocracy, the leaders are chosen because they are the wealthiest citizens. Nazi Germany may have been a brutal regime, but its leaders were the ones with a certain ideology, not the greatest wealth.

13. **A** Choice (A) is a pure definition of monarchy: rule by king or queen, usually power passed down in family groups.

14. **D** You don't have to know anything about Andrew Mellon to realize that, in this statement at least, he is on the side of the people. He writes that "unwise" public officials "fall to these interests of monopoly as against the welfare of the people of whom they are supposed to serve." So we are looking for an answer choice that is sympathetic to the people and critical of officials who lose sight of the people's welfare. Choice (A) seems possible at first, but goes too far: Mellon doesn't suggest that public officials who profit from a monopoly shouldn't run for office. Choice (B) goes too far, because Mellon never says the profits of monopolies should be shared by all. Choice (C) is wrong because it sides with the public officials over the interests of the people. This leaves us with (D), which is a simple restatement of what Mellon says in the passage.

15. **D** The federal government oversees tasks that involve multiple states and any tasks specifically enumerated in the Constitution. Declaring war (A) affects all Americans and is a responsibility delineated in the Constitution. Interstate trade (B) affects more than one state, so is regulated by the feds. Post offices (C), although they exist in local communities, are part of a federally regulated organization, the United States Postal Service, and are managed by the Postmaster General of the United States. So, that leaves you with (D). Civil matters such as marriages and divorces are handled at the county or state level and are not managed by the feds.

16. **D** The highest concentrations of recent immigrants tend to be on the outside edges of the country, (think California, Arizona, Texas, and New York) not in the interior. Question 16 asks you to pick the best geographic explanation for the areas that have the highest numbers of non-English-speaking children. Choice (B) is irrelevant because we aren't concerned with the total number of children in the country—only the children who can't speak English. Choice (C) is irrelevant because these people *do not* speak English. Choice (A) seems possible at first, because lower income taxes might attract new immigrants, but then again, wouldn't they attract just about everyone? Let's hold onto this as we look at (D): If recent immigrants settled in border and coastal states, wouldn't that be a pretty logical explanation for why these areas contain the most non-English-speaking kids? Choice (D) is a much better answer than (A).

17. **B** All of the answer choices would have an effect on the distribution of immigrants EXCEPT (B), climate. In general, new immigrants would seem to make decisions based more on the availability of job opportunities, immigration laws, social services, and even migration patterns (where immigrants have gone before) than on climate. One of the states with a long-standing tradition of immigration is New York (which has a colder climate) while others include California and Florida, with warmer climates.

18. **D** To answer this question, you have to consider each answer choice in turn. Are immigrants evenly distributed across the *entire* country? Even in Alaska and North Dakota? No way. Eliminate (A). Are there more of Spanish-speaking immigrants in Arizona than in California? (B). Maybe, although California has a much higher population. And while Texas and California *do* have high levels of kids who are illiterate, could that really mean that they have more kids who can't speak English than kids who *can*? We don't have clear evidence for this, so eliminate (C). The correct answer is (D) because immigrants do tend to settle in certain coastal states.

19. **A** Lowering the speed limit, limiting senators to two terms, or reducing pollution—none of these deprives people of their constitutional rights. However, prohibiting protests by a union takes away fundamental rights guaranteed by the Constitution: the right to free speech and the right to assembly. Thus, the correct answer is (A).

20. **B** Freedom of religion is a fundamental right guaranteed by the Constitution—so we can eliminate (A). A right to a trial by jury is also guaranteed by the Constitution—so we can eliminate (C). The right to vote is also guaranteed to citizens by the Constitution—so we can probably eliminate (D), because even if they don't speak English, people can be citizens. The correct answer is (B).

21. **D** The timeline states that the Berlin Airlift was "in response to Soviet Premier Joseph Stalin's attempt to block supplies to Berliners." This is closest to (D). Choice (C) is tempting, but the creation of the Warsaw Pact happened *after* the Berlin Airlift. Choice (A) is unsupported by the timeline and (B) does not work, since if the Marshall Plan had been completely successfully, Berliners would not have needed assistance.

22. **A** According to the timeline, the Warsaw Pact was created after the formation of NATO. All remaining answers include events that happened before NATO.

23. **A** "Communist expansion" would be a common threat.

24. **B** As you may know, World War II ended in 1945. World War I (A) ended in 1918. The Korean War (C) was later in the 1950s. Vietnam (D) did not end until 1975.

25. **D** A couple of these items are not on the timeline, but if you remembered that "containment" pertains to the attempt to stop Communism from spreading throughout the world, then you will notice that the Berlin Airlift was more of a humanitarian effort in a region that was already Communist, not a direct effort to "contain."

26. **C** Because so many different factors can affect stock prices, there can be no guarantee that two companies producing the same goods will do equally well—so we can eliminate (A). While amateur investors are certainly an economic factor, their behavior is not the most important factor in a stock's success—so eliminate (B). Amateurs may do as well as a professional stock trader, but they will not always do better—so we can eliminate (D). The best answer must be (C), because past success does not ensure future performance—a concept always mentioned in stock prospectuses, but often forgotten in practice.

27. **A** Since laissez-faire economics is free from government restrictions, labor laws, building codes, and antitrust laws would all be incorrect choices.

28. **C** What caused the end of the era of transatlantic ship-crossings? Do you think it was a series of accidents, a major war that disrupted routes, the cost of travel by boat, or the fact that sea travel fell out of fashion? Nope, it was something much more basic—the airplane. The correct answer is (C).

29. **A** No, you don't have to memorize the entire agricultural history of the United States! This question asks you to remember a Big Picture fact about the colonial South: namely, that its economy was based on tobacco sales to England.

30. **C** The term "muckrakers" refers to a group of journalists whose work revealed widespread corruption in urban management (Lincoln Steffens's *The Shame of the Cities*), oil companies (Ida Tarbell's *The History of the Standard Oil Company*), and the meatpacking industry (Upton Sinclair's *The Jungle*). These books and others like them outraged the public, who in turn called for widespread reform.

31. **B** Of the four groups listed in the answer choices, only the socialists had any desire to "destroy all enslaving and degrading capitalist institutions." Radical Republicans (A) sought to punish the South after the Civil War; isolationists (C) wished to avoid military and political involvement in Europe; New Deal Democrats (D) sought to resuscitate the economy by means of aggressive government intervention.

32. **B** During the Eisenhower administration, the government began developing the Interstate Highway System. Interstates were initially developed to assist in troop mobilization in the event of war; however, their most important benefits were to the civilian population. The new roads sped interstate commerce, thus lowering the cost of goods. They also facilitated speedy travel in and out of cities, allowing city workers to move to the suburbs.

33. **D** The American System (A) was an 1820s program designed to strengthen the national government; the New Deal (B) was implemented in the 1930s by Franklin Roosevelt; the New Frontier (C) was the name of John F. Kennedy's agenda.

34. **A** In this cartoon, the two Civil War veterans, one African American, one white—each missing a leg—are shaking hands. Always read the caption carefully in a cartoon or photograph. The two soldiers are calling each other comrade and saying they each lost a leg for a good cause. The best answer is (A), which reflects what the Civil War was fought over: the right of all men to be free and equal to each other. Both (C) and (D) suggest information that is impossible to know about these two individuals, while not reflecting the point of the cartoon. Choice (B), while true, again did not reflect the larger point behind the conflict.

35. **B** Congress (the legislative branch) is responsible for passing laws. They do not veto (A); that is the president's role. They do not oversee the Supreme Court directly so eliminate (C). Choice (D) is tempting, but the president does this, not Congress.

36. **D** Jefferson states that "judges as the ultimate arbiters of all constitutional questions" is "a very dangerous doctrine." He made this statement in response to *Marbury vs. Madison*. The quote also indicates that "their power is… dangerous." This matches best with (D). Choices (A) and (C) are too positive in tone to match with the Jefferson quote. Choice (B) is close, but *Marbury vs. Madison* pertains to the Judicial Branch, not the Executive Branch.

37. **A** Jefferson is using negative language, such as "dangerous." The only negative word in these answers is "tyranny." It is not a literal definition of "oligarchy," but is the only word that captures the spirit of Jefferson's opinion regarding *Marbury vs. Madison*.

38. **D** Read *all* the choices before you make up your mind. Although it is possible that the authors of the amendments were legal scholars, this isn't knowledge you are required to have, so (A) doesn't seem likely. The First Amendment prohibits government interference in religion, so you can safely eliminate (B). Choice (C) says that the writers of the amendments believed in government with ultimate

authority—but that seems to go against the idea of granting citizens rights that can't be taken away by the government. The writers didn't want to give the government too much power. The best answer is (D).

39. **B** At first glance, *all* of these answer choices seem to be things people wouldn't like—but only one of them doesn't violate the Fourteenth Amendment: Choice (B) requires all citizens to pay taxes, regardless of their beliefs. Choices (A) and (C) deny equal protection under the law. Choice (D) denies due process under the law.

40. **A** Amelia Earhart made her historic flights in an earlier era when women were often expected to take a backseat to men.

41. **B** This is a tricky question. You must read the statements carefully. Notice the graph measures only *union* employees, *not* total numbers of employees. Thus (B) is unsupported by the data. Choices (A), (C), and (D) are consistent with the data given.

42. **D** Always read the chart first; in this case it shows changes in employment in a number of fields. Now, go through the answer choices. Was there an increase in agricultural jobs? Actually, no, there was a decline, so eliminate (A). Was there more growth in administrative support than in any other occupation? No, services had more growth, so eliminate (B). Was there more growth in administrative support than there was in services and technicians and support jobs combined? No, services *alone* had a bigger increase, so eliminate (C). Was there less growth in precision production than in professional specialties? Well, yes, as a matter of fact, there was! The correct answer is (D).

43. **D** Indentured servitude differed from slavery in one important respect: Indentured servants were set free after serving their terms of duty (usually five to seven years), while slaves served for life (or until they or someone else could buy their freedom). Europeans were sometimes forced into indentured servitude (A); indentures made up the majority of British immigrants to the South (B); those who survived indenture usually received property along with their freedom (C); and most indentured servants had much better working conditions than African slaves (D).

44. **A** The concept of federalism is central to the Constitution. The term *federalism* describes a system of government under which the national government and local governments (state governments, in the case of the United States) share powers. Under our federal system, the national government provides defense, regulation of international trade, and other important services. The states control licensing, intrastate roads, and many other government responsibilities. The two levels of government share powers in such areas as roads, taxation, and law enforcement. Other countries with federal governments include Canada, Switzerland, and Australia. In comparison, a centralized government is one in which the national government maintains all power. Both Great Britain and France have centralized governments. Choices (B), nationalism, and (C), idealism, are not governmental systems. Choice (D), autocracy, refers to a government that answers only to itself; usually this describes a dictatorship.

45. **A** Believe it or not, the government imprisoned a large number of its own citizens during World War II. Paranoia that Japanese Americans, even those born in the United States, would help the Japanese war effort led to the drastic measure, which relocated West Coast residents with Japanese ancestry to prison camps, primarily in the South. Most lost their homes and possessions as a result of the internment. A 1944 lawsuit concerning the internment, *Korematsu v. United States*, reached the Supreme Court. The Court upheld the government's right to take such drastic measures during wartime.

46. **D** For obvious reasons, the U.S. government declared the war effort the nation's chief priority. As part of the effort, the economy was retooled to support the war. Manufacturers and producers of raw materials gave top priority to military shipments, resulting in a sharp decline in consumer goods for those at home. The situation grew so bad that the government had to ration such items as gasoline and meat.

47. **D** The key line from this quote is the last one: "I shall resign from the presidency, effective at noon tomorrow." To date, there has been only one president to resign from office, President Richard Nixon. Connect him to the era of the 1970s and you should be able to pick the right date, 1974 (D).

48. **C** Do not let the academic language of the prompt throw you off. While it may sound intimidating, GDP is just a measure of wealth. For this question, the definition does not even matter because it asks you to select the *opinion* from among the facts. Choices (A), (B), and (D) can be verified from the data in the graph. They do not express personal opinions. So long as the data from the graph is accurate, they cannot be disputed. Choice (C), however, expresses a political opinion, not a fact.

49. **A** The belief that God ordained the expansion of the United States from the Atlantic Ocean to the Pacific Ocean is known as "Manifest Destiny," (A). Choice (C) is not quite right, since imperialism implies interfering in the politics of other nations. Choices (B) and (D) are irrelevant.

NOTES

NOTES

NOTES

NOTES

NOTES

NOTES

International Offices Listing

China (Beijing)
1501 Building A,
Disanji Creative Zone,
No.66 West Section of North 4th Ring Road Beijing
Tel: +86-10-62684481/2/3
Email: tprkor01@chol.com
Website: www.tprbeijing.com

China (Shanghai)
1010 Kaixuan Road
Building B, 5/F
Changning District, Shanghai, China 200052
Sara Beattie, Owner: Email: sbeattie@sarabeattie.com
Tel: +86-21-5108-2798
Fax: +86-21-6386-1039
Website: www.princetonreviewshanghai.com

Hong Kong
5th Floor, Yardley Commercial Building
1-6 Connaught Road West, Sheung Wan, Hong Kong
(MTR Exit C)
Sara Beattie, Owner: Email: sbeattie@sarabeattie.com
Tel: +852-2507-9380
Fax: +852-2827-4630
Website: www.princetonreviewhk.com

India (Mumbai)
Score Plus Academy
Office No.15, Fifth Floor
Manek Mahal 90
Veer Nariman Road
Next to Hotel Ambassador
Churchgate, Mumbai 400020
Maharashtra, India
Ritu Kalwani: Email: director@score-plus.com
Tel: + 91 22 22846801 / 39 / 41
Website: www.score-plus.com

India (New Delhi)
South Extension
K-16, Upper Ground Floor
South Extension Part–1,
New Delhi-110049
Aradhana Mahna: aradhana@manyagroup.com
Monisha Banerjee: monisha@manyagroup.com
Ruchi Tomar: ruchi.tomar@manyagroup.com
Rishi Josan: Rishi.josan@manyagroup.com
Vishal Goswamy: vishal.goswamy@manyagroup.com
Tel: +91-11-64501603/ 4, +91-11-65028379
Website: www.manyagroup.com

Lebanon
463 Bliss Street
AlFarra Building - 2nd floor
Ras Beirut
Beirut, Lebanon
Hassan Coudsi: Email: hassan.coudsi@review.com
Tel: +961-1-367-688
Website: www.princetonreviewlebanon.com

Korea
945-25 Young Shin Building
25 Daechi-Dong, Kangnam-gu
Seoul, Korea 135-280
Yong-Hoon Lee: Email: TPRKor01@chollian.net
In-Woo Kim: Email: iwkim@tpr.co.kr
Tel: + 82-2-554-7762
Fax: +82-2-453-9466
Website: www.tpr.co.kr

Kuwait
ScorePlus Learning Center
Salmiyah Block 3, Street 2 Building 14
Post Box: 559, Zip 1306, Safat, Kuwait
Email: infokuwait@score-plus.com
Tel: +965-25-75-48-02 / 8
Fax: +965-25-75-46-02
Website: www.scorepluseducation.com

Malaysia
Sara Beattie MDC Sdn Bhd
Suites 18E & 18F
18th Floor
Gurney Tower, Persiaran Gurney
Penang, Malaysia
Email: tprkl.my@sarabeattie.com
Sara Beattie, Owner: Email: sbeattie@sarabeattie.com
Tel: +604-2104 333
Fax: +604-2104 330
Website: www.princetonreviewKL.com

Mexico
TPR México
Guanajuato No. 242 Piso 1 Interior 1
Col. Roma Norte
México D.F., C.P.06700
registro@princetonreviewmexico.com
Tel: +52-55-5255-4495
+52-55-5255-4440
+52-55-5255-4442
Website: www.princetonreviewmexico.com

Qatar
Score Plus
Office No: 1A, Al Kuwari (Damas)
Building near Merweb Hotel, Al Saad
Post Box: 2408, Doha, Qatar
Email: infoqatar@score-plus.com
Tel: +974 44 36 8580, +974 526 5032
Fax: +974 44 13 1995
Website: www.scorepluseducation.com

Taiwan
The Princeton Review Taiwan
2F, 169 Zhong Xiao East Road, Section 4
Taipei, Taiwan 10690
Lisa Bartle (Owner): lbartle@princetonreview.com.tw
Tel: +886-2-2751-1293
Fax: +886-2-2776-3201
Website: www.PrincetonReview.com.tw

Thailand
The Princeton Review Thailand
Sathorn Nakorn Tower, 28th floor
100 North Sathorn Road
Bangkok, Thailand 10500
Thavida Bijayendrayodhin (Chairman)
Email: thavida@princetonreviewthailand.com
Mitsara Bijayendrayodhin (Managing Director)
Email: mitsara@princetonreviewthailand.com
Tel: +662-636-6770
Fax: +662-636-6776
Website: www.princetonreviewthailand.com

Turkey
Yeni Sülün Sokak No. 28
Levent, Istanbul, 34330, Turkey
Nuri Ozgur: nuri@tprturkey.com
Rona Ozgur: rona@tprturkey.com
Iren Ozgur: iren@tprturkey.com
Tel: +90-212-324-4747
Fax: +90-212-324-3347
Website: www.tprturkey.com

UAE
Emirates Score Plus
Office No: 506, Fifth Floor
Sultan Business Center
Near Lamcy Plaza, 21 Oud Metha Road
Post Box: 44098, Dubai
United Arab Emirates
Hukumat Kalwani: skoreplus@gmail.com
Ritu Kalwani: director@score-plus.com
Email: info@score-plus.com
Tel: +971-4-334-0004
Fax: +971-4-334-0222
Website: www.princetonreviewuae.com

Our International Partners

The Princeton Review also runs courses with a variety of
partners in Africa, Asia, Europe, and South America.

Georgia
LEAF American-Georgian Education Center
www.leaf.ge

Mongolia
English Academy of Mongolia
www.nyescm.org

Nigeria
The Know Place
www.knowplace.com.ng

Panama
Academia Interamericana de Panama
http://aip.edu.pa/

Switzerland
Institut Le Rosey
http://www.rosey.ch/

All other inquiries, please email us at
internationalsupport@review.com